JOHN LOVEDAY
of Caversham
1711 – 1789

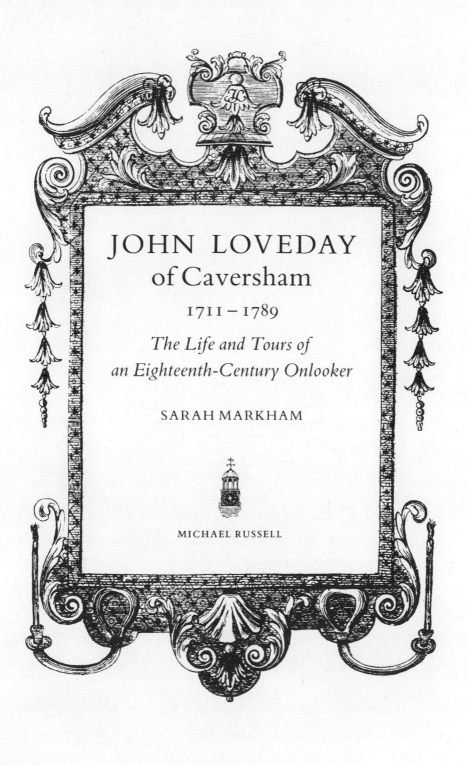

JOHN LOVEDAY
of Caversham
1711 – 1789

*The Life and Tours of
an Eighteenth-Century Onlooker*

SARAH MARKHAM

MICHAEL RUSSELL

To the memory of my father
THOMAS LOVEDAY, LL.D.

© Sarah Markham 1984

The British Academy generously
contributed towards the cost of
including the Appendix

Indexed by the author
Maps drawn by Denys R. Baker

First published in Great Britain 1984
by Michael Russell (Publishing) Ltd,
The Chantry, Wilton, Salisbury, Wiltshire

Printed and bound in Great Britain
by Biddles Ltd,
Guildford, King's Lynn and Dorking

Contents

CONTENTS

Family trees of the Loveday, Lethieullier and
Goodwin families will be found between pp. 302–3

Author's Note

John Loveday has a niche in the *Dictionary of National Biography*. He is known to have been a friend of Thomas Hearne and Daniel Waterland but is more often thought of as he appears in the diaries of John Byng or William Windham – a benevolent old gentleman keeping open house at Caversham. He is also remembered for his diary of a tour in 1732 which has been of use in the restoration of certain houses and which was published in 1890 by his great-great-grandson, J. E. T. Loveday. The descriptions of houses visited on that tour have not been repeated in this volume.

The diaries of his other tours were mislaid for the best part of a century and were never seen by my grandfather. Unlike the 1732 tour, which was bound, they were written on odd sheets of paper which were often used again throughout the years. When I transcribed them I found they covered a period from 1729 to 1765, varying from day visits to journeys of several weeks. The descriptions of houses are quoted in full and paintings, sculpture and tapestry which he recorded are listed in an Appendix. Any significant changes to cathedrals and churches included in the diaries have been extracted from his lengthy accounts.

Throughout his life he built up a notable library which is still largely intact and well cared for at Pennsylvania State University. He never wrote a book himself and his contributions to learned journals were almost always under a pseudonym. He became, however, a highly valued consultant on theological, antiquarian or literary matters to a number of authors. Thomas Warton might have spoken for them all when, two years before he became Poet Laureate, he wrote:

> I know not how to thank you sufficiently for the many useful Corrections and excellent Hints, which you have so repeatedly communicated. I only wish you would give me Permission to take the first opportunity of acknowledging this kindness in a public Manner. The Public have a right to know by whom they have been obliged.

With the help of his diaries and correspondence and with the new light thrown upon them by the diaries of the tours and by other researches, I have followed him through his early years and middle age and have also attempted to reconstruct to some extent the lives of his numerous friends. It is partly due to the care with which his daughter, Penelope, and her first husband, William Benwell, preserved so many of the tales of his youth that this has been possible.

In quoting selectively from the sources I have retained John Loveday's original spelling but have as a general rule set out in full those words he customarily abbreviated.

My first thanks must be to friends who have supported and encouraged my efforts from the beginning. Mr Jeremy Gibson, Mr Nicholas Cooper and Dr Frank Lewis all read the original drafts and gave me valuable advice at many times. I am also grateful to two other readers, Mrs Pamela Allen and Miss Diana Wilbraham. Dr Molly Barratt guided my researches in the Bodleian Library with the utmost patience and much useful information. Professor Charles Mann, who has charge of many of John Loveday's books at Pennsylvania State University, has been most generous in giving me information from those sources, strengthened by his own scholarship. I am extremely grateful to Dr J. D. Fleeman and Dr J. F. A. Mason for their interest and support and am greatly indebted to Dr David Fairer to whom I have often turned for advice. Mr Jeremy Cater helped me with some early research and Mr Nicholas Bagshawe gave me useful information about his family and other matters. I thank Dr John L. Abbott, Miss Margaret Toynbee, Dr G. L. Harriss and Mrs Valerie Jobling for expert advice and Mr S. P. Beachcroft for his special help.

I am particularly indebted to Mr Gervase Jackson-Stops for his help and support and to Mr Robin Wright for his kind encouragement. I also thank other members of the National Trust, especially Mr G. M. Trinick, Mr Christopher Rowell and Mr Anthony and Dr Brigitte Mitchell.

I have been fortunate in receiving some expert advice about paintings and wish to thank Sir Oliver Millar for his comments on the accounts of those in royal houses, Mr John Kerslake for his helpful interest, Mr Francis Greenacre for his kind assistance with the index to the Appendix and Professor A. Smart for further information about Allan Ramsay. Mr David Alexander has been most helpful to me and I also thank Mr John Harris, Mr Jacob Simon, Mrs Cynthia Carter, Miss Wendy Hefford and Mr Howard Mann for information and suggestions.

In Berkshire my thanks go especially to Canon J. G. Grimwade, Mr H. Godwin Arnold, Miss Mary Kift and Mr John Finch. No one could have been more generous with his knowledge of Warwickshire people than Mr Anthony Wood and I thank him and also Mr M. W. Farr for all their help. I am grateful to Lady Hamilton, Mrs Nan Clifton, Mr Eric E. F. Smith and to Mr Victor Churton who, with the kind cooperation of Mr W. W. Inge, has given me much useful information from his splendid researches. I also thank Captain J. B. Morison for practical assistance on various occasions and Mrs Janetta Lee for her valuable advice. I remember with gratitude the late Mrs Gwen Beachcroft and the late Mrs Joan Berkeley who took so much interest in the work. My obligations to other people are mentioned in the footnotes, though not, I fear, to everyone who has so kindly answered a query during the last few years.

I express my special thanks to those owners of historic houses with whom I have been in touch and to their librarians. I am most grateful to the Keeper of Western Manuscripts and members of the staff of the Bodleian Library, several of whom have given me assistance, to the Keeper of Manuscripts and the staff of the British Library and particularly Miss Anna Simoni; to Mr J. H. Hopkins for allowing me to work in the Library of the Society of Antiquaries, and to Mr Norman Higham and his staff at the Library of the University of Bristol – the facility of being able to work there frequently has been invaluable. I also thank the Keeper of Manuscripts and Records and Mr D. E. Williams of the National Library of Wales, Mr A. Giles Jones of the University College of North Wales and all University and Cathedral Librarians with whom I have corresponded. I wish to pay a tribute to the many County Librarians, Record Officers and Archivists who have unfailingly answered my questions with the utmost speed and efficiency.

In thanking members of my family for their encouragement and support I must mention first the work done by my father, the late Dr Thomas Loveday, who catalogued many of the letters and also the researches made by my great-aunt, the late Miss Marianne Loveday. I thank especially my sister, Mrs Charity James, who has given me the greatest possible support from the beginning, and my uncle, Bishop D. G. Loveday, who has helped me in many ways. I am also grateful to my cousin, Mr T. T. Loveday, for his very kind cooperation, to Mrs Norah Nicholls both for research and wonderful encouragement and to Mr Anthony Loveday whose wise suggestions have been invaluable. I thank my sons, Francis and John, for all they have done in many ways to help, and my husband, Gervase, who welcomed John Loveday as an extra member of the family some time ago and has unfailingly done all he possibly could to lighten the labours.

SARAH MARKHAM

may. 6. 1732. ~~Saturday~~ Dyd will: ~~Hawles~~ B. D. having been a little diforder'd in his senses.

Nov. 1. dyd will: Muffendine, M. A. Sup. B. of Law.

—— 3. Beaver elected.

~~May~~ June ^Monday^. 5. 1733. Dr. Holloway dyd at Witney betw. 6 & 7 in ye Evening, of a violent fever wth Convulsions occasion'd by stopping a Loosenefs.

Jan. 8. 1733-34. Tuesday. The Coll: presented Thos. Bowles, B. D. ~~to ye Living~~ of Aston cum Tubney, void by ye death of Ralph Webb.

July. 29. 1734. Monday. The Coll: presented Christopher Willoughby D.D. to ye Rectory of Sanderton in Com. Bucks. void by ye death of Mr. Vaughan. It is worth 7score £ p Ann.

~~Sa~~ Feb. 1. 1734-5. ^Saturday.^ The Coll: presented Phanuel Bacon, B. D. to ye Rectory of Bramber cum Botolph V. in Com. Sussex. void by ye death of Mr. Cooper, formerly fellow of Magd:Coll: It is said, yt if he does not reside upon it, but pays a Curate., it will not yield him clear above 100 £ p Ann.

April. 1735. The Coll: presented William Swinburne B. D. to ye Vicarage of Willoughby in Com. Warw. void by ye cession of P. Bacon. It is tena= =ble wth. a Fellowship.

June. 10. 1735. Tuesday. Dyd John Palmer, D.D. Rector of Appleton, at Appleton, in Com. Berks.

Jan. 29. 1735-6. The Coll: presented George Knibb, D. D. to ye Rectory of Appleton; William Vedcocke, B. D. had a prior Presentacon from ye Society, but Bp. Sherlock would not accept of it, would not institute him. Dr. Knibb resign'd his fellowship on Febr: 10. 1736-7.

Jan. 31. 1735-6. The Coll: presented William Swinburn B. D. to ye Rectory of Swaby in Com. Lincoln, void by ye cession of James Fynes D. D.

April. 12. 1736. The Coll: presented Richard Jackson, A. M. to ye Vicar= =age of Willoughby in Com. Warw. void by ye cession of W. Swinburn.

May. 19. 1736. Wednesday. Died Jonathan Kimberley, B. D. fellow of Magd: Coll:, in ye Countrey, of an apoplectick fit.

An example of John Loveday's handwriting. The college referred to is Magdalen College, Oxford.

THE TWO JOURNEYS
OF 1730 AND THE
JOURNEY OF 1731

Walsingham

King's Lynn

Norwich

Yarmouth

Shrewsbury

Birmingham

Northampton

Huntingdon

Bury
St Edmunds

Newtown

Coventry

Saxmundham

Ludlow

Warwick

Cambridge

Newmarket

Tregaron

Worcester

Bishop's
Stortford

Cardigan

Hereford

Chipping

Colchester

Brecon

Norton

1730

1731

St Davids

Carmarthen

Pen yr
Heol Vawr

Gloucester

Thame

Haverfordwest

Oxford

St Albans

Pembroke

Swansea

Reading

1730

Bromley

Rochester

Sunninghill

Canterbury

Maidstone

Dover

Petersfield

Dymchurch

Buriton

Chichester

Lewes

Hastings

Portsmouth

Miles 0   25   50   75   100

Kilometres 0   40   80   120   160

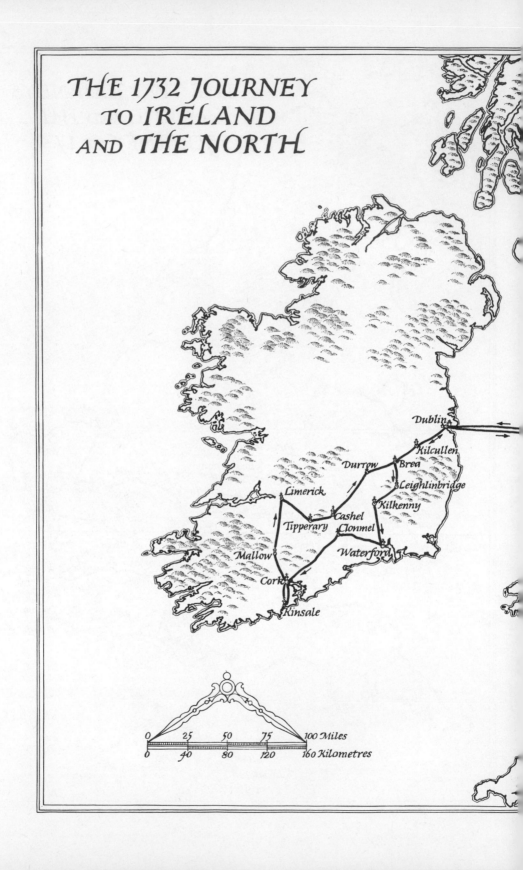

THE 1732 JOURNEY
TO IRELAND
AND THE NORTH

Dublin

Kilcullen

Durrow   Brea
Leighlinbridge
Limerick   Kilkenny
Cashel
Tipperary   Clonmel
Mallow   Waterford
Cork
Kinsale

0   25   50   75   100 Miles
0   40   80   120   160 Kilometres

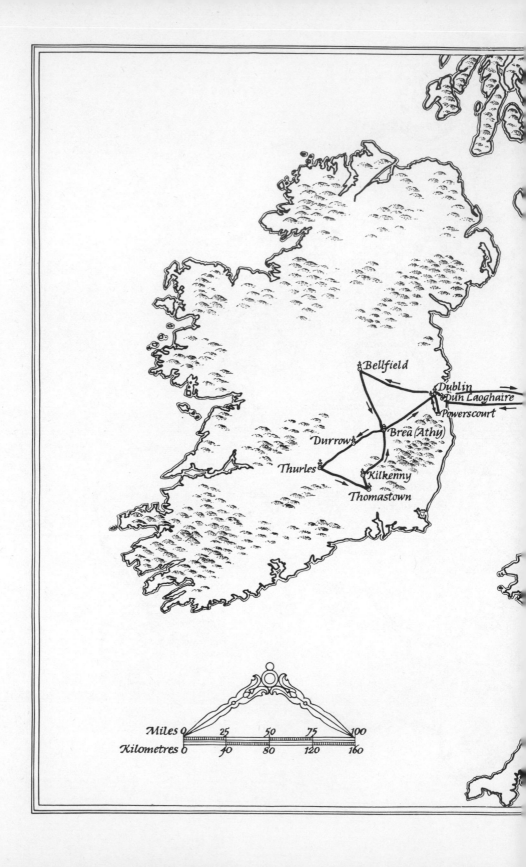

Bellfield

Dublin
Dun Laoghaire
Powerscourt

Durrow
Brea (Athy)

Thurles
Kilkenny
Thomastown

Miles 0   25   50   75   100
Kilometres 0   40   80   120   160

THE 1733 JOURNEY
TO IRELAND

yhead
Beaumaris Denbigh
Ruthin

Shrewsbury

Bridgnorth

Worcester

Chipping Norton

Oxford

THE JOURNEYS
OF 1735, 1736
AND 1765

York

Beverley
Hull

Leeds
Wakefield

Sheffield

Buxton   Edensor   Lincoln

Malpas

Derby   Nottingham
Newport   Burton-   Sewstern
on-Trent   Stamford
1765   Lichfield
Wolverhampton   Shenstone   Peterborough

Hagley Hall   Coventry   Kettering

Warwick

1735   Stowe

Fairford   Oxford
1736   Reading

Holt   Newbury

Wells
Barnstaple   Bridgewater   Stockbridge
Dulverton
Torrington   Hinton St. George
Stratton   Crewkerne   Lymington
Exeter   Honiton   Christchurch
Camelford   Launceston   Wareham
St. Columb   Powderham Castle   Melcombe
Plymouth   Chudleigh
Redruth   South Brent
St. Austell   Lostwithiel
Falmouth
Penzance
Lands End

Miles 0   25   50   75   100
Kilometres 0   40   80   120   160

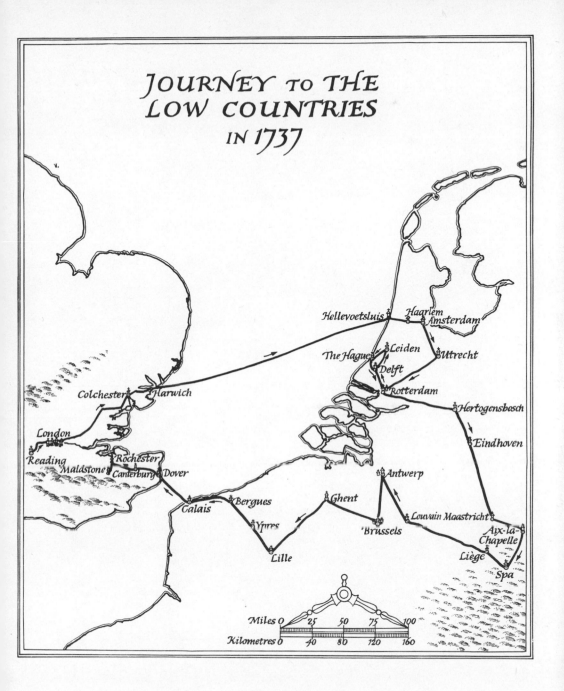

JOURNEY TO THE
LOW COUNTRIES
IN 1737

Miles 0   25   50   75   100
Kilometres 0   40   80   120   160

Maps drawn by Denys R. Baker

Childhood and Schooldays
1711 – 1727

'My Grandfather was an Officer in King Charles's Army, 'prenticed himself to a Goldsmith and married his Master's Widow.' So John Loveday summarized his grandfather's career and provided two known wives with a predecessor.

Thomas Loveday came from a family of mercers at Atherstone in Warwickshire. While his brother John continued the family business, he, with little more in 1646 than his captaincy,[a] apprenticed himself to Richard Hill, a successful goldsmith in London. There he remained for his seven years and in 1653 was admitted to the Freedom of the Goldsmiths' Company by service and was able to claim the Freedom of the City of London. By 1660 he must have been a man of some standing: he was elected in that year to the Livery of the Company and in 1679 he achieved the distinction of the Fourth Wardenship.[1] He remained meanwhile on good terms with his Warwickshire relations and owned property in Atherstone himself, including eventually the house in which his brother John lived; but it was his nephew John, also a goldsmith in London, and Matthew, an Oxford innkeeper,[b] who were his more intimate friends.

The date of his first marriage is obscure, but it may well have been to the widow Mrs Hill, and it seems likely that he was in search of a family home when he came out of London in the year of the Great Plague to look for a house in the country. He settled on the old parsonage house at Caversham,

---

[a] He styled himself captain for the rest of his life.
[b] He kept the Blue Boar Inn in St Aldate's, Oxford.

ideally situated on the river he knew so well and within fairly easy reach of
London; for Thomas may have liked the idea of establishing a gentleman's
seat in the country (in common with many others who, having made their
fortunes, had joined the general exodus), but he was still a man of business
and kept his London properties until he died.

The timber and stucco house nestling beneath the church of St Peter was
owned by Christ Church, Oxford, and Thomas took up occupancy in
February 1666 under a lease dating from the previous Michaelmas. It was even
then very old, having belonged to the Augustinian priory of Notley before the
Reformation. Built round inner and outer courts and partly balustrated, its
chief feature indoors was a low gallery running the whole length of the house.
The grounds sloping down to the river contained only a few trees, but the view
of the historic town of Reading was partly obscured by a thick hedge along the
river bank. To the east the Reading road crossed the river over the ancient
narrow bridge. Two years before Thomas's lease a summer-house[c] with a
boathouse below had been erected, its weather-vane bearing the date 1663.
This fine example of a Thames boathouse was a symbol to his descendants –
often mentioned in their letters and journals and a place where many happy
hours were spent.

In 1669 Thomas took a second wife twenty-two years younger than himself
– Letitia, daughter of Clement Throckmorton of Haseley, whom he had
probably met while visiting his relations in Warwickshire. She brought him a
dowry of £1,400 and, perhaps as important to him, a link with an ancient
family. They were married in London at St Martin-in-the-Fields,[2] he being
described officially as a 'widower [aged] about thirty-five', though he must
have been very much older than that. They had a daughter, also named Letitia,
in 1671, but three years later Thomas's wife died, leaving little by which to
remember her save a small picture of her father and a memorial in Caversham
church.

It seems that Thomas spent a good deal of his time in London and he was
living there when he courted and married his third wife, Mary North.
Everything about Thomas points to his having been a robust opportunist, but
in Mary North he met his match. She brought him a dowry of £3,000 on
condition he agreed not only to give her a jointure of £400 but to purchase land
in Berkshire and Oxfordshire to the tune of £200 a year for her eventual use.
They were married in the Charterhouse chapel in May 1677. The witness or
alledger, a fellow goldsmith,[d] gave Thomas's age as about forty; the captain
must have worn his fifty-three years with a flourish.

Mary was the youngest of the three daughters of Michael North, who had
been Master of the Society of Apothecaries. The elder girls had married[e] and

[c] Restoration of the gazebo began in 1979. Caversham Court, as the house was eventually
called, was demolished in 1933. The grounds are now a public garden; the stables are still
there and traces of the site of the house can be seen.

[d] Robert Cuthbert, citizen and goldsmith of London.

[e] Sarah North married into the Cox family, brewers of Southwark, from whom was

when her father died in 1674 he left her as his executrix, having every confidence in her sound business head. Michael North had suffered in the Civil War and had never regained his health; though elected Master in 1663 he had been unable to take up the appointment, but he did so when re-elected in 1666 – the year of the Great Fire; in which the Society's portrait of James I was destroyed. To commemorate his mastership he commissioned an artist, Matthew Snelling, to paint the reproduction of the lost portrait which now hangs in the Great Hall; and so that there should be no mistake about it left them a legacy of £20 to be paid a year after they had

> sett up the picture of King James in a most convenient place in their Hall and shall have putt underneath it within the said frame these words and letters following, – ex dono Michaelis North, Societatis Pharmaceuticae Magistri, Anno Salutis humanae MDCLXVI: and a sufficient security to my Executrix that the said Picture shall soe continue and remain.[3]

It has remained so, but the receipt for the legacy of £20, duly paid by the Master and Wardens on 3 November 1676, was only found recently, placed in John Loveday's account of his visit to the Great Hall in 1746. It proved also that this painting had been the gift of his great-grandfather.

Mary gave birth to a son in 1680, but it is significant that the terms of her husband's will, made some time before his death, did not leave Letitia to her care. He appointed instead his uncle Matthew's son,[f] whose wife, Frances, was descended from Charles I's Secretary of State, Sir Francis Windebank. Thomas may have conjectured some social advantages, or possibly he entered into a property deal, for he seems to have come to an arrangement with this Matthew that his son should marry Letitia as soon as the pair were old enough. All his plans came to nothing, however, for his daughter died suddenly in Matthew's house near Oxford when only ten years old. Her father survived her by but a few months and Mary was left to bring up her little boy, Thomas, alone. By the time John Loveday grew up he knew of scarcely any relations on his father's side of the family. Matthew's son had died and all communication with the goldsmiths, John and his son Joseph, ceased after the death of his grandmother, Mary, who was much more interested in the Norths.

Thomas had arranged an impressive funeral for himself and was buried in his own vault in St Peter's Church, Caversham, in 1681. Mary lived in some affluence, partly in the old parsonage and partly in London. Young Thomas grew up to be the weak son of a domineering mother and this in the end was his tragedy.

---

descended the famous Lady Cathcart of Tewin Water (who corresponded in her old age with her cousin, John Loveday). Judith married Matthias, the unsatisfactory brother of Antony Scattergood, the divine and scholar. See p. 268, n.z.

[f] The second Matthew matriculated at Oriel College and was admitted to the Inner Temple in 1673.

A near neighbour of Mrs Loveday was the famous preacher and divine, Dr Robert South. On the surface they were on good terms, but it is not surprising that two such indomitable characters should occasionally like to get the better of one another. John Loveday's daughter Penelope[g] recalled two anecdotes which she was told his grandmother had enjoyed recounting.

> When the celebrated Dr South lived at Caversham, he and my Great Grandmother Loveday were very intimate; and I have heard my Father mention her having told him that in the first year of her widowhood,[h] during the troublesome times, when the loyalists were at times equally burdened by King Charles's and the Rebel armies, – a regiment of the former marched into Reading, and were to be quartered there, at Caversham and other neighbouring villages upon private families as well as publicans. After their departure, Dr South called upon her to inquire how she had borne the trial, complaining at the same time of the noise and disturbance made in his house by the six turbulent soldiers who had been quartered upon him; and he was astonished at hearing her in return assure him that she and her family had been perfectly quiet, informing of her method of effecting it. My great-grandmother was very much the gentlewoman, and had ever a happy forecast of thought, so that she no sooner heard of what was impending than she wrote a well bred note to the Commanding Officer stating that as she was a widow, and the chief of her domestics were female, she had a great objection to admitting common soldiers alone into her house; but that she should be happy to receive as many Officers as her house would contain. In consequence of this, the Commander accepted her invitation, and one officer with him; and brought a couple of soldiers to attend upon them to spare any avoidable trouble in a private house; behaving at the same time in the most polite and considerate manner.

Her other story was rather less well bred.

> My Father heard from his grandmother Loveday that Dr South was travelling in a Stage Coach with a deformed woman who abused the Clergy in a most unqualified manner and said she would rather marry a Tinker than a Parson; to which Dr South replied 'Madam, you have made a very wise choice – you have brass enough to set him up and back enough to carry his pack.'

Dr South was not altogether the kind neighbour that he seemed and he was well aware that Mrs Loveday, who appeared to be doing very well for herself was paying only a small sum to Christ Church, his own college, for the lease of the rectory and the adjoining property, Toots Farm. In 1702 he handed

[g] Penelope Loveday, eldest of John Loveday's four children by his third marriage, married the Revd William Benwell in 1796 and the Revd Dr John Hind in 1808.

[h] It seems probable that the year was 1688 and the king James II.

some information about her affairs to John Brooks, the chapter clerk, 'in my Large Dining Room in Christ Church'. It included a very exact description of her estate and was entitled 'Some Writings concerning the Impropriate Rectory of Caversham in Oxfordshire held by Mrs Mary Loveday, relict of Mr Thomas Loveday, Citizen of London'.

> The Parsonage consists of tithes, glebe, large mansion house with summer house and orchard; another handsome house with a walled garden, large barn, stable, coachhouse, pigeon house, yards, and benefit of burial in the Chancel.

Mrs Loveday lived in the large mansion house, said he; the other house she let. Her portion was worth about £24 per annum as she made at least £10 or £12 yearly by the sale of fruit from her orchard. Also, he added,

> Hardly any Pigeon house (especially if but lately built as hers was) can be rated under £5 per annum.

He went into further details and considered that the fine should be £200, the previous fines of £100 and £120 having been a 'Scandalous under-rate'. He continued:

> I hope there will be some Course taken to prevent these and such-like Practices again in future; and if not it must be openly Protested against in Chapter, and the Protestation entered in the Chapter Book . . . there seems to be a Deeper mystery in this matter than I am aware of.[4]

A week later[5] he put the sum up to £250 as he had discovered she had 'screwed up to £15 per annum more' on her rents; but nothing was done to his satisfaction and it was actually nine years later than he sent another account of her estate with increased valuations, saying that 'In most Abatement of fines College and Church are generally much laughed at by the Tenants'.[6] Nevertheless, unperturbed by all these protests, the College remained a benign landlord. It really received (at any rate later in the century) a fine of about a year and a quarter's computed value of the property; the actual rent was nominal. In 1619 it was £18 a year. In 1799 it was £12 in money, nine quarters of wheat and twelve quarters of malt at their full price in the Oxford market.[7]

Mary had been left very well provided for and she was also a good manager and expected to get fair rents for her two farms, Toots and Lower Street, and to make a profit from her fruit. Perhaps the good doctor was a little jealous of her success. A note written by John Mead, her overseer or bailiff, in 1696 reads:

> When Mr Manesfild under tooke to looke after Madam Loveday's Garden thear was then standing and growing sixtey aprey Cock trees

with peaches and nectar a Boute all the Wales in the great Orchett and garden in the back sid of the house.[8]

Mansfield and his son Paul, were faithful and greatly respected members of the 'family of servants', with a span of service between them of over seventy years.

In 1703 Thomas Loveday married Sarah, daughter of William Lethieullier, one of a family of rich merchants trading with Turkey. They were descended from Huguenots who had come to Britain from Frankfurt about a hundred years earlier. One of William's brothers was the 'Sir John Lethulier' mentioned by Defoe in his *Tour through the Whole Island of Great Britain*,[9] a sheriff of London and grandfather of Smart Lethieullier, the antiquary and collector. Another brother, Sir Christopher, who married Jane Ducane, was the grandfather of Sarah Fetherstonhaugh of Uppark and of Sir James Burrow, Master of the Crown Office. William, who pronounced his name Letha*lear*, was the sixth of seven surviving children when their father died in 1679 leaving them jointly £38,071. 19s. 4d. He lived, rather more modestly than some of his brothers, with his family of two sons and five daughters until marriage removed most of them from the parental home at Clapham.[i] His wife, Mary, came from a background steeped in civic affairs; her father, Henry Powell, had been a merchant and John Loveday was intrigued when he came across some of Powell's letters to his father-in-law, Alderman William Daniel of London Bridge, in Hooke's *Philosophical Experiments and Observations*;[10] they gave graphic accounts of earthquakes at Balasore in India which had caused great damage to his ship and destruction inland on a vast scale. If there was a dearth of Lovedays there were Lethieullier relations in profusion – so much so that John and his sister, in spite of family gatherings, were never to know or even hear of many of their kinsmen.

Thomas and Sarah settled at Feens Manor in Berkshire, a property bought under the terms of the marriage settlement. Some time after 1711, the year of John's birth in London, they came to reside permanently at Caversham, while Mrs Mary Loveday moved to another house in the village.

If John had inherited from his paternal grandparent his independence of mind and positive and decisive attitudes to life, it was his mother who showed him both by example and tuition how to apply them within a Christian concept of thought and behaviour. From her he acquired those traits of honesty and fidelity which were always so apparent in him. Sarah had undergone some sort of conversion the year before he was born and the account of this period of her life is best told in her own touching words.

I Sarah Lethieullier was married on Thursday July 6, 1703, and was

---

[i] The house, known as Sir Peter Daniel's Great House, was rebuilt by him in 1690 and leased to the Lethieulliers by his widow after his death in 1700. Grafton Square was eventually built on the site. See Eric E. F. Smith, *Clapham*, 1976. Sir Peter was a son of Alderman William Daniel and half-uncle to Mrs Mary Lethieullier.

twenty years old the February before. Mr Loveday lacked a small matter of twenty four years of age. I and my husband went to Feenes to continue there on March 1, 1704. I count my life from on Good Friday, 1710, I then did promise to cast away all vanities and wholly to put my trust in God . . . I lay in of Jack at Cateaton Street over nigh St. Lawrence's Church by Guildhall on the fifth of February, 1711.

August 15 1711. After a long illness I on that day mended. My illness began a week after Jack was born. I give to the poor every year in memory of the great mercy I received from in recovering from so severe an illness. I do here set down what I have promised to my God, that by his help I will perform, lest I should at some time or other be drawn from it; which I hope I shall not so readily be, when I have under my own hand-writing . . . to keep every year a day about the middle of August with fasting and prayer; and I pray God that I may never forget the blessings I then received. The last Lodgings we had in London were taken in September, 1711 . . . Jack had the smallpox at these lodgings. Mr Loveday died the 6th of June, 1720. If he had lived to the 6th of July we should have been married seventeen years. I have had six boys and four girls; none lived beyond two years except John and Martha, Martha (Patty) was the only child that was christened at church which I think was a very great fault and I pray God forgive me that the rest were not. This was the youngest child born in 1717.[j]

John was baptized at home by the minister of St Lawrence, Old Jewry, two days after his birth.

It would be unfair to Thomas to portray him as a man devoid of religious feeling. His first present to his wife was Robert Nelson's *Feasts and Fasts*[11] (a suitable gift as Nelson's father had also been a merchant trading with Turkey), and his volumes of William Sherlock's works on Death and Justice were marked in many places with his private notes. But there can be no doubt that, apart from the misery caused by the deaths of eight of their children, something had upset their marriage, possibly his addiction to strong liquor. The only other explanation for the extraordinary will he made in 1716, four years before his death, must be the extreme domination over him of his mother. It may have been because Sarah was already provided for that he left her only the contents of the houses and her jewellery, 'coach, horses, harness and furniture thereof', while his property and all his securities were to go to his children or his mother and after them to his cousin Joseph and other relations in London; but what must have been deeply hurtful to Sarah was the fact that he not only made his mother executrix but gave her sole guardianship of the children, which was to pass on her death to a man quite outside the family. In a codicil added in 1719 he revoked this clause and made

[j] Sarah's early diaries were transcribed by her granddaughter Penelope and the original spelling is lost.

Sarah executrix and guardian 'in the room of my honoured Mother Mary Loveday who is now very antient and not able to undertake the trouble'.

The cause of Thomas's death in 1720 in his forty-first year was said to be dropsy and yellow jaundice, but hard drinking had undermined his health; the truth was eventually made known in those indiscreet diaries of Thomas Hearne, the Oxford antiquary,[12] who became a great friend of John. Sarah's problems, however, were not yet over. Her mother-in-law so distrusted her that she had made a will in which, should the children not survive her, everything, including the old rectory, should go to her own kinsmen in London. The only mention of Sarah was that she should hold the plate, linen and jewellery for Martha and the old gold for John. A codicil seems to have been prompted by panic; if Sarah remarried, the items she held in trust for the children must be delivered at once to Mary's cousin and executor, Cellus Thornbury.

The conclusion of this tale of jealousy and suspicion was happier: the old lady – perhaps after tears and reconciliation – added in 1722 a further codicil which made Sarah executrix jointly with their attorney, Alexander Staples of New Windsor, who was to be a firm friend and adviser for many years. Mary died in London in 1724 'of an asthma' and Sarah was free at last to take entire charge of her family.

The practice of keeping children in their place undoubtedly screened them from much that went on, but John must have been affected by the continual illnesses of his parents as well as their sorrows. He left no criticism in writing of his father, but no words of praise either; the subject was a closed book except for his one confidence to Hearne. He seems to have had a happy relationship with his grandmother; of his mother, his friend and counsellor until her death in 1759, he could never speak too highly.

One of his earliest memories – he could not have been more than five years old – was of meeting Dr South, 'who lived in the same village'. His parents had probably moved to Caversham about this time, for when he was six he was sent to Reading School as a day boy. An anecdote of his early childhood was told by William Benwell,[k] the young protégé who acted as a sort of Boswell to him in his old age and married his daughter Penelope after his death.

> I have heard him relate with great pleasantry that when he was a very little boy, his mother had a great intimacy with a Mrs Kent, of whose son he had frequently heard mention as a very *wild* young man. This lady being one day at his mother's house, he took an opportunity while there was a silence and asked her 'Pray Madam, how does your wild son do?' His mother was in great confusion at such a question and was going to beat him but was stopped by the Lady who said she knew the reason of

[k] Benwell collected many anecdotes from John Loveday himself and the family, as well as from his own observations.

the question and asked him if he had not been reading *Valentine and Orson*. He owned he had read it the day before, and from having heard her son called *wild* he concluded he must be the same kind of being as Orson.

(In the early French romance Valentine was brought up as a knight at court while his brother Orson was reared by a bear to be a wild man of the woods.)

Although John was a day scholar at Reading School for a year or two before he became a weekly boarder in August 1718, he did not travel to and from Caversham every day; this might have been difficult, if not dangerous, as the road, before it was improved in 1724, was in places lower than the River Thames.[13] When the locks were 'flashed' the water was so deep that the horses had to swim and when the floods were out the road was sometimes impassable for days.

It may seem strange that his parents, having lost eight children, should send such a young son to be cared for outside their jurisdiction, but they had every confidence in the headmaster. As John was not old enough to board at school he lodged in the house of Mr Thomas Glory, a master in charge of writing. Glory was still teaching John this subject ten years later, for he was paid for a year's writing in May 1727 by his pupil himself, who was said by his grandson to have 'treated his old master kindly by occasionally inviting him to Caversham'. Glory's charge for board and lodging was £3 a quarter.

Reading School was endowed by Henry VII as a Free School in 1486 when it may have replaced a school even older than the Abbey. Although its fortunes have fluctuated throughout the centuries, often in conjunction with the abilities of a particular headmaster, it has survived all reverses and now has excellent new buildings on a different site. At the time of John's arrival its star was in the ascendant under the efficient direction of Mr Haviland John Hiley. Kindly and imaginative, he was also a good business man and some time after his arrival in 1716 he realized that it would advance the progress of the school and his own pocket if he were to set up a boarding house for the sons of the local gentry. This project is said to have met with some criticism from the natives of Reading who thought he was taking places in the school from their own children, but this does not seem to have been the case. Hiley still took day boys and simply enlarged the school to include his own boarders. When John arrived Hiley was living in a small house on the north side of the Forbury, but later he built a much larger one, still in the Forbury but situated on the Vastern Lane. As soon as he was old enough John became a boarder in Mr Hiley's house and was very happy there. Mrs Hiley, a daughter of Alderman Terrell of Reading, was a friend of Sarah's; at this time she had a nursery full of small children, but though several of them lived for some years only four grew up and of these three died before their parents. The years John spent with the Hileys brought about an intimacy with that pleasant family which lasted all their lives. He himself was a bright intelligent boy, rather small in size. A German artist, Schwartz, who painted him in 1721 at the age of ten, caught the alert expression in his blue eyes in spite of the disadvantage of a flowing wig beneath which his head had been shaved for the occasion. Patty, who was only four, was dressed in a low-cut gown and there is not much life in her bewildered little face.

The schoolboys were surrounded by scenes of antiquity – the ruins of the Abbey, the Forbury itself which had been one of the great courts, the Plummeries, formerly Abbey meadows, and not least their lofty old schoolroom built on the site of the Friary. Close by was the church of St Laurence where Mr Hiley's pupils sat in the north chancel as according to tradition they had always done. Later the headmaster and his boys were allotted seats in a new gallery[14] and so were the girls at the school run by the Misses Anne and Elizabeth Eades which was also situated in the Forbury on the same side as the Infirmary. Patty became a boarder at this school as soon as she was old enough. There seems to be no connection between this establishment and the famous Abbey school to which Jane Austen was sent towards the end of the century and which was over and adjoining the Abbey gateway. Mr Hiley told John in 1734 that the girls' school had been the house of the King's Equerry and his own house the stables belonging to the Abbey which was renowned for its great horses.

Archbishop Laud had appointed three Visitors to the school, the Vice-Chancellor of the University of Oxford, the President of St John's College and the Warden of All Souls, and had left money to defray their expenses. Here they came every third year to hear speeches and see a play performed by the scholars. This was always a great event and John must have felt proud when he and his friend Charles Hopson were chosen to read speeches on 27 October 1725 which Mr Hiley had wisely written for them. Even the fact that Dr Delaune of St John's was absent and Dr Gardiner of All Souls was known to be a Whig did not detract from the occasion. Hopson, who lived at Beenham, near Reading, was John's closest friend until his early death in 1749.

John was confirmed in 1726 at Checkendon by Dr John Potter, the Bishop of Oxford, and this was probably the year in which the school put on a performance of *Cato*[1] in which he took the leading part. William Benwell remembered a story he used to tell about it.

> One day while this Performance was preparing, a Gentleman happening to come into the hall where the boys were dining and Mr L's plate being well filled as he always had a great appetite, the Master immediately put his hand on Mr L's head and repeated the following lines from his part in the play:

[1] Addison's tragedy, first produced in 1713, had become very popular.

> Dost thou love watchings, abstinence and toil,
> Laborious Virtues all? learn them from Cato.

This account of himself I have heard him relate with great pleasantry.

Now that he was growing up he needed suitable clothes and his mother kept a careful account of her expenditure on his wardrobe. Her spelling was unique.[15]

May 17. 1726. Boight for Jack a Sute of Druget.

for 13 yards of Druget at 2s. 8d.	1	14	8
for 6 yards of Shalloon at 1s. 8d.	0	10	0
for 4 yards & a half of dimity	0	4	6
for 1 yard of Wading	0	0	9
for a pocket skin	0	1	0
for buttons silks & Mohare &c.	0	13	8
The taleer had for making it	0.	12.	0
	3	16	7
for helepeceing 3 pare of shues	0	1	7
for a pare of glowes	0	1	2
For riding stockings &c.	0	2	4 ½
for putting new tungs to a pare of buckles	0	0	4
for new strops to a pare of shoes	0	0	3
for soleing to pare of shues & Helepeceing one pare	0	2	6
for a Pome for a wig	0	0	3 ½
for a new wig	1	10	0
for new mounting a wig	0	2	6

It was in February 1727 that John began to keep a diary, written in small pocket books known as Rider's Almanacks which he used till his death. He left directions for them to be burnt, an order which his son John, finding it hard to obey, left to his own son Thomas to carry out.

> But I would wish them to be first carefully looked over by my son Thomas who may wish to collect from them anecdotes of his never to be forgotten Grandfather; and then by all means let the said volumes be burnt.   1808.

Fortunately Thomas only obeyed the letter of the law. He carefully copied out the diaries and the notebooks containing lists of books and pamphlets given and received over the years, and then he destroyed them. Even so, finding himself unable to deny them to posterity entirely, he kept a few pages. From these remnants it can be seen that he did not copy the items of national and political news with which John began each day and which showed that his mind was not entirely concentrated on antiquities. The news entries in a few early pages reveal a mature understanding of current events at the age of sixteen: he was especially interested in the disposition of troops, the deliberations of the European allied heads of state and the revenues of the new king, George II. This concern with financial affairs, inherited from both his Loveday grandparents, was part of his make-up and explains his future preoccupation with the salaries and stipends of the clergy.

Three events now occurred which were indicative of the shape his life was to take. He was sent on a preliminary visit to Oxford, he went to the West Country with his headmaster and he wrote his first letter to Thomas Hearne.

He rode up to Oxford with his schoolfellow Thomas Baber, whose father, 'an admirable Grecian and polite scholar', lived at Sunninghill.''' They lodged at the Greyhound and were shown the sights by several Reading friends who were at the University. Two of these, Peter Zinzan and Phanuel Bacon, were older than John. Zinzan, six years his senior, had been a pupil at Reading School, his family, originally Italian, having lived in Berkshire for several generations. A little shy with strangers he was fluent and entertaining among his friends, who, while sometimes deploring his natural indolence, were devoted to him. Phanuel Bacon, a Fellow of Magdalen, was the son of the vicar of St Laurence and well known to the boys. They could not have wished for a more amusing companion that 'Phanny'; he had already gained a reputation as a wit and at the age of twenty-seven was known as a writer of light verse. His poem 'The Snipe''' recounted a day's shooting with Zinzan (disguised as 'Peter' with himself as 'The Friar') who had slipped a snipe into his friend's pocket of which he was unaware and it lay there undiscovered for several weeks. 'The Friar' was just about to commit suicide owing to the inexplicable ostracism to which he was subjected by his friends, when he luckily discovered the cause. Phanny was an unashamed punster with a talent perhaps better appreciated by his own generation than it would be today. His later comedies are not remarkable but he had a lively mind and was not the 'weak man and liar' that Hearne called him after only one meeting. Pope admired him and is known to have thanked him for his poem 'The Kite', while suggesting a few alterations.[16] Perhaps his reputation can be enhanced by a letter which John Loveday wrote in 1756 to the girl who was to become his third wife, Penelope Forrest.

My delightful Pen, I bless God that you gather strength; may you go on from strength to strength! As to myself, I doubt not but to receive

---

''' John Baber inherited Sunninghill Park from his father-in-law, Sir Thomas Draper. Thomas Baber sold it in 1769.
'' One of the poems included in *The Oxford Sausage*, ed. Thomas Warton, 1764.

improvement both to my body and soul by an union with you. My best services to your good mother. Mr Pope thanked old Mr Bacon of Reading for begetting such a son as Phanny, who cut that joke on our loves which Jenny Birt told you of; why should I not follow Pope's example and thank your mother for bearing you? However I honour her on that and many other accounts. [17]

Besides these older men there was Charles Hopson who was already at St John's and who took them to see the great new palace at Blenheim on the first of many visits. There it stood in all its Baroque glory, an incredible sight to John who had never seen anything so grand. After visiting the Theatre, where they heard the Professor of Music, Richard Goodson, play and listened to a speech by Zinzan as Senior Collector, the boys returned to school to find the floods between Caversham and Reading higher than ever before. John applied himself to his work with increased vigour and began to buy books in earnest. It was only now, by borrowing his works from Mr Hiley, that he was introduced to Shakespeare and he began to read Homer and *Macbeth* at the same time. Antiquarian works by Peck and Kennett, Collier on the English stage, [18] Cumberland's *Essay on Jewish Weights and Measures,* [19] Walker's *Sufferings of the Clergy* [20] and Latin and French dictionaries, together with books on the classics, geography and theology, were the beginning of his celebrated library and cost him at this time over five guineas.

It was not very difficult in those days to procure an extra half-holiday at Reading School. All a boy had to do was to present a book to the library.

Feb. 9. Had an holyday in the Afternoon for Plato's Book on the Immortality of the Soul, given by Mr Peareth.
Sept. 13. Had an Holyday in the Afternoon upon Keatinges Junior giving 1os. 6d. to buy a book – Gay's Fables.

There were holidays for Camden's *Britannia,* Gordon's *Geographical Grammar* ('Richards's Book') and on another occasion when 'several of the Monitors joyned Money to buy a book for the Library'. When Ben Burton gave the issues of *The Spectator* John spent the whole half-holiday reading them in school while the others went out to enjoy themselves at play; he was blissfully happy and certainly did not think the occasion wasted. The arrangement was a clever move on the part of Mr Hiley. Holidays were harmless and the parents could well afford to stock the library. The visitation of the Vice-Chancellor was also an obvious excuse for a holiday and so was the going-out feast for the mayor. Then there was the commemoration of the Reading Fight when King James's troops were defeated, and the bells of the three churches rang out as they had done since the year 1688, [21] This always earned a holiday as well as the task of describing the incident in blank verse.

In March 1727 Mr Hiley asked Mrs Loveday if he might take John to Bath and Bristol for two weeks; Charles Hopson was down from Oxford and would accompany them. Hiley was born in Stapleton, then a village near Bristol, and had some land in Somerset. He was also the pluralist vicar of Saltford and eventually died there. He took the boys to Keynsham to meet his patron, Mr Bridges of the Priory House, and then to visit his various relations and friends. It was John's first taste of the joys of riding thirty miles or so on consecutive days.

His sights were now fixed on Oxford. On his return from the Bristol trip he asked Peter Zinzan if he would be his tutor the following year and then on 13 April he wrote for the first time to Thomas Hearne the antiquary at St Edmund Hall, Oxford, of whom he had heard a great deal. It was almost certainly Hopson who afforded him the excuse for writing.

> Sir, The Gentleman who took in for me a subscription of the work you are now publishing, acquainted me with your desire to know something concerning the quondam Chappel on Caversham Bridge. I can give you but a very imperfect account of it; but such as it is I willingly submit to your perusal. The person who can best inform you is Mr Brigham of Canon End in this parish whose ancestors were once in possession of the greatest part of it and from whose writings we might (as I am very well assured) have a satisfactory account of it. But as long as county squires are suspicious of every one, and especially of the curious inquirers, you must not expect any information from that quarter. The father of the present possessor I once asked about it, who told me briefly, that it was dedicated to St. Ann, and that from thence the Religious went at certain times to a well now in a hedge between the field called the Mount and the lane called Priest Lane, which is supposed to have its name from their going through it to this well . . . He likewise informed me that there was in the memory of man a large ancient oak just by this well which was also had in good veneration. This is the whole of his answer, and the son inheriting his father's suspicious temper as well as his Estate, it is vain to desire a more particular account from him. About twelve years since an inhabitant of the Parish observing what a good foundation there was still remaining of the Chappel built him an house upon it. As pitiful as this account is, I rely upon your good nature to a young lover of antiquities, who is far from thinking what he has said will be any satisfaction to you, but whose only motive to trouble you with this letter was the observance of your commands, though at the same time he was sure to expose himself as an ignorant schoolboy . . .

He concluded by sending Hearne a few more notes and by offering to consult old people in the parish if he was told what to ask them.[22]

If Hearne was surprised to receive this letter he must at least have known who John was. Feens was in the parish of White Waltham where Hearne had been brought up, and where his father had formerly been sacristan for many years. He replied on 21 April but the lettter has not been preserved. John had·

laid the foundation of an association which was to mean a great deal to them both.

The school holidays fell in May. With no worse task than the translation of Psalm 68 into blank verse, John took himself off to stay with his schoolfellow John Peareth, whose father held the living of Aldworth in Berkshire, having come originally from Northumberland where he still had many connections. He had an odd way of ending every sentence with the sound 'hugh', a habit which amused John but passed unnoticed by his friend. They listened to the sermons in church surrounded by the famous 'giants', the effigies of the de Beche family which had been defaced by Cromwell's men but which are still so remarkable. These certainly appealed to John's growing taste for antiquities, but it was the oyster fossils on Lowbury Hill which really fascinated him and he went back to see them whenever he was in the vicinity. John Peareth, sound, practical and entertaining, was to be his companion on some of his tours.

In June an event occurred which shocked the whole school. Robert, a younger son of Sir Robert Rich of Sonning, was drowned in the river where the boys were playing. His brother Daniel jumped in after him but was unable to save him and was brought out himself 'near to death'. Mr Hiley did not help matters by swooning away on the bank. Robert's body was not found for twenty-four hours and he was buried the following day, six of his schoolfellows, including John, acting as pall-bearers. More happily, in ten days' time the bells were pealing out to celebrate the accession of George II and it was on this auspicious day[o] that Mr Hiley suddenly realized that John had a turn for antiquities; not that he had a great deal of time for them as, besides the normal classical curriculum, he was now studying French with the new master, Giles Bellai, attending lectures and learning to dance. He was old enough to make firm and lasting friendships with two of the ushers – Richard Wooddeson, who became the well-known headmaster of the school at Kingston-upon-Thames, and Deodatus Bye, who later followed the same profession at Maidstone.

There was plenty to do during the holidays. John was frequently to be found in Benjamin Shirley's bookshop where he was a very good customer. Shirley, who was also an auctioneer, was getting old and John would help him out by writing his letters. Another favourite haunt was the barber's shop belonging to Simon Walcroft, the parish clerk of Caversham. There were purchases to be made there too, such as a bottle of scent for Peareth after his visit, but what he most enjoyed was listening to Walcroft play on his pipe and tabor and he often went there just for this purpose.

Church of course he never missed and Saturday and Sunday evenings were usually spent with the curate of Caversham,[p] Richard Jekyll, a man he

---

[o] 16 June 1727.

[p] Caversham, a Christ Church living, had a perpetual curate for many years – sometimes called vicar. The parish obtained rectorial rights in 1916.

respected. On one of these occasions Jekyll said to him, 'My dear boy, I have been in sad spirits and strongly tempted to make away with myself.' John knew that he had mentioned these fears to other people and he had his answer ready. 'Indeed, sir,' he replied, 'why I think there are many more agreeable ways of going to the devil than that.' This had the intended effect of startling Jekyll into a more rational frame of mind and giving his young friend a thoughtful look he relapsed into silence. Possibly he had been depressed by an affair of the heart, for later that year he married. He continued to tend his parish for a further two years and was then presented to a living in Lincolnshire.

John's mother realized he needed masculine society and he was encouraged to bring his schoolfriends home. She herself moved in a comfortable social circle; she had her own coach, a luxury not enjoyed by every widowed lady in those days, and she was able to go about freely – calling on her friends Lady Rich, Mrs Lybbe or Lady Cadogan at Caversham Park. She was an excellent housekeeper and her books of recipes and cures for various ailments suggest an original mind. She liked to keep open house (a characteristic of Caversham as long as the Lovedays lived there) but, apart from John and Paul Mansfield, it was a feminine establishment. This was apparently too much for one of John's friends, who liked coming to the warm room over the kitchen, but only on certain conditions. Benwell recalled:

> While he was at Reading School, under Mr Hiley, he had a school-fellow named Alexander, the son of a butcher in the town, whom the boys nicknamed 'Ogles' because he had a power of seeing on each side of him without moving his head and would often take an opportunity of looking over the boys who were writing their exercises next to him, in order to see if they had made any mistakes; and if they did, being himself an excellent scholar, he would always set them right. One day Mr L. says to him 'Ogles, you must come over to Caversham and dine with me.' 'No,' says he, 'I won't, – you have women there.' 'Well,' replied Mr L. 'and have you no women at home?' 'None,' said Ogles, 'but my mother; I do not mind her, but other women I'd rather not see.' At last, however, he agreed to dine with him, on condition that they should dine upstairs and that the servants should not bring the dinner into the room, but should set it down on the outside of the door. This was accordingly done and our young heroes conveyed it into the room and enjoyed a comfortable dinner without interruption.

> Though this Ogles was beloved by the whole school, yet they were continually obliged to complain to the master of him, and to have him turned out in the middle of the room. The case was this: Ogles' father in the summer nights would always keep his shop open for the benefit of the cold air, and have his meat watched. Ogles was often appointed to watch with the men, and as he lay upon the shop-board, he would come

to school in the morning with pieces of fat and blood sticking to his cloaths, which caused such a smell that nobody would sit near him. He was afterwards apprenticed to a Bookseller, but died early in his apprenticeship.

John was a devoted and popular member of the Lethieullier family circle. His mother's closest sister was Mrs Mary Tooke, whose husband, Edmund, was Clerk to the Salters' Company; through the marriage of their daughter Anne with Robert Bootle they were to be ancestors of the notable Bootle-Wilbraham family. Then there was Aunt Anne who had married the immensely rich Sir Richard Hopkins and lived at Low Leyton in Essex; they were extremely kind to the children, having none of their own, and Patty really had a second home there. Sir Richard was Governor of the London Assurance Company and a sub-Governor of the South Sea Company as well as being an alderman of the Lime Street Ward in London. The fourth sister, Elizabeth, was unmarried and popular with her nephews and nieces. Martha, the youngest, was married to the rector of Tooting, the Revd Nicholas Brady. Old Mr and Mrs Lethieullier must have missed their son John who had settled in Ireland after a career in the army[q] but young William was a different consideration altogether. Like his father he was trading with Turkey but there the resemblance ended. He was always getting into scrapes and his behaviour in Aleppo in 1724 had occasioned the following letter from Abraham Stanyan, formerly Envoy Extraordinary to the Porte, to Robert Walpole. He wrote from Constantinople on 15 February 1724:

> I have received the honour of your Letter of the 13th December about Mr William Lethieullier of Aleppo, and shall always obey your Commands with Pleasure. But as to this particular Case, I find you have heard but one side; for I have been obliged to take Cognizance of this Difference and do assure you that Mr Lethieullier has been egregiously in the wrong in his behaviour to the Consul and that what the Consul did, was only in his own Defence. This appears by Mr Lethieullier's Declaration under his own hand, wherein he confesses himself to have been in the wrong and desires the Consul to forgive what is past, which he accordingly did, and so their Difference was made up and they are good Friends again. However you may be assured I will do all Friendly Offices to any Person you shall please to recommend to me and be glad to give you a proof of the perfect Respect with which I have the honour to be, Sir, your most humble and most obedient Servant.[23]

Whatever William may have done there was a great family welcome awaiting him when he returned to England in September 1727. John went up to London for the occasion and after staying at Clapham he went on to visit the

[q] He had been a captain on half-pay with the regiment commanded by the Duke of Ormonde in Ireland.

Hopkinses at Low Leyton. He had been given complete liberty at school and
during his last term he was allowed to go to Caversham whenever he pleased.
Uncle William came down by the stage coach in October and was met at The
Cardinal's Cap in Reading by his nephew. The next week was a social whirl as
William insisted on calling on all their grander acquaintance and as a final fling
took the family to the Reading Assembly. This slightly disreputable but
affectionate uncle was probably rather good for John, who was after all soon to
leave the tender care of his mother and his headmaster to fend for himself at the
University. In December he heard that he was now the tenant of rooms which
Zinzan had procured for him.

So 1727 drew to a close, a happy year in which there was much to remember:
the bustle of the by-election when Lord and Lady Fane had been in and out of
the school and the neighbouring houses gathering votes for his lordship who
was defeated by Mr Recorder Pottenger; the time when the school was
measured for enlargement and the Recorder had personally solicited a holiday
for the boys; natural phenomena such as strange lights in the sky in March and
the earthquake which John recorded at Reading on 1 October at 3 p.m. There
had been the boys' nutting day in August, the fire on Knowle Hill in November
when he had watched the glow of the burning furze, and the homely
excitements at Christmas when the village women came 'a-gooding'. Besides
all this there was the interest of his ever-expanding library which had
substantially increased in size by the end of the year; Among the volumes was
his first gift of a book from its author – *The Noble Race of Shinkin*, in English,
Latin and Greek, which Tom Baber had brought as a very special present from
his father.

Oxford and Hearne
1728 – 1729

Early on the morning of 11 February 1728 a small cavalcade set out from
Reading and took the road for Oxford. Mr Hiley, devoted as ever, was on his
way to deliver John Loveday into the arms of his future Alma Mater. For good
measure he took along with them his own son Thomas, an engaging and
whimsical lad of thirteen who was to enter Magdalen College three years later.
The party also included Charles Hopson and Dr John Merrick of Reading,
friend and physician to them all. In spite of the rigours of the wintry day
Merrick was determined to put them on their way as far as Benson where they
would stop for refreshment.

By a fortunate chance John's seventeenth birthday had fallen only six days
before his departure for Oxford, so that the new clothes which his mother
considered suitable for his age could also do justice to his status as a gentleman
commoner of Magdalen College. His slight figure was clad for the first time
in a red-rug greatcoat; his boots at fourteen shillings were not as expensive as
his manly new wig which cost thirty-seven and sixpence, but they were
worthy of the solid silver spurs which embellished them. As the party rode
along he had time to contemplate the excitements of the next few days; they
were to lodge at the Greyhound inn that night, after he had visited the
President, Dr Edward Butler, to be entered at his college. Next day Lady
Rich would bring Daniel from Sonning to be entered at St John's and on 13
February they would attend the matriculation ceremony together before the
Vice-Chancellor, Dr Mather. Then he would move into his new rooms in
college where Zinzan would join him. During the previous month two of the

Fellows, Dr Thomas Jenner and Philip Vaughan of Reading, had visited Caversham and had given his mother and himself all the necessary instructions as to procedure; so he had few problems, there was no need for apprehension and he had enough friends at Oxford already to ensure him plenty of congenial society.

Uppermost in his mind was the thought of meeting Thomas Hearne in person. During December he had read with care the Preface and Appendix to Hearne's *Adam de Domerham*, published that year and on 9 January he had written again, not forgetting to remind him of his own imminent arrival at the University.

I have took all imaginable Pains to get the Queries you sent me answered; but the oldest People in the Parish are intirely in the Dark as to that Respect; none but Mr Brigham can give an account of 'em, whose Character I sent you in my Last; I can but own myself extremely obliged to you for taking Notice of that impertinent Epistle; had I not Hopes this might be of some Service to you, I would not have troubled you with it. You must know then, Sir, the Charters you published with *Adam de Domerham* have put me upon an Enquiry after such like Writings; one I have already got, relating to the Priory of Merton in Surrey;[a] a Copy of which I now send you and will bring you the Original with the next Lent to Oxford, when I shall be proud of waiting upon you with that and a few Grecian and Roman Coins which I have collected upon reading your Preface to the 2nd vol. of *Ductor Historicus*.[1] Here follows the Charter . . .

John then described the seal and concluded

But of this enough. If the account of this Writing does not detain you from things of greater Moment, I shall think myself very happy in having an opportunity to subscribe myself – Your very humble Servant, John Loveday.[2]

Hearne had replied on 17 January:

I was very glad to find in your Letter of the 5th the Copy of an old Charter relating to the Abbey of Merton, especially since I think that it is not already printed. 'Tis a common thing to have Charters without dates . . . I am well pleased, that you are in quest of other Monuments of this nature, and that you also lay out some part of your time in picking up old Coyns, by the help of which many particulars in History may be settled, tho' not so well as from Marbles in which there's more erudition. As you are near Reading, I could wish you would, (at least by way of diversion)

---

[a] This had been given to John by a schoolfellow, William Grover. It came from the papers of John Deane of Mattingley. The name is given as Groves in Hearne's *Collections*, vol. IX, 5 January 1728.

get what historical Accounts you can (if not already printed) about that
Town and the famous Abbey where there are many Registers of the
Abbey, but I know not whether there be any in the Hands of the
neighbouring Gentry. King Edward IV soon after he had married with
the Lady Elizabeth Wyderville, appeared in the Abbey Church of
Reading, and his Queen was led through the Church in a publick manner
by two Great Nobles; after which there were publick Rejoycings in
Reading. If there be any historical Notes concerning the Affairs of that
time (when there was a Parliament also held in Reading) in any of your
Friends' Hands, a short detail of them would be acceptable to, Sir, Your
most humble Servant Tho: Hearne.[3]

When all the arrangements were completed and John had settled into his
rooms, he was able early on 19 February to knock on Hearne's door at St
Edmund Hall, bearing with him the Merton Charter. Face to face with the
antiquary who had been occupying his thoughts for nearly a year, he saw a
middle-aged man of a rather corpulent figure; his face was wide with strong
features, a slightly tilted nose and a generous mouth. The eyes were dark and
alert and he wore his own hair, thick and dark, to his shoulders.

Three days later John was searching every bookseller's shop in Oxford in
order to buy all his works. Quick on the mark, Hearne had already contrived
the boy's subscription to his lately published *Thomas de Elmham*[4] and had sent
the book round to John's rooms on the 20th. That night he described their
meeting in his diary.

Last Saturday called upon me, and staid with me a great while, in the
forenoon, Mr John Loveday, Gentleman Commoner of Magd. Coll.
Oxon, of which he was entered this Lent Term. He was born at
Caversham in Oxfordshire, where his Father, Mr Thomas Loveday, is
buried, having shortened his days by hard drinking as his son told me.

The said young Mr Loveday is an ingenious Gentleman and takes
great delight in Antiquities. He hath a Collection of old Coins (some of
which he shewed me) and collects curious Papers and Books. He went to
School at Reading, his Master being Mr Haviland John Hiley, who took
his Master of Arts Degree as a Member of Balliol College May 27. 1714.
He said he believed his said Master (whom I know not) is as good a
Schoolmaster as any in England. Mr Thomas Loveday (Father of this
young Mr Loveday) was several years at Feenes in the Parish of White
Waltham, near Maidenhead in Berks, having bought that Estate, which
(as his Son told me) is now the joynture of his Widow, the mother of this
young Loveday.[5]

Two days later John was back again in order to lend Hearne Francis Peck's
Academia Tertia Anglicana which had appeared in 1727 and which the recipient
now declared to be 'one of the most strange, injudicious, conceited

Rhapsodies that ever I saw in my Life'.[6] Hearne was in good form and as John
talked with him on that warm and sunny February day he fell even further
under his spell. He was shown all his medals, found himself subscribing to the
Black Book[7] and stayed even longer than the time before.

Whatever it was about Hearne that so fascinated his young admirer it cannot
only have been respect for his undoubted gifts as an antiquary. There must
have been something in the man's character which induced John to confide the
secret of his father's death upon so slight an acquaintance. Some quality in each
of them appealed to the other, but the older man – now in his fiftieth year – was
rather more wary of embarking on a new friendship. He has been called by one
of his biographers[b] 'a hearty friend, a hearty foe and a hearty worker'. He did
not lack friends; indeed he had several in high places in Oxford alone and he
needed them to bolster up his self-esteem which had suffered many reverses
during his life at the University. That he was a hearty foe is evident from the
invective in his pocket books, though his letters and probably his conversation
were civil enough. He thought of himself, and not without reason, as a much
maligned man; sensitive and nervous, he kept his wounds open with constant
attention.

Hearne's ability as a boy had earned him the patronage of the antiquary and
non-juror Francis Cherry of Shottesbrook, who sent him to school and then to
his own college, St Edmund Hall. Hearne was deeply grateful and always
thought of that brave and charming man as the greatest friend he ever had.
With the help of Bodley's Librarian, John Hudson, he was appointed
sub-librarian at the Bodleian and found it his spiritual home, holding
simultaneously the offices of Superior Beadle and Archi-Typographus and
working tirelessly at cataloguing the books and coins; but when it became
necessary for him to take the Oath of Abjuration on the accession of George I
he utterly refused to do so as it entailed renouncing his non-juring principles. In
order to get rid of him it was decreed that his two posts could not be held
simultaneously. He immediately resigned one of them, but Hudson was now
determined to force him out of the Library. He changed the locks so that
Hearne could not get in and then accused him of failing in his duties. Hearne's
career as a librarian was finished, but he had his own resources and friends who
offered him other appointments. These he refused as it would have meant
taking the hated Oath; he retreated to his rooms in college and other men 'ate
his bread' in the Bodleian.

No one was a more faithful friend to those who liked and trusted him and
only those who had strong Tory principles did; to Hearne these were the
honest men and no invective was bad enough in his secret diaries for Whigs or
courtiers – categories which included most of the bishops. None of this was
likely to trouble John who had been brought up as a Tory and would remain
so for the rest of his life; the fact that the University of Oxford was at this time

[b] Dr H. E. Salter.

still a great Tory stronghold suited his political outlook very well. Gradually he was to be drawn into Hearne's coterie and to consort with men older than himself – a piece of good fortune which did not come the way of every youth in his first year at Oxford.

Hearne must have felt gratified by John's obvious admiration; and he saw, too, that he could become a very useful companion. He himself was ageing and could no longer walk thirty miles or so to look at a ruin or read an epitaph. Here was a young enthusiast who, if encouraged, might well take over a great deal of this kind of research. Friendship, cooperation and assistance had been offered on the scroll of the Merton Charter and these Hearne accepted. John visited him again in February and March; in April he 'wrote over some books in the Library for Mr Hearne' and then the term was over and he had to return to Caversham.

Meanwhile he had been making friends of his own age as well as buying books, attending auctions and settling into his new way of life which according to his grandson he did 'without the least agitation owing to his enviable disposition'. The first of his new Oxford friends who remained so for life was Robert Lowth, later Bishop of London, who came over from New College to drink tea with John and his companions and stayed on to read sermons to them, a not unusual form of entertainment among the young demies with whom John, although not one himself, associated. William Derham of St John's (and later its President) was soon a constant companion although he was older; born in 1702 he had been up for seven years and was working for his M.A. degree, which unlike the B.A. degree entailed a certain amount of application. A less reliable acquaintance was Henry Dodwell who had been admitted gentleman commoner from Magdalen Hall some two years earlier. He was about ten years older than John and well known to Hearne; his father, the non-juror and scholar Henry Dodwell the elder, had been one of Hearne's heroes. The son Henry, unlike his brother William who was entirely estimable, had embraced with fervour the controversial heresy of deism which denied the revelation of God in Christ. Two years later he and his associates carried their beliefs to a point of blasphemy which resulted in their expulsion;[8] but at this stage he was so well thought of in the College as to have been invited early in May to use the Fellows' Common Room instead of that allotted to gentlemen commoners.[c] John must have felt complimented when Dodwell invited him to 'drink a bottle' in the Fellows' Common Room to celebrate the event on the very first day. If his real intention was to convert John to deism he was in for a disappointment; John was always a committed and faithful son of the Church of England even though, being as Hearne said a curious young man, he wanted to understand all opinions and doctrines. But Dodwell may have had some influence on his reading, which included John Edwards's works against

[c] Henry Dodwell was not a Fellow.

atheism and controversies between Hoadly and Snape. On the assumption that a non-juror's son could not be wholly corrupt Hearne blamed the Magdalen librarian, Henry William Cane, for misleading Dodwell, saying that he put 'vile scandalous books . . . into the Undergraduates' Library of Magdalen College on purpose to seduce and pervert young men'.[9] This was probably unfair to Cane who shortly afterwards was presented to the living of Selborne. John, spending so much time in the library, saw a good deal of him. He himself was buying books on orthodox theology and by the end of the year he was busy sorting out his volumes 'against Arianism'.

His classical education was merely formal and he did not occupy himself with it unduly; but the facilities were there for educating himself in other ways if he chose to look for them in books and conversation. Zinzan, his tutor, was easygoing and the only treatise John is known to have written for him was a mathematical one, though no doubt there were others. His private reading soon included Pope, Swift and Voltaire and when in April he and Lowth began to read the second book of Euclid together no one could say whether it was for duty or pleasure.

On 11 April he rode back to Caversham with Hopson and Zinzan for three weeks' vacation and at once began to sound his friends about the history of Reading. This was for Hearne, but there was really no time to deal with it. He was also a little tired (he had been suffering from fainting fits during March), though on the whole he had an excellent constitution and more than his fair share of energy. He had kept in touch by letter with his schoolfriends and they were all invited to Caversham – ushers and boys alike. Then there was the excitement of Princess Amelia's arrival on her way to Bath when she stayed at the house of Mr Reginald Fellowes[d] and everyone turned out to see her. A few days later John rode down to Mattingley with Deodatus Bye to visit Mr Bryan Richards who had been steward to the 2nd Earl of Clarendon and who possessed a number of Clarendon manuscripts.[e] There they copied letters from Charles I to Windebank, inspected other manuscripts and were allowed to take one away with them for Hearne.[f] This first mission in the cause of research was followed three days later, on 25 April, by the

---

[d] Fellowes is mentioned as host in John's diaries.

[e] A note by the younger John Loveday says that Bryan Richards was formerly in the 'Royal Regiment of Dragoons' commanded by Lord Cornbury, later 2nd Earl of Clarendon. I am obliged to Mrs W. Nowottny for the information that the statement that he had been a steward comes from John's note on a copy he made of Dr South's letter to Queen Anne when it was in Richards's possession. The five additional volumes VII–XI of South's sermons, collated by John Loveday, are in Pennsylvania State University Library. According to the *Catalogue of Western MSS.* in the Bodleian Library, *vol. III. B. 1767*, Richards was given some Clarendon papers by the 3rd Earl (d. 1723) and is said there to have been a first cousin of the 2nd Earl's second wife, Flower, formerly Lady Backhouse.

[f] The paper was lent to Hearne and later returned to Richards. See p. 25.

forerunner to his numerous tours, though this time he had a very short way to go – simply up the slope behind the house to the church. It suddenly occurred to him to take a pencil and a sheet of paper, and there, in that familiar church, he wrote down nearly all the inscriptions he could find, including those on the marbles by the chancel door which related to his own family, buried in a vault under the Communion table.

Over the altar are two Flags of the Lovedays' Family, one quartered with the Throckmortons, the other with the Norths, of which Family was Mary the Relict of the said Thomas, who put up the Inscription.[g] She dyed December 14th, 1724, in her 77th year and was buryed at Christ Church, London . . .

Over the Singer's Gallery 1605, the oldest Date in the Church, being upon the Timber-Work of the Tower, 'tis supposed to relate to the Erection of it then, tho' it has since been rebuilt, being altered from a wooded Spire to a wooden four-square Tower . . . There is a Tradition in the Brigham's Family that they were akin to Chaucer; I know one Nicholas Brigham put up a Monument for Chaucer . . .

Describing the six bells with 'Praise God' upon the second and 'Honour God' upon the third, he added:

There is a Tradition that a Brigham gave one of the Bells, perhaps it was the Treble Bell and the Donor Brigham who dyed in 1696 who was a great lover of ringing.

Over Mr Smith's Pew is an Hatchment for Dr South . . . Mr Smith marryed the Person the Doctor left his Estate to.[h] There is a Gravestone for [one] of the Stewards of the late Earl of Kildare who lived at the House, now Earl Cadogan's; his name Bradley, dyed about two years since, almost 100 years old, they say he was an Officer in Oliver Cromwell's Army. The Chancel on the inside is apparently older than the Church as appears from the Pavement, but Pillars chiefly. There is in the Pulpit Pew an Holy Water Hole[i] for the Priest to cross himself (as I suppose) at some time of the Service. There is in the Cupboard by the Altar a piece of Marble which by the hole in it seems to have been for the Holy Water perhaps, on the right side of the Altar as you enter by the Folding Doors and walk up . . .

He made a neat copy of all his notes which he took to Hearne in June, together with the 'old Writing of Edward VIth's time' which he had brought from Mattingley. He had something to offer even if it was not the history of Reading and he had described the first of about 250 churches on which he was

---

[g] On the memorial Mary Loveday had erected to her husband, Thomas, his wife, Letitia, and their daughter.

[h] See p. 106.

[i] This was a piscina for cleaning the Communion vessels.

to comment during the next thirty-five years. He had already given Hearne a number of silver medals on his return to Oxford early in May as well as presenting nine others to Dr Richard Rawlinson of St John's College who had just been consecrated a non-juror bishop. Most of his diary entries for the summer term concern presents or errands for Hearne. A typical example reads:

> June 2. Robert Cane[j] brought me the MS. (from our Archives) which is *Sermo de Sacramentis Dedicationis*, falsely called William of Worcester's. Mr Hearne took a copy of the Letter prefixed against the Title-page; he examined the MS. again whether he could find the author's name, but he could not.

Not only could Hearne now see manuscripts from Magdalen College Library but John could actually take him round it – a pleasure conferred on 23 May and often repeated. Since his expulsion from the Bodleian it had been virtually impossible for him to visit any of the college libraries and he had had to rely increasingly on his friends to bring him information. It was not only ancient texts that he needed; there were other lists to be consulted both for his publications and his pocket books. Among the volumes, pamphlets and parchments which John showered upon him either as gifts or loans were to be found the names of all the members of the Society of Magdalen College, the names of the Fellows of Wadham, a complete list of the gownsmen at Magdalen Hall and a recipe for the ague which John had no doubt gleaned from his mother.

In Magdalen on 24 June, John the Baptist's Day, Phanny Bacon preached the University Sermon and according to custom he stood in the stone pulpit in the quadrangle on the site of the old Hospital dedicated to St John in the time of Henry III. The walls of the chapel were always decorated externally with grasses and rushes on this occasion and the members of the University enjoyed the joke that they were all going to Magdalen to enjoy 'bacon and greens'. Unfortunately John kept no record of this sermon, but a note in his diary saying that Mr Bacon preached in the stone pulpit on this day confirms a story which has been thought possibly to be apocryphal.[k]

Back at Caversham for the long vacation he began to develop some new interests. He was to be found at a number of musical parties and he enjoyed the legal battles at the Assizes, especially one which was lost by the Dowager Duchess of Marlborough;[l] but the innovation which was to give him the greatest pleasure as far as Reading society was concerned was the new French

---

[j] Cane became Master of Magdalen School from 1745 to 1752. John said he never received a Fellowship in spite of having an unexceptionable character.

[k] *Magdalen College Register*, first series, vol. VI, states that 'It does not appear, however, that Dr Bacon ever preached on that occasion.'

[l] At Reading Assizes, 31 July 1728. Duchess of Marlborough *v*. Grey before Justices Denton and Pengelly.

Club. This had been organized by the volatile M. Bellai with the popular proviso that there should be a new patroness every year chosen from among the sisters of his former pupils. It may have been a mixed club and certainly Patty, when she was old enough, was an even better French scholar than her brother. The young men tended to go along in a group and if the girls were present they must have been escorted by chaperones. John's interest in French led to his learning Saxon French the following term; he had begun to study Saxon English that summer.

Two of his Oxford friends, Sir William Bowyer and Edmund Lambert, came down for the Reading Assembly; otherwise August was a quiet month given to religious reading – on 1 September, more than two years after his confirmation, he was to receive the Holy Sacrament for the first time. From then on he was very regular in his attendance.

No sooner had he and his mother returned from the usual autumn visits to their relations than word came of the death of his grandfather, William Lethieullier, and they had to go back to London. John escorted the Tooke family to Clapham where they saw old William buried on 1 October in the new vault he had erected in Clapham churchyard. This vault was to accommodate a number of his descendants during the next thirty years and to cause some problems for their survivors who had to maintain it. John then returned to Caversham where there was only just time to hear his friend Thomas Bonney declaim his own composition *Monasterium Readingense* to the school before he was riding back with Zinzan to Oxford. They were greeted by a violent thunderstorm which, according to Hearne, caused great apprehension.[10]

He had already warned Hearne of his return.

Good Sir
The MSS I promised to send you were not retarded out of Forgetfulness, but only for want of a good opportunity to speak with the Possesor of 'em, who has now promised 'em to me against October the 10th when I design for Oxford . . . notorious Omissions in the Disposal (or rather the non-Disposal) of Corporation-Charities have been a long while complained of there and their Shyness in granting a Perusal of their Papers gives me Reason to believe the complaint not altogether groundless; so that what with Frowardness in some (as was Brigham's case) and guilt in others, many Monuments of value are lost to the curious . . I have been at London and there picked up a few Curiosities, as well as in the Country, among which I reckon the Great Bible, published at London in 1549, with Wooden Cuts and nothing wanting, but the second Leaf of the Calendar. I bought all Shirley's Auction-Catalogues, at little more than Wast-Paper-Price; but Creech's is lost. I was looking in the 9th Chapter of Plot's Oxfordshire t'other day and casually met with William Wyrcester's name, at the 222nd Page, where

he has the Character of an eminent astronomer; and is said to have 'wrote a verification of all the fixed Stars as to their Longitude and Latitude for the year 1440 . . . with some other Astronomical matters at the instance of his Patron Sir⌊John Falstoff`, (for so Plot spells it). This I took down for fear you should have passed it over; 'tis 33 Years, I think, from the Date of this Tract to that of *Sermo de Sacramentis* in Magdalen College Library. I have an old English Chronicle Imperfect; so that I can't learn the Author, though I presume it is Stowe; But of this enough, since when I come to Oxford, I shall be proud of laying my little Treasure before you, with the Master of it. Your very humble Servant and hearty well-wisher . . .[11]

It was surely tactless to suggest that Hearne could possibly have overlooked anything. The antiquary's reply on 3 October was a little peevish.

I am sorry you met with such disappointment with respect to your Reading Antiquities. Methinks they should be glad of any opportunity of communicating what would tend to the honour of that place. Nor should any private Interest hinder the Service of the Publick. I find you sped better at London and elsewhere . . . [going on to say that the catalogue of Creech's books would have been useful to him].

I am well acquainted with what Dr Plot observes about William Wyrcester and I have often looked over the MS. he refers to in the Bodleian Library, before I was debarred that Place. I suppose the Dr. might have the first hint of it from Mr Wood with whom he was well acquainted, and they used to converse together almost every day when they were in Oxford. I cannot judge of your Chronicle without a sight of it, tho' 'tis very likely to be Holinshed's. I have printed your old Charter and have taken occasion to mention your Name in the *Black Book* more than once, for what you have been pleased to impart to, Sir, your obliged humble Servant, Tho: Hearne.[12]

In his third term John began to see a little more of Oxford's night life.

Oct. 17. Went with Zinzan and Lambert to the Mitre by 7 where was Daintrey . . . the Company being gone by 12, we with Derham, Taverner and Daintrey stayed there till 2.

This was the first recorded supper party among his own personal friends. By December he had begun to join Hearne and his circle at the club in Cat Street, and evenings spent at the inn there became his chief pleasure. He attended whenever he could, enjoying meeting men of varying ages from other colleges. Sometimes he came away disappointed at finding no company, as happened on three consecutive evenings after the Christmas gathering, but this was unusual. The two pillars of the club were Hearne himself and the

Revd Dr John Whiteside, fourth Keeper of the Ashmolean, who lived in Cat Street. The following April John and Bowyer began to attend his course of Divinity lectures.

It was William Benwell who said that he had heard John speak in very high terms of Hearne's moral character and blame Thomas Warton for his insinuation of drunkenness in the story of the tessellated Roman pavement. In the *Companion to the Guide* (1760)[m] Warton made great play over an alleged incident at the inn known as Whittington and His Cat. Hearne he claimed, had mistaken the floor for a Roman pavement whereas it was neatly lined with sheep's trotters. He said Hearne, encouraged by a companion, drank too much in his excitement and spent some time sleeping on the floor; and the bookseller Daniel Prince, by providing a sketch of Hearne being escorted home the worse for wear, added credence to the tale. This was supposed to have taken place shortly after Hearne had published his *Discourse* on the Stonesfield Pavement. Although we have John's word for it that the antiquary's behaviour was impeccable during the years of their acquaintance, he cannot have been sure about this incident, since the Discourse appeared in 1712. But if hard drinking was as universal at Oxford as it is said to have been it is odd that Warton should have made such an issue of it or that John should have been so annoyed with him. He would not have denied that his friend liked his ale or the fact that he himself did not drink it (though he took wine) caused Hearne some amusement.

> With this man [said Benwell] he passed many of his evenings at a little tavern[n] where Mr Hearne would go to smoke his pipe and drink his ale. When he had drunk he would give the cup to Mr Loveday, who though he never drank, would always hold it some time to his mouth, with which his companion was much pleased, though he sometimes detected him and watched him more closely the next time.

It was during his third term that two men came into his life who were to be of great importance to him. One was John Audley, a Magdalen demy and Bachelor of Arts whose home was in Birmingham. Later on as a Fellow he was to spend a large part of his life at Magdalen and a not inconsiderable amount of it at Caversham. The other was Thomas Bagshaw, whose father held the living of Bromley in Kent and was chaplain of Bromley College. Bagshaw, who is best known for having performed the burial service for Dr Johnson's wife, Tetty, was to become John's beloved brother-in-law when he married Dorothy Bagshaw as his second wife.

When John was older he was asked why so much of his life had been spent in the company of the clergy. He replied that as a young man he had particularly sought their acquaintance, thinking (as his daughter Penelope

---

[m] A skit on Oxford guides.
[n] When not in Cat Street they frequented Shepherd's Inn in Coach and Horses Lane.

put it) that in their company 'there was not that improper licence allowed in conversation as was too commonly the case among the laymen at Magdalen'. Not all his college friends, however, were destined for the Church – in particular the Lambert brothers, Edmund and Edward (known respectively as Mun and Ned), Sir William Bowyer and William Courtenay, who all had considerable expectations. Neither rank, money nor age seem to have raised many barriers in the friendly intercourse of John's University life. In April he had begun to dine with the Masters of Arts and had continued to do so until the end of May, presumably a regular practice in order to help the new members of the Society to integrate freely. As to the pattern of his life, it was his habit to go to bed at ten o'clock and to arise at five so that he could make the best use of the daylight. All his life he kept fast days when he would eat no more than an egg and drink only water. He was from childhood a very self-disciplined person.

On 6 November he narrowly escaped an embarrassing situation. The previous evening Hearne had been praising John Urry's edition of Chaucer° and when John asked him where it could be bought he replied that he thought all the copies had been left with the Dean of Christ Church. The Dean, Dr William Bradshaw, was also Bishop of Bristol and was a Whig for whom Hearne had nothing but contempt – he 'cringed to the Duchess of Marlborough as if he had been her footman'.[13] John persuaded John Audley to accompany him, dressed himself with particular care, and set off to buy the book from Dr Bradshaw. They presented themselves at his door and were shown into his parlour where he was standing before the fire.

> John addressed himself to the Bishop [says Benwell] saying that he was come to purchase a copy of Urry's Chaucer; the Bishop stared at him very attentively and asked him his name and college, which he took down in his pocket book. After eyeing him for some time and being convinced that he was not come by way of a joke, but through ignorance, he very politely sold him the book and insisted upon sending his own Servant home with it, which he did and attended Mr Loveday himself to the door.

Benwell evidently thought the blunder was caused by the young man visiting the Bishop without an introduction in order to buy a book; perhaps John thought so too when he retold the story many years later at his dinner table; but could not the reason for Dr Bradshaw's hesitation have really been a political one and was Hearne entirely innocent in the matter? For John Urry had been Hearne's friend and a staunch non-juror and his edition of Chaucer, which was not a good one,[14] had been promoted by Francis Atterbury when he was Dean of Christ Church – and he, after all, had been imprisoned as a bishop for his Jacobite sympathies. Bradshaw, who three years earlier had

° Urry's work was completed by others and published in 1721.

accused a non-juror[p] of corrupting the principles of young gentlemen,[15] was active in Oxford politics and represented everything that Hearne disliked. Hearne was not above scoring off the Bishop at John's expense. Fortunately the Bishop's perfect manners saved the day.

William Derham was as much interested as John in the practices of other denominations and they attended a Quaker meeting together early in December. John's interest had been aroused two years earlier when Mr Powell, a Quaker in Reading, had been christened by old Mr Bacon at St Laurence's and provided with two rather unusual godparents – namely Mr Recorder Pottenger and Mrs Watts, the wife of the mayor. On another occasion Derham and he attended a meeting of Dissenters. Benwell wrote:

> 'Speaking of Coventicle preachers, I went once' said he, 'at Oxford with Derham, the son of the Physico-Theologist, to hear a hedger and ditcher preach. We had not been there long before he addressed himself to us, telling us we had the seal of the Whore of Babylon in our foreheads. Upon which Derham said to me "We should make way for others now we have been sealed" and accordingly we went out; but we did not laugh. For my part I wonder how people can: to me nothing is more shocking as to hear men say they are inspired by the Holy Ghost to talk nonsense.'

Deodatus Bye, preparing to move to the school at Maidstone, came to stay in November. This was an excellent excuse for visits to Clements the bookseller and to one of John's favourite haunts – the Theatre Printing House run by Joseph Brookland.[q] Thomas Bonney had been another visitor and he had been entertained by a visit to Blenheim. John had a tiresome habit of making 'bonfires' of his friends' letters at this time – always excepting Hearne's which were tied up with copies of his own replies. A macabre note which escaped the flames was from his crony Jonah Chesterman, the assistant curate at Caversham, who wrote on 15 January 1729:

> The Lady that was to be buryed today at Causham will not be brought till next Wednesday, by reason her son lies in Wales and has been dead about seven years, is to be brought with her. Her name is Mordaunt. Your Aunt Betty is here. I am, Sir, Yours affectionately . . .[16]

Chesterman was a Balliol graduate who was well thought of and often returned to preach before the University.

Another fragment survived, this time from Thomas Bonney, John's old schoolfriend and a great favourite. John had remained in Oxford for Christmas so they had not met since his visit. Thomas came of a humble and

[p] William Oldisworth.
[q] Brookland, manager or head printer, was Hearne's printer and agent. The University Press, originally housed in the Sheldonian Theatre, was by this time in the Clarendon Building which had been built for it (1713).

impecunious family (his father, Charles Bonney, was a Reading tradesman) and his only hope of getting to the University was by becoming a servitor to one of the Fellows. This was quite usual in the circumstances, but there was a certain amount of snobbery attached to it and gentlemen commoners were not supposed to consort with servitors in public. Bonney was undergoing some heart-searching and did not know whether to approach Phanuel Bacon or Philip Vaughan. He was now an assistant usher at the school and he wrote on 22 January to put the problem before John.

> . . . and that is whether Bacon will as readily assist me, if I should be Mr Vaughan's Servitor, as he would if I was his own; or in other words whether Phanny will not take it ill that I should rather apply to Mr Vaughan than to him. But I think I almost resolved this Question myself, by telling Mr Hiley that you, in one of your Letters, told me that you had mentioned the affair to Phanny and afterwards that you seemed to hint that if Mr Vaughan would not, Phanny would. But he answered me that was only innuendo and we had better be certain of such things before we proceed too far. So to oblige Mr Hiley pray send me word whether Phanny will not . . .[17]

The matter was not settled until March 1730, when Phanny at last took Bonney on as his servitor, perhaps as a result of a letter from John the previous September. Meanwhile Bonney settled in Oxford, encouraged as usual by his friend, who did everything he could to assist him. He kept up his studies and matriculated on the day he began his service. This menial state only lasted for a year as John tackled the President on his behalf in order to procure him a clerkship in the College. He shared John's enthusiasm for archaeology and was frequently his companion on afternoon rides.

John spent his birthday with Hearne and then returned home for a few days during which time they exchanged letters. He wrote on 12 February sending notes relating to Feens, and added:

> The Mapp of Feenes Manor I bring with me to Oxford. Mr Archdeacon Rye is an agent for Browne Willis among his clergy here to perfect his List of the Dedication of Churches. What a great value Willis has for Curll you may see in the inclosed Advertisement . . .[18]

The advertisement was a recommendation put out by the antiquary Browne Willis to Dr Charlett, Master of University College, many years before. Hearne had an affectionate disdain for Browne Willis's work which he thought, very often with some reason, was hastily and inaccurately put together. For Edmund Curll, the unscrupulous bookseller, he may have had the measure of respect which attends fear; though it was not until after his own death that Curll made his worst attack on him.

Hearne replied on 20 February.

I am glad you have revised your Evidence relating to Feenes, and corrected two of the Observations you made to me. Perhaps I may have occasion to take notice of this hereafter. When you come to Oxford again, we may have a proper opportunity of talking about the Copies of the two Inquisitions you sent me, as also about your Mapp of Feenes Manor which I long mightily to see. My friend Mr Cherry (whose Memory hath been stained since his death by his nearest relations) being present at and concerned in the Survey, as I think I have several times heard him say. I am obliged to you for the Advertisement. I knew before what a value for C . . . ll one of the persons had, but then I did not know, that Br . . . W . . . llis had a like value, since I have several times heard him condemn those very books, that are mentioned in the Advertisement, a thing I could not but take great notice of, because I knew at the same time, that the things published by himself (barring what some body else took care of)[r] are lyable to the very same Exceptions. I have delivered your Trokelowe[19] to my binder, as you desired . . . Some of our Oxford Scholars, in the old Broils between the University and City, aimed at making Reading a University. If you could light upon any ancient Memoirs upon that head, they would be welcome to, dear Sir, Your most obliged and humble Servant.[20]

The short term was soon over; John spent two days at the Oxford Assizes, heard Phanny preach before the judges and on 11 March paid the College Steward[s] a year's rent for his rooms, which were leased from Dr Edmund Isham. Robert Lowth came round that evening and they talked until 11 p.m. but in spite of this John was up early and reached Caversham by mid-morning. As his horse clattered into the great Court, passing by the farm horses who used the same entrance, he must have felt elated. He was just eighteen, he had enjoyed thirteen months of bliss at the University and his name had appeared in the preface to Hearne's *Liber Niger Scaccarii*, where his friend had most generously acknowledged his obligations and had described him in words which would always be remembered – 'Optimae spei juvenis, literarum et literatorum amantissimus.'[t]

[r] Hearne was referring to himself.
[s] Dr James Fynes.
[t] 'A young man of the highest promise, devoted to letters and to men of letters.'

The First Ride to Wales
1729

Mrs Loveday might have been a little put out if she had known that she now occupied a permanent place in one of Mr Hearne's pocket books, thanks to further family revelations made by her son on his birthday. But at least he had obligingly removed a few years from her age.

> February. 5. Mr Loveday of Madg. Coll.'s mother's maiden name was Lethullier [sic] and Mr Lethullier (late of Trin. College, Oxon) is related to her. This Mr Lethullier is a worthless vain man, whom therefore Mr Loveday hath a very mean opinion of, and yet some in Oxford used to cry up this Lethullier, notwithstanding he despised true Learning, but 'twas merely to flatter him. [1]

In May he added

> So Mr Loveday is second cousin to Mr Lethullier that was lately of Trin. College and is now a married man, his lady being a very pretty Woman. This Mr Lethullier, who very lately entered a brother at Trin. College, is looked upon (as I am told by impartial men) as a very great Coxcombe. [2]

Smart Lethieullier was a grandson of William Lethieullier's elder brother Sir John, and was about ten years older than John Loveday. Hearne's note is the only firm indication that they ever met and they had evidently not taken to each other. Smart lived in the world of fashion and may have found the younger man's homespun honesty a little naive. Whatever the cause of the rift it seems to have been permanent, which is a pity as they were both gifted antiquaries and collectors who might have found they had a good deal in common. Smart was one of Hearne's subscribers and could well have expected to earn a little more good will from that quarter. His brother Charles was younger than John who had probably met them when staying with the Hopkinses in Essex. Smart had inherited Aldersbrook House, near Ilford, in 1710.

Hearne was having quite a busy social life of his own while John was away, but if he did not miss him he was not allowed to forget him. Only a week had passed before he received a very long letter and a parcel.

> You'll oblige me if you'll favour Sir Thomas Elyot's *Castell of Helth* a place in your Study; the Author seems to be a Learned and a Pious man . . . I am sorry to hear that the greatest Divine in these parts, Dr Stapylton, is very ill; there is a Notion that he has been about some great work a considerable time . . . I sent t'other day to Staples our Attorney in Windsor (who was Brother to the Minister of Shottesbrooke) to enquire whether Eaton College Statutes mention a Boy-Bishop. His Answer I expect shortly . . . if you come on this Side the Countrey you'll call and see King Charles's picture.[3]

This painting was one of several reproductions of the Van Dyck school which graced the gallery at Caversham. Hearne replied on 27 March thanking him for his present of the three little books and other enclosures.

> . . . Sir Thomas Elyot was a very great man. His *Bibliotheca* was always much admired and Leland made great use of it as appears from his *Collectanea*. Cooper's *Dictionary*[a] is nothing but Elyot improved . . . Mr Lewis was nettled at my Letter and returned it again. I hear enough of his Character. I find that there was printing Temp. Henry VIII at Greenwich. Mr Beckford, a Paper Maker at Wolvercote near Oxford, had a Book printed there; but what became of it I know not. I mention this, because in your searches after old Books, it may be proper to pick up such as you shall meet with printed there . . . Richard Beauchamp, Earl of Warwick, lived often at Caversham. His Will bears the date there Aug. 8. 1437 not, as in Dugdale, 1435. If you meet with any tradition relating to this Family, particularly to this great Earl, you will be pleased to communicate the same to, Dear Sir, Your obliged and humble Servant . . .[4]

It was hardly surprising that the Revd John Lewis, a well-known antiquary, was nettled. Hearne had intended it. Lewis had written rudely, criticizing Hearne's accuracy and had been repaid by receiving his own letter quoted word for word in Hearne's hand. Lewis had returned it with a note on

[a] See p. 256 n.*h*.

the outside saying that as Hearne had misrepresented him he did not wonder at his misrepresenting dead men. This kind of controversy was the breath of life to Hearne and he wrote in his diary:[5] 'I knew he would be angry as he most certainly is'; but poor Lewis, who was a reputable scholar, took it all very seriously. How much John enjoyed this side of his friend's character is uncertain, but most of the vitriol was in the notebooks and only a few enemies received draughts of it in his letters. Years later John was asked to comment on Hearne's manners and would only say that he had always been very civil to him.

On 9 April he set off with Charles Hopson who was staying with him to find out whether there had ever been at Eton one of the medieval boy bishops. According to custom they were elected from St Nicholas's Day until Holy Innocents' Day and went round the town in bishops' clothes blessing the people as well as performing all the ceremonies except Mass. The young men breakfasted at Bracknell with Charles's uncle Richard Hopson and reached Windsor by midday, spending the rest of it with the genial Alexander Staples. But the attorney's consultations had proved fruitless. John wrote to Hearne the same day.

> . . . I went to Windsor myself to Staples to enquire about the Eaton Boy-Bishop. He consulted Dr Sleech upon it, who is Fellow of Eaton and manages Affairs for the College; he told him that there was no mention of any thing like Episcopus Puerorum in Eaton College Statutes, nor did he ever hear it hinted by any one that there was; the Statutes call the Provost Gubernator and the Master Informator Puerorum. I find that they will not let any one search their Statutes, which indeed in this Case I think there's no occasion for; it being very strange that Sleech should not know it, was there any such thing there . . . I design for Oxford next Thursday Se'nnight where I promise myself great Happiness in your good Company . . .[6]

He avoided any mention of the commissions which Hearne had suggested; there were limits to even his enthusiasm. Besides he had some researches of his own to attend to – another visit to the church and some notes on Caversham and Reading to which he added more in the summer; they were a patchwork collection varying from comments on the interest paid to poor housekeepers of Caversham which had sunk very low, to notes from Bonney on the Reading streets:

> One Lovejoy, a Maiden they say, gave £2 15. 0. Simon Wallcroft has paid interest for it these eight years.

> That which is now called Rotten-Row was before the Pestilence called Little Silver Street but from their throwing their Dung out of Window into Street (by which the Pestilence was stayed) it was called Rotten-Row, quam Stinking-Row.

There was also a nice rhyme about Oxfordshire villages:

> Finstoke upon the hill
> And Fawler down Derry
> beggarly Stunsfield
> and lowly Charlbury
> Hayley, Crawley, Curbridge and Cogges
> Witney poor Spinners and Duckleton Dogs.

John was naturally shortsighted and on 12 April Thomas Birt, who among other things was the Reading undertaker, 'came to the Coffee-house with a glass for me from Steropes'. The Birt family are often mentioned in Loveday diaries and Thomas married Henry Dodwell's sister Monica the following year – as his third wife though he was still fairly young. According to Hearne he was a complete non-juror[7] and would not attend churches where the 'Usurpers' were prayed for, which cannot have been very good for business.

On his first night back at Oxford John went along to Cat Street and who should be there with Hearne but the 'Dragon of Whaddon' himself – Browne Willis. Hearne had seen a good deal of him during the vacation and had come to some private conclusions.

> Mr Willis always talks of his own performances which are (excepting his View of the mitred Abbies in Leland) meer Rhapsodies. He usually takes any thing upon Trust, and runs thereby into thousands of errours, which he takes little or no care to correct.[8]

Though proud in many ways, Browne Willis – for all his natural enthusiasm – was in fact relatively humble about his work. No doubt he was grateful for Hearne's assistance, which the latter never let him forget, and he put tremendous effort into his detailed researches on the abbeys and cathedrals and also on county histories; but absolute reliance could not be placed on all his assertions. Indeed, his personal appearance and slovenly habits, which became more marked as time went on, were perhaps an indication of his unmethodical mind. But while it was one thing for Hearne to jeer at his old friend, it would hardly have been respectful for a boy of John's age to criticize a man then in his forty-seventh year. Nevertheless he and Hearne shared the same feelings on this subject and when John came to write the diaries of his tours his frequent exasperation at Willis's blunders was partly rooted in the past. All the same it must be conceded that he seldom went anywhere without consulting Browne Willis's volumes first.

So, with Lowth coming to breakfast on the first morning, life at Oxford settled into its pleasant routine – one which could be adapted at will though with John it was in order to pack more into every crowded day. There was still time, however, to absorb the beauty of the surroundings. After their frequent visits to the College Library Hearne and he would walk in the serenity of the grounds where the browsing deer and the sunlight filtering through the leaves to the dark pools of the Cherwell were the background to their earnest conversations. In the evenings he would sometimes foregather with his young friends at the Tuns or accompany Hearne to another inn, Shepherd's in Coach and Horses Lane, though the Cat Street fraternity was still flourishing and Phanny Bacon had taken to joining the gathering there.

Mun Lambert gave a party on 27 May as a 'Treat for his Examining Master – Townsend' three days after he had sat for his M.A. degree. John found most of his usual companions there; like young people of any period, they tended to go around in a group. He had been seeing a great deal of Lambert, often reading to him in French, and though Mun was to leave the University the following December their friendship continued into later life.

In June John twice set out from Oxford on new expeditions. He had read on the 3rd some comments of Hearne's on Roper's account of Fairford.[9] On the 4th he was on his way there, with Daniel Rich as a companion, to see the glass for himself.

> *Fairford.*
> There is a Chauntry on the East side of Fairford Church still remaining. If you lift up the Seats you see strange Figures of a Woman beating her husband with a Ladle, pulling him by the hair of his Head &c. At Shottesbrook there is such a Chauntry remaining. So said in 1729.
>
> Mrs Fermor left 300£ to wire the Glass at Fairford, which was done about 9 years since, and the Glass took-down, cleaned and leaded broader.[b] She left 1000£ for an Afternoon Sermon. and 1000£ to a School to teach to write, read and cast Accounts.
>
> A Journey-man Sadler gave 40£ per annum to the Poor as the Stone over his Body tells you, by the step to the Altar. He gave one of the Sconces and Sir Thomas Delves (who married a Barker) the other. The Living is about Seven Score Pounds per Annum including the money for Afternoon Sermons. . . .

This was the first of five sets of notes on Fairford church. The second expedition was quite different. He had always been fond of hearing Simon Walcroft play his pipe and tabor or tabret, Simon now introduced him to another exponent of this kind of music – John Boulton of Eynsham, always known as Jack o' Stunsfield (now called Stonesfield) where he had been born. Benwell wrote:

> There lived formerly at Ensham in Oxfordshire a curious person who

---

[b] Elizabeth Fermor (d. 1706) was the unmarried only child of William, 1st Baron Leominster and Jane, daughter of Andrew Barker of Fairford. In *The Ancient and Present State of Gloucestershire* (1712) Sir Robert Atkyns said Mrs Fermor left £1,000 to be laid out on lands for maintenance of an afternoon lecture from which £10 per annum was to be paid to the schoolmaster. £200 was to be spent on mending and wiring the windows. John's is the only intimation that they were 'leaded broader'. The saddler was William Butcher.

went by the name of Jacky Stunsfield, being some foundling child of that parish . . . This man having from his youth been employed in keeping sheep, had by his own ingenuity made a Pipe, which he taught himself to play upon, and by constant practice had arrived at such a degree of perfection in the tabor and pipe as to be reckoned the best player in England. He gained so much by his performances in this way, that for some time before his death he was worth fourscore pounds a year. To this curious man Mr L. was introduced during his residence at Oxford by Simon Walcroft, formerly Clerk to the Parish of Caversham, who was a great friend of the bard. After this introduction Mr L. would frequently go over to Ensham and would often take some friends with him, one of whom was Mr Holdsworth (the Commentator on the Georgics) to hear his inimitable performances. One day Simon Walcroft called on Mr L. at Oxford and they both went over together to Ensham to pay a visit to their old musical friend. He was then near eighty years of age, but his health was still entire and his senses vigorous and unimpaired. In the course of this visit he took Mr L. by the hand and addressed him as follows 'You, Sir, perhaps may not know that you are remembered in my will. I will read you the passage. "I give and bequeathe to Mr Loveday my best pipe, bound round at the top with a coger's end, for the use of my old friend, Simon Walcroft, during his life." As I have now an opportunity I cannot do better than deliver it into your own hands. I have been long a practitioner and made some progress; I am now old, my breath fails me and it is time that I should leave off. Here, Sir, take this pipe, I have had it from my youth, I made it myself and it is the sweetest pipe I ever played on.' This account I had from Mr L's own mouth and it seemed to me to have so much of the pastoral in it and so much of the spirit of *Damoetas dono*[c] that I could not forbear taking this notice of it.

It was some eight or nine years later that John was given the pipe as a symbol of the friendship which had developed between the performer and his admirer. On this first occasion he dined at the Angel with John Boulton and learned all about him. There was another attraction, as Hearne soon found out.

John o'Stunsfield is the most famous man for musick on the Tabour Pipe that hath been for ages. He was born at Stunsfield near Woodstock and being a Bastard and a Foundling, they gave him the sirname of Stunsfield. He used to be sent for far and near, and he got a great deal of money, so that growing rich he married a Wife (an Eynsham Woman) and then removed to Eynsham where he now lives and hath done many years and seldom now takes journies in order to play, but keeps for the

---

[c] Echoing Virgil's *Eclogues* II, 37: 'Fistula, Damoetas dono mihi quam dedit olim' ('The pipe Damoetas once gave me as a present').

most part at home, being (as he says) 70 years of age, though his house is
still pretty much frequented by Gentlemen, partly for the sake of himself
and partly (and indeed more) for the sake of his neece, a young pretty girl,
to whom he designs to leave what he hath, after a proper provision for his
Wife by whom he hath had no children. [10]

Except for being 'jobbed' for not 'capping' 'Edmunds of Oriel, Pro-
Proctor, under the Turle', John recorded no personal misdemeanours. Early
in July he spent some time writing letters for Phanny whose quips had been
temporarily silenced by illness. Then on the 13th he went with his friends
Sir William Bowyer and Mun Lambert to visit Lord Cobham's gardens at
Stowe; but beyond remarking that they found 'T. Bowles[d] there with Rand,
Lord Cobham's Chaplain'[e] and that there were forty acres of grounds, he
made no notes on this occasion. He had taken Virgil's *Aeneid* VI with him
which possibly distracted his mind from the sight of Bicester and Barton
churches; and in any case this was only the curtain-raiser to his first real
'ramble'.

A long tour without any adúlt interference – that was the plot which the two
Johns, Loveday and Peareth, had been hatching for some time. Old Mr Peareth
had offered his blessing and whatever Mrs Loveday may have felt privately she
too had given her permission. They intended to follow much the same route as
that which John had taken with Mr Hiley, but to include Glastonbury, Wells
and even Cardiff in the itinerary. So on 17 July the pair set off for their first
objective, Shrivenham.

> In the Road to Shrevenham we met with a Man, who told us there was a
> Priory at Creeklade where he lived and on which his Father had built
> several Houses; that the Chappel, or at least the Chancel part of the
> Chappel, was standing not long since, but this his Father took down and
> built a House upon it; there was then, he said, remaining in the Chancel the
> Holy Water Hole and the Pope's Chair, so he called it; but these were then
> broke to pieces; he said the Chappel was called in Writings the Free
> Chappel of St. John Baptist.

Like many young enthusiasts John kept a very thorough record for the first
few days, though he managed after this to ride through Wells, Bath and Bristol
with scarcely a mention of them. At Shrivenham, however, he took down
some epitaphs and was especially attracted to the memorial to Sir John
Wildman, the politician and master of intrigue who was sent as a prisoner of
State to the Scillies after the Restoration.

> 'tis said upon Sir John's part of the Marbles that he was not guilty of what
> he was confined for.

[d] Thomas Bowles became vicar of Brackley in 1729 and was known to John as a Fellow of
Magdalen.
[e] Conway Rand was appointed chaplain to Lord Cobham's regiment, the 1st Dragoon
Guards, in 1723.

His son John, who 'chose confinement with his Father rather than Liberty' was also memorable for another reason –

who approving the Roman Custom of Adoption adopted John Shute of the Inner Temple Esq.[f]

The clerk's children were very communicative. The boy showed him the date of the church in the north aisle with the names of the churchwardens and assured him that what appeared to be the figure of a woman lying prone was really a friar. 'The Clerk's girl' told him there had been a very good scholar in the parish called William Hoare and their vicar, George Stephens, had got him a place at Oxford. The altar, said John, stood in the middle of the chancel with seats all along the east side.

They went on to Avebury[g] where in a little ground floor room at The Catherine Wheel they found drawings by the antiquary William Stukeley[9] and[h]

an Oval in which this Legend, 'Ruben Horsall Clark of Abury and Antiquarian July 22. 1722.' This Horsall's Son is Clark now in 1729. July 18 . . . The Son, the present Clark is a shoemaker as his Father was who dyed in January, 1728 aged 77.

The Truslow monument in the church pleased John so much that he copied it all out. This is part of it.

John Truslowe here interred is and lyeth in his grave
Which unto me large benefits most bountifully gave
The race he lived here on earth was threescore yeares and seven
Deceast on April, 93 And then was prest to Heaven.

He having then no Issue left for His living wholy gave
To Richard Truslowe of his name for so he would it have
Who in remembrance of the gyver this tomb hathe caused to be
Within this Church of Avebury erected as you see.

The Clark says, that about 20 years ago one of the Truslowe's (which Family is now extinct with regard to Legitimate Issue) sold the Estate to Esqr. Holford.[i] This Truslowe has left several Bastards.[j]

[f] Shute was also the heir to Francis Barrington and took that name in 1716. He was created 1st Viscount Barrington in 1720.

[g] Notes on Cricklade and Avebury which Hearne took from John's accounts are in the Bodleian, MSS. Rawl. lett. 7. f. 183.

[h] For details of Stukeley's drawings see Appendix No. 17. A sketch he made of Lord Hertford's house and garden appears in his *Itinerarium Curiosum* published in 1724.

[i] This was Sir Richard Holford, a Master in Chancery, who died in 1718. The son, Samuel, who erected a monument to his mother, Susannah, was living at Avebury Manor, but died the following year – 1730.

[j] The Truslows are said to have left Truslow Manor early in the eighteenth century. In 1884 Charles Truslow of New York sent money from his family to construct choir stalls from the seventeenth-century pews, 'being descendants of the former occupants' – *A Guide*

Among the inscriptions was one to the predecessor[k] of Mr Mayo, the present vicar. 'Mayo lives at Calne; Presbyterians increase here,' wrote John, thinking perhaps that the two statements were not entirely unconnected.

On their way to Bath they stopped at Lacock, but he did not describe the house in his diary. However he told Hearne about it later when he gave him many of the inscriptions he had already copied.

He brought his pen and paper out again at Glastonbury, having read up the history of the place before they set out.

> Brooke at the Crown, and Downe at the Kings-Head, rent a considerable part of the Inclosure of the Abbey. Mr Prue, a Presbyterian, has had the Abbey-Inclosure for about 20 Years. The first Street in Glastonbury, East and West to the Market-Cross, six furlongs long, leading to Bridgewater is called the High-Street. The second Street from West of the Market Cross, South and almost North, being the Road to Exeter, 2 furlongs long, is called Magdalen Street. The Market at Glastonbury is on Tuesday. The George is called the Abbots-Inn . . . there is the Abbot's Bed-Chamber and Bed. The Slip of the Thorn at the White Hart has been gone about ten years. The Wallnut Tree in the Holy Church-yard blows[l] at the same time when other Wallnut Trees do. So said the Woman who shewed the Abbey.
>
> The Almonry has been down some years by leave of the Duke of Devon. Mr Prue has this Estate upon two Lives, from the Duke of Devonshire, who, they say, is going to sell the whole Estate.

He added a little note about the famous thorn.

> A Slip of the Thorn is now in a Butcher's Garden; it blows every Christmas Day. It is like other Thorns only the leaf is larger and it has no prickles.

The notes became haphazard again. The money arising from showing the 'Wookey Holes'[m] had been given to several poor people the year before; Chewstoke paid as much tithes to the parson of Chew as the parson of Chewstoke received for himself – about £30 per annum; and he copied the Latin inscription over the parsonage house door. Then he wrote:

> Bath lies low, Wells lower; Bristol low upon the side of a Hill. We saw

---

to the Church of St. James, Avebury. The brass plate with the verses which John saw against the east wall to the left of the altar is now on the south wall of the chancel which was reconstructed in 1878–9.

  [k] John White, vicar of Avebury, died in 1712.

  [l] sc. blooms; from the Anglo-Saxon.

  [m] Wookey Hole and the manor of Wookey were owned by the Bishopric of Bath and Wells. John had some doubt about his statement that the owner was Lord Newton – of whose existence there is no trace.

upwards of 40 Glow-worms down the Hill from Chuton to Wells on Saturday night. July 19.1729. Enquire what soil they like best.

Vast quantities of flies about Bristol (this perhaps owing to the season.)

They stopped there all the same to call upon Mrs Hiley who was staying with her relations and was no doubt glad to send reassuring news to theirs. Now they were to go into unknown territory over the Severn; they crossed by way of the Aust Passage.

Newport in Monmouthshire. You enter over a long wooden-planked Bridge with Ridges that you mustn't slip, under which runs the River Usk; on your right hand as you come off the Bridge are the remains of a great Castle, which, a man told me, was said to have belonged to a Duke of Buckingham. It now belongs to Squire Herbert of Oakley-Park; 'twas (if I understand my Informer right) garrisoned in the time of the Civil Wars when the town was burnt."

This town formerly had a Church next Door to the King's Head; now by Agreement with the Parishioners of St. Woolo's, it belongs to that Church which stands on your Right-Hand as you go out of the Town towards Cardiff.

He made numerous notes here, including:

The present Vicar is Bouchier, a Gloucestershire Man. At the West-end of the Church is a Chappel; 'tis now only used for Burying, 'tis not floored, any more than some part of the Church which is to be floored; the part which is floored was done lately. The Clark said there was a Friary on this side the River, by the Water-side.

On reaching Cardiff they put up at the Angel.

Though Glamorganshire is farther in Wales than Monmouthshire yet there is more Welsh talked in the Latter than the former. Several at Newport understand Welsh so that about once in two Months, or thereabouts, the Minister changes with some Welshman who reads prayers and and preaches in Welsh which pleases the Inhabitants who do not like their having an English Minister. Now at Cardiff they have had no Welsh Service in the memory of Man; not one in an hundred there understanding more of Welsh than is just sufficient to go to market with . . . on Saturday.

" In 1578 the Castle was leased for 300 years by Sir William Herbert of St Julians. His granddaughter, Mary, married Edward, 1st Baron Herbert of Cherbury. Henry Arthur Herbert of Oakley Park, Shropshire, was created 3rd Baron of Cherbury in 1743 and 1st Earl of Powis (1st creation) in 1748.

He described the monument in the church to Sir John Herbert, who died in 1617, saying he was of the same family as the Earl of Pembroke.

The Heir who is now in London is a Minor; his Grandfather stabbed a Man just by his house called the White Friars in the suburbs of Cardiff, because his Wife said that the Man's Horse, as she was going by, trod upon her. He was tryed but did not suffer. There is an Organ in the Church, a very good one they say and the Organist is allowed 30£ per annum by the Parish besides Perquisites. There was another Church (which was the Mother Church) called St. Mary's;[o] it was pulled down in the Civil Wars, there is little more than the East Wall remaining. The River Taaf now runs by it, having forced its way far into the Church-yard, so it runs close by the East Wall of the Church. The Clerk of Cardiff said that the River did not run by here till after the Church was destroyed; some of the Poor whose Ancestors were buryed in this Church-yard (St. Mary's) chose to be buryed here too. If the wind be fair the Passage from Cardiff to Bristol is about 4 or 5 hours; This accounts for Glamorganshire being more English than Monmouthshire. Mutton at Cardiff 3d. per pound.

The Town is walled, though now much ruined, as are the towers upon it. Here is a Castle, though much defaced ever since the Rebellion. It belonged to the Pembroke Family, being their chief Seat, then it came to the Jessenes whose it was till Lady Jefferies [p] (of the Pembroke Family) marryed to her second Husband, the Lord Windsor, who has sold much of the Estate, as did also some of the Possessors of it before him, so that much within the Memory of Man the Estate is reduced from 30,000£ per Annum to 1600£ per Annum. 'Tis said that Talbot, the Sollicitor-General, is about buying the Estate. He has an Estate at Castle Monnock [Castell Menich], about 5 miles from hence in the right of his Wife of the Matthews family.

Cardiff standing commodiously nigh the Sea, trafficks with Bristol, which the Rustics of Monmouthshire do not. . . . The Minister of Cardiff is one Colerack; his Predecessor was Andrews, a man in great esteem for an admirable delivery of his Sermons, as was his Son also, both now dead.

The Holmes belong to the Castle Estate. Flathome is cultivated . . . St Mary's Chappel at Llandaff is new paved, white-washed &c very lately. They are going to seat it and to pave part of the Church.

Caerleon lies in a Bottom, on the right hand as you go from Christ-Church to Newport. They have a wooden Planked Bridge here

[o] Although the old church of St. Mary was damaged in the Civil War it is generally agreed that its decay was brought about gradually by flood water. It was roofless in 1678. The last known burial was in 1709.

[p] The widow of the 2nd Baron Jeffreys (son of the notorious judge).

as well as at Newport. Caerleon stands on the River Usk. There are the poor Remains of a Castle towards the northern end of the Bridge as you enter the Town; 'tis the Duke of Beaufort's; the Church here was new pewed, paved, whitewashed &c, in 1725, when they took up all the Gravestones, putting some in the Church-yard and some in a little Room for Lumber in the Church;[q] they have made an order that none should be buryed in the Church, except in their Pews where they might have a Monument against the Wall.

How excited he would have been if he could have known of the future discoveries of the Roman barracks and amphitheatre there.

I was told that Tyler made all his own Relations (Herefordshire men), Prebendaries of Llandaff. There is but one Welsh Prebendary now, viz. Mr Maddocks. The Skeleton in Stone in Llandaff Cathedral was (as the Virger informed me) in Remembrance of a Skeleton found in the Body of a Tree hereabouts.

Their route back lay through Chepstow, Newnham-on-Severn and Northleach.

I was told at Newnham, in Gloucestershire, that about fifteen years since the town was a Corporation, but one of the Mayors sold the Mace and so they have had none since. They have a sword carryed before their Mayor; –that Wilcocks, Bishop of Gloucester was born here, though Willis says at Bristol; –that the Town's Trade is now chiefly sending Casks of Cyder to London. &c. It formerly subsisted (if I'm not mistaken) on Glasshouses, though at present there is not one in the Town.

John's account of the tour ended on a practical note:

At Cardiff salmon is 4 lb. 5 lb. and 6 lb per £. They serve Bristol and Bath. A side of a kid for 2s. Shrimps two years ago as many as you could eat for a half-penny. 'Tis now there but one fish Monger who does not think it worth while to bring any to this place.

They reached Oxford on 31 July and two weeks later John went home to Caversham,

It has long been my opinion [he wrote later in life] that the more modern languages we understand, the better we shall understand the antient languages. The difficulties which are in some degree relative being the idioms, perhaps at this time, of the English tongue, though by no means so of the Italian or French. In which case such passages of the

[q] The late Revd D. Morgan Jones kindly told me that when the church of St Cadoc was rebuilt in 1867 these gravestones may have been used to pave the aisles.

Antients shall be clear to an Englishman which gravel a Frenchman or Italian. Hence an Englishman wonders to see a foreign Critic, of great natural and acquired abilities, laying himself out in explaining a passage which to him is self-evident; and on the contrary taking no notice of passages which our countrymen can make nothing or little of; this latter case to be accounted for, from the antient passages in question falling-in with the idiom of the annotator's native tongue, whether Italian or French.

John himself might have been a suitable student for the new school of modern history and languages with its young Regius professor, David Gregory. The chair had been established some years earlier by the reforming bishop Edmund Gibson who was one day to become Patty's father-in-law. John would not have qualified for the other requirements – Whig tendencies and an ambition for diplomatic preferment.' He did in fact meet Gregory's elderly assistant, M. Louis Baillardeau, at the lodgings of a mutual friend, William Johnson of Queen's; but the lack of further tuition did not deter him and he applied himself to studying French with even greater enthusiasm, though it had nothing to do with his curriculum. He could speak as well as he wrote and Lambert and Audley often asked him to read aloud to them. When he was at Caversham he not only attended the French Club meetings but also studied privately with M. Bellai.

Another regular member of the Club, having joined earlier that year, was his friend and schoolfellow Richard Simeon, who could as easily be found with him at The Mitre or the coffee house in Reading. They would foregather in a group which included all ages, Dr John Merrick, the clergymen, Whitehead and Beaulieu, and Dick Wooddeson, the school usher. It was Wooddeson with his talent for verse who this month had written some lines about the old cleaning woman at Reading:

> On Goody Biddice, who cleans the Church and the Assembly-Room.
>
> What mighty jarring Interests may we see
> Obsequious Biddice reconciled in thee?
> Who to adorn hast equal skill bestow'd
> The House of Mammon and the House of God:
> Still studious to oblige the righteous few,
> You set the Hassock and you dust the Pew;
> Nor with less Care you rub the shining Board,
> Where Widows worship and Spadille's ador'd.[11]

Richard Simeon, who was descended from the Simeons of Pyrton, became an attorney and when Alexander Staples gave up he took over the affairs

---

' Bishop Gibson and Lord Townshend founded the Regius chairs at both universities in 1724 to further the Whig cause there. The plan was not well received at Oxford. See W. R. Ward, *Georgian Oxford*, p. 132.

of the Loveday family. One of his four sons was Charles Simeon, the well-known evangelical leader.

Hearne, who lived very much in the tradition of Anthony Wood, was a great collector of epitaphs, most enthralled by those of people he had actually known. With this in mind John and Thomas Bonney rode over late in August to the beautiful church at Shottesbrook, close to the house where Hearne's hero, the fearless and talented Francis Cherry, had lived and died in 1713 before he was fifty. His widow, Elizabeth, daughter of John Finch of Feens, had long survived him and had died only a few weeks before this expedition. It is easy to imagine the young men taking their notes in the church or wandering under the shade of the trees in the parkland, for this is one of those places which seem unaffected by time. Close by was the church of White Waltham where John's parents had worshipped and the names on the gravestones were almost as well known to him as to Hearne; indeed land in the parish was being held in trust for him. He found memorials for Cherry's daughter, Sarah, and for Alexander Staples's brother Edmund who had been rector of Shottesbrook, but nothing for the Revd John Griffyth who had held the living of White Waltham and whom Hearne had known well. He wrote on 25 August:

> I went on Monday with Mr Bonney to . . . White Waltham and Shottesbrook Churches. Mr Griffyth has not so much as a Stone over him to let you know where he lies . . . His Mother-in-Law's[5] Epitaph I took down and here send you. I suppose you have his Wife's, if not I can help you to that. There is nothing yet put up for Sir Constantine Phipps . . . I have got Mr Staples's Epitaph at Shottesbrook and Sara Cherry's . . . These, if you have not them already are at your Service. To be sure you have heard that Mrs Cherry dyed suddenly at Mr Hayes's of Holyport-Green in Bray Parish. She was buryed (if my Information is right) on Friday August 8th at Shottesbrook in the Family Vault. Sir C. Phipps was born at Reading and educated at the Free-School there, his Father (as the Report is) keeping the Golden Bear in that Town. I should be glad to know for certain where the Founder of St John's [Sir Thomas White] was born; we are not positive 'twas at Reading, tho' Dr Merrick remembers an old man who used to name the very House of his Birth, a Building since taken down in the Butter-Market; upon the spot there now lives John May, an Undertaker. Sir T. White's father, who was a Clothier, was born at Rickmansworth in Hertfordshire[f] . . . 'tis a very sickly time about us; several are down with the Small-Pox and Fever; if any of our Family

---

[5] Mrs Jane Rudge.
[f] Charles Coates's authority for the site of Sir Thomas White's birth (see *D.N.B.* and Coates's *History and Antiquities of Reading,* p. 405n) must have come either from this letter to Hearne, from John's copy in which a note was added to say that Dr Merrick had given him the information on 20 August 1729, or from a note in John's original diary.

should be taken ill I shall be with you before October 9. But let that be as it
will . . .[12]

The only person to catch the disease in his immediate circle was the sister of
his former schoolfellow John Hocker, so he did not have to escape. In any case
he had had smallpox as a child.

> I wanted Madam Rudge's Epitaph [wrote Hearne on 4 September] and I
> thank you for sending it me. I shall also be obliged for Mr Griffyth's Wife's
> Epitaph, as I shall likewise if you will be so kind as to communicate that to
> the Memory of Mr Cherry's daughter Sarah . . . I had heard of Madam
> Cherry's Death, but I knew not the day. The Founder of St. John's as I take
> it was born at Reading. I know some have scrupled it, but I think that
> Matter hath been cleared . . .[13]

Hearne ended his letter with the usual sort of request. This time it was for
information on a tournament which had taken place at Reading in 1307.
Replying on 11 September John made no reference to this but added a note to
his copy to say that Hearne had the only account of such a tournament in a
Garderoba. He sent the epitaphs, saying that he wished he knew who had
composed Sarah Cherry's as it was so well done. The last letter between them
for almost a year came from Hearne, written on 18 September.

> I thank you for the Epitaphs. But I am so far from knowing who the
> Author of that on Mr Cherry's Daughter was, that I never heard of any
> Monument to her, 'till you told me . . . Whoever 'twas I take him to have
> been of a different Persuasion from Mr Cherry (as Mr Staples indeed was)
> otherwise he would have mentioned in it Mr Cherry's integrity, which (as
> well as his other Virtues and great Learning) made him so deservedly
> respected. Some time after Mr Cherry's Death, I remember some body
> told me, that a Monument was designed for him in the Church, with an
> Inscription (different from what had been put by his own order over his
> Grave in the Church-Yard)" agreeable to what I have wrote of him in my
> Preface to Leland's Coll.[14] but I heard no more of it, and perhaps no more
> was meant, than what was said of him in his Daughter's Epitaph. I have
> not so much as one of Mr Griffyth's Things. Nor did I know that he had
> published any other Piece beside his Sermon, 'till you lately informed me.
> I should be glad to have a List of every thing he published. I knew him full
> well. He was really a great man, and 'twas a Scandal that he was neglected.
> He expounded the Catachism in White Waltham Church (in the
> Afternoons) many Years, to the great Satisfaction and Improvement of
> his Auditors. I hardly knew one that excelled him in the Duties of a
> Parochial Priest.[15]

John did not neglect his mother. He enjoyed accompanying her on polite

---

" 'Hic jacet peccatorum maximus.'

calls, particularly when it was to their near neighbours at Caversham Park, Lord and Lady Cadogan. She was a daughter of Sir Hans Sloane and as kind as she was intelligent. The usual visit to London was made in September. Aunt Hopkins was with the Tookes but he missed seeing the kindly Sir Richard this time as he could not be found when searched for in the South Sea House. Sarah had been asked rather urgently to come to town as Edmund Tooke was unwell and when John returned home she stayed on at Tooting. Little is known of Edmund Tooke beyond his having been Clerk to the Salters' Company, but a portrait thought to be by Kneller shows him as a handsome man. He died in November and was buried beside his father-in-law in the Clapham vault.

Meanwhile John went to stay with the Hileys and the following year he gave a present to Thomas in order to repay his parents' kindness.

July 24. 1730. Gave to Thomas Hiley the sum of VI Guineas to buy him books in consideration of the great Favours I had received from his Father, and particularly that of allowing me to live with him Part of the Long Vacation.

Wooddeson was preaching in Goring in September and John went with him on a short trip to Streatley, Newbury and Hungerford and on to Littlecote Park where he saw Mr Popham's tessellated pavement. On 23 September workmen began to take down the timber at the southern end of Caversham Bridge (the northern end consisting of stone arches). The road to Reading had been improved the previous year by the progressive mayor, John Watts. John recorded some of his remarks in August 1731:

Alderman Watts said that when Causham-Bridge was last built-up, above half a year since, they light upon the old Foundations of the Bridge and upon a Stone with an ancient Inscription which workmen let slip; that the first mention of the Bridge was in Temp. Stephani; that the Road before [was] at Norcot Scower; that a Chappel was upon Caversham-Bridge dedicate to the Holy Ghost, as says Queen Elizabeth's Charter; that the Chappel of Our Lady was at Benwell's, Caversham Farm . . .

Hearne was planning his *Historia Walteri Hemingford* (which came out in 1731) and the first few days of term were entirely taken up with helping him. In John's son's[v] words

He transcribed from the Reading Mercury concerning Reading and communicated it to Hearne; for whom on October 11th he collected from the College Archives part of an MS. of Hemingford's Edward III which he almost daily compared with Hearne; who was frequently with him in the afternoon as he was with Hearne in the morning.

John did not complete this copy until 22 October having applied himself to

[v] Dr John Loveday, D.C.L. ('Jack').

it 'very eagerly and carefully'. On 12 May 1730 he gave John Dart's book on Westminster Abbey[w] to Magdalen College Library in gratitude for the use of the Hemingford manuscript.

John Whiteside died unexpectedly in October, his illness partly caused, according to Hearne,[16] by drinking bad small beer at Christ Church. The Cat Street evenings continued for a month or two but the convivial spirit had gone out of them and Shepherd's became the usual rendezvous for Hearne and hs friends. Death seemed to be in the air as the winter crept on. John received the news from his mother of Uncle Tooke's demise but he was not expected to leave his studies for the funeral. Another fatality was a highly respected resident of Caversham, Henry Benwell, whose grandson William was to be John Loveday's son-in-law and chronicler. The funeral at night was unusual in that loaves were distributed by 'the Overseers' according to the will of the deceased. In December came the loss which most affected John, that of Benjamin Shirley, the bookseller whose correspondence he had dealt with whenever he was at home during the last two years. Shirley left a widow and daughter with whom John always kept in touch.

Indefatigable as ever and fired by indignation, he was now busy with a new ploy – that of removing all the heretical books from the Little Library[x] at Magdalen. Whether or not Henry William Cane was responsible for putting them there, he certainly remained on very good terms with the President and Fellows after he had gone to Selborne. Since Hearne was now so frequently in the Library it may have been due to his influence that on 15 October John took the 'offensive' books from the shelves himself, sent a list of them to Philip Vaughan, who happened to be at Reading, and spent some time next day walking the Margaret Professor of Divinity, Thomas Jenner, round the grounds while he told him all about them. Whether his protests ever penetrated the comfortable lethargy of the Fellows' Common Room (where Henry Dodwell was still acceptable) is doubtful – but at least he was not told to put the books back. Besides all this he had set apart Fridays to 'settle the College Writings for Zinzan', presumably in some sort of voluntary capacity.

In spite of his many occupations he was reading for his own benefit and interest harder than ever. The authors he tackled in November alone comprise a formidable list – Leland, Browne Willis, Richardson, Clarendon, Anthony Wood, William Lowth (Robert's father), Swift, Robert Boyle, Henry Wharton, Thomas Smith, John Bearblock,[17] William Fulke, Nicholas Fitzherbert, Sir Philip Warwick, Peter Barwick – as well as studying Dacier's Horace. This list of a month's reading (and the actual works are all recorded)

---

[w] Dart's *Westmonasterium* is thought to have been published in 1723, although R. Watt, *Bibliotheca Britannica* gives the date as 1725. The book was reissued in 1742, the only date in the *D.N.B.*

[x] The 'Little Library' was probably the small room adjoining (or a subsidiary of) the main library.

is all the more startling as apparently he found it hard to apply himself. Benwell wrote:

> I have heard him declare that when he was young it was with great difficulty that he could bring himself to attend to any book which he sat down to read and notwithstanding all his endeavours to the contrary, his mind would be straying several times in the same page. How well his application surmounted this is clearly demonstrated in the vast stock of erudition he now possesses; and this may serve as a useful hint to those who from discovering in themselves an inattention of mind, with want of memory, are too apt to despair in the pursuit of learning and give up the point from a fear of those obstacles which application might easily remove.

Unfortunately neither of them explained exactly how it was done.

Over the Brecon Hills
1730

The following March (1730) Bonney rode back to Oxford with John to enter
Bacon's service. As he was now to live in college he was able to repay his
friend's assistance by helping him with the transcriptions of the Magdalen
documents. John, now nineteen and entering on his third year at the
University, was thoroughly well established and had no qualms about
confronting the President or Thomas Jenner, who was next in the hierarchy,
on Bonney's behalf. He had become a favourite with the authorities with
whom he mixed freely, even walking in procession with the Proctors. A series
of visitors came to see him during the next few weeks. Mr Dore, the dancing
master from his school, was the first, bearing a letter from Mr Hiley and
delighted to be made welcome in the Common Room; then came a number of
Reading friends to hear Joseph Spence, the Professor of Poetry, preach at New
College and to dine with John; and they were followed by Jonah Chesterman
when he preached before the University. But the most exciting visit was on 18
April when John's mother, sister and Aunt Betty came to see him at Oxford for
the first time. This was an occasion of great importance to him and he rode
down to Benson with Charles Hopson to meet the coach half-way and escort it
back to the city. The family stayed for four days, saw the colleges and
Blenheim and met both old and new acquaintances. Mrs Loveday in her tactful
maternal way gave John twelve guineas 'for the charge of treating' and Aunt
Betty presented him with a handsome silver kettle to grace his rooms. It must
have been a wonderful outing for Patty who was now thirteen years old. John
escorted the coach back to Benson where they all dined together before
parting.

Mrs Loveday knew her son was planning another ramble and no doubt wanted to discuss it with him and perhaps to stipulate that he should be accompanied by his tutor, who was a full six years older than he; but be that as it may it was Zinzan who was the chosen companion for a ride into the heart of Wales. To travel on horseback over the Brecon Hills and on into Pembrokeshire was no small undertaking and much time was spent in planning the route, part of which would be along rough tracks. They made inquiries of Philip Whitehead, the curate at St Laurence's, Reading, who knew the country well. His crumpled letter with John's pencil marks on the back has obviously travelled many miles in a pocket.

> Let Mr Whitehead be a guide to the Gentlemen to St. David's Church, there turn short on the left hand; from thence the great and public road to Pont y Cynedir, and on up Bwlch y Van, and a Bridge called Pont ar Daf— the great and Common road you are to ride to Pont y Stickill. An Alehouse 8 miles from Brecon. I recommend you to take a Guide from thence to the top of the Coal Pit and you from there will readily find the road to Pen yr Heol Vawr and with great ease from thence to Cardiff.[1]

Though these explicit instructions might have made more experienced travellers think twice, they felt sure they could follow the route. This time John kept careful records, the route and mileage always preceding the accounts of the places. They set off from Oxford on 25 May and reached Gloucester the same evening, a distance of thirty-three miles according to John's reckoning, though he added

> The Miles are so long between Burford and Gloucester that to every third Mile we may add one.[a]

It is hardly surprising therefore that they only paid a short visit to the Cathedral before finding their lodgings at the Swan. Poor Zinzan, never very energetic and now tired after having carried the baggage on such a long ride, still had something new that night to learn about his young charge. Benwell writes:

> . . . as they travelled on horseback without a servant, it was agreed that one should carry the Portmanteau for the day and the other should see the horses taken care of in the evening, and this alternately. Dr Z.[b] carried the Portmanteau the first day and in the evening Mr L. took charge of the horses and staid near an hour in the stable while they were fed and littered. Upon his return into the Room the doctor inquired if it would be necessary for him to pay as long attendance in the stable in his turn and

---

[a] The distance from Gloucester to Oxford is forty-nine miles, though the route differed at first. John was using the old mileage of 2,428 yards to the mile.

[b] Benwell knew Zinzan as a man who had practised medicine. In 1730 he was known as Mr Zinzan.

being answered in the affirmative, said that he would rather carry the Portmanteau every day, if Mr L. would every evening take charge of the Horses; which plan they practised through the whole of their Tour.

Possibly the reason John had chosen Peter Zinzan as his tutor was because he knew how to manage him. Zinzan no doubt had a good working knowledge of the classics but his real interest was in medicine and he eventually returned to Reading to practise for a short time as a physician until marriage made it unnecessary for him to work at all. Meanwhile he was a cheerful and amusing companion, though the entertainment he provided was sometimes unintentional.

They rode into Hereford next day through 'pleasant suburbs' and visited the Coningsby Hospital for twelve men.

1 Chaplain. 1 Corporal and 10 Servitors. The Servitors have 4s. 10d. per Septimanam, besides an allowance of 9s. per Hyemem for Cheeses and Fuel. This Salary is but ill-paid by their Steward, Mr Carpenter. Their Commander was the late Earl Coningsbye, some Rules of whom are hung up in the Chappel dated 1716. They are to attend Sermon and Prayers every Sunday Morning in their Habits in the Cathedral, in the Afternoon at their own Chappel; as also on Monday, Wednesday, Friday and Saturday. This and other Orders to be obeyed under the Penalties of Fines. In the road and suburbs nigh Hereford we saw Barns wattled with Planks of Wood between the Timber-Work and we met with more of this afterwards in the Road. In Hereford we saw some Women wash Clothes thus; they wetted the Linnen very much in the River, then folded it together and laying it upon a Stool, beat it very hard with a flat wooden Instrument on both sides; then wett it again and beat it again, till the Water drove through every thread of it cleanses it entirely.

Both at Hereford and at Gloucester John, with the dislike of Norman Romanesque architecture typical of his generation, thought the pillars of the naves too large. His description of Hereford Cathedral was almost entirely confined to the tombs and monuments.

Bishop Francis Godwin's recumbent Statue is basely used; the Head beat off and otherwise mutilated when that part of the Church was made a Stable in the troublesome times. There are two recumbent Statues in different parts of the Church, over both of which is the same writing in modern Text-hand . . viz Dominus Robertus de Losinga, Episcopus and Dominus Reynelmus, Episcopus. So that it is doubted which is Losing's and which Reynelmus. Bishop Booth's Monument is lately by a Relation cleaned and otherwise adorned, as is Alexander Denton's and his Wife by Judge Denton, a Descendant of theirs . . . There are Persons buryed in the Chapter-house in one part of which is the Library.

The Vicars-Choral have a College to themselves and are buryed in the Cloysters of it. They have a common Refectory with Offices and a floored Room called the Chappel with an old Desk in it, but now disused and running to decay. These Vicars that are marryed do not live in the College, and (if I mistake not) let their Rooms to any Gentleman that will take them.

They looked at the palace, restored by the previous bishop and with a room still waiting to be made into a chapel, and they visited the three other churches. Next day, after an uneventful ride to Brecon on an easy road, they stopped for two nights at the Great Bear and John made extensive notes about the four churches. Of the town itself he said:

There are some Remains of the Town Walls, the Gates standing entire. We see here without the Walls the ruin of a Castle and the Mount belonging to it . . . The Great Bridge . . . over the Usk is without the Gate and is a fine piece of Stone-arched Work. There are no Brick Buildings in the Town; the Streets are pitched. They say that within 4 miles of the Town is a Pool called Llangos of large Extent, through the middle of which runs a River of reddish Colour which never mixes its Waters with the Pool. But we did not go to see.

They set off on 30 May, with a real sense of adventure, to ride over the hills to Pontstickill and Pen yr Heol Vawr.

The Road along this Journey very mountainous and stony. We went nigh a Bridge called Pont y Cynedir . . . then our Road was up Bwlch y Van, on which is the highest Mountain in South Wales called Beggans, 3 Miles from Brecon. This we crawled up, fastening our Horses to a Stone below. Fern grows on some part of it. The Day was very cloudy so that we lost a very extensive Prospect. We were sufficiently wet with the Mist, though our Horses' Saddles entirely dry below. It was pleasant when up the Hill to see the Clouds below us slide along the Sides of it, as it was also when on Bwlch y Van, (which by the by is an hill itself, a Valley running considerably below it) the Clouds then seemed to cap the Hill, rowl backwards and forwards along at top of it and down the Sides. The continual Mists filled all the Cavities here capable of holding Water. Rills of Water are perpetually trickling down the sides of the Hill, several of them meeting together in the Valley give rise to the River Taff which waters Cardiff and there meets the Sea.

Benwell has an account of this ride and the clearest picture emerges when it is compared with John's diary. He says:

Their journey lay over a high mountain in the wild part of Brecknockshire, where were numberless mines and pits on all sides which rendered the riding very unsafe. As they rode along they espied a very

stout man coming towards them, very raggedly clothed and carrying in
his hand a long staff with a huge knob on the top. At this sight they began
to apprehend themselves in some danger, but as they could not ride off
without great hazard of falling into some of the chasms, they judged it
more adviseable to shew no signs of fear, but to approach and address him
civilly. Mr L. enquired of him if that was the road to some town where
they proposed to stop. He replied, it was, but the way was very difficult to
find. Mr L. asked him if he would be willing to go with them and direct
them, adding that if he would, he would make it worth his while. 'Yes, he
said – he would shew them the way. Accordingly he turned back with
them; Mr L. entered into conversation with him and to his great
astonishment found him one of the most intelligent men he had ever
conversed with.

In his written account John said that the guide told them that in Castell
Murglas, which they passed, there was still one room left with pillars and
curious arched work – the rest was a ruin. He said

that the best Welsh was spoken in Carmarthen and Cardiganshires, the
worst in Monmouth and Glamorganshires . . . that the people of Rhysky
in Monmouthshire are the Jest of the Welsh for their Stupidity – called the
Fools of Rhysky; several such stories are told of them as of the Men of
Goatham. He said that the Welsh Judges had 1000£ per Annum (its false –
about 500£) . . . He mentioned Caerphilly as a noted place for Strumpets;
gave Moses Williams the character of a conscientious as well as a learned
Man; but for the generality of their Clergy, complained of them as a
druken set of People, drawn through the Universities (this was his
expression) with small Improvements in anything but Debauchery. He
finished them with telling us that they spoilt their Parishes. He told us that
Mr Rees Prichard (Author of the admirable Welsh Hymns) left Lands at
Llandovery for the use of the Poor of the Place; but they receive no Benefit
from them, being withheld by Captain Manwry [Mainwaring], a
descendant of Prichard's,[c] who left but one Child, a Daughter. He
remarked that the River Towyn had encroached upon great part of these
Lands, which was looked upon as a Judgment for their misapplication.

According to Benwell the guide then turned to matters of religion.

'We have got, said the Stranger, 'among us a most odd set of men who

[c] Were it not for the fact that John misheard the name and added his own contribution –
that the flooding was looked upon as a judgment – he might have taken this story from
Anthony Wood's *Athenae Oxonienses*. The vicar, Rhys Prichard, had also a son, Samuel,
whose daughter, Elizabeth, married Thomas, son of his friend and executor, Roger
Mainwaring, Bishop of St Davids. In 1729 the charity was deemed lost and the school lands
were in the possession of Anne Mainwaring, widow of Thomas's son, Roger. See A. T.
Arbor-Cooke, *Pages from the History of Llandovery*, 1975.

are for subverting all right Religion. They even go so far as to deny the reality of original sin. It is impossible such people as these can believe the Bible . . .' Mr L. and his Companion stared with amazement at their wonderful guide. He continued this strain of discourse the whole way.

John wrote in his diary that after they had passed the most dangerous bogs and coalpits

we called for Drink at a lonely House upon the Heath, but might have called in vain, had not our Guide spoken Welsh, which gained us the privilege of a Mug of Ale. The People of the House seemed to be in a fright at seeing anything unlike a Shepherd or Drover, confessing to the Guide that they were at the Door when we called, but should not have opened if they had not heard Welsh.

The story is finished by Benwell.

At last, coming to the strait road, the guide put them in the way and turned to depart. Mr L. entreated him to accompany them to the town and spend the Evening with them, adding that it would cost him nothing and that they would provide him a bed there and when the morning came he might return. He replied that he should be very glad to do it, but that it could not well be as he had a wife and five children at home who would be very uneasy at his absence. Mr L. then took out his purse and offered him some money for his services. He started back with some anger and said 'Have you so bad an opinion of me as to think that I won't put strangers and wanderers in the way without being paid for it?' Dr Zinzan told him that he was sure his friend would not have suffered him to come a step of the way with them, if he had not meant to reward him. After much solicitation they at length prevailed upon him to accept of a small present and having taken leave of them he turned back. Mr L. forgot to ask his name and was never afterwards able to learn any accounts of a person whose figure had inspired him with so much terror and whose abilities with so much admiration.

On Sunday 31 May they were at Caerphilly.

Carphilly Castle is called by the Welsh the blue Castle of Wales; it belongs to Mr Powell who lives hard by.[d] It is vastly large, the Walls excessively thick and strong and has been double-moted. A round Tower in it inclines too much to stand long. There is a covered way remaining pretty entire. The Pillars in the Hall . . . are for nothing but

[d] There is no other evidence that Roger Powell of Energlyn (sheriff in 1707) or his son owned Caerphilly Castle, but his wife was Ann, daughter of William Herbert of the White Friars, Cardiff, and the castle had been in the possession of the Herbert family since 1550. See also *Caerphilly Local History Society Journal*, no. 1, 1968.

ornament, the lower part of them being a good way from the Ground . . .

As they passed Lord Mansell's seat, Margam,ᵉ they admired the thick oak woods 'whose even Tops look at a distance like the greensward of the Mountains'. They crossed the River Neath at Briton Ferry and rode along the sea side to Swansea which was clean and pitched and had only one brick house. Salmon was scarce

> though they abound in Shuin which is neither in Taste or Look discernible from Salmon, but the Fishermen will have it of a different Species. 'Tis Salmon-peelᶠ perhaps. They have excellent French Wines here.
>
> There is a Ferry over the River Logher [Loghour] which we crossed and then were in Carmarthenshire. A great Colliery about this Countrey. At Llanelly we were told that 7000£ per Annum went one year with another to the Crown from that Parish only. The Duty upon Coals here is 5s. per Chaldron. We were told here that they feed their horses with Fuss Tops, having ground or pounded them, when green, to a Pulp. They mix a small quantity of Oats with it and give it their horses. An Arm-full of Fuss (we were informed) was Meat enough for an Horse for 24 Hours.

Several years later John noted that Mr Hiley had told him that the colliers of Kingswood, near Bristol, fed their horses in the same manner. They reached Carmarthen on 3 June.

> The Gateway of the Castle and the Tower on the Mount (which is all remaining) are used for a Prison; it was never, I believe, an handsome Building, the work of it looking but clumsy. One Perrot keeps a Dissenting Academy here. There are several Coffee-houses and Taverns in the Town; in the Winter is a large Assembly, the Gentry (all the Summer at their Countrey-Seats) then residing here. Salmon at Carmarthen is at 6d. or 7d. per pound.

At the palace he noticed that the chapel 'above Stairs new-Pewed by Bishop Ottley' had recently been painted by Bishop Smalbroke 'who lives here sometimes a Quarter of a year'.

They left the Red Lion at Carmarthen next day and travelled on 'as fine a Road as any in England' to Pembroke, pleased to find that the people spoke English. A glance round Carew Castle showed a few rooms still remaining, some above stairs and some underground. There was also 'a Bog-house very entire'. Pembroke Castle was ruined, but they visited the Wogan –

> a large Room hewn out of solid Rock for a Storehouse. A Pistol fired

---

ᵉ This house was demolished at the end of the eighteenth century.
ᶠ Salmon weighing less than two pounds.

here makes as great a report as a Cannon. In the middle of it was a Well now filled-up. The Site of the Castle and Mannor there is Mr George Langton's of Hurst, Berkshire.[8]

They saw the ruined church of St Daniel with a steeple which was a landmark for sailors, St Mary's with its tower damaged by Cromwell's men and the 'Mountain-Church' of St Nicholas on the site of an old monastery. They were told Sir Arthur Owen's seat, Orielton, a mile south of the town, was the best in the county. It was Cromwell again who was still a source of gossip in the town.

Pembroke Town and Castle (says a Barber that was my Informant in some of the foregoing particulars) held out so strong against Cromwell that he left the place for Tenby; but a Soldier, getting from the Castle and informing him that their Ammunition was spent and they reduced to 5 Beans a day, he returned and the place surrendered; but hung up the Informer at the East Gate, saying he hated the Traytor though he loved the Treason.

On 5 June they travelled on a very fine road to Haverfordwest, 'commonly called Harford'. The new stone bridge had been erected only four years earlier by Sir John Philipps of Picton Castle.

The Priory, just out of the Town, belongs to Campbell, Knight of the Shire who would not suffer the Ground of it, because Consecrated, to be turned into a Bowling-Green. The Pigeon-house belonging to it is now a Barn, the rest in Ruins. Harford is a Town of great Trade, chiefly malting. The best Welsh-Ale is sent from hence; one man here brews 100 Barrels a Week. The Assizes for the County are kept here. Our Landlord at the White Hart, Mr Blundel, is a Dancing Master. He told me that Carew Castle surrendered to Cromwell and was destroyed and that Cromwell, upon consultation what to do with the Castles about this Countrey said he would send a Drove of Hogs to root up Carmarthen Castle, alluding to its Foundation on a Sand. Seagers are taken and sold for 2d. a piece. They call them in other places Sea Cray-fish or Sea-Spiders.

As John's interest in architecture was not yet fully developed he had less to say about the structure of St Davids Cathedral than about the peculiarities of its clergy, about which the landlord was informative; he was after all only making notes for his own (and Hearne's) amusement. They had come past Roch Castle

[8] Nicholas Lewes of Hean Castle bought the lordship of East and West Pembroke, including the castle, in 1661. George Lewis Langton, stepson of Walter Pryse, was a descendant as is shown in a pedigree in 'The Lewes Family of Abernantbychan', an article in *Ceredigion* (Journal of the Cardiganshire Antiquarian Society), vol. VI, no. 2, 1969 by Daniel Huws. See also p. 103 n.*l*.

which belonged, with its estate containing 'a good Colliery', to the son of Sir Richard Walter (who had died the previous year).

He was knighted by King William – a Nonjuror till the Act for registering Estates, and upon his taking the Oaths made High Sheriff of the County.

There was a new monument at St Davids for William Needham, who had been Chancellor there for forty years and had died as recently as 1727. It stood against the south wall of the chancel which was paved with painted brick. The nave acted as the parish church. Bishop Smalbroke, a Magdalen man and a great fighter of heresies, was apparently not very popular here.

The Ruins of the Bishop's Palace are very grand; it has the finest Vaults I ever saw ['and a noble Kitchen,' he added later]. The People have a silly Notion that if the Bishop should come here at St. James's Tide, when the Audit is, the Chapter can oblige him to rebuild his Palace. Bishop Smalbroke is in no good understanding with the Chapter. He has obliged them by law to reside here two Months in a Year; in this undertaking he had the concurrence of the Chantor; the Chapter fills up their own Vacancies. Blundel told me that the Bishop interested himself in Parliamentary Elections, but that the Generality of the Clergy voted contrary to him; that Impropriators generally gave their Clergy 5£ per Annum; the most generous 10£. One half of the Clergy hereabout have never been at an University. The Chantor, Chancellor, Treasurer and the Archdeacon have Houses standing now. Dr Davies, the Chantor, has laid out money on his House; he is very hospitable here . . Medley, the Archdeacon has never been here but once . . .

Culm is much burnt in the Countrey; 'Tis a kind of Dust-Coal and this mixed up with Clay in Balls, makes a strong fire, does not smoak but emits a Sulphurous Smell; sometimes found in Pits with Coal and sometimes by itself.

They rode back into the country around Haverfordwest where English was spoken and then out of it again as they approached Cardiganshire.

Bwlch y Guent is the highest Hill in the County; over part of it our Road lay, but (as at Bwlch y Van) we fastened our Horses to a Stone and mounted the Top of it; the Mist indeed spoiled our prospect; on the sides of the Mountains are several great Stones and at Top a large Heap lie all together; and so on in the Road farther. Not coming down the same way I climbed up, I lost sight of my Horses and concluded them stole by some Welsh Men.

Fortunately it was a false alarm and they made their way to Cardigan which they considered to be very mean. On 8 June they arrived at the little town of Tregaron.

We took up at the best house in Tregaron which is a poor straggling place. Here we had Oat-Bread served up to us, made in form of Pancake, of Oatmeal and Water; and our Provision and Lodging altogether was the worst I ever met with. We were taken for Officers employed in the Wine Licence.

The memory of the appalling conditions at Tregaron remained with John for the rest of his life and were well known to his children. Benwell fills in the details:

In his Tour through Wales with Dr Zinzan, his Tutor, he stopped one Evening at an Inn at Tregaron in Cardiganshire, where he had not been long before he observed great numbers of the inhabitants collected round the window. Upon enquiring the reason of this of the Landlord, he replied 'I b'live, Sir, tha thinks ye be Custom-house Officers.' 'Custom-house Officers or not' says Mr L. with his usual spirit. 'tell them if they don't separate this Instant I'll fire among them.' Though he had in reality no fire arms with him, this menace had such an effect that they all immediately departed with the greatest order.

Their discomforts, not to say dangers, were by no means over.

At Tregaron they were obliged to sleep in the same bed at the Inn, for want of better accommodation. In the morning he observed the Doctor getting up very early and seemingly in a very ill humour. Upon being asked the reason of this he replied that he had been terribly bitten by fleas and besides had been in great danger of falling out of bed. Mr L. expressed much surprise at this answer as the Doctor had laid next the wall the whole night, when the other drawing aside a blanket discovered that the wall of the house was entirely down on that side and that this blanket had been the only partition between them and the street.

On leaving Wales John made a few general observations which were not entirely laudatory.

We were asked at Inns what we would have for Dinner and what time; what we bespoke was put upon the Table, and perhaps two other Dishes besides; the House dined with us, and without ceremony eat of our Dish; and we made no distiction of 'This is my Dish and this is Yours', but eat indifferently of either; and for such a Meal the common Price was 6d. a head, sometimes a Shilling. At Supper indeed no more than what you bespeak is dressed, but then you don't pay for all the Joint you bespeak but only 6d. or so for eating of it. A Goose was sent up at Haverford-West with the Neck and Head on; with Pinnions and Liver and Gizzard under 'em; Chickens in the same manner throughout Wales, as were ducks, except that they had no Heads. Black Oats all through Wales. We were asked at every Inn whether we would not have our Horses put to Grass. We met with Numbers whose only Answer was Stim Sasnach i.e.

No English. If we pointed with our Whips towards the place we would
go to and named it thus – to Tregaron? – we were answered perhaps
with Ye-a, Ye-a. The common Welsh Women were neither Shoe nor
Stockings; their Garments are full short; their upper Covering a dusky-
coloured Stuff, over that a Night-Rail of the same sort or sometimes of
a Red Colour. A Piece of Black Gauze, or Crape (as I take it) in form of
Scull-Cap comes over the head and is pinned close under the Chin;
over this a Man's Hat lopped. You often see them with a long Pole in
their hands driving half a dozen Pack-Horses, loaden with Coal. The
wheat-Bread was so wretchedly made here that we always preferred
Rye when we could get it.

   The Maid at the Inn at Cardigan being dressed because it was Sunday, in
the Evening put-on her every-day Cloaths and laid-by her Shoes and
Stockings (waiting upon us as usual bare-legged) only, I presume, to be
worn on High-Days.

They took two days to ride back over the hills, stopping the first night at the
Excise Officer at Newtown and reaching Shrewsbury on the next. The scenery
was romantic but the tracks were stony and the bread was poor for most of the
way. No doubt they were glad to arrive at the Gullet Inn and have a quick look
at Shrewsbury town. It possessed such large suburbs, John said, that it was, all
told, the biggest town he had ever seen. The brick houses all looked new but
there was a good deal of old building intermixed.
   He admired the handsome church at Ludlow.

   The Body of the Church is as at St. David's, a Choir and in the Nave a
Parish Church; in the former there is now never any Service. Relievo
Work under the Stalls in it and Painted Glass in the Windows. The Hon.
Mr Herbert, Member of Parliament for this town[h] is going to put up an
Altar-piece here. Sir Littleton Powys gave the Engine and Buckets here in
consideration that the Town assisted at a Fire at his House a mile
hence . . . The Castle is decaying apace and falling down. In the
Court-Yard before it is the Gaol for the Welsh Counties, their Court of
Justices and Stables. At Ludlow is a new long and very handsome
Brick-arched Market House; over it a sashed Room; one end of it the
Town-Court, t'other the Council Chamber; the long Space between
being made use of for an Assembly which is not now in its Lustre . . .
Here we eat Bread made half of Wheat and half of Rye, called Munkunn
Bread.

Compared with Shrewsbury, Birmingham, reached by way of Kidderminster and Halesowen, did not seem unduly large, handsome as it was –

---

[h] Henry Arthur Herbert, created Lord Herbert of Cherbury in 1743 and 1st Earl of Powis
in 1748, represented Oakley Park interest for Ludlow jointly with his younger brother,
Richard, from 1727 until 1741. *V.C.H. Shropshire*, vol. IV.

much the greater part of it new-built and Brick. The Streets are strait and regular. Here is a small, but very regular Square having four Entrances into it from four Streets . . The new Church is built of a whitish Stone and is a very neat and beautiful Structure . . . Bishop Chandler consecrated St. Philip's and presented Mr Higgs, formerly of Wadham College, to the Benefice, who now enjoys it. The Parishes are still very large. The most genteel Houses are in the new Parish out of the Trading part of the Town. The Free-School here, a pretty, late Brick Building, was founded Anno Edward VI. The Iron-Slitting Mills at Birmingham are very curious, but we did not see them working. They want a River to export their Iron-Ware . . .

April 15. The Black Bull at Meriden is absolutely the grandest Inn I ever saw; a new, large, regular Brick Building, sashed. Coventry Streets are narrow and the Houses for the most part old. Though not nigh so populous, it stands upon about as much Ground as Birmingham. There are but small remains of the Town Walls with Walks on them.

Three Churches here, the Cathedral being destroyed. St. John's is now out of use being unglazed and decayed, so that its Parishioners go to St. Michael's. About 5 years since, as I was informed, a Breve had been procured for it, but the Bishop and the Government of the Town disputed the Presentation to the Benefice. St. Michael's is a magnificent Building; a handsome Tower and upon it a Spire of different Ages . . The Pillars here are very beautiful, being taper and the intervening Arches sufficiently wide. . . . There is a small Room called St. George's Chappel which is the Taylors and Sheermongers Hall;[i] over the Chimney-piece is 1623 carved out, with the names of some of the aforesaid Fraternity. There was a Pulpit here in the Memory of Man and a Marble Grave-Stone, as they say for St. George, but this Sir Russel Skipwith bought of Alderman Distans about twenty years since. They shew here part of a Coat of Mail, a Target made of small Iron Bars and lined with Bone with other parts of Armour, belonging also to this Saint, together with an old-fashioned Elbow-Chair and a large Wooden Trunk, barricaded with Iron; St. George triumphing over the Dragon hangs up here, carved in Wood. Against the East Wall on the Outside, hangs up a Bone of some Fish (as it should seem) but they tell you 'tis the Spade of the Wild Boar killed by St. George . . .

He could hardly leave Coventry without mentioning Lady Godiva.

On the Friday after Whitsun-Week, their chief Fair, a poor Girl is set on horseback and rides through the Town, in remembrance of Godiva, the Corporation attending here. There is now looking out of the window of a house in this Town the Effigies of the Man that saw the

---

[i] There were a number of guild chapels in the parish church of St Michael's which was a cathedral only from 1918 until 1940. 'Sheermongers' dealt in shears and scissors.

Countess ride naked. On the same Fair Day a Man is dressed up in a
Bishop's Habit and attended in a Procession, representing Bishop Blaize[j]
with a Bible in one Hand and Wool Comb in t'other; he being, they say,
the Inventor of that Instrument. Woollen Manufacture, such as Coventry
Stuffs, Yard-wide, and Ribbands, are the chief Trade of Coventry.

The road to Warwick was a good one 'with very short miles'. There John
saw the Castle which he was often to revisit.

The Stables are in the outward Yard, where they shew a Pot which upon
gauging was found to hold more than 87 gallons[k] and is 700 Weight; this
they tell you was Earl Guy's as also some Armour. Before that part of the
Castle which is a Dwelling-house are two round Towers, one on each
side, a convenient distance from the long Gate-way. There is a very
beautiful Vista of Rooms in the Castle . . Here is some of Van Dyck's
Painting . . I was told that Bodwyn, near Green's Brew-House,
Westminster, was copying all Van Dyck's Pieces, and that with Success.
A Room here is hung with Tapestry, curious for its small Figures and the
Variety of them.

St Mary's Church was, they say, built out of the Church-Yard except
the Pillars the Tower stands on, which are harder Stone: there are large
Pillars just within the Church, which 'tis reported, the Tower was to have
stood upon, but the Stone was found to be too green for the purpose . . .
One Mrs Leveson[l] of Lord Gower's family left, about the year 1673, 40£
per Annum issuing out of her Estate at Foxley in Northamptonshire, for
the Repair of decayed Monuments in this Church and the Overplus to
Dudley's Hospital.[m] St. Mary's Parish design with some of the Overplus
to pave their Altar with Marble and otherwise adorn their Church. And
they have repaired those Monuments hurt by the Fire, one of which was
Thomas Beauchamp's, (grandfather to Earl Richard) who lies before the
Altar. Nothing was remaining of the Monument of Thomas Beauchamp
(Richard's Father) but his and his Countess's Brass Effigies which are now
inserted in the East Wall of the South Cross and a Marble is put up with an
Inscription. They have also built anew the Seats in the Choir; . . . I was
told that the Rebel Soldiers would have destroyed the Monuments here,
had not one of them pretended that they belonged to the Ancestors of their

[j] 'Bishop Blaise' or St Blasius, patron saint of woolcombers.
  [k] John added a note in 1762 to say that it was now said at the Castle that the pot held ninety-
two gallons. The porridge pot was really a fourteenth- or fifteenth-century pot of cast brass.
Earl Guy was the legendary hero from whom the earlier line of Beauchamp Earls of Warwick
were said to have descended.
  [l] This was a mistake. Katharine Dudley, granddaughter of the Earl of Leicester, married
Sir Richard Leveson and was thus Lady Leveson. He was descended from Sir John Leveson of
Haling whose daughter Frances married Sir Thomas Gower, 2nd Baronet.
  [m] Lord Leycester Hospital.

Officer. Alderman Oken buryed here, besides considerable Charities, left 5s. per Annum to be spent between persons reconciled. Robert Dudley, Earl of Leicester founded in this Town an Hospital of 12 Men with a Salary of 10£ (now near as good as 30£) per Annum each. They have the Presentation to Hampton in Arden. There are two Chappels in Warwick, one belonging to this Hospital which is in use, the other is now a Charity School. There is an handsome new Stone Building here for Mayors' Feasts."

Zinzan must have cast a longing glance at the road south to Oxford but John had set his heart on 'taking-in' Worcester though it meant a long detour. They were disappointed in the Cathedral:

. . . Nothing strikes one . . . the Pillars are large . . . the Choir is large and long – under the Stalls Relievo work . . . The Bishop's Palace is an handsome Building of Brick, very much improved by Hough, who lets it to Mr Bromley,⁰ living himself at Hartlebury on which he has laid out a considerable Sum; he was very charitable to the Poor of Worcester last Winter. There is here a very grand and beautiful Brick Structureᵖ of about 6 Years' standing; in the Lower Room are the Courts for the Judges of the Circuits . . . there are Private Rooms besides for other Conveniences . . . Over this large Court is a Room made use of for the Mayor's Feasts. Two houses built as Wings to this Hall are let out by the Corporation; in one the Judges lie. Offices of all kinds there are behind this Building. The Corporation with the Assistance of the Gentlemen of the County erected it . . .

Two days later, on 20 June, they were back at Oxford having spent twenty guineas on the tour, including hire of the horses.

" The fire occurred in 1694. I am grateful to Dr Gilbert Cope for his comments on points in this and later accounts of Warwick by John Loveday which produce new information. These include the story of the rebel soldiers and the paving of the chancel from Lady Leveson's bequest. See also p. 191 n.e. The building for the Mayors' Feasts no doubt refers to the Court House.

⁰ There is no record at Hartlebury Castle of Bishop Hough having leased out the Palace, but the lessee was probably William Bromley of Abberley (son of Francis, d. 1703) or one of his sons of whom only Robert survived him.

ᵖ The Guildhall, built 1721–23 and designed by Thomas White.

The South Coast

1730

By some ironic coincidence the four people to whom Edward Gibbon referred specifically in his famous denunciation of his school and university education[1] – and of Magdalen College in particular – were all close friends of John Loveday. Had it been published in his lifetime John would surely have spoken out against the man who reviled his beloved college and scorned his lifelong companions.

The first of the four was Richard Wooddeson, who had the doubtful honour, in 1746, of becoming Gibbon's first headmaster at Kingston-upon-Thames. The impression is given that a brutal Wooddeson was responsible for the 'many tears and some blood' contributed by the poor child towards his improvement in learning; but another of his distinguished pupils, Gilbert Wakefield, said of him: 'His whole conduct indeed was so engaging in all its circumstances, as to make every scholar happy under his gracious and gentle reign.'[2]

The next on the list was the only one of the four who had not been educated at Magdalen. Robert Lowth was by then a bishop so renowned for his scholarship that Gibbon could hardly fail to commend him for that. However he quoted Lowth's own description of his happy days at Oxford,[a] criticized the bishop for not explaining the benefits he received there and denounced Lowth's claims in the light of his own trials.

[a] Robert Lowth's *Letter to the Author of the Divine Legation of Moses Demonstrated*, 1765. Warburton had attacked him and the University in an appendix added to the fifth volume of the fourth edition. Lowth gives an attractive picture of the days when he and John Loveday were undergraduates.

The third victim, Dr Thomas Waldgrave, his first tutor, was damned with faint praise and perhaps more justification. Kind, mild, erudite and godly as Waldgrave undoubtedly was, no one could have accused him of being a strict disciplinarian and it was of discipline as well as tuition that Gibbon felt he had been deprived. The second tutor, Thomas Winchester, was damned completely though his name was withheld by Gibbon's biographer, Lord Sheffield, when the memoirs appeared in 1796. Those of Winchester's friends who were still alive sixteen years after his death[b] may well not have realized who it was whose, 'literary character did not command the respect of the College' who 'well remembered that he had a salary to receive and only forgot that he had a duty to perform'. Yet this 'contemptible' Winchester was the man who, from the moment he came up from Magdalen College School in March 1730, walked straight into John Loveday's circle and remained one of its best-loved members for the rest of his life; to whom Caversham was a second home and who was married from that house to Lucretia Townson, herself as fine a character as her brother Thomas. Was the College really lacking in respect for a man whose theological studies demanded it from Archbishop Secker and Dr Glocester Ridley or whose *Dissertation on the XVIIIth Article of the Church of England*[3] was later widely praised? This was the man, too, who was so much loved by young people that John Loveday's son would ride out from Oxford or Caversham a dozen times in the year to stay with him at his living in Appleton, while Penelope, John's daughter, could write:

> Dr Winchester was a zealous friend and there was an energy in his manner that was peculiarly prepossessing from its so evidently arising from the honesty and warmth of his excellent heart. No man had, in the number of their acquaintance more friends . . . we thought of him as a tender father and next to our own beloved as such.

It could be enough to say that John Loveday, who always dealt summarily with any kind of imposture, would never had made a friend of such a man as Gibbon described. This was a case of blatant character assassination which has too often been cited to support criticism of the University. Gibbon was only fifteen when he came under Winchester's tutorage for a short time before being removed from Oxford. He was a precocious, unattractive youth, not ready for college life, who appeared to have settled in for several years as a rich gentleman commoner with plenty of time to find his level. He should at this stage have been under the direction of a private tutor or understanding schoolmaster as Wooddeson with his love of elegant prose might have been if the boy had remained in his charge. It is true that Winchester failed to discover his genius and unfortunate that he did not spare him the extra attention accorded to some young men under his care; but, whatever the defects of University life as it then was, such a personal attack was quite unjustified. It is sad that the feelings of a discontented child, swollen through thirty years to an

---

[b] In particular Dr John Loveday ('Jack') and Ralph Churton.

outrageous animosity, should have prevailed rather than the solid, honest loyalty of Thomas Winchester.

Winchester came down to Caversham for his first visit soon after John's return there. They were already firm friends and had walked together through the villages near Oxford, ridden down to Eynsham for musical evenings and worked at their studies in John's rooms. At Caversham he tasted the delights of Mrs Loveday's table and went shooting with that inveterate sportsman Zinzan. One morning they attended the opening of the new shop which John Hocker had set up in the market place in Reading. It seems to have replaced Shirley's bookshop and became an even more popular meeting place. There Hocker sold prints, medals, coins and anything the young collectors went in for. Simeon, Bonney and young John Merrick were also there and having made their purchases they left Hocker to his customers and climbed Catsgrove Hill to the south-west of Reading, where they could see the fossilized remains of innumerable oysters. They ended up by playing like children in the chalk holes underground.

The popular theory according to Mrs Lybbe Powys,[4] writing when she was still Caroline Girle, was that the oysters had been buried at Catsgrove 'at the Deluge'. Other remains, too, were to be found there: in 1757 John Hocker sent John Loveday a packet with an account of his discoveries.

> These Teeth I found at Catsgrove in the same beds, in which the Oisters lie. The upper bed is of Sand, of a sea-green colour, of about ten inches thickness; the lower bed is about fourteen inches thick, of a sort of bluish clay, interspersed with thin layers of the same sand; the two beds make together much about two feet in thickness, where ever I could measure them; which I did in different places; in some, the bed of Sand was not quite so thick; tho' taking the whole together, I believe the above to be pretty exact. I examined different places to the distance of four hundred yards, and found the same appearance; the teeth are very sound which lie in the upper bed; those in the lower are much decayed and of a yellowish colour; most of them will not bear handling; two of this sort I have herewith sent, which are the soundest I have seen of the kind. Under these two beds you come to chalk; above them are beds of Clay, Sand, Fuller's Earth, &c to the height of seventy or eighty feet. I also went under ground in one of the chalk Pits a considerable way; and found the same beds continued, where ever, part of the top of the pit being fallen in, one could get a fair sight of them.

John was eager to be off on another ramble and the amiable Zinzan was easily persuaded to join him. They planned to ride through Kent, Sussex and Hampshire, calling on the Bagshaws at Bromley and the Lowths at Buriton. Before leaving, John wrote to one of his female relations, probably Aunt Betty or Anne Hopkins, and kept his rough copy.[5] Trifling though it is, it has a certain whimsical charm.

Dear Madam, I had not deferred an Answer so long to your last Favour, could I have found Matter for an Epistle of any tolerable Length; for, you know, I have been taught that the Respect the Writer bears to the Person he writes to, is to be estimated by the Length or Shortness of the Letter. I fear you'll reply to me that want of Matter has hitherto been no Hindrance to my writing very tedious Epistles and why should it now? My best Answer is, that to write upon Nothing is very difficult and my often writing in that way has entirely exhausted the subject. I am now to beg a Favour of you and that is to excuse my waiting so long for a Subject and at last writing without one; which I chose to do, rather than putt it off' till something offered to write upon, when possibly my own Incapacity to handle it might make you commend me with better Success to my old Theme – Nothing. Little more than Nothing is it to tell you that on Monday Fortnight my Tutor and I set out for Maidstone.[6]

Hopson joined them for the first two days and they left Caversham on 31 August. The road from Reading to Sunninghill, where they were to spend the first night with the Babers, was of course well known to them.

The Ridings in Windsor Forest for the convenience of the Royal Family's hunting are just finished by the Soldiers; the work was little else than clearing the Ground of Fern &c. Mr Baber's Seat[c] is situated in a Park out of the Jurisdiction of the Forest: 'tis an handsome Brick House, built by Sir Thomas Draper who pulled down the old Seat which stood on an Hill and erected this in a Flat just by. Ascot Heath runs by the Park Pales. We saw the Chalybeate Well at Sunninghill; it lies in a bottom; the Water of it leaves a Taste upon the Palate not unlike the Spaw Waters.

They rode to Bromley next day, parting temporarily with Charles Hopson at Southwark and finding time for a brief visit to Hampton Court.

The Road lies in the Forest almost to Egham; you have some beautiful Views of Windsor Castle from it. Several handsome Seats along the Road, as Brigadier Honeywood's on the left, General Hill's, the Dutchess of Marlborough's (as Ranger) on the Right . . .[d]

Hampton Court is beautifully situated by the Thames; it is a Brick Building of three Quadrangles; the two first Cardinal Wolsey built, the third King William. You have fine Vistas of Rooms here; a Glass is so contrived over the Chimney-Piece of one of the Rooms as to reflect the whole Vista. The Cartons (so-called because painted on thick Paper) of Raphael D'Urbin are now copying by Sir James Thornhill and Le Blon.

After describing some of the pictures John continued:

[c] Sunninghill Park.
[d] Windsor Lodge.

Here is some Cieling-Painting of Thornhill's and some of Verrio's who has painted the Grand Stair-case. The Guard Room here is large and the Arms beautifully disposed . . .

Lewisham, where Sir John Lethieullier[e] had a Seat, was the first Village we came through in Kent. Bromley Town is so called from the very great quantity of Broom once growing here-abouts. The Bishop of Rochester's Palace here is moted. It is an old Building and has been beautified by Bishop Atterbury. St Blase's Well is still kept open for the convenience of the Palace.

They did not stay in the chaplain's house at Bromley College but put up instead at the White Hart, where Thomas and his father, Harington Bagshaw, joined them for dinner.

Harington, also educated at Magdalen, was the perpetual curate of Bromley parish and chaplain of the College. His grandfather, a great Royalist, had been the politician and writer Edward Bagshaw, one of whose sons, also Edward, was that strange, pathetic figure who was ejected from his position as usher of Westminster School and became a noted controversialist. Harington's mother was a daughter of Sir Sapcote Harington; her brother, James, wrote *Oceana*,[7] the model for a new republic. With his son Thomas and his daughters Elizabeth and Dorothy now the only survivors of a large family, Harington had lived at Bromley for many years. His wife, a daughter of Sir John Busby of Addington, had died in 1713. In 1735 he was to hand over the living and chaplaincy to Thomas but he lived on until 1739. They were a good-looking family. The girls were pretty and Thomas had sensitive clear-cut features. He was never in his life known to show any signs of agitation; and allied to this absolute composure he had a nice humour, a mind as clear as a bell and the same enthusiasm for philology as his friend John Loveday.

The College, founded in 1666 by Bishop John Warner

for 20 Clergymen's Widows, with an Allowance of 20£ per Annum each, is a large and handsome Brick Building with two small Wings, one of which is the Chaplain's Lodging, who is chosen by the Governors from Magdalen College in Oxford (the present Chaplain Mr Bagshaw) the Preferment tenable with a Fellowship; in the other Wing is the Room where the Governors meet about the College Affairs. The Gate in the middle of the Front opens to a Quadrangle, where the Widows lodge, who are allowed to keep but one Woman to wait upon them, be it Daughter, Neice or Maid. There are 2 Kitchens which they make use of upon occasion. They have Prayers in the Chappel twice a day, except when there is Service at the Parish Church. In the Chappel, which is very neat, is a Picture of the Founder, Bishop Warner kneeling, but there is no likeness between this Piece and those in Magdalen College. One of the

[e] See p.6.

Widows, a young Woman, is marryed lately and so makes a Vacancy, a thing scarce known here.

The little River Ravensbourne runs by Bromley; the Head of it is from a Well about 4 miles from the Town near Caesar's Camp in Keston Parish, but in the Summer time the River received no supply from hence; 'tis a good stream for Trout. Upon a Common on a Hill is Caesar's Camp, as 'tis commonly called; it seems to be an Oval and that a very extensive one, so more probably Danish Work. About the same Distance from the Town, though another way, is Addington where (I am told) is a Camp on an Hill and that there have been several Tumuli there; that a man digging one, and finding an Urn with Coyns, was encouraged to digg all the rest, but found nothing but Ollae Ostiariae.

After riding round the countryside with Thomas and his father's curate, Mr Higgins, John and Zinzan left for the Black Bull at Rochester.

We come through Stroude [Strood], a pretty large Place before Rochester, which is divided from it by the bridge. This is a noble Work, standing upon 10 stone Arches over the very wide Medway; 'tis railed with Iron Rails (within these few Years I am told); a strong Tide here. To secure the Arches, they have drove in Wooden Piles standing close together; . . . the intervening Spaces break the Force of the Water. You call this Frame a Stirling-head or point.

Chatham is divided from Rochester by a Guttur only, which crosses a Street above 2 Miles long; this Street is narrow; it runs the whole length of Rochester and Chatham and is almost the Breadth of both, there being little else but Allies in either of these Places. In the old Dock at Chatham they now lay up the Guns of the Ships. Within these ten Years the New Dock has been enlarged and made more commodious and 'tis still improving; very handsome Houses built here for the Officers. Here are two Rooms for the making of Cables nigh a Quarter of a Mile long each. We went aboard the Britannia, a First Rate, carrying 110 Guns. In the long Street in that part belonging to Rochester, is a Building with an Inscription in English over the Door, which tells you that any six Travellers, not exceptionable, may have Lodging there for one Night and also receive Four Pence each.

John was not impressed by Rochester Cathedral, which he described only briefly, calling it a 'very mean' building in a 'slovenly condition'. He added that the Chapter was still under Bishop Atterbury's injunction to spend £200 per annum on the church and was talking of settling £150 per annum for ever on repairs. The register had been lost in the Civil Wars and many monuments had been destroyed.

They left on 4 September for Maidstone where they were rejoined by Hopson. With Bye and the Revd Samuel Weller, the incumbent, both Reading men it was a great reunion of old friends. Weller lived in the part of the house which had once been a place for the Archbishops of Canterbury and now belonged to Lord Romney.

While they were at Maidstone they rode out to Mereworth Castle.

Colonel Fane,[f] Brother to the Earl of Westmorland, has built an Italian House at Merryworth,[g] with great expence. You ascend to it by a great flight of Stone Steps, under which are part of the Offices. A vast Portico on every side the House, so that there are four Fronts exactly alike, but Steps up to only one. The Windows are very small. A Cupolo very large, seemingly too large for the size of the House, as are also the Porticos. The Rooms below are lofty, above very low. The Servants lie in the four Rooms over the Porticos. Above there are some of the Bed-Chambers, others below Stairs. The Passage, and Hall under the Cupolo, have a Floor of Red Plaister. There is no Grand Stair-Case; two go up from the Hall and lead you to a Gallery round it, in which are the Passages to the Rooms. You see no Chimnies on the Outside, for the Smoke is conveyed through Leaden Pipes, which are as Ribs to the Cupolo; at the top of which the Smoke of the whole House goes out.

They left Maidstone for Canterbury on 8 September.

Boxley is a pleasant Village. The inclosure Walls of the Abbey remaining, but every part of the House I take to be of a later Date than the Suppression. Kitscot's House [Kit's Coty House] stands in a field by Boxley Hill . . . two Stones set on end with another across between them, and a very large Stone at top . . . a plain Structure[h] by no means grand or magnificent. There are a great many Cherry-Orchards and Hop-Gardens about Maidstone.

In Canterbury Cathedral Bishop Warner's font was the most handsome he had seen, but there was now no sign of Pope Alexander III, Louis VII or Thomas Becket in the Dean's chapel and the monuments for the bishops were in a very filthy condition.

In the Space behind the High Altar stood Becket's Shrine, but there is now no Footsteps of that or any other Monument to his Memory.

It was one of the 'noblest Gothic Buildings', however, and he would return. He noticed the Archbishop's Palace was let out to a great many families.

So far they had ridden through narrow lanes with high hedges, but they

---

[f] Colonel John Fane succeeded to the Earldom of Westmorland as 7th Earl in 1736, having been created Baron Catherlough in 1733.

[g] Designed by Colen Campbell and based on Palladio's Villa Capra at Vicenza, Mereworth Castle was built in 1720 – 30, replacing an earlier house.

[h] The remains of a Neolithic burial chamber.

found the journey to Dover next day full of interest. They rode through Sandwich, past Sandown Castle, to Deal, where they watched the women laying out their linen to dry on the beach. John described Dover as being like a half-moon with a street behind it, all the buildings being on the sides.

The Castle stands upon a very high Hill over the Sea; 9 Gunners and Porter kept here; there are near 30 Acres within the Walls; the greater part of the building in Ruins. The Governor's Apartment was partly new fitted last Winter, wainscotted, sashed and is still improving. I was told that in the Well for the use of the Castle it was 66 fathom to the Water. The Case only of the Castle-Chappel is remaining; an Inscription against the Wall informs us that the Earl of Northampton's marble Coffin is removed to East Greenwich[i]. . . Over the Cliff here is mounted a Brass Piece of Ordnance, made at Utrecht and given by the States to Queen Elizabeth. It is very curiously wrought and of very great Length. It carries but a 12 pound Ball, with 15 pound, 2 ounces of Powder. At Bredenstone, vulgarly called the Devil's Drop, (where stood a Roman Pharus) not far from the Castle was a Tent erected for the Duke of Dorset's taking the Oaths, upon his being made Governor of the Castle.

Their ride took them through Folkestone to Dymchurch and Romney.

This ride had been very Pleasant (for the Road lay upon a high Ground just above the Sea) had it not been for the most stormy Weather I ever knew, considering that it continued from Morning to Night. Full Gales of Wind coming perpetually from the Sea drove a thick Rain full upon us, so that we were wet through long before we put in at Dimchurch. The Bank raised to keep Rumney Marsh safe from the Sea begun about two Miles and a half before Dimchurch. Just as we came upon it my Horse's Girt broke and I was obliged to walk the remaining part of the Journey. There is now an Impost of 2s. upon every Acre in the Marsh for the maintaining the Bank, which was formerly much more chargeable . . . Rumney Marsh which is firm Ground, famous for the best Sheep (for a Rot was never known among 'em) ended at Rye. We stayed before Rye for the Tide's going out. At Rumney I left my Papers at the Inn, but missing them at Rye I sent a Letter to the Landlord, who made a Packet of them and directed them to Caversham where I found them.

On 14 September they took the ferry at Shoreham and passed through Arundel, where a fair was in progress, to Chichester.

The four Streets in Chichester may be seen from one point in the Town.

[i] The 1st Earl of Northampton was buried in the chapel of Dover Castle in 1614 as Warden of the Cinque Ports. The memorial over his grave was removed to the chapel of Norfolk College at Greenwich in 1696 by the Mercers' Company. (*D.N.B.*)

There are six small mean Churches here and no River. The beautiful Spire to the Cathedral is lately cleaned. Some out-parts of the Church are decayed.

After making further notes on the interior, including the famous paintings of kings, John continued:

> The present Bishop Waddington has laid out a great deal of Money on his Palace and Gardens. He is much beloved here, for he spends the whole Revenue of his Bishoprick (about 1200£ per Annum) at Chichester, being very hospitable, keeping a public Table once a Week. He is a Fellow of Eaton and they say has 2000£ per Annum, Temporal Estate. He could never agree with Dean Sherlock who would not allow the Virger to go before the Bishop, since which time the Bishop has a Man on purpose. Sherlock rebuilt the Deanery. He was counted a proud Man here. From Chichester to Petersfield at the Red Lion, 12 Miles. The Road very bad from the Earl of Tankerville's Park[j] about 4 Miles hence. We were benighted in this Road.

The Sussex roads were notoriously bad in an age when few were good. The chief complaints were usually about the liquid mud[k] and for many years there was little improvement. However the travellers were now close to their destination and the Lowth family were waiting to welcome them to Buriton Rectory in the same village where later on Edward Gibbon's father came to live.

> This Village lies in a bottom with hills all about it. Lowth the Commentator (at whose House we were) is Rector here. This is the Mother Church to Petersfield. Mews, Bishop of Winchester, to whom Lowth was Chaplain, presented him to a Living which he changed for this, the Minister here before him not agreeing with the Parish. He was made Prebendary of Winchester by the same Bishop.

William Lowth's appellation 'Commentator' derived from his *Commentary on the Prophets*,[8] his most notable work. Though he never achieved the eminence of his son, Robert, he was an even greater scholar. The elder son, William, who had just sat for his M.A. degree at Magdalen, was less distinguished. He was to take the living of St Margaret's, Rochester and John often saw him in the future when he visited Bromley and Maidstone.

Instead of staying quietly for a day or two the visitors were suddenly whisked off to Portsmouth at a moment's notice, escorted by the entire Lowth family. They all put up at the Fighting Cocks.

---

[j] The Earl of Tankerville's house was Uppark. He sold it in 1747 to Sir Matthew Fetherstonhaugh who married Sarah Lethieullier, granddaughter of John's great-uncle Christopher.

[k] See Esther Moir, *The Discovery of Britain*, 1964.

This is a very foul stinking Town; one Church in it. The Dock here is very large and commodious. We went aboard the Royal William, the largest Ship in England, built about twelve Years since and never out of the Harbour. The Length of her Keel is 146 foot, the Gun-Deck 174 foot, the Middle Deck 182 foot . . . from Head to Stern 215 foot, the Breadth 50 foot and a half. The Length of her Mast 115 foot and 40 Inches through it. Her tunnage 1984. She carries 112 Guns, some of them weigh almost a Tunn; her Complement of Men 880 when there is no Admiral aboard, about 1200 Men when there is. This Ship cost about 90,000£ the Building, as much more the Furnishing. We were aboard the Kent, a 3rd Rate, now the Guard-Ship; Admiral Wager was on board her at the Siege of Gibraltar.

Benwell told a story about this visit to Portsmouth, but he was mistaken in thinking they had had two days' rest at Buriton.

In one of his tours with Dr Zinzan they called and spent two days with Mr Lowth, the father of the Bishop of London, at his Rectory of Buriton in Hampshire, and afterwards made a party with the family to some of the dock-yards . . . They slept one night at Gosport and as the Inn was very full, Mr Robert Lowth and Mr L. chummed together. The room in which they slept was a scullery which had in one side of it a small recess, boarded and furnished with a bed. In the morning the sun shone full upon a bright copper kettle, and both happening to wake at the same time and casting their eyes at once upon this object, it had such a ridiculous effect that without speaking to each other they both burst into a loud fit of laughter.

For once Lowth overcame his tendency to melancholia.

Portsmouth is moted; the Draw Bridge taken up every night, a Guard placed at the Gates to examine the Coaches, who are in 'em, from whence they come and what Inn they lodge at. A Brazen (as I take it) Statue of King William was erected before the Officers' Houses a few Years since by Richard Norton Esqr. but the Face is very unlike any I ever saw before of this Prince. I was told that almost all the Cannon and Balls are made at Woolwich; that if over-heated Iron Cannon will split, whereas Brass melts; but Iron carries farthest, which (I suppose) is owing to the Elasticity of the Metal. We returned to Mr Lowth's at Buriton. The Ride to Portsmouth was entirely out of our first design.

They left for home early on 19 September. It was a long way and there was no time for sightseeing as they pressed on through Alton and Odiham to Reading. It had been a very successful tour and had cost, including hire of horses, a total sum of twelve guineas.

A letter from Hearne dated 17 September was all about Dr Abraham Woodhead, an Oxford theologian, long dead, whom I take to have been one of the greatest Men ever produced in England and I should be very glad to have a more distinct and particular Account of him than that in Athenae Oxon.,[9] which notwithstanding is very good and much to be regarded.

Hearne wished he had remembered to ask John to inquire about this good man as he thought some 'gentlemen in Kent' had some memoirs that Anthony Wood had not known of and there was a design currently in Oxford of writing his life.

I understand Mr Topham of Windsor is dead. He had an extraordinary Collection of Books,[l] such a one as would be worth seeing and perusing if one could have an opportunity. I suppose you may easily learn how he hath disposed of them. I hear Dr Wall's Study is not worth above twenty pounds in all,[m] which is remarkable for so great a Man.[10]

John's first thought on returning home was to visit his sister at Mrs Eades's school. Then, taking young John Merrick and Charles Hopson with him, he went off to Aldworth. They wanted to see John Peareth and also to compare the oyster beds of Lowbury Hill with those at Catsgrove.

On 4 October he was back at Magdalen. As Zinzan was not returning immediately, Winchester, who was looking for rooms, came to stay with him, sleeping in Zinzan's room. 'Read in the Greek Testament with W. as I shall do for some time. He was also able to help the younger boy with his 'theme'.

It was during this term that he received a most welcome letter from his friend Edmund Lambert who was now living in the Isle of Man. It intrigued him so much that he thought seriously about going there – indeed he tried to do so in 1732 on his way to Ireland – but there was never enough time.

I met with many troublesome accidents since I left Kertlington, the most tedious of all was staying at Liverpoole 5 weeks waiting for a fair wind to carry me to the Island.

The first night we were at Sea, we weathered out a smart Storm, but not without some damage to the Ship's rigging; about 5 in the morning, the winds being at West, we were obliged to alter our Course and run for Beaumaris in Wales where we stayed 5 days waiting again for a wind; from thence we set sail about 11 at night and were in sight of the Island by 12 next morning; just as we stood in for Douglass harbour, the wind blowing violently against us, we were forced to come to an anchor and put out the signal of distress for a boat to come to our assistance,

---

[l] The books were bequeathed to Eton College but not received from the executors, Dr Richard Mead and Sir Thomas Reeve, until 1736 when the Library was ready for them. See Robert Birley, *The History of College Library*, 1970.

[m] According to Hearne, William Wall was too poor to purchase books. (Hearne's *Collections*, vol. X, 17 September 1730.)

which carried us in much confusion and no small danger, safe a shore. So much for sailing, which I am not a little pleased I have done with for some time. The Island in some places is very mountainous and barren, tho' some of the Vallies are fruitful enough, both in grain and pasture, but altogether destitute of timber, chiefly occasioned by the unfruitful blasts from the sea air, for this reason they are entirely Strangers to all Wall fruits. Instead of Hedges they fence their lands with turff and stone which they gather from the sea side; the former makes pretty good fewel mixt with coal. Butchers meat is much cheaper here than in England, fish and tame fowl plenty enough, a fat Goose may be bought for tenpence, a Cod of 8 pounds for sevenpence and a penny is the common price of a Lobster. Liquors are not dearer, the same measure of ale you pay twopence for in England may be had here for a penny and this as good. We drink a small French Wine for 8 pence a bottle, the best French brandy and Jamaica Rum is sold but for two shillings a gallon, the duty to the Lord Derby being no more than a penny per gallen. The trade of the Island chiefly consists in this last article; many English, Irish and Scotch and Welsh boats trade here in that commodity and is the reason why Ships passing to and from these places generally make the Island in their way. I have been more particular in relation to provisions, that you may judge by the by whether it would not be more convenient for me to stay here till some Friend in England shall make it worth my while to return; but be this as it will, notwithstanding this appearance of plenty, there are some things necessary for house keeping, dearer than in England, for they are entirely obliged to Strangers for their Sugars, Salt, Coal and Iron; Salt they have had a great demand for since they have got their Herring fishing again, which they had lost for twenty years past, not by any encroachment of their Neighbours, but the fish leaving their coast; they are now plenty, insomuch that I have seen 150 boats coming in, in a morning, and their fish sold for 5 pence a hundred; that the Fishery has been for many years the support of the place is plain from this; that they always pray for it in the Litany under the title of the blessing of the Sea; as also for the Lord Derby. Here I cannot omit a story of a Mare-maid, or rather of a Mare-man as they call it, which was credibly reported to have been seen since I have been here; it appeared in a moon light night within 3 yards of one of their boats, the same is testified by many people in 20 others; from the breast upwards it resembled a man, with long black hair, of a dark olive complexion, not unlike Dr B − − −e[n] of St. John's. The Bishop[o] seemed to countenance this story by producing the history of one taken at Haarlem in Holland, and was to be seen there publickly for many years, a brass figure of it still

[n] Dr William Bridge.
[o] Dr Thomas Wilson, Bishop of Sodor and Man.

remains in that place. Perhaps you will give less credit to this story when I tell you the Manx-men are exceedingly superstitious, but this we must leave to the Naturalists. But to return, the poor people live chiefly upon dried fish, salt Herrings and Potatoes, and drink butter milk; Gentlemen's Servants are not often fed with any thing better and have no more than 20 shillings wages; in short the English Servants live in perfect luxury in comparison to these. The poor natives are much like the Welsh in their manners and Customs and are altogether as choice of their shoes and stockings; living among themselves, good-natured enough to Strangers, but cholerick; those that have plenty have generally hearts to make use of it, I wish I could say with moderation. The Gentlemen that reside here are Scotch, English and Irish and there are but few. Woolston's[p] Pamphlets have been very lately brought over, and I am told industriously spread abroad by a person of loose life and character; I am sorry to say they have met with too much encouragement among some of them. Excuse this imperfect and trifling account of the place I am in; I have only mentioned such things as are beneath the notice of an Historian; it would look like folly in me to pretend to give you any account of the Model of their Government, either Civil or Ecclesiastical, when by turning to your Study you may be so soon acquainted with both. One thing I must observe to you, that this Island that formerly was so remarkable for peace and tranquillity as to be known by the name of the little quiet nation, has now nothing left of that Character, but the honour of being once called so, but miserably torn into publick divisions and private resentments; this makes the little company we have troublesome and hard to be pleased – if you are familiar with one you affront another; more I could say of this unhappy place and hard it is to forbear, did not the practice here of opening Letters forbid me; but should I offer to go any farther, I should rather excite your indignation than please your curiosity. You may well expect I should before this time have taken notice of the civility you shewed me at Oxford; I gratefully acknowledge it; but too much complaisance is as troublesome as ridiculous, and ceremony from a Friend is as cruel as from a Mistress. I have not heard what answer my Aunt gave Mr Prouse[q] therefore cannot yet determine upon any thing. I must own I am not at all inclinable to orders and hope that by my brother's assistance and my own industry, I may be able to do something in another capacity, but must own I cannot put so much confidence in my own judgement as to believe I cannot be mistaken. Let me have your thoughts upon this, and

[p] Six discourses on *The Miracles of Our Saviour* were published by the free thinker Thomas Woolston between 1727 and 1729. He was fined and imprisoned for blasphemy in 1729.

[q] Prouse was probably an attorney. Edmund Lambert inherited Boyton Manor in Wiltshire from his uncle Edmund Lambert whose wife (born Sarah Blake) was the aunt referred to in the letter. Another uncle had been Thomas, rector of Boyton, whose wife, Jane, died in 1742.

whatever news you can send me relating to the government, affairs of the University, either publick or private, in short any thing that in some measure I may keep pace with the rest of the world and not be altogether ignorant of what is doing in it. Consider we see but very few news papers and hear less; whatever expense you are at shall be faithfully repayed you by my Brother or myself. Perhaps you will ask why you have not heard from me sooner; I must confess I cannot offer you any sufficient reason, the novelty of the place and some other interfering accidents, improper to mention, made me neglect my Friends longer than I ought, or indeed was willing; but pray let not my delay occasion any in you; remember the uncertainty of wind and weather may a long time interrupt our correspondence. Whether I continue or not in the Island I have no thoughts of coming to England 'till next Summer when I hope to be happy again in your company, the loss of which I do assure you is much and often lamented by your affectionate Friend and Servant, E. Lambert.[11]

Edmund did not explain what he was doing in the Isle of Man. He was living at Scarlett with a Mr Seddons and he sent details of bankers in London and Liverpool on whom he could draw. His younger brother Ned was still at Magdalen.

In December Zinzan began to lecture John and Robert Lowth on 'the globes', a subject they enjoyed as much as he. It was no special part of their courses but, as John had made a classical declamation, it could be justified as a minor digression. On Christmas Day the President dined in Hall and another year drew to its close.

A Taste for Country Houses
1731

Within the circle of John's Oxford friends, one small group had included the Lamberts, William Derham and Sir William Bowyer, who left in January to return to his Buckinghamshire estates having obtained his M.A. degree the previous October. Another of his more influential companions, William Courtenay, received this degree in January and came of age on 11 February when, as John wrote in his diary, 'his Father[a] gave him Powderham and the Estate belonging'.

At the lower end of the social scale Thomas Bonney ended his term as servitor and was made a clerk; but John had now found someone else in need of help, a Magdalen chorister called William Pennington. This young man's father, when a curate, had fallen in love with his servant maid and had married her on obtaining a living. She had helped him to get out of debt, but on his death she married again and her second husband took all her savings. When she herself died, young William was left destitute. John had befriended him at Oxford, taking him to Cat Street and later inviting him to his rooms and helping him with his work, besides providing him with books. Eventually William became a curate at St Mary's, Reading, and later their two sons were at Magdalen together.

John was pursuing his studies 'partly on design, but more on the inclination of the moment' – to quote his grandson's words. In his spare time he was continuing to digest set after set of College papers for Zinzan

---

[a] Sir William Courtenay, 2nd Baronet.

who was in some way responsible for them. Some of them he took to Hearne so that he could take transcriptions. Zinzan himself was preoccupied with his efforts to procure a Fellowship and was busily persuading the Fellows to vote for him.

Just before the close of the winter term John described the traditional commemoration of John Higden, John Claymond and Robert Morwent in Magdalen College Chapel:

> This being the first Monday in Lent, while Sternhold's Benedictus is singing after the second Lesson, the Bursars go about the Chappel with silver-Groats, the President has so many; the Fellows too; all the Chappel, the Choristers too, the Demies have one groat and of late the Gentlemen Commoners enjoy the same Gratuity.[b]

He had now passed his twentieth birthday and on his return to Caversham he began to exchange more visits with his established neighbours. Lord Fane of Basildon, Philip Powys of Hardwick and other older men called on him and received him for the first time. Later in the year Lord Cadogan invited him to dinner instead of the usual polite call – 'Her Ladyship's sister Rose there and an Officer of his Ship'. It was when dining with Walter Pryse of Hurst, an eminent attorney, that he first met Henry Jennings of Shiplake, the father of that eighteenth-century eccentric, 'Jennings the Virtuoso'.

His visit to Lady Rich at Sonning at the end of March was much less formal, for Daniel had come over to the French Club and taken John back with him. Lady Rich, now widowed, approved of his curiosity and showed him round her house and grounds so that he saw them with new eyes. Sonning House had been built in the seventeenth century by Sir Thomas Rich using material from the old palace of the Bishops of Salisbury.[c]

> Lady Rich had since Sir Robert's Death, enlarged the Gardens by taking in the Dog-Kennel, which began on this side the Mount, (of her Ladyship's making) and took in that Building which consists of two Rooms, one above the other, and which stands by the side of the Canal. It was bounded towards the Church-Yard by the now Garden-Wall. I am so particular, because D.Rich tells me on that Spot of Ground stood the Bishop of Sunning's Palace, and that, upon turning the Ground into a Garden, they met with Foundations and Pavement-Tiles now in the House . . . On one side of the great Mansion-House

---

[b] The money came from rents at a manor at Standlake which the three friends gave to Magdalen College in 1483. The benefaction, paid in terms of pence, included all members of the Society present at the service as explicitly stated, but gentlemen commoners were not mentioned. See *Magdalen College Register*, first series, vol. IV, p. 6. A groat was worth fourpence.

[c] The house built by Sir Thomas Rich was demolished in 1796. Bishop's Lands Farm is still standing.

occurs 1638 L^HL i.e. says her Ladyship, Laurence Halsted.^d Lady Rich has a Farm . . . called Bishopsland.

On 24 April John and several of his friends were examined for their B.A. degrees. They included Thomas Bagshaw, Edmund Crynes, James Webb and William Payne, who was a cousin of the poet William Collins. Examinations were often quite festive affairs, particularly if the candidates had chosen the examiners (as on this occasion seems pretty certain). They could hardly be intimidated by William Derham, young John Merrick and one other, 'Watkins of Wadham', while the Collector who had arranged the preliminary Determination was Peter Zinzan. However, these young men were serious about scholarship, even if the examination was entirely oral and merely a formality, and John and Thomas Bagshaw had been studying schemes of ethic and logic together for some time.

John kept a careful account of his expenses. They involved a good deal of conviviality, particularly if everyone provided as many bottles as he did.

Expenses of a B.A.'s Degree.	£	s	d
To the Register &c. University Dues.	1	3	10
To the Dean	1	11	6
To the Moderators	1	3	0
To the Bell-Ringer		1	0
To Major for a Hood		1	0
To Proctor's Men		1	0
To 23 Bottles at 1s. 8d per Bottle	1	18	4
To man carrying my Gown		1	0
To the Common-Room Man		1	0

Now that the formalities were over he felt that a long journey on horseback was a necessary compensation and that having had satisfactory dealings with his own University it was time to see what the other place looked like. It was also an excellent excuse for a detour through Essex and Norfolk – an unusual route from Oxford to Cambridge but none the less attractive.

Hearne always approved of John's tours if they would bring him more information. He wanted to know more about Dunmow and he probably hoped for more Cambridge gossip than he actually received. He gave John a letter to deliver into the hands of that most lovable of all the scholars of those days – old Thomas Baker of St John's, antiquarian and historian of the University.

As usual John read up his Leland and Camden; he also studied Thomas Tanner – possibly *Notitia Monastica* which the future Bishop of St Asaph

^d Laurence Halstead, merchant, part-owner of the lease of the palace, bought it in 1629 with the Messenger family as tenants; 1638 was perhaps the year he moved in. He conveyed Sonning Manor to Thomas Rich in 1654. See Angela Perkins, *The Book of Sonning*, 1977. Rich was created a baronet in 1661.

had brought out in 1695. They had met two years earlier in Hearne's rooms and being sometimes in Oxford as a canon of Christ Church Tanner may have let John see some of the notes he had made while living in Norfolk.[e] John's own notes from other writers[f] were always written on long narrow strips of paper which would fold neatly into his pocket. These notes are quite distinct from the diaries of his tours which he usually wrote out on his return from his own memoranda – written at night in the inns and later destroyed. As he grew older he frequently looked through these diaries and added to them from new information, but as his writing changed, the additions which he often dated can always be discerned.

On 3 May, accompanied by Edmund Crynes and Sam Gurney, the servant, and with Thomas Winchester putting them on the road for the first day, John set off for Thame. There he found the neatest church he had ever seen and read the inscription in modern letters on the tower – 'The church built 1138 repaired 1726.' Inside the chancel had been repaired by Viscount Weymouth in 1707 and the noble tomb of 'Judge Williams and his Lady' was washed once a quarter. One of the aisles was in great decay.

It belongs to the Herberts of Kingsey. . . the Heir of which family who will be of age shortly, proposes the refitting of it, his ancestors lying there in a vault.

The Road from Tame to Tring was for the most part chalky; Hills on one side and a delightful open Countrey on t'other, made more beautiful by the Prospect of Villages thick set, each having an handsome towered Church.

They reached the White Hart at St Albans next day. In the Cathedral, which was then the Abbey church, he could see the marks of destruction caused by Cromwell's men on their way south in 1647.

The Cieling of the Chancel is adorned with the gilded figures of Lambs and Eagles. . . the Parliamentary Soldiers have shot it in several places. . . there is yet remaining intire (and the only one I ever saw) on the Floor of the Chancel an inlaid Brass Monument for Bishop Thomas de la More [Mare]; he is habited in his Religious Dress, Saints adorning the Edges of the Tomb; the People of the Town, turned it, upon the Parliamentarians coming hither, by which means, though broke in two, 'twas saved from the common Destruction . . . There is a Wooden Font representing the shape of a noble Brass one, which the Parliamentarians broke to pieces and sold; on the top is still a Brass

[e] Dr Tanner left Norfolk, where he had held the archdeaconry, in 1731 and was consecrated Bishop of St Asaph in January 1732.
[f] He read extensively among historians and antiquarians, but surprisingly never mentions Defoe's Tour.

Dove, the only Remains of the old Font, which the Parson's Daughter is said to have begged from the Soldiers.[g]

He made further notes[h] and after seeing the exhibition at the Crown Inn of antiquities which had been dug up at Verulamium or in the garden of the monastery, they visited the first big house of the tour.

Gorhambury, the Lord Grimston's, built by Sir Nicholas Bacon, is two short miles from St Albans; 'tis a very large Building. Two round Towers at the extremities of an extended Front. The Hall adorned with Paintings (as indeed the House very plentifully throughout) . . . The Gallery here is a noble Room, Pictures at length in every Panel . . . In the Windows on one side is most curious painted Glass in little Panes, representing Birds, Beasts &c. in lively colours; a larger painted Window at one end. In one of the Rooms are Sir Nicholas Bacon and his Wife. In a Closet is a very beautiful Mary Magdelene (they said) reading. A very good Piece in another Room drawn by Sir Nathaniel Bacon[i] who was no Limner, but took a fancy to the Cook-maid of the House; whom he draws sitting, a Fellow behind her who has brought in Fowl, the several kinds of which are exactly represented. In a Room above Stairs is a good piece of the Prophet fed by Ravens. Paintings of the Grimston Family in the Library. A Table in this House of above 100 different sorts of Marble Squares.[j] There is no Water nigh this pleasant Seat.

They visited Hatfield the same day.

A very large and grand House of the Earl of Salisbury's at Hatfield, but now almost unfurnished; every part of it very well supplied with Water. The Rooms are lofty and spacious; a Gallery here and a pretty Chappel with an Organ. In one of the Rooms a Painting of the late Earl of Thanet. This was a Royal Palace, till James 1st exchanged it with Robert Cecil for Theobalds; At the distance of half a Mile from the House through the Park is the Vineyard; so they call it, but 'tis a lovely

[g] John gave as reference Thomas Staveley, *The History of the Churches*, 1712, which gives the story of the font until it was 'washed away itself with the late Deluge of Scandalous Avarice', but does not mention the story of the parson's daughter. It had been taken from Holyrood Abbey and given to St Alban's Abbey by Sir Richard Lee. See also Thomas Fuller's *Worthies of England* (1662) which bears out the statement that the brass font was destroyed.

[h] John wrote: 'About 27 years since Captain Polehampton of Cow-Lane London – Coach Stainer – gave a good Painting by his own hand of the last Supper. 'Tis inserted just above the Table which is very ancient.' Edward Polehampton (d. 1722) was a painter and benefactor to churches and hospitals. The painting of The Last Supper at St Albans now is, I understand, by James Thornhill.

[i] Sir Nathaniel Bacon of Culford, the painter, was a grandson of Sir Nicholas Bacon, the Lord Keeper, who built Gorhambury. His daughter married Sir Harbottle Grimston, great-uncle of the 1st Viscount Grimston.

[j] This table had been thought to be post-Grand Tour. (From information kindly given.)

hanging-Garden, the River Lea, that waters Ware, running through it. The Prospect is perfectly pleasant from the highest walk of the Garden. London and Wise laid out the Ground, which takes up 12 Acres.

At Hertford the castle was now a gentleman's seat and there was an assembly once a fortnight at The Glove and Dolphin for the gentry. The gaol had a good front and they also admired the fine Bluecoats' school, where the children were 'well grounded' before being sent on to Christ's Hospital in London.

The church at Ware very neat, the church-yard perfectly pleasant with a walk under an arbour of rows of trees. Six bells are putting up today, being founded at London; they had but five before. At the farther Crown is the great Bed of Ware, an antique carved piece of work, twelve foot square.[k]

Great Dunmow is no inconsiderable Town. . . the Lady of the Mannor is Mrs Hallet, Widow of the son of Sir James Hallet of London, the King's Jeweller. No Bacon has been demanded here since 1701, when Mr Reynolds, a Gentleman, Steward to Sir Charles Barrington and Parsley, a Butcher, carryed off two Gammons. The former is now alive, the Widow of the Latter married again.

After passing through Coggeshall, 'a large town' where women, boys and little girls stood spinning before their doors, they reached Colchester three days after their departure from Oxford. Next day after visiting the castle with its house of correction and admiring Charles Gray's handsome house[l] nearby, they turned north for Saxmundham. Three miles out of the town[m] they saw the oyster pits where the oysters were kept in flat baskets in water about two feet high. Colchester was also remarkable, said John, for 'bays and says'[n] and for candying eringo roots.[o]

The beautiful church at Blythburgh[p] where they found a clerk who had known Peter le Neve, the Herald and antiquary who had died two years earlier, was a respite from the dreadful roads – all on heavy sand. They passed

---

[k] John also said that the organ-loft in the church at Bishop's Stortford, 'before slovenly enough', had been built from a £60 per annum fund which had caused a Chancery suit between the parish and the late minister. Lord Chancellor Macclesfield had decreed it must be spent on beautifying the church.

[l] The Hollytrees, now a museum. In 1755 Gray married Mary, daughter of Randle Wilbraham of Rode Hall, the sister-in-law of John's first cousin once removed, Mary Wilbraham-Bootle.

[m] Brightlingsea.

[n] Colchester bays (or baize), a coarse wool cloth. Say was a finer serge. Bays manufacture was begun by Flemish settlers.

[o] This manufacture was described by Camden and Fuller.

[p] John described the church at Blythburgh at length. A law suit, he said, had taken place between Sir Charles Blois who provided a fortnightly preacher at £20 per annum and the Bishop of Norwich (William Baker), who 'insisted on Service every Sunday, but could not bring it to bear'.

Lowestoft where Bishop Tanner's brother had been vicar for twenty years and came next to Gorleston.

which has born the character of a debauched Town, insomuch that they have a Proverb:– if a good Woman falls down here, there'll never be another to take her up.

At Yarmouth they lay at the the Three Wrestlers and John thought the Market place was the finest and most spacious he had ever seen. He noticed the Yarmouth coaches which were like very light drays and he also observed that all round Lowestoft and Yarmouth the women wore close hats like bonnets.

May 9, We descended a steep Hill to Norwich, much as we do at Worcester . . . It being a Sunday morning and in Sermon time, the Gate was shut and a Porter planted at it.

Of the many churches in Norwich the only one to which he paid much attention was St Peter Mancroft where a new altarpiece was proposed.

The Pillars remarkably lofty and taper the neatest I have seen. They have here a most curious Communion Chalice, double gilt, enchased with fine large Figures in strong Relievo, representing a piece of Scripture-History. An excellent Organ, the Loft very neat, and an incomparable Ring of Bells. An Inscription here against the Wall on Isaac Fransham, an Attorney, who is not dead; but being apprehensive that his Executors will not bestow a Monument on him, has erected one here and at London (leaving a Blank for the Date of his Age and Death) that in whichever place he dies, he may be buryed and have a Monument.[q]

There are Hospitals of all kinds and workhouses at Norwich. Several thatched houses in the Lanes and some in the streets of this City; an Act of Parliament (I'm told) forbids the thatching of houses again, when the Spears have once failed. . . The Duke of Norfolk had a fine House[r] in this Town of 50 years standing, but not finished; this the present Duke pulled down 20 years ago upon a quarrel with a Whiggish Mayor; the Latter refused to give some Players leave to act in the City, though they had his Grace's Licence; upon which the Duke let 'em act in his own House and afterwards pulled it down. This was very much to the Town's loss, the Duke's Family laying out a great deal of money in Norwich. His Grace has

[q] Isaac Fransham, an attorney of the Court of the King's Bench, died in Norwich. It is recorded in the registers of St Peter Mancroft that he was buried there on 11 May 1743. (PD 26/17 (S)). His mural monument and a silver cup inscribed to him are mentioned in *An Essay towards a Topographical History of the County of Norfolk* by Francis Blomefield.

[r] This house was called the Duke's Palace. It replaced an old palace demolished in 1602 and Thomas, Duke of Norfolk, pulled it down when it was barely finished. See also Blomefield's *History* above.

now no grand Seat. The Government of the Town is among the Whigs; to preserve their Interest a few years since a Journeyman-Weaver was made Mayor. Dr Sam Clarke's Father was a Weaver in Norwich, as was his Brother the present Dean of Sarum who is commonly called here 'Dr John Clarke the Weaver.' He had Cole the late Dean entirely at his disposal, who was so violent a party-man as to fly in Passions at those of contrary Sentiments.

From Norwich to Walsingham

These Miles were very long of which we complained for the two last Days, the Road still upon an heavy Sand. There is at present no Saffron growing at Walsingham, but some Grounds still retain the name of Saffron Closes.

They visited the Abbey house and the ruins of the Abbey church with its east window still standing and its chapel now called 'Glutton's Barn'. There were two holy wells and a bathing place.

Now they were to leave the antiquities of the Norfolk churches for a spate of modern building which had even involved, in two cases, the removal of whole villages to sites where they would not spoil the views from Palladian windows. The first of these houses (on 11 May) was Raynham Hall, which had been greatly altered.[5]

> Rainham-Hall, the Lord Townshend's, stands in an handsome Park, a River flowing by it. His Lordship has expended such large Sums on the House that it looks new; 'tis a Brick Building faced with Free-Stone. We could not see the whole House, but it appeared grand and commodious. The Rooms are gilt and elegantly furnished; one hung with the Pictures of famous Admirals in Queen Elizabeth's time; in another a very fine Picture of blind Belisarius, given to Lord Townshend, as I understand it, by the King of Prussia.[t] There are no Gardens here. His Lordship orders particular Civilities to Strangers.

They were probably unable to see all the rooms because William Kent was still in the process of redecorating them; but his work at Sir Robert Walpole's great new mansion, Houghton Hall,[u] built to the design of Mereworth's architect, Colen Campbell, was now complete.

> Sir Robert Walpole's Houghton (or as 'tis pronounced Holeton) Hall stands low and is a large, heavy Building of Free-Stone; not nigh so spacious as Blenheim, yet seems to have more room in it. The Hall is adorned like Italian Halls, a large Gallery at top, from whence the Doors

---

[5] Raynham Hall was begun in 1619. See Margaret Jourdain, *The Work of William Kent*, 1948.
[t] Frederick William.
[u] Houghton Hall was begun in 1722.

into the Lodging-Rooms, and to every larger Room belongs another
for a Servant; a fine, gilded Lanthorn hangs in the middle from the
Cieling. The Salon is hung with Scarlet Coffoy,[v] and Paintings of
Snyders, &c. the Room gilt. A great deal of Tapestry, representing
rural life at Houghton. All the Doors and Windows in this House are of
Mahogany; one small Bed-Chamber wainscoted with it. The Grand
Stair-case, the grandest I ever saw, is all Mahogany; 'tis of great width,
the Stairs Free-Stone. The Gardens plain, much like those at Blenheim;
Sir Robert has removed above 20 houses of the Village to a
considerable distance and he proposes to remove the rest. The new
Building they call Newtown.

The use of mahogany in this way was new to John. The wood was scarce as
very little was imported from Jamaica at that time and in other houses was
chiefly used for furniture.[w]

The accepted way of discovering whether there were houses to be seen in the
vicinity was to ask the landlord at the local inn. Occasionally such information
was not forthcoming and nothing annoyed John more than to miss seeing a
house because he had not known about it. This happened at King's Lynn where
he was not told about Sir Andrew Fountaine's 'elegant box'[x] a few miles away.
Unspecified 'accidents', of which he had extraordinarily few on his tours,
prevented their seeing much of the town and on 12 May they took the road for
Bury St Edmunds, stopping on the way to inspect Euston Hall, a much older
house than Houghton.

On the right as you go out of Thetford for Euston is an huge Mount of
Chalk cast up to a great height and fortified with Trenches; from hence
you have a pleasant view of Thetford, which looks as much like a Garden
as a Town. Euston-Hall, the Duke of Grafton's, stands low in a Park; 'tis
an old Seat[y] built of Brick and consisting of three sides; the Furniture for
the most part old. Charles II kept Court here . . . In one of the Rooms a
Painting in several divisions said to be done as a Trial of Skill by several
painters. The Cielings are painted by Verrio. The Gallery is repairing so
we lost sight of the Pictures there. Tapestry here of the Duke of Newcastle
instructing his Son in Horsemanship. The handsome Gardens were made
by the present Duke and are very well watered; a Wooden Bridge here
built about 2 years since is 60 foot long without Supporters. There is a
large Kitchen-Garden.

[v] Furnishing material sometimes patterned like damask.
[w] Lord Oxford considered the use of so much mahogany at Houghton 'most
monstrous'. See James Lees-Milne, *Earls of Creation*, p. 211.
[x] Narford Hall.
[y] Great improvements were made by the 1st Earl of Arlington (see John Evelyn's
Diary), whose daughter married the 1st Duke of Grafton, son of Charles II and Barbara,
Duchess of Cleveland.

They spent a long time examining the ruined abbey at 'Bury'.

Much within the memory of man the public Refectory, the Kitchen and
Offices were standing; but Major Pack, having bought the Estate at
2,800£ pulled 'em down and then sold the Estate for 1,400£ to Sir Jermyn
Davers. Some of the Walls are now pulling down for the Stones. . .

Chippenham had belonged to the Earl of Orford who had made many
improvements.

This Seat came into the hands of Mr Sandys of Worcestershire in right
of his Wife.[z] It stands in a Park and is a Brick Building very much
improved by the Earl. The Hall, wainscoted with Juniper and adorned at
the top with Paintings of Kings and Queens and Queen Consorts from
Edward VI to George I, as also with the Pictures of some of the Rebels, as
Cromwell, Ireton &c. The Stairs are Oak. A great deal of Tapestry with
small figures in the Rooms above. In another Hall on t'other side the
Green-house is a Piece representing at full length the Earls of Orford and
Hallifax, Duke of Devonshire, Lord Sommers, Lord Wharton and the
Earl of Sunderland. The gardens are all his Lordship's making; they are
very handsome and well-watered, taking up 53 Acres, Water and all. The
Earl removed the village of Chippenham to some distance.

They reached Newmarket that evening and lodged at the Ram.

Newmarket is a pleasant airy place; one street and new Brick Boxes on
each side, where the Noblemen live during the Races. In the Duke of
Bolton's and Devonshire's are Pictures by Wootton of famous Racehorses. One Church here.

The road to Ely was over heaths. When they reached it they found it a 'small
mean place . . . the Minster which is fine, its only Ornament'. In spite of the
Norman nave John had nothing but praise for the Cathedral which was 'neat'
throughout – especially the 'spacious' Gothic choir. They rode on through
'fenny' country with flag grass growing all around until they came in sight of
Cambridge, though at first all they could see was King's College Chapel
through the mass of trees. Having deposited Sam Gurney with the baggage
and horses at the Rose Inn, they lost no time in making themselves known to
old Mr Baker at St John's College.
No one could have given the travellers a more genuine and courteous
welcome than Thomas Baker. Horace Walpole later described his character as
'beautiful, amiable and conscientious'[1] and he was more than generous to other
scholars. He was a friend of all that group of antiquarians of whom the pivot
was Edward Harley, 2nd Earl of Oxford. Baker had suffered deprivations
through his indomitable refusal to take the Oaths of Allegiance to the

[z] Through Letitia Sandys's maternal grandmother, Letitia Cheek, who was heiress to
the Russell estates.

Hanoverian Succession. He resigned his living, but when later he was deprived of his Fellowship it was a blow from which he never really recovered, though he bore it with dignity. At least his personal standing was such that he was able to live in college for the rest of his life. John fell immediately under his spell and from that time on they constantly exchanged complimentary messages through Hearne.

Mr Baker showed them the Public Library, 'which will not hold the Books since the Addition of Bishop Moore's', the Theatre and the most important manuscripts in the College.

> St. John's has 3 Brick Quadrangles; the Chappel very mean. In the Library hang the Pictures of Bishop Morton, Archbishop Williams, Sir Ralph Hare, Mr Prior (his Picture not like others I have seen, – an Original – under it the Books he gave), Lord Malton, Dr Gower, a Master here (not an Original), the Countess of Richmond, Bishop Gunning, Bendloes the Poet and some others; a good Collection of Medals and all Queen Anne's (I believe) in Copper. Among some Curiosities they show a Folio of ancient illuminated Pictures of Sacred History; also the Greek Testament that King Charles I used at Chappel. Among the MSS. is the very Book that Archbishop Laud used at the Coronation of King Charles I and his Queen; the Book (as is most probable) that Charles I had in his hand at the Coronation, as also the very Book that Archbishop Sancroft used at the Coronation of King James II and his Queen . . . here is also a Collection of Prayers in Sancroft's own hand, which is small, neat and close written; . . . Mr Baker informed me that Sancroft's Printed Books are in Emmanuel College Library, the very neat Chappel of which College was built by Contributions from him and other Benefactors. His Manuscript Papers are in the possession of the Earl of Oxford and these Mr Baker has had the perusal of and also Dr Tanner . . .

John and Mr Baker may well have discovered that both their grandfathers had been Royalists.

They had other acquaintances at Cambridge where they spent four days. Matthew Nicholas of their own college had recommended them to Thomas Johnson of Magdalene, a Cambridge divine and scholar. He dined with them and invited them both to supper where they met the philosopher John Rowning of Magdalene. He in turn gave them breakfast on 17 May and showed them Pepys's Library.

> The Bibiotheca Pepysiana [in Magdalene] is distinct from the other Library and may not have a Book added to it or taken from it; the Presses, just as they stood in Pepys's House, are very elegant with Glass Doors and Pannels of Glass between Press and Press; the Books gilt, Pepys's Arms on the Binding and his Picture in the inside.

John made as many notes as he had time for here, but there was so much to see and other people to meet. Crynes knew Bishop Hoadly's son, Benjamin, and he dined with them at the Rose in a party which included Johnson and James Bate of St John's, the Moderator. They studied Cambridge customs with as much interest as if they had been those of foreigners, noting the many comparisons to be made with Oxford, such as the word moderator for proctor and the proper or waiting sizars, pensioners, fellow commoners and so on.

There were also the other colleges to be visited.

The Senate house of Portland Stone, when another Wing is up, will with the Schools make a very good appearance; it has a neat Cieling of Plaister of Paris, but not high enough for the Dimensions of the Room.

Trinity College Quadrangle is the largest in Cambridge; larger, they say, than Christ Church at Oxford; the Chappel, which has not long been fitted up, is the neatest in the University, a sizeable handsome Room, wainscotted with Oak, the Altar-Piece of the same, the Cieling Painting looks like carved work; the Library, a new Building, is very beautiful, wide and long; the Library at Queen's in Oxford is like it, but not so long any way . . . there is an Observatory at Trinity to which Sir Isaac Newton has made some Presents.

The new Portland-Stone Building at King's College is perfectly neat and elegant; two more sides are designed, which with the noble Chappel will make an handsome Quadrangle . . .

Trinity-Hall is a Foundation for Lawyers, their Master Sir Nathaniel Lloyd, seldom resident, but he has been a good Benefactor. Caius College is for Physicians; Dr Gooch, the Master. Pembroke-Hall Chappel was the first public work of Sir Christopher Wrenn's; the Master, Dr Hawkins upon a quarrel with the House, will not live with 'em, so that several Fellowships are vacant and can't be filled up. In the area of Jesus College is a remarkably large Walnut-Tree. Beyond Magdalene College, on the Right, is the Gateway of the Castle, with an artificial high Hill remaining. Only King's, Trinity and St. John's Colleges have Choirs, and the two latter but at Surplice-Prayers: the Choristers wear flapped Hats and no Bands. The only Distinction a Proctor has is that he wears his Master's Hood (not like the Oxford Hoods) the different way over his Shoulders. A Pudding Sleeve, or as the Cantabrigians call it a Tucked-up-Gown, is an Undress for almost every Degree; they are worn by Doctors, Masters, Batchelors and Fellow-Commoners. Hats with Silver-Lace, or a gold Loop and Button, common here. There are no Seats at St. Mary's for Batchelors and Under-Graduates except Fellow-Commoners; the Masters sit in the Isles. Their Taxers answering to the Clarks of the Market at Oxford, are remembered by the Preacher in his Prayer, as is the Corporation of Cambridge; The Fellow-Commoners at Trinity wear a finer habit than at the other Colleges and the Under-Graduates wear purple Gowns. Cambridge and the Places hereabouts smell strongly of Turf which the common People burn. The Streets are narrow and old. The River flows pleasantly and is of good width under Stone Bridges behind some of the Colleges where are Walks under Rows of Trees. Cambridge Butter is made in Cylindrical form, scarce an Inch thick but of great length.

On the final day they visited Thomas Baker to take their leave and to collect a letter for Hearne. He had found several more curiosities to show them before they left for Huntingdon, thoroughly satisfied with their kind reception.

Huntingdon was chiefly remarkable for having four churchyards, three steeples, two churches and one minister, but they took the opportunity of riding a mile or two out to Hinchingbrooke Cattle, the Earl of Sandwich's seat,

> formerly belonging to Oliver Cromwell's Family and once a Nunnery . . . the House is of Brick but has no Front; the Rooms in it large; in the Chappel are preserved the Heart and Bowells of Admiral Montague, as I remember. In the Hall a wooden Man in a Boat, representing a wild man taken by the Admiral; in a spacious Room above Stairs is a very lively Tapestry of Raphael's Cartons, and I think more exactly taken than any Copies either in Colours or on Copper-Plates, which I have yet seen.

The road to Northampton was once again through 'fenny' country and watery lanes. At Higham Ferrers they found that the castle was now largely in ruins and all that remained had been converted into the Sergeant's Head alehouse; but at Chichele's 'Hospital' just south of the church, there was more to see.

> Mr Dacres of Hampshire refuses to pay out, as he ought, to the Foundation for which Lord Malton is suing him as I understand.[a] Twelve Men should be maintained here, but there is not above half the number. They are allowed 1d. per diem and Fire and a Washer-Woman. They have a Chappel but not now used.

Northampton was pleasant and airy, much of it resurrected after the disastrous fire of 1675, and John very much admired the restoration of All Hallows Church. They missed Althorp on this occasion, and also Holdenby House, through lack of information, but in any case the chief excitement of

---

[a] The advowson of Higham Ferrers was granted to Robert Dacres of Cheshunt in 1543. His lands were charged with a payment of £24.10s.0d. The advowson passed down (with one recovery) to his descendant, Thomas, who was patron in 1726. He seems to have sold the advowson to the Earl of Malton within the next ten years and is said to have sold the College Estate to the Earl in 1734. See Whellan's *History of Northamptonshire* and *V.C.H. Northants*, vol. III.

the journey home was always intended to be Easton Neston with its great collection of statues belonging to the Earl of Pomfret. John had discussed them with Hearne and had consulted notes on them made by the late Dean of Christ Church, Henry Aldrich.

The Earl of Pomfret's Seat is delightfully situate; there is a Vista just in the front, terminated by a Church. The House was built in 1702 of a fair white and durable Stone and is now compleating . . . the Stair-Case painted by Sir James Thornhill . . . Above Stairs is very fine Tapestry, the design of Raphael of Hercules's Labours, the Temple of Victory &c. Good Tapestry of Alexander's History. A most curious Cabinet adorned with the History of Moses, painted on Copper by Rottenhamer in Colours.

He described more paintings before turning his attention to the statues.

The Garden-Front is set off with antique Statues; there is a Building designed where they are all to stand on Pedestals.

There were others in the 'Garden-house' and in the park – 'The Tully declaiming with an angry look, the Handkerchief in the right hand, a Roll in the left' – and so on.

Stowe was the last of the great houses to be seen on this journey and this time John was more communicative.

Lord Cobham's at Stow is a Brick Seat, placed commodiously for good Prospects. There is a Vista through the House of great length; the House is elegantly furnished; here is Tapestry of a Battle Lord Cobham was engaged in; in other Rooms, an original Picture of Oliver Cromwell in Armour with his Page; two Paintings of Van Dyck and his Wife both by Van Dyck himself, a painting of Joan D'Arc. The Rooms above Stairs were beautifying, so that we lost sight of the Pictures there. The Gardens lie most on the right of the House; no one part of them answers to another, but yet you perceive no Irregularity for the View is confined to as much only as is regular within itself; several beautiful Vistas here over an open Countrey; several Buildings, but heavy and clumsy, end the Walks, one to the memory of Sir John Vanbrugh; yet there is no Walk round this Garden; not a great deal of Water here.[b]

Expressions always interested John and at the end of his notes, he wrote down a few new ones which he had come across. The 'Generals' was how they described the Archdeacon's visitations at Ipswich; at Blythburgh an honest person was called 'square' – whose 'actions are fair and square'; and at Higham Ferrers a 'ditch velley landed' meant a 'ditch well-nigh

[b] I am indebted to Mr George Clarke for information on Stowe. John Loveday provides the only description of paintings in the 1730s besides other points of interest in house and garden. See pp. 204–5.

stopped up with earth'. 'Velley' also meant 'well-nigh' at Birmingham, he remembered.

The journey, for which he paid all the expenses, had cost this time about sixteen guineas, including hire of horses and servant. It had lasted seventeen days.

On the afternoon of 15 June he dropped in to see Hearne and found there Robert Fysher, Bodley's Librarian, with an inscription he had taken from an old altar stone which had been dug up, while he watched, at nearby Dorchester. Hearne was not satisfied with the accuracy of Fysher's transcription and asked John to have a look at it next time he rode down to Caversham. John went to Dorchester a week later and riding straight back to Oxford wrote the following note for his own use.

> As they were digging a Saw-Pit in the back yard of the Red Lion in Dorchester (June 14) they light upon a Roman Altar above four foot underground. The next day Fysher, the Librarian, brought Hearne an imperfect copy of it and said that some Horses' teeth were found with it, one of which he had with him. I heard that human bones were found there. This is an exact copy of it as I took it on the spot.

Next day he took his version round to Hearne and it is now in the Bodleian with Hearne's note on it.

> It was dug-up at the west side of the Red Lyon . . . in the Close called Court Close . . . Mr Loveday's is the best copy.[2]

But Benwell supplied a postscript to this story.

> The following circumstance he related of himself and Mr Thomas Hearne; there was formerly a Roman Altar dug up in some Inn yard at Dorchester; a copy of the inscription had been sent to Mr Hearne, but so ill taken that it was quite unintelligible. 'Mr Loveday', says he, 'you go by there in your way to Caversham, will you call in and take a copy of it for me?' Accordingly I did and carried the paper back with me to Oxford and gave it to him. 'Ay', says he 'I can understand your copy very well, but I have got a plain country man with me who can copy letters very well, but as he knows nothing of these matters, he has no Hypothesis to serve; I'll send him if you please and he shall take a copy for me.' 'Do Sir,' said I; 'but however I assure you I have no Hypothesis to serve.' I said no more, but a few days after when I called on him, he began without my mentioning a word; 'Well, Mr Loveday, I have sent, and find my friend's copy of the inscription agreeing exactly with yours, but I could not help being a little suspicious as I never yet saw in any inscription the words *cum cancellis* added after *hanc aram*.'

This was probably as near an apology as Hearne ever made and was certainly as close as John came to any criticism of him. No wonder it had rankled a little –

he was not on his way to Caversham but had gone down specially, though he had delayed for a few days because he was so busy with the College writings, many of which he read to Hearne and allowed him to copy.

John, meanwhile, was spending all his spare time in the Library and on 2 July he gave the College the nine volumes of Hottinger's ecclesiastical history[3] which he had bought from Deodatus Bye for fifteen shillings. This was quite a high price in those days when you could, as John did, buy a Caxton for six shillings and eightpence.[4] Over the years he made many more gifts of books to Magdalen.

John Audley was due to return from Birmingham and John decided to ride as far as Banbury to meet him on 15 July. He collected his notes from his usual sources and set off by himself.

> We descend to Banbury which lies for the most part in a Valley. . . Much of the Building here of the Stone of the Countrey. 'Tis a very dirty Town. There are four Stone Gates in this Town, yet, says Leland, no Token that ever it was walled. There is only a very small piece of the Castle standing; 'twas destroyed (they say) in the Civil Wars; within this last Year above one hundred-weight of Bomb-Shells were dug up in the Castle Garden. The Castle Gate is now two Miles off at Broughton, Captain Twistleton's. The Church is one of the largest; the middle Isle in a very dangerous condition;[c] 'tis not cieled; the black Marble Tomb of William Cope, Cofferer to K Henry 7 is very much abused and broken, no sign of any Inscription remaining. In the Chancel are the very mutilated figures of Judge Chamberlayn and his Lady (so I'm informed) on their Knees; she was a Dashwood of Wickham in this Parish . . . On the Chancel floor are several Stones for Presbyterian Ministers, called Ministers of the Gospel. Here is a Stone with A P on it; the Clerk told us it was a Queen buryed there and the Register mentioned it. The Register says: 'August 1682.6. Ann Peregrine of the Kingdom of Pomunkey in the East Indies baptized at the age of 16 or 17 years in the parish Church of Banbury by Mr Jo. Knight.' I suppose she was Slave to some Gentleman here, though vulgar tradition has in so short a time made her a Queen. In the Church is a Monument for John and Joan Knight (He several times Bailiff of Banbury) who from 3 Sons and 10 Daughters, 9 marryed, saw 84 descended from 'em; he dyed 22 Nov, 1587, she 26 December 1590. They have both extraordinary Characters in the Inscription. On the floor of the Church are several Inscriptions wrote in an Oval. This Parsonage is not now a Prebend of Lincoln, but yet a Peculiar of that Church. The Tower was rebuilt after the Civil Wars, the old one being quite destroyed. On the Right, just as you enter the Town is a large Barn; the Inhabitants say it was St. John's Chappel, but it has no appearance of its ever having been anything but

[c] It survived until 1790 when the fine old church was demolished after much neglect. Most of the monuments disappeared with it.

a Barn; no sign of Chappel windows. This Town is full of Sectarists of all kinds.

The castle gate was certainly not the famous gatehouse at Broughton, but it is just possible John was referring to the actual gate itself.[d] On the other hand he may have been given some faulty information. This occasionally happened, particularly in the case of paintings in country houses when some uneducated housekeeper was the guide. He used to tell his children about one of these old dames who pointing at a picture said 'This is the gulf Sir Martin Frobisher shot and that is the gun he shot it with.'

He was intrigued by the reference to Ann Peregrine but he had to wait until 1751 to hear the whole story when the Revd John Gibberd,[e] son of a baker in Banbury, wrote it down for him.

January 12. 1682–3. Ann Perugrina of the Kingdom of Pomounchy in the East Indies.

> Supposed to be the Sovereign
> of Pomonqui, taken by Pirates
> as she was walking on
> airing with her maids,
> some of whom were taken
> with her, Lord Rochester
> of Adderbury, pitying her
> condition, put her to a
> Boarding-School at
> Calthrop nr. Banbury
> where Mr Jo: Knight
> converted her to Xtianity
> and where she dyed soon after.

How did the libertine Lord Rochester come to know the child who was only thirteen or fourteen at the time of his death in 1680? Had he a hand in her abduction or was he in some way responsible for her pitiful condition? It is hardly likely that she was kidnapped or bought later by one of the sober sectarians of Banbury and much more probable that she was brought down from London. Possibly it was an act of clemency, a first intimation of the change of heart which caused Rochester, in the final year of his life, to repent of

[d] I am grateful to Mr D. E. M. Fiennes for the suggestion that John may possibly have meant the actual wooden gate or a previous one which has now gone. He cannot have meant the present gatehouse or another which is shown in Buck's engraving of 1729.

[e] John Gibberd, curate at Whaddon and popular with Browne Willis, became vicar of Sharnbrook, Bedfordshire in 1766. His brother, according to William Cole (*Blecheley Diary*), was a baker in London. The brother, William, settled at Sharnbrook in 1774 and became a sheriff for Bedfordshire in 1785 and a J.P. of the Borough of Westminster among other distinctions. The name became Gibbard.

his former excesses. At any rate it was kind to send her to Calthorpe, which at that time seems to have been a school for girls of gentle birth.*ʃ* Sadly she did not long survive. Perhaps the change to the cold North Oxfordshire climate was too extreme for a young lady from Pomonqui.

John and John Audley returned to Oxford. 'July 20th. College alarmed by Burslem' wrote the former in his diary. Thomas Burslem, who held a B.A. degree at Christ Church, had applied for a Magdalen Fellowship on the grounds that he was a Lincolnshire man and the Statutes prescribed a certain number of Fellowships for each county. Of the seven for Lincolnshire only one had been taken whereas the three Berkshire Fellowships were all filled. As Zinzan had procured the promise of the Fellows' votes, it was proposed that he should have a Lincolnshire Fellowship and – according to tradition but not the letter of the law – should transfer to a Berkshire one when a vacancy occurred. History does not relate why they should not both have held Lincolnshire Fellowships, but Burslem was refused and Zinzan, who was very popular, was elected. The President and Fellows then realized that they could well be accused of twisting the rules, so to help their case they elected Zinzan Lecturer in Moral Philosophy – rather remote for someone who really wanted to practise as a physician. Burslem appealed to the Visitor, Bishop Richard Willis, and less than a year after his election Zinzan was to have the mortification of finding his Fellowship nullified. The cup which he now presented to the College was to be returned and though his expenses would be refunded it was all to be a great misfortune. He had the consolation of knowing that the President and Dr Jenner were his most fervent supporters from the beginning to the end, becoming deeply resentful of the Visitor's interference. Hearne, who could not bear either of them, took Burslem's side in this affair in spite of the fact that Zinzan was John's tutor and close friend. John himself did not disclose an opinion on paper. He must have gone along with the Establishment, but he was such a stickler for propriety in matters of this kind that he must also have felt that the Bishop had some justification for his action.

However, Zinzan still had ten happy months as a Fellow before him when John set off on another ramble with Thomas Bonney and his servant, Michael Welman. Excited by the marbles at Easton Neston he could not wait to compare them with the collection belonging to the 8th Earl of Pembroke. He was on his way to Wilton House to see for himself.

They left on 28 July, sleeping at the Bear at Hungerford 'chiefly famous for Trout and Crawfish' and rode next day through 'fine corn countrey' to Stonehenge.

> The Duke of Queensburgh [Queensberry] has a Seat at Ambresbury [Amesbury] chiefly remarkable, they say, for the finest Dairy in England.

ʃ This was Calthorpe Manor. See D. M. Barratt, 'A Presbyterian Preacher' in *Cake and Cockhorse*, Banbury Historical Society, vol. 6, p. 30. Anne Peregrine is mentioned in Banbury records, but there is no account of her.

We were alarmed at the Church here, for looking in at the Windows, Mr Head, the Schoolmaster (a Native of the Town and a very worthy man) appeared solitary in the Pulpit repeating his Sermon.

His description of Stonehenge was orthodox enough, except for an additional note which would shock modern conservationists.

An old man that sells Drink here, above a year since digging him a Hole for his Liquor within the inmost Circle, discovered a Stone (was it the supposed Altar-Stone of Mr Jones,[g] which according to Gibson[h] is now gone and in Jones's time appeared much above the Surface of the Earth?) which he tells me, with all the rest that are visible, compleats the number of 94 Stones.

At Bemerton they stopped to see the chapel – 'much the meanest I ever saw' – and were surprised to find that there was no inscription for the divine and poet, George Herbert, who lay under the same stone beneath the altar as another scholarly rector, John Norris – yet there was a marble on the wall for Norris.

They had spent the night at Salisbury and were now approaching Wilton House.

'. . . The Earl of Pembroke's one mile farther than Bemerton. 'Tis an old Stone Quadrangle, built out of an Abbey of Benedictine Nuns, which was granted to this family at the Suppression. In the Court before it a Porphyry Pillar from Egypt. There are no fine Beds, Chairs, Glasses &c. here. The Wainscot common, small Pannels and of a lead Colour. The Tapestry of which there is no great quantity, has all small Figures. In a lower Room is a Marble Bass Relieve with a Greek Inscription.

This inscription puzzled John and he made several notes about it for Hearne.

'His Lordship has with his Pencil on the Wainscot remarked upon this Marble; from whence I observed as above. He has wrote by several others in the same manner. In the same Room a large and valuable Bust of Caracalla in Bass Relieve. There are several very fine Tables at Wilton, as Granite, Porphyry and other curious Marbles, and a large Table of Lapis Lazuli. Two black Porphyry Pillars in a Room below.

He wrote down descriptions of most of the statues above, below and on the stairs – just as he had at Easton Neston.

---

[g] Inigo Jones's theory that Stonehenge was a Roman temple founded by Agricola, or soon afterwards, was published posthumously in his account of it, *Stone-Heng Restor'd* (1655).

[h] Bishop Edmund Gibson's edition of Camden's *Britannia*, vol. 1, second edition, p. 172 – '. . . no Cross nor any other token of the Christian Faith.'

Above Stairs are a great number of antique Busts of all sizes, a few for Colossus's, others of the living size, others for the closet; most of them stand on Marble Pedestals . . . the very fine head of Julius Caesar is just as it were transparent . . . Socrates is perfectly homely and has a very deep Dent on the top of the Bridge of his Nose . . . we saw a smaller Hercules moriens, Paeas supporting him, his Body admirably swelled and distended with the working poyson.

These were but a few of his numerous comments and he was equally painstaking about the pictures. When he came to Wilton House again in 1738 he found that many of these paintings had been moved to different positions by the 9th Earl.

There are three very fine upper Rooms, the Cielings painted; one is a Cube of 30 foot; another 60 foot long, 30 broad and high. In these are busts of the Caesars, all but Otho and Tiberius, which being of the Closet-size are in a third Room. The White-Marble Chimney-Pieces curiously wrought, are by Inigo Jones; over, but behind, one of them is a large Window. Above are two of the Cartons in Tapestry, but I can't think them comparable to those at Hinchinbroke; a Room below is set off with Horns. Two sets of Elks' Horns found in the Bogs in Ireland, the Earl brought with him from thence. His Lordship made a Present some years since to Sir Robert Walpole of a gilt Roman Gladiator, exactly like that in the Vatican. The Building in the Bowling-Green contains some Antiques . . . at the upper end of the plain Garden here is an equestrian M. Aurelius in Lead, like that in the Capitol. Among several foreign Plants and Trees in this Garden is a Tulip Tree near 30 foot high; I take it to be just the same as that at Swallowfield House; an Arbutus Tree, a Cork Tree &c. Here is a Water-house with no small variety of Water-works, an Hare-Warren and a Park.

From Sidney's *Arcadia* painted on the lower panels of the Cube Room to the 'iron Cuzule Chair' embossed with silver studs, everything he saw intrigued him. The 8th Earl might not have very fine furniture but as a collector he had a great reputation. Still it was Lord Pomfret who in John's opinion finally won the day.

However Lord Pembroke excels all others in Busts; yet Lord Pomfret's Statues vastly exceed his; Pembroke's chiefly consisting of fictitious Persons, – Heathen Deities, such as Hercules &c. yet finely cut; whereas Pomfret, besides a good shew of these, has the Statues of real and great men such as Tully, G. Marius &c and those excellently performed too.

Back in Salisbury with time to look around, they noticed first of all that the river water had to be used in rivulets to clean the streets and the gutters sometimes overflowed for want of clearing. The market place was very spacious and airy – 'new Houses in it would make it perfectly grand'. John had an up-to-date outlook and liked to see new buildings rising, with stonework, stucco and glazing all still untouched by the effects of climate and weather. But here it was the 'most beautiful Tower and lofty elegant Spire – just as high again as the Monument in London',[i] which inspired him. As usual he described the interior and took down the inscriptions on the tombs in the Cathedral.

> The Pillars here are neatly taper and proportionate. . . round each Pillar are four Pillarets of a finer Grain, which till lately have passed for Artificial. The Tradition is that this Church had as many Windows as there are days in the year, as many Pillars and Pillarets as there are hours and as many Gates as months. The Church is lofty, the Roof Stone-work plaistered over in Brick fashion.

He was pleased to find a monument for a boy bishop behind a grating and an ancient round table from Old Sarum, but regrettably they could not see Bishop Jewel's library. However they were able to visit Bishop Ward's Hospital for ten clergymen's widows and to compare it with Bromley College.

On 1 August they rode through lanes and over commons to Southampton, stopping to inspect Romsey Abbey which he was told had been sold by Henry VIII for £100. He did not admire it but heard that it was thronged every Sunday. Of the six churches at Southampton the French one 'makes a considerable part of the inhabitants'; St Mary's had been in such a ruinous condition that only the chancel could be used, but Dr Brideoake, the rector, had recently rebuilt much of it on its old walls.

It was a short ride to Winchester so, though they had only one night there, John had time to take even more extensive notes than at Salisbury. Foremost among the monuments, of course, was that for Bishop Waynflete, the founder of Magdalen College –

> His Figure with his Heart between his Hands, in Plaister of Paris, the work clumsy and materials coarse; this, I'm told, Magdalen College (as obliged) visit every year in their Hampshire Progress and propose to adorn it.

Another interesting inscription written by William Lowth, the Commentator, was for Bishop Mews whose 'neat marble Monument' had just been erected and paid for by President Butler, whose family had been 'under obligations to the bishop'.

Here was no Library , I'm told, till Bishop Morley left his Study with

---

[i] Wren's fluted Doric column in Fish Street (1671) commemorating the Great Fire of 1666.

an order that it should be a public Library; but since it has been abused considerably they have shut it up . . . Under the Presbytery are Vaults where the Prebendaries store their Liquor.

Everything here was admirable and John was by now able to discuss the architecture with more discernment. After examining Morley's Hospital for clergymen's widows where 'fewel and a Nurse in common' were provided, they went on to look at Winchester College, though how this was arranged is not explained.

Just in the South Suburbs stands Wickham's College, a Stone Building but by no means elegant. On the left as you enter, are the Warden's Lodgings of Brick; he only is allowed to have a Wife in College: Farther on, in the Quadrangle and above Stairs, are the Lodgings for the School-master and 10 Fellows called the Masters. The Lower Lodging-Rooms, of which there are seven, have ten Beds apiece for the seventy Scholars, or the Children. The School-Boys, not upon the Foundation, are called Commoners. The sixteen Choristers, who go to School and wait in the Hall at Meals, do not lodge in College: the Usher has no Lodgings here. The Masters only at particular times dine in the Hall; they make use of one Room entirely for that purpose. The School-Master in Chappel sits next to the Warden in the right-hand Stall. The painted Glass in the East Window was the subject of Mr Robert Lowth's Poem.[j] Wardens Braithwaite and Cobb have Monuments in the Ante-Chappel. They bury too in the Cloysters, in the Area of which is a small Library. The School, which stands backwards, is a late handsome Brick Building, the Founder's Statue over the Door; it is full of Boxes for the Boys to write on &c.

Their final visit was to St Cross.

. . . 13 Brothers are maintained here: they wear long Black Gowns, with silver Crosses on the left Breast, given them by Bishop Compton; before they had Purple Crosses worked into the Gown. Four of these Brothers live now as Out-Pensioners and are allowed 10£ per Annum. Cardinal Beaufort made up their number 36 but Henry VIII's avarice has reduced 'em to the primitive 13; so that there is a great deal of vacant Room here but all kept in good repair.

There was more to say about the Brothers of St Cross, who had 6d. a week,

[j] John did not read Lowth's poem on the genealogy of Christ as displayed in the east window of Winchester College chapel (written at school) until 22 November 1730. In a note in the Bodleian (MS.Rawl.J 4°.5.f.54) he explained that it had come out in London in 1729 as a 22-page pamphlet without the author's consent. See the preface to Lowth's pamphlet (1729).

8s. a quarter and '2d. apiece poundage out of Fines'. Their chapel was also the parish church for the inhabitants of St Faith's whose own church had fallen down. Then there was the 'Unfinished Palace of Charles II on arches' designed by Wren and 'not suffered to run out of repair' and the fine room used for Assizes. They saw the round table, but did not connect it with King Arthur – 'the figures of a King &c painted on it – used probably in Entertainment at Tournaments'.

On 3 August they rode north through 'dirty' Whitchurch and Kingsclere and stopped at the Pelican and George in Speen.

Most of the Road was open, part of it through Warrens full stocked with Rabbets.

And so from Newbury, which smelt of peat and turf and had an 'exceeding neat Spanish Oak altarpiece' in the church put up by the miller[k] who had won £1,000 in a lottery, they returned to Oxford. They had seen a great deal in a week and it had cost eleven guineas.

John had barely time to do more than take to Hearne the Wilton House inscriptions which had puzzled him, together with John Norris's epitaph from Bemerton and two stones of portable dimensions from Stonehenge, before he was on his way again to Cambridge. Accompanied by Ben Dye, his servant, he went as fast as possible and twenty-four hours after his departure he was handing another letter from Hearne to Mr Baker of St John's. This time these worthy gentlemen were of only secondary importance, for that evening his enterprising mother and Aunt Betty arrived at Cambridge, not in their comparatively comfortable coach, but 'in the Stage'. The stage coach at this time was not much more than an unsprung wooden wagon without proper windows, and could only average about forty miles a day, frequently sticking in the muddy or sandy tracks.[5] The journey therefore, though they had probably come from London, must have been tedious as well as uncomfortable; yet here they were for a stay of four days and one can only assume they were possessed of unparalleled moral fibre and well-padded clothing. John's friends, Mr Johnson and Mr Thompson of Magdalene, assisted him in showing them the University and on 14 August they returned as they had come, while John rode back to Oxford to put the finishing touches to his account of Wiltshire and Hampshire. He made one more trip, this time to Faringdon, a town 'decayed upon the turning of the Western Road through Burford' and notable now for manufacturing 'rubbers for scythes'; but the Faringdonians could tell him nothing about their old Cistercian abbey and did not even know where their castle had stood. With this disappointing news for Hearne, tempered by the loan of a manuscript from Magdalen College Library, he took his leave of Oxford once again and rode down to

[k] William Cundell, mayor of Newbury.

Caversham with Bonney and young George Langton (step-grandson of the attorney Walter Pryse*l* of Hurst), the latest Reading schoolboy to become a gentleman commoner at Magdalen.

l Walter Pryse, the rich lawyer and governor of four hospitals in London, came from Painswick (though of Welsh descent) and died at his house at Woodstock in 1745. He married Elizabeth, widow of John Lewis of Hurst. Her daughter Catherine and son-in-law, John Langton, had died early. See p. 59 n.g.

To the Defence of Hearne
1731 – 1732

During the summer at Caversham John made many excursions to places nearby, including Silchester. It was not for another ten years that John Stair, the parson's servant who was the first to excavate there, was to make his plan of the street system by watching the parched bands in the crops above.[1] Looking at the site in 1731 with Mr Hiley and Tom Bonney, John merely said that the church and farm stood just within the space where the south gate to the Roman town had been; a deep ditch surrounded the walls on which trees were growing and which were almost level with the ground they enclosed; fragments of bricks and tiles lay about in the fields. He would come back again. 'Onion's Hole still here – or Inian's as they pronounce it.'

On 4 September he and his mother left Caversham very early in the morning for the Mermaid at Windsor where they signed a new lease with Farmer Dell of Feens and his nephew and bondsman, John Hatch. They spent the rest of the day with the Stapleses and John took the opportunity of investigating St George's Chapel and taking more notes in the Castle. He also paid a visit to Eton.

> Eaton College is a Brick Building. You enter into a Quadrangle – on the right is the Chappel of Stone; here are two Schools, the Upper and the Lower and a long Room in which 48 of the 70 Foundationers lie in single Beds. Through this Quadrangle you enter by a great Gate, like that at St. John's, Cambridge, into Cloysters. The Fellows' Wives here live with 'em in College. At the High Table in the public Refectory the Fellows dine.

The carved woodwork of the stalls in St George's Chapel was 'wondrous curious' and the brass plates nailed on the back of alternate stalls with the titles of the Garter Knights intrigued him. As a devoted Royalist, he looked in vain for a remembrance of Charles I. In the Castle, however, he found the original portrait by Van Dyck of Henrietta Maria in a grey silk gown and cherry-coloured ribbons from which his fine copy at Caversham had been taken. As usual he enjoyed comparing the paintings with others he had seen: the Schalcken nightpiece at Wilton House was better than this one; the portrait of Charles II when a lad was similar to that at Euston Hall; Holbein's Erasmus was like one in the Oxford Picture Gallery,[a] and so on. He confined his notes to the paintings and the needlework of Mary, Queen of Scots. At five o'clock he and his mother left for home, driving round by Feens to have a look at the farmyard.

His time was occupied to the full, not only with expeditions and the round of social visits, but also with public occasions which often included a dinner. After Mayor Iremonger had 'gone out' to a sermon preached by Dick Wooddeson, Mayor Thorne had come in with a feast attended by the gentry and townsmen of any 'tolerable fashion', as Mayor John Watts had observed three years earlier.[2] It was then that Watts had had to eliminate the ladies: so much offence had been caused in his earlier mayoralty because there was not room for them all that with some regret he cut them out entirely in 1728, replacing them with well-dressed townsmen. For some reason which Watts had taken to be political the clergy stayed away with the ladies, but their absence was only temporary. In any case they had a dinner of their own preceded by a sermon known as 'The Lecture'. John invariably attended this sermon when he was at home. Charles Coates in his *History of Reading* said that it took place on the first Tuesday of the month at the church of St Laurence and was supported by a society of the clergy. In a letter to John's son, Dr John Loveday, of 14 April 1805 he enlarged on this statement:

> I believe the Lecture is revived, having been a Sermon advertised by the Rev. Nathaniel Gilbert, preached at Archbishop Laud's Lecture[b]. . . By the way the Archbishop had nothing to do with *this* . . . He had an antipathy to Lectures.

When John dined with the Visitors to the school in October they included his own President, Edward Butler, who was now the Vice-Chancellor. One of the performers was Dr Merrick's youngest son, James, a boy of eleven. He was to play an important part in John's life.

When Dr South died in 1715 he left his house, The Priory, to his

---

[a] Portraits from the Bodleian Library were hung in an upper storey of the Public Schools called the Picture Gallery. See *A Pocket Companion or Guide through the University*, new edition, 1768.

[b] 'The Forbidden Tree'. *A Sermon (on Gen. II, 16–17) Preached at Reading Oct. 2, 1804*, published London, 1805.

housekeeper, Mrs Margaret Hammond, the widow of his curate at Islip. After her death it was to go to Christ Church; but in spite of the Doctor's exhortations to her in his will to continue in a state of widowhood

> and that for her own Sake and Interest as well as my Satisfaction. For that otherwise neither she nor I can tell what Havock an Husband will make upon the Premises, nor what (if there be no such check on him) can prevent his making it,[4]

she had married again. It had apparently not occurred to the Doctor that she might move out, but this she did when she went to live with her second husband, Henry Smith, a man of substance and high standing in the county, at The Grove, Emmer Green. She died in 1731 but Henry Smith lived on, surrounded by relics of Dr South and with a store of anecdotes with which he would entertain John, who enjoyed walking up the hill to hear them and to look at the pictures.

> Henry Smith said that Dr South had no great notion of the Earl of Rochester who published, or of Bishop Spratt who corrected, Clarendon's History – for Spratt was an airy man and South extremely rigid; that South had wrote in his Copy against some of the Characters in this History thus – this (or that) Character was meant for such a one; that he (Smith) has Sermons of South tyed up in five Volumes designed for the Press,[5] but Mrs Smith was so troubled with publishing the 5th and 6th Volumes that she could not think of going any further; that Mrs Smith had burnt a vast number of Papers, wrote by South, at his command; – that King James II sent for South, thinking that he would come into the Penal Laws[c] &c. He refusing, said the King 'What, does Dr South refuse me?' He answered 'Sir, I can't do it: I would sooner turn my Religion than betray it.' That when South was at the last he was writing a letter to William Shippen to thank him for some bold Speech he had made in defence of the Church.

The Dorchester altar stone had been causing much speculation and a number of people had been there to copy the inscription, including William Derham. John heard in August that Sir George Oxenden had ordered it to be taken into his house nearby at Wittenham. He wrote to Hearne[6] to say he thought it might be seen as well there as at Dorchester, but Hearne jibbed at paying a visit to such a well-known reprobate as Sir George whose dissolute character was a byword. As Lord Egmont said of him, he was a 'proud conceited lewd man' who was only out of gaol because he was a Member of Parliament.[7] Hearne replied on 26 August

> I thank you for what you write concerning the fate of the Stone. Had it continued at Dorchester I designed to have been there this Week. I know

---

[c] Against Protestant nonconformers.

not now where to follow it. Nor indeed am I inclined to make inquirie at the place specified in your Letter. All things have happened just as I at first expected. Sandwich, I told you, is the place whither 'twas intended to be conveyed. I am well enough satisfyed with the Copy you took; only the points must be altered . . . which change the Countryman's Copy seems likewise to justify. I wish, however, you had seen it again your self for your own satisfaction, especially since 'tis pretended that the Variations have arose from washing and cleansing the Stone. Which if true, perhaps upon a new washing other differences may appear.[8]

John replied[9] that he would go there on his way back and tried to cheer Hearne up with information about the grave of Robert Betham, onetime rector of Silchester, which he had seen there. Betham, who had once been tutor to Mr John Baber of Sunninghill, had been drowned in the Fleet ditch in 1719. This lugubrious information, together with a couple of epitaphs, had the desired effect and Hearne's reply on 23 September was placid, not least because John had been mistaken in thinking that William King, the Principal of St Mary Hall, had bought Betham's library for Sir Thomas Sebright when he had actually kept it all himself.

They used at Silchester to carry all the Coins found there to Mr Betham, who kept only such as were fair, and always returned the rest. What became of his collection of coins I cannot say . . I am glad you design to review the Dorchester Stone if you can have a Sight of it. I do not know but I may print it, and should be willing to have it pretty exact, though I believe there is nothing material omitted even in the Copy I before had from you.[10]

Nothing was too much trouble if it was for Hearne. John and Bonney had arranged to ride back on 8 October with John Spicer, a schoolfellow, and Simon Walcroft, who was on some business of his own; but on reaching Dorchester they left their friends and made their way to Sir George's house. There they asked if they might see the stone, but it was 'denyed'. Hearne was indignant when he heard about it.

. . . Tho' Mr Loveday offered a Crown to the Servants he spoke with . . . they said had he come half an hour sooner he might have seen it, it being then in the Kitchin, but it was now conveyed to some Upper Room . . . of the House. Sir George is an ill-natured man. Mr Loveday called purely on my account, who suggested a Review to him.[d][11]

He had the last word as he so often had about his fellow men, who had no

---

[d] Oxenden's family home was at Dene, near Wingham, Kent. He was M.P. for Sandwich for many years. The house at Little Wittenham came to him through his marriage to Elizabeth Dunch. Hearne's criticisms were corroborated by Lord Egmont, Lord Hervey and Lady Mary Wortley-Montagu.

idea their peccadilloes, or worse, were being collected for posterity. By refusing to cooperate Sir George had delivered himself into Hearne's pocket book, where he received no quarter.

John's final expedition in 1731 was to Shotover House, the home of Colonel (later General) James Tyrrell, son of James Tyrrell, the historian.

> November 12. Colonel Tyrell's Seat in Shotover-Forest commands a good Prospect; it is a late elegant Building of Stone, the Rooms small; in one of them an ancient Shield (Wooden I take it) on which are the Devil, a Man and a Woman, with an old French Inscription. Several good Paintings here – Earl Cadogan at length, an half-piece on Wood of Ann Bolen with black Hair, and of a Duke of Buckingham. The three lengths of James I, his Queen and Prince Henry seem to be good Copies from those at Hampton Court. 'Twas observed that the lower part of the Prince's face is not unlike T. Garrway's . . . Here is a good Painting of a Nymph extracting an Arrow from another's Breast. There are Family Pictures of the Grandfather, Sir Timothy Tyrrell who married the Primate's Daughter^e – the Father of James Tyrrell the Writer, and himself among the rest. Charity with her Children is no mean Performance. Good Tapestry here and a Table and Chest made of a Plane-Tree that grew in the Grounds.

He frequently found likenesses between people he knew and the subjects of portraits. Thomas Garway (*sic*) was a demy at Magdalen.

Four days after his return to Oxford on 8 October, John went to the President 'for Grace for a B.A. degree'. On the 16th Phanuel Bacon and William Payne came to his rooms to read the Articles with him and he was then presented for his degree in the Convocation House. Two days later he called at Edmund Hall to collect Hearne at four o'clock in the afternoon and they went off to Shepherd's to celebrate the occasion with a number of other friends, staying there until ten o'clock that night. During the evening John regaled the company with accounts of his summer expeditions and anecdotes he had heard on his visits to Hurst with Mr Hiley and Bonney. They had made friends with a group of gentlemen there which included Walter Pryse, who, as Hearne pointed out, was a very High Tory

> and hath abundance of MSS papers relating to the late horrid Revolution, more he saith than any one hath besides.[12]

Next day there was an informal celebration in the Senior Common Room when John was 'treated on becoming a member' and at the end of the month he gave the College Library a beautiful edition of John Barclay's *Argenis* (1621) – a political satire. He was also invited to sup with the President to meet Mr Hiley, with Phanny, Joseph Andrews the Proctor, and Thomas Jenner,

^e Elizabeth Tyrrell, daughter of Archbishop James Ussher.

the Vice-President. He now faced nearly three more years of study before receiving his M.A. degree but it was a way of life he found entirely satisfying. In three months' time he would come of age; he was unambitious and wished only to fulfil his desire for knowledge; yet he was undoubtedly an enthusiast—a word which was unacceptable in the Age of Reason when its exuberance was identified as curiosity or ingenuity. Besides he was interested in many other aspects of life, not least the oddities of his fellow men.

His faith in God who watched over his every action was unshakeable and his whole life and conduct were based on this unquestioning conviction. He did not doubt that his ability to make quick and sensible judgments or to take the initiative in a dilemma was due to constant prayer and the admission of God's will at all times into his life. On a less exalted level he was very fond of reading or listening to sermons, though his favourite preachers were two whom he had never actually heard, South and Swift, both vigorous and intellectual exponents of the Christian faith and both men who appealed to him for their formidable command of language and a certain derisive humour.

Every Sunday he went to service in Magdalen College Chapel or St Mary's and frequently took short notes on the substance of the sermon. Among those whose themes he recorded are the names of such well known University figures as John Conybeare, Rector of Exeter, Theophilus Leigh, Master of Balliol, Joseph Smith, Provost of Queen's, and Thomas Cockman, Master of University College.

He was equally at ease with people at all levels of society though with that healthy respect for the aristocracy which was almost universal. Usually tolerant, he could be very forceful if his anger was aroused and nothing annoyed him more than miscarriages of justice or dishonest tricks; but in relating the following story from his undergraduate days he was as amused by the transparency of the rogue as he was shocked by his depravity. Benwell heard it from John's son Arthur.

One morning during his residence at Magdalen College, having some very ill-tasted butter brought him for breakfast, he sent for the butler in order to reprimand him. The man begged his pardon for the mistake he had committed, saying he made it a rule to leave all the bad butter for the Demies, reserving the good for the Gentlemen-Commoners. At this he was much more incensed and gave the man a still severer reprimand for his injustice in reserving the best accommodation for the independent members.

He could lose his temper and one of Benwell's tales, about an evening at an Oxford inn, reveals also that he could not always take a joke if it offended his personal dignity, though perhaps this can be attributed more to his youth than his pride.

Though a man of the strictest piety, he was always of a warm temper. As he was sitting once with some of his acquaintance, one of the Company watched the opportunity of his rising from his seat to remove it from under him, so that when he attempted to sit down again he fell backwards. Upon this, getting up again with some indignation, he addressed the gentleman thus: 'Sir, I'm not fond of your practical jests; the next time you serve me so I'll knock you down if I can; – if I can't you must excuse me.'

The civility at the end of the ferocity was due to his very moderate height of which he was always conscious. His physical courage was never in question. Even when he was a frail old man he astonished his frightened household by separating two huge drunken ruffians who were fighting in his courtyard.

It was now that he found himself involved in an affair which called for all his powers of tact and judgment.

Thirty years earlier the young Thomas Hearne had sent to his patron, Francis Cherry, a 'Vindication of Those who Take the Oaths of Allegiance'. It was not a personal letter but a long and thorough essay dealing with all the Whig arguments and approving them. Cherry wished to understand the young man's reasons for taking the Oath which in fact he had done three times: first when he was made Bachelor of Arts, then Master of Arts and finally when he was made Beadle

and I paid those to whom I took it all the Allegiance (that is just none) that was due to them. All this I readily acknowledge, but when the Abjuration Oath was imposed I utterly refused it. [13]

Hearne had repented his youthful heresy long before he had refused to take the Oath of Abjuration ^{f} in 1715 and had become one of the staunchest of non-jurors. On several occasions he asked Cherry to return the manuscript, which he looked on as his private property, but though his patron promised to do so it went on his death to his widow Elizabeth and there it had remained until her death in 1729. Early in 1730 Hearne was told that the daughter, Anne Cherry, had on the advice of a family friend, the Revd Samuel Parker, given it with the rest of her father's manuscripts to the Bodleian Library.

This was distressing news to Hearne, who feared that some unscrupulous person might find it there and use it to his disadvantage; but by trying very hard to recover it he drew attention to its existence and must therefore have whetted the curiosity of his enemies. Those who professed themselves his friends were too weak or double-faced to exert their influence. Robert Fysher, the Librarian, thought it should be returned to Hearne, but was ineffective. The ultimate decision lay with the Vice-Chancellor, Edward

^{f} The Act of Abjuration repudiating the Pretender required an oath of loyalty of all official persons after August 1702.

Butler, who had little reason to be sympathetic as Hearne had strongly disapproved of the appointment of a layman to the Presidency of Magdalen. Anne Cherry had never liked Hearne, but on hearing of his distress she felt enough regret at her action to let it be known she would like the paper to be returned. As for Samuel Parker, he blew hot and cold; he went to the Vice-Chancellor, ostensibly on Hearne's account, but his main concern was to get his mentally retarded son accepted as a clerk at Magdalen.[g] The influence of Francis Wise, who had succeeded Hearne at the Bodleian and whose hopes of the highest appointment there had been defeated by Fysher, was paramount. Hearne visited Butler twice to plead his cause but found it was as impossible to get his essay out of the Bodleian as it was to get himself in, though the Library could prove no right to the manuscript and it had not even been catalogued.

Hearne may have exaggerated the potential ill effects a mere mischievous pamphlet might have on his reputation or on the sale of his books, but his apprehension was to some extent justified. In spite of the ignominies he had suffered in the past, he had now at least succeeded in living in some kind of dignity, respected for his scholarship by a considerable number of people. Sensitive and vulnerable in private, he was controlled, decorous and authoritative in public. That he might now be made to look a great fool in the eyes of the academic world had also occurred to John Bilstone, the chaplain of All Souls, when he read the 'Letter of Vindication' in the Library. He decided to use it, not only to score off Hearne, but also to increase his income. He felt sure he could write a satirical pamphlet based on Hearne's 'Letter' which everyone in the University would buy. Accordingly he consulted two friends, Robert Shippen, the Principal of Brasenose and 'Jolly' George Ward of University College. Hearne knew they had been seen together in Ward's rooms in the summer of 1730, apparently concocting the publication of his letter. Then Bilstone published, anonymously, proposals for printing it by subscription, though it was not until 16 November 1731 that it appeared with his lengthy unsigned preface.

Hearne's real friends were incensed when they read it, but they were intrigued by a letter which appeared in the London *Grub Street Journal* in December. It was a satirical attack on Bilstone disguised as a defence of his publication. Dr Richard Rawlinson wrote in a letter to Hearne:[14] 'The Grubb Street is full of a piece said to be published concerning you by Bilstone, despised by your friends.' Hearne replied:

> I never saw the piece you speak of . . . but I met with the Grubstreet put under my door. Grubstreet does me justice and it vexes them. They, particularly B., are scouted as scoundrels by men, women and children . . .[15]

[g] Samuel Parker, Junr., 1704–67.

Another of his friends, the collector James West, wrote from London:

The low scandalous Memoirs of you, as they are called, meet among all understanding Persons here the contempt they deserve, and the Grub Street Journal hath been rightly thought the only proper way of chastising both the folly and impudence of the Publishers. [16]

When John had acquired Bilstone's pamphlet he had read it with increasing fury. Superficially it was ingratiating and facile; without going deeply into any of the points Hearne had made, Bilstone managed to convey the impression that he himself was extremely well informed. Not only did he criticize Hearne's inconsistency in this matter, but he accused him of errors in his later publications. The whole production was a mixture of satire and sympathy. Hearne was depicted as an unfortunate scholar for whom everyone should feel sorry, but each sentence had a sting.

There are notes in John's handwriting on almost every page of his copy. [17] The first of them reads:

This Performance, resolved upon August 3. 1730, was with all expedition finished and then published November 16. 1731.

From the first page until the end he carries on a one-sided conversation with the unsuspecting Bilstone. Many of his notes are corrections to the unscholarly conclusions in the preface, but others are replies to unscrupulous remarks. By the end he is addressing Bilstone as if he stood before him: 'this formidable criticism', 'this sad dilemma', 'these curious remarks' give way to such plain speaking as 'He will not, my sweet Mr Bilstone' (in reply to a suggestion that Hearne would thank him for setting him right), 'thou art too contemptible.' To the notion that Hearne had a little surliness of temper which it was thought he had brought into the world with him, John replies:

Happy those of a more humane and kind Temper, though there are more than two Persons who know what inconvenience it has sometimes brought upon the Possessor of it.

Bilstone had at one point claimed he was 'considering our Antiquary's Character by setting him right in his mistakes': John expresses his reaction in three words – 'Poor vain Animal'. It seems a pity that Bilstone never saw that particular copy of his work.

Something had to be done quickly before Hearne was made a laughing stock, for enough was already known of his odd habits. John was aware how deeply his friend was hurt, but realized it would never do to mention it to him. He decided to take his own course of action. The only person he consulted was his friend William Johnson of Queen's, though not one of those closest to him; but he admired Johnson's style of writing and wanted his comments on this first letter to the press. It is all in his diary:

November 16. Today was published Bilstone's Life of T. H. Read Bilstone's Life of H.

November 20. Wrote a Grub Street concerning H's Life. Johnson drank tea here congratulating about the Grub Street.

November 21. Wrote over a fair Copy of the Grub Street. .Went to Johnson's at 9, correcting and writing over the Grub Street for the Press.

December 11. Read the Grub Street on Bilstone.[18]

December 12. Put the Grub Street under Hearne's door.

No one except Johnson of Queen's ever knew that John was the author; even Benwell did not hear of it. This was an act of considerable self-discipline for in fact 'the Grub Street' was a clever piece; if Bilstone could write in the manner of Swift, so could John. He adopted the same technique of commiserating with his victim, but he was not savage and wrote with a gentle irony. It goes without saying that, being so conversant with Hearne's work, he knew all the answers to Bilstone's accusations. He decided not to discuss the unfortunate 'Vindication', which was open to criticism, but to concentrate instead on the chaplain's lack of learning and his real reasons for the attack. Bilstone himself was the subject of 'the Grub Street' and the tables were turned. John's long letter begins:

As your writings shew you to be the friend of mankind, they are an encouragement to apply to you in behalf of an injured Individual, whose case is this. Some uncharitable persons in this University have more than insinuated, that the object, Mr Bilstone of All Souls College did maliciously, slanderously and moved by an evil disposition, publish (a day or two since) *a few memorials of the life and some observations on the writings of T. Hearne of Edmund-Hall*. These, Sir, are hard sayings, and what the Author's ingenuity was before a stranger to. For he is not ashamed to own in the said performance, all evasion aside, that his motive arises from a much kinder principle; 'Auri sacra fames'[h] was the forcible inducement, and 'conscientia mille testes'[i] (his motto on the title page) that he says true. How strong must be the prejudice his enemies have conceived against him, when not satisfied with this frank declaration, – and for those in *Oxford*, when they so well know what the poor man has to live upon. It is but a small Chaplainship, a poor pittance for a growing family. But to wave this; there are several marks in the work itself, which plead strongly for its innocence of envy, hatred and malice, several marks which 'tis plain the Author was not aware he stamped. Before I instance, I would ask whether had those inhumane qualities moved him to write, he would not have guarded against the gross misrepresentation of his subject; certainly to lay

[h] 'The accursed hunger for gold.'
[i] 'A thousand witnesses share this knowledge.'

himself open to every boy's observation, to be so surprisingly unguarded, would defeat such a design, his blows rebounding with additional force upon himself. But as his only view was 'quocunque modo rem',[j] it mattered not whether truth guided his quill, if the subject of his work was so extraordinary as to engage the 'totus orbis litterarius'[k] to come in to his subscription. Now with your leave, I would lay before you some passages which will admit of no defence, but upon the footing I have been endeavouring to place 'em.

He then proceeded with authority and acumen to demolish most of Bilstone's arguments and continued:

From these instances, Sir, the world may be convinced what an object of pity this Gentleman is, whose cause I am defending. As I have vindicated him from malice, let me obviate another objection, that the vanity of shewing his parts was a prime inducement to his commencing Author. This is scarce worth the notice, since the above-quoted passage, full fraught with human frailties, make this accusation impossible to be credited; tho' indeed some expressions at page 35, 36, seem to go far in providing the allegation, as that he does not doubt but Hearne *will make a public retraction in his next work, and acknowledge him his friend*, forsooth. Now tho' this may have the face of conceit, as if his Memoirs could be worth the answering, yet his meaning is no more, than that if *the Antiquary* will deign 'em an answer, *that answer* will be worth *his* answering. And as Hearne is inflexible in barbarously despising these *Memoirs* and therefore will not answer 'em; I am to beg of you, Sir, to recommend to your readers the subscribing to *Bilstone's Answer to Bilstone*, with his picture prefixed, for he proposes to take up the cudgels against himself, as Daniel de Foe did before him. I am Sir, your most humble Servant, Phil-Bilstone.

If Hearne guessed who the author was he never said so, but he expressed his pleasure in his diary.

[These memoirs] are so low and scandalous that they meet among all understanding Persons with the contempt they deserve, particularly in London, where a paper called the Grubstreet Journal hath taken notice of them, and done Justice to the Writer of these Accounts, and it hath been rightly thought to be the only proper way of chastising both the folly and Impudence of the Publisher . . .[19]

He also confided to his diary that he knew not who had written the letter, but Providence, he was glad to observe, soon brought retribution to his enemies. Samuel Parker grew 'melancholy and hippish' and died even

---

[j] '(Do) the job in any way (you can).'
[k] 'The whole world of letters.'

before the publication was out; Bilstone's confederate 'Jolly' George Ward succumbed to a violent fever and the chaplain himself took to his bed for some time; and after all, Hearne reflected to himself, was that essay of 'Vindication' really the silly childish performance he had once called it? Although he had felt bound to despise it

> yet it was commonly said, that in it was great Reading, Skill and Judgment shewed, far beyond his years, and some declared that they defied any one in the University of so tender an age to compile such a Tract . . .[20]

In January 1732 Peter Zinzan went to live in his own rooms and soon after this John celebrated his twenty-first birthday, very quietly as he was ill with a cold in the head. He was very much occupied with his will, seeking both Hearne's and Zinzan's approval of it. He had made a draft for his mother four months earlier, but it was not until January 1733 that Crynes, Bagshaw and Edward Lambert witnessed the final document. He was also working hard for his Determinations. He had to take part in two Disputations during Lent, on grammar, rhetoric, ethics and politics or logic and there were other Declamations to be made. The charge for the first Determination, with his friend James Webb as his opponent, was 4s. 6d. Bonney was the 'Under Bachelor' and there were no 'Officers'. On the second occasion Crynes was opposing and the cost was 2s. In April he took 'Austins',[1] with Webb in opposition again, under the Revd Isaac Griffith of Magdalen. None of this was unduly arduous.

Deodatus Bye came to stay with him in February. He was always badly off and he told John that his salary as an usher at the Free School in Maidstone, combined with the stipend of his curacy, only brought him in £110 a year. He was taken to see Hearne who was interested in his efforts as an amateur archaeologist – Bye was always hunting round vaults or graves on the lookout for Roman relics, which he sometimes found. Scale drawings would then be sent to John on which Hearne was to be asked to pronounce an opinion.

The only other notes this winter were on the Corpus Christi College Library and the music room at Magdalen.

> With Johnson of Queen's to Corpus to Gibson's, a Gentleman-Commoner. Drank tea there. He shewed us the illuminated Books in their Library and some of their Medals. The emblazoned Books at C.C.C. are two large Folios in French, being an History of the Bible; they were given to the College by Mr Oglethorpe. The particular Distinguishment of them is, that their buildings are formed well and the Furniture of the Rooms with the different Greens of Trees in admirable colours, especially blew.

---

[1] 'The Disputation *apud Augustinenses*.'

In Mr Hecht's music room there was a very large painting of six ladies and gentlemen and three dogs, all 'as large as the life'. The name 'Lady Isabella Turnor' was inscribed round the collar of one of the dogs and 'in Essex' round another. John was surprised and pleased to see this picture again on a visit to Salisbury in 1738. It was then hanging in the rooms of Thomas Hecht's nephew, Edward Thompson, who was the organist at the Cathedral. Hecht died in 1734 and was succeeded at Magdalen by a better-known organist, William Hayes.

The spring vacation was marred by a tragic death. Charles Hopson's brother Kit, aged only twenty-one, died in his uncle's house at Bradfield of hard drinking. The funeral was at Beenham for the body had been brought home accompanied by the family and the rector of Bradfield. John, who was one of the pall-bearers, drove there in a mourning coach with Thomas Birt, the undertaker. Soon afterwards Charles, who was only a year older than his brother, came to stay at Caversham. In times of trouble he and John invariably found comfort in each other's company.

A memorial to Sir Constantine Phipps had at last been erected at White Waltham and John went there to copy the epitaph for Hearne. He thought it very paltry and by no means equal to the man. Moreover it was at some distance from the place of burial. He added a postscript to his letter[21] to say that he had heard that a statue of Apollo, lately found at Cirencester, was now at Oxford. Hearne replied that he thought Sir Constantine would have approved of the Latin words used as he was all for keeping to old law terms. His letter contained the usual kind of request – this time it was for prayers printed in the time of Henry VII but actually addressed to Henry VI as the people believed he wrought miracles. He wondered if Magdalen Library could provide such a book, but feared not as they were very scarce. As for Apollo,

> Here was a Statue from Cirencester shewed about for Money. And the Persons concerned (one of which I had seen more than once before) had a great number of coins said to be found there, and he offered them to Sale. But I am not ready to heed Stories of that kind unless well attested . . .[22]

Later he said he thought the statue was a modern thing. In 1769 John saw it in the possession of Bodley's Librarian, the Revd John Price, at Jesus College.

He rode back to Oxford on Easter Monday for his Austins and then took three days off work to see Faringdon and the surrounding country. First he visited Faringdon House, the home of Henry Pye, which had been rebuilt after the Civil War. It was to be destroyed by fire some thirty-four years later and the present house completed by Pye's grandson, the Poet Laureate, in 1785.

> Mr Pye's House is a very large old Building, the Dining-room very spacious and that as well as the other Rooms lightsome and pleasant,

it being a pretty Situation. Good family pictures here. There is a Park belonging to this Seat, descending from it every way. Faringdon Plush is famous.

A mile away he found the notable Coxwell Barn and spent some time measuring the walls and dimensions in great detail. The arched entrances, like porches to a church, were

> not large enough to admit Waggons, which makes the Tradition probable that originally this Building was not a Barn; a Stable 'tis said and that King John's. In the Roof there is much Wood-work (probably in Irish Oak) supported on 12 Stone Pillars; without are large Buttresses. There still remain three Stone Crosses over the West Entrance and South and North Ends; that over the East Entrance is now gone. To the North of this Barn stood a Chappel which was pulled down and the Parsonage-House built with the Materials. Near this Chappel was also much within the Memory of Man a Great Kitchin and a fine Dining-Room over it; the present Farm House is partly the old House patched up. From hence they tell you is a subterraneous Passage to the Church. To this Farm belongs about 7 score Pounds per annum.

He also visited Winchcombe Packer's house at Shellingford[m] – 'an old House pleasantly situate on a Rise above the Gardens, where is a fine Head of Water and a great number of Wild-Ducks on it'. Packer was descended from John Winchcombe, alias Smalwoode or Jack o'Newbury, whose memorial John had seen in Newbury church the previous summer when he had said that it

> not long since, lay flat on the Floor just by, but for the better Preservation of it, they have placed it where it is now . . . by a North-East Door inserted in the Wall . . . He built the Church from the Pulpit Westward, Tower and All.

The portrait he saw at Shellingford of a man of sixty-one must certainly have been a picture of the benefactor's son[n] as the dates conflict. He described it as painted in 1551 of a man dressed like the mayor of a town, full-faced and short-necked.

Among other paintings in the house was a small piece of St Matthew at the receipt of custom which he thought was copied from Van der Hagen's large picture belonging to Lady Rich. In the Hall was a portrait of the Duke of Buckingham,[o] 'his hair-curled – the Navy out at Sea', and also to be seen was an old English bible dated 1556 and printed at Rouen, interesting because it was divided into paragraphs rather than verses.

In the church at Lechlade he noticed

[m] Near Faringdon.
[n] John Winchcombe of Newbury (1489–1565).
[o] Admiral the 1st Duke of Buckingham (1592–1628).

two Stones over Baronets of the name of Bathurst; in a Cottage in Lechlade lives the present Sir Francis, who once had an Estate of about £40 per annum which is now gone, he having been a debauched man in his time; he now teaches a few Children their A.B.C. which is his only means of subsistence except from Gentlemens' Benevolence; he marryed the Sister of Peacock, Fellow of Magdalen College. He is of an elder Branch than Lord Bathurst; his Lordship took Sir Francis's eldest Son[p] and would have given him the same Education as his own Children, but he grew loose and my Lord has entirely discarded him.

William 'Dizzy' Peacock had no better reputation than his brother-in-law. Hearne called him a 'great sot' and a 'blockhead'[23] and he died in a pothouse near Hinksey in 1735. John himself said later that Bishop Sherlock refused to initiate him to the living of Appleton. Sir Francis's fate was to be packed off to Georgia in 1734, where his property was to depend on the number of servants he took with him − fifty acres to a servant. His sixteen-year-old son had one servant, but he had to 'carry' his daughters. As Lord Bathurst only gave him £100, life cannot have been much more agreeable than when he was teaching the alphabet. In the end he made such a fuss that the Georgia Board granted him 200 acres.[24]

Finally John revisited Fairford church. He had seen the clerk in Oxford the previous October and had made the following note:

> The Clark at Fairford called upon me and observed upon the Account of the Painted Glass in Fairford Church Windows, which is printed in Roper's More, that in the 7th Window is Peter, James and John and the three Tabernacles, not taken notice of in that Paper, as also that the 14th Window is broke, but yet has remains of more than there observed; and that in the 16th Window there are, he thinks, 2 Priests and a remarkably fine Crucifix not here set down. There are small Figures over these larger ones, and writing in the Windows, left out there also. He told me that Rencomb [Rendcomb], about eight or nine miles from Fairford, was the Village which had the Overplus of the Glass, too much for Fairford Windows; but he has been told 'tis not comparable to theirs. Doubtless they put up the Best.

Now he saw the windows again, noted the representation of the Trinity in brass inserted over the inscription to Edmund Tame and had further conversation with his friend the clerk.

> The Clark observed on April 14. 1732 that in the 5th Window is omitted Judas hanging by the Neck and 3 Persons digging his Grave.[q] 300£ to wire the Windows. A fine Wood-work Screen to Chancel.

---

[p] Later Sir Laurence Bathurst.
[q] Omission in William Roper's *Life of Sir Thomas More* (1626).

Among the Relievos a Dog's Head in a Porridge Pot, the Woman beating him with a Ladle.

Revd Mr Huntington told me that Fairford offered to new-glaze the Rencomb Windows, if they would let them have the Fragments of their Painted Glass, for the sake of the Colours, to mend their Windows, but they refused though they have no compleat Figure.[r]

[r] This information suggests that the vicar, Edward Shipman, and churchwardens had not been so thoughtless as has been supposed when they repaired the windows with plain glass after the storm damage of 1703. See Oscar Farmer, *Fairford Church and the Stained Glass Windows*, 1955. Frampton Huntingdon was vicar from 1711 to 1738.

To Ireland and Scotland
1732

The last Disputation took place on 26 April 1732 and cost John ten shillings. He now had barely three weeks in which to prepare for a four-month ramble to Ireland and Scotland.[1] His chosen companion was the dependable John Peareth who shared so many of his interests and would have a cure for every possible malady. The main object of the tour was to visit John's uncle and godfather, Captain John Lethieullier, who had settled at Brea, near Athy, in County Kildare. He had married his wife, Catherine Ricklesey, in 1712 and they had lived on her family property ever since the days when he had been a first captain (on half-pay) of the regiment commanded by the Duke of Ormonde. He was now a man of about fifty with an only son, William, who was a student at Trinity College, Dublin.

The plan was to ride through Wales to Bangor and then follow the coast to Anglesey; they would then take the packet boat to Dublin and spend most of June with the Lethieulliers, making their house a base for further explorations. On their return to Wales they could expect hospitality from Lord Bulkeley at Baron Hill, near Beaumaris, and later from Bishop Tanner at St Asaph. Then they would ride north as far as Dundee and return down the East coast through Newcastle and York.

It must have seemed a hazardous undertaking to John's less adventurous friends, but everyone admired his spirit and they rallied round to help in any way they could. While he himself was preparing his long strips of notes in his usual careful way, Zinzan chalked out the route and at the last minute Hearne thought of writing to his old friend Dr Richard Richardson, the Yorkshire antiquary and botanist, to inquire about possible dangers of exploring the Picts' Wall.[a] As the travellers were to leave two days after the dispatch of the letter, he promised to send on the reply.

> . . the occasion of my writing now is this [wrote Hearne on 13 May]. A friend of mine designs in a little time to go into Scotland; and desires to know whether in such a journey it may be safe travelling for two or three persons out of the high roads, if they have a mind to seek antiquities and to go into bye-roads; and particularly if they have a desire to trace the Picts Wall from one end to the other. He is a young gentleman that is inquisitive and curious; and being satisfied that most Antiquities lye hid in bye-places, he hath a desire of seeing what remains there are at the Picts Wall and in some other bye-places; but is willing first of all to be satisfied whether there may be danger in such sort of travelling out of the high roads. My friend put another query to me viz. Is it best to go by land or water from Edinburgh to St. Andrews and Aberdeen? My friend's name is *Loveday* and you will find mention of him in 'Hemingford,'[2] which I suppose you have received before this time . . .[3]

They set off on 15 May accompanied by Zinzan and Bagshaw who parted from them next day at the Rollright Stones. It may seem strange that they had not got further on their way, but typically John was determined to see everything *en route* so the first visit had been to Cornbury Park at Charlbury only a few miles from Oxford. They all knew their man, Peareth not least; it was only very occasionally that he dug in his toes.

On the journey to Holyhead they visited, during the first four days, Elmhurst, Beaudesert and Ingestre, the Staffordshire seat of Lord Chetwynd with 'the stateliest trees imaginable, hares in abundance about this woody Garden' and a room hung with Lady Chetwynd's 'curious Needle-work'. John was even more delighted by Powis Castle (now much altered) and described the gardens laid out thirty years earlier. As for the towns, Lichfield, Shrewsbury again and Bangor received full treatment. There was an assortment of human quirks to record – from the people of Machynlleth who would not bury north in the churchyard till their minister ordered his own grave to be dug there, to the justices of the peace at Tan y Bwlch who drank everything at the inn, leaving nothing but milk for the two Johns. It was further on at Bangor that they had good 'French claret', oysters at twopence a hundred and horn-fish known locally as 'sea needle'.

After leaving Shrewsbury the road became more difficult. 'A causey wide enough for one horse runs from Shrewsbury with some Interruption for about 8 miles' on the way to Welshpool and the road was bad and rocky. Next day they found the road to Machynlleth 'very tiresome, being continually up and down, very miry and stony'; they had to cross the rivers Vyrnwy and Dovey

---

[a] Hearne and his friends invariably called Hadrian's Wall the Picts' Wall.

repeatedly 'sometimes on bridges'. It was a relief to stop when in passing they heard a Welsh harp being played in one of the houses, many of which were built of hurdles and mud and thatched with fern. With difficulty the musician was prevailed upon to appear and play, 'being diffident at first of our paying him – or, as a Welshman expressed it, was afraid we were deceitful.' They had set out early in the morning and reached Machynlleth late at night. 'A long day's Journey,' said John and it is astonishing that they managed it in one day under such conditions.

On the next day they were joined on their ride by a Presteigne clergyman called Griffiths who went with them to Dolgellau. Refreshed with claret, John and Peareth set out with a guide at 7 p.m. to climb Cader Idris on foot, 'three long miles' from the town to the top. The final ascent was as perpendicular 'as was possible for a Man to crawl up' and they could just see the mountains to the north and the sea at Barmouth. John told Benwell that they had passed over the top of the mountain about four hours before sunrise.

> He fain would have walked about and waited for its rising, but his companion, Mr Peareth, being violently against it, he gave up a sight which of all others he said he longed to see. [b]

It was not unreasonable of Peareth to resist this suggestion; indeed they were back at Mrs Owen's lodgings by midnight, having hobbled over the stones through a slippery dew by the light of the moon.

Mr Griffiths left them next day at Tan y Bwlch, but his friend Richard Hughes, a cattle dealer, took his place and pleased them by giving them the side of a kid for breakfast and 'two Wooden Spoons made by the Hinds of Merionethshire to eat Curds and Whey with'. It was raining so hard as they approached Snowdon that no suggestion of climbing it was broached to Peareth. Hughes, meanwhile, regaled them with local gossip and with information about Henry Rowlands, the Anglesey historian, showing them a house he had built near Caernarvon. John stored it all up in his mind for Hearne.

They reached the port town of Holyhead (then called Caer Gybi) on 30 May and left Wales with only a few comments.

> Some of the ordinary Women in N. Wales wear Stockings without feet and no Shoes; so do several Boys. The Women all wear black Hats (Several such we saw in Shrewsbury); in the other parts of their Dress, much superior to the Sex in S. Wales . . . They say *big* for *great* . . . their Oath is – Name of God.

The weather was so calm that the packet boat took twenty-six hours to cross the Irish Sea and the crew amused themselves profitably by catching

[b] William Benwell's anecdotes.

fish. John was 'excessively ill' the whole time and did not enjoy his first voyage at all.

They did not stop at Dublin but took the good wide road to Kilcullen on which the only turnpike charged a mere halfpenny for a horse. They noticed the great number of people walking in the road and the bare feet of the children. In the country the older people had also discarded their shoes and stockings and carried them on their shoulders. As they passed the cottages or cabins by the way, they saw that every one had its own calf. The following day they reached the old plastered brick house at Brea where the family was waiting to greet them.

Five days were spent in meeting the neighbouring gentry, some of whom were related to Mrs Lethieullier. Pleasant as this was – and John always enjoyed himself on these occasions – there was no time to waste if they were to see Kilkenny, Waterford, Cork, Kinsale, Limerick and Cashel and all the intervening places and be back at Brea by 22 June. With several cathedrals as well as many churches to visit, John had every opportunity to indulge his interest in architecture, which was now more mature, and his notes were made at great length and with his usual attention to detail.

Two days before their return to Brea they called on Mr George Mathew of Thomastown whose grounds were renowned for their plantations. He was away for the day but received John's letter of introduction on his return and sent a servant after them to beg them to come back. There was no time to alter their plans but John resolved to try again if he visited Ireland. They had in any case been held up by bad weather the previous day and had had to stop the night at a place some two miles from Thomastown (near Tipperary). An incident had occurred here which impressed itself indelibly on John's mind; Benwell's account is even more graphic than the diaries of the tour. They had already been rather shocked to see a Catholic child buried in a Protestant part of the country with no more than an Irish howl. Now they were to hear the howl again in more macabre conditions.

As they were sitting together in the Evening, they were suddenly surprised with a violent howling and going to the window they saw a numerous body of the rabble attending a corpse, which they were carrying, enclosed in a rough box and covered with a sheet, and which they saw them convey into a kind of barn. Upon enquiring of the Landlady the meaning of this Sight, she replied that they were a party of people who were waking the dead; that it was the custom of the Country, when any one died, to invite all their friends and to have a merry-making all night over the deceased; that their cottages being too small, these people had begged the use of her Malt-house for the Evening, and were preparing to have a kind of feast there, with some tobacco and beer, which they had got from the house. Mr Loveday asked if he and his companion might be admitted. She answered that she believed the party would

behave very civil to them and accordingly conducted them to the place
and introduced them.

John described the scene where 'everything was preparing for the
Solemnity'. At one end of the room was a table spread with a white cloth; on it
were lighted candles and sprigs of rosemary, some stuck in the candles.
Benwell continues:

Immediately upon their entrance the whole company set up a most
violent howl. In the middle was the corpse covered with the sheet, in one
part candles, in another some beer and tobacco and on a stool near the
entrance stood a large wooden bowl with some halfpence in it. They took
out their purses and put some silver into the bowl, upon which the
assembly, surprised probably at the sight of so large a contribution, set up
another hideous yell. They then sat down and observed the manners of the
company; who continued to smoke and drink and to howl at intervals. Mr
L. would willingly have spent the night with them, but Mr P. whose
spirits were much fatigued and whose curiosity was never very great,
desiring to retire, he with great reluctance left them and withdrew to
bed. The next day he was informed that after depositing the body in
the church-yard, they had all retired in good order about six in the
morning.

The slight discrepancy about the money between Benwell's version and the
diary of the tour can only be attributed to the passage of time. John's
contribution was certainly only a penny. As for Peareth's alleged lack of
curiosity, Benwell must have confused him with Zinzan. He was only fifteen
when Peareth died in 1778 and never knew him well. It was not the first time
Peareth insisted on his sleep; few of John's friends could match his energy.

After four more days at Brea they had to leave the affectionate family and
their hospitable neighbours, but there was no doubt John would return. They
left on 29 June and that same day they visited Mrs Conolly's house,
Castletown, built only in 1725 and still without its great staircase. John was
amused that so many of the houses were called castles and had some other
pertinent comments on the Irish.

According to the grand way in Ireland they call it Castle-Martin, the
general affectation to call their houses Castles.
The Irish Gentry are an expensive People; they live in the most open
hospitable manner, continually feasting with one another. They are well-
bred, obliging, but proud enough. They always praise the Dishes at their
own Tables and expect that the Company should spare no words in their
commendation. The common-people are notoriously idle; but few of the
meaner Sort (and among these most Gentlemens' Servants) which are not
Romans, most implicitly obedient to their Priests . . .
In the Country-places you'll meet with persons who can talk Old

Irish . . . Even the Gentry, when they are speaking to you will call you
'*Honey*' . . . Even the Ladies make use of Expressions, bordering too
near upon Swearing . . . So great is the Pride of these common People that
if a woman be of the same name as some noble Family, she'll retain it in
marriage unless her Husband has as distinguished a name . . . All the
People in general are very suspicious (and often express it) that their
Countrey and their Good-Breeding are represented to disadvantage in
England.

John's first thought at Dublin was to approach Henry Rowlands's son at the
Auditors' office to find out where he could buy a copy of the *History of
Anglesey*. He also called on the Revd Mr King, the Under-Librarian of
Marsh's Library,' and Henry Ware, the grandson of Sir James Ware, the
seventeenth-century historian of Ireland: but the most satisfactory visit of all
was to William Perceval, Dean of Emly and minister of St Michael's, Dublin,
who also held the living of Bellfield in the county of Westmeath. He was an old
friend of Dr Merrick from their university days and had another link with
Berkshire in that his stepfather had been an Aldworth of Standlake, a family
John knew well. He was also a cousin of Lord Egmont who called him a fine
scholar and a noted preacher, who took great pains in his parish. He
immediately invited them to dine and there was little he could not tell them
about the people of Dublin.

They had four days in which to see the churches and Trinity College and then
they were at sea again on the *Grafton* – the same boat which had brought them
over. Once again they were becalmed but at least the crossing took only
nineteen hours. They had meant to leave earlier, but

> some Dispatches from the Castle kept us in Dublin so long, otherwise
> we had set sail on friday night; from that time we were kept in hopes of
> sailing every Tide, so we packed our Cloaths and all this while were unfit
> to see or be seen, for Things could not be got ready till the Sunday
> morning.

Richard, Viscount Bulkeley was a cousin of John's Oxford friends William
and Henry Courtenay of Powderham Castle in Devon. They had told him in
the spring that the two Johns would be passing through Beaumaris on their
way back from Ireland and he accordingly invited them to stay at Baron Hill.

' In 1733 John visited Archbishop Marsh's Library again and said 'the late Librarian has
been the most considerable benefactor to this Library.' Information kindly provided by Miss
M. McCarthy shows that this was Robert Dougatt who repaired it from 'a miserable
condition . . . out of his own pockett' (Letter from his uncle, Archbishop William King,
1727). The Revd James King (D.D. in 1743) was a cousin of Dougatt. He was an executor to
Swift who was fond of him. Henry Rowlands's account of the origin and formation of fossil
shells (1705), which John saw in 1733, has been missing from the Library for a long time. It
was anonymous; John said "Someone has wrote in the Title Page "Auct. Hen. Rowlands".'

Although he had made arrangements for them were he to be absent, both he and his wife, to whom he had been married for a year, were there to greet them.

> Lord Bulkeley is a gentleman of the best good temper, obliging and friendly, does not take State upon him, yet lives like a Nobleman.

The domestic chaplain was a young graduate of Jesus College called Lloyd and Lord Bulkeley's gentleman in attendance was, rather surprisingly, Richard, the second son of Samuel Parker who had been such a poor friend to Hearne. Richard had left his scholarship at Lincoln College as he would not take the oaths and Hearne had said disapprovingly that his father should have put him in trade and not let him have to pull off his gown. He died ten years later at the age of thirty.

For three days the travellers relaxed. From the house they could see the ships passing between Dublin and Chester; by day they could go three miles to Lord Bulkeley's 'little place by the sea-side', Penmon, eat a cold collation and watch the seaweed being burnt on the shore to make kelp.[d] There was of course the usual throng of visitors to join them in these pursuits or to drink with them in the afternoon on 'a romantic seat of turf under a rock and a large encroaching elder' from where they could watch the cataract on the opposite mountain. This was a place to come back to in the future.

To crown this peaceful interlude there was a letter from Hearne awaiting John at the post house at Beaumaris which enclosed a copy of Dr Richardson's reply. John had written from Holyhead a short note[4] to say they had been well entertained at Bangor by the Master of the Free School, that he had seen so many Binsey towers he thought they must represent the true British tower and that Hearne had never told him about Henry Rowlands's *Antiqua*.[5]

Dr Richardson had, as Hearne said, sent his best advice and directions. Hearne copied his spelling exactly.

> 'If he intends to spend some time in viewing the Picts Wall and the Country about it, he must go directly to New Castle, and take Yorke in his way, where the octangular Roman tower in Mint yard will be wel worth his seeing, and some other Roman Antiquitys stil remaining in and about that City. One Smith, a Baker in Grape lane has pickt up a great many medals in that place. Mr Francis Drake a Surgion there, who is now writing the History of Yorke, has some Curiouse Manuscripts by him. Though Dr Steukly and Mr Gordon have taken much pains and been very Curiouse in theire Inquirys about the Picts Wall and the Country adjacent and have made very considerable discoverys there, as wel as in Scotland, yet there is stil some left for a curiose

---

[d] Carbonate of soda was obtained from the calcined ashes of seaweed and used for making glass and soap.

Inquirer to spend some time there with much satisfaction. About ten years agoe I was at Chevot Hills in Northumberland, in quest after plants. Upon the very top of the largest of those hils I met with three large heaps of Stones, called the three Kairns. These must have been Funeral monuments, perhaps of the highest antiquity. The same observations I have made of these heaps of Stones upon the highest hils in other places, one upon the top of Boulsworth nigh Coln in Lancashire, called Lad Low, which by the name semes to be of later date than the former, and several others I have seen. Though I give no great Credit to the account of Chevet Chase, yet that the Country there about has been a place of great action, the remains of instruments of war daily dug up there sufficiently make out. I was shown heads of Spears, broaken Swords, heads of arrows of a larger size than usual, and a short sort of Dagers with Buckthorn handles which stil remained uncorrupted. Upon inquiry I find that upon improving the ground adjoyning, these remains are frequently found, and in great quantitys. I was never farther in Scotland than Glascowe, where the inhabitants are very civile, and I do not doubt your friend may travil through any part of Scotland with safety. My old friend Mr Ed. Lhwyd who obliged me with severall letters in his travels through Scotland, not only from the Highlands, but from other places, gives frequent accounts of the Civility of the Inhabitants, but being pretty much a stranger to the language, he could not have that satisfaction in his inquirys he desired. If your friend designes to trace the Picts Wall from New Castle to Carlile, he must hier a Guide, for a great part of that Country is very thinly inhabited as wel as in Scotland and places of good accomodation not very frequently met with.'

These are curious notes [wrote Hearne] and I believe will be of Service to you. I am sure I am much obliged to the Dr. for them, both upon your account as well as my own. I mentioned your Journey to another affectionate Friend, Mr Baker of Cambridge, who is pleased to write thus in his Letter of the 30th of last Month – 'If Mr Loveday designes to visit the Picts Wall, I think he may do it very safely. I have been there many years ago, and found it as safe travelling there as in any other part of England. I presume he takes a Servant with him . . .' I thank you for your notes. Tho' I have not got Rowland's *Monaantiqua,* yet I am not a stranger to the Character of the Book. I formerly just turned some leaves of it over, but it was so cursorily that I am not able from thence to form a Judgment of it. It is spoke well of by his Countrymen. And there's a laudable Account of it in Nicholson,[e] whose Accounts, however, in many particulars are not to be relyed upon. Dr Tanner, I think, went for Wales on the 5th. He will be glad to see you. Adieu my dear Friend.[6]

On 7 July Lord Bulkeley sent them to the mainland in his pinnace with a

---

[e] Bishop William Nicolson wrote extensively on the Northern counties.

guide to help them over the sands and rocks and past 'a dreadful precipice' to
Conway. There they were shown round by his friend Mr Coytmore and the
inn provided the first port they had tasted for a long time, a welcome change
from claret. Their ride next day to St Asaph was very pleasant, being chiefly on
the good public road between Holyhead and Chester.

Bishop Thomas Tanner, who was now to be their host, was one of the few
bishops Hearne could tolerate; indeed he owed a good deal to this profound
scholar who generously made available to him his researches into the legal
aspects of Roman antiquity. Tanner had also counted himself a friend of
Anthony Wood and shared Hearne's affectionate but sceptical regard for
Browne Willis. He was not in any way hidebound and was also closely
associated with the Whig Bishop Gibson through their antiquarian pursuits.

> We came when he was at Dinner and met with a very hearty reception;
> after Prayers at the Cathedral we drank Tea with his Lordship but refused
> his kind offer to lie at the Palace since he had not been so long there (we
> imagined) as to have proper convenience for it. On the Sunday we dined
> with him and drank Tea as before . . . It would be utterly inexcusable if the
> Bishop did not live in an hospitable manner, for the Countrey is
> continually sending him in Provisions of all kinds, as they do to the Bishop
> of Bangor.

Among the local clergy in attendance they particularly liked Josiah
Babington, the vicar general and schoolmaster, and a young man called
Paynter who was steward to the Davies family of Llanerch; John continued to
correspond with them both. Babington who was small and lively took them
walking and told them all the sorts of things about the diocese that John
loved to hear and store up. Paynter invited them to sup with him at Llanerch
and showed them the fine library collected by the late Robert Davies. The
gardens descended in 'plats' and had pretty waterworks in miniature which
John in a romantic mood compared to the notes of a nightingale. His
occasional poetic descriptions of the beauties of nature – as also at Brecon,
Cader Idris and Penmon – were rather unusual so early in the eighteenth
century.

'According to those Directions I shall steer my course,' he told Hearne when
thanking him for Dr Richardson's advice ''Tis no small pleasure to me that Mr
Baker confirms the safety of the Journey.'

There was much, too, to tell his friend about Ireland and especially about the
various people he had met. He described his visit to Henry Ware who had
£3,000 worth of books, though none of his grandfather's – Sir James Ware's
books were almost impossible to find in Dublin. Mr King had settled Marsh's
Library in the most excellent order and Dean Perceval was

> a very fine Gentleman, as lively and good Company as ever I met with; he
> has the greatest Respect imaginable for Mr Dodwell's memory . . . my

Uncle detained me longer in Ireland than I intended, so that I had not time to wait upon the Lord Primate, when Dean Percival offered to introduce me. Bishop Milles I saw at his Cathedral, but did not wait upon him . . . I purchased Rowland's Mona [Antiqua] in Dublin; to be sure it is a great Performance considering the Author had no learned education, nay (I'm told) was never out of Anglesey . . . We came time enough to St Asaph yesterday to dine with the Bishop who received us with the utmost civility; your Health was the very first that was drank. Probably will do so again today when we dine with him again. Tomorrow morning we proceed through Denbigh and Flintshires to Chester . . . Strange Doings I hear at M.C . . .[7]

(The 'strange doings' at Magdalen were in connection with the Burslem affair which was now flaring up and in which Zinzan was so deeply involved. No doubt John had heard from him or from Audley who had become rather friendly with Hearne.)

The pace to Wrexham was slower; there was a good deal to see on the way and the weather had deteriorated. As they approached the town John's horse went lame and, as had happened before on this tour, he had to lead it through a great storm. From Wrexham they visited Erddig. Though the house was altered by Philip Yorke in the 1770s, some of the furniture there now is that which John saw in 1732 when the house belonged to John Meller, a Master in Chancery.

They reached Chester on 15 July and stayed there for two days exploring the buildings; John did not approve of the Rows which he thought by no means an ornament to the town, but he was more appreciative of the Cathedral. Two days later they saw Knowsley Hall which the then Earl of Derby had partly rebuilt and which was still incomplete. John admired it though he thought the front was like a greenhouse. The gardens were not yet laid out but he was intrigued by a hot wall for vines where coal fires were lit every night.

After so long in the country it was a change to 'descend to Leverpool' where the 'River Mersey brings up Vessels of great burthen into the Town-Docks' and where the Freemen had the distinction of having also the Freedoms of Bristol. Waterford and Wexford; but after only a night at the Golden Fleece they went on to Manchester – 'perhaps the best inland Town in the North for trade in spite of its narrow streets'. They spent two nights there and John admired the Collegiate Church and the College for sixty Bluecoat schoolboys, but found the three-storey spire above the tower of St Anne's Church the most disagreeable piece of building he had ever seen.

They were always glad to be joined on their rides by other respectable travellers and one of these, an attorney called Highmore, offered them hospitality when they visited Carlisle. They were bound first for Lancaster, accompanied by the Recorder, Joseph Harrison, whom they also met by chance – 'a young Gentleman, very agreeable in his Person and Carriage and has the farther Character of an ingenious Lawyer'.*f* As the posts were more reliable than is commonly supposed, Hearne's letter was awaiting John at Lancaster just two weeks after his own was posted from St Asaph. Hearne reported that Burslem had been entered a Fellow at Magdalen; he thought that Rowlands, being a man of observation, had probably managed to work quite easily from translations and was possibly well versed in ancient British. His geography went a little amiss when he asked John to search for manuscripts in the Manchester Library. He was also determined that Hadrian's Wall should not be forgotten.

When you are tracing the Picts Wall (which must be a usefull Diversion) you will find many of the neighbouring Villas and Houses built, in some measure of the Stones taken from the Wall. I desire you to note whether any of the Stones are flint. . .

When Birmingham School was void many years ago (by the factious Townsmens' turning out the worthy Mr, afterwards Dr John Hickes, Fellow of your College) the Townsmen, thinking themselves not proper Judges of the Qualifications of a Schoolmaster, referred the choice of one to Dr Tillotson, Archbishop of Canterbury. This Prelate, having Liberty to chose out of the University and all the World besides, could not think of any Person to prefer to this Place but one Parkinson, who was expelled the University of Oxford for Fanatical Anti-Monarchical Principles. I should be glad to know how he behaved in the School and what became of him.*g*

The rest of his letter concerned sixteenth-century ladies, who having survived several husbands were buried in quite different places from any of their spouses.[8]

They decided to reach Kendal by way of Cartmel which entailed a difficult journey, crossing the Keer and Kent rivers. Their landlord, whose varied career had included the office of gentleman to Bishop Nicolson and an appointment as 'officer of Excise' before running the Mermaid inn at Lancaster, was very helpful. He saw them across the sands to Cartmel, a distance of over twelve miles. When they came to the wide estuary of the River Kent they were guided across on horseback by a patent officer of the Crown.

f There is evidence of a Harrison being Recorder of Lancaster in W. O. Roper's *Materials for the History of Lancaster* (1907). The Recorder for 1731–47 is listed as Allan Harrison. The burial of Allan Harrison, gent of Lancaster is recorded in the Clitheroe parish register (PR. 1859) on 15 April 1753. The dates would reasonably fit John's acquaintance who apparently changed his name or used both Joseph and Allan.

g James Parkinson remained as headmaster for thirty years. Hearne acknowledged he was a man of parts in his letter to John at Newcastle 'tho he made (as many have done before) a very ill use of them.' (L.F.P. 5 August 1732.)

It was not until they reached Whitehaven on 28 July that there was an opportunity to reply to Hearne. By then they had wandered round the Priory church at Cartmel, visited Kendal and climbed the mountain road over Shap. It reminded them of Wales and so did the toasted oaten bread covered with melted butter at the inn. Another obliging landlord had taken them from Penrith to see the Giant's Cave –

> just by is a place where Sir Christopher Musgrave[h] sometimes drinks a glass with his friends – a round open Room in the Rock, the Seats all round out of it, and a large stone lying in the middle for the Table.

John had seen the valuable collection of books at Manchester, he told Hearne, but had been unable to look at the manuscripts as the Library keeper was not at home.

> Tomorrow we hope to see Carlisle and on Tuesday shall set-out for Scotland; if we like the Countrey we shall go from Glasgow to Stirling, Perth and the two Northern Universities and so to Edinburgh. As I am obliged to be at home by the third week in September to sign a Lease, I much suspect whether I shall now have time to trace the Picts-Wall throughout. This too will depend very much on the weather, which hitherto has not been very favourable to us. I have not been at Birmingham this time, but sure Mr Audley can inform you about Parkinson . . . the Bishop of St. Asaph is wondrously beloved there.

It was apparently unknown at the time that Dr William Stanley, Dean of St Asaph until 1731 and formerly Master of Corpus Christi College, Cambridge, had written *Faith and Practice of a Church of England Man* and John continued his letter with information on this point which he had received from the 'very sensible Gentleman, Mr Babington, Vicar General of the Cathedral'

> The Doctor told Babington so himself, who farther informs me that it was wrote in Holland, when Stanley was Chaplain there to the Princess of Orange; moreover after Stanley's Death, Babington saw in his Study – a printed Copy of the Book with some of his own Writing in the Margin, as if he had designed a 2nd Edition. This Gentleman tells me . . . he kept as good an house as the Bishop.

He also described the Llanerch Library where Bishop Tanner would soon be looking through the catalogued manuscripts and concluded by asking Hearne to write to him at Newcastle upon Tyne.[9]

It was not until he wrote again from Whitby at the end of August that he explained why his hopes of tracing the famous wall had finally been defeated.

> As for the Picts Wall, besides want of time to see that also, moreover

[h] The grandson of the statesman of the same name was M.P. for Carlisle.

upon view of it and farther Consideration, I found it impracticable to think of tracing it on horseback, it runs so through Inclosures, far sometimes from public Roads. If God gives me Life 'tis my full Intention to walk it on foot in another Summer or two; *Now* I had not Things proper for a journey of that kind. Not a mile from Naworth Castle in Cumberland, I saw the Wall about 10 foot high (as we guessed), the Ashler was gone, the Stones not laid carefully One upon the other, but some of them pitched edgeways as they do Flints; except this one Patch, I saw no more standing, but then the Ridge runs most visibly on and has a wide Ditch (just by it) to the North of it. [10]

They spent three days at Carlisle where Mr Highmore was as good as his word, entertaining them and showing them round the ancient town. On 1 August they crossed the border into Scotland 'as the houses could easily have convinced us, being some of 'em mud cots covered with turf, laid-on the grass side lowermost'. Riding in and out of corn country and over moors, they came next day to Drumlanrig Castle, the Duke of Queensberry's great house some miles north of Dumfries where John for once made more notes about the grounds than the pictures. A little further on they mistook the Earl of Hopetoun's house at Leadhills[i] for a 'pretty tolerable house-of-Entertainment' but were soon better informed. They found that the village could provide no food:

> We encountered great hardships to day, for setting out early in the morning, without having eaten or drunk anything, as we thought to breakfast at Lead-hills, and that affording no Entertainment that we could digest, we were forced to travel-on with empty Stomachs to Douglass-Mill where it was after 12 before we arrived; the Landlord and his Wife were at Kirk, it being a solemn Fast, as the Sacrament was to be administered on the Sunday following, so the Wheaten-bread and Wine was locked up, and the good people did not come home 'till the evening, when we met great numbers on foot or horseback, returning from Kirk.

However when they did get something to eat it was good Scotch broth made from a shoulder and neck of mutton and no doubt Mrs Loveday was told how to make 'this truly Scotch dish' when they returned home.

John had nothing but praise for Glasgow; it was 'delightfully situate in a plain and fruitful country' and you could walk two abreast under the handsome piazzas, sheltered from rain or sun. If only the streets had been straight 'no place would exceed (as very few do even now) the beauty and grandeur of Glasgow'. Indeed so much did he admire the city that almost his only other criticism was the blocking up with pews of the cathedral choir, stopping all communication with the nave, an arrangement which he

---

[i] The 1st Earl inherited the house and valuable mines through the marriage of his grandfather, Sir James Hope of Hopetoun, to Anne Foulis.

attributed in unflattering terms to 'these Scots'. The greatest attraction was of course the University, but as it was vacation he did not see many students in their red or black gowns and had to learn about them from a young gentleman from Halifax who happened to be staying at the Red Lion. Some of the conditions with which they had to put up were revolting, but on the whole the city streets were clean. They attended services in the Meeting House, a private room where the Jacobite prayers were not so heavily disguised as to fool two members of the University of Oxford – 'It was, I suppose, to pray for the safe return of their Country-men who are outlawed by the present Government.' The minister, Mr Graham, accompanied them on an uncomfortable ride to Stirling. There were no special incidents until they took the road from Kinross to Perth, where they were really in difficulties: darkness was falling, they had lost their way and were riding through bogs. Feeling apprehensive, they stopped at a lonely cottage and knocked. A woman appeared at length who tried to direct them back to the road, but without success as they could not understand each other's speech. Eventually, consenting with many complaints to trudge along beside the riders,

> she let us know *en passant* that she never got out of her bed before for man or woman, and that she had left her Bairns there by themselves.

The poor woman had to stand in a ditch in order to get them and their 'cattle' over it and deserved rather more sympathy than she seems to have had from John.

If Perth, Scone Palace and the Earl of Kinnoull's seat, Dupplin, were pleasant or interesting places, Dundee turned out to be very different. It was so full of trade, said John, that it entirely neglected to keep itself clean; 'for needs must I say that many places in this Kingdom are nasty enough, but this exceedeth them all.' What the Highlands would have offered they never knew for this was the turning point and their horses' heads were facing south for St Andrews on 13 August. Here they were much happier, though a vein of criticism runs through the account indicating that the place was now a shadow of its former self. Still there was a great deal to see and James Angus, the Public Librarian and Clerk to the University, was an excellent guide and host.

It was here that they decided that the Scots were 'excelled by None' in the exact observance of the Sabbath, for when they invited Mr Angus to dine with them on the Sunday, their landlord told them that he would certainly not come as it would be noticed. 'Yet he took an opportunity to slip-in to us Unseen in the afternoon, when Kirk was over.' They had made friends quickly and continued to correspond.

Edinburgh was of course the Mecca of the Scottish tour and came up to most of their expectations. Although they had only two days there they managed to see the Castle, Holyrood Palace, the Chapel Royal and the

University, besides many other buildings. John's copious notes included an excellent description of the whole plan of the city. Hearne had given him an introduction to Thomas Ruddiman of the Advocates' Library who was kind and helpful; they also met old Robert Henderson who was Librarian to the University. He showed them his rare books, but talked so much at breakfast that they thought he was crazy.

They left Edinburgh on 18 August for Haddington, spending a long time at Newbottle, the Marquess of Lothian's fine house and at the Palace of Dalkeith; but on reaching their destination a shock awaited them.

> I spent no time with so little pleasure as whilst I was at Haddington, and upon the Road from thence to Belton-Ford, for my Boy with the Portmanteau stayed behind in Edinburgh upon some occasion, and was to meet us again at Haddington; there we expected him in vain, apprehensive that the Servants at the Red Lion had directed him purposely in a wrong Road. However we were informed that Belton-Ford lay in the immediate road from Edinburgh to Berwick, which Haddington did not, and therefore he might keep in the great road and so miss Haddington. In short at Belton-Ford we found him with as much satisfaction as he had before found the house, for a Scotch ugly-looking fellow had met with him by the way and had asked some questions; better answered within sight of an house than in a bye-place . . . We must do Belton-Ford – a single house – the justice to say that we had here much the cleanest accommodation of any place in Scotland except at Perth, but that was an English-house.

This was the only time throughout his tours that John referred to anyone even remotely resembling a highwayman. It was also the first time he mentioned this boy and it is not clear whether he was his own or a hired servant.

Their experience at the Red Lion at Edinburgh, though less worrying, was annoying enough, for they had been charged a shilling apiece for their beds which they thought outrageous. On being told it was the custom, they had in John's words introduced another – not to give the servants one halfpenny for themselves. On 19 August they reached Berwick and so ended John's only visit to Scotland which, like Dr Johnson, he left with mixed feelings. As he said to Hearne in his letter written ten days later from Whitby:

> I found that Countrey as Dr Richardson represented it; the Inhabitants civil, Travelling safe; no fault to be found but their consummate Nastiness. [11]

Apart from their unclean habits he had liked the Scots in many ways. On the whole they were people of good taste, their clothes were good and so was their butter, but their cheese was eaten too soon and their meat was burnt to a cinder.

As for religion, apart from a few Episcopalians, he termed most of the people lukewarm Christians, torn between the Kirk and the non-jurors.

All in general with the utmost freedom damn the *Union*; as unanimous, in saying no good of King William; all remember the *Darien* affair and the Massacre at Glencoe.

On the whole, however, the Scots were a good-natured, lively, active sort of people who always gave you clean sheets even if they never washed the rooms and took snuff at a 'most immoderate rate'.[11]

The only adventure on the road to Newcastle was to be nearly caught by the tide at Lindisfarne. They had ridden south through Berwick and Bamburgh to Warkworth where they looked at the Castle and Hermitage. They had another day's ride to Newcastle itself where John Peareth really came into his own. His family had lived there for generations and his father still owned a house in the town. They were people of some account, his great-grandfather having been Sir John Marley, a Royalist in the time of the Civil War, who had been made mayor in 1644. Peareth's cousin, William Peareth, had married Ann, youngest daughter of Mrs Susanna Jennens of Weston Hall in Northamptonshire and both these ladies were there with him to greet the travellers. Besides being shown the town they were treated with the utmost hospitality by the Peareths' friends and relations - Dickenses, Russells, and Ords; they also met Walter Blackett[j] and saw his interesting house, Wallington. They were taken to see the Blackburn Colliery and went on a family expedition to North Shields in the mayor's boat, though they could scarcely see the 'Sheales' for smoke from the salt-pans. All this was quite a new experience for John Loveday, but he was just as interested and full of inquiries as he was on more familiar matters.

Hearne's letter was waiting for him at the post house. He was a little put out at John's failure to conduct his tour exactly as *he* would have liked, for besides missing the manuscripts at Manchester John, had signally failed to look over those at Llanerch in enough detail. He had a lot to say about Robert Davies, who had collected them, as well as other antiquaries and historians, some with praise, others with mild disparagement. He was also anxious for John to find a Caxton, particularly the Chronicle printed by Caxton himself and not by Wynkyn de Worde.

It is a Book that was very much used formerly by Buchanan and other Scottish Historical Writers, though they took occasion often to confute it. You may also enquire after other Books printed by Caxton, particularly Chaucer. I mention Caxton's Chaucer because a perfect one

---

[j] Walter Calverley took the name of Blackett and married his cousin, Elizabeth Ord, thus inheriting Wallington on Sir William Blackett's death in 1728. He inherited the Calverley baronetcy on the death of his father, Sir Walter Calverley, in 1749.

is extremely scarce and 'tis very difficult to tell all the pieces of Chaucer that were really printed by Caxton. Mr Bagford[k] had an imperfect Chaucer printed by Caxton given him some time before he died, but notwithstanding so imperfect that it did not appear how much it originally contained, yet he was (for he was a modest man) very thankfull for it.

He was surprised to be told Dr Stanley was a generous man as he was sure he had often heard he was very covetous. He concluded:

> I fear you will not now have an opportunity of seeing the Isle of Man, the present Bishop of which place, when at Oxford in 1707 was very curious in seeing our MSS. and other Rarities and he then told me there had lately been found several Urns in that Isle under Barrows, full of Bones and that no Coins were found near them. Without doubt they were Danish, the Danes using to burn their Bodies . . [Axes and Runic inscriptions had also been discovered.][12]

Durham was one Romanesque cathedral which John could not fail to appreciate, though with certain reservations. The pillars of the nave, in spite of being of the very largest size, were so well proportioned that they did not seem at all clumsy. The choir, which was being paved with black and white marble, was very handsome and apart from anything else 'no Church can be kept cleaner and more decent than this'. He made extensive notes as indeed he had done in every cathedral he had visited. In his letter from Whitby he told Hearne about the alterations he had seen.

> You'll not be pleased with what the Dean[l] and Chapter are doing at Durham Cathedral; the Choir is new-paving and the old Tomb-Stones are removed; the same was done in the other parts of the Church about three years since, when it was new-flagged.[13]

They saw so many places in the next three days that it is hard to believe it was only 30 August when they rode into Whitby, having come through the little village of Staithes where the waves continually breaking on the rocks with noise and violence 'always affords one of your pleasing dreadful Scenes'. John posted off his letter to Hearne asking him to reply as usual, this time to the post office at Nottingham. After seeing the church they pressed on to Scarborough through rather desolate country, the road rising and falling 'with small, easy unevenesses . . . continually in view of the German Ocean'.

Two days later they were at Castle Howard[m] where John made some of his most detailed notes on a house. 'It altogether pleases me more than any I have

---

[k] John Bagford was notorious for mutilating books for his collection, but evidently was not responsible for the Caxton's imperfections.
[l] Dean Henry Bland.
[m] Built chiefly for the 3rd Earl of Carlisle.

yet seen,' he wrote. He understood Vanbrugh's magnificent Baroque palace which reminded him of Blenheim.

In spite of the most explicit instructions sent to him from Berwick, Peter Zinzan did not succeed in finding his friends until the day after their arrival in York; his failure was logged in the diary of the tour, but it made no difference to their eventual reunion. They had a great deal to tell him and wanted to hear all the news about Burslem and the Fellowship. They spent three days at York, charmed with everything they saw except the Cathedral library, a dirty old room with few books. The Minster itself surpassed all expectations. They then rode from York to Selby in one day and to Hull in another, stopping to see Beverley's beautiful Minster on the way. On 8 September they reached Lincoln, where they stayed for three days. William Hasledine, a young Magdalen demy and a particular crony of Thomas Bagshaw, lived there and he showed them the town and entertained them at his home. They saw two other familiar faces, Coningsby and Humphrey Sibthorp. Humphrey later became the Professor of Botany at Oxford.

'The Prospect of Nottingham is really grand' as seen from the bridge and this in spite of the fact that rain and high wind had entirely spoilt their ride that day. There was not much to see and the Castle only boasted a single picture; but Hearne's letter had arrived. It was chiefly taken up with an attack on the defunct Bishop Nicolson who had forsaken his good honest principles and 'courted the favour of great men at Lambeth'. In Hearne's opinion this had had a very adverse effect on his scholarship. He also spoke of the loss he had suffered by the death of his friend, the Hon Benedict Calvert, an accomplished young man who had died of consumption in June and had been buried at sea. It was a real grief to Hearne who was as sincere in his friendships as he was stubborn in his dislikes. [14]

Having visited Lord Middleton's house, Wollaton Hall, and the town of Derby where the art of twisting silk was so secret that they were unable to see the silk mills, they came to Leicester on 14 September. After crossing the Trent, Zinzan and John had left Peareth to his own devices and, loyal Magdalen men that they were, had paid a call on their President, Edward Butler, at his country seat, Burley Hall. It was an old house, covered by stucco and sashed, so that it looked respectably new. Dr Butler, who was already entertaining his nephew and general steward, Dr Richard Good, and the librarian Dr Paige, hospitably included two more for dinner.

After an interesting day at Leicester they soon found themselves in country they knew. From Northampton they rode out to Althorp, but the Earl of Sunderland" was entertaining company so they could do no more than notice the handsome new offices of squared stone which he was building. They could

---

" Charles Spencer, 5th Earl of Sunderland, became the 3rd Duke of Marlborough on the death of his aunt Henrietta, Duchess of Marlborough, in 1733. By agreement he surrendered Althorp to his younger brother John.

not resist a return visit to Easton Neston and John used the notes he had made the previous year as a basis for many additions.

They returned to Oxford on 18 September. John went straight to Hearne and spent the evening with him at Shepherd's. Next day he was back at Caversham recounting his adventures to the ladies, who included his cousin Sally Tooke as well as Patty and his mother. During October he received a letter from John Audley who was in Birmingham – or 'Bromichan' as he called it.

> Your last brought me the agreeable news of your safe arrival at Caversham. My hearty wishes attended my Friend throughout his long journey, tho' I was so unfortunate as not to be able to travel any part of it with him. You give me no account of Scotland, not a word of the usage you meet with there. Pray be a little particular in your next. I am concerned to hear you were resolved to go among this puritanical folk, not knowing but they might make you or your Companion undergo the discipline of the puritanical stool. If Johnny hath brought any Snuff with him from among the Scots, I desire he will send what he designs for me by the Carrier, perhaps it may be sent more conveniently by Jo. Steel. Mr Steel will enjoy his Living (I hope) very peaceably; it is reported that the Patron [Sir William Compton] will give him no disturbance. I doubt not but you have heard of a famous book lately published (it being advertised in almost every newspaper) called divine inspiration. I can, perhaps give you a more exact account of these Prophets (for that's the name they go by) than you otherwise can have. Hannah Wharton, by whose mouth these manifestations are said to be communicated to mankind, is wife to a patten-ring° maker in this town and hath for many years rode about the Country prophesying with a married man. She hath drawn a few disciples after her. The impudence and effrontery of these deluded people is very prodigious; for they have not only printed two volumes of their manifestations (as they call them, tho' by the way nobody can understand one sentence of them) but have also sent the title of the book and a letter (a copy whereof I have sent you) to every Bishop in England and every Clergyman in London and Westminster and to all the neighbouring Clergy here. It is a gainful trade to the good woman and therefore she will be unwilling to leave it. She is one of those prophets that prophesy deceit. About twenty years agoe we were disturbed at this town with this very woman and the rest of the present cabal. They would then have done a great deal of mischief had they not been dispersed by the care and vigilance of the then worthy Rector and Constable. You may see a full account of what they did in Dr Hickes's history of Montanism. . .ᵖ

° Clog or overshoe mounted on an iron ring.
ᵖ *The History of Montanism* 'published by a lay-Gentleman' was published with Dr

On an inner sheet was copied the letter to the bishops and clergy signed by twelve 'prophets', including five members of the Wharton family.

John Hocker was married to 'the Widow Hiley' in October. She was probably a relation of the headmaster and it was at his house too that John met the Misses Fane, one of whom was 'the Queen's Laundress'. But it was soon time to return to Oxford and on 10 October he rose early and was on the road by five o'clock. He went straight to the President with a letter from Mr Hiley and there he stayed, for the congenial company included a most interesting man – John Baskett, the King's Printer. From 1709 until 1779 the Baskett family held the patent to print Bibles and John's recent visits to several important libraries must have been of great interest to John Baskett, who had himself produced the Vinegar Bible in two volumes in 1716–17, but had unfortunately gone bankrupt in 1731.

Now that he was twenty-one, John's financial affairs had kept the Staples, father and son, busy for some time with all the legal transactions attending his coming-of-age. Indeed the amount of business it caused seems excessive for a young man of moderate possessions, but preoccupation with land was an important part of country and family life. Paul Mansfield, the old retainer, came up to Oxford three times with the Christ Church lease and bonds to be signed and he was then petitioner on John's behalf in a common recovery of property. It was a relief during a few days at home in November to ride over to Fawley Court near Henley. This house, built by William Freeman fifty years earlier, was eventually to be restored by his great-nephew, Sambrook Freeman. John saw it in the interim period and all was elegance.

> November 2, 1732. Mr Freeman[q] of Fawley Court had that Estate left him by his Uncle Freeman for which he changed his name by Act of Parliament – before it was Cooke. The compact House has a great deal of Room; 'tis built of Brick, the Windows and Doors faced with Stone. The Rooms are large and well-proportioned; some wainscotted with Oak, others with Wood painted like Marble, others hung with good and lively Tapestry, the Furniture answerable. In one of the Rooms are the Usurers – a Copy from Windsor Castle with other Copies from thence. In the Hall are three antique Statues, one of a man – very large, its Drapery most exquisite and bold, but it has a modern head and hand . . . The Gardens are beautiful and have pretty Canals; at the end of a close Walk between the trees is a Ruin of Flints erected about an year since, with a very good effect; it represents the Eastern or Western Windows of a Chappel, on each side are two really antique and

George Hickes's *Sermon on the Spirit of Enthusiasm Exorcised*, 4th edition, and the *Discourse Occasioned by the New Prophets' Pretensions to Inspirations*. None of the signatories to the Whartons' letter to the clergy are mentioned in these earlier accounts of Birmingham 'prophets'.

[q] John Cooke took the name of Freeman on inheriting Fawley Court from an uncle, William Freeman, who built it in 1684.

mutilated figures, the Drapery of one very good, the other more defaced
has its head lying down at the foot; behind this is an arched Room, the
outside of it has in Niches some Busts of Antiquity and some of the
Ornaments are the Bowls of Tobacco Pipes, ranged in Rows. Beyond this
and the Garden flows the Thames, a remarkably long reach and of noble
Breadth. The view of Henley, about three-quarters of a mile off, adds
much to the beauty of the Place. A large Kitchen-Garden. Several Ever-
Greens of different shades grow close together as one Tree in the chief
Garden. A Countrey well-wooded rises about here. There is a great
variety of Marble here, none English that I could find, the Slabs in the
Windows of Marble as well as the Chimney-pieces.

This was an early example of a flint grotto and John Cook Freeman was
evidently a pioneer of garden fashion. John learnt more about him the
following year from Michael Blount of Mapledurham who told him that the
owner of Fawley Court, who had married Sir Jeremy Sambrook's aunt, had
sunk the ground about his house towards the water side (it having previously
been on a level with the water). He also said that Freeman had a painting of the
Duchess of Richmond whose waxwork figure was in Westminster Abbey. In
1734 John went there again, and mentioned the 'wretched glass' in the
windows. In February 1738 he made his final notes about this house:

Nothing can be neater than the back-stairs; the great staircase takes a
large Sweep, but the bare Walls of it stand in need of Paint. The very many
fruit-trees in the kitchen-garden are a wondrous sight; they are so
curiously cut and spread; Mr Freeman of Gloucester's[r] trees are (for
number) a very miniature of these. The Manor House called Fawley
Court was built in 1684.

The winter of 1732 was drawing in when John paid Zinzan's fees of £21 for
the last eighteen months. More than once he visited Bishop Tanner who had
returned to Oxford. In November he had an affectionate letter from Deodatus
Bye:

Yours, the one from Dublin and the other from Causham, I received;
and should you wonder that you heard not from me long before, impute it
to any thing but the Forgetfulness for or Disrespect to my best Friend. I
had the unexpected pleasure of seeing Mr Hopson the other day at
Maidstone and had Mr Loveday been with him, my pleasure had been my
Happiness. Believe me, Sir; for there is no one whom I entertain a greater
value for, than the person that deserves it, or whose Friendship I more
greatly esteem, than that which is so long standing as ours, and will be (I
am persuaded) as lasting as our Life . . . Considering my Cure, the

---

[r] Anthony Freeman. See pp. 218–19. A relationship between the two Freemans is a
possibility but not, to my knowledge, proven.

School, my former poverty, my present want of Books, with other difficulties and cares that surround me, expect not Letter for Letter, nor Learning for Learning; this I rejoyce in, that with the same chearfulness wherewith I formerly would have instructed you, I am now instructed by you. Write soon and often.[15]

Uncle William Lethieullier suddenly appeared in Oxford on 20 December and put up at the Angel. For once John had to excuse himself to Hearne who called to see him at the same time. He might have asked him to spend the evening with Uncle William but he spared himself possible embarrassment, though which of the two might have caused it is open to conjecture. In any case his uncle was only there for one night as he had come to Oxford merely to see how his nephew was faring.

There was little left for the diary now but a few random thoughts concerning expenses. A hat had cost 12s. 6d, a pair of shoes 4s. 6d. and he had spent 2s. 7d. on a cauldron of coal. A charge for transcriptions from the Cotton Library was quite expensive at 1s. 6d. a sheet. He noted that Audley's Birmingham curacy was worth £30 per annum and he must have reflected on his own comfortable income as well as the pleasant memories of a year in which he had seen nine cathedrals and over thirty country houses.

Return to Ireland
1733

John's circle of friends at Oxford had not greatly changed in the last four years. A few of its members had left and some of the original companions had proved incompatible after a while; but most of the close friends were as agreeable as ever, though Derham was becoming a little pompous. John confided as much to Mun Lambert, who replied from the Isle of Man on 31 January 1733.

> I acknowledge two or three very entertaining Letters from you; 'tis with pleasure I have your repeated good opinon of my Brother which was always agreeable to my own. Our Governor, Mr Horton of Chederton in Lancashire, was formerly Gentleman Commoner of Brazen Nose, I have received many favours from him. Yours came to hand just as we came in from hunting, he obliges me with a Horse whenever I have a mind to divert myself that way; after dining with him I communicated the most material part of your Letter which was news to him, his own, which came by the same Ship not having some articles yours contained; for this reason I took the Liberty of sending it this morning to a worthy Friend of mine in Douglass; in return I had Dr Conybear's book[a] and a Cask of fine olives, this last I suppose, hastened to me for the entertainment yours gave him, pray divert us in this manner as often as you have matter sufficient. 'Tis with pleasure I

[a] John Conybeare's *Defence of Revealed Religion against the Exceptions* came out in 1732 and was well received. He had become Dean of Christ Church in this January, 1733.

survey the good fortune and preferment of my Friends; tho' Mr Derham is grown grave, I am sure not proud, he will accept of my Service. You have given me much inducement to see Oxford once more, if I can continue in the same resolution as now, I may be in England in the Spring and if possible embrace your offer. I dare to say my Brother will be as well pleased with the opportunity as myself.

You must expect no news from this part of the World, but of Storms and Tempests; we have now a large wreck lying in the Bay. 'Twas dismal to see 8 bodies drove a shore, and only two alive. Have you ventured yet on that Element? My Brother has given me no reason why you went by me, if you have been in Ireland. The right of Succession is dubious; the Governor tells me he thinks Lord Derby has consulted Lawyers upon that head and that the best of the Profession give it in favour of him; if so Sir Edward Stanley[b] stands fairest for it, he being much in my Lord's good graces, 'tho most are of opinion it will be publickly disputed. He is now calling in the copper coin of the Island in order to give us new, which is to be coined in the Castle here; they'ill not deserve a place in your Collection, yet, out of curiosity I may keep one or two. The Governor having hinted to the twenty four Keys that it would not be unacceptable to his Lordship to be addressed to have his face placed on one side the coin, it was voted[c] but carried in the negative; the reason you will say is somewhat merry, for fear of being all hanged. But perhaps they think an act like this would make the World believe they were under great Obligations to his Lordship and took this way of shewing their gratitude, when I believe in their hearts they are far from acknowledging any. The Twenty four Keys have met often for this year past in order to revise and correct the Laws of which they say there is great occasion, but are so divided amongst themselves that they cannot agree upon one particular, but like men walking in Sand lose almost as much ground as they get; they are almost the subject of ridicule. I am glad to hear the Dissenters have met with so much contempt from above; those in Ireland have looked upon the point as good as gained and are not yet without strong hopes of it . . . Our Bishop is well, he wears more the Garb than the Face of old age; he has a cheerfulness and freedom peculiar to himself and agreeable to his Friends, yet becoming his gravity. What is the opinion of Father Girard?[d] Which way is the World inclined to believe? By the tryal it appears to me he was guilty and La Cadiere, if executed, unjustly. I thought Sir William [Bowyer] had left you. Pray my humble respects to him.[1]

[b] On the 10th Earl's death in 1736 the Earldom reverted to a cousin, Sir Edward Stanley, who became 11th Earl of Derby, but the Isle of Man devolved upon James Murray, 2nd Duke of Atholl.

[c] Meaning 'put to the vote'. Note by John Loveday.

[d] Father Girard was acquitted of criminal seduction in October 1731. Marie Catherine Cadière's story was published in memoirs of them both (London, 1731). Her ease, presented to the parliament at Aix, was published in 1732.

Edmund came to Oxford, staying with John, during the following May, and his brother Ned spent all the time he could with them. It must have been Mun who gave John his manuscript account of the trial and imprisonment of the much-loved Bishop Thomas Wilson in 1722. Although the vicious Governor of those days, Alexander Horne, had gone, the Bishop had still been involved in controversies with his successor, Thomas Horton. Horton acting on claims made by the Earl of Derby, had refused to recognize the ecclesiastical laws as approved by the House of Keys and the Bishop. By now he had suspended the whole code and nothing was revised until he was replaced by a more constructive Governor in 1736. Lambert, being a friend of Horton's, saw things his way up to a point, but the brave and stubborn Bishop was regarded as a hero by John and his friends. As Edmund talked, John – listening with the greatest interest – jotted down brief notes on the conversation.

> Mun Lambert said that there was good agreement between the Bishop and the late Governor of Man, [Horne] till the Governor's Wife, an inquisitive Woman, scandalised two Persons, upon which the Bishop sent a Soldier to commit her to the Castle; the Governor sends a Soldier and actually commits the Bishop there; the King and Council set him free ... .

(In fact Mrs Horne had been told to beg forgiveness of those she falsely accused and the Bishop had been imprisoned under dreadful conditions.)

Edmund continued to pour out information about life on the island: the Governor did not live in his house by the Cathedral – it was only partly roofed; the late Earl had often lived in the Castle; the Manx people were very flattering when you met them, but hollow and deceitful – one Englishman could do as much work as four of them; the only taxes were those to the Earl of Derby who had an income of not less than £1,500 per annum as compared with the bishopric worth £400 and the Governor's post at £200. There was one 'Mass-house and no other Meeting houses; penance in a white sheet was common. The Bishop was a very credulous man, said Lambert, thinking perhaps of the 'Mare-man'. Clap bread was eaten and brandy was drunk at twenty pence a gallon.

Another friend who was never forgotten was Bonney and in the January of 1733 John went to the President to ask if Bonney might be allowed to return to Reading School as assistant to Mr Hiley; Richard Wooddeson was leaving to take over the Grammar School at Kingston-upon-Thames. Evidently Bonney thought a petition on his behalf from John would be more effective with Dr Butler.

In February the College was startled once again by Burslem. Shortly after his hard-won contest with Zinzan he had suddenly expired at Montpellier, where he had gone for his health. Hearne, who could never resist a dig at the President, chiefly because he had taken office without being ordained, lamented the loss of an 'excellent scholar and a man of a working politick head'. Burslem could hardly have proved popular with Dr Butler, being the cause of his censure, but though Fate had removed him it was some time before Zinzan could be reinstalled.

In spite of Derham's increasing gravity, he still enjoyed expeditions with John and late in March they met at Windsor to look at the pictures together. Derham's father, the 'Physico-Theologist', as he was called, was a canon of Windsor and had compiled a catalogue of all the paintings in the Castle. After their visit William lent this list to John who lent a copy to Hearne and it was eventually published in the *Collections*.[2]

The statesman and politician, Dr George Clarke, who was Burgess for the University, had built a house for the Warden of All Souls on the condition he himself should occupy it until his death (which occurred in 1736). John described the paintings in 1733 and in December 1736 he added to his original account a note on the bequests in Clarke's will.

Saw Dr Clarke's house which he built. In the first Room is an original (and the only one that was ever sat for) of Dr Radcliffe by Kneller (bequeathed to his Library when built.) A picture of Dean Aldrich, the only marks of Age in his Grey-hair, for the face is smooth and the Eyes remarkably lively and sparkling; of Dr Blechynden, the present Provost of Worcester College . . . [and so on].

In another room

the inimitable Charles I in black Velvet sitting in a red velvet elbow-chair, his Beard grown over his face in which there sits Grief and Majesty, nobly proportioned; the face longer than the wretched Prints from it and much more sallow than that that at Causham; but this was drawn when in greater extremity; witness the Beard; 'tis a wretched copy at Lord Bulkeley's from hence (bequeathed to the Warden and College of All Souls as being one of the pictures over the Doors and Chimneys in the three Rooms below Stairs . . .) In the Study a half length of Prince George of Denmark robed and Dr Clarke, his Secretary, sitting. I don't admire it, especially the Prince, very sallow. An odd piece of the Doctor's father and mother and himself, an infant. On the top of the Stair-case a picture of Fuller, the Painter of Magdalen Altar-piece and at All Souls; drawn by himself, a very remarkably ugly man . . .

And there was always Hearne: Hearne with Browne Willis, who was in trouble with the Earl of Oxford for 'reflecting' on one of the Harleys;[3] Hearne with George Vertue the engraver, and a great supper party at Shepherd's attended by John and Audley; Hearne still producing endless books so that

John, when collecting his copy of *Thomas Otterbourne*[4] on his way
down to Caversham, reminded himself that 'Mr Hearne's books including
and concluding with Otterbourne have cost me £38–12–6'.

There was some excitement at home, for Patty, now sixteen, had been
elected Patroness of the French Club, still the chief rendezvous of the
younger set in Reading; but John was only there for a short stay and on 19
April he was back at Oxford. A cryptic entry in his diary for this month
reads 'Gave M. W. a silver Chamber-Pot which cost me £7.14.6.' This was
probably a rather handsome present to his servant Michael Welman, who
had accompanied him to Stonehenge and Wilton House. Not very much is
known about his ménage except that he insisted on his servant wearing a
wig as he himself always did.

The chief event that spring, though John was not present, was the
marriage of Uncle William to Kitty, the third daughter of a London
alderman, Sir John Tash. She brought a dowry of £6,000 to her rather
impecunious bridegroom, who had only managed to save £2,000 himself;
but her father was heard to observe that if God spared his life a few more
years another £5,000 would fall to Kitty's share when he died.

John still had some interest in Loveday property at Atherstone and it was
agreed he should now make it over to a distant cousin called Loveday
Rollestone. He took Alexander Staples with him to make the transactions
and, with William Payne and Thomas Bagshaw joining them, they stopped
at Coventry on the way.

> . . . At the Entrance into this Close towards the West-end was a large
> Arch leading to it out of the Oat Market; it lately fell-down; not far
> hence still stands the lower part of a great Tower or Steeple which was
> one of the Steeples of the Western front, now a Dwelling-house. The
> Site of the Church is now a Garden, so [also] where the chief
> Habitations of the Monks were; several apartments probably buryed
> underground as appears by the Door-cases, yet visible at the end of the
> Buildings next the River. A mean house called the Bishop's Palace.

Staples and John left the others at Warwick and made their way to
Atherstone, the home of the Lovedays when they had been mercers. After
the business arrangements were concluded John did not quite lose touch
with his Rollestone relations. In December 1737 he wrote:

> John Rollestone of Atherstone who lives by the Jacket-block in
> Gosford Street, tells me that he is 33 years old, his brother Loveday
> two years older, his brother Thomas not so old.

In 1748 he sent John Rollestone two guineas by the hand of John Audley
who was on his way to Birmingham and that seems to have been the last
time he had any dealings with members of his father's family.

As soon as Lambert had left him he went off with an unidentified companion on a short tour of great houses. He had to pass through Windsor so, predictably, they stopped first at the Castle, where John noticed especially a portrait said to be of Luther and his wife hanging in a gallery water closet. The man's face reminded him forcibly of his friend Thomas Hearne.

His visit to Eton College Library on 8 June 1733 is an early example of a stranger being allowed in; though he may already have known Stephen Sleech (later Provost), whose father, Richard, had died in 1730.

> The Library lately erected, very elegant; much carving chiefly out of public Stock. Waddington the Bishop of Chichester's books stand by themselves;[e] vast substantial Mahogany Tables. Desks not half filled. Among their Manuscripts is (says Sleeche) part of Homer A. B. &c, with a Critique upon it said to be Longinus's; t'other part is in St. Mark's Library at Venice, now out of order, t'other part at Leipzick Library.

He saw the Library once again in October 1737, a year after the arrival of the books bequeathed to Eton by Richard Topham.[f] They numbered nearly 1,500 volumes and John said they 'well-nigh filled the Library'.

After stopping for a night with Sir William Bowyer in his 'old brick house by the Coln', Denham Court, they saw Hall Barn at Beaconsfield from the outside.[g]

> Mr Waller, Son of Dr Stephen Waller of the Commons, Son of the Poet, lives a little distance Westward of the Church; the House called Hall-Barn is brick and stands low; he has built a very fine Room of Stone at a distance from the house called the Poet's Room; it is of Stucho Work, Poets' Heads fronting a long Bason of Water. Many most lovely Walks in the Woods which rise high . . .

Undoubtedly the most breathtaking place he visited during this week was Cannons. Built at Edgeworth by the first Duke of Chandos, who was now living there, its magnificence was described by Defoe in terms of ecstasy. John in his matter of fact way was equally impressed.

> Cannons is of Brick, the Grand Front and that towards the Garden being cased with Stone, the Offices of bare Brick . . . the Hall too low, paved with Marble, at the farther end of the Stair-case; the Cieling is Stucho-Work and Painting. Two Chimnies right and left opposite; over the right a bust of Oliver Cromwell. Over the left an antique bust of Plato. The Stairs of grey Marble, the ballisters of cast Brass and of Ebony and Mother of Pearl inlaid; Venetian Windows on the Stair-case; part of the Stair-case upheld by eight Corinthian fluted Pillars.

[e] Edward Waddington's collection of over 2,500 volumes had been left to Eton College and was received there in 1731.

[f] Topham's will stipulated that learned persons must have access. See Robert Birley, *The History of College Library*, Eton College Collections, 1970.

[g] See p. 303 n.*a*.

Bolusis [Bellucci] painted the Cielings in this House. Marble tables inlaid with cards &c.

After describing some of the paintings and tapestry he continued:

In a Closet some of the Dutchess's Painting. In his Grace's private Study, a long good Room, the Painting of the Apostles finding the Money in the Fish; good carving here; the grand Apartments above:. all the Rooms but small. The Cielings are beautiful of Stucho and gilding, the Rooms low.

A Gold and Velvet Bed, Coronet at the Bed's Head, with precious Stones, Pearl, Emerald, Garnet; rich embroidered Carpet, Chairs and Curtains the same as the Bed; marble Table inlaid with Stones of natural colours resembling flowers. Silver bottoms and cheeks to the Chimnies. Next to the State Room, another – the Bed Curtains and Chairs of Silver and Velvet. Polished Silver bottoms and cheeks to the Chimnies here. Length of Lord Treasurer Goldophin by Lely; table the same as the last; a Length of Charles the Prince by Van Dyck they say. The Locks to this grand Apartment are Silver . . . A Picture of the Dutchess marrying the Duke, ill-performed, the Duke very ugly. A large Room has the Cieling painted by Thornhill very well. The Chappel a good Room paved with Marble – painted Windows by J. Price. The Roof is painted by the same Italian hand as those in the house, but it is better, gilded also and Stucho. The Organ is behind the Altar; a Gallery over the Entrance where sits the Duke supported by Marble Pillars. 100 acres for the Gardens – plain and well-watered. Coffee-Trees, redberries, India Pine-apples.

In 1747, three years after the Duke's death, this splendid place was destroyed. Parts of it were sold in lots and the rest pulled down.

The next stop was at the Bell in Kensington in order to see Kensington Palace, one of George II's residences.

The House of Brick, the best Front towards the Garden, has but one Wing. Kent has painted the Stair-case and some of the Cielings very well. The Stairs are of Black marble. We only saw the Apartments above. The Gardens stand very high so as to command fine Prospects towards London with fine high hedges and long Walks. The Mount commands Hyde Park and is separated only by a Haw-Haw so that the Coaches seem to go into the Gardens.

The rest of John's notes were concerned with the pictures.

Hampton Court, the King's favourite country abode, was of course not new to John; but as at Windsor there was always something fresh to absorb.

Through a Range of Offices you come to the House with an extended regular front. The whole Building looks much like a College. In the second Court on the left hand are some Cloisters upheld, not by Arches, but by Pillars of the Ionic Order two and two together; the opposite side is now almost built up new by George II. The 3rd Quadrangle, which contains the State Apartments, was built by King William – 'tis perfectly elegant, cloistered, Brick as the rest except the Cloisters and the Windows (all Sashed) are faced with Stone. Most of the Apartments are wainscotted with Oak, some hung with red Damask as at Kensington. Verrio painted the Stair-case and truly 'tis the best Wall-painting I have seen, and admirably fluted Pillars in it, infinitely exceeding his Performances at Windsor. *Now* I'm informed, he was older, this being painted in King William's time and Verrio himself, when he grew old, despised his Performances at Windsor. So Wanley.[5]

Perfection was achieved, in John's view, by accuracy and realism in the great religious paintings and never more so than in Raphael's Cartoons. He would criticize too any shortcomings, as he saw them, in the interpretation of character or the portrayal of natural phenomena. In Mantegna's *Triumph of Caesar* 'the Painter by avoiding an ostentatious swelling Pride in the Victor, has made him stupidly unconcerned' or in the Cartoon of *The Draught of Fishes* – 'an Inconsistency here; the Wind blows the Hair of one of the men a different way from the smoak of a Chimney in Prospect and the Birds are too near the Boat.' Sometimes he would gaze at length at a great work and, lost in admiration, carry on a dialogue with himself which he later transferred to paper.

> In the Healing of the Importuner he is ordered to arise up and walk, How can he? for many years he had been brought thither to his begging Station and could never move hand or foot from the place they put him in; extravagant Pain ever attended the least tendency to the most cautious and gentle Motion of a Limb; only how should he then think of rising thus at once and use those Limbs so long disused; this and how much more expressed in his face, in every part.

Wandering outside in the gardens, 'chiefly two fine Gravel Walks, one by the Thames Side' with a Bowling Green at one end, he looked across the river to 'the most rural Prospects'. Iron rails separated the gardens from Hampton Park.

> In them at proper distances are mock Gates, most admirable Performances in Iron work and various – one higher in the middle. Those on one side this middle Gate are the same as those on the other side of it. The Wilderness-Garden we did not see . . . Along the Wall between Bushy and Hampton Parks is a most elegant Gate to the latter, neat plain Boys, supporting Baskets of Fruit, happily imitated.

Lord Halifax's brick house in Bushey Park and his 'neat box' near a cascade, which in the front presents you with a Rock of Stone and burnt-Iron, on each side Canvass painted to represent the perspective of Caves – with success[h]

completed this tour and John had to hurry back to Oxford to prepare for his next; for in three weeks' time he intended to leave for Ireland once again. He had been corresponding with people he had met both there and in Wales and one of Dean Perceval's sons, Will, had now arrived in Oxford and was lodging in Corpus Christi. He was also putting the finishing touches to his long account of his 1732 tour which was to be bound up in one volume.

On 27 June Charles Hopson, now a barrister of the Middle Temple, wrote to him from Tunbridge Wells.

Dear Jack,
    I have been at this place a fortnight this day and am heartily tired of it; but my Sister has received already so much benefit by the Waters, that I shall with the less uneasiness attend her here a month or six Weeks longer. I desired Mr Potter[i] when I left Town to send you down by the next Parcel *Blount's Tenures* and the plainest Jacobus[j] I could get at the Custom-house; the Book cost me 2 shillings and the Broad-Piece 25s. 8d.
    In my way to Tunbridge I saw the Duke of Dorset's House at Sevenokes [Knole]. It is an old Built House, much like the outer Quadrangle of St. John's College; situated on the highest Spot of a very pleasant Park about 7 miles round; the Rooms are adorned (after the old-fashioned way) with large Marble Chimney-Pieces up to the top of the room and whimsical Figures painted on the Wainscoat, which gives it an agreeable Antique look. In it are two night-pieces by Schalken; one is a copy from that in Windsor Castle Gallery; the other a Fryer tempting a Nun with Gold, which I thought a fine Painting. There is a Bacchus in his Cups by Titian, a Great Number of old Family Pieces and the Heads of most of our English Poets; there are also Copies of the Cartoons of Hampton Court taken some years since.

Zinzan had to wait until 1735 for his Fellowship and on 2 July he left Magdalen to become tutor to Sir Lister Holte of Aston in Warwickshire and his brother Charles. A day or two later the University plunged into the excitements of the 'Act', then the forerunner to the Encaenia, which had not been held for twenty years and which was enriched by the arrival of Handel with his orchestra and oratorios. Serious music was not of great importance to John except perhaps on this occasion. His daughter told a story which

[h] See p. 245 and n.*p*.
[i] Thomas Potter of the Inner Temple (d. 1741).
[j] A gold coin worth 20–25 shillings struck in the reign of James I.

bears this out and also illustrates the unequivocal manner in which he could sometimes refuse a quite harmless request.

When a young man in Oxford my Father was never inclined to attend the publick Concerts; but he always subscribed to them, from thinking it right to encourage Music as one of the Sciences. As he was known not to go to Concerts his acquaintance sometimes asked him for the tickets he did not use himself; but he told them they must excuse him as they could afford to purchase them and he always gave his to the Choristers.

Probably the most often quoted passage from Hearne's diaries is his description of Handel 'and his lousy crew, a great number of forreign fidlers';[6] but, whatever he thought of them and however little inclined John was in the ordinary way to attend concerts, Hearne had no influence over him on this occasion. On 5 July he joined the large audience at the Sheldonian to hear *Esther* at five o'clock with a five-shilling ticket.[7] The next two days he spent in the theatre at the Act. On 8 July he heard Handel's 'Utrecht Te Deum'; the next day he was at the Act all the afternoon and on the 10th, after a visit to Bishop Tanner in the morning, he listened to another oratorio, *Athaliah*, composed for the occasion. Then it was time to leave the world of Oxford, the elegant disputations and speeches of the Act and the irreverence of Terrae Filius with his earthy, disrespectful allusions to his instructors. The Act was not over but on 11 July John and Thomas Bagshaw had set out for Ireland.

Their first stop was at Cornbury Park where nothing much had changed. At Evesham John pondered for a while on the two churches in one churchyard, All Saints and St Laurence which was

so much decayed that it has not been used above these three years, a Breve has been out for it. There has been one Minister to both Churches these many Years, one Church having been used in the Morning and the other in the Afternoon. There is a side-Chappel with a stone carved Roof in All Saints Church built by Abbot Lichfield who is buryed under a Stone now broke and pillaged of its brass which lies at the entrance of it . . .

The bells of both churches were removed, he said, to 'Lichfield's Tower . . . a strong piece of work' which the people did not think had ever belonged to the Abbey church. A rugged stony road took them on to Pershore where the Abbey churchyard and another were as near together as those at Coventry.

One was the choir part of the Priory-Church, This was dedicated to the Holy Cross; it has a stone arched Roof, good pillars and Arches and wants paving much. The large substantial tower is still standing in the middle of the cross-Isle, the South part of which is still also standing, but the North is down as is all the West-end from the Cross-Isle. On the ground just north of the altar lies a Knight-Templar. Just above it is a carved partition of Wood-work on which the Inscription printed in Hemingford. .It parts from a Chappel (in which is an old raised Tomb with recumbent Effigies) which for these many years has been turned into a school; it has a Chimney in it. . . . On the outside of the Church at the East end you see an Arch stopped up. I easily believe the Clark that the Church itself never went any further that way, but that it was the Gate into the Cloisters now demolished . . . The outside of the South Cross they have finished with plaster-work lately. One Yeend lives in the New-House called the Abbey-house. It is his free-hold, he purchased it of the Lawrences. It stands South-West of the Church. As for the old Abbey-House it is all down . . . and Yeend's house was not built upon the spot, yet he is Lord of the site, so I'm informed.

They reached Worcester on 13 July and John was able to add to the notes he had made in 1730. He was told that there were ten churches and two chapels and that St Nicholas's church was not yet finished. 'The wondrous taper-ribbed Spire of St. Andrews was damaged by lightning last Midsummer Eve, as I'm informed.'

He made intensive notes on the Cathedral where some alterations were taking place:

The body, Cross-Isles and Presbytery are paved with Brick, now 'tis old and in bad condition; the Choir Pavement is of Black and White Marble Squares. . . . The Pillars in this Church are large, not to say clumsy; those of the Choir, its Isles and Chappels, have little Pillars of grey Marble interlaced with the main Pillars and fastned to 'em with rings of copper gilt. The two Arches of different form at the very West end were the addition of Bishop Wakefield, who also built the North Porch; there are Snail-shells by way of ornament over these two Arches, therefore you are told that one Bishop Snell[k] built this part. Here the early Prayers are said; the place for which in other Cathedrals is generally at the East end of the Nave. In this place is an old stone carved Pulpit. They are now new-roofing the Western part and chipping part of the North. The East has been fitted-up of late – they intend to whitewash the Church. The Altar-piece was erected about 12 years since, of oak, neat but plain . . .

After describing the tombs and monuments he continued:

There is but little painted Glass intire in this Church . . . On the East side over the Gate of an ancient Tower, lately chipped, under which is the entrance into the College-Green, are the Statues painted lately, of King Edgar[l] (his right leg over the left knee) with his two Queens Aethelfleda

[k] Evidently a fictional character.
[l] I am grateful to Mr R. J. Collins and Mr David Whitehead for information on Worcester.

and Aethelfrid. On the West side the Gate is a Bust of George II. Dr Birch
has not yet finished his Prebendal house, which will be the very best of
'em, of brick; there are other houses in the Green besides the Prebendaries,
neither are *they* all here . . . the Chapter-house is now a Library, but
notwithstanding used also as a Chapter-house.

Once more he described the 'Town House' or Guildhall with its 'Groupe of
Warlike Instruments' over the great door.

Although the route they now took to Anglesey was a little faster than the
previous year's, it was still arduous after they left Droitwich, or ' 'Wich so they
always call [it]'.

'Wich stands in a hole, is old built, nor is there a good house in the town.
There are but three Brine Pits of much account. Now they pay the
Government about 50,000£ per annum. The Coal they use in boiling their
Salt comes from Stourbridge and that Countrey.

Kinver was approached through lanes – 'I never travelled in a more Bye-road
than was this after Harvington.' In the church he found a vault under the east
part of the south chancel

in which it does not appear that any have been buried. The People call it the
Dungeon; they have a notion that this town had once the privilege of
trying and executing within itself and about half a mile hence, in the road
to Bridgenorth is a place called Gallow Tree Hill. We came upon a
Common just after Kinfare [Kinver] where Rock prevailed much, though
sometimes concealed by deep Sand. The Morse is a great Heath at least
three miles over; it ended not a mile before Bridgenorth.
July 15. Bridgenorth, consisting of the upper and lower town, is so
divided by the Severn, but again united by a stone-bridge on which are
some houses. The upper Town stands secure upon a very steep Rock of
Reddish mouldring Stone. Yet the chief of the buildings are of brick; 'Tis
a difficult breathing Ascent (as at Newcastle upon Tine) to the Upper
Street which is of a very handsome width, some of its houses of wood and
Plaister, the View of the Street intercepted by the Town house in the
middle of it. Several houses are built in the rock of the ascent and there are
Gardens and Passages over several of them . . . there are Brick Piazzas to
some of the houses and also some old ones of Wood . . .
     . . . a large piece of the Castle still remains and seems by its inclining
to threaten a terrible fall, had it not (as we were told) stood just in this

---

The legs of the statue of King Edgar were cut off in 1801 by a mason who used them to
'exhibit a paltry transparency at the illuminations to celebrate the Peace of Amiens' – from an
annotated copy of V. Green's *History of the World* in the Birmingham Reference Library.
The figures were all replaced by others made of terracotta in 1912–13. The bust of George II
by Thomas White disappeared.

manner ever since the destruction of the Castle in the Civil Wars. There
are hooks fastned onto this Ruin on which the besieged hung bags of
Sand to receive the Enemies' Balls, or rather [he added later] phassocks
filled with wool which were loosely suspended from the Wall. There is
a Hill thrown up by the Parliamentarians to annoy the Castle. Nothing
can exceed the pleasant walk all round the Castle hill, which is of great
extent; hence you see that the Countrey rises more or less, nearer or at a
greater distance, every way about Bridgenorth and the greater part of it
is well inclosed; indeed one of the Views is upon Morse, abounding
with Rock – its verdure fern but affording Pasture for Sheep. You may
descend steep from this hill . . . into the lower town, by steps cut
through the rock of it; the more private Passages between the two
Towns being cut through the very main rock. But what adds to the
view of Morse from the hill is the high rock in it of the reddish stone
and also the Hermitage, a groupe of Cots, six or seven in number,
nestled into the rock; we walked to see 'em; upon the hard Stone above
some of 'em there hangs-over a more loose Compound of Pebbles,
hardened Mould &c which sometimes falls down in great pieces and
threatens yet more destruction.

They left this romantic spot for Shrewsbury on 16 July

altogether on close Lanes and for the first part on a Clay; we went up
hill and down hill often. On the road we met several carriages drawn
by Oxen and Horses.

Two places which especially attracted their interest on the way from
Shrewsbury to Ruthin were Oswestry and Chirk Castle, the only country
house they visited on this lap of their journey. Of the former he wrote:

Its Walls are now decaying, the Gates are standing. 'Tis an old-built
place of Wood and Plaster – the Church standing without, the Castle-
hill remaining ditched and on it are some fragments of the Castle itself.
The church is a very large building and handsome . . . the Walls are
adorned with texts of Scripture . . . the Church is full of pews . . .

It was out of the way to Chirk Castle to go by the village

which stands on an hill; just before we ascended which, a bridge over
the river divided England from Wales. The Castle, Mr Myddelton's
built by Roger Mortimer, stands in a Park on uprising Ground; built of
a Free-stone, the front has two round Towers at the Extremities and
another in the middle; the entrance is between two of the towers;
entering the quadrangle, on the left hand are Cloisters; an Inscription
says that Sir Thomas Myddelton, Knight, rebuilt great part of the
Castle in 1636. The Stair-case with a Gallery round it is in one of the
round Towers; in the Gallery are some views of the Castle. The Dining

Room has an old fret-work Cieling, very rich. In it, with several others is a small-life-piece of King Charles I on a dun horse, such an one as at Brancepeth;[m] Prince Rupert in the Garter Robes . . . The Gallery, a very well-proportioned room, has among other paintings one of Lord Keeper Bridgeman[n] sitting, of Sir Thomas Myddelton with many other family Pictures; in this room are two curious Cabinets; one has some Lapis Lazuli in the front of it, the other represents several Beasts and that by means of several kinds of stones, advantageously inlaid according to their native colours. In another Room is a Cabinet, whose front represents on copper the Miracles of Christ painted and is also adorned with silver carving. In a Closet is an excellent painting of a Burgomaster reading and meditating by Brugen; of Grapes full ripe by Schalcken. An Altar-piece also. Tillemans and Dahl have Pictures in this house. There is a Painting of a fine Cascade in one of Mr Myddelton's Lordships.

There are no Gardens laid out. The back View is very delightfully extensive, upon the fine Inclosures in Shropshire. The Iron Gate to the Castle is an exquisite piece of carved Work, performed by Persons of this countrey.[o] The two Sisters, Lady Myddelton and Lady Whitmore, were so much alike that it is not easy to distinguish 'em; the former is one of the Royal Beauties[p] – so is also Lady Denham whose Picture they have here.

Llangollen is no inconsiderable size, the Church is something large; the bridge of good free-stone Arches over the Dee; I have seen many Rivers before which passed over a Rocky bottom, but this has something peculiar in it; the rocks are so even just under the bridge that you would imagine the channel paved by art, but the Pavement is something out of repair.

From our Entrance into Wales till we came to Ruthin, the Road was never on a level, but continually up and down; among Mountains we were all the while and travelled over some of them; they were clothed with fern and furze; goats we saw by the way; sometime before we came to Ruthin a Prospect opened of the Vale of Clwd; when we came

[m] John had noticed the miniature of Charles I on horseback at Brancepeth Castle on 28 August 1732. The Chirk picture is still there.

[n] Sir Orlando Bridgeman.

[o] The gates were made 1719–21 by the Welsh wrought-iron smith, Robert Davies, and his brother.

[p] It seems that John had confused the relationships in the portraits. The two sisters were Frances, Lady Myddelton and Mrs Dorothy Langley. Their mother, Lady Whitmore, and her sister, Lady Denham, were two of Lely's Beauties and renowned for their looks. Frances Myddelton was one of Kneller's Beauties.

The cloisters under the Long Gallery were removed in the nineteenth century, but the inscription survives. The cabinet with the Miracles of Christ was given to the 1st Baronet of Chirk Castle, Sir Thomas, by Charles II and is still there. Ten years later the gardens had been laid out.

near the town the Soil was Red, sometimes a Red Rock . . . we met with several carts of the English kind in Wales today.

They stayed the night at the Red Lion and next day examined the church – 'entirely new West, South and East except where the old Tower makes part of the East' – with its interesting carved roof.

. . . Over one Grave in the Church are laid Laurel, Rosemary, Thyme and some flowers. These are renewed against every Sunday, till the Tomb-Stone is laid and this is the Custom always. The Minister is called Warden of Ruthin which is but a Chapelry. We saw this morning several coal Carts in the town, some drawn by oxen and horses; the Coals are brought from the Countrey about Wrexham and sold by the Load.

On 19 July they crossed the water from Conway to Anglesey and came once again to Beaumaris and all the joys of a seaside holiday. At Baron Hill they were welcomed by Lord and Lady Bulkeley whose house as usual was full of company.

On the friday we went aboard a Sugar Ship and afterwards went a fishing with Nets and caught Thornbacks – rather Skates, here they call them Rays or Cats – Floukes or Flounders as we call them, and Oysters. On the Saturday we dined at Penmon and then went to Preston Island to catch Puffins, a fowl that breed in Rabbet-burrows out of which the dogs draw 'em. . . They are good potted, collared or pickled. We all returned, as some of us came, by Water. Lord Bulkeley has, by a grant from the Crown, all the Water from Preston-Island to Abermenai beyond Caernarvon.

John spent some time examining Lord Bulkeley's pedigree as well as his house and Beaumaris chapel.

In the Area before the Altar is an high raised Tomb of Alabaster having on the top two large recumbant Effigies of a Man and Woman. This, tradition says, was brought from the Church of Llanvaes Priory together with three more, one of which is in Penmynydd Church in this Island. Against the North Wall in the Chancel is a brass-Plate for the Bulkeley family with the usual representation of the Trinity. Mr John Williams, Curate here, dined with us today as we had been in his company before. The two Maces belonging to the Corporation of Beaumaris were given by Henry Bertie, their representative under the Crown; in each a Pint Cup is contained.

They left on Sunday for Caer Gybi where they were to spend the night at the Widow Jones's lodgings before embarking for Ireland.

We cut off something from the length of this journey by going over the sands before Holyhead. Lord Bulkeley sent his Groom with us beyond Bodedern from whence a Tenant of the Lady Dowager's shewed us to the Head. Long before we came to the Head we saw (or were strangely deceived) some Mountains which must be in Ireland. The Sun set fair upon them from Baron Hill till 4 o'th'clock in the Afternoon.

John's old acquaintance Captain Quiltra was ready with the same 'Pacquet Boat, the Grafton' to conduct them over the Irish Sea. As before they were becalmed and the voyage took twenty-seven hours. They landed at Kingstown and were soon installed in that rather unsatisfactory Dublin inn, The White Hart, which provided no meat. It took three days to show the sights of the town to Bagshaw to whom the experience of touring in this way was quite new. John still had a few notes to add to those of the previous year.

Stephen's Green, an very high situation, one side built completely and that admirably well with fine houses. One Side, almost open, gives a View of the Wicklow Mountains (as I'm informed.) There is a pleasant Walk all round this very large Square and between Trees. Within it is a Meadow where Horses graze, round which is also a Grass-Walk. . .

The Castle Apartments are unfurnished in the Lord Lieutenant's[q] absence. The Rooms are not large, the Wainscotts painted, but there are good Vistas of the Lodging Rooms. In one Room is the Duke of Bolton at length, but very ill-painted. In another Room where is good Tapestry, is a Length of Queen Anne. In the Presence-Chamber are two Chairs for the Duke and Dutchess of Dorset under a Canopy.

At Christ Church Cathedral he found that the south aisle of the nave was closed up and 'the Chappel North of the Choir is now fitting with Deal Seats whereas last Summer it was a very Nasty Place.' Among the many epitaphs which he copied down he found some for members of the Cadogan family. One of these was for Ambrose Cadogan who had died in 1713 and he wondered how he was related to Lord Cadogan who had succeeded his more famous brother, the Earl, one of Marlborough's generals; he must remember to find out more about Ambrose.

One day they rode out to Powerscourt which Mr Wingfield, later the first Lord Powerscourt, was rebuilding.

It commands no kind of Prospect but Mountains rising close about it. In the Deer-Park is a Water-fall down a Rock; at the bottom are vast fragments of Rocks, among which it empties itself. I think that I have seen many such as these as I have rode in a gut below; sure that opposite to Penmon Island in the Isle of Anglesea exceeds it.

Dean William Perceval had invited them to stay with him at his country living, Bellfield, and they arrived there on 28 July having made the journey through Clonard and Kinnegad in one day , thanks to an excellent road. The

[q] The Duke of Dorset.

Dean was waiting to welcome them with his three sons, Kene, Will and Charles, and his daughter Catherine. He had lost his wife three years earlier.

The Lord Chief Baron Rochfort was the Dean's Patron here. He built the Church where had never been one before; indeed 'tis within a neat and elegant Structure, wainscotted and gilded at Top. The Dean was the first Minister of this Parish in which Mr Rochfort's[r] house, Golsalltown [Gaulstown] is situate; the Gardens are well laid out and have a fine head of Water. There is a most wonderful Echo here, but it never answers except in the stillest Calm. The Speaker makes use of a Speaking-Trumpet, which situate at one end of a great Length of Water throws the Voice upon a building in a small Island which is almost at the farther end of the Water. T'other way repeat two Hexameters at least, and about the space of a minute after you have done, the Echo begins and you perceive no difference between your own voice and the Echo of it, but that the Echo takes off every harshness of sound. This we had from the Dean's Information for the Weather was not calm enough for our making the Experiment.

They stayed there two nights. When they left, the Dean with two of his sons put them on their way for six miles or so. As they rode along he regaled them with anecdotes as he had done during the whole of their visit.

He tells me that Swift was to have been made Dean of Wells, but Archbishop Sharp hearing of it gave such a character of him to the Queen that she resolved never to prefer him; his only hopes then were in Ireland where the Duke of Ormonde, Lord Lieutenant, might prefer him without the Queen and so he did to the Deanery of St. Patrick. His living of Laracor, not far from Trim, is worth 120£ per Annum.

John and Thomas, on their way to Brea after leaving the friendly Percivals, had to labour through an almost continuous bog as far as Maryborough. On arrival they found that Billy was at home and the Lethieulliers had another guest staying with them, Mr Kean O'Hara[s] of Trinity College, Dublin, a nephew of George Mathew of Thomastown, whose house John had failed to see on his previous visit. They spent five congenial days at Brea and were introduced to the Wednesday Club at Athy. Then the whole family set out for Thomastown 'breakfasting at Mr Welche's of Ballikilcavern about 8 miles away – an handsome and pleasant Seat'.

There were 'very pleasant prospects' along the road to Durrow and 'Gentlemens' Seats thick set'. They revisited one of these – Castle Durrow, the home of Colonel Flower (later 1st Baron Ashbrook). Next day the journey was poor.

---

[r] The younger Robert Rochfort became Viscount Bellfield of Gaulstown (later called Belvedere).

[s] Kean or Kane O'Hara became a well-known figure in Dublin and produced a number of burlesque plays.

O'Hara says that Longford-Pass was so called from the Earl of Longford's gaining this Countrey from the Irish and making a Pass through it. It is all an uncomfortable Bog. . . and the Causey through it is ragged and broken. Bad weather and want of Provision sent us to Thurles, which is out of the way.

Bogs and bad weather, however, were soon forgotten when their party of six joined the company already assembled at Thomastown. There were a number of ladies, one of whom was Mrs O'Hara, sister to Mr Mathew and mother of Kean. The son of the house, Toby Mathew, and his wife,[t] who lived about two miles away, were also there for most of the time.

There is always an abundance of Company at this house, who lie here. Amongst others while we were there was the Earl of Barrymore whose great good nature and easy carriage cannot fail to recommend him strongly; the Lord Kingston; Mr Butler,[u] eldest Son of the Lord Mountgarret, Colonel Butler, Colonel Magrath, Dr Winter of Kildare, Hort, Bishop of Kilmore – an Englishman, he appears to be a sensible well-bred and good-natured Man; Mr Clarke, Fellow of Trinity College, Dublin; the Countess of Rosse, who has been a very fine Woman and is still extremely agreeable; Mrs Segrave. . . Our Mr Mathew is a convert from Popery.

George Mathew was not only improving his house, but took the greatest interest in his estate and plantations which must have been very fine.

Mr Mathew has finished the Portico of his house which has a very good effect; there are handsome Apartments in this Seat, which is very old, though fitted up by Mr Mathew. There is a fine broad and long Avenue to the front, with Water-Works in the middle, the Cascades falling both ways meet in one common Bason. The leaden Statues in the Garden are very well-performed, as are also the Busts in Stone of some Poets; the little Boys in Lead are deservedly admired as is the Gladiator in the front of the house. There are handsome Vistas from the Garden, upon a fine Sheet of Water and upon an old ruin of a Castle. There are neat buildings – one a shell house – at each end of a canal in the Garden.

But his improvements over above 2,000 English Acres exceed Admiration.[v] Oak, the two kinds of fir, Beech, Hazel, Arbute and what not are the substance of the Plantation, and all these disposed in the most

---

[t] George Mathew and his son Theobald (Toby) both died in 1736. George was known as 'Grand George' on account of his acquisitions and style of living . Toby's son, George, died in 1738 when the estate went to his maternal uncle. Toby's widow then married Kean O'Hara. She was cousin to both her husbands.

[u] Richard Butler succeeded as 7th Viscount Mountgarret in 1735.

[v] John added a note later – 'See what Lord Bathurst has done at Cirencester.' Though he went there in 1736 he left no account of this house. See p. 218 and n. *l*.

elegant manner; here is a very fine Labyrinth with only one way out and in, comprehended in a square, a Danish Court and many other figures. Through the thickest woods fine Vistas are cut, terminated by some pretty building or other. One is often surprised when in a lonely walk between Trees to drop all of a sudden upon a green Meadow or Plantation. Here are two fine Parks. One is well stocked with Deer of various colours and there is an admirable covert for them. From this Park (which has also some of Mathew's Plantation) you have a fine view of a good Countrey, well set with good houses. But which mightily sets-off the whole is the vast high ridge of the Galtees-hills (they part the Counties of Limerick and Tipperary) which seem to be the magnificent termination of these Improvements, Though indeed there is a large intervening Tract of Land. The Decoy is very beautiful and far removed from any noise; it has four Pipes in it. There is no part of this large Plantation but a Coach may turn in.

After an eight-day visit the family had to tear themselves away. They left Kean O'Hara with his relations and a Captain Paul joined them as escort. At Kilkenny John had a brief look at the Castle to see what changes had taken place in the last year. Its owner, the Earl of Arran, had not been there since he was a schoolboy some fifty years before; he had purchased it from his brother, the 2nd Duke of Ormonde, and it was inhabited by his agent. There was none of the old furniture there now except for tapestry which the Earl had bought when it was sold in England and had returned to the Castle. Captain Lethieullier could remember a fine portrait of the Earl of Strafford and his Secretary and John wondered whether this was the actual picture which now hung at Blenheim. (Later on, in 1738, he saw such a painting at Eastbury Park in Dorset.[w]) Kilkenny itself was delightful and in an imaginative moment he said that with the trees all around it and the river close by one might think that a much larger town was concealed there. The way back to Brea was 'altogether pleasant through a Countrey well stored with Gentlemens' Seats'.

He had managed to send a letter[8] off to Hearne from Clonard, apologizing for the paper 'for this town affords none'. Except for telling his friend that the crossing had been so calm that none of the Passengers had been disordered and giving him more information on books and libraries, he had had time to say little but that good Lord Bulkeley was an honest man, which Hearne would take to mean that he was a strong Tory if not a Jacobite. 'Mr Bagshaw, a worthy demy of our College, is my fellow-traveller,' he added, making them sound rather like a couple of elderly divines. Hearne's reply[9] duly arrived during the next ten days at Brea. It was a long letter, dated 7 August with an interesting suggestion that if John could get into Trinity College Library, which he had so far failed to do, he might obtain some useful

[w] See p. 296.

knowledge by simply turning over the books. For Archbishop Ussher 'had a Privilege of writing whatever Notes he thought proper in any Book, MS or Printed, in Trinity College Library'.[x] After touching on the 'Chronicle of Olney', the writing abilities of Henry VIII and Charlemagne and other interesting but rather obscure matters, Hearne jumped back to the present day by saying there was great talk of the designed new building at Magdalen College[y] and that the Master of University College[z] had promised to do what he could to arrange for the Act to take place every year.

On 28 August Captain Lethieullier and his family packed up again for a trip to Dublin where Billy was due back at college. The road lay through Chapelizod where John had a mission to perform:

> I called on the Lord Primate[a] at Chappel-Izod to know whether he had any commands to the President of Magdelen College in answer to his letter which I left at his Grace's house in town. The Primate had great Company with him, so I only saw Mr Charles Moran. This house belongs to the Government, it makes no figure at all, being a very plain single brick house, but pleasantly situate. The Wall of Dublin Park is close to the left hand of the road from hence.

Back they went to the White Hart where the Captain had taken rooms for them all including his wife's half-sisters, the Misses Berkeley. John and Thomas spent the evenings with Billy and his student friends in college; there was plenty to do by day but it was only the lack of a boat that kept them waiting in Dublin for the next ten days or so.

> The winds were stormy and sat full for England and so detained the Vessels on that side the Water.

Dean Perceval called on them as soon as he heard they were in Dublin, as friendly and communicative as ever. Another noteworthy visitor was Mrs Mary Barber, the poet 'wife to Barber the Drapier' who, aided by Swift, was preparing her *Poems on Several Occasions* for publication in England the following year. But to meet Swift's friends was by no means enough for John; it was intolerable to be in the same city as a man he so much admired and not to have even a glimpse of him before returning to England. Yet as his son Arthur eventually told Benwell he was to be disappointed.

> When he was in Ireland he had a great desire of seeing Dean Swift. For this purpose he attended regularly at the Dean's Chapel for a week in the

---

[x] The learned Archbishop's library was bought by the State in 1756 for 2,000 guineas and deposited in Trinity College Library in 1761.

[y] The original designs by Edward Holdsworth would have destroyed a great deal of Magdalen College and were fortunately restricted. Sir William Bowyer was one of four people who laid the foundation stones of the New Building the following year.

[z] Thomas Cockman.

[a] Hugh Boulter.

hopes of seeing him there. Being disappointed in this expectation, he resolved to make a farther attempt and waited on the Dean at his own house, but to his unspeakable regret was informed that he was too ill to see Company.

However he had better luck in other directions. The Primate sent him a letter for Dr Butler, coupled with an invitation to dinner and on 30 August they were allowed into the Library of Trinity College.

We saw the College Library by favour of Mr Thomas Loyde, M.A. They have not books enough to fill the half of it; the Library will not be opened yet awhile, for the books are not catalogued. Archbishop Usher's are to be by themselves, so Palliser's, Archbishop of Cashel by themselves, who was also fellow of the College. The MSS in great disorder are in a large room at the farther end below Stairs, in the wainscot of which are inserted two ancient Greek Stones. The room over, not yet wainscotted, is for a Museum of Rarities. Though there seems to be too many windows on the outside, yet when you go in you perceive that they are not more than is absolutely necessary, there being a Window between each Class. The Wooden Pillars within are Corinthian. The Garden front is best, for here no buildings jut against the Wings; here are also Piazzas, as in the other front. The old Library was in a vile garret and everything there in the greatest confusion.

One of the fine outlets in Dublin is the Strand, of several miles length; to the landwards there is a fine Countrey and Houses of Entertainment continually occurring. The City Bason is within its own Wall, 'tis an ill-shaped Head of Water, yet much advantaged by the thick Willows that grow on its banks, for they hide the odd figure of the Bason; all around it are fine grass-Walks between Hedges, out of which grow pretty Elms. The Park of Dublin is the most delightful Outlet; it stands high commanding a Prospect of the City and Countrey; in its Woods is a beautiful Ring with four Vistas from it; there are handsome Lodges about the Park. Ormanstown-Green is just by the Barracks; there the Soldiers are reviewed in the Winter Season, as in the Summer in the Park.

At last on 7 September the sloop *Carteret* bore them away to England and John took leave of his uncle and aunt for the last time. The Master, Thomas Hughes, made the crossing in twelve hours and to improve matters still further there were congenial people on board, some of whom John already knew. Now they had to return to Oxford with all possible speed. Stopping for only one night at Lord Bulkeley's on 8 September and another at Denbigh, they reached Shrewsbury on the 10th. One night at Worcester and another at Chipping Norton and they were back at Oxford. This must have been the fastest journey John ever made and the only one on which he stopped to look at nothing. Almost his only comment was on posts marking parish boundaries near Shrewsbury and Welshpool which he thought very unusual.

He had expressed his views on the Irish fairly cogently the previous year, regarding them as he did with an elegant distaste for their lack of restraint and devious ways but affection for their warmth and originality. He was interested in their government and laws, their diocesan and parochial arrangements and any more trifling differences between themselves and the English, not least their manner of speech:

'I'll do it now' for 'immediately'. 'A Key', meaning a place where Ships load and unload, they always spell Quay. To stink for to make to stink – as 'you stink the Room.' They call the Ague the 'Shake', 'Unwell' for not very well, 'Speak small' for speak low, 'Setting a house' for letting it. An haggard is a place to stow Hay or Corn in. Very few of the Irish gentlemen smoak. Most of the men of ordinary rank wear black Irish Frieze. We observed that the very poor Irish have (for the most part) sore Eyes.

The ordinary people in common speaking to you give you the title of 'Your Honour.' 'Tis the custom here to salute one another at every Visit, or whenever they meet elsewhere – and this amongst the Men as well as the Women.

As we came from Brea to Dublin we saw great numbers upon the road being loaded with Kilkenny coal. Some of them were fastened behind one another . . . The public roads about Dublin exceed any in England; they are pitched and bind well with their Gravel, not dusty as with us. There is more Bare[b] than Barley in great disproportion in Ireland. I don't remember to have seen one Countrey-Seat built of brick; they are all plaistered over; in short every house is white so they are all either faced with stone or plaistered.

The Mass-houses in Countrey-places are in fields, just large enough to contain an Altar and Priest, the Congregation attending whilst in the field; such as one we saw within a very few miles of Bellfield. . . In the last session of Parliament the Bishops endeavoured at an Act to make every Clergyman who had several Parishes united, to build a Parsonage-house in each Parish and settle a resident Curate in each; and to enable them (the Bishops) to take from one Living and add to another; it was in great want of it.

The rest of his notes chiefly concerned the power of the Irish Council, so much greater than that of the English Privy Council,

for though Acts run in the name of King in Council, yet they are seldom called together till the whole Affair is concerted and agreed upon in the Cabinet Council and then they are not to consult and debate the matter,

[b] Bear (Anglo-Saxon 'bere') – bindweed or convolvulus.

but only to give the formal Sanction to it. It seems reasonable the Complaint of Ireland against the Laws enacted relating to it in the Parliament of England for it never consented to such Subjection as that.

Four days after his return to Caversham on 14 September John dined with Lord and Lady Cadogan; but although his Lordship was quite expansive on the subject of his late brother, the General, saying that he had bought Caversham Lodge[c] for the sum of £15,000 and had spent £23,000 purely on the buildings, the subject of Ambrose, whose memorial John had seen in Dublin, does not seem to have come up. It was not until 1746 that he told John that Ambrose had been the middle one of the three brothers and that he had been a seaman.

Michael Blount of Mapledurham was a near neighbour whom the Lovedays knew quite well and on 23 September John went there to make some notes on the house. It was many years now since Mr Blount's sisters, Teresa and Martha (so celebrated for their friendship with Pope), had left Mapledurham on their brother's marriage. They moved in the world of high fashion outside John's orbit.

Mr Blount's of Mapledurham. Brick. Most regular front. A large Hall, adorned with great variety of Horns and foreign Curios, more than I have seen elsewhere, Among other Paintings in it, are two small half-pieces of Philip of Spain and Queen Mary. In the best Parlor are several family-pieces drawn by Holbein, Lely and Van Dyck; over the Chimney a very fine Holbein of not much more than the head of Sir Thomas More, much sagacity and judgment is expressed in his features, his Complexion brown. In the withdrawingroom is a large Painting of Albert Durer's representing St. Jerome sitting with his books before him, and an Angel by him. An Enamell of Galba's Bust.

The great Stair-Case is handsome; there is a noble large Room above-Stairs admirably proportioned, well-lighted, a fretwork Cieling;[d] but its most observable beauty is the Wainscot of Irish Oak, most curiously carved, with great taste, representing Ionic Pillasters. Higher than this is the Chappel,[e] in which are Paintings; the Altar-piece (no large Painting) is by Paul Lorain of a dead Christ. There is a Van Dyck of Christ afflicted, the Crown of Thorns upon his head. At the top of the whole house is a Room the whole length of it. From the first Story you command the Thames just by it. The house is situate on a

[c] Caversham Park.

[d] I am grateful to Mr Marcus Binney for the information that this account shows that the ceiling of the Saloon is probably the original one. For further conclusions he made about the pilasters and their resemblance to those at Hardwick House, see his letter to *Country Life*, 22 July 1971.

[e] The chapel in the house was hidden upstairs. The unknown painter, P. Lorain, may possibly have been Nicolas Lorain who painted in churches in the seventeeth century.

dead flat, yet the View from it is not unpleasant. A Stork here. Reading seems to be just in front of the house, especially St. Mary's Tower.

He went to Silchester again on 4 October.

Kemp, the old farmer who rents Silchester walked with us about the Place. The Church and his farmhouse stand just within the East Gate, being the only building now remaining within the Walls. 'Tis not long since the Church has been cieled and pewed. The farmer imagines that the Walls may be about two miles and a half in cirquit, but they contain 100 Acres; the figure of the inclosed Ground is irregular, neither square nor round, being an irregular Polygon. The materials of the Walls are flint and large Slade Stone; of either of which my Informer says there is no Quarry within many miles. He tells me that towards the North Gate many Streets met. There were four Gates. The Ground within the Walls is higher than the Countrey about it so that when you are without the Walls and they appear in some places to be about 20 foot high, yet on the inside, 'tis but here and there that you see anything of them. . .

Last Winter they discovered two Pavements in the fields; the Tessellae are red (of brick) and white, bigger each than two Dice and not representing any regular figure, so that probably it was the Pavement of the Ground-floor in the houses of the town; it was fixed upon a bed of sifted Gravel. What content each Pavement might have, no one knows; for neither are pursued as far as they will go. In the slopes just by the Wall they sometimes dig mens' bones, I saw some sticking in the bank. There was a scull also which I saw dug up not long since. Before Christmas last, as they were grubbing a Crab-Tree, which grew upon the slope at the top of the Wall, West of the North Gate, they found a rugged mouldring kind of free-stone, with an Inscription, now to be seen at the Parsonage-house. Dr Paris designs to remove it to Cambridge. His servant (a Native of Silchester, John Stair, Junior) has several coins found here. . . But as for the Roman Silchester, there was a Ditch round the Walls, not close under them but at some distance, some part of it still remaining and holds water to this day. The Walls may be at the foundation about 12 foot thick as the Farmer says. There are no great Oaks now growing upon the Walls, as formerly there have been, some so large as that there were three or four Load in a Stick. There is one Spring within the Walls which might serve the whole town with Water.

The Farmer shewed us at his house an entire Roman Brick which he had dug-up himself. It was near 17 inches long; the Breadth and Depth was not the same throughout . . .

On the following day John went to see Englefield House, some miles to the west of Reading and owned then by the Wrighte family. The Englefields themselves now lived at Whiteknights having left Englefield House many years before, as John explained:

'Tis said that Sir Francis forfeited the Estate before he had finished the house; that afterwards it was Sir Peter Vanlore's and then came to the Paulets.*f*

Englefield House is built of Brick chiefly, yet some Stone in the Front. You ascend much by Steps to the house, which is seated on the side of an hill, commanding the View of an open Countrey, appearing woody. There are some Escutcheons of Arms in the stone-work of the front and also the date of the Building twice occurring – 1555. There is a large Hall, hung with good Lengths of the twelve Apostles. A small Parlor has in it very ancient and uncommon Tapestry, also a Painting of Lord Keeper Wright, sitting. A Stone Stair-case and noble large Dining Room, hung with Tapestry. A Picture in one of the Rooms, very valuable, of the Priest of Jupiter sacrificing to Paul and Barnabas; 'tis a miniature. . . The Gallery up two pairs of Stairs is built on an Arch, the Road lies under it. Having been much rebuilt, however much repaired, of late years, it is not wainscotted or anyways furnished; it lets you out into the Park which here rises very high above the house, a Mount at the top of it, from whence are several Views. A large Kitchin with three Chimnies. The Gardens are in hanging Walks, one under the other and may be much improved. There is a fine Head of Water upon the flat below the house.

Hearne wrote on 27 September to thank him for some epitaphs and the copy of a sermon which he pronounced to be 'a strange, immethodical, rambling Discourse without Divinity'. But though the author, unnamed, had 'exhausted his whole stock of learning . . .', he had at least exploded the story of a legendary female Pope – Pope Joan. This, thought Hearne, was a good thing – 'Many Books have been written on this subject, but I think 'tis quite exhausted and that 'tis time to give it up.' Hearne's letters tended to be about librarians and this was no exception: it was concerned with the efforts of Dr Drake to give an account in his forthcoming book of the manuscripts at York Cathedral 'which,' as he concluded sadly, 'I am told are in great confusion and disorder'; but none in that place had been curious in MSS. since the death of Dr Thomas Gale.[10]

Unfortunately John made very few observations on the Oxford colleges but he wrote down one or two brief remarks after trundling his Brady aunt and uncle round them when they paid him a visit that autumn. The rector of Tooting seems to have been a rather tiresome person and less interesting than his father who had been chaplain to William and Mary, Queen Anne and the Duke of Ormonde's Regiment of Horse and had also collaborated in a

f Sir Francis, a Roman Catholic, fled the country soon after Queen Elizabeth came to the throne. The estate was eventually forfeited and most of it, with the house, was given by Elizabeth to the Earl of Essex. It was acquired by the Norryses of Thame and later by the Paulet family. Paulet Wrighte, son of the Revd Nathan Wrighte and Anne Paulet, was the owner in 1733. His widow married Richard Benyon in 1745.

metrical version of the Psalms. Aunt Martha, unlike her Lethieullier sisters, was nondescript. However they kept in touch with John, but in spite of their visits to Oxford they sent their own son[g] to Cambridge.

Among Dean Aldrich's Prints in Christ Church Library is a night-piece of Godfridus Schalcken drawn by himself, the Print taken at London in 1694. A Book of Mrs Esther Englishe's Writing. A small Picture set in gold of Bishop Sancroft when aged, a bloom in his face, inclining to a blew as if occasioned by the cold – Two Mandrake Roots.[h]

He noted the windows at Queen's College chapel, Thornhill's altar piece at All Souls and Archbishop Marsh's portrait at Exeter College. He also made additions to his extensive accounts of Blenheim.

Having packed the Bradys off to Caversham he was free to accept a very pleasant invitation from Lady Ashhurst of Waterstock. She was a daughter of the late Sir Thomas Draper of Sunninghill and sister-in-law to that polite scholar John Baber. Her husband, Sir Henry, had recently died but, though the estate had passed to a cousin, Lady Ashhurst was still living there. In future years John was to be connected through marriage with the daughter of the heir,[i] Elizabeth Ashhurst, who became a devoted friend to his daughters.

He rode there on 29 October with Tom Baber and a new friend, Richard Congreve of Christ Church, first cousin once removed to the dramatist. He is already known to history for his habit of drinking herbal tea for breakfast, using sage, colesfoot or balm in this very year, 1733.[11] He was two or three years younger than John and remained in the close circle of friends. The Babers were staying with Lady Ashhurst and after they had dined she showed John the house which had replaced an earlier one in 1695.[j]

At Waterstoke, the Lady Ashhurst's the House is large, built of Brick in the figure of an H. The Tame runs just by. The Church is close to it. The Hall is lofty, in it thirteen good Paintings of Christ and the Apostles; an original Length of King William. Pictures also of Philip of Spain, Husband to Queen Mary and of the Duke d'Alva. The Rooms are handsome and well-sized. Some have family Paintings, several belonging to the Earl of Uxbridge's family which are Relations, one of him that was Ambassador to the Porte.[k] In one Room is a Painting of

---

[g] Nicholas Brady.

[h] These objects can still be identified in Christ Church Library. The mandrake roots or rods were left in a silver box by Dean Fell.

[i] Thomas Ashhurst succeeded his kinsman Sir Henry as owner of Waterstock House in 1732, but the baronetcy became extinct.

[j] This house and its predecessor were close to the river. The third house, built in 1787, was higher up the slope. It was pulled down in 1953, the servant's building being converted into the present house.

[k] William, 6th Baron Paget. The Sublime Porte was the name once given to the government of Turkey (deriving from the high gate giving access to the principal government block in Constantinople).

Robert Boyle. . . it is said on the Picture that the first Sir Henry Ashhurst
of Waterstoke was Executor to him. Mr Baber tells me that Mr Boyle's
Sister was a Dissenter and so commended Ashhurst to her brother.[1] He has
a lank yellow look, truly a very ordinary man, like the Prints of him. A
Painting of the Earl of Holland. Tapestry – the Colours wondrous lively.

One last fling before the winter set in took him to Eynsham to look at the
stone cross and the gates of the Benedictine monastery, of which only one
remained. Then it was time to settle down. Early in December he received a
letter from Charles Hopson.

'Dear Squire,' he wrote, 'Here is an incorrect copy of Lord Pembroke's
Remarks on the Tabulae Votiva, but 'tis easy to amend this when you revisit
Wilton House.'

'This of Jupiter', the Earl had stated, 'proves 8 remarkable things' and he had
proceeded to explain these points at some length. Hopson had copied it all out,
adding, 'I wish you may be able to make more sense of these Remarks than I am
able to do.' He also sent John some descriptions of pictures in the Princess
Royal's apartments at Windsor and with his mind on royalty added a morsel of
London gossip:

The Prince of Orange is upon the mending hand: the Queen stuffs him
with Asses Milk and Wine Broath incessantly. . . Mr Lethieullier has
been so taken up with visiting Relations that I never saw him till the latter
end of last week; he drank a dish of Tea with me yesterday; he comes to live
in Chambers the beginning of next week and then, I hope, we shall be
better acquainted.[12]

This must have been Charles Lethieullier, brother of Smart, who was called to
the Bar in 1734. John evidently knew him and he had been at All Souls for
several years, but there seems to have been no friendship between them.

[1] Probably Robert Boyle's devoted sister, Catherine, Lady Ranelagh, with whom he
lived.

The Waterland Conspiracy
1734 − 1735

The year 1734 was a quiet one with no major adventures and only a few mild sorties to nearby places. This was partly because John was committed to obtaining his Master of Arts degree in June and was determined to allow the proper amount of time for his studies before the examination in April. To this end he went through the course of six Wall lectures, so called because they were usually delivered by the aspiring candidate to the four walls of an empty room. They were looked upon as a mere formality and if read at all some sort of crib or set piece was used. John thought this unethical and was determined to perform the exercise as it was originally intended – as Benwell explains:

> I have heard him declare that while he was residing for a Master of Arts degree at Oxford, his Conscience would not suffer him to omit those six exercises commonly called the Wall lectures, which students are by oath engaged to perform before their admission to that degree. He therefore determined to compose them himself, and for that purpose bought books on the subject to a considerable amount, in which number was Ray on the Creation[1] with many others; and he assured me that by studying the subject on this occasion he became acquainted with many parts of natural history and philosophy which he should otherwise have remained ignorant of all his life.

John entered this achievement in his diary, either with pride or astonishment, and in April, with his friends Thomas Bagshaw and Thomas Bonney, was examined for his Master's degree. On 12 June, as Hearne put it,

Mr John Loveday of Magd, Coll, had his Grace for the Degree of M.A. and was presented to it the same day in the convocation house, a dispensation for Circuiting and Visiting being granted.[2]

During his preparations he had managed to fit in various visits, starting the year off with another look at Fairford church on 9 January. After contemplating the glass and comparing the figure of the Trinity on a brass plate with one he had seen in Beaumaris church, he wrote:

> The Clark says 'tis a tradition that J. Tame built also Rendcombe Church and moreover that he built Barnsley-Inn, about 4 miles off, where he used to refresh himself in the road between Fairford and Rendcombe; one Lambe,[a] a Dissenter belongs to the great house at Fairford.

It is a pity he did not visit Pusey on his way back – so little is known about the house in which the Pusey family lived before the present one was built in 1746–48. He might too, have discovered a distant connection with Mrs Pusey, a daughter of Sir William des Bouveries; John's own great-grandfather's[b] sister, Catherine Lethieullier, had married Jacob Desbouverie in 1630. But all he did was to question the landlord at the inn where he dined. He wanted to hear more about the Pusey Horn which, according to tradition, King Canute was supposed to have given to a Pusey with all the land over which its sound could be heard.

> Mr Denman of the Dragon in Farringdon tells me that the Estate in Pusey held by the Horn is not that which was the Dunches, now in the possession of Mr Nicholls, but an Estate belonging to Pusey of Pusey,[c] whose House (having Brick about the Windows) is near Nicholls's and to which belongs an Estate of about 6 score £ per Annum. More was once held by this horn . . .[d] Denman also tells me he thinks the Barn at Caldecot near Tetbury to be larger than that at Coxwell, but nothing like it for magnificence or elegance of work.

In April he went to Easthampstead to compare the fortifications in the Roman camp with those shown on a copper plate which John Bridges, the Northamptonshire historian, had prepared for Hearne. At Windsor once again, he concentrated particularly on the Tomb House – the chapel built originally for Henry III and restored by Henry VII (now the Albert Memorial Chapel). Many monarchs had tried and failed to put it to some use and it was now at a dismal stage in its history. 'It belongs to the Crown,' said John, 'so the

---

[a] James Lambe, a Presbyterian, married in 1730 Esther Barker of Fairford Park, granddaughter of Andrew and cousin of Elizabeth Fermor.

[b] John Lethieullier (1591–1679).

[c] John Allen Pusey of Pusey House.

[d] John referred to George Hickes's *Thesaurus* in which is a detailed description of the horn (now in the Victoria and Albert Museum).

Church must not be scandalised for the nasty condition in which it now lies, or for its broken Windows.'

On 8 June, just before the Degree ceremony, he spent a day at Ewelme and another at Islip. At Ewelme he added to the notes he had made there in 1733 when he admired the carved woodwork in the roof and the splendid tomb of the Duchess of Suffolk – 'the finest Alabaster and best wrought that I have ever seen'. Islip was the parish where Dr South had lived and for which he had done so much and was also the place from which he had imported Mrs Hammond, later Mrs Henry Smith; so it was of especial interest to John and it was probably not his first visit.

As you go through the Meadows to Islip, the Cherwell affords a beautiful Reach of Water for some time before you cross the bridge at the entrance of Islip. Fronting the bridge is the beautiful Parsonage-house of stone built by Dr South. Islip stands pleasantly on the top and sides of a little rising hill . . . a Throughfare between London and Warwickshire. It is a very good Church, the Chancel built in 1680 by Dr South in a very decent manner. He also founded a Charity-School here for 21 blue-Coat-and-Cap Boys, to be taken out of Islip Parish, if it can find so many; otherwise out of that part of Noke Parish that belongs to Islip or from other neighbouring Parishes; three of the Boys to be prenticed out yearly, 7 pounds to be given with each of 'em; if not so many to be found, fit to be prenticed, the overplus to be bestowed on poor Widows frequenting the Church. The Rector of Islip is Super-visor of the School; but the grand Visitors are the Bishop of Oxford, the Dean and the Senior Prebendary of Westminster. The Statutes of the School, dated 1712, are hung-up in it, ('tis a Stone building). They are most wise and prudent Orders . . .

After quoting the inscription to Dr South over the school door he described Edward the Confessor's stone chapel a little north of the church –

. . . it being 15 yards long and a little above 7 broad. It is now a Barn. The North West corner of it is in a very bad condition. From an Inspection of the East end of it, it seems plain to me, and others, that the Roof of the Chappel was raised when converted into a Barn; and that the Chappel-Roof did not reach so high as the 3 angular Hole, which appears to be made only for owls to go in and out; at present it has no border of Stones round it, as in the Cuts; Concerning the Font that stood in the Chappel in which Edward the Confessor was baptised – see Plot's *Oxfordshire*.

On the North-East part of Islip, low in a bottom is the Court-Close in which stood the Manor-house; the Mote round it, though in most parts filled-up, is still very visible in others. A little higher than the Court-Close is Mr Dickenson's, a Clergyman's, house. He holds an Estate here from the Church of Westminster. Every three years, the

Dean with a Prebendary or two holds Court at Islip. The Estate here was given to the Church of Westminster by Edward the Confessor.
June 11th Mr Hearne says that Edward the Confessor did not build this Chappel.

John had no thoughts of leaving Oxford where he was happy and comfortable and enjoying congenial company. Some of his friends, including Bagshaw, departed (though not out of his life), but among those still there were Winchester, who did not receive his M.A. degree until 1736, William Payne, Pennington, with whom John read classics, and Hasledine. There were new faces too: Matthew Horbery, a clever but modest young divine, was to remain always a close friend; and John had come to know Thomas Tanner on his visits to his father, the Bishop. He also entertained Thomas Waldgrave (later Gibbon's tutor) for the first time this year.

There were comings and goings in the family as well. The marriage of his favourite cousin, Anne Tooke, to Robert Bootle, a captain with the East India Company, had brought a whiff of sea air to the polite villages of Tooting and Clapham. On 23 January Bootle, according to John, had

sailed from the Downs commanding the *London*, a Ship in the Service of the East India Company, of 490 Tons, carrying 98 men and 32 Guns to make one voyage to Canton, China.

It was a long separation for a newly wedded couple. That other connubial pair, Uncle William and Aunt Kitty, had most rashly produced a daughter[e] in April – a girl who was to inherit all her father's waywardness and be more trouble to him than he had ever been to his own long-suffering parents. John met his new aunt and cousin at Caversham for the first time in August and again on his annual visit to his grandmother when his ever-generous uncle presented him with a fine French Psalter. It was Billy Lethieullier who crossed the Irish Sea this year, bringing with him all the latest news from Dublin including the foundation of a new printing house by the benefaction of the Vice-Chancellor.

Before going down at the end of the summer term John wrote a very long account of Oxford Cathedral, conscientiously transcribing every inscription he could find and commenting on the state of the building. Most of the painted glass was broken, the windows were decaying and the church was badly in need of whitewash – 'This and more was sufficiently done in 1736.'

On 28 June he rode, with a companion, to Edgehill on a three-day trip, taking in three country houses on the way. The first of these was the great new mansion at Ditchley recently built from designs by James Gibbs for the second Earl of Litchfield. Kent and some Italians were responsible for the decorations.

---

[e] Catherine Lethieullier.

Ditchley House, the Earl of Lichfield's, stood formerly much lower, where now the Menagerie*f* is, over the old Ditch called Grysne's Ditch; Mr Hearne has been in the old house, in which there was a very long Gallery hung with Pictures.

This house stands high in a Park on the left hand of the Road commanding in full front a good Prospect of Blenheim. 'Tis built of Stone. It is a very neat plain Building; there is a rounding Wall on each side the front and then the offices, on each side also. The Hall is adorned with Stucho-Work, Lord Lichfield's Picture here; 'tis something uncommon to find the Nobleman's Picture in his hall, or indeed Paintings of any but fictitious Persons. The Rooms are not large here; one half the house below Stairs is not yet fitted up. In one of the lower Rooms is a good Piece of James II when Duke of York and his Dutchess and their two daughters . . .

Among a number of portraits he noticed one of Henry VIII – 'his Beard would have been shaved closer by our modern Painters' – and another of Charles I with his eldest son which exactly resembled a picture at Newbottle House. 'There is a most charming Painting in Miniature of the lovely Dutchess of Cleveland and her little daughter*g* by King Charles II who was Mother to the present Lord Lichfield.' But on this occasion he did not mention the Duchess's full-length portrait or that of Charles II. Here too was the famous picture of Queen Elizabeth standing on the 'Carpet Map' of England and some good coloured tapestry.

Some extremely neat and plain fret-work Cielings to the Rooms below. In the making of the Stair-Case they have well avoided the grand schemes on the one hand and the pitiful new-fashioned Italian Stair-cases on the other; this is not wide or grand at all, but wondrous neat and pleasing, particularly for that it takes up the least Room that I ever saw, though it reaches to the top of the house, where a Window from the Leads affords it a sufficient Light. Here is a Cabinett curiously inlaid with different stones in such a manner that their native Colours represent Birds, Beasts, Fruits &c. The Furniture, as the Beds and Chairs, of Mohair, Coffoy, Worsted-Damask &c. Some Chairs of my Lady's Work. The Chimney-pieces are all of different kinds of Marble. Some are of Derbyshire; there are some curious Marble Tables. In the little Chappel, the Altar-piece is a dead Christ. There are good Offices under ground. There are no Gardens here, but a very pretty Terrace is almost finished to a back-front, separated from the Park.

(His comment on Italian staircases did not indicate a dislike of Palladian

---

f This seems to be the only reference to a menagerie at Ditchley at this time.
g Charlotte Fitzroy married Edward Lee, 1st Earl of Litchfield.

architecture but of the inferior designs which were often reproduced in order to be in the fashion.)

Having dealt with Ditchley Park he went straight on to the house only half a mile away which belonged to the Brownes, an old Roman Catholic family. George Browne did not succeed to the baronetcy until the death of his father, Sir Charles, in 1751. He was the model for Sir Plume in Pope's *The Rape of the Lock*.

> Mr Brown, son of Sir Charles Brown, Bart. has a large old Stone Seat at Nether Kiddington. It stands upon a little Hill, close surrounded by rising Grounds; it is a most retired Countrey-Place; the Church stands just by the house, the Browns are Roman Catholics. In the Gardens on a Pedestal stands the Font[h] in which King Edward the Confessor was baptised. It stood in the Chappel at Islip; there is a modern Inscription on the stand of the Font (but now with great difficulty legible). It is printed in *Robert of Gloucester*[3] and there is a draught of it in Plot's *Oxfordshire*. The Outside of the Bason-part is (as there represented) Octagonal, but the Inside is not so but circular. We saw some of the Rooms below Stairs in which are some good family Pictures . . . Contemplation is finely described in the picture of a Nun of this family.

On they went, having presumably stopped to sustain themselves, to Heythrop, which was then owned by the 13th Earl of Shrewsbury, a Roman Catholic priest who did not live there. This house was burnt down in 1831 and rebuilt in 1870.

> Haythorp, the Earl of Shrewsbury's, stands in a pleasant Park. It is reckoned to have as elegant a front as most houses. It is built of Stone and by the look of it it cannot be many years since.[i] There are 11 Windows in the front, which is adorned with Corinthian Pilasters, and the Portico upheld by 4 easy light Pillars of the same Order. The Building is not high, it is much ornamented, even to the very Chimneys. A Ballustrade of Stone on the top of the house. In the same Line with the front, and on each side of it, runs a Wall which has four openings in it, discovering a very large View of the adjacent Countrey towards Enstone &c. for the house stands very high on the edge of an hill. The Beauty of these Openings is discovered when you approach to the front through the Park; there you have in View the most elegant Work of Art and at the same time view

---

[h] In his *History of Kiddington* (1738), Thomas Warton described the font and thought it was of a later date. He too criticized the engraving by Michael Burghers. The decorations of fourteenth-century character might have been cut on an older tub. The modern inscription was put there by the Brownes (*V.C.H., Oxon*, IV). The font was taken from Islip to Kiddington in 1666 by Sir Henry Browne and presented to Middleton Stoney about 1866.

[i] The Duke of Shrewsbury bought the manor and estates in 1697. Building of Heythrop Hall began in 1705 and was completed in 1716.

Nature in great Variety, each adorning the other. But to this open Wall there joins at right Angles (on each side also) another Wall of the same height and length with the open Wall, but it is closed, yet has 4 blind openings in it; from this Wall (on each side) in a line are the Stables, built in a rougher Stile, but proper to the occasion.

John and his friend put up at the inn on Edgehill kept by Mrs French and Tom, probably her son. This was the Sunrising, well known to travellers in later years. The French family were to become good friends to John and he was to stay with them frequently.

> Mother Frenches is in Tysoe Parish, the Church we were at. It stands in the Vale on the left hand as you descend from Edge-hill, whence one may see Warwick, Coventry, the Malvern hills in Worcestershire and the Clee hills in Shropshire with the Wrekin, as the People say. There do not seem to be many villages in the Vale, yet there are several which lie concealed among the Trees. Great part of the Vale is called the Vale of Red Horse, the Soil being red hereabouts. The Barn in the Lane a furlong before Sunrising (so Mother Frenches is called though there never was any Sign) is in Gloucestershire.

The final port of call was Brackley, a place of special interest as the school in the ancient Hospital of St John and St James was annexed to Magdalen College.

> Leland says 'There is a Church as a Chaple of Ease of Seint James in the South end of the Towne, an old pece of Worke.' The Minister (T. Bowles) has shut up this Church, refusing to perform Service here as was used to be done once a Sunday and once a Sunday at St. Peter's.

Leland had called it a poor town and it was still poor enough, said John, but he admired the 'very good Stone Market-house and Town-house over it supported on Arches'. He added, 'There is but one Dissenter in the Town and that is a Presbyterean.' He did not have strong feelings about dissenters – indeed one of them, Professor John Ward of Gresham College, was to be one of his dearest friends. It was the number of isolated zealots to be found that was surprising, for only a man of very deep convictions, or an exhibitionist, could in those days have lived in a community of opposing views.

Most of his account concerned the old Hospital, or College. Of its present state he said:

> One of the old College Rooms below Stairs is the School-house, where 6 Boys (if I mistake not) are taught to write, read and cast accounts gratis. The People say, that they ought to be taught Latin. Magdalen College joins the Schoolmaster's Place to the Living of Imley [Evenley] a mile off; Dr Knibb receives £13. 6. 8. per Annum for the School. He puts in a Schoolmaster who lives in the School-house and has that and the Garden

belonging to it for his trouble. The Schoolmaster's house is a good one.
There is an Hall and Parlor in the Old Buildings where Magdalen
College keep Court and are entertained by their Tenants once a Year.
The hidden foundation of the old Buildings extends over a large Spot
of Ground.

The paving had gone in the College church and some of the tombs were
robbed of their brass.

About half a year ago a Gentlewoman was buryed here when they let a
little light, or rather gloom, into the Church; before the Windows were
altogether stopped up close . . . There was a Bell in the Tower, but it was
removed to Oxford when Magdalen College newcast their Bells into
eight, not many years since.

William Payne came down to Caversham in September and was taken to
dinner with Mr Pryse of Hurst[j] and shown the portrait on wood of Walter
Devereux, Earl of Essex, which hung in the parlour. 'His hair upon the head is
black, upon the beard 'tis red,' said John, inspired by an excellent meal. Next
day he took his friend to see the pin manufactury at the Oracle in Reading, a
building which consisted of workshops and tenements. He took the
opportunity of adding to his Reading notes, most of which have been used by
Charles Coates in his *History of Reading*; but Coates only used a part of those
which emanated from a conversation with Mr Hiley when John took Payne to
see his old master – probably because they applied to 1734 and the people in the
houses were long dead when Coates wrote his book. He did not always
attribute the statements to John but anything from the mouths of Mr Hiley or 'a
very accurate observer' were taken from these scraps of paper.

Mr Hiley said that . . . the Infirmary stood along that side of the Forbury
where Mrs Eades's house is and that the round Tower and the Lodgings
belonging to it were part of it. The Area of the Abbey Church is now a
Garden belonging to the house that Mr Betterton, the Actor, lived in and
where now lives Mrs Vaughan.[k] The Garden is terminated by the East
Wall. The Cross Isle is stopped up on both sides. There seems to have been
a great Door into the Church in the North of the Body. There was a
smaller Door in the same Wall near the very East End. How far the Church
extended Westward is not known; Willis imagines it to have been built in

---

[j] From information kindly given by Mr John Finch it is clear that Pryse's house was not
Hurst Grove. This belonged to John Dalby, who was a guest with John, H. J. Hiley, Zinzan,
Jennings and others on 31 August 1731. The house must have belonged to Mrs Pryse or her
grandson, George Langton, who left his property to his step-grandfather when he died in
1738. See p. 59 n.*g.* and p. 103 n.*l.* It cannot have been Hurst House, as other people are
known to have lived there.

[k] Philip Vaughan had died on 5 March 1734, aged forty-six, and his widow had left
Basildon Rectory. He left money to St Laurence's and to St Giles's churches in Reading.

the form of a Cross with a tower. The shell of the Refectory is standing. Hogs are now kept in it . . .

The final visit, and one of the most interesting which John made in 1734, was to Cliveden. He rode there from Caversham on 10 October.

Cliffden, the Earl of Orkney's is in Buckinghamshire and Taplow Parish. It was built by George Villiers, Duke of Buckingham who dyed in 1687. Buckingham House in the Mall built by the Marquis of Normanby[l] seems to be very much on the Plan of this. The Materials of it are Brick chiefly. It is situate on a very high Hill, much higher than that on which Windsor Castle stands. There are 3 Stories to the grand front and 9 Windows in a Story; the Building seems full high for the width of it; it was surely monstrous before a 4th Story was taken down. From the house on each side runs a rounding Colonnade of Stone in the Ionic Order, at the end of which is a smaller and low House built of Brick. The Stables and other out-offices are long Buildings on each side yet farther distant from the Body of the House and sealed more backward. The House is exposed to the Winds every way. The Garden-Front has a grand appearance; it appears higher than the grand Front as the Garden-Ground is there considerably lower than the Ground on the other side, except towards the front where you see a ridge of the Berkshire Hills.

The Prospect from the Garden is most unbounded, the Thames flows at the bottom of it, but it is at a great Distance from the higher parts of the Garden; in some Places the Descent to the River is almost a Perpendicular and very terrible. The good large Village of Cookham (where the Church is also large) lies on the other side of the Water, just upon it. The Trees in the Garden are forced to be upheld by Ropes, otherwise the Winds would tear them down, On both sides the Garden there are Woods; one of them is within the Garden-Pales; there are several Walks in it and Vistas cut through it. The whole of the Garden (excepting the Wood itself but not the Walks in it) may contain 100 Acres.

As for the inside of the house, most of the Rooms are wainscotted with Spanish Oak. Several have fret-work Cielings. Here is a Picture of that Duke of Hamilton that was beheaded. It looks exactly like that piece at Windsor Castle which Hanneman painted.

A list of portraits follows, one comment being that the Countess of Orkney had a 'lewd look',[m] and then John continued:

[l] John Sheffield, Earl of Mulgrave and Marquess of Normanby, built Buckingham House on land granted by the Crown in 1703, the year he was created Duke of Buckinghamshire and Normanby.
[m] More probably due to her having 'squinted like a dragon' according to Swift (D.N.B.) than to her having been William III's mistress.

I know no Tapestry that excells Lord Orkney's; 'twas made at Brussels on purpose for him; the Colours are extremely lively, yet that is the least commendation of the Arras. 'Tis of the Siege of Lisle, of the Battle in the Woods &c. In the latter, the old Miller that was so good a friend to the English, is sitting smoaking his pipe . . . [and so on].

The Stair-Case is very handsome, the Stairs are of Walnut-Tree and the Landing-Places are of Walnut-Tree inlaid.

John's account confirms the existence of a fourth storey in the original house." He returned in September 1737 when it belonged to the Countess of Orkney, wife of the Earl of Inchiquin.° Surprisingly he did not mention the temples erected by Leoni in 1735 but he saw the 'noble Gravel-Terrace, to be ascended by many steps', from which you could see Windsor Castle.

Yet high as this house is situate, you look down on it from Pen in Bucks. One might . . . expect a View of many Villages and Churches, but 'tis not so. The Wood without the Garden-Pales towards Taplow is said to have fine Walks in it, whence a rather finer View than from the Garden.

The summer feastings and functions had continued as usual, but this time when John and Charles Hopson attended the school speeches there was a stranger present, though he was not unknown to Dr Merrick and Mr Hiley. He turned up for tea at the headmaster's house and they discovered that he was a Spanish gentleman called Don Lewis des los Torres and that he was extremely popular with everyone. They learned that he had been chaplain to the Spanish Embassy but had only the previous year renounced the errors of the Church of Rome before Dr Zachary Pearce at St Martin-in-the-Fields.[P] He was now out of a job and had come to Reading with Dr Holmes, the Vice-Chancellor. This supporting role was very pleasant but not much use to a man who had nothing to live on. However, the Vice-Chancellor had become a strenuous champion and shortly after their return to Oxford he issued a printed statement extolling Don Lewis's virtues and explaining that several 'good hands' and particularly Dr Daniel Waterland (the Master of Magdalene College, Cambridge) and the Bishop of London[q] had judged him worthy of officiating as a Minister of the Church of England. He had apparently translated the New Testament into the

." The original house built by the 2nd Duke of Buckingham was bought in 1696 by George Hamilton (later Earl of Orkney). He talked of lowering it in a letter to his brother of 1705. The greater part of the house was destroyed by fire in 1795. See Gervase Jackson-Stops, *Cliveden*, The National Trust, 1978.

° The Earl of Orkney's daughter, Anne, succeeded as Countess of Orkney on his death in 1737. She was the wife of the 4th Earl of Inchiquin. In 1739 she leased Cliveden to Frederick, Prince of Wales.

P Information in a notice written by the Vice-Chancellor, Dr William Holmes, recommending Don Lewis; transcribed by John Loveday, 5 November 1734.

q Edmund Gibson.

Minorcan language, hoping to be sent there as chaplain, but at the moment he was 'destitute of any subsistence'. However, he seemed to be doing quite well on charm and John was captivated by it. Over the following months he and the Spaniard met or wrote to each other at every opportunity.

So 1734 petered out with nothing much else to record except one undated entry in the diary:

Sam. Johnson, one year at Pembroke College; Son of a Bookseller in Lichfield, now living in Birmingham.

There was no fame attached to Samuel Johnson in those days and there is no evidence that John had met him; yet he thought it worth while to make this note. He had probably heard about Johnson's abilities from Richard Congreve, whose brother Charles had been at the same school at Lichfield.

Early in 1735 John entered upon a correspondence with the Master of Magdalene College, Cambridge which lasted until the latter's death in 1740. It may seem strange that Dr Waterland, then in his fifty-fourth year and a scholar of great repute, should wish to write regularly to an unknown Oxford graduate aged twenty-four, but the fact is that he was coming, slowly but surely, to appreciate John's own scholarship – his attention to detail, his meticulous references as well as his familiarity with all matters concerning the Anglican faith and the heresies perpetrated against it. There was also a comic side to the whole Waterland affair, not only because of the part played in it at first by Don Lewis, but also because of the subterfuges to which the participants resorted to conceal their collusions. Nearly all Waterland's letters to John were published by William Van Mildert in his *Works of Dr Daniel Waterland* in 1828 but the full story of Don Lewis was not told.

It was probably through his talks with Don Lewis, who seems to have been acting temporarily as a secretary to Waterland, that John conceived an idea whereby he could assist an important theologian and promote a promising one, while satisfying his own desire to be useful to each. Waterland, who has been called the most learned of contemporary divines[4] and who was greatly encouraged and protected by Bishop Edmund Gibson, published his pamphlets from a deep sense of commitment to the established church. He had replied to Matthew Tindal's *Christianity as Old as the Creation*[5] in 1734 with *The Importance of the Doctrine of the Holy Trinity Asserted*. For this he had been attacked in print by the Yorkshire rector of Rossington, John Jackson, who had been the mouthpiece[r] of the Arian Dr Samuel Clarke and was now a prolific writer of undistinguished tracts. The religious arguments are well known and this is not the place to discuss them in detail. Waterland, of course, did not really need any defence against an adversary whom he could have dispatched with ease, but he was a man of some dignity and preferred not

[r] See *D.N.B.* Jackson had published criticisms of Waterland from 1723.

to demean himself. All the same it was tiresome not to be able to refute Jackson's arguments, and when John's plan was unfolded he was undeniably acquiescent.

It all began when John wrote to Don Lewis, probably on 16 December 1734.

If you have seen a Pamphlet wrote by a Country Clergyman against Dr Waterland's *Importance of the Trinity*, I doubt not but you think with your friends here that had the Author left out Scurrility and personal Reflections his Pamphlet had been reduced to much smaller compass; upon the whole it appears so despicable a performance that some persons make, 'tis said, a doubt whether Dr Waterland will himself take any notice of it. If the Doctor should take it into consideration, you may save yourself the trouble of reading the remaining part of this Letter; otherwise 'tis observed that such Books are industriously spread about where those Treatises that might be Antidotes to 'em may never have appeared. But this we do not presume to judge of. It may be necessary that some short strictures be made upon this Piece.

A Gentleman of my Acquaintance has lately read all Dr Waterland's works upon the Trinity and is well satisfyed that the main Objections occurring in the Country Clergyman's Pamphlet have been obviated long since in the Doctor's works. Now it would very much expose the Pamphleteer's disingenuous way of proceeding to draw out his main arguments and subjoin Answers to them in the very words of Dr W. referring to the pages of each book from whence they are extracted. This my friend has thoughts of doing if no notice should be taken of the Piece by any other hand; but even in that Case he will not presume to do it without leave first obtained from Dr W. And also the farther favour of revising the Piece before it be put to the Press. I beg of Don Lewis to mention the Contents of this Letter to no Person but Dr W., and not to him if you think the Proposal impertinent; in such case I will give you my word that the Design shall be entirely dropt.[6]

The scene was set. Having been apprized by Don Lewis, the worthy Doctor now entered the stage with all the assurance of the principal actor.[7] On 1 January he wrote to John to say that though he had no thoughts of taking any public notice himself of Mr Jackson's 'romancing and railing' he should not be sorry to have some strictures made upon it in such a way as John had hinted. He then proceeded to 'make a few observations' on Jackson's piece at great length, with directions as to how it should be tackled by John's unknown friend, and concluded:

If the gentleman pleases to write but on one side the papers, and to have a Blank page all the way, and will afterwards favour me with a sight of them, there will be room for me to supply any thing material upon the Blank pages.[8]

A day or two later another letter arrived from Don Lewis which John found rather annoying. Again he kept a copy of his reply.

Revd. Sir – I received two letters from you last week; Dr Waterland also honoured us with another, which by no means requiring an answer – for it would be superfluous to say that his Directions shall be obeyed in every particular – we judged it might be impertinent and presuming to trouble the Doctor with one –. . . now I am writing to you to return our humble thanks for his Observations which my friend has now lying before him; to whom whatever farther the Doctor shall send shall be faithfully transmitted which will be a very great Assistance to him. You desire to know his name; I have not his leave to divulge it; so you will agree with me that 'tis a point of honour not to mention it. The Contents of this Letter you perceive must not be mentioned.[9]

Here was the first hint of perfidy and when Dr Waterland heard of it he was furious, for it was of the greatest importance that he should not know who was so faithfully copying his notes and writing on one side of the paper. He wrote from Windsor where through Bishop Gibson's influence he held a canonry.[s]

I intend, God willing, to send you what I promised by the Return of the Carrier; or else by Don Lewis if he should meet you sooner. I was not well pleased that he had been enquiring after the Gentleman's name, and was glad you did not oblige him in an imprudent Request. I had rather not know, that I may afterwards safely and truly say that I do not know who or what the gentleman is. If he has any occasion to write to me, he may write without setting any name, and I can direct my Answer to you with your good Leave.

He hoped the gentleman would not mind receiving further notes which he could eventually consign to the flames and concluded with many instructions as to how to crush Jackson.[10]

The gentleman in question, who was soon to be known simply as 'Mr Anonymous', was none other than John's shy friend Matthew Horbery. For all his fine figure and excellent voice in the pulpit – and his considerable intellectual ability – he was completely unworldly and needed someone to push or pull him in the right direction. He had learnt to rely on John (who was four years his junior) ever since he had first drunk tea in his rooms the previous summer.

From his copy of his next letter to Waterland it is clear that John wrote at first in a flowery – almost fulsome – way; but on reading it through his common sense seems to have prevailed and he crossed out the affectations. Rather pompously, he said that his friend would take farther occasion to animadvert on the Adversary's frequent breach of moral probity,

---

[s] He was also vicar of Twickenham and Archdeacon of Middlesex.

decency and veracity as he found that to be a method which the Doctor approved.

The moral attitude displayed by the three conspirators was disingenuous to say the least. Compared with Don Lewis, admittedly, they were virtue itself, but for all their honourable intentions they thought nothing of deceptions that would mislead their acquaintances without quite ranking as lies. Waterland himself, as the plot developed, revealed a talent for turning one blind eye while maintaining a vigilant supervision with the other. He was soon assured that he might delete anything he said 'in a heat' before the work went to press.

When he wrote from Twickenham in March Don Lewis was still in favour.

> Poor Don will find it hard to get a comfortable subsistence amongst us. I perceive that his Top-friends in Town think of nothing higher than a Curacy for him in England (when such a Thing can be had) and as to the Minorca-affair there is no liklihood of its succeeding while Mr Achmooty has no prospect of moving to a better Preferment. Mrs Titchburne [Don Lewis's Patroness] is continuing to send Don Lewis into Suffolke, to board with his countryman Dr Brugatts and to exercise himself there for a twelve-month in Parish Duties.[11]

Perhaps Don Lewis decided himself that if it meant being immured for a year in a Suffolk parish, the game was hardly worth the candle. He had been petted and spoiled in the social and academic circles of both the Universities and was hardly the man to visit the poor at the behest of a rich old lady – at least not for so long. The denouncement came in a letter from Waterland dated 28 March 1735, which Van Mildert did not print.

> I was sorry that your Carrier failed us here (at Windsor) last Tuesday. Otherwise I had sent up Wesseling' as I promised. I think of returning to Twickenham tomorrow and there to stay some time. If I can contrive to send the Book by London I will. The chief design of my writing now is to give caution about Don Lewis. Mrs Titchburne, his chief Patroness, and Dr Pearce who reconciled him and who both recommended him first to me, have discovered him to be a very ill man and given me notice of it. He went up to Town some weeks agoe, and there he is; I do not expect to see him any more. Probably, he will make off in a little time. By the Accounts sent me, he has a Wife and Children in Westminster and seems to have pretended himself a Convert only for a Screen to himself, and to sharp money where he could. I have had suspicions of him for some Time, but charitably believed the best as long as I could. I helped him at Cambridge, having then a very good opinion of him. I began to doubt a little of him when

---

' Peter Wesseling's work *Probabilium Liber Singularis &c.* (Frankfurt, 1731) was evidently used to correct Jackson's interpretation. See William Van Mildert, *The Works of the Rev. Daniel Waterland, D.D.* (1735), vol. X, p. 415.

he went to Oxford, but could not charge any thing upon him. He made use of my Lord of London's and Dr Pearce's and my name there; as he had deceived us all; but now he is detected I shall take the best care I can to prevent my name's being any more used in his favour . . .[12]

This crossed a letter from John informing him that the papers were now ready and would be sent by the Oxford coach to Mr Warcupp's at the White Lion near Charing Cross.

[The papers] are now, Sir, with the utmost deference to be laid before you with sincere acknowledgment that whatever shall be found good in them my friend can pretend no claim to. If the manner in which he (who is but a young Writer) has drawn them up, be confused, Repetitions too often occurring, if the Language in the general be juvenile and unbecoming the gravity of Subject, if there be many other great faults (as we are apprehensive there may be) it would be unreasonable to trouble you with so thorough a correction of them as is requisite. As Mr Anonymous enterprised this matter (I dare answer for him) it will be entirely agreeable to his way of thinking to smother the Piece if it shall be found inadequate to the designed effect; in short if you disapprove of it in whole or in part, my friend will be very content to lock it in his Box without any inclination to impose a crude Scribble upon the world.[13]

One can imagine that Horbery dictated those words. Next day John wrote again:

We are amazed at Don Lewis; we cannot fathom his Scheme, if he really was Chaplain to the Spanish Embassy and threw himself out of his place by declaring himself a Protestant.[14]

That was all he said about Don Lewis. The man had been his friend and in the first shock he wished to withhold his comments. Instead he asked Waterland about another fraud which had been played on them both. A woman had called on him in 1732 and again in 1734 with a long story of poverty. Her mother, she said, was a daughter of the deprived Bishop Mackenzie of Orkney and she subsisted on little more than £4 a year paid by Dr Waterland from the Earl of Thanet's" charity. John had given her two moidores out of pity, but the second time she came with an even more elaborate story. Hearing that she had previously begged at Bath and Marlborough and even from Mr Finch of Trinity College, he became suspicious. The Doctor had no illusions: the mother had been an impudent cheat, he replied; her name was Douglas and she had left the real Mrs Mackenzie to 'starve like a jay' after stealing her papers. If the daughter troubled John again he should put her into the hands of a constable; and Don Lewis was no better, said Waterland, warming up to the scandalous truth. He was only waiting to see Mrs Titchburne to get the whole

" The 6th Earl of Thanet was a benefactor, while living and in his will, to many charities.

story. Don Lewis had never been a chaplain and the charges against him now were

> running after women, telling of many extravagant lies, frequent swearing and using many sharping Tricks to get money and contract debts. I have a letter from Don this very morning, protesting his Innocence, and begging me to suspend my judgment.

The Doctor now knew that he had been cheated of £40 and, even worse, the culprit had been charged at Windsor with two bastards, though the case had not been proved.

> It is certain he loves to be toying with young girls and I know that he almost inveigled a young Women to be in love with him at Windsor, for I saw and read one of her Love-letters to him. Such conduct of his is very odd, especially when he has a wife of his own.[15]

John replied that Mr Baber, with whom he had been staying, would be shocked at the account, having been a good friend to that 'abandoned Spaniard'. He added a paragraph which he decided not to sent to Waterland after all:

> The Don told us himself that he was twice charged with Bastards at Windsor; then I was entirely inclined to think it a Calumny of the exasperated Papists.[16]

So Don Lewis disappeared into the side streets of London and out of Waterland's life, but not quite out of John's. The conspirators returned to the exciting prospect of the pamphlet's publication.

There had been some hitches, John reported:

> Mr Anonymous, because he was anonymous, met with some difficulties in the publication . . . however it is now finished at the Press . . .[17]

and he ended his letter with a hint that a prelate had taken notice of Anonymous. Waterland, who was by now ready to learn his name, caught it beautifully. He was highly pleased with the finished work which showed 'the gentleman and the scholar' and inquired to which 'great Prelate' John referred.

> I will tell you whether it be proper for Anonymous to own his Performance there. I know pretty well how men stand affected, having a general Acquaintance.[18]

The Bishop, replied John, was Smalbroke of Lichfield[v] 'but be it ever so proper to own this Performance there, I so well know the excessive modesty of Mr Anonymous that he would never be able to open the matter to his Lordship.'[19] By 15 July Waterland was able to say he was glad that Mr A. was so

---

[v] The bishop had been translated from St Davids to Lichfield and Coventry in 1731.

happily fixed with a person who would 'esteem his merit' and hoped 'his Lordship might discover it publickly'; but he added a few words to intimate that he would now like to learn his identity and to meet him.[20] This gave John the lead he wanted and he wrote in September, after his summer ramble, to disclose Horbery's name; but only Waterland, and if possible Bishop Smalbroke, must know. The curtain must not fall too quickly; Horbery should wait on the Doctor when he passed through Oxford on his way to Bath. But Waterland had come to the conclusion that it was safe for the world now to know the name of his defender. He wrote from Twickenham:

> I see now no reason for keeping it secret; the end I had in view is already answered by concealing it hitherto. However I have discovered no farther yet to anyone but that he is a Fellow of a College in Oxford. One Gentleman told me the other day that he heard his name. I asked him to tell it me, but he said he had forgott; so the discourse ended . . . Every Body that has seen the Book speaks well of it and none can justly do otherwise. Jackson has seen it and calls it mine, which is his way. He was told that I neither was the Author nor knew the Author . . . he referred to the Preface as discovering private things. The gentleman told him in return that he saw no discoveries in the Preface more than had been made long agoe in a Printed Preface of mine; as indeed there are not. But that raving Creature loves to ascribe to me every Thing written on my side; that the orthodox Cause may be represented as resting upon a single man . . .[21]

The achievement was Horbery's, but as the shrewd Jackson suspected the material was nearly all Waterland's. So a happy ending was secured for the trio – Waterland was vindicated, Horbery got his prebendary stall, John had pulled off a *coup*; and if Jackson was crushed it had no effect at all on his literary output.

The winter of 1735 followed the usual course at Oxford. The weather was very bad in January and the high winds damaged the house at Caversham and tore a gallows tree out by the roots. At the end of the month a letter arrived from John Peareth in Newcastle full of that ingenious youth's tittle-tattle. The good companion of the 1732 tour had decided to go to London.

> The reason is this. I'm resolved to study the Law and by taking a Master of Arts Degree may have the privilege of being called to the Bar in three years after I'm entered, tho' I'm not actually Master of Arts when I enter. Now after I had made the resolution I thought 'twould be very foolish to let one term slip and if an actual residence, which I find by my Friends is not, had been absolutely necessary for my keeping the term I must have been in town before the latter end of the month. I can't say but I was in some sort of a Panic on the account of travelling now the roads are so

extremely bad, and the waters overflowed to such a degree. The poor Boy last week run in imminent danger of his life, for he waited six hours longer than his usual time on account of the floods at Ferry Bridge, yet I saw that the letters were quite wet that he brought. Mrs Peareth [his cousin] has gone through her salivation and both the maid and child; the last two are perfectly recovered and Mrs P., except a few red spots in her face which the Doctor ascribes to the Calomel having sharpened and violently agitated her blood.

Peareth was fascinated by medical details and parts of his letters are almost unreadable. John must be told about the 'poor child swelled by quicksilver', but 'saved by a dose of Manna', and Mrs Russell whose bones looked rotten, but who had kindly lent her 'Paraphernalia of flannel to a Lady who took to her chamber the latter end of last week'. Without going into further details, as Peareth did, it would appear that the infection was not smallpox but a pox of a different nature. Having dealt with these intimate matters concerning the ladies, he switched suddenly to poetry and archaelogy. Of George Lyttleton he wrote:

I like Littleton's poem much.[w] I fancy he will be a very good Poet for he seems to improve. I hear Pope has published one or two things lately but I have not seen them yet. Pandon Gate is almost in a line with St. Nicholas so that the Picts Wall, if it went through St. Nicholas Church yard must almost necessarily run along near Pandon to Tingemouth [Tynemouth]. I have not spoken to the Sexton, for . . . 'twould be a foolish question, for 'tis doubly improbable he should dig to any remains of the Picts Wall when we consider how prodigiously the ground of the Church yard must have been raised since the Church was built. I know not whether you was told when you was here that the upper town is by far the oldest and that the Sandhill and other parts of the lower town were a sand bank and overflowed whenever the tide was in, many years after the upper town was built. I saw the other day the Church which is the Mother Church to these four. I hope you'll excuse my forgetting the Name, though I'll take care to ask it again and set it down in black and white.

He had a good deal to say about the Cartmel well where a man had told him he had been cured of the itch three times by drinking twelve to fourteen gills and where his friend Mr Russell had once been sent with a sore on his leg the size of a large pin's head 'and in a short time, I can't say whether by inward or outward application, or by both, he was perfectly cured'. This reminded

[w] George Lyttleton's poem *The Progress of Love* (the first eclogue dedicated to Pope and all four corrected by him for the press) came out in 1732, followed in 1733 by *Advice to a Lady*.

him that John and he had missed seeing a pitch well when they were in Shropshire and he had lately heard that

> in the summer time there is a sort of slimy substance which swims on the surface of the water. – this the People skim off and make Pitch of. The well is 6 or 8 miles from Shrewsbury.

Peareth came now to the real point of his letter – he had been crossed in love. He had been in the habit of calling on the Clavering family who lived at Axwell Park, a castle in County Durham. This time he had been refused admittance on account of the desperate condition of Lady Clavering which he described in detail:

> I have not seen her or either of the young Ladies since I have been here, she has been so very ill, yet for all that a lover who came about the same time I did was admitted and 'tis reported exceedingly well liked; he is the only child to the Earl of Shelbourne, perhaps you may have heard something of him; he was in the Bastille some years ago on account of a Murder that was committed where he was in company though he was perfectly innocent of the fact; yet it cost his father a deal of money to get him out of Limbo, besides the King's own Letter to demand him as a Subject of England. He is by all accounts a meer toupèe, all dance and song. I should be glad if you know or have heard anything of Lord Shelbourne if you would give me his Character – here are such opposite and different accounts of him one does not know which to beleive . . .[22]

Elizabeth Clavering married the notorious Lord Dunkeron three years later, shortly after he had cut his valet's fingers off in a rage.[23] She was said to be a most unhappy bride[x] and only lived five more years. She would have had a much better chance of survival with Peareth.

---

[x] *Wentworth Papers, 1705–39,* p. 529. See also *The Complete Peerage* under 'Shelburne'. Lady Lucy Wentworth, in a letter dated 8 January 1737 wrote: 'The most unhappy body I know is Miss Clavering who was married yesterday to my Lord Dunkerrin [Dunkeron] for I never heard any man have so bad a character; he has lately almost killed his servant.'

North, East and Farewell to Hearne

1735

February 5. 1735. This day the Fellows received their Fellowships; the very Junior Class had a demand of 55£, baiting 5s. besides a Room and Battles. The very Senior Fellowships were not above 10£ better, for the revenues of the year were chiefly in Fines in which the whole Society bear an equal share. [Diary.]

Hearne's health had been worrying his friends for several months. He himself thought he had 'the stone', but there were other possibilities and he went into some detail describing his symptoms. Certainly he was unable to digest his food properly and suffered permanently from gastric disorders. He had become more of a recluse, locking himself into his rooms at Edmund Hall for hours at a time, but this could be partly explained by the nature of his illness. His idiosyncratic behaviour had always caused comment and there is no real proof of the suggestion that he had become even more peculiar.[1] Unfortunately Dr Richard Mead, who acted as his consultant, could not come as far as Oxford to see him at this time and his prescriptions could only be sent from London by post. His personal physician, Dr Frewin, did all he could but there was no improvement.

Anxious as he was about his old friend, John can have had no idea of any imminent danger when he made his plans for his next long ramble. After hearing Mr Seed of Queen's preach the Easter sermon he paid the visit to the Babers at Sunninghill that he had mentioned to Waterland. He returned to Oxford and left again for Caversham on 30 April. He wrote to Hearne on

4 May, a letter which has not been preserved but which it is evident from Hearne's reply of 8 May accompanied a present of marmalade – about the most unfortunate gift the poor man could have received in his condition. This is one of Hearne's last letters and shows that mentally he was still alert, though unable to write at length because of pain.

> I received your Antiquity from London, and I heartily thank you for it, as I do for your Letter. I have eat of it and believe it may be very good, but indeed I am not (that I can perceive) any thing better than I was. Dr Frewin is expected constantly in Town. Both he and Dr Mead sent me new directions, and I now follow them, but the effect does not yet answer expectation. The Marmarlade (it seems) is fourteen years old. I thank you for your intelligence about Scurlock and Dart, with whose characters I was not unacquainted before.
>
> Mr Baber (to whom always my most humble Service) being curious in the old Greek Authors may have made it his business to have furnished himself well with the ancient Greek Lexicographers and I believe he is very capable of improving and correcting divers of the corruptions that have crept into them. The Etymologicon Magnum[2] is one of those books, but it is scarce, and should be reprinted. Great Improvements might be made to that work from the Baroccian MSS and other unpublished Greek Pieces that lie hid in Libraries. Marquardus Gudius was admirably furnished with things of that kind, and he was willing enough to communicate what he had to persons, whom he judged capable of making a right use of them . . .

Hearne elaborated on this theme still further and described how learned Greek grammarians and critics had collected glosses from the margins of old Greek manuscripts and turned them into one common alphabet,

> an undertaking which proved of signal service. The like method was taken among the Latins. For many Latin Classicks being glossed, the Glosses were in length of time gathered into one alphabet, and gave original to the Catholicon and our common Dictionaries. The consideration of which hath oftentimes made me take pleasure in turning our oldest Latin Dictionaries, where I have sometimes found explications very diverting tho' uncommon. But my pains will not permitt me to be larger. . .

Busy as he was with preparations for his tour to the Peak country it was a relief to John to know he would be able to stop for the first night at Oxford and see for himself how Hearne was faring. Meanwhile, ten days before his departure, a new visitor came to Caversham. The Revd John Burton of Corpus Christi College, Fellow of Eton and newly appointed vicar of Mapledurham, was to spend many days and nights there in the future. John knew him slightly and gave him a warm welcome. Although Burton was some fifteen years older, in terms of classical scholarship they were not so far apart and though he spent a good deal of time at Eton he was an acquisition as a neighbour.

Charles Hopson had elected to come the whole way with John while their companions, whose presence was rather more spasmodic, were to be the Hileys and Peter Zinzan. Mrs Hiley was the only woman ever to go on one of John's long tours and presumably travelled in a coach with her husband. The party set out on Monday, 19 May, picking up Tom Hiley at Oxford. His parents took him to spend the first night with the Revd Mr Lee at Wootton but John and Hopson stayed in Oxford in order to see Hearne, visiting him twice that evening. Then they joined the others for breakfast and spent the second night with Mrs French and Tom at the Sunrising.

The house John especially wanted to see was Compton Verney. His is the last known account of the church while it was still in use; a new chapel replaced it in 1772.[a]

Just on the right of the road between Little Keinton and Wellsburn [Wellsbourne] is the seat of the Hon. Mr Verney,[b] belonging to his Ancestors Lords Willoughby de Broke. It stands low and is built of Stone; the front is towards the Garden and has 11 Windows; part of it was built by the late Lord that was Dean of Windsor.[c] Below there is an handsome Gallery or Dancing Room, the Ornaments to it are of the Doric Order. Several family Pictures well painted . . .

There are Chimney-pieces of Derbyshire Marble in this house. The Gardens, with the room taken up by the house contain 20 Acres. The Gardens rise up an hill, and are well-contrived for Use and Convenience. There are Views down to a Pond; of these Ponds there are 4 in a string,[d] which make a mile in length. . . . The Chappel near the house has Service performed in it when the family is here; and here (and in the Cemitery to it) the Verneys are buried; one of their Monuments consists of two Alabaster figures of a Man and Woman on a raised tomb. Old painted Windows here; the East Window which is the newest (as it seems) bears date 1634.

Nothing that John had seen already on the way north was to be denied to the

[a] There is no reference given for the statement in an article in *Country Life*, vol. 34 (see E. M. Mills, *Historical Notes on Compton Verney Church*, 1932) that George Vertue and the Earl of Oxford saw the old glass stored in the house. In fact a window was dedicated to the memory of John Verney in 1741, the year the Earl of Oxford also died. A slab in the churchyard stating that the old chapel was taken down in 1772 is described by E. M. Mills. The old glass was put up in the new building and sold through Christie's in 1931.

[b] Although the eldest son, Richard, inherited the title in 1728 on the death of the 12th Baron, it seems that it was the younger brother, John Verney, who lived in the house. He was Master of the Rolls in 1738. See previous note and p. 332.

[c] George, 12th Baron Willoughby de Broke was installed Dean of Windsor in 1713.

[d] An estate map of 1736 shows five lakes, but the uppermost is very small. See R. Chaplin, 'The Landscape Lakes at Compton Verney' in *Warwickshire History*, vol. I, no. 1, 1969.

Hileys. At Warwick they were making 'an elegant Altar-piece in the Lady Chappel of 4 or 5 sorts of Marble'.[e] In the churchyard were the wood and plaster buildings of the Deanery and College. There were more pictures to be seen at the Castle and then there was the town itself.

Several of the houses in the great street are sashed. Over both the Gates are Chappels . . . one belongs to Dudley's Hospital which consists of a Master and 12 Brethren; the Master is a Clergyman and reads Prayers here twice a day, except when there is Service at the high Church, for so they call St. Mary's. This is St. James's Chappel: St. Peter's over the other Gate is now a mean school for poor Children; 'tis commonly called the Hanging-Chappel from its situation, probably.

They went on to Coventry the same day, stopping to admire the gateway to Kenilworth Castle where they saw several stone balls 'which were slung in the Barons' War with Henry III'. Some of them were more than sixteen inches across. At Coventry John added to his earlier papers, describing the 'regular and beautiful' church of St Michael and some of the ruins. The red stone St John's was 'now fitting-up'. On their way out of town they passed the long red stone building of the White Friars near Midgford Street Gate which was now used partly as tenements; then they rode out on to the Lichfield road through an arch 'within it a barn, once a Chappel, called Pond-Gate Chappel from a Pond just by'.

There was no time to see Packington Hall, the Earl of Aylesford's 'elegant brick Seat' as they had spent it in Coleshill church surrounded by the alabaster tombs of the Digbys and the 'exquisite fine faces' of the effigies.

There is a most elegant Urn erected for a Monument. The Inscription wrote by Bishop Hough on part of it is for the present Lord Digby's Mother[f] and a most elegant English Epitaph it is.

They soon had to leave the Knights Templar, the ancient iron helmet under the northern arch and the crocketed spire for the long ride over the heath to Lichfield[g] and a night's rest at the George where the party was to be increased by the arrival of Peter Zinzan. By the next evening they were in Burton upon Trent—'as dirty as any paved town can be'. However the church was 'neat' and there was the great curving bridge with its thirty-five arches and a warehouse at one end which had once been a chapel. Riding over it into Derbyshire they made at once for Bretby Hall which belonged to the Earl of Chesterfield, passing his 'pretty whimsical brick-house'[h] on the way. It was delightfully situated.

[e] This is the only information of four or five sorts of marble being used for the altarpiece which was replaced in 1775. See Gilbert Cope, 'The Beauchamp Chapel, Warwick' in *Warwickshire History*, vol. IV, no. 2, 1978/9. See also p. 65.n.n.

[f] Mary, Lady Digby.

[g] John added to his notes on Lichfield Cathedral, made in 1732.

[h] Probably Brizlincote Hall.

His Lordship's great house is of a yellow Stone, being three sides of a Square; there are four Corinthian Pilasters in front, with a Cupola over it; there are two Turrets in each of the sides. It is but a single house. The Chappel is an handsome lofty room, the Ceiling of fret-work consisting of admirable fruit &c. 'Tis paved with large squares of black and white Italian Marble. The Altar has a grave solemn Monument look.

There are many excellent Paintings here, but who painted them or of whom the Portaits are we could get no information. There are many Paintings of Birds, Beasts and Flowers and these most excellent in their kind . . . Reading of Derby[i] painted some of the Cielings; others are rich fret-work,[j] but in some decay. There is some Variety in the Tables here, some of artificial Marble, one of Agate, one of Silver with Stands &c. There is little good furniture here considering how old it is and what condition it is in; it has been good.

In spite of what he said he was able to recognize some Stuart portraits.

We crossed the Trent 3 miles before Derby in a Ferry-Boat which had no sides to it. From hence to Derby the road was extremely rotten, moorish and full of Water.

On 26 May the party left the King's Head Inn early for a long journey from Derby to Edensor, travelling on 'causeys' through the Peak country which began, said John, at Cromford:

. . there being very considerable Rocks about the Place and there is a smelting mill at it . . . there are large new buildings to this Bath. The Clock belonging to the house is moved by Water. . . Matlock is in a very romantic situation.

So was the scenery as they followed the banks of the Derwent and passed by the High Tor. After a night spent at the Duke of Devon's Arms they were ready for one of the most important highlights of the tour – Chatsworth.[k] It fulfilled all their expectations.

[i] Jonathan Reading, a Derby painter, is known to have worked on St Werburgh's church. There is no other record of his having worked at Bretby Hall and John's evidence implies that he was a decorative painter. The name Jonathan occurs in a mortgage deed dated 1725 describing him as 'painter' and the St Werburgh's Parish Register – burial 1746. Considered opinion now agrees that 'John Reading' who worked for Francis Smith of Warwick (see accounts of expenditure, Bodl MS. Eng. Misc. f. 55) was the same man. Bretby Hall, built about 1610 and improved in the late seventeenth century, was demolished and replaced in 1777.

[j] In a later note John said he had seen similar fretwork (or plasterwork) ceilings at Ditchley, Northumberland House and Syon House.

[k] Chatsworth was then owned by William Cavendish, 3rd Duke of Devonshire. Information kindly given shows that John's account provides new information on the location of pictures and furniture, the size of the gardens, the stabling block and the height of the fountain which was replaced by the Emperor fountain.

Chattesworth House is built of very good Stone of a yellow colour. The house is by no means an exact Square; the grand front has 9 Windows with fluted Ionic Pillars and Pilasters and is admirably finished in a neat and elegant taste, without the affectations of extraordinary Ornament. To the grand front of the Gardens there are 12 Windows; and the Windows in both these Fronts are of Looking-Glass and the Sashes gilt. There is a great Kitchen here. The Hall is painted by Verrio; at the upper end are 2 pair of Stairs winding round to one common Landing-place; behind which is a large Area from whence the Stair-case ascends; Verrio painted the Chappel with the Miracles of Christ &c. exquisitely performed. In those Parts where there is no Painting is a Wainscot of Cedar.[1] The floors of several Apartments are inlaid with Walnut-Tree (which now grows old) and the Cielings painted by Verrio. Excellent tapestry here, of several kinds, some are of Raphael's Cartons at Hampton Court. In the long Gallery, which we scarce gained a view of, is some Point in Wood-work. A Chest of drawers, made of Tortoise-shell inlaid with Brass curiously. A Bass-Relievo Bust of King Philip, husband to Queen Mary, in Marble. There are few Paintings here; one is of Judith and Holofernes, she has the Sword in her hand ready to execute her great design. . . Holofernes in a deep sleep lies – very convenient for Judith's purpose. Lengths of William Earl of Pembroke, he that was Chancellor of Oxford and some of the Cavendish family. The Japan of the Duke's Closet in the old house is turned into Chests of Drawers. There are some antique Busts here. In one of the Rooms is a large Pannel of Glass, set opposite to the Doors of several other Rooms, so that it reflects a long Vista. . .

Sir James Thornhill has some Performances here upon Stucho; he also painted the Wonders of Castleton. The Furniture for Chairs and Beds is very grand here, being of the richest materials in very good condition. The stabling &c. are built of brick and take up three sides of a Square. 'Tis a plain building and is sunk below the house. The Ground taken-up by the house and gardens is 133 Acres. The Waterworks here are esteemed the best in England. As the Gardens rise very high behind the house they give room for an amazing Cascade, near 200 yards long; the perpendicular fall is 57 foot. There is a noble Canal 325 yards long, in which is a jet d'eau of 100 foot in height. The resemblance of an Olive-Tree, waters from every Leaf. The View from the Gardens is on enclosed Valleys, beautiful and fruitful, rising into Hills no great distance off. Another way, there is a succession of hills beyond hills. On the top of the Garden-hills is a building like a Church Tower called the *Stand*, from whence you have a large View of the Countrey. Nothing, in short, can be more grand and elegant than Chattesworth.

[1] In a later note John said that White Kennett, in his *Memoirs of the Cavendish Family*, 1708, called the wood cyprus.

It was at this point that Mr and Mrs Hiley left the party for several days in order to pay some private visits of their own. The four young men rode on north to Buxton, a place about which no one in those days ever had anything good to say. John was no exception. 'Buxton is no pleasant place,' he remarked, adding that the Bath House could find accommodation for a great number of persons and that the bath was hot. In fact they appear to have stayed at the Bath House themselves for two nights, making local expeditions by day.

The party was now further depleted by the departure of Peter Zinzan, possibly because he was in disgrace. Somewhere between Cromford and Buxton he had committed an almost unforgivable sin. The story of this misdemeanour is told by Benwell though his geography does not quite match that of the diary. It concerned some miners who were staging a dramatic performance and as lead mines were dotted about the Peak country it cannot be placed exactly.

> The incuriousness of his companion, Dr Zinzan, was wonderful beyond measure, but this he did not confine to himself, but would often prevent others from seeing as much as they desired. Mr L. had been once with him and some more company on an excursion to the Peak in Derbyshire and on their return, about twenty miles distance from the place, Zinzan at last informed them that the tragedy of Cato was to be performed that Evening by the miners, that he knew it when they were there, but was afraid to acquaint the others with it, lest they should be tempted to stay and see it. Mr L. would have given any price to be present at the representation, but it was then too late to return and he was obliged to content himself with threatening the Doctor that he would 'cut his ears off if ever he served him such a trick again'.

To be deprived of this interesting spectacle, and a performance moreover of the very play in which he had taken the leading part at school, was infuriating. So Zinzan departed, with ears intact but, one assumes with head bowed, and was not seen again until they returned to Oxford.

Next day, 28 May, the three survivors took the Sheffield road. They saw the Ebbing and Flowing Well, but as it had failed to flow for a month it was hardly worth seeing. Eden Hole made up for it.

> Eden-hole is on the wild hills, very cautiously inclosed, with a Wall; 'tis a vast and terrible Chasm, as of a great massy rock split in two; at top it is wide and craggy, some of the inward recesses are contracted and intricate; others may very reasonably be concluded large and spacious; for throw-down a stone here; when it has gone such a depth it jars in such a manner as anything passing through vaulted rooms must needs do; the sound at last dies away by degrees; in all liklihood then, the stones descend much deeper than we can hear the sound of 'em.

Mam Tor is a very high Mountain which deceives those that travel at the foot of it, for it rises higher and more contractedly so that not near the height of it could be guessed at but by those that have climbed it. Towards Castleton it is a monstrous rocky Precipice; the view from hence is upon beautiful inclosed Valleys – together with high Hills. Mam Tor seems to have been fortifyed for there is a kind of Ditch drawn round it; under this Mountain are Lead Mines. From the foot of this Mountain to Castleton is a great descent through a narrow Valley one mile deep between two vast high Ridges, out of which often appears an impending craggy Rock, horrid enough.

Stony and uneven as it was, it was still the public road which took them on to Castleton and then to Sheffield. It was dangerous too where the rocks projected – 'covered thick with Stones falling'. But it was wonderful country, said John in a brief summary, with excellent bridges and good churches, though there were but few of them. As for the dialect he noticed that the wild hills were called 'mores' and that 'nay' was used for 'no'. It seems surprising that either word was unusual.

Sheffield is pitched upon a gently rising hill, which it seems to cover for the most part, 'Tis of brick chiefly and old. The Duke of Norfolk is Lord of most of the town which is a Staple for knives, Scissars, &c. great numbers of which are transported beyond Sea to Dantzick &c. There are Coal-pits within 1 mile of the town. The Church[m] stands at the top of the town and is a large building, but irregular; the Steeple is a crocketted Spire out of a Tower. The inside is crowded and darkened with old Lofts and Pews like a Scotch Kirk. There are many modern brass-plates here, one in 1732 and an Epitaph on Wood like an Hatchment in 1708. The oldest Epitaph in the Church is on a brass-plate in the Chancel and bears date in 1510. . .

Leaving the old church, with its monuments to the Earls of Shrewsbury, they found also a new church[n] built by subscription:

Mr Downes, a Tradesman of the town, now living, gave 1000£; the Date on the Leads is 1723. 'Tis not yet paved and some few Ornaments are still wanting, it not being consecrated; for there is a great dispute concerning the right of Presentation to it, which is now before Parliament. The East end is a round, the Pulpit stands with the back to the Altar, the Pillars are on Pedestals as high as the Pews. Galleries here.

The Sheffielders themselves were not thinking about their churches or their

[m] The parish church became the Cathedral Church of St Peter and St Paul in 1914.

[n] St Paul's Church, Pinstone Street was completed in 1723 but not used until 1740 owing to a dispute over right of patronage between the vicar of Sheffield and the benefactor, Robert Downes, a goldsmith. It was demolished in 1939.

cutlery on this light-hearted occasion – it was Oak-apple Day and Charles II's escape at Boscobel some seventy-five years earlier was still a good excuse for a festival.

This being the 29th May it was not sufficient to wear Oaken-boughs in their Hats and deck their Shops with 'em; for they cut-down large limbs from Oaks and planted them in the Streets. Garlands hung across the Street some decked with Eggs, small Pictures &c.

They rode through Rotherham to Wentworth Woodhouse, the great mansion which belonged to Thomas, Earl of Malton, who in 1746 became the Marquess of Rockingham. It was a brick house

but cased with Stone to the grand front, which is unfinished; when finished it will be 606 feet long – that is with the offices, which stand on each side in one line with the grand house, but something retired behind it. The offices are finished. The Garden-front is compleat, partly of brick, partly of Stone. From the house there is little of Prospect. In it is a very curious Cabinet of Tortoise-shell, Ebony and Ivory. A Conversation piece consisting of 13 persons, one of which is the present Lord Malton.

They were unable to see the finest portrait of the Earl of Strafford in the dining room, but the Earl of Derby, who was also beheaded, and his wife 'that held out Lathom' were shown.[°]

The Chimney-pieces are very neat. The Library is a very neat and handsome Room, the cieling of coloured fret-work. So is that of the neat Chappel now building.

The Gardens rise behind the House. In them are many fir-trees and a Mount of above 100 foot high perpendicular; but then great sums must be laid-out to make this Mount anything Ornamental; at present 'tis a great dirty Hill, irregular and misshapen. The Gardens are to be altered, Walls to be taken-down; the old Park, at a distance from the house, is partly disparked and Ground much nearer taken-in. There are Prints representing the grand-front of this house as if it were finished; 'tis by no means so, nor is it to be finished entirely according to that Plan. The Bathing Room is lined with Dutch tile.

In spite of some alterations and the addition of a number of follies it was not until 1790 that the grounds of Wentworth Woodhouse were transformed by Humphry Repton from much the same bleak condition in which they were to be seen in 1735.

They stayed that night at Wakefield. The church was fine and airy and the south side had been rebuilt in the last twelve years, but Edward IV's chapel on

---

[°] Charlotte, Countess of Derby, defended Lathom House in 1644. See p. 396.

the bridge over the Calder was badly defaced and the room was full of rape seed. Two nights followed at Leeds with its old brick houses and slated roofs.

It must be owned that there are several exceeding good houses scattered-about here, belonging to the Merchants of the Town; the Woollen Manufacture flourishes here in a very high degree. Every Tuesday and Saturday are Cloth Markets. They are held in the great Street from the King's Arms to the bridge-foot; the Wares are set-out upon 4 rows of Stalls, open to the weather and the whole business is transacted without any noise or disturbance. About 6 in the morning the Market opens and holds above an hour; till 1684 it was kept upon the bridge, which is strong built. The river Are [Aire] is so calm and smooth that it can be discerned to flow, 'tis truly a dull Stream withal. In 1698 it was made navigable by Act of Parliament.

There were three churches to see but the Sacrament was only administered in the mother church, St Peter's.

. . . The King's Arms are in Bass-Relieve; the figures of the Lion and the Unicorn so contrived as to appear in a right situation in both parts of the Church. The Altar-piece is very handsome, of right Wainscot, the Intercolumn is Purple Velvet with gold fringe, over all is a good Painting of the Last Supper by Monsr. Parmentier. The Canopy to the Font is very lofty and has been a fine thing. . . There is no memorial for Ralph Thoresby, who is buryed here; and who (in his Ducatus Leodiensis[p]) speaks so magnificent things of this town as are not reconcilable with the strictest truth; for, if so, stately, magnificent and grand must sometimes mean no more than scarce ornamental, nay but tolerably neat.

He said as much in a letter to Hearne which he wrote next day at York. It was a short note for, as he said, he did not wish to tire his friend about whom he was increasingly anxious.

I am very desirous to hear from you; if the Prayers and best wishes of your friends can prevail, you will send me good-tidings concerning your Health. Favour me with a line or two forthwith, directed to me, to be left (till called for) at the Post Office in Northampton . . .[4]

He sent this letter to the manciple at Edmund Hall, thinking that this was the safest way of ensuring that Hearne read it.

They had spent some time at Kirkstall Abbey[q] and came to York eventually on 'Causeys like the Pavement of Streets' until they actually approached the city when the surface changed to sand. Later on that evening at the Black Swan they were reunited with Mr and Mrs Hiley, and at supper they were all joined

---

[p] Ducatus Leodiensis was published by subscription in 1713. When St Peter's Church, Leeds was rebuilt (1838–41) a mural tablet was erected to Thoresby's memory.
[q] John said the pronunciation should be 'Chirstal'.

by 'Mr Johnson, the Collector who had been in that capacity at Reading',[r] and they breakfasted with him next day.

John had said so much about York in 1732 that there was not a great deal to add now. He mentioned three patterns and chalices found in the tombs of William de Melton, and Archbishop Greenfield and others made of lead from the 'graves of inferior persons'. It was Dean Finch, he said, who had put the altar so far back. Among other details which he noticed was the 'picture on wood by way of Monument' in the choir for Edmund Bunny.

> The King's Palace, called the Mannor-house, is now divided into lesser houses. It stands out of Boutham-Bar and is granted by the Crown to Gentlemen for their lives as now to Alderman Robinson.
>
> The Assembly-house:– the room used for common Dancing – is at the race-time, for service of breakfasting and for Tea and Coffee in the afternoon; for by means of a partition of Wood between this and the great Room which takes-down upon these occasions, this opens into the great Room.

Return visits were made to Beverley and then to Hull where

> one of the Gates is barred and nailed-up; some say it is that which Charles I commanded to be opened to him and which Hotham refused to do; therefore, they say, it was stopped-up when the fortifications of the town were dismantled. . . In Trinity Church they have lately reared the Pulpit upon a kind of wooden Arch in the mid-Isle, which is a very burlesque situation for it. This Church is of very great length, extremely disproportionate to the breadth of it, which was the reason that after-times have done their best to cramp the length of it on the inside; for within there is a large space left at the West-end like a Chancel; the Altar-piece of the last Supper was painted by Parmentier. . .

Leaving this well-paved town they went on to another place John had seen before – Lincoln. The choir of the Cathedral was 'new-pewing in a neat manner' and a monument for the late sub-Dean Gardiner had been erected within the iron rails which enclosed that of his father, the Bishop. At Newark they found the library which had been left to the Town by Thomas White, deprived Bishop of Peterborough, in very great disorder – though kept in a room belonging to the church.

> Mr William Warburton, who assisted Theobald in his edition of Shakespeare,[s] was a Native of this town, had no University Education, but was Clerk to an Attorney; he may be about 35 years of age, is Minister of

[r] Formerly a tax collector in Reading.

[s] Lewis Theobald's edition of Shakespeare had been published the previous year, 1734, and well received.

Bruton,' near Newark – a Living of about 6 score £ per annum in the gift of Sir Robert Sutton.

Southwell was the only town between York and Nottingham that was new to him, so anxious was he the Hileys should see all these places he had found interesting. Here his notes were fairly predictable, The Minster was not at that time a cathedral and though he admired the choir he had certain criticisms.

The Body and Cross seem to be built at the same time and are certainly no credit to the builder. The Pillars are exceeding thick, massy and clumsy, the Arches low. . . the present roof of the mid-Isles and Cross is flat, consisting of large wooden Pannels, very neat and handsome, leaded at top; in 1711 Lightning set fire to the roof and this is what was made after that accident. . .

Besides his usual descriptions and measurements his eye was caught by the loft over the third prebendary's stall where the Prior of Thurgarten used to sit, Archbishop Sandys's alabaster tomb, much 'abused and defaced' and 'a small dirty space behind the Altar'. For the chapter house he had nothing but praise –

Indeed the very best part of the building and truly 'tis a neat piece of architecture; a small Octagon, with no Pillars to support the stone-Arch; some remains of painted Glass are well-disposed up-and-down in the Windows. There is excellent carved stonework to the Door.

John was interested in the fact that the prebendaries, who had only to be in residence for three months in the year and who received between ten and fifty pounds, seldom lived in their houses but let them out, sleeping themselves at the inn. The Residentiary's house was furnished but he had to supply his own plate and linen and to keep a public table for the clergy every Sunday and Thursday. Prayers were said three times a day throughout the summer season.

Nottingham, they all agreed, was the best-built town they had seen on their tour.

That brick building which, besides the Town-house, includes some Shops is a great Ornament to the very spacious Market-place. It contains 12 Windows in front and is built upon Pillars. The East end of St. Mary's Church is rebuilt in a new taste without any regard to the other parts of it. . . Some of the old Walls of the Castle are standing. . . the room in which Queen Anne lay is floored with Cedar. Several of the Rooms are wainscotted with Cedar, but painted over to prevent the smell. The Vaults in the White Lion Inn, hewn out of the main rock, are sunk a great

' Sutton presented Warburton to the living of Brant Broughton in 1728.

depth under the house; they run-out into several Lengths and contain a great number of Vessels of Beer; one holds 14 Hogsheads, another 17, another 21 and another 24. This rock, like all the others in Nottingham, is of a soft stone so that it is very easy to dig into it; these Vaults at the Inn have been enlarged very lately; at the end of one of the Lengths they dig the rock into Sand for the floors of the house.

Passing by Mr Musters's house, Colwick Hall, next day, they came to Holme Pierrepont, the Duke of Kingston's seat and saw the tombs of his ancestors in the church; but they did not have time to visit his house as they were going to Belvoir Castle and the road was 'bad enough'.

The Castle is seated on the top of a steep high hill that commands a most unbounded flat Prospect, yet Water is wanting in it. Lincoln Minster, 23 miles off, is very visible from hence. At the foot of the hill stand the Stables, 3 sides of a Square, built of stone; here also are the Bakehouse, Laundry, Granaries, Smithy &c, Just-by too is the Kitchen-Garden. The Stables and Castle are in different Counties. The Castle is no regular Pile; the grand front contains 9 Windows and is an half H . . . The Court within the building is a mean thing, like the very irregular area of some old Colleges. The Staircase is as particular in its kind as anything I have seen; after it has risen such an height, turning short, a double pair of Stairs ascends from it; each of which ends in one common landing-place, which is very spacious, and in which are two noble bufets" of Marble to answer one another; yet after all, the Staircase does not please. In the Gallery are Lengths of the Peers of this House beginning with the first Earl of Rutland and continued without any interruption to the present Duke.ᵛ Some of these are painted excellently well; and what family can shew so fine a series of Portraits belonging to it?

After describing other paintings he concluded by saying

The Chappell is a crowded Room but has an Organ in it. The Gardens are laid-out in Walks between Trees. The Castle stands in an open Chase; the Park is 3 miles from it.

Continuing their weaving route down the centre of England, the party stayed the night of 9 June at Sewstern on their way to their next objective, Lord Winchilsea's house in Rutlandshire – Burley on the Hill, which had been built by the late Earl,ᵂ starting in 1696 while he was Earl of Nottingham.

This Place, with several Lordships now belonging to the Earl, were once the Estates of Villiers, Duke of Buckingham. The house is built of

<hr />

" Chests for the display of plate and china.
ᵛ John Manners, 3rd Duke of Rutland.
ᵂ Daniel Finch, 7th Earl of Winchilsea and 2nd Earl of Nottingham, died in 1730.

good white stone. There are 15 Windows in the Front and 4 fluted Ionic Pilasters in the middle. From the front there runs on each side a small rounding Colonnade of 5 Tuscan Pillars, which joins at the farther End to the Offices, from whence on each side runs-on a sweeping Colonnade of 34 Tuscan Pillars, which ending the Stables begin – long buildings. No area can be disposed more beautifully. The Labours of Hercules in water-colours are painted in the Hall. The admirable coloured Tapestry, some of the Cartons, were covered from view.

Among other portraits was one of George Villiers, Duke of Buckingham.

and a very singular look he has, a baby face; the Robes hang on him as they would on a Skeleton, his legs are remarkably long and lank; here is much the best piece that we ever saw of Charles II. The Colours are wonderfully lively. The front of a Cabinet of inlaid Stones in their native Colours representing flowers and birds. Above Stairs is one very large most magnificent Room, admirably proportioned and painted all over by Lanscroon in 1711. 'Tis the History of Caesar, his death, apotheosis &c. This Room echoes to a very great degree; 'tis, in short, the grandest painted Room I ever remember to have seen. The Chappel is plain and neat. The Stair-case is grand and solemn, the Stairs of inlaid Spanish Oak. There is a Park belonging to the house. The view from this house to the front is on wretched thatched Cottages; the back view is on part of the small, but fruitful Vale of Catmose; hence you see also 2 fishponds in a line.

Oakham he thought a mean town with the church in a bad state of repair, the roof and floor dilapidated 'and as for Pewing it is most grievously bestead'. The north side of the chancel was diminished as a floor had been laid over it for a small library. The school had been repaired in 1723.

There is nothing remaining of the Castle (besides the Walls) but an old room now used for the County-hall, upheld by two rows of Pillars. 'Tis a Royalty belonging to the Castle to demand an horse-shoe of every Peer of the Realm the first time that he comes through the town in his Coach. Several horse-shoes are accordingly nailed to the Castle-gate and to the door of the County-hall; the names of the Peers are cut on the horse-shoes; some of the shoes are vastly large and are gilt. There is a prodigious large horse-shoe fastened at one end of the County-hall; the people say it was given by Queen Elizabeth[x].

After a night's rest at the George at Stamford and a quick look at the town, they presented themselves next day at the Earl of Exeter's mansion, Burghley House, which stood in 'a well-wooded park'.

[x] The horseshoes are still to be seen in the Castle where the Norman Hall is still the County Hall.

'Tis a very large magnificent old Palace built of Stone; it does not indeed command any great View. The Chimnies in the form of Pillars with Chapitors, are an ornament to the house. There is a fine Iron-gate to the Porch of one of the Fronts. The Kitchen is a good arched room. Much the finest Apartments in the house were painted by Verrio, but they are not fitted-up, nay not so much as floored. The Paintings in this house are without number, all most excellent in their kind. Of Portraits indeed there are few here except family-pieces. The Cielings of the Rooms are of fret-work, not very much laboured. The Cieling of the Hall is curious pendent wood-work.

John described a number of classical and religious paintings in his own way, dwelling on the exact representations, the emotional scenes and the looks of horror or surprise so often portrayed. Some of the most incomparable, he said, were in the closets.

Christ's Agony in the Garden . . . improves upon the Eye, discovering continually some new beauty. But the most inimitable Piece for exquisite soft touches is Carlo Dolci's Institution of the Sacrament. . . 'tis an half-piece of Christ only. . . There is some very curious Carving in wood here[y] some miniature. Statues in Box are esteemed Master-pieces. There is a large Chappel here adorned with paintings of Scripture History. The Chappel with its Steeple stands at one end of the house and is a prejudice to the regularity of it.

All this had taken place on Sunday, 8 June, and they had slept at St Martin's. John and Charles Hopson left the Hileys to get their breath and went off to visit Thorney. Now they were in the fens where 'Kine, Sheep, Horses and Geese were feeding in abundance'. First they had to see Crowland Abbey, which did not arouse great enthusiasm, then they were in Cambridgeshire.

The Flat in the road to Thorney shewed us good Pasture and Arable land. Willows grew all along by the Water-Courses, which, as they approached nearer to Thorney, enlarged to so great a degree as to admit some small boats to the very Town. It was a delightful ride to Thorney, which belongs to the Duke of Bedford. He is making it a very pretty little Country-town. A very large Inn is built there, though it stands out of all great roads. The new buildings in Thorney are of brick. Some persons of fashion live in this market-town. . . The West front with the middle-isle only of the Abbey-Church is now standing and used for the Parish Church as perhaps it always was. This front is regular, neat and grand, and very considerably lofty, adorned with 9 Statues; it has 2 round Turrets at the Angles. Willis says that all this was repaired in 1636; but sure it is a mistake, for 1638 is the date over the West Door. But the Body is

[y] A later note attributed the carving to Grinling Gibbons.

neither wide nor long, and is clumsy enough; it is indeed lofty and has a
wooden-bowed roof. Here is an Epitaph for Ezekiel Danois, first Pastor
(as it says) of the French Congregation here, which begun in 1652. There is
no such Congregation now, yet the chief persons in town are of French
extraction, and there are many Tomb-stones for French-men in the
Church-Yard.

They met the rest of the party at the Talbot Inn at Peterborough, 'a good
pretty City' where the Cathedral demanded John's entire attention.

The Minster looks grander without than it does within, for the Pillars
and Arches are excessively clumsy and vast; there is great variety in the
form of the Pillars, but in all this not one approach to Elegance and
beauty. . . the bowed roof of painted Wood is very venerable and
striking. That of the Cross being also Wood painted is nothing
extraordinary and both are out of repair; but the Dean[z] and Chapter are
laying out large Sums in repairing and adorning this Church. . . The
roof of the Choir is very curiously and beautifully carved and painted.
The Throne, Stalls and Pews are just made new, of deal painted, they are
very plain and decent. . . But the most Eastward Piece in the whole Pile,
is what they call the New Building, which is really very elegant, more
than can truly be said of any other part of the Church. . . The Eastern
part of it is inclosed by partitions of Deal from the rest and is used for
a Library, one side of which is entirely taken-up by Bishop Kennet's
books . . .[a] Mr Deacon's is the only modern Monument in the Church;
he in a tie-wig leans on a Cushion. This is in the new building where is
also an ancient Monument shaped like some Trunks, and ridged at
top . . . it is esteemed one of the most ancient Christian Monuments in
the world. 870 in modern Characters is insculped at one end of it, for 'tis
said to be in memory of the Abbats and Monks of this place, massacred
in that year by the Danes. . Against the West wall of the mid-Isle hangs
an old Canvas Picture, in full proportion, of Robert Scarlet, the Sexton.
The brass-Plates are stripped off the Tombs here. There is a Cope
preserved in one of the Vestries made of Purple Velvet worked thick
with Gold.[b]

The Cathedral was gradually recovering from the terrible scars inflicted on
it in the Civil War, when many of the secondary buildings were destroyed.
John saw that the chapter house was now a dwelling house for 'Mr Kennet,
who is the late Bishop's son' and that the Infirmary was used for houses for

[z] Francis Lockier.
   [a] Bishop White Kennett, who died in 1728, founded an antiquarian library in
Peterborough Cathedral and gave about 1,500 books and tracts.
   [b] I am indebted to Canon A. Gribble and Mr T. Christie for information on Peterborough; the original function of the ancient monument described is unknown. The purple
cope has disappeared.

minor canons and 'Singing-men'. Critical though he was of the lack of a fourth steeple on the west front, he thought it the most beautiful he had ever seen. He made many further notes before leaving.

Hearne's letter was waiting for him at Northampton. It had been written on 6 June and was very short.

Dear Sir,

I make shift just to write, to thank you for yours of the 1st inst. and to acquaint you, that tho' I am generally pretty easy in the night time, yet in the day I am often painfull and I am really extremely weak. I thank you for your fresh Marmalet, and am, dear Sir, Your most obliged humble Servant, Tho: Hearne.[c]

Poignant as this brief note was, it did not alarm John unduly. Except for one deletion the beautiful script was as clear and concise as ever; it did not cause him to curtail his journey and rush back to Oxford and he dawdled round Northampton, even making another visit to Easton Neston where, among other things, 'The Cicer once so visible under Tully's eye can scarce be seen since the face was cleaned, by which it has suffered considerable damage.' It was his third visit and this time he concentrated on the pictures rather than the statues. On Friday 13 June he found himself once again at Stowe where a number of alterations had taken place.

Lord Cobham's Gardens consist of 60 Acres actually improved and kept in order; 40 acres more are also taken-in, but are not yet disposed of; the Church, Church-yard and Parsonage-house are within the Gardens. There is now also an irregular head of Water in them. Gibbs and Kent have been the Architects for the buildings in the Gardens since Sir John Vanbrugh's death. The House, as well as the Gardens, have been improved since I was here;[d] to the middle of the Garden-front they have added a double Colonnade, one over the other, consisting of 4 Pillars each, the lower row is Tuscan, the upper Ionic; this has had a very good effect, which cannot be said of the four blunt Turrets, one at each corner, which is also a late addition. The inside of the house is wondrous elegant and is furnished accordingly. Here is excellent Tapestry of the Battle in the Wood, the old Miller appearing in it; it differs something from the Tapestry at Cliefden House, the Earl of Orkney's. Here are Tables of the Giallo antico, Paintings of Rubens's wife by Rubens, of Joan d'Arc supposed by A. Durer, of Moses burying the Egyptian by N. Poussin; of the marriage in Cana by Bassano; of the Duke de Sully, French

---

[c] L.F.P. 6 June 1735. In his Preface to vol. XI of Hearne's *Collections* H. E. Salter states that Hearne could do no more than write the date on 2, 3 and 4 June and could probably not leave his bed. His last published letter was to George Ballard on 22 May. However, his letter to John written on 6 June is in his usual beautiful handwriting.

[d] In 1731. See p. 93.

Ambassador[e] to Charles I, a Length by Van Dyck. Four Pictures in low life, very well done by Ciperi,[f] now living (if I mistake not.) Oliver Cromwell and his Page was copied by Richardson from a Painting at the Earl of Oxford's. The Marble Bass-Relieve of Cyrus's Camp is one of the most exquisite pieces of Sculpture that I have ever seen. Sisygambis is a Master-piece; the Sculptor's name appears on it.[g]

John returned to Oxford the same day to be greeted by the news that Hearne had died on 10 June while he had been occupying himself with Peterborough Cathedral. He found himself immediately engulfed in a sea of speculation and rumour. Hearne alive had provoked criticism enough, unfair at times, though justifiable at others; but in death he had provided enough ammunition to keep his enemies busy indefinitely. The chief accusation was that he had refused to allow the Revd John Ball to pray with him on his death bed although he himself regarded him as an 'honest' man. Worse still, a Roman Catholic priest had been admitted and had stayed for an hour and a half. A man was expected to proclaim his faith when he was dying and Hearne's reputation would suffer if it were thought he had gone over to Rome – even though he had not been inside a church for years. John wrote at once to Bishop Tanner (who must by then have gone to St Asaph), but it was not until 9 October that he set the whole facts before him. During that four-month period the gossip had evidently not much abated.

> I did imagine [he wrote on the Bishop's return to Oxford] that you would soon hear of the common report concerning Mr Hearne's exit, of which I will faithfully relate the very truth. That he refused the Principal's[h] Ministerial Office, no one wonders but the Principal himself, who has been a main Instrument in spreading the common report. As to his not admitting Mr Ball, the Nonjuring Clergyman, I have no more to say than this, that (to my certain knowledge) Ball was a man that Mr Hearne had very little personal regard for. But as to the admitting of Sir Fra. Curzon's Priest I have something to say, that, I trust, comes up to this point. . .

He had returned on 13 June, he continued, and hearing the common report wished to discover the truth. He had therefore visited the Manciple of Edmund

---

[e] The Duc de Sully is not usually remembered as an ambassador but the French *Dictionary of Nobility* says that Henri IV sent him to England as an ambassador extraordinary in the reign of James I.

[f] John wrote 'Ciperi' and later added 'Chipari'. The artist was Giacomo Francesco Cipper; the four paintings were in the sale catalogue of 1846, and described as having been 'very old pictures at Stowe'. See 'The Picture Collection at Stowe' by Colin Anson (*Apollo*, June 1973), to whom I am grateful for further information. See also p. 93 n.*b*.

[g] See p. 93 n.*b*. The fact that John made a return visit only four years after his previous one adds to the knowledge concerning alterations etc. at Stowe.

[h] Dr Henry Felton, Principal of St Edmund Hall.

Hall, Mr Johnson, and had made a memorandum 'from Johnson's Mouth'. From this it transpired that the priest had left Hearne in a very uneasy and choleric condition as if he had been in a great passion. Johnson also avowed that Hearne had invariably read the Psalms and Lesson for the day and that for the last two weeks he, Johnson, had at his request, often read them to him. In John's opinion it was not unusual for such priests to try to reconcile to Rome those in a weak physical state.

> Now had this Priest actually administered to him, I presume that the Satisfaction of Mind upon having received the *Viaticum* would naturally (in the Condition he was in) have afforded him a serene Repose; to be sure no reason can be assigned, why it should so immoderately have ruffled his Temper, as Johnson testifies. In truth it looks as if the Priest had been attacking him and as if too my good friend had withstood his Attacks and with more than common Zeal defended the Protestant Religion. . . I am persuaded that for some Years before his Death, few knew his sentiments more intimately. . than myself, for he was always very open to me and without reserve. From the uniform tenor of his Conversation and from what I have offered to your Lordship, I presume to think the Principal, Mr Ball and the other reporters, have not in this matter acted the Christian part, so well as Mr Hearne ever did the stanch Protestant. . .[5]

John was not alone in thinking himself Hearne's most intimate friend. It was common knowledge that he, of all people, would be most conversant with the intricacies of Hearne's study. So it was that on that same summer afternoon of 13 June, having scarcely had time to absorb the sad news, he found himself – with Thomas Winchester in support – face to face with the executors, Hearne's brother Edmund and his sister, Anne Dean. He had been summoned to meet them at Manciple Johnson's rooms so that they could request his assistance in cataloguing and sorting the innumerable books, papers and manuscripts. It was not surprising that it was quite beyond them: both were country folk with little knowledge of scholarship. Although he had lived so long in the academic world Hearne had always been a loyal son and brother and all his property was to be shared between them and the small son of his deceased brother William, with the exception of the books, coins, medals and manuscripts. These were left to William, eldest son of Hearne's old friend the non-juror divine, Hilkiah Bedford. Neither John nor any of his other friends were mentioned. Bedford was supposed to help the family, but though he corresponded with John he did not come to Oxford until the end of the month. He subsequently sold all Hearne's papers to Dr Richard Rawlinson for £100 and so they eventually became the treasured possessions of the Bodleian Library which had once closed its doors to their original owner.

Unfortunately John did not take to the executors, but he agreed to carry out this formidable task. He then retired to bed, only stopping to write a few words to Dr Richard Mead. Next day he attended the funeral and made his visits to the Manciple to ascertain the truth as far as was possible. That evening Charles Hopson and Tom Winchester decided he needed cheering up and took him off to the Greyhound Inn where he was able to relax and discuss the last two days' events with his two closest friends. There were other people to whom he felt he should write, among them Thomas Baker at Cambridge and James West, lawyer, politician and antiquary – still a young man and the most urbane of Hearne's friends. It seems probable that John was worried about the rights of the little nephew and had consulted him in his legal capacity. West replied on 19 June, writing from the Inner Temple.

> I am very much obliged to you for your kind Letter which I received yesterday with the Will enclosed. 'Tis happy for the Memory of my worthy friend, and for Mr Bedford, that you are so kind to assist in the preservation of his Papers. I never saw Mr Bedford till this Morning who acknowledges his great obligations to you as will every one who loved and respected Mr Hearne. I am very sorry to hear so indifferent a Character of his Executors and of the Mother of the Child. The fortune will be too inconsiderable to bear the expense of throwing it into Chancery; I should therefore think that if Mr Bedford or yourself would secure the Executors to pay the Child's share into your hands it would be very safe and highly beneficiall to the interest of the Infant; Tho' this should be done before Probate be granted for afterwards it will be in their power pretty much to squander it away; Pray what hath he died worth?
>
> I doubt it will be very difficult to wrest the Child out of the Mother's hands whom Nature and the Law have made the properest Guardian; I am glad of this opportunity of corresponding with a Person my friend used always to mention with respect. . .[6]

However altruistic John's thoughts may have been, the idea that he should be responsible for the child's share was certainly not one that appealed to him, nor was it the kind of scheme with which he would want to involve himself. Besides, the fortune was not nearly so inconsiderable as Hearne's subscribers might have been led to expect by his modest way of life. There seems to be no doubt that the rumour that over £1,000 was found in his rooms was a true one.

John at once threw himself into the business of sorting the papers and he must have been one of the first people to see the famous diaries. No doubt he was surprised, if not a little shocked, by the revelations and invective in the pocket books which were all carefully indexed by Hearne. Insertions had been neatly pasted in, several of them from John himself. He made a list of his own letters, noting the fact that he had or had not kept copies and it does seem that he pocketed one or two. He had an assistant in the main task,

Samuel Speed of New College, who was a few years older than himself.
They soon struck up a lasting friendship. Later on Speed became an usher at
Winchester College.

At the end of the month John received a letter from Thomas Baker.

Worthy Sir, By the last Post I received the favor of your Letter with an
account of the death of our worthy Friend Mr Hearne; and tho' the
news was very melancholy, yet you were kind in imparting it and I
heartily condole with you, for our common loss, as well as for the
greater loss to the public. I oftened cautioned him against fatiguing
himself too much, but he was not to be advised and so he dies a Martyr
to Antiquities and it was not in my power to prevent it. . .[7]

There was another duty to perform for the sake of Hearne's reputation
and John was soon to find himself in print again. Of all the literary vultures
the printer and publisher Edmund Curll was one of the most reprehensible
and scurrilous. He had enjoyed the appetizer of Bilstone's 'Vindication';
now he was able to swoop down for the feast. John read his advertisement
and wrote to him on 30 June.

As you intend to publish the Life of that eminent Antiquary, Mr
Thomas Hearne, it is to be wished that it might be compleat and just; not in
that Manner in which it was set out about four years ago by a Chaplain of
All-Souls College, which was intended rather as a sneer upon Mr Hearne
than to give us an impartial Account of his Life and Writings.

Curll published the correspondence;[i] and added a note to this letter to say
that far from being a sneer Bilstone's account had contained many judicious
remarks and was a full detection of 'Our Antiquary's gross Errors'. He
evidently asked John to contribute something about his friend, but this John
declined in his second letter, saying he had promised not to do so. He hoped
that Curll would do Hearne honour and that nothing trifling or injurious
would be handed to the world. Two days later, on 10 July, he wrote again, very
much in his own style.

As to the Gentleman's Character you intend to attack, I must desire to
be excused, if I don't concern myself: he is dead, and has answered
elsewhere, and how far his Censures are just, I know not; he cannot now
defend himself; *De Mortuis nil nisi bonum.* As to the Gentleman to whom
the MSS. are left, I will not encourage you, or any Body, to apply to him.
By the Will you'll find he had Directions from the Testator as to that
Affair, and he is a man of too nice Honour not to strictly adhere to them; so
that all manner of Application, there, will be ineffectual.

Our Correspondent [wrote Curll] is very tenacious of the Antiquary's

---

[i] John's letters were signed P.Q. and A.B.

Character. We hope he will not find any Thing mean, trifling, or injurious; unless doing Justice may be mistakenly so deemed.

Curll had some justification for saying that Hearne had had little regard for the characters of the living or memories of the dead. Where he was despicably unfair was in denigrating his work as dull and useless and in the unpleasantness of his attack so soon after his victim's death. Pope, to whom John also wrote at this time, had made a similar misjudgment in *The Dunciad*.[j] However, John had done all he could. It was beneath his dignity to continue the discussion and he meant it when he said he would not concern himself further. Hearne's name would be dragged through the mud and the public would be interested to see just how far Curll would go; but in the end it was Curll's name which would suffer the most; better to ignore the matter than to continue a wrangle with such a shameless opponent. His letters, of course, had no effect on Curll, who published them, albeit unsigned, as a foreword to his *Life of Mr Thomas Hearne* which appeared anonymously in 1736.

At the beginning of July John was at last able to go home to Caversham, taking Winchester with him. Apart from a brief weekend his mother had not seen him since early May and he found his favourite cousin, Anne Bootle, had come to stay as Robert was away at sea. He was very much occupied with his Waterland correspondence and with adding to his notes on Reading with Mr Hiley's help. At the end of the month Peter Zinzan was reinstated as a Fellow of Magdalen to the delight of his many friends. There were the usual summer festivities in and about Reading and then John was away again on a tour to Kent and Essex.

'I set out upon a Journey,' he wrote in his diary on 8 September, but it was really a round of visits beginning with his grandmother at Clapham. Crynes and Bonney rode with him on the first day and they all breakfasted on the 10th with the genial Richard Wooddeson at his school at Kingston-upon-Thames. It was only three miles on to Wimbledon House, recently built by the Dowager Duchess of Marlborough. It was well situated

upon an Elevation commanding a view of the fine Hedge-row Inclosure, but no Water. 'Tis built of the pale Brick called Greystock. The Window-Cases of Stone; the third is an Attick Story. The Grand Entrance is into the second Story, the lowest Story being under Ground. Some of the Locks are inserted within the Wood of the Doors. In the Sallon are family-Paintings of the Duke and Dutchess, their Children, Sons-in-law and Grandchildren. Wood [Whood] painted the present Duke and Dutchess of Bedford, his Drapery and Manner imitate Van Dyck very well.[k] Seymour painted other Pieces. In this house are Paintings of Sidney, Earl

---

[j] Wormius in II, 85, though not to be taken too seriously as Pope intimated in his note.

[k] The Duchess had bought the estate from the bankrupt Janssen in 1723 and was furnishing it in 1734. Writing to the Duchess of Bedford on 17 July 1734, she had said

of Godolphin, Queen Anne, of Daniel, Earl of Nottingham &c. Here are two fine rich Statues of Blacks, made of different kinds of Marble . . . Some most excellent Tapestry here, wherein Lions, Camels, Crocodiles seem alive. Sir Theodore Janssen has an house in Wimbleton Village; it was of him that the Estate was bought on which the Dutchess built her house.

Crynes left the others at Croydon and they spent a long time making notes in the church and the Archbishop's Palace, in which, John remarked, Laud had delighted.

'Tis a very irregular building, chiefly of brick; the Hall is just like a College-hall and has a great wooden roof. There are many good plain Rooms here, unfurnished, wainscotted in large Pannels considering their age; such is the Gallery and that called the Guard-room. The Chappel is a plain large room, in which Bishop Juxon's Coat of Arms often occurs which consists of four blackamoors' heads. Here is a very good Kitchen, Pantries &c but all this lower floor is very damp. These Apartments are (most of them) fronting you upon entering the Court through the Gateway, in which is much room, where the Chaplains and Secretary are bestowed. The buildings on the right and left hand are for Servants as at Hampton Court.

It was a feat of endurance at that time to cover the twenty-eight miles (in John's reckoning) between Bromley and Maidstone in one day. The road to Farnborough was a 'great' road, but after that it became very narrow,[1]

So much so that two horses could by no means pass one another; it was also on very uneven stony Ground, continually up and down hill. A View sometimes opened to the right hand. Chalk prevailed very much today, but a sand the nearer we approached Maidstone of which I had a very good View from the Road and which I entered over a stone-arched bridge.

He had parted from Bonney at Bromley, no doubt after seeing the Bagshaws, and his only companion now was his servant. He had a special purpose in this journey, since he planned to spend the next two weeks or so studying Hebrew with Deodatus Bye. He boarded his man and the horses at the Rose Inn and lodged himself with Bye's landlady, Mrs Bishop. Conviviality by night and study by day was the usual practice at Maidstone; the Revd Sam Weller entertained the scholars as before in the part of the

---

that 'with the help of Vandyke's postures and clothes' the portrait would be 'an extreme fine thing'. (*Letters of a Grandmother*, ed Gladys Scott Tomson, 1943.)

[1] Travelling the same road in April 1744, John noticed a number of 'Eugh-trees' (yews) in the hedgerows shortly before Wrotham.

Palace, where he lived and there John met Lord Romney[m] (who owned all the buildings) and his sisters. Evenings were spent at a tavern with Weller and Bye and a young clergyman, John Oare, who had been a gentleman commoner at Magdalen.[n] During the daytime John made notes on Maidstone itself, admiring its wide and very clean streets. The church housed the library which consisted chiefly of the study of Dr Thomas Bray, who had himself composed a method for strengthening parochial libraries.

On arrival at Rochester he put up at the King's Head but dined, supped and breakfasted with William Lowth who was now in charge of St Margaret's parish. To his delight Robert was there too with a pupil, Mr Peckham of New College. He stayed only two days during which time he wrote a long account of the Cathedral, which he disliked, calling it the 'clumsiest Cathedral and the meanest in the Kingdom'. It was as usual the pillars of the nave which caused this harsh verdict and it did not prevent him from commenting on every detail in his usual careful way – and on Browne Willis too, 'who blunders every step almost in his account of this Church'. The library was kept in the chapter house –

> a small Collection of Books, however here is a fair Copy of the Complutensian Edition of the Bible; in a Chest here is preserved Textus Roffensis which Archdeacon Denne shewed me in the Sunday afternoon . . . It is wrote in a fair, good hand and is handsomely bound; it was lent by Dr Harris, Author of the History of Kent, who bringing it home by Water, stained it much. The Arch-Deacon also shewed us a small MS. wrote by a Monk, containing the Consuetudines of several Manors and Estates belonging to this Church.

John's next host was his old undergraduate friend John Cleeve, who now held the living of High Laver in Essex.

> It was a very good Road to Gravesend; on the right hand runs a fine length of the Thames with Ships on it. The Church here is built of the same Greystock white brick as Wimbleton-house, the outward Ornaments are of Stone . . . Sure, I was not above ten Minutes crossing from Kent into Essex where the Water is one mile over. For some miles after I got into Essex it was a bye Road, very deep; three miles before Brentwood we rode by a Church not quite finished on the Inside; 'tis neatly built of the red brick; a Latin Inscription on the Tower informs me that in 1734 this St. Nicholas Church was built by Lord Petre for the Parishioners of West Thorndon and Ingrave, which Parishes were united by Act of Parliament. Some time before I arrived at this Church, Lord Petre's house[o] appeared on

---

[m] Lord Romney lived at Mote Park. A year younger than John, his interests were similar. He became a Fellow of the Royal Society and a Doctor of Civil Law.

[n] Another companion was the Revd John Fuller, who was vicar of Yalding.

[o] Ingatestone. Lord Petre also owned Wirral Park.

the left hand. From Brentwood to the end of this journey a very woody Countrey was in View; this part of Essex is perhaps as wood-land a Countrey as any in England.[p]

In High Laver church he saw the Latin inscription on marble to John Locke, the philosopher, and his burial place under the south wall. He walked with Cleeve to Otes, Lord Masham's[q] house, where Locke had lived and died.

Sir Francis Masham and his Lady, father and mother to the present Lord, were Dissenters; this Lord told Mr Cleeve that his Mother-in-law [stepmother] used to read the Bible to Mr Locke; he desired her Ladyship, who was reading to him, to withdraw, for his time was come; she went out and he died presently; he used to attend a Dissenting Teacher's Lectures on a Thursday, but he went to Laver Church upon Sunday.

Among the pleasant expeditions (which included a visit to another University friend, Thomas Velley, at Chipping Ongar), one of the most delightful was to Greensted. John Cleeve's father lived there in a charming house next to the ancient timber church which has scarcely changed with time.

It is built of Oak-trunks uphewn, the Bark only stripped off; these are pitched on end and by tenons fastened at bottom into a tree which has the Bark on, and lies just below the Surface of the Ground. On the inside the Walls are plastered-over as in other Churches. Mr Deputy Cleeve,[r] my friend's father, was at Grinsted-hall, his seat just by the Church. He said that Domesday Book mentions a Church in this Place; by the simple inelegant taste of this building it may perhaps be older than the Conquest.[s]

On leaving High Laver John made one last stop before going home. This was at Waltham Abbey and it was a disappointment. The church was at that time in a very bad state of repair and the Abbey house 'partly vamped up'.

---

[p] An additional note reads 'every Land being separated from one another by Hedge-Rows'.

[q] Samuel, 1st Baron Masham was the eighth and only surviving son of Sir Francis by his first wife, Mary. His stepmother, Damaris, daughter of Dr Ralph Cudworth, was a scholar of whom Locke had a high opinion. Lord Masham's own wife was Abigail Hill, who supplanted the Duchess of Marlborough in Queen Anne's affections.

[r] Deputy probably referred to a position as deputy Alderman of the City of London and one of who was a member of the Common Council. Alexander Cleeve was a merchant pewterer. The Cleeves and Velleys were related. See also P. J. Budworth, *Memorials of Greensted, Budworth &c*, 1876.

[s] The date of the oldest wooden church in the world is A.D. 845. Some of the timbers were saved from an earlier church built A.D. 650–60. Those lying under the surface of the ground, which John described, rotted and were replaced by brick plinths in 1848.

There was nothing to linger for; and he and his man put up at the Crown at Uxbridge and were back at Caversham next day.

There was another family visit to Oxford late in October when Aunt Tooke with her daughters Anne Bootle and Sally came up with Patty to see the sights. John loved these occasions. He rode down to Benson to meet them for dinner at the Red Lion and escorted them to Mrs Wickham's lodgings in Oxford. That night he gave the four ladies supper in his rooms and next day took them to Blenheim. He never went there without finding something new to say; this time it was that the marble in the Gallery and elsewhere was 'most exquisitely polished, glaring against your eyes'. The company for supper that night included his uncle Brady with one of his sons, and the visit concluded with a tour of the colleges and chapels. Then it was time to accompany the family as far as Dorchester where he made more extensive notes.

Back at Oxford Sam Speed was waiting for him to continue the tremendous task of sorting through Hearne's pamphlets and revising the catalogue of the manuscripts. He also spent as much time as he could with Bishop Tanner, whose life was drawing to a close and who died in December. The loss of this affectionate and scholarly friend was another severe blow to John and he ended his diary for 1735 sadly:

He was buryed privately in Christ Church just by the Pulpit (as he himself ordered) after Afternoon Prayers, Mr Allen making the Speech.

Devon and Cornwall
1736

The year 1736 came in mournfully with a death in the family. Sir Richard Hopkins had caught a cold in the Sessions House which turned to a fever from which he did not recover. He was only fifty-nine years of age and it was a great shock to everyone. Lady Hopkins continued to live alone at Low Leyton, but relied more than ever on long visits from Patty who had always regarded her aunt's house as a second home.

At the beginning of February John called on Lord and Lady Bulkeley, who were spending a few nights in Oxford at the Angel Inn. Probably he had met them already at Wytham Abbey where Lord Bulkeley's uncle, the Earl of Abingdon,[a] had a secondary establishment. As John's friend Sir William Courtenay was also Lord Abingdon's nephew, it was a natural courtesy for John to be invited to Wytham. He had been accompanied there by a member of the College, Dr James Fynes, who later that year was to be presented by Sir William to the living of Moretonhampstead and whose father had been steward at Powderham.

The Earl took to John and suggested he should pay him another visit in two weeks' time when he would be in residence at his house at Rycote. So it was that on 15 February John and Fynes rode eastwards over Milton Common to spend three nights at the magnificent mansion where many illustrious guests,

---

[a] Bridget, sister of Montagu, 2nd Earl of Abingdon married Richard, 4th Viscount Bulkeley and her sister Anne, married Sir William Courtenay, 2nd Baronet in 1704; Abingdon was therefore uncle to John's friends, the 5th Viscount Bulkeley and Sir William Courtenay, later 1st Viscount, who were cousins.

including Queen Elizabeth, had stayed in the past.[b] So it was, too, that John's account of the house, much of it recollected from Lord Abingdon's words, may have been the last that was written; for nine years later the whole place was destroyed by fire, the little heir,[c] who was the Earl's great-nephew, perishing in the flames. In the winter of 1736, however, all was hospitality and good cheer. The Earl had now no children, but some of his young nephews were staying with him.

This house belonged to the family of the Quartermains; 'tis situate in a Park; just within the Park-Gate is Albury Church. The house was situate very unwholesomely, Bogs all about it; this Earl has in great measure, and proposes entirely, to cure this Inconvenience and at the same time make an addition of beauty to the Seat, for some of the Bogs are already very fine regular Ponds. To secure the house from a mischievous wind, a large and long Mount (as they call it) was reared up parallel with the length of the house, Gardenwards; Inigo Jones has contrived to make it wonderfully ornamental by designing a light, open kind of Alcove on the top; on a lower part making proper Ornaments for an Approach.

He added a note later to say that this design was executed in 1656.[d]

The large old Seat is built of brick, the front very regular. The long Gallery of very great length, but not proportionably wide, is adorned with very good Portraits. In this Room and the Billiard-Table Room are Paintings of the Chief of this family from Richard Bertie . . . who was Gentleman of the horse to Catherine, Dutchess of Suffolk; who for him (though by his Picture no personable man) refused the Elector Palatine of the Rhine, and Casimire,[e] then upon the election for King of Poland; afterwards elected, he invited the marryed Couple into Poland and made Richard a Count there . . . In the long Gallery there is a Length of this Dutchess who was (in her own right) Baroness Willoughby of Eresby; Peregrine[f] who succeeded to that title is in the Billiard-Room compleatly armed.

[b] I am indebted to Mr A. Clifford Morris and to his book *The Rycote Yew*. See also a manuscript by the Revd Thomas Delafield, Bodl. MS. Gough. Oxon. 31.

[c] James Bertie, Lord Norrys, was the son of Willoughby, 3rd Earl of Abingdon, who succeeded on his uncle's death in 1743. The 2nd Earl's only son, another James, Lord Norrys, had died in 1718.

[d] This can be seen in Kip's engraving of 1709. The statement that Inigo Jones had worked at Rycote must have come from the Earl.

[e] It was not Casimir, but Sigismund, King of Poland who saved them from danger in Germany by inviting them to Poland, where he made Richard Earl of Kroze. They returned to England on the death of Queen Mary.

[f] Peregrine became 11th Baron Willoughby de Eresby on his mother's death, she holding the title in her own right. John related the well-known story of his having been born abroad in a church porch.

So he continued describing the portraits[g] until he arrived at a painting of General Monck:

. . . he has a remarkably sleepy, dull look. Lord Abingdon, who told me several of the particulars above-mentioned relating to his family, said that the General was imagined to be the father of Dr George Clarke of All Souls; his reputed father, Sir William Clarke being Secretary to the General, he a poor weakly Man, his Wife a beautiful Woman.[h] Here also is an head and shoulders of Colonel John Cromwell, a Relation of Oliver's – who not prevailing in his endeavours of making Oliver Cromwell alter his Conduct, out of detestation of that man's Practices changed his name to Williams.[i]

Next John was shown the little chapel[j] in the house:

A little kind of Closet, not unlike that at Naworth Castle, remains in statu quo, which was that of a Popish Chappel; the small Window above the Table is painted in very lively Colours and much expression, – the Crucifixion of Christ; over the Table there is still spread a green-Velvet Covering with Gold Lace; round the Window is much Shell-work, beautifully disposed; the holy-water Bottle, just on the right hand, is in a Case of Shell-work; I think it is not unlike the Shape of a large Tea Chest; the bottle has three necks; there are beads hanging near the Window; on the Table is a wooden Chalice, dated 1624. Here is a Copper Censing Vessel. The Chappel in which the Family attend Divine Service is just by the house; it has a Tower; it consists of one Isle and has *now* the small remains of painted Glass in the Windows; it was of the twelve Apostles with their particular Articles of the Creed. The

[g] Many of the portraits, including those of Lord and Lady Williams who entertained Henry VIII and Queen Elizabeth at Rycote, must have been destroyed in the fire of 1745. John's appears to be the most complete account. See Appendix 150.

[h] This description of Monck is similar to that of John Aubrey who calls him 'slow and heavy' and implies that his wife Anne, 'his seamstress', had been his mistress. Monck spoke highly of Sir William on his death in action and commended his widow and child to the favour of Charles II. She later married Samuel Barrow, physician to the King and to Monck's army.

[i] Colonel John Cromwell's nephew, Henry, is known to have resumed the family name of Williams but it is more difficult to confirm that John did so. None of the references given by John Loveday (see Appendix no. 150) are relevant to this point, though Echard in his *History of England* III, 638 describes a visit in 1649 from John to Oliver Cromwell in which he threatened that the relations would be forced to change back their name. However, according to H. R. Knight, *Historical Records of The Buffs, Formerly The Holland Regiment* 1905, John who had formerly been Colonel of an English regiment in the Dutch service did in 1658 ask Charles II (before his accession) for permission to change his name to Williams. His death in Holland is apparently unrecorded. John Loveday's statement suggests that his information came from the Earl of Abingdon. See also James Heath, *Flagellum*, 1663.

[j] This appears to be the only description of the chapel inside the house. The other chapel is now a national monument.

Chancel, in which sit the Chief of the family, is paved with marble; in the body, which is something lower, sit the Servants; the family are buryed in the Chancel, but there are no Monuments. The Cup for the Altar is of massy Gold; the Chappel, (as the Earl assures me from the original papers in his hands) is dedicated to St. Michael and All Angels; so correct B. Willis's 2nd Quarto.

They rode back to Oxford on 17 February stopping at Mother Pert's on Shotover Hill, one of their favourite haunts – though not for much longer as Mother Pert was to depart this life on the following New Year's Eve.

The next trip at the end of March was to Gloucester, with Thomas Waldgrave who was living at Faringdon playing host to John, Tom Winchester and William Payne. Winchester's own home was in the same town and his father came round to see them twice in the evening. Next day they rode through Fairford where John's old friend, the Clerk, was ready with more information about local families.

The Impropriation here belonged to the Oldisworths; they never had to do with the Mannor; that, from the Tames, came down to the Untons, so to the Lords Tracy, then to the Barkers, and so by marriage to Lambe, a Presbyterian.

Once again John described the glass, remarking that there was not one black devil in the church, and then they took the road to Cirencester on which

at every mile's end a Stone set-up in the Road tells you the distances. In Amney Park is a small Cottage where Mr Gardiner, a nonjuring Clergyman, lives a truly Hermitical life.

One might imagine the early eighteenth-century landscape littered with milestones, but it was not until the Turnpike Trust Acts from 1744 that they became more or less obligatory.

Cirencester, (pronounced Ciceter), is a considerably large town still, next perhaps to Gloucester in this County, though Leland observed that more than three parts of the old Town was in his time Meadow. It is no compact Town, built chiefly of the Stone of the Countrey. The mitred Abbey of Canons Regular founded by Henry I has not one Stone remaining upon another. Mr Master's handsome house[k] (and there may be three or four more very good houses in the Town of the same materials) is built on the site of the Abbey . . . St Cecilia's was 'clene down' in Leland's time; the name of Cicely Hill still remains.

---

[k] The site of the Abbey having reverted to the Crown, it was given by Queen Elizabeth to the Master family, who built the Abbey House. Thomas Master, who inherited it in 1710 and died in 1769, was living there in 1736. He made over the estate to his son in 1738 when he was twenty-one (see settlement of Abbey Estate, Gloucester Record Office).

There was much to admire in the church, which John called 'an elegant and grand Structure'. He liked especially the roof of 'pannelled wainscot' and the remains of painted glass in almost all the windows and especially that in the Trinity chapel. He noted that the order for 'Singing-Psalms throughout the year was hung up in this church as it was in St. Mary's at Nottingham, evidently an unusual practice.

The walls of the town had now quite disappeared, while

The Wool-Market on Fridays is still very considerable, though their Woollen Manufacture is not so great as it has been . . . Lord Bathurst's house is on one side the town, a plain Structure of Stone with a long front, built by his Lordship. The old house[l] was built by the Earl of Danby, Founder of the Physick Garden in Oxford. The Park rises behind it inclosed within a Wall which also encompasses Oakley Woods where are many Vistas . . .

Now it was time to set out for Gloucester, for though he had been there before he had not had time to consider the Cathedral properly. They rode north-west up Ermine Street (which he thought was the Fosseway) and down the steep hill at Birdlip.

The Descent is of great length and curves much from Burlip-Hill. The Steep is almost perpendicular on the left side of the hill and clothed with trees.

John Byng said in 1787 that no other turnpike road was as bad as these last six miles to Gloucester – narrow, wet and stony. In 1736 it can only have been a track, for the Roman road, said John, had become quite lost. This was one of his few rides in the Cotswolds which regrettably he never really explored.

On reaching Gloucester they put up at the Swan and went at once to call on the Revd John Newton[m] whom they had known at Magdalen. He was about a year younger than John and like his father before him was a minor canon of Gloucester. 'He afforded us his good Company, shewing us the place and we breakfasted with him.' In return John paid the first instalment of five shillings on old Mr Benjamin Newton's sermons which his son was publishing.

They also had an introduction to Anthony Freeman, a Gloucester merchant who had built Eagle Hall in Lower Westgate Street within the last ten years, having bought the property in 1724.[n] He had made a beautiful garden, though

---

[l] According to K. J. Beecham, *History of Cirencester* (1887; reprinted 1978), the tradition that this Lord Danby built the original house has not been proved; it is thought he must have destroyed an earlier building if it was he who put up the house Lord Bathurst removed. John Loveday reflects local opinion in 1736.

[m] The scholarly John Newton lived in Lower College Yard. He published his father's sermons in two volumes in 1736.

[n] Eagle Hall, or the Spa House, is said to have been built between 1724 and 1750 (*Gloucester Community Council Local History Bulletin, no. 39, 1979*). John's account shows that it was

his fruit trees were not as fine as those belonging to Mr Freeman of Fawley Court:[o]

Mr Freeman (an hearty, hospitable man we found him to be) has a most elegant house in this Street; the front is of Stone, not large; backwards to the Garden 'tis of brick, and there too uncommonly finished; Florists and those that understand Gardening would meet with high Entertainment here. But sure the Summer-house in the Garden is the most complete thing, both inside and outside. On the very top of it in the middle of the Cupola is a flower-Basket in Stone; through this great Ornament the Smoke is conveyed from the Chimney within. The shape of this little Room is, I think, an Octagon; out of each Window you have the Steeple of a Church, some near, some at a considerable distance. One is that belonging to the Cathedral. On one side the uneven ridge of Malvern hills terminates the View, the space between being an extensive Flat of many miles. The Room is elegantly wainscotted. The ceiling was painted by Casteels (still living) in about twenty-four hours; it represents the day in its Glory, Birds and Fowl of various kind flitting through the air. Others settled on the Rim of the Wainscot, where is also a Monkey or two. The air is not unnecessarily charged with Fowl; the Painter has evidenced as great a skill in nature in every part of this Performance. In the house itself are two Pictures by the same hand in still life, of Fowl, an Hare &c. exquisitely finished and laboured.

They looked at the Bishop's Palace which 'made no figure at all' on the outside, but had very good apartments and the remains of the White Friary 'vamped-up and made use of' as well as the neat new church of St John; but it was of course the Cathedral they had really come to see. Though John could only find beauty in the west front if seen from a distance, so that the tower was a part of it, and though he thought the pillars of the nave too 'massy' in proportion to their intervening spaces, these were only minor quibbles. 'Take all the East end together,' he wrote, 'you shall see nothing more striking and august.' One or two extracts must suffice from his very lengthy account.

Upon Sundays they have very fine Velvet to insert in the Pannels over the Altar. The Altar-piece, made probably at the same time with the Throne, is of Oak; the Segment of a good large Circle bending in the middle. Just behind this is one of the largest and stateliest East Windows in England . . . this reaches up to the very Roof, which throughout the Choir is of most curious laboured workmanship in Stone . . . in the 15th century Our Lady's Chappel was erected, a long but proportionable

---

inhabited in 1736. His is also the only description of the summer-house. In 1798 the house was let to the 11th Duke of Norfolk when he became mayor for the second time. Thereafter it was known as 'The Duke of Norfolk's Lodgings'. It was demolished in 1971.

[o] See p. 140.

Room entered under this great Window . . . though there be an Altar in the Chappel yet it is never used. The Chappel itself is used for early Prayers . . . in the North Chappel is buryed Bishop Goldsborough . . . in the South Chappel, against the East Wall, a plain mural Monument for Bishop Nicholson . . . [no Memorial] for any Bishop prior to him . . . there is not one Brass remaining in the Cathedral whilst it was a Monastery and few Inscriptions before the year 1660. . . Robert Curthoise's Tomb is placed so as to advantage the View of the Choir; it is on the rise to the Altar in the middle at an equal distance from North and South. . . the present figure is very large, lies cross-legged; the Wood is very light: 'tis inclosed within a lattice of wire . . . Perhaps the noblest Cloisters in England . . . they open into the large old Chapter-house, now the Library which is well fitted-up, though as yet it has no very large collection of books. . . It is doubted whether the famous Whispering-place was designedly or accidentally what it now is. . . You stand on one side of the great Window; the Person that speaks to you stands exactly opposite on the other side; the Voice passes behind the curving Window, being conveyed from angle to angle and on and on quite round the back of the Window. . . . From the East side of the South Cross projects the Stone Figure of a Workman's Square under which. . are the figures of two men; they have this Saying concerning the figure: 'John Gower built Gloucester College and Campden Tower.'[p]

'No Church is kept more neat and clean than this,' he concluded.

They saw the gaol, once the home of the Black Friars, and looked at the Cross with its figures of kings and queens.

There are two or three Statues of our Monarchs in this City, but all in a most astonishing degree deplorable. The Pin-making trade is carryed on here. . Here we ate of Shad, a large Fish in taste something like a Mackerel, but nothing near so strong. Ray calls a Shad the Mother of Herrings. . .

Thursday April 1. The Road was the very same that we travelled over on Tuesday, till we came almost to the foot of Burlip-hill when we took the left-hand Road, going-up Crickley-hill, easy ascent, remarkable Rocks about us; it called to mind the more pleasant parts of North Wales. Before Frogmill,[q] on the left hand opened a most lovely Prospect of the Vale of

[p] John Gower was, traditionally, the mason who built the great tower of Gloucester Cathedral about 1454–57 and the nave and tower of Chipping Campden church, built c. 1450–60. John Harvey in *English Mediaeval Churches* (1954), says there is no justification for saying the master mason figured on the mason's bracket was Robert Tulley (master of works). According to John Loveday he was thought in 1736 to be John Gower. The bracket dates from about 1337.

[q] After 1747 when the turnpike road from Gloucester to London passed through Shipton, the Frogmill Inn there became the first important staging post on this run.

Evesham, incircled with hills, well inhabited and as well-watered. Almost from Frogmill the Road lay through a very open Countrey. On the right of the Road lies Sir John Dutton's[r] large Stone Seat at Sherborn, situate very low.

It was not unusual to ride out from Oxford in order to see the Priory at Burford and particularly the famous painting of Sir Thomas More and his family which hung there. It is surprising that John had not been there before during his eight years at Oxford especially as this picture interested Hearne. He found now that it did not altogether tally with the account in Hearne's preface to Roper's *Life of More*. There were some other good portraits but they were all in some danger.

Perhaps most of the Pictures in this house may be something the worse for the damp-Walls, yet no Dauber has been repairing here.[s]

The house belonged to John Lenthall, a descendant of the Speaker who had built the chapel with its 'fretwork roof of Scripture history'. They thought the church a handsome pile and admired the magnificent monument to Sir Lawrence Tanfield and the memorial to John Harris; but they did not think much of Burford itself.

It makes but a mean Appearance; the main Street, long and very wide, runs down the steep side of an hill and continues on the Flat; 'tis built of the Stone of the Countrey. You will not see Publick-houses thicker anywhere.

Robert Lowth was particularly interested in this tour and when John and Audley drank tea with him in Oxford a few days later he was promised a copy of the account which John, with help from Crynes, would write up.

The only other incidents of any consequence that spring were the arrival of James Merrick at Trinity College and the death of George Beaulieu, the amiable curate of Caversham, at the early age of fifty-two. Dr John Merrick was indignant at the failure of the burgesses of Reading to elect his youngest son to a place at St John's College; James was by far the cleverest boy in the school, but–possibly because one of his brothers had been elected previously– they had chosen another boy, Thomas Sharpe. Dr Merrick's expostulations, attached to an old copy of *Cato*, are still in the school library. He wrote for redress to Bishop Hoadly who at once recommended James to the President

[r] Sir John Dutton's first wife was Mary, daughter of Sir Rushout Cullen of Upton, Warwickshire. The Cullens were friends of and possibly related to Abigail Goodwin who became John Loveday's mother-in-law in 1739.

[s] John Lenthall owned the Priory from 1686 to 1763. Things had evidently improved by 1753 when William Borlase, on a visit to Oxford, said it was in perfect repair (B. L. Stowe MS. 752.ff.156r–157v. Borlase to Charles Lyttelton; undated but written on or soon after June 30, 1753). There is a misattribution in R. H. Gretton, *The Burford Records*, 1920. Lenthall's character was apparently 'precise and exacting' (Gretton).

and Fellows of Trinity. There, though he could not follow the family and school tradition, he found a very happy niche for himself – one of the first of 'these Trinity College Poets' as John Loveday later called them, thinking also of Thomas Warton and William Benwell.[t]

The death of Beaulieu was a great loss to Sarah Loveday. With John so much away she had very little masculine companionship and had to rely on her own judgment in matters of house and estate management. However she had a good friend in her attorney Alexander Staples, as a letter he wrote from Windsor on 18 May 1736 shows:

> Honoured Madam,
>   I take it as a great honour, to be favoured with this Correspondence with so ingenious and fine a Lady about matters relating to my own Profession. The life of Copyholds is Custom. Originally Copyholders were bare tenants at Will, according to the strict sense of the word; but now by time and Custom, they have a fixed and dureable estate, though still called tenants at the will of the Lord according to the custom of the Mannor. As to the Surrenders made out of Court into the hands of two tenants, they are made without the knowledge of the Steward; he knowes nothing of them till they are brought into Court. As to Conditional Surrenders they are Mortgages for money and the Lord has no fine upon their being brought into Court untill the person that lends the money coines is desired to be admitted (which seldom happens).

After explaining the system of fines to the Lord of the Manor upon surrender or death as it affected her tenants, he concluded:

> Pray Madam read your Book. I hope to have an opportunity of waiting on you before the Summer is over and shall then enquire what progress you make in the Study of the Law of Copyholds. . .'[t]

A new perpetual curate called Francis Gastrell was appointed by Christ Church to St Peter's; he remained there for four years and soon got on well with John and his mother.

> April 30. 1736. The double gilt Bowl at Jesus College contains 10 Gallons, the Ladle about half a pint. Parry, once a Fellow here, now living at Shipston-upon-Stoure,[u] has wrote upon Vellum the Statutes of the College, in folio, and the life of Dr Mansell, once Principal, from an MS. in the Museum in Quarto. These are wrote in such a manner as by no means to be discerned from the most clear and beautiful Print. I have never seen anything equal to them. Sure one of these was wrote in 1722.

---

[t] To whom must be added the name of Henry Headley. William Lisle Bowles, though also under the influence of Thomas Warton, did not write verse early enough to be noticed by John Loveday in this way.

[u] William Parry was presented to the living of Shipston-on-Stour in 1729.

This was John's only descriptive note during the spring; but he was busily preparing for his next long tour and consulting the works of past travellers, particularly Leland.

No one, it seems, has ever had anything interesting to say about Dr Thomas Jenner, D.D. His only distinctions were the Margaret Professorship of Divinity, a post which he held from 1728 for forty years, and the Presidency of Magdalen College from 1747 until his death in 1768, which in his case was hardly a claim to fame. He was, however, a central figure in college life during John's ten years or so at Oxford, being closer to President Butler than most other members of the Society. He owed his Professorship to Butler who had manoeuvred it with Trinity College; it was indeed because of this that poor Dr Fynes had failed as a candidate for the Keepership of the Ashmolean, as Butler supported a Fellow of Trinity in order to repay that college for its help over Jenner. Jenner was neither more nor less than mediocre, but probably not a dull companion or the astute Butler would never have permitted such a close association for so long. Jenner was Vice-President in 1730 and Senior Fellow when Butler died.

Let it now be stated to his credit that in the summer of 1736 he rode on horseback through Somerset, Devon, Cornwall and Dorset and followed this feat the following year by travelling the Low Countries in a variety of conveyances.

It seems unlikely that John would have suggested such an expedition to the older man and Jenner probably broached the matter himself, inviting another member of Butler's clique, the Revd William Haward, to be the third member of the party. John being the youngest cannot have been in charge of the expedition, but the fact that they stopped to look at almost everything points to his having had some influence on the arrangements and must also mitigate to some extent the charges of lethargy which have been levelled against Thomas Jenner.

After a night at Fairford and another at Holt they reached Wells on 3 June. They had visited Malmesbury Abbey on the way where, as was to be expected, John thought the pillars bulky and the proportions spoiled by the blocking up of the nave. On the other hand there was the beautiful porch and the ruins at the east end were magnificent.

As to the West front, nothing Northward of that Door is remaining at present. That Door is not large; just south of it is standing part of a large square tower . . . there are two brass plates here, one bears date 1660, the other 1661. On a plate of copper, framed and hung up, is an Epitaph in 1732 . . . The lonely Spire – Steeple of St Paul's Church still stands in a corner of the the Garth; here the Bells hang; the Church itself, as Browne Willis observed, has been long since a dwelling for poor people.

The next two nights were spent at the George Inn at Wells.

Wells in the roots of Mendipe hill in a stony soil and full of Springs, whence its name, is built chiefly of Stone as in Leland's time, yet makes but a mean appearance. Streams for these Springs run in almost every Street . . . the beauty of the Cathedral is the West front, which is one entire Pile of Statues, every nich filled but those towards the bottom. The two West Towers do not stand over the Isles of the Body, but North and South of them; if they were higher, as well as the Tower in the middle, it would be an addition of beauty to all. It is very good Stone that the Church is built of . . . the Walls within are suffered to be too green – the Pillars are not clumsy in the Nave; the Pavement is in some meagre old gravestones.

It might be concluded from his long and careful but prosaic description of a cathedral which has so often been praised in the most exalted terms that he was insensitive to its glories or unaffected by its spiritual beauty. However, this was not the occasion for superlatives; he was taking notes for his own future interest alone. One does not forget feelings of rapture, but distances between arches or the exact words on inscriptions are not so easy to remember. The cause of one criticism he made was removed in 1758 when the high altar was taken down.[v]

The persons that made the Altar-piece did not consult the architecture of the Church which designed three open Arches under the Window and over a low Altar-piece to give a View into our Lady's Chappel, a lower building, the most Eastward of the whole; the painted Window of which should have terminated the View through the open Arches as is done with great good effect in Gloucester Cathedral.[w]

Looking at a marble slab for William Healy[x] in the Lady Chapel, he remembered a description in Hearne's *Adam de Domerham* of the discovery of Bishop Bytton I's coffin twenty inches below the pavement on the same spot, a gold ring on the finger and a small silver cup with the bones:

This large Coffin, with much such another, (which was found I am told when Bishop Hooper's grave was dug) is still to be seen in a place (which they tell me was once the Vestry)[y] to be entered out of the N. side Isle. In the side of both these Coffins there is an hole cut for the reception of the Cup.

[v] I am grateful to Mr L. S. Colchester for his comments on John's account of Wells Cathedral. See also L. S. Colchester and J. H. Hervey, 'Wells Cathedral', in *Royal Archaeological Journal*, vol. 131.

[w] The view is now as he would have wished; this reredos was taken down as unsafe in 1758.

[x] William Healy's slab probably disappeared when the floor was tiled in 1843.

[y] The coffins were in the Undercroft, formerly the Treasury, and are now in the south walk of the cloister.

After John had recorded the position of all the monuments, some of which have now been altered, there was only time for a quick glance at the rest of the town. They admired the gatehouse to the Palace, the Deanery and the 'Close for Minor Canons'.[z] John praised Bishop Beckington's 'Twelve Houses',[a] but was not much attracted to Bishop Bubwith's Hospital which he said was like that at Newark but not quite so mean.

It was seven years since his last visit to Glastonbury and he was now able to devote more time (as well as experience) to his explorations. He wanted to compare the facts with Hearne's *History and Antiquities of Glastonbury* published in 1722, in which he had incorporated Charles Eyston's *A Little Monument to the Once Famous Abbey and Borough of Glastonbury* (1716) because of their friendship. 'The Quadrangle Inclosure is said to contain 60 Acres by Mr Eyston, but they tell us here that there are 67 Acres within the Inclosure.'

He described St Joseph's Chapel and the Abbot's Kitchen, which according to tradition, he said, was built by Abbot Whiting who was martyred on the Tor, but which is now known to date from the fourteenth century.

> Dr Plot and Mr Eyston are mistaken when they say there are no tunnels to the [four] Chimnies; they do not indeed appear on the Outside; there is a stone Lanthorn at top to convey away superfluous smoke; it may perhaps be 80 feet high to the top of the roof.

Mr Prue was still living in Glastonbury;[b] they came upon his house just within the enclosure on the south-west side of the Abbey grounds –

> ... a neat little box built in 1714 (as the date upon it shews) the front set-off with Coats of Arms from the Abbey. Here lives Mr Prue, a Presbyterian, who has this Estate upon a lease of two lives; the Duke of Devonshire was Lord Paramount here, but he lost it gaming to Colonel Bladen.[c] Just opposite to Prue's house, on t'other side Magdalen Street, is an Almshouse with a Chappel for ten men. 1512 is the date in the stone-work over the Gate of it. Such another for ten women stands at the North part of the Abbey and this is undoubtedly Abbot Beere's Almshouse mentioned by Leland, which very assuredly Eyston makes out to be St. Margaret's Chappel as if such an Almshouse did not now exist in statu quo.

[z] Vicars' Close.

[a] Known now, as it was originally c. 1453, as The New Works.

[b] It seems that the only other mention of Thomas Prue or Prew is in the diary of John Cannon (Somerset Record Office DD/SAS–C/1193/4), a Glastonbury schoolmaster who disapproved of Thomas Prew's having blown up the vaults and pulled down the hall, selling some stones and using others for his dwelling house near Magdalene gate.

[c] Information kindly given shows that transactions preserved at Chatsworth do not mention gambling debts, but that large sums changed hands between the 3rd Duke and Bladen in 1735 and 1738. Property is not shown to have been involved in these MSS. but gambling may have been the reason for the Duke's debts.

They spent the night at the Swan but it was the George Inn which John described, saying that it was thought to have been the Pilgrims' Hospital;[d] the Abbot's bedstead was now taken to pieces. After seeing the two churches and, as it was a Sunday, no doubt attending service in one of them, they left next day for Bridgwater.

They had a guest for supper that evening, a man in whom they were all greatly interested and whose name reminded John of his tour into Wales with Zinzan in 1730. For this was the Revd Moses Williams, the renowned Welsh antiquary whose praises had been sung so forcibly by their strange guide over the mountains. He was now the vicar of St Mary's at Bridgwater. John may have met him when he visited Hearne not long after their return from Wales. Hearne had liked him when he had been a sub-librarian at the Ashmolean, but though conceding that he was skilled in modern Welsh had thought him indifferent in ancient British.

> The River Parret is a thick muddy stream, like the Avon at Bristol . . .
> Leland mentions the Castle all going to mere ruin . . . They are now
> pulling-down the Castle, but we reckon it to be a building erected since
> Leland wrote this, taking up no large compass of ground; it seems to be a
> dwelling-house built castle-wise; it stands fronting the haven at the top of
> a new Street built of brick, of no great length . . . Ships of above 100 ton
> ride at the bridge, 36 sail belonging to the town. Sull, (pronounced Zull),
> an Anglo-Saxon word, signifies in this Countrey a cart and plough or
> waggon.
> Monday June 7. The journey today [to Dulverton] was upon uneven
> ground; sometimes upon considerable high hills; on the right before
> Stoke Gomer [Stogumber] we had a view of the Sea with the Stepe
> Holmes and Flat Holmes; on the left-hand a pretty Countrey . . . Stoke
> Gomer is one of the vilest, most contemptible Market-towns in the
> Kingdom; there are not many Villages but what exceed it much. In our
> ride today we saw several walls built with Slate-Tiles pitched edgeways
> and covered at top with turf. We had one exceeding steep descent. Some
> river runs in the Valley between two very high hills covered with
> hanging-woods.

Thirty-four miles over the Quantocks (twenty-seven in John's mileage) was very good going. The journey next day was nearly as long but it brought them into Devon.

> Three miles beyond South Moulton . . . lies Lord Clinton's Seat, no
> large place, the Outside of Stucho, the ballustrade of wood painted in a
> stone colour; the upper is an Attick Story. The situation is on something of
> a rising ground, as good as the Countrey just hereabouts will afford.

---

[d] The almshouses and the George and Pilgrim Inn still stand. Medieval pilgrims often came to Glastonbury from Winchester and Salisbury.

This Lord has made a very good Road for a considerable distance in our tour.

This was Filleigh Manor and Lord Clinton (who was created Baron Fortescue and Earl of Clinton in 1746) was devoting his life to restoring the old house. He renamed it Castle Hill and it was eventually a much larger and grander building than when John passed by in 1736.

They spent a night at the Fleece at Barnstaple and John praised the town for its beautiful situation and the fine lawns across the river no less than for its 'sumptuous' bridge. Then they rode south to Torrington, but first they had to see Bideford with its splendid ancient bridge –

a very notable work of 24 arches of stone (the arches not so high as those in Barnstaple) fairly walled on each side. It is excellently well paved and there is great care taken to keep the bridge clear of all filth. The Key here is much finer than at Barnstaple as is the trade – to Virginia chiefly.

Although they had been into a number of churches it was not until they arrived at Kilkhampton that they entered a country house. Stowe[e] had been rebuilt in 1679 and now belonged to Countess Granville. It was, said John, 'the finest Seat in these Western parts', but its situation was bleak and isolated and only three years later, partly due to the expense of its upkeep, it was demolished.

'Tis a large Square Pile projecting two Wings which are not longer than to contain one Window on a Side, but they have each two in front; which added to the others make the whole number of the Windows in the front to be twelve. 'Tis a brick house . . . Several family Pictures, among others Sir Bevil Granville – a red-haired man; . . . Charles II riding over the Sea in a triumphal Car drawn by Sea-horses, Dolphins attending.[f] The Picture that strook me most was Christ's Agony in the Garden. . . . Fretwork Cielings, elegantly performed to some of the Rooms and very good Carving in Wood to adorn the Chimney-pieces of fruit, flowers and fowl. The Chappel[g] is wainscotted and fitted-up with Cedar, the Pavement of black and white marble. The grand Stair-case[h] is adorned on the three broad sides with Views of this house, Plimouth and Biddiford. In one of the Rooms is the Bed that Charles II dyed in, of crimson Velvet;[i] the Earl of Bath, as Groom of the Stole, claiming it as his Fee. The house is very dark

[e] See G. M. Trinick, 'The Great House of Stowe', in *The Journal of the Royal Institute of Cornwall*, new series, vol. VIII, part 2, 1979. John's account of the house, mentioned here, is thought to be the most accurate contemporary description.

[f] Now in South Molton Guildhall, it was sold to the Corporation for seven guineas.

[g] The chapel was very probably taken to Stowe, Buckinghamshire by Lord Cobham who certainly bought some of the panelling. His sister married Richard Grenville of Wotton, Bucks.

[h] The staircase went to Cross, Little Torrington.

[i] The fate of this bed is unknown.

because the Panes of Glass are remarkably small. The Gardens in decay. One way the house looks upon the open Sea, the other way upon a narrow Valley between, and bounded by, rising hills cloathed with low Wood, the tower of Kilkhampton Church almost in the front. This Seat has been inhabited but one year since the rebuilding of it;[j] it now belongs to the Countess of Granville (Daughter to the last Granville, Earl of Bath) and the Lord Gower.[k]

At Launceston there was not a complete street in the town though there were some very good houses. He found the well-known exterior of the church, its granite surface carved with coats of arms or other devices, 'extremely curious' – as indeed it is. He took particular notice of the effigy of Mary Magdalene.

sleeping or weeping, the Stones about her carved with the figures of musical Instruments. Willis was too full of Epithets when he applyed 'beautiful' to this Statue and 'high and handsome' to the tower which stands at West. On the South and West sides the view of the Church is spoiled by houses built-up against it; 'tis a handsome Church within . . . they have with good success added Stucho between the wood-work of the mid-Isle and propose to do the same with the side-Isles, the Rafters of which are well-worked . . . Against the wall of the South Isle is King Charles I's letter to the Cornish in 1643 wrote in Golden Characters on a wooden table; over it was a Painting of Charles I and the Earl of Strafford which Bishop Weston ordered to be taken-down . . .

Leaving Launceston next day (12 June) they headed west to the coast and after seeing Tintagel returned to Camelford for the night.

Our Road was extreme good today, part through Lanes, but chiefly over Heaths called 'Mores' here, which in the West-Countrey seems to be a common name for an open Countrey whether high or low situated – the miles too were short.

He was interested in the fact that many small villages were boroughs in spite of their size. Newport at Launceston had been one of these and now they rode through two more which together constituted a borough – Bossiney and Trevena in the parish of Tintagel ('pronounced Dundagel').

There are at present about 22 Voters;[l] they have no Charter but they

[j] By the Earl of Bath (d. 1701).

[k] John was mistaken in thinking Lord Gower owned half the property. It belonged solely to Countess Granville (Grace Carteret) after the settlement of a lawsuit in 1720, having originally been inherited jointly by her and her sister, Lady Jane Leveson-Gower, who died in 1696 and who was Lord Gower's godmother.

[l] Sixty years later there were only about six voters (W. G. Maton, *Observations on the Western Counties*, 1794–96).

have by prescription a Mayor annually chosen; the town-hall is a neat room enough in Trevana Village where is also an annual Fair; no Market held in the Borough. There are not near 40 Dwelling-houses in both Hamlets taken together. There is one very handsome new house at Bossinney, otherwise the houses in both Hamlets may be termed Cottages, though they be covered with Slate-Tiles.

Quoting Leland's description of Tintagel 'on a great and high terrible Crag', John continued

It is now extreme difficult to mount this steep rock, which contains about 30 acres of pasture and has fresh water on the top . . .

But, apart from stating categorically that King Arthur had been born there in the year A.D. 500, his description of Tintagel was unromantic – nor was there much to say about Camelford save that Browne Willis had not allowed it enough houses and King Arthur had been slain there in A.D. 542. At Bodmin, a much smaller place than it once had been, they visited the Priory church of St Petrarch. Here Browne Willis was in trouble again for having mixed it up with the Bowry church.

. . . Just West of the Chancel stands the tower, broad and strong; much within the memory of man there was a Spire on it, thrown-down by a Storm of Thunder and Lightning. . .

The ride over Bodmin Moor presented few difficulties; most of the way the road was very good. Their destination was the Red Lion at St Columb, but a few miles before they reached it they turned off to visit Lanhydrock. Any expectations they may have had were daunted, for the place was desolate

Llanhidrock – the Earl of Radnor's is in a Park, no View from it and no sight, sure, in itself; 'tis all built of Stone; there is a large Gate-house to it built later than the house.''' The house itself is an old low Quadrangle, like some little College. The Gallery is a long and well-proportioned Room with a bowed fret-work Roof performed in a Gothic taste. The house is extremely out of repair and utterly destitute of furniture; we saw one family Picture.''

As they rode south to Redruth on 25 June they came into the tin and copper mine country, many of the mines being by the side of the road. To the

''' The 2nd Lord Robartes began building the gatehouse in 1636. It was completed in 1651. The house had been begun by the 1st Lord Robartes who died in 1634.
'' The Robartes family had become Earls of Radnor. They lived at Radnor House, Twickenham, neglecting their Cornish home. John's account provides further evidence of this.

south-west they could see the great rocks of Carnbrea (or 'Karn Bre Castle' as John called it). Next day the conditions changed again.

> The Road for a few miles was up and down and something rough and in lanes; then we had an open Countrey, then on the Shore of a Creek near great heaps, perfect hills, of white Sand blown-up by the Winds from the Sea; it has destroyed some good Land and we saw it piled up very high against Lelamp Church, about 5 miles from Penzance . . . to which we rode partly on the Sea-Shore on an hard white Sand.

Dr Jenner was a long way from Oxford and the comfortable life of a Senior Common Room. No sooner had he dined at the Ship and Castle (dinner was always the daytime meal) than he found himself sitting in a boat and heading for St Michael's Mount.

> From Penzance in the afternoon we took a boat for the St Michael's Mount, an high and craggy Rock encompassed with Water when the Tide is in, joined to the main-land when out. Leland says that 'tis not half a mile round the root of the Mount, but truth 'tis very near a mile. There are, all the way up, many fragments of Rock, much of 'em covered with Moss; in one part they seem in the very action of falling as naturally as a horse seems yet running in Picture; in another part a very large Stone projects, scarce any thing to support it, and forms a Cave underneath. On the top of the Mount was a Benedictine Cell to St. Michael's in Normandy and a fortification.
> Sir John St. Aubyn, to whom this Island belongs, has fitted-up some of the ruined buildings, and therein resides sometimes, his chief Seat being 7 miles distant . . .[o] The East Window of Our Lady's Chappel still remains. St. Michael's Chappel is roofed; it is one length, has no Isles, no Cross-Isle, yet the tower in the middle with five tunable Bells in it; in the Chancel are Stalls with Relievo-work. From the Stone roof of the tower is an amazing large Prospect towards the Land, the Mount's-Bay makes a glorious View; 'tis a large Semicircle, an easy descent from the Countrey to it – from a good Countrey, not Rocks; four towns on the margin viz. Market Jew[p] just by, Mousehole, Newlyn and Penzance; several towers of Churches in View; hence you also see the North Sea too and hence the Lizard Point . . . at 7 leagues distance to the South, it being the most Southern point of England. Out of one of the Parlour-Windows you see nothing but the spacious Sea; the Hall was the old Refectory of the Religious house; 'tis cieled with Rafters of Irish Oak; at the upper end is, and ever was, a Chimney; now indeed it is contracted. Sir John has planted some Scotch Fir, Dutch Elm and Tamarisk here, which, if the plantation succeeds, will be a great addition to the Island . . . There is a large number

---

[o] This was Clowance in the parish of Crowan.
[p] An old name for Marazion.

of fine Rabbets in this island but there are no Cornish Choughs here now. There are several Dwelling-houses on the shore of the Mount and Sir John has made a little haven in it.

Sir John (whom we met with on the Mount) is a Gentleman of great good Sense, good nature, affability, modesty and fine breeding; he spared us no Pains to shew us the Curiosities here and afterwards entertained us very handsomely; his good Lady was with him, (she is Sir William Morris's Sister)[q] and Mr William Borlase, a Clergyman in the neighbourhood. Sir John is a little Man, about thirty years of age,[r] one of the Knights for Cornwall. He told us that upon a computation, the fishing-nets belonging to this Bay would stretch (if spread-out) from Penzance near as far as the Isle of Wight. He said that some Land, near about here, was let for 4 or 5£ an Acre.

Of Penzance itself John had not much to say except that it was now very populous, that St Maddren's Well was 'sovereign for the cures of some distempers' and that the town was excellently well supplied with fish. 'Mr Gwavas, a Gentleman of fortune here,[s] is said to understand Cornish the best of any man.'

They stayed for two nights having planned an expedition to Land's End.

The first part of the ride was up and down in stony Lanes; we saw a very barren Countrey today. Before Land's-End was Chappel Karn Bre on an high hill, a Ruin whence a good View of the Countrey; west of this hill runs a Slip of improved Corn-Land, which bending with a sweep to the South reaches to St. Buriens, belonging to the Deanery. We saw St. Just's at a distance on the North Coast; where at Newlyn also and Mousehole, there are some that can talk the old Cornish tongue. Sennen Chappelry is the most Western Village of England; the Chappel consists of two Isles, has a bowed, raftered Roof and is not paved. The font stands on a Stone round the borders of which is an ancient Inscription. The tables which represent the Kings-arms and the ten Commandments on the West side have on the East side King Charles Ist's letter. The Land's-End thrusts into the Sea very high and horrid Rocks, the level of the Countrey far above the Water. The Rocks opposite, some distance off, are called the long Ships; the coast along here is armed with Cliffs to withstand the violence of the North and South Seas rushing into one another here.

On their way back they saw the church at St Buryan with its screen 'carved,

[q] Catherine Morice.
[r] Sir John was then forty years of age.
[s] John may have been referring to a chancery suit which Gwavas, a lawyer, inherited with the rectory of Paul on the right of the rector to take certain fish. It had begun in 1680 and he won it in 1727. Edward Lhuyd also referred to his having the greatest knowledge of Cornish. Cornwall had its own language until the sixteenth century.

painted and gilt'. There were a few stalls in the chancel but the place needed paving and new pews. John called it 'desolate', though 'lightsome'.

On 18 June they went on to Falmouth, travelling on a brick road after Helston. The town consisted of one long, fairly narrow street with some brick houses – the first they had seen for some time. Pendennis Castle, where a small garrison was kept, was 'out of repair' and though they went up there they could only admire the view.

Penryn they thought was a considerable town though chiefly in one broad street. Truro was 'a fair well-traded town, as much talked of as any in Cornwall', but they could do no more than look at the church as they had to reach St Austell by evening. Probus had the best church tower they had seen in Cornwall. The next day was a Sunday and the ride to Lostwithiel was pleasant.

> Just beyond St Austels we saw the Sea . . . and some Creeks afterwards . . . We descended sharp upon Lostwithiel which is most delightfully situate in a Valley bounded by Several small hills all covered with a profitable Verdure, several Orchards about the town. The River Fowey (over which is a bridge) is a very clear Stream . . . still the Election of Knights of the Shire is made here. In the Shire-Hall the general Quarter-Sessions is held twice a year – once it is at Liskerd, once at Bodmin. Leland mentions Ruins of the Dukes of Cornwall's house by this hall; they now appear – one part seems to have been a great hall; another is now used for a Prison for the Tinners that are Debtors. This is one of the Coynage-towns. The Church is no extraordinary Building, the Pillars not neat, the side-Isles very low, an awkward raftered roof . . . One of the Insignia of the Mayor is a silver Oar shewing his Authority upon the Creek; . . . the Town now again flourishes by means of the woollen manufacture – not twenty years since it was very poor.

They climbed the hill to inspect the ruins of Restormel Castle, once the seat of the Dukes of Cornwall:

> It was a round building as the outward shell remaining evidently shews. The Parapet remains. One Room was a Chappel, the holy-water hole remains. Part of the Stone was carryed off years ago to build at Llanhidrock above one mile off; this is so strong a Building that the very Finishing remains.

They passed through 'the Lows, pronounced Loos' on their way to Plymouth which they reached on 21 June.

> Out of Eastlow we ascended a very high steep hill, the Road lay on the top of it and at first on the edge of the Cliff open to the Sea; for four miles it was troublesome riding, continually ascending and descending steep hills, much in narrow lanes and every now and then on the very edge of

the open Cliff as before. At eight miles distance we saw Plimouth-Dock, the Road for some time on red Sands. One mile before the Crimble-Passage [Cremyll] we came through Milbrook, a fishing town and then by the side of Mr Edgcumbe's' Park . . .

Now that they were leaving Cornwall John had some general comments to make about the Duchy and its inhabitants.

As for Cornwall in King John's time there was more Tinn in Devon-shire than this County. The most valuable Copper-mine belongs to Mr Basset. They improve the land with Sea-Sand; the Persons who carry it about the Countrey are called Sanders, whence perhaps that Surname; though it be generally esteemed the nick-name or abbreviation of Alexander. They carry it on horses, two small Sacks being the loading of an horse. The Language is more pure and refined than in Devon and Somersetshire; when they answer affirmatively to any question they join 'sure' to the affirmation, as 'yes, sure'. They say the same when they would tell you that they will do as you order them. This Phrase, in both cases, is used in Devonshire. Here are 27 Market-towns; for most of the Parliamentary Boroughs Cornwall is obliged to Edward VI and Elizabeth. 'Tis about 70 miles long from East to West, forty broad in some places, five in others. For Provision the Mutton is very sweet and fine-grained, the heaths of this Countrey well-agreeing with Sheep. Bread they are utterly ignorant of the art of making – here and in other parts of the West. To make Sampson take 1 Bottle of Cyder, a quartern of brandy, some fine sugar and you may add Lemon; you may colour Sampson with half a Pint of Port.

In the West part of Cornwall the hedges are of Furze, as in Ireland. There is scarce a tree to be seen in that part of the Countrey; there the rich mines are. The Miles are but short in comparison of the neighbouring Counties. A Cornish Stile is not ladder-wise, but is formed thus:– they dig an hole; over this from right-hand to left they pitch four or five long Stones, an Interstice between each Stone wider than the Stone itself; sometimes instead of Stones there are pieces of Wood placed edgeways; sometimes this Stile lies level with the Ground, sometimes is something higher. In the East part of this County the very vile Cottages are healed (as they call it in Cornwall as well as elsewhere) with Slates – a beautiful as well as a strong Covering, of which there are Quarries in Tintagel Parish. In the West the Cottages are thatched; in some of them the thatch is bound-on with Ropes of Straw; these Ropes cost a mere trifle of expense and are renewed about once a year. Several thatched Cottages have sashed Windows, but few brick houses and those tiled with Slates after the Scotch mode. One Complaint we made through the County, that for want of Casements

' Richard Edgcumbe became 1st Baron Edgcumbe in 1742.

in the Rooms they smell too hot. There are large commodious Butcheries in the towns. The Churches are in good measure alike" and indeed are neat and well-proportioned . . . There are very few Monuments in the Churches, either ancient or modern; in some of the Churches the Clerk reads the 1st Lesson; the Cornish Crosses are particular – a Stone pitched up on end, smooth on each side; the top of it is formed in an oval shape, having the figure of the Cross in Relievo upon the side of the Oval; many of the Crosses lie broken in the way; some that are erected are so very low that one may suppose them to have been broken-off and then re-erected. The Cornish are, many of 'em, black-haired; the women too are very fair. The lower rank of women wear black-hats like the Welsh and they smoak as in Devonshire. A Cornish Daw has a red bill and red feet, his feathers are glossy black. A Cornish Chough is a less bird, nothing observable in the bill and feet, the head of a blew or different black from the rest of the body.

They had company that night as Dr Jenner had a friend who was now a lecturer in Plymouth, Mr Robert Forster, once a chorister of Magdalen College. His son, Nathaniel, later a well-known scholar who edited Plato's Dialogues but now a boy of eighteen, was with him. They joined the trio for meals, dining with them at the George and entertaining them at home. This was a pleasant change and two nights were spent at Plymouth where there was plenty to do.

We took a Boat to Mount-Edgcumbe, the Seat of Richard Edgcumbe Esqr. It stands in a Park on the gentle Ascent of an hill, the green hill rising beyond it; through a fine, wide Avenue taking-in the whole front, there is an extended View of the Countrey across the Passage; long since the house was built the View from it is much mended by the building of Plimouth Dock; Stonehouse Village is also just in the front with the Harbour. The house is old, built castle-wise of rough Stone plastered; it is not very large – the front is handsome, round towers at the extremity. The house is in bad repair and wants furniture. In the hall (among other Paintings) are those of Prince Rupert in a black wig with a truncheon . . . of William, Prince of Orange (afterwards King) in his own hair, armed, an handsome likeness. . . Opposite to one another out of this Room are two very plain Stair-cases; the pleasantest Rooms are those angular ones in the towers which also take-in a View of Plimouth-town in a Valley. The modern Offices stand on one side. The Wilderness and Gardens lie below the house; the Views through Walks in the Gardens are terminated, each very happily. Though on the West side of the Tamar, yet this Seat is in Devonshire, yet it is subject in Spirituals to the Archdeacon of Cornwall. Baronhill, Lord Bulkeley's, is very like Mount Edgcumbe, but this exceeds all for situation.

" 'coped raftered Roofs, neat pillars and those of the same make too' (John Loveday).

In our way to this place we sailed-by the Isle of St. Nicholas,[v] of two acres or more says Camden. Plimouth-Dock is 2 miles from the town; it is a growing place still; it has two or three good streets. The rope-house about 180 fathom long is well built of brick; it is two Stories high; they spin above and twist below. The natural Rock has been cut-away to make room for the Dock; what remains is a Wall to it to landwards; what is thus cut-away is used for building here. An handsome range of building has in the middle the Commander's-house; joined to it on each side are other Officers'-houses. Sir William Morris[w] is Lord of the Soil here, which was once worth scarce anything.

The growth of the dock had, he thought, reduced the number of people in Plymouth which had once been as large as Exeter. It was still a very close-built town with narrow streets and many houses. An organ was being erected in St Andrew's church where 'Zachary Mudge is Minister, who was educated a Dissenter at Exeter'.

John quoted so many former visitors to Plymouth – Leland, Willis and Dr Thomas Smith in particular – that there was little more to add from his own observations except that he preferred the view from the garrison 'manned with Invalids' to that from 'the How' which lay so low.

There followed a night at South Brent, another at Chudleigh and then on 25 June – a Friday – the tour became more exciting again, for they had been invited to spend two nights at Powderham Castle with John's old college friend Sir William Courtenay. They were by no means the only guests: besides the family they found Sir John Morgan, the Member for Hereford, Dr Williams, a physician at Exeter and formerly a member of Exeter College and Proctor of the University, and Mr Brudenell, Collector of Excise at Exeter. The clergy too were in full force, for there were not only Mr Chute, the rector of Powderham, and Dr Charles Bertie, a cousin of the Courtenays and rector of Kenn nearby, but also Dr James Fynes himself, now duly installed as rector of Moretonhampstead since 13 June.

Three of the Sisters are married to Messieurs Ilbert, Basset and Langdon. There are two maiden Sisters and three Brothers.

Powderham Castle is a large, strong Seat of Stone and ancient. One Wing was built by the late Sir William in 1717, a Chappel below, a Library above; there is another Wing designed to answer it. The Hall was originally extremely large; it is now contracted to a very moderate size, a noble Stair-case and several good Rooms made out of it. Sir William's best Paintings are at Ford[x] by Newton Bushel[y] ten miles off; yet here are some well worth noting as a three-quarter piece of the Duke

[v] Drake's Island.
[w] Morice.
[x] Forde House – a Jacobean building.
[y] An old name for a district in Newton Abbot – formerly a separate town.

of Albemarle in armour, his Robes over it . . . A Length of Peregrine
Bertie, another of his Wife . . . a fine Portrait of Lady Anne Courtenay,[z] a
beautiful Person. There is an old Gate-way and Wall before the house . . .
through the Park which is not above one mile and a half in compass, you
have a pleasant walk to the Sea, or rather the River Ex; on t'other side of
which there is a pleasant Country and an house of Sir Francis Drake by the
Sea-shore. Dr. Fynes's father, the late Steward here, gained (within these
few years) many acres to Sir William from the Sea. Powderham Church
has a bowed, coped roof, plastered between the wood-work; in a Window
on the North side lies Isabella de Fortibus, no large figure, the hands
joined, the head-dress like Queen Philippa's; the Courtenays bury here
now; there are tomb-stones for some of them, as also a mural Monument
for Lady Mary Bertie. The great-Grandfather of Sir William was offered
by King Charles II the Earldom of Ockhampton and Barony of
Powderham. The Surveys of Sir William's Estates are very curious.
Those in Ireland are drawn-out in a large folio on Vellum; on the opposite
leaf in different columns are Tenants' names, the number of acres, the
Rent &c. Some of his English Estates are drawn-out by Wittlesey in 8vo
very neatly.

When the time came for them to leave, Henry Courtenay – a younger
brother who was also an old friend of John's – and Mr Brudenell accompanied them along the sandy lanes to Exeter and spent the evening with
them at the New Inn. Henry stayed with them all the next day and took them
to drink tea with his eldest sister 'Mrs Anna Sophia Courtenay' who had a
house in Exeter.

They had two days there and John spent most of the time in the Cathedral.
He admired the town immensely with its gentle slopes to the hills 'rich with
verdure and rising with all ease and beauty'.

Leland speaks of the Walls as newly made in his time; they with the
Gates are still standing. The East Suburb is biggest . . . It is chiefly an old-
built town and the houses of Timber and Plaster, yet very good. The high
Street . . . is very noble – though not so wide it is much longer than the
high Street in Oxford and much better built if you consider the Dwelling-
houses only. The Cross-Street at the Conduit, as the rest of them, is but
narrow. It is reckoned one of the most considerable Cities in England. In
the highest part between the East and North Gates the Castle stands stately
commanding the City under it and the Countrey on all sides. There is a
very good gravel-walk, carefully maintained under the Castle-Wall on
the Outside, whence the Prospect is beautiful. The Cathedral was
compassed with many fair houses in Leland's time as it now also is; the
Area is planted with Trees which make pretty Walks . . . several houses

---

[z] She was Sir William's mother, Anne, sister of the 2nd Earl of Abingdon and died in 1718.
See p. 214 n.*a*.

are built up against the Church hindering the view of it. The buttresses supporting it are massy and vast . . .

Inside he was appreciative of the pillars and arches and the beautiful roof but critical of the dimensions – 'the Cross Isle (take it all together) is the most blameworthy part of the building' – and the lack of grand windows. The eastern had the most perfect glass and the western the finest workmanship.

Though this Church was about 400 years in building yet the symmetry is such that it might pass for the work of one man.

He summed up his mixed feelings as best he could:

'If there are few beauties to strike you there are on t'other hand perhaps as few Improprieties to disgust as in any Cathedral at all.'

Of particular conditions at the time of his visit he said:

Early Prayers are performed in the Nave which is very handsomely fitted-up for that purpose. The Bishop's Court is a small space by the West door out of the North Isle . . . the Ornament of this Church is the beautiful and stately Throne, and the ancient Canopy of Wood-work. . . reaches near as high as the Roof. . The old Table of Latin Verses is also renewed and appears here just North of the Altar. Behind the high Altar appear two open Arches which the Wood-work of the Altar has very preposterously stopped-up; when open the view of the Church was terminated Eastwards by the Window of Our Lady's Chappel. You ascend to the Chappel by seven steps, which is now a Library well fitted up; no long Room . . . South of the Nave is the Cloister . . . and it is very mean and paltry. They often bury here. The Chapter-house in the Cloister is a Parallelogramm, having nothing remarkable in it; 'tis paved with painted brick and has some painted glass and a good roof of Irish Oak.

His descriptions of the tombs and monuments were as careful as ever, their positions exactly placed and every detail noted.

On Monday 28 June they rode to Honiton, passing through Ottery St Mary where the church received much praise. The roof reminded John of the Divinity School at Oxford; the painted stone figure – 'and truly not ill done' – of John Coke of Thorne had been beautified by his grandson, John Misson, ten years earlier. The manor of Honiton belonged to the Courtenays, as it had done since the reign of Edward III.

At Axminster they were joined for dinner by Nathaniel Forster, the brother of Robert whom they had met at Plymouth. He too had been a chorister at Magdalen and was later at Magdalen Hall. He now held the living of Crewkerne and before joining them for the evening at the George he took them to see Forde Abbey not far off.

Ford-Abbey is the Seat of the Gwyns. It came to them by marriage from the Prideaux. An Ancestor of the present Possessor about seventy years since, repaired and enlarged the house[a] which is now 300 feet long, a venerable, irregular front of Stone; 'tis seated low. But one side of the Cloister remains which is very remarkably neat and elegant. The Courtenay's Arms, among others, appear on the Outside of the Building, being probably benefactors to the Abbey. In the Chappel are two mural Monuments. 'Tis so dry a situation that the Fret-work Cielings, though of so long-standing as seventy years are still as good as new. And such Cielings there are in every Room. The Hall is a large handsome Room, though some Apartments have been taken out of it. The Rooms are large; a stair-case opens into a most magnificent Room, exactly proportioned – it is longer than broad; such a grand Room you may see at Wilton house and Burley on the Hill; this fine Room is sometimes hung with Tapestry of the Cartons. Here is a good Library of English history. The Dormitory,[b] or part of it, is still remaining; such cells you may see at Ailesford Priory in Kent. Of Portraits here are Chancellor Clarendon and his Son the Earl of Rochester, a Length of Sir Edward Seymour in his Speaker's Robes, Judge Popham as at Cornbury house . . . Francis Gwyn is (as yet) fellow of All-Souls College; with thorough good nature he shewed us his house. He has the Leiger-book of the Abbey. The Gardens are well laid-out, there is one very long walk in them. If there had been full light we had seen the glorious Prospect in the way to Crewkerne which exhibits Glastonbury Tor.

Devonshire is the second or third County in England for bigness. It has in it more Rivers perhaps than any other County and 166 bridges. . . In the North the Roads are very stony and up and down. They ride much in Gambadoes[c] here.

They saw Mr Forster's church which was 'handsome and lightsome', and breakfasted and dined with him. He then took them on another expedition – this time to Earl Poulett's house, Hinton House at Hinton St George, 'seated in a Park'.[d]

'The front is old, but not very regular. The Wings which project great

---

[a] Forde Abbey was a Cistercian house founded in the twelfth century. While under the ownership of Sir Edmond Prideaux, Cromwell's Attorney-General, it was enlarged and improved by Inigo Jones.

[b] John added a note to say that the Dormitory was called the Monks' Walk in William of Newburgh's *Historia Rerum Anglicanum* (c. 1197).

[c] Gambadoes were leggings.

[d] I am obliged to Mr Colin Winn for information about Hinton House and to his book *The Pouletts of Hinton St. George* (1976). John Loveday's visit has produced new evidence about the building and the Grand Room – probably the state drawing room – the staircase and the gardens. His is the only reference to a banqueting room within a maze.

lengths at right angles are newer; all but the higher part of these is built of round Stones. The Wings only are sashed. The grand Room below Stairs is considerably long and proportionably wide, but not high; the gable-ends of Glass communicating here with another Room, there with the Garden, as it makes this Room appear longer, so in proportion it takes from its height.'

There were a number of fine paintings – a woman shifting herself he had seen also at Shotover and Mr Baber had, at Sunninghill, an identical picture of boys with a pitcher. From the walls the Pouletts, Herberts and Berties looked down on the visitors. Leading out of the Grand Room was

the Chappel where the Altar-piece and Chimney front each other, they are each in a corner of the long sides. The sides of the Stair-case are of blue Stucho streaked with Gold; it looks not unlike the Lapis Lazuli or a Sky richly spangled; the light at the top of the Stair-case gives an Eclat to it; altogether it has a very good effect and is entirely new to me. The Rooms are large and very well furnished. The very good Tapestry of Darius's Tent is formed (as I take it) upon the design of Le Blon . . . The Gardens are very pretty; by the help of an Haw-haw you take-in a good View for a low Situation, particularly an hill at a proper distance, beautifully cloathed with Trees. The Wilderness and Maze are in the Park, the hedges of it are in great perfection, the building within serves as a Banqueting-Room.

Next day they turned south again for Weymouth and the coast, stopping on the way to see Colonel Horner's house at Melbury.

Melbury, Colonel Horner's by marriage with a Strangeways,[e] is a large Stone house of 11 Windows in front, commanding no great Prospect. It looks new except that part which Leland mentions[f]. . . In the Hall are Paintings of Charles I, Charles II and James II with their Queens. Among the family-Pictures is the present Duke of Hamilton who married Mrs Horner's Sister for his second Wife. The house is set-off with new furniture, very rich, Velvets and Damasks.

From Maiden Newton to Abbotsbury was all cross the Countrey. This is a poor nest of thatched Cottages in a bottom, yet 'tis called a Market-town. On one side out of the town, are the Ruins and Shell of a Religious

[e] Melbury House was built by Sir Gyles Strangways c.1530. Colonel Thomas Strangways Horner married Susannah, daughter and heiress to her father, Thomas Strangways, and to her sister, the Duchess of Hamilton. Their daughter, Elizabeth, had married in 1735 Stephen Fox who became Stephen Fox Strangways, 1st Earl of Ilchester.

[f] Mr Strangeguayse [Sir Gyles] hath now a late much buildid at Mylbwri avauncing the inner part of the house with a lofty and fresch tower.' From *The Itinerary of John Leland*, ed. L. Toulmin-Smith. (Tour begun 1538.) See also Mark Girouard, *Life in the English Country House*, 1978.

house; on an hill just by is an old building they call St. Catherine's Chappel, now disused . . .

The noble Swannery in a Creek just by here now belongs to Colonel Horner of Melbury;[g] we saw great numbers of Swans; 'tis said that there are 800 or 900 in all, belonging to the Swannery. They are no expence to the Proprietor who sometimes kills of 'em for potting. Just by, the Decoy for Ducks has four Pipes. Hence to Weymouth we coasted, the Sea within View and the high Cliffs of the Isle of Portland, for so it is still called. . . it is now joined to the Continent by a bank of gravel and pebbles several miles long. Our Road was much over Downs today.

Weymouth in those days was much smaller than Melcombe which is now part of it. It had not yet gained the popularity it had later in the century as a resort. They put up at the Three Crowns at Melcombe where the chief interest in the church was James Thornhill's altarpiece representing the Last Supper and dated 1721. 'Great attention is differently expressed in every face. In Judas you see a lurking, ill-natured, mischievous villain.' They went on next day to Wareham, riding at first on sands until the road became 'excellently good over Downs'. Lulworth Castle they noted but did not enter. They spent some time at Corfe, remarking that the village had a Corporation and a market day, but never a market.

The Castle was garrisoned for King Charles I by the possessor, the Lord Chief Justice Banks, and defended by his Lady. It held out a long Siege and the Rebels got it by treachery, stript it of the timber and lead and attempted to blow-up several of the Walls with gunpowder; so this noble and stately Seat was reduced to ruins which are vastly large; great part of them are fallen-down the sides of the hill on which the Castle stands; the hill is Rock-cloathed with Grass near half a mile round; 'tis encompassed with two dry Ditches over both which the bridges yet remain; the outer has four Arches; the situation of the Castle makes it visible at great distance Northwards, to the other points the view is closed by ridges of hill . . .

Wareham had three churches, but only one parson. He officiated at the great church, St Mary's in summer and at Trinity Church in the winter. St Martin's he seldom used, but the roof, which was in a wretched condition, was being repaired. The next objective was Wimborne Minster to which they rode on 3 July over 'heathy' country. In spite of having lost its spire some hundred years earlier, it came up to John's expectations and he meant to be complimentary when he said that the arches were 'preposterously worked and carved'.

---

[g] The land properties both at Melbury and Abbotsbury remained in the hands of the succeeding Earls of Ilchester.

Through a door in the South Wall of the South Isle you enter the
Vestry out of which a Stone pair of Stairs leads-up to the Library. The
East Window of the Choir has three good lights; there are but 9 Stalls
of a side; to this Church, which is the only Choir in the County, belong
3 Vicars, 3 Clerks, 3 other singing-men, 4 Boys (so in both cases correct
Willis) and one Organist. There are Prayers twice every day; the Vicars
take their turns to officiate weekly; the officiating Vicar sits in the first
Stall on the South side; there he reads Prayers turning himself Westwards
to the Congregation; the Lessons are read at Desks placed at the rise to the
Choir; the Clerks read the 1st Lesson in which they take their turn
weekly as the Vicars; the Pulpit is in the Body which is fitted-up for a
Congregation.

He added that one of the vicars lived in the official house and paid the other two
for the privilege.

They rode on gravel lanes to Christchurch where Dr Jenner had another
friend, an elderly clergyman called Bowen. Once again John was unapprecia-
tive of Norman architecture and typical of his age. In his view, as usual, it was
the pillars which were clumsy.

However they attended divine service and observed among other things that
the clerk wore a surplice.

A row of Pews runs along in the middle of the great Isle . . . In the
North side-Isle is a Chappel built with a fine white Stone and the
workmanship is very exquisite and laboured; it reaches from the floor to
the roof of the side-Isle; it has another front in the Choir just North of the
Altar which is equally curious and high. . . There is no Window over the
Altar; it is all a representation in Stone painted of the root of Jesse;
. . . though clumsily performed, yet the loftiness of it, set-off with lively
Paint, had a good effect at a distance. This representation is made partly in
Glass, partly in Stone.

He remembered similar representations at Dorchester Abbey, Winchester
College Chapel and St Chad's at Shrewsbury.

They said goodbye to old Mr Bowen who had spent the day with them and
reached Lymington on Sunday 4 July, where another acquaintance, John
Pearce, an apothecary, joined them for their meals at the Nag's Head. Dr
Jenner disappeared for the whole of the next day, probably on business which
had brought them there, and there was nothing much to do but wander about
the quay and look at the salt pans close by. The little town was 'wholesomely
situate and very airy' and the one street up the hill had a few old houses and
some new brick ones. On 8 July they turned north, through Lyndhurst,
passing another new brick house belonging to the Warden of the New Forest.
The first miles were through gravelly lanes until they reached the forest itself.

At Romsey John was impressed by the interior of the church though he felt it was not as long as had been originally intended.

> Except the Plaster or stone-Roof of the side-Isles, the Roof of the other part is Wood-work; that of the Choir is painted Wood-work. How much of the Church might have this stone-Roof I can't tell, for part of the Roof of the Isles has now fallen down, discovering the upper wooden Roof. The Pavement is of Brick.

He did not mention the Saxon sculptures at Romsey though he said there were ancient tombs on which he could scarcely make out the figures. A stone on the floor was inscribed 'Here layes Sir William Pety'—this is all that is yet erected to the memory of this considerable man.'[h]

When they reached the Swan at Stockbridge in the evening they received a great welcome from three good friends who had come there to greet them. Jonah Chesterman, once curate of Caversham, then Silchester and now at Kingsclere, was there with Dr Joseph Andrews, the bursar of Magdalen, and a friend of Jenner's, Dr Slococke of Pembroke College, whose home was in Newbury. One can imagine the cheerful meal at the inn and the rush of conversation as the three travellers recounted their adventures; and though he was by a long way the youngest, John was on easy and equal terms with his five reverend companions.

Stockbridge was just 'a poor street of scattered buildings' depending chiefly on the inns, as it was in a much-used thoroughfare. It was governed by two men– 'He that is Constable one year is Bailiff the next.'

Joseph Andrews rode with them to the Pelican at Newbury, passing 'Lord Limington's' house, Hurstbourne Park.'[i]

> It stands low, a beautiful Park rising above it; 'tis a large brick Seat and looks rather new. Most of the Road today was in an open Countrey, sometimes over fine Downs but ever and anon wading through Water; but the watery Countrey was all before Husborne.

Their final ride, through scenery they knew well, brought them back to Oxford by 7 p.m. on the evening of 8 July. There had been no mishaps, they had met interesting people and seen some wonderful places and John had a very much clearer picture of the South-West. Now, for the rest of July, he remained at Caversham with Winchester, Ned Lambert, William Payne and John Audley all there as guests.

[h] A monument was not erected to Sir William Petty until 1868.

[i] John Wallop was created Viscount Lymington in 1720 and Earl of Portsmouth in 1743. A plan by Thomas Archer for a Baroque house does not fit either John Loveday's description of a large brick seat or the pictures by John Griffier as explained by John Harris in *The Artist and the Country House*, 1979. I am obliged to Mr Harris for the further point that the wings or office blocks are more consistent with Archer's style than the main body of the house.

At the end of August, which had been a fairly quiet month, John put away his Hebrew books and took a short trip into Surrey with Hopson, Winchester and the curate of St Laurence, Reading, Philip Whitehead. It was not an attractive ride. Ten years earlier Defoe had described the country north-east of Farnham as a sandy desert, barren, 'horrid and frightful to look on'[2] and there had been little improvement. It had to be traversed however if one wanted to see Moor Park, the home of the Temples. They came upon a sort of oasis just before Bagshot, called Bagshot Park.

From Ockingham [Wokingham] to Farnham the Road was almost in a continued open Countrey, heathy and barren. The Earl of Arran's house is about half a mile on this side Bagshot Village. It was about thirty years since the Seat of Jones, Earl of Ranelagh. It is Crown Land. The Gardens, which contain above seventy Acres, want nothing but Water. They are laid-out in fine carpet Wood-Walks; some of the noble Hedges, which are kinds of Wood not all of the same, may vie with those at Ingestre, Lord Chetwynds's for height and compactness; this is certainly a noble Improvement in a barren, dreary Country. About two Acres of the Garden are in Berkshire; the rest with the house in Surrey.

They spent two nights at the George in Farnham and first of all visited the Castle. Since it was the residence of the Bishop of Winchester it was especially interesting to Magdalen men, as he was also the Visitor to the College. They found that it was

all in very good repair, except that part which was designed purely for defence; for the Castle is a perfect Citadel commanding the town and adjacent Countrey. It is built chiefly of Stone, one Tower is of brick. The front-View is immediately down the North Street and upon a great Extent of Hop-Gardens. A side-View opens into Farnham Park belonging to the Castle and upon the same Eminence with it. The Offices are very good here, a fine Kitchen &c. . . There is an handsome Room for Entertainment on public days; the Chappel is next to it, both above Stairs, the Wainscot of the latter carved and painted . . . the old Chappel was below Stairs; it was found too cold and damp for use. We saw no Paintings in the Castle. The Library is an exceeding good long Room; the Bishop's books (which he brought with him from Salisbury)[j] take-up full one side of it; here are the most classical books in Divinity, the Fathers, the English Divines in Queen Elizabeth's and James I's times. History and what are particularly called the Classics. There is a Ditch about the Castle. The Hops are reckoned the best in England, very clear.

Moor Park, where the statesman Sir William Temple and his wife Dorothy

<hr />

[j] Bishop Benjamin Hoadly had been translated from Salisbury to Winchester in 1734.

Osborne had come to live rather late in life, was a Mecca for such an ardent Stuart historian as John. They rode there next day passing by the ruins of Waverley Abbey where some of the walls were still standing.

Not far hence, and just within Moor Park, is Mother Ludlow's hole, an open Cave at the bottom of an hill; through it runs a very cold Stream. The water is confined in a Gutter made of diverse kinds of Marble; 'tis not unlike the Giants Cave by Penrith; here are Seats placed within the Cave, which is paved with small brick. Upon all four one may creep into the Hole whence the Water comes out, though the Rock at the farther end is open no great height above the Pavement. Hence 'tis a pleasant Walk of about three-quarters a mile, all through the Park, to Mr Temple's – whose brick Seat stands wondrous retired at the bottom of the Park. This John Temple Esq. is the younger Brother's Son (second Son of the great Sir William).[k] He marryed Sir William's granddaughter, Elizabeth, the Daughter of his Son. In the Hall is an antique Bust of a Moor, the face and neck of Touchstone, inimitably soft and finished; a Room next to this has several antique Marble Busto's placed here also by Sir William . . . In a Parlor are several family-Pictures, half proportioned, by Sir Peter Lely, as Sir John Temple . . . Sir William himself – and just like the Prints –[l] and his Sister, Lady Giffard. This is judged to be a finished Piece. An half-Piece of the Earl of Northumberland, Admiral in Charles Ist's time, with an Anchor the Symbol of his Office; there is a Painting of this Earl at Cornbury. In a kind of withdrawing-Room, out of this, is a small Busto in Ivory of Tully, as we imagine, for 'tis like the face at Lord Pomfret's, but here indeed is no Circe. Above Stairs is another half proportion of Sir William when he was a younger man, his hair and eye-brows jet-black. There are Mottoes in Latin and Italian over the Door-cases of the Hall and of other Rooms, one is Horace's 'modus agri non ita magnus',[m] well-describing this Seat.

The small square Garden was all that was here in Sir William's time; in the middle of it stands a Dial on a Post, under which Sir William's heart is buryed. Two antique Statues here are much admired; on the Pedestal of one is written *Papirius*; the Boy has a Bulla on his neck; on the Pedestal of t'other *Comes Papirii*, this Lad has no Bulla. The larger Garden in all Privacy is sweetly laid-out; the fine Canal at the bottom runs between two rows of fine Plane-Trees, which open opposite to the middle Walk of the Gardens. Not far behind the Canal is the River Stoure that supplies it by a

[k] John was mistaken in this. Sir William's son, John, committed suicide in 1689. Elizabeth, John's daughter, married John Temple (d. 1753), second son of Sir John Temple, Sir William's younger brother.

[l] This portrait, now in the National Portrait Gallery, was engraved by a number of people. John had no doubt seen engravings by George Vertue, Jacob Houbracken. George White or Peter Vanderbank.

[m] 'A portion of land not so big.'

very simple Machine; the Water of the River moves a large Wheel that is in it; on one side of the Wheel at convenient distances all round, are fastened small Wooden Buckets, which, as the Wheel turns down, fill themselves with Water and again on the rotation of the Wheel empty themselves into a Receiver, out of which are Pipes leading to the Canal.

Back at Caversham John took notes on some places nearby before making his usual autumn visit to London. One of these was to the ancient Manor of Pangbourne–Bere Court. It was the home of John Breedon, whose family had bought it in 1671."

> Bere Court, Mr Breedon's, is a large brick Seat in a dry bottom. Mr Breedon thinks that the Mansion has been all rebuilt since the Reformation. The consecrated Chappel is detached from the house, a building by itself; 'tis one length, has no Pillar or Arch; in the East Window is painted Glass of Christ crucifyed. In the West – *HF* twice occurs painted, as also on the Arms of Reading Abbey, quartered (as is imagined) with this Hugh Faringdon's,° whose Arms (Mr Breedon says) occur also in other Windows of this house. In one of the Windows of the lofty and spacious Hall are the Arms of Denmark; probably that part of the house was built in James Ist's time, who married a daughter of Denmark.

In Pangbourne church he saw the monument of Sir John Davis whose family had owned Bere Court before the Breedons. It was entirely 'made of Chalk; they say it was dug from Shooters-hill just by.' He also looked at the church at Sulham (rebuilt in 1838) and described it as extremely neat within and well fitted up since Mr Turton had been in charge. There were no old monuments in it now.

Early in September a Magdalen friend Richard Lluellyn, rode over from his home at High Wycombe and it may have been then that they conceived an idea for a tour abroad the following year; but that was for the future – the immediate plan was for John to go up to London with Whitehead, Bonney and Winchester and to pay his respects to the family from a base at Richard Wooddeson's school at Kingston-upon-Thames. By so doing he could include a short tour of some of the villages around the metropolis.

On 7 September the four friends went to Bushey Park, which was 'laid-out in fine Walks'. It was a return visit for John who wanted to have another look at the strange artificial caves he had noticed in 1733,^p close to the Earl of Halifax's old house.

" The 2nd Sir John Davis sold Bere Court in 1671 to John Breedon whose nephew, John Breedon, sheriff of Berkshire, left it to his kinsman, the son of Thomas Breedon, rector of Pangbourne. This John Breedon was living there in 1736. See *V. C. H. Berks*, vol. III.

° Hugh Faringdon was the last Abbot of Reading (1368) and was hanged after the Dissolution. Until then the Manor of Pangbourne was held by Reading. (Ibid.)

^p This appears to be the only description of the painted caves.

Here are fine pieces of Water. A Cut from Uxbridge (winding over Hounslow Heath to supply the Canals at Hampton Court) serves this Park also; for the noble Canal which at last rolls-down a Cascade of five high Steps into a large Basin, comes from that Source; the Basin again supplies another Canal by Pipes. In the Rock-work on each side the Cascades are two Stone-Basins which weep when the Cascade is full. Aloes appear as growing on the top of the excellent Rock-work of the Cascade; when on the backside of it, you see that they are placed in Pots, but these do not appear in front. The two painted Caves on Canvass have these words on them – 'Ts. Carwitham Fecit 1736.' They are done inimitably well to deceive; and very judiciously the Caves are of a different size and unlike one another; for Nature, which these are designed to exhibit, always affects a beautiful Irregularity. The Gravel-Walks round the Basin are continued in these Pictures as is the Rock-work in the Painting of the Roofs of these Caves; in the smaller Cave at the Entrance a Bough is described hanging-down.

This is by the old house, the motto on which is '*Simplex Munditiis.*'[q] It has two Stories with dormer windows. There is a noble Walk of Trees to the front of it, the Walk running on before; the house is on one side bounded by the Cascade, on t'other by a long Canal.[r] The new house is larger, in which the Earl resides.

It was not far to Hampton Court which John wished his friends to see and enjoy as much as he did.

Gibbons has some exquisite carving about the Chimneys and round the Borders of some of the Rooms. Rich Tapestry of the History of Abraham &c. Some Perspectives of Rosso's [Rousseau's]. A Painting of Charles I, Mr Vertue says (as I am informed), is the only one of that Prince in his Parliamentary Robes. It is said to be the last that he sate for . . . One Gallery is called the Admirals' Gallery because adorned with the Portraits of fifteen Admirals painted by Dahl and Sir Godfrey Kneller. . . On the new Stair-case is a large Emblematical Painting of Charles I and his Queen etc.

They saw more pictures and then the 'neat Chappel', King William's Court and the room used as a playhouse which John took to have been the refectory and so past the 'much admired brass Gladiator in the garden to the Wilderness garden laid out in Walks between Wood-Hedges'.

John dined next day with his grandmother at Clapham where he found his aunts Tooke and Elizabeth and this was followed by a call on the Bradys

[q] 'Neat but not gaudy' – Horace, *Odes* I, 5, 5.
[r] George, Viscount Sunbury and Earl of Halifax (d. 1739). An Earl of Halifax closed the gates to the public but a shoemaker served him with a notice of action saying that the people had always had access to Bushey Park and won the day. See Norman G. Brett-James, *Middlesex*, 1951.

at Tooting; but he was soon back with his friends and ready for more explorations.

The way to Richmond is over Ham Common where is a Walk of Trees leading to the Earl of Dysart's.[s] The other Walk . . . before you enter Petersham, is cut so as to meet at top Archways. In a Garden at Petersham belonging to the Dutchess Dowager of Rutland is a lofty Eugh-tree, like a ribbed Cone, having Branches out of it at top. Lord Harrington's house[t] in the modern taste here, built of brick Stuchoed, stands where the Earl of Rochester's was burnt down. Richmond Hill rises just beyond Petersham – there are houses on the top of it . . . The View hence is deservedly admired on Petersham and Montpellier Row which is a fine Row of brick houses in Twickenham Parish, a Chappel belonging to them.

At Isleworth[u] and Twickenham there were many handsome seats all in fine woody country with the Thames running through it.

Richmond Green, regularly disposed, is pleasant with the houses round it; one is what remains of the old Palace of which the Gateway is still to be seen; low Buildings. It was last built by Henry VII who dyed here as did Queen Elizabeth. It is of Brick and seems to have been plaistered-over. Another house belongs to Duke William.[v] One mile further on is a Park by the Thames side in which is Richmond Lodge, the Kings's house, once the Duke of Ormond's upon a Grant from the Crown. Almost opposite to it on the Middlesex side the Water is Sion-house.

On Friday 10 September John went with Bonney to see Kingston church and the very old chapel of which only part of the walls were remaining. 'The town itself is a dirty place, but the outlets very fine.'

The next day, being a Saturday, Richard Wooddeson, was able to leave his pupils and ride with the others to Kew Green.

A fine irregular Spot of Ground where (among others) is the Prince's Seat,[w] a brick house with a Stucho front having three Stories in the modern taste; in the two lowest there are long Windows – the highest is an Attick Story . . .

They crossed over to Brentford in a ferry in order to see Syon House which

[s] Ham House.
[t] The 1st Earl of Harrington's house, built about 1733 at Petersham on the site of New Park House, built for the 1st Earl of Rochester.
[u] 'Pronounced Thistleworth – the Isleworth' (John Loveday).
[v] Prince William Augustus, Duke of Cumberland.
[w] White House – also called Kew House.

belonged to the Duke of Somerset.[x] After giving some facts as to its earlier history, John wrote:

The house is a large Square built of a white Stone, a square Turret in each Angle; within, it constitutes a quadrangular Court, five Windows in the second Story of each of the four sides . . . here are seven Windows in front but the grandest View of this house is on the Surrey side of the Water where you may see two sides of it at once. No View from this house is more agreeable than that on the King's Park.

The Hall is a spacious Room with a Chimney in it; 'tis paved with Marble; in each Angle is a Door to be ascended by Steps. Almost all the Rooms have plain-fretwork Cielings. Of Paintings here are a good head and shoulders of James II when a Boy, but the chief Pictures are in the long Gallery which a Glass at one end makes appear yet longer.

Among the pictures he found one of Charles I and James II of which he himself had a fine copy at Caversham. Another he compared with similar paintings at Bretby Hall, Burford, Ditchley and so on. He said no more about the house itself, save that there was no park, and they went on to visit a place which was famous for its garden as well as its owner – Pope's villa at Twickenham.

Mr Pope's house makes no manner of figure next the Road. You enter the Garden on the opposite side the Road; it contains about six Acres, but is laid-out in such Variety as to appear much larger. At the upper end is a most plain Stone Villae, the Inscription in Capitals round it – 'Ah Editha Matrum Optima Mulierum Amantissima Vale'–.[y] A piece of Water was in vain attempted in one part. By the banks of it lies a Nymph sleeping in Stone; of this the point of view is at a distance least you disturb her Slumbers. There are two small Mounts shaded very much, only one Opening to each about a Window size, exhibiting something well worth the View. Nature reigns in these Mounts, and indeed throughout this Garden, at the lower end of which is a large Grass Area where Chairs are placed; from whence through an open Temple and long Arched Passage you view the Thames and some little of the Meadows beyond it. The Temple is made of Shells, extremely curious; it consisted of Pedestals supporting a Roof; the latter being blown-down by the Wind, there are only now the main ribs going across, so that it does not look unlike a crown; when a complete Roof was on it had a better effect – the Ornament seemed then to have some use in it and did not look so wild and indeed ruinous. The arched Passage goes under the Road (the Rising in the Road itself shews it) and the house; about the midway is a Part, the Walls

---

[x] Through his marriage to Elizabeth, heiress to the Percy estates, the 6th Duke also owned Alnwick Castle, Petworth and Northampton (later Northumberland) House.
[y] 'Ah, Edith best of mothers and most loving of women, farewell.'

whereof lined with pieces of Glass, called the Grotto. There is a small green Plat before the River; the house this way has an appearance of elegance; It is Mr Pope's only for life.

It was probably Richard Wooddeson who explained the original design of the temple as they walked round.

Who should come into John's life again the following day but Don Lewis des los Torres. Evidently he came to Wooddeson's school to see John and probably by arrangement. There is no record of their conversation, alas, but one thing is certain – no mention of their meeting was made in any of those long letters to Dr Waterland.

On 13 September John rode to Low Leyton to stay with his Aunt Hopkins for the first time since Sir Richard's death. He had to make haste as Sir William Thompson, Judge, Baron of the Exchequer and Recorder of London, was coming to dinner. Patty was staying there too and next day John took her on a fruitless journey to see Uncle William Lethieullier who was not to be found at his home at Tottenham. They returned to Low Leyton and together visited a neighbour, Sir Fisher Tench, former sheriff of Essex, who lived at the Great House. He died a month later.

> Sir Fisher Tench's Garden contains fourteen Acres. Here is a fine Canal; there are two Mounts opposite and a long Gravel-Walk between them. All this on one side the Canal. The Wood on the Mount and t'other side along the Canal – a great deal in all, shaded with much judgment. There are some Statues here and here are Arbour-Walks striking from one Center. In the Inclosed Garden is a Walk between Eugh-Hedges in which Horses are represented in strong Relieve.

Another day was spent in the company of John's friend Dr Ernle Bertie, who was staying with relations at Low Leyton. John noted paintings there on the staircase and in the parlour. Together they paid a visit to Earl Tynley's house, Wanstead; it was not until 1739 that John actually went inside to take notes.

> This is in Epping Forest; the Paddock is but small that it stands in; the house is built of Portland Stone; to the front of it is an Octangular Basin of very great circumference. It is a noble front containing twenty Windows. Two flight of Steps meet at one Landing-place in the middle of the front; upon this is erected a Colonnade of Corinthian Pillars supporting a Pediment; there is a door below as well as above upon the Landing-place; the middle part of the building is higher than on each side; There is an Attick Story in the middle part and a Ballustrade on the top all round. The Wings for Offices are not yet begun upon. The Garden-front has the same kind of Steps up to it as the grand front; but here is no Colonnade and Pediment; in the middle of this front there are Corinthian Pilasters; the Windows all along have Rustick Work. And

the Garden just in view from the house is truly wild and Rural, a very
spacious Lawn just before the house – Woods about it – Water at the
bottom of the View; the River runs through the Water. Here are fine
Walks under Arbours of Trees, Statues placed in other parts. Woods and
the River bound one side of the Garden, a fine Prospect of a woody
Countrey every way.

On his departure his aunt presented him with a copy of John Ogilby's maps.
It is hardly conceivable that he could have managed for so long without them as
they were almost essential for travellers once the complicated system of tables
had been mastered; but this was a pocket edition which would be easy to carry
about.[z] He made his farewells to her and returned to London to stay with his
cousins, the Bootles, and to have the excitement of dining on Captain Bootle's
ship, the *London*. Finally, to round off his holiday, he went back to his friends at
Kingston. On 21 September they were joined by Thomas Bagshaw who had
ridden over from Bromley to see them all and go with them on a visit to
Richmond Old Park.

Richmond Gardens contain 537 Acres; they are laid-out in a most rural
taste, widely different from those open Gardens at Kensington. There is a
large Cover within the Gardens for Game. That part toward Kew is held
by Lease. The Cave, seated by a piece of Water, is thatched; the Door-way
to it is in the old Gothic Taste, so are the Windows – they are glazed in the
old way. Within 'tis a rough-cast Cieling. Here is a Collection of Books in
Divinity, History, Poetry all bound-in or covered with Vellum. The six
waxwork figures,[a] all *actually* cloathed, are Merlin, the Boy his
amanuensis, Queen Elizabeth, young, and her Nurse, an Amazonian
Lady, and a Prophetess; the latter is ill-performed. Merlin's face is
admirable, the lively attention of the Boy is surprising. . . the main
exception to this Place is that they call it a Cave, for 'tis above ground. Call
it then a Cottage or Cell.

The Hermitage you descend-to by winding Walks through Woods;
on the opposite bounds of the Grass-Area before it are large Stones cast
to make the situation more natural; for the front of the Hermitage consists
of large Stones thoroughly rustic and unadorned. Within are five Marble
Busts; that in the principal Place is Robert Boyle; the others are Wollaston,
Dr Clarke, Locke and Sir Isaac Newton. The Terrace towards the
Thames commands a long Reach of that and a View of Sion House and
Brentford.

[z] *Tables of Measured Roads of England and Wales with Maps* came out in 1676. This copy was
sold by Robert Paske, bookseller. The larger publications were easier to follow.
[a] Queen Caroline often stayed at Richmond Lodge and amused herself by erecting a
grotto and cave filled with lifesize wax images of historical persons. See Janet Dunbar,
Prospect of Richmond, 1966.

They left for home two days later, Wooddeson saw them as far as Egham where they saw in the church 'a strange Monument for Sir John Denham, the father of the Poet', with another against the south wall for his two wives. After that there were no more delays and, parting from Bonney in Reading, Winchester and John clattered in to the courtyard at Caversham before dark.

Back at Oxford he and Sam Speed were still occupied with Hearne's affairs and had to testify Memoranda in the Manciple's office. On St Cecilia's Day, 'the first day of Audit', the new organ was heard in Magdalen College chapel. There were musicians from London and a public entertainment in the Hall.

John had been away so much during 1736 that he had not had so much time as usual for serious study; but a letter in November from Joseph Trapp, the Professor of Poetry, shows that he was still submitting classical translations for inspection. Trapp's rather obsequious tone was not entirely out of keeping with his character[b] but he does seem to have had a genuine respect for John's ability.

> Though without taking the Liberty I have done with your Translation, I could not have obeyed your Commands, nor indeed have been Faithful and honest; yet, I know not how it is, upon Reading over what I have scrawled out, I seem to have taken too much Liberty. I set down things as they occurred to my Thoughts, without any Formality; nor did I mean my Questions in the captious way, but purely as Queries proposed to yourself, and submitted to your own Judgment. You will make such use of them as you think proper; or none at all.[3]

The year closed with a visit to 'Pinchbeck's Machines', which were often shown at fairs throughout the country and had come to Oxford. These were probably the mechanical singing birds. barrel organs and astronomical clocks which the elder Christopher Pinchbeck had invented in addition to his zinc and copper alloy for making toys and sham jewellery.[4] They cannot have been the 'machines' which his son produced later in the century – though such novelties as patent snuffers, improved candlesticks and nocturnal remembrancers for those who wished to write in the dark would surely have found a ready customer in John Loveday.

He still had no thought of marrying or of leaving Oxford, but the final quotations in his diary for this year suggest that he was less impervious to the opposite sex than he allowed his journals to know:

> 'How Polite was the plan of Pagan Theology which made the Graces and the Muses of the Fair Sex and exhibited Apollo, the Deity of Science and the Belles Lettres, without a beard.'
> 'Do but convince a Lady she is a Goddess, out of gratitude she will soon convince you she's a Woman.'

[b] See his character in the *D.N.B.* I am indebted to his descendant, Mr Douglas Trapp, for further information.

Holland and Flanders
1736 – 1737

Except for the Waterland correspondence John preserved very few letters at this time. Thomas Bagshaw, fortunately, was less drastic; he kept, among others, a number of letters from two of their College circle – William Hasledine and Thomas Hiley. Hasledine had been a Fellow of Magdalen for two years and was, at twenty-five, tutor to a wild undergraduate called Cheale. This was how he came to know Mrs Lintott of Shermanbury Place in Sussex who was young Cheale's aunt. His delightful letters to her, written a year or two later, have been published.[a]

In March 1736, he wrote to Bagshaw from Magdalen.

You must know my wild young Squire has lately had two or three intolerably extravagant frolicks and would submit to no Discipline, nor even the President's authority; and indeed had reduced himself into a dangerous state of Health; upon which I thought proper to acquaint his Mother[b] with the Case and at her desire have been to wait on him into Sussex to breathe the Country Air for some time. I have had a tolerably

---

[a] *Sussex Archaeological Collections*, vol. XXII, pp. 170–7; letters written in 1738–39 while Hasledine was curate at Withington in Gloucestershire. He later became rector of Corberley in the same county and vicar of Dinton in Wiltshire. See p. 137.

[b] Mrs Cheale and Mrs Lintott were the daughters of John Gratwick of Shermanbury Place, Sussex, which Mrs Lintott inherited. They were both widows. Letters from Hasledine and others to Mrs Lintott show that her nephew, Philip Cheale, was impossible to control. He died early, apparently unreformed. The Cheales lived at Shiprods, Henfield, Sussex.

pleasant journey, though with severall dirty plunges into quagmires and clay-Pits and a most painful Distemper upon me ever since Thursday se'ennight, which they tell me is the Shingles . . . My neglect of them 'till this time and the violent agitation I suffered from my horse, which is none of the lasiest, have made them desperately bad indeed.[1]

However, depression was not one of William's characteristics and he cheered himself up by sending Bagshaw a ribald satire written by that unassuming scholar who was to tutor Gibbon, Thomas Waldgrave. Hasledine himself was an engaging extrovert destined to become a highly respectable divine and in the running for the Presidency of Magdalen. He wrote well and enjoyed discussing poetry with Bagshaw who was considered to be a good critic. He was also very fond of him. One of his letters concludes:

I am – Revd. Sir I should say in answer to your 'Dear Sir' – but rather as my heart dictates – dear Tom, your most sincere Friend.[2]

In October 1736 he wrote a long letter which Thomas must have greatly enjoyed.

In my present happy Situation, tho' I don't forget my absent Friends, I can't so readily oblige them as at another time I should be glad to do. Business and the Ladies, you must know Sir, command all my time. But lest this should seem too pretty an Air, it mayn't be amiss to explain myself a little. My Guardian and I never had an opportunity till now of clearing up some very intricate Accounts that have been depending these four years and he has not the quickest hand, tho' a very safe one, in despatching Business. But he is in that part of Life in which Horace, in his Characters of our different Ages, has long ago taught us to expect, and therefore to excuse – Dilatoriness and what young Fellows are very apt to blame as over-great Caution and Circumspection. As for the other part of my Time, that I mean which is spent much more agreeably to my Taste, among the Ladies, Fortune has been so vastly indulgent to me as to place me in a Family with two of the most charming Girls you ever saw, of Wit and good humour in great abundance, and so much Beauty that was you in my place but for half an hour, I'll engage, it would set thee a Sonneteering for a twelvemonth after; to the happy production of that Celata Virtus which the Divinities of Parnassus seem at present to have quite thrown away upon thee.
For my own part I have kept pretty clear of Rhyme hitherto . . . but then I have made it out another way which you will not be less surprised at. Such Flanting, Gallanting and Janting, Such Frolicking here I see, That I ne'er like a Clown, shall quit this polite Town but live in mine own Country. Now if you should be unacquainted with this modish Song, the Joke is quite lost upon you: therefore in plain Prose I have, by the polite-ness of the place and the encouragement of my two good-natured

Ladies, been entered among the Men of Gallantry, the pretty Fellows of the North, have thrown off that silly Bashfulness which makes the Gown and Cap Gentry look so extremely awkward, appeared at most publick Diversions, and, what is most extraordinary, given a publick Specimen of my Activity in French as well as Country Dances, in an Assembly of Ladies as famous for their Censoriousness as their Beauty. Can their be a greater Instance of the Power a pretty Woman has over us, except in Tales and Fables? Don't you almost suspect me of a certain Figure in Rhetorick, called Amplification or Hyperbole? I really believe you must; yet I insist upon it, this Anecdote is almost literally true . . .

William also had been on a tour and included a detailed account of it in his letter. He had visited Burford, seen the painting of Sir Thomas More, looked at the Fairford glass and then taken the same route as John through Cirencester and Gloucester, which he thought had the finest cathedral on their tour, though the tower inferior to Lincoln's. At Worcester he said 'the College', as they called their cathedral, was a very plain old building and the town, in spite of its fine situation on the Severn, had very little trade, 'only what it owes to their present Mayor[c] who has set up a Linnen Manufacture there.' This at least, he thought, was better than Gloucester which had no trade at all. Hereford had an indifferent appearance and its cathedral was 'very antique, all except the Quire which has been lately beautifyed and made very neat by Bishop Bysse'.[d]

He called at Hampton Court[e] and saw, among many paintings, that of its first builder, King Henry IV. He was quite impressed by Wrexham where the tower of the church was 'reckoned one of the wonders of Wales'.

This grand Metrop. as I believe I may not improperly term it, is somewhat more populous than Woodstock, but for the Buildings, I think they are much upon a Par. The Manners of the People and their wretched Poverty, you are too well acquainted with to want any of my Observations upon them. Perhaps it may be as unnecessary to tell you that it cost us a bottle extraordinary at this place to drink to all Friends in England. From Wrexham we made a visit to Sir J. Glynne,[f] an acquaintance of Mr Bertie, at Hawarden in Flintshire, about four miles

---

[c] This appears to be the only evidence that Moses Winsmore, the mayor from November 1735 until November 1736, was a linen manufacturer.

[d] Philip Bisse.

[e] Hampton Court, Herefordshire. Hasledine added: 'Sir Michael Newton, by marrying Lady Coningsby, is now Master of the Seat.'

[f] Sir John, who succeeded his brother in 1730, went up to Queen's College the same year. In 1734 he was reputed to have spent £35,000 in an unsuccessful election contest. See 'Welsh', D.N.B. Mr Bertie was Charles Bertie, rector of Uffington, Lincs., and a former Magdalen demy.

from Chester, where we were detained very agreeably three or four days, in which time Sir John favoured us with his Company in severall Excursions round that Neighbourhood to shew us the Curiosities of the County, such as the Fire-Engines to pump out the Water from the Coal-Pits and Lead-Mines, which are very frequent there; the Smelting Houses, Wire-Mills and St. Winifred's Well, at a good pretty little Town called Holy-well, famous for the coldness and quantity of Water that rises there continually not less than an hundred Tun in a Minute, and the great Cures performed on all that have bathed there . . .

My greatest Danger was from the too great Hospitality of the Welsh Gentry; but to enliven this part of my Letter a little, let the Scene change to the Mayor of Chester's Venison Feast, to which most of the Parks within severall miles contribute and where almost all the Gentlemen, all of honest Principles,[g] are present. 'Tis an Annual Feast, of no less, I believe, than 80 or 100 Dishes, there may be more; the first Course is nothing but Venison in all the different Shapes and Manners of Dressing that you can imagine, except roasted Haunches which, with a Pudding between every two Dishes, make the second Course, and that succeeded by a Desert. This I presume is something new to you, tho' not the most extraordinary thing to a perfect Stranger in this fine large old City. Imagine the first Story above Stairs of every House laid open, above the breadth of a common Piazza into a Thorough-Fare, and you may have a notion of what they call their Rows: Here are all the Shops and Crowds of People elbowing one another continually, while the Streets are quite clear and scarce a Man to be seen in them, except here and there one crossing over from one side to the Stairs which lead up to the Rows on the other; the Castle and Fortifications are very good, the Walls strong and perfect quite round the City; they are the only publick Walks for the Ladies and very much resorted to in an Evening. The Cathedral is very old and very clumsy, all except the Chapter-House, which is reckoned a neat, regular piece of Gothic Architecture . . .[3]

William's pen failed him after that and he told Bagshaw that he must suspend his curiosity about the next eight counties. In spite of his criticisms of the 'Gown and Cap Gentry' he was soon to set out for Oxford, joining the College Progress at Stamford.

Tom Hiley was equally articulate and light-hearted, but his letters are the more touching because he was so soon to die of consumption. He usually wrote to Bagshaw in Latin, sometimes addressing him as 'Timmy'. He had stayed at Bromley and had come to know the pretty sisters, evidently having a very soft spot for Dorothy. One of the poems he offered up to his friend – a cynical reflection on the state of matrimony – ended

[g] Tories if not Jacobites.

For fear of exposing my Madness and Folly
I heartily beg you'll not shew this to Dolly,
No, nor yet to Miss Betty, but in burning it slyly,
You'll oblige your Poetical Servant, Tom &c.[4]

Soon after Bagshaw had left Oxford in 1734 and settled in Bromley, Hiley, who was a few years younger, had written.

Why do you tell me what the famous men are up to in London? Why don't you tell me what work you yourself are doing – or do you eke the hours out in cruel loneliness? – or do you pass the time in taverns while both your sisters mourn the brother they have lost and the moist tears fall down their pretty cheeks? Nevertheless let not their grief eat into their gentle breasts and let not sorrow harm their precious eyes. It is you alone who can remove the cause of so much grief just as much as you are the cause of it . . . if Dorothy asks after me you should reply – 'He languishes for love of you' – my inner self is dead; my spirit does not regulate my limbs, nor is there warmth within me while my love is absent . . .[5]

Do not make haste slowly as is your wont [he wrote a month later], but if you wish to prove your friendship don the wings of Mercury and fly hither in response to our beseeching pleas. Lambert wants to see you. Crynes wants to see you. If only you would cast off that unfriendly modesty towards your friends and wish to be seen yourself. Oh how much better it would be for all of us if you wanted us more or we wanted you less. Spare us your unmannerly reply for in fact your friend Thomas Hiley has managed to write these words in Latin even though he is deprived of the aid of Cooper or Littleton,[h] and of the other experts in Latin, – Thomas Hiley, whose shade you will find with Mrs Beech at the Ethiopian's Head in Cheapside.[6]

His last letter, written on a New Year's Eve, probably in 1736, gives an irreverent picture of life in College.

Please listen to the story of how this poem came to be written which I now hand to you either, if you wish, to be read or, if you prefer, to be burnt. Lately in that publication, which rejoices in the name of the *London Magazine*, were included four types of poem illustrating the styles of four of our most famous Poets. As ill luck would have it our Dean, the very Revd Tobias Payne A.M.[i] came across this publication, for they were

---

[h] Dr Thomas Cooper, Bishop of Winchester (at one time Master of Magdalen College School), published his *Thesaurus Linguae Romanae* – known as *Cooper's Dictionary* – in 1565. Adam Littleton's *A Latin Dictionary in Four Parts* came out in 1673. See page 33.

[i] This must have been a private joke as no one at Magdalen was called Tobias Payne. The Deans of Divinity were Joseph Andrews (1735), said by Hearne to be good-natured and George Knibb (1736). The *imprimatur* was signed (31 December) by Stephen Niblett, as Vice-Chancellor (1735–38). Tobias Payne was an Oxford councillor for many years till his death in 1739. He was mayor in 1715.

always lying open in the Common-Room and could be looked at by any one. Enthralled by this beautiful imitation of styles – alas too much enthralled – he betook himself off to Evensong; as usual I was not there. The Dean was beside himself; next day he came to me expostulating on my disgraceful behaviour – I was absent from Evensong last night; my impromptu reply was that I was aware of that and I hoped this was not a sufficiently strong reason for him to chide me. He insisted and he then orders me as being one of the cleverest young men at Magdalen (which you have known for a long time) to write a poem illustrating the style of some Latin poet. Finally he left me still denying the weight of his accusations. This, then, is the story behind the poem and here then is Ovid duly mangled.[7]

John Loveday did keep one letter from a youth at this time, but surely only as an awful example of cringing, since he of all people detested anything that smacked of flattery. It came from his cousin Nicholas Brady, a schoolboy at Westminster, who had taken great trouble over its composition.

Dear Cousin, Since you have so far honoured, as to receive these Trifles and to correspond with so unworthy a Person as I am, partly with fear, partly with Joy I make bold to write. With fear lest these lines may disoblige you (but that your good Nature washes away) with Joy that you think me worth your Observance. To you I am doubly bound by Affiance and Gratitude. Your Candour, Humanity, Affability and Learning gain you friends into which Number that I may be received is my constant wish, and being conscious to myself, that nothing but merit bears a share in your Affection, I shall strive to attain it to the utmost of my power and not endeavour to be learned only, but to be virtuous. – For what does Witt, Education, Affability avail; if by Vice, Witt degenerates into Profaneness, Education draws us into bad Company and Affability enjoyns a Compliance with the most detestable Actions; but thus wandering I forgot to enquire after your Health. Indeed I have, and am still, been pestered with a Cough. I hope my Aunt is well to whom I desire my Love . . .[8]

He enclosed a long poem in Latin for good measure.

Even allowing for schoolboy gaucherie this sanctimonious epistle seems out of harmony with the easy camaraderie of John and his friends. Young Nicholas never attained his desire to be one of them; but no doubt John continued to be affable to the Bradys while keeping a strong curb on his actions.

In March 1737 there was a good deal of political activity at Magdalen as Dr Edward Butler, the President, was elected Burgess for the University on the death of William Bromley. Like others, before or since, who have entered public life, he had to suffer an attack in the press. John did not enter into the

open ring, but he wrote a defence of his President to Dr Waterland with whom
he was having a learned theological discussion.

> I cannot take my leave till I have borne my testimony against a late letter in
> the Whitehall Evening Post[9] reflecting on the Character of the President of
> this College: it is in every Particular utterly false and groundless; the
> Person very strongly suspected to be the letter-writer cannot forgive our
> most worthy Governour for exerting a proper zeal (some few years since)
> when the Gentleman and a friend or two of his appeared in their proper
> Colours blaspheming Deists.[10]

John evidently thought the anonymous writer was Henry Dodwell. The
article written in the popular satirical vein was clever enough; the charges
varied from the opprobrium of ridiculous nicknames to those of dullness and
bad behavior. All these accusations can be discounted, but possibly that of
causing divisions in the College, as a party man, might not be entirely
unsubstantiated; John was in Butler's set without experience of being outside it
and his alliance was by no means passive. Meetings were held, votes were
canvassed and into all this John threw himself with great zeal. Dr Waterland
replied obligingly that he would take care to do justice to the worthy President
if ever he heard him reflected on.[11]

There was a little trip to the Sunrising in April with the particular purpose of
seeing Compton Wynyates.

> In the week before Palm-Sunday, on the side of the hill towards the top,
> (not far from Mother French's) the figure of the Horse on that red Soil is
> new-cut every Year; 'tis said that the Earl of Northampton holds an Estate
> by that Tenure; Thomas French says that upon the hill within Tysoe
> Parish there is a Mote and foundations of some considerable Building; he
> has since seemed ignorant of this.[12]

> Two or three miles from Mother French's, not far out of the way to
> Oxford, is Compton Wynyate, the Earl of Northampton's ancient brick
> Seat, (from which place he also borrowed his Name;) 'tis situate in a
> bottom almost surrounded with Hills; it is a most retired Place, Fishponds
> about it and a Rookery; the Garden rises from the house; the Church just
> by is small but very neat consisting of two regular Isles, the Roof coped.
> Here are some very mutilated recumbent Effigies in Alabaster; also a
> Mural Monument of later date for one of this family; for in the Vault this
> family bury.

After a fortnight at Caversham John was ready for his next adventure – his
first and last visit to the Continent. The plan was to cross over to Holland and
spend the next two months following a tortuous route which would take them
through most of the cities in the northern and southern Netherlands.

Peace at that time reigned throughout the Low Countries just at it had in
England under the administration of Sir Robert Walpole for nearly as long as John

could remember. There was a pleasant feeling of stability in 1737, especially in the Dutch and Flemish territories with their tradition of friendship for Britain. Moreover there were many English residents and a number of children from well-known Roman Catholic families were being educated in Flanders, particularly in Brussels.

John Peareth rode up to London with John on 19 May and wished him well at the White Horse in Fetter Lane, the rendezvous with his two fellow travellers, Dr Thomas Jenner and Richard Lluellyn. They were to have another companion as far as Amsterdam in the person of Samuel Buckley, the printer and gazetteer. John said he was

> a man that has seen a great deal of the World, has a large fund of humour, is a good Scholar and a thoroughly good-tempered man. It was our good fortune to travel as far as Amsterdam [in his company].[13]

The other three left for Colchester in the stage coach, but John, thankful to have his horse as long as he could (and in this case it was his own) rode there by way of Chelmsford, which he carefully inspected. Even the prospect of greater excitements in store did not deter him from noting down his impressions of the town with its pretty meadows about it. The road was in lanes practically the whole way and Colchester was the only town in Essex which had any pavements. Manningtree was the worst of all, being 'situate on a stinking Strand' on which they had to drive the next day. There was time to look at the church at Harwich where the tombs were made up of bricks in the shape of coffins.

> The Kings-Yard here has not been made use of these many years. No Ships built or refitted here; but small remains of the Town Walls.

Remembering Camden's description of the streets being pitched with the blue clay falling from the cliffs, John added:

> and so indeed we found it by the Cliffs, about half a mile from the Town; it seems to be a sort of Fuller's-Earth; just over it there is usually a yellow Stratum. Harwich is almost surrounded with the Sea; there is no fresh Water in the town, but among the Cliffs we found a good Spring . . .
>
> The Pacquet-boats go from hence to Holland on Wednesdays and Saturdays in the Afternoon; the Passage hence to Helvoetsluys is 32 leagues. About 2 o' th' Clock in the Morning of Sunday May 22, we set sail in the Dolphin, Captain Deane commanding. What with contrary Winds and Calms we did not make the Port of Helvoetsluys (at the Golden Lion) till Tuesday May 24 almost 6 in the Evening. On this day we observed numbers of white Butterflies about the Ship and Sea and many Porpoises rolling in the Water . . . Helvoetsluys would demand an

Englishman's notice, if not satisfyed what a Nothing it is in comparison of almost every place in this Countrey . . .

One of the novelties of this tour was that it was frequently to be made by public transport, either on land or water. They travelled north to Haarlem in a wagon on the first day, having crossed the Maas by boat. At Maassluis they saw the most ornamented and noble organ in the church that they had ever seen – a good beginning to the day, which was only partly spoiled by the weather.

From Delft our Road lay much between Rows of Trees and hence to beyond Leyden fine Seats occurred continually and fine-planted Gardens; the whole Countrey was a Garden. In the latter part of the journey the Road was exceeding deep in Sand; we sometimes saw little Boxes with holes in, fastened to trees . . . in these the Postmen put letters for the Gentlemen whose Seats are just by; and also we found Turfs laid at such distances in the very Roads; they shew that the Gentlemen who are Surveyors of the Roads have been there surveying. Some miles before Haarlem a most shocking Storm of Thunder and Lightning broke just upon our Waggon; by a wondrous Providence no Mischief ensued; it was attended by a heavy and severe Rain and Hail, extraordinary in so sultry Weather and what added to it was the exceeding largeness of the hail-stones.

They spent the next four days in Amsterdam staying at the inn in Warmoes Street called the Bible and Orange and kept by Mr Saunders. (This may have been its usual name, but John often translated the names of inns into English with some odd effects.) Wherever they looked they could see ships and windmills in the distance. He thought the view of the Stadhouse was in some measure blocked by the Weigh House standing awkwardly in front of it. Its stone casing was decaying, but the great room upstairs was magnificent:

'tis lined with Marble not far above reach and there Paint on Stone (I suppose) imitates Marble. The Hemispheres in the Pavement are worn much by the Mob of People walking here upon every occasion, 'tis open to the Children to play in; possibly this may be a very valuable part of the Liberty of the Amsterdammers.[j] The Paintings and exquisite Sculpture in the Chambers here seem well adapted to the places that they adorn

Although the churches were dedicated to saints they were not called by their names. In the New Church[k] near the Stadhouse they saw the finest screen they had ever seen anywhere 'massy, yet elegant and well-wrought' and a pulpit with

[j] Amsterdam received its first charter in 1300 and in 1342 received further privileges including freedom from certain tolls.
[k] Dedicated to St Catherine.

such exquisite Carving, especially of Perspective, that it can scarce be matched in Wood. The Sounding-board is of prodigious circumference, on it a Canopy rises high, tabernacle wise. The human voice in the Organ is much admired.

He added a note later to say that his friend Professor John Ward who had made a tour of Holland in 1733 was sure it had cost £10,000 and that John Ray's estimate of £1,000 was wrong. Ray's *Observations* published in 1673[14] was John's chief guidebook to Holland.

The country at this time was governed by an oligarchy of Regents who had kept it without a Stadholder since the death of William III. They ruled with justice and discipline, even in Amsterdam which had a history of independence. Some of the effects of this régime were indicated by John in a letter he wrote to Thomas Bagshaw.

Yours of the 30th April I answer from Amsterdam on Whitmonday. Count Lluellyn and Baron Jenner often join with me in drinking your health. London I did but just call at in my way to Harwich; as we return by Calais, sure we shall contrive to shake hands with you at Bromley; but this not yet awhile. Mr S. Buckley, the Gazetteer has been our Companion for the last week, a good Scholar, one of great humour and great humanity. On Saturday some Criminals were publicly whipt here on a Scaffold erected for that purpose against the Stadthouse; the Magistrates attended in great formality; the great Solemnity of the business is thought to deter more from flagitious Courses than the dread of corporal pain.[1] Yesterday we saw near 40 Couple married in a great Church here. Brides and Bridgrooms all in black, a very serious business; those that dissent from the established Religion are marryed before the Magistrates in the Stadthouse; the English Episcopalians are only excused. Within this hour the Treckschuit[m] scts out for Utrecht, so excuse brevity; you shall have more *ex ore proprio*. I cannot conclude till I mention a Painting in the Stadthouse here, representing 'Markus Kurius Burghomeester van Rome'. Yours (dear Sir) bona fide J.L.[15]

He said later that according to Professor Ward all the couples married in church had first to be examined by the magistrate; and he himself observed that the members of the English community had to meet in a garret. Only the churches on the establishment were allowed bells.

They also visited the Physic Garden:

Besides Curiosities in Botany there are within a building several Reptiles kept in Glasses; among them is the Worm that eats through the

---

[1] In his diary John observed that the statue of Justice was set on the whipping-post and that the magistrates watched from the windows of the Stadhouse.

[m] The boat for public transport.

Piles; it is long and flattish, has two Horns out of the head and is armed on each side with an horny Substance which saws the way farther and farther; one should dread no great matter from the contemptible appearance this little Worm makes; but a specimen of the Wood it found its way through is preserved here too.

Another famous garden belonged to the house which in 1651 had been restored in the Italian manner by Isaac de Pinto, a wealthy merchant.[n]

We rode in a Phaeton six very short Miles to Pinto the Jew's Gardens; they are close to the Canal that leads to Utrecht; here on a small spot of Ground a great deal of money has been expended with what taste I can't say; here is a fine Alcove of Marble and Shells – Beasts &c. made of the latter. Basins on each side all the way down the Alcove; Migdol David in Hebrew characters over a building and here we saw white peacocks.

They had good company in Amsterdam and were especially grateful to a merchant called Wilkinson to whom they had been given a letter of introduction by Henry Pye[o] of Faringdon. He was, said John,

a Gentleman of great humanity, sound understanding, plain like a merchant, wanting in no point of behaviour, but generous to his friend and performing real acts of friendship. We were treated handsomely by him and assisted in Purchases where we wanted Assistance.

The Minister of the Episcopalian Church, Mr Widmore, and his wife even went so far as to travel with them to Utrecht and to show them round the town. They stayed at the New Castle of Antwerp in the Gaans market.

Today being Whitmonday and so an Holyday (one of the few observed here) we saw from the Treckschuit several of the Boors and their Vrouws dancing and making merry. Soon after Nieurfluys the banks of our Canal were continually set-off with fine Plantations of Gardens, but not exceeding what we saw on the 25th;[p] though that, being a Road seldom travelled on, is not so well-known. We were shewn Corn growing here as a Rarity – but it was none to us who had travelled on the 25th. These fine Plantations were in the Province of Utrecht.

Utrecht is reckoned an healthy situation for it stands higher above the Water than most of the Towns. In some of the Streets where are Canals, the Houses of some Mechanicks are under the Streets, close by the sides of the Canal, opening upon it. The Domo is of brick, the Nave in Ruins except the South Isle . . . The Silk-Mills are nothing comparable to those

---

[n] Built about 1601, the house was plundered in 1669. Isaac de Pinto, who bought it in 1651, altered it in 1680 and decorated it with some ostentation. It stands on the Antoniesbreestraat.

[o] Henry Pye's son, Charles, was apprenticed to Wilkinson. (Diary.)

[p] 25 May – the road from Hellevoetsluis to Haarlem.

at Derby; the Gardens belonging to them are very pretty, but here, (as through all this Countrey) you must dispense with Sand instead of Gravel. Here is a Grotto made of Shells very artificially, much excelling the Shell-work at Pinto's . . . There is a very pleasant Mall without the town; some Gardens open into it, the Walls of which have half-Moons in them, for the better raising of fruit by the reflection of the Sun . . .

After a night at Gouda they drove in a wagon to Rotterdam,[q] thereby nearly completing a circular tour.

The Bomb-key is the finest part of Rotterdam, for the Merchants' Houses there are very handsome; before them is a Walk half an English Mile long between Trees; the Maas with Ships on it runs by the Walk and there is a View of the Countrey across it.

John's observant eye noticed that here, as in other Dutch towns, prostrated buttresses sometimes shelved against the houses in order, he thought, to prevent the rain from running down to the foundations.

They saw the great church with its fine brass-work screen set in marble and the 'neat' English church which boasted an organ and a bell to ring to prayers. Then they visited the Exchange,

a very neat and elegant Structure, a Parallelogramm, the front of Stone built not long since; the Pillars are not numbered here as at Amsterdam (where each Merchant keeps to his Pillar and the Area is full crowded;) . . .

Still in a wagon they drove to Delft on 6 June along a wet, muddy road. In the Old Kirk they saw the interesting monuments to famous men and found here, as they noticed later to be the case everywhere, that the finest monuments were erected to the admirals, only exceeded by those of past Stadholders. It was apparently rather unusual that in Delft several gentlemen lived upon their private fortunes without trade. The manufacture of china was still flourishing at this time, but John did not mention it, though he remarked on its popularity with the Dutch in his general account of Holland.

Back in the *treckschuit* again they went on to Leiden,[r] a city famous for its university which had produced so many scholars of repute in its past 170 years.

The place is extremely still and quiet; the Physick-Garden of the University is lately enlarged considerably; at the Entrance is a Palm Tree; in a Building within the Garden they shew Curiosities; here is a Rhinoceros, an Hippopotamus from the Cape of Good Hope, stuffed, the Body is vast, the legs very short, the Nose exact like an Oxe's, the

[q] At the Ham in Wine Street, Mr Cater's. (Diary.)
[r] At the Golden Ball, Mr Clarke's. (Diary.)

Teeth a very Ivory. They shew a Toad of very great magnitude here. You enter the Physick-Garden through the Area of the Publick Schools, an high brick Building and old, it having been a Convent. The Anatomy-School and publick Library, both under the same Roof, are quite on t'other side the Street and on the Outside resemble much the Publick Schools; in the former are curious Injections. The latter contains a collection of most valuable books. Joseph Scaliger's MSS. are here and Gerhardt J. Vossius's MSS. Here hang the pictures of Lipsius, Joseph Scaliger, Erpenius, D. Heinsius, Isaac Casaubon, Sir T. More, Bishop Fisher, &c.

Although they were only in Leiden for a day and a night they managed to hear lectures given by two of the professors. They were fortunate to meet Herman Boerhaave, once Rector of the University and Professor of Medicine, Chemistry and Botany, for he was to die the following year at the age of seventy. The fame of the University was largely due to his genius and reputation.

They have the most eminent Professors at Leyden as Albert Schultens, Gravesande, Peter Burman, Vitriarius and Boerhaave; we heard the two latter give private Lectures in their own houses, where is a Room fitted up with Seats and a Desk for the Professor; the former of these two, the present Rector Magnificus, is a very great Civilian; he read on Grotius; he is a well-bred personable man, is above seventy though he looks strong and florid and has a very long white head of hair; his father was a great man and an Author in the same faculty. Boerhaave is full as much like Horn, the Glover in Oxford as he is like his Pictures, a florid plain man and has a very intelligible way of delivering himself. . . .

Here we had the good fortune to be all day in Company with the Revd Mr Ezekiel Hamilton, a Nonjuror, brother to Archdeacon Hamilton of Ireland.[5] We spent the Evening at his Lodgings; he is well in years yet sprightly and entertaining; he has seen most parts of Europe and is ingenious, well-bred, humane. He said that Mr Downes of Balliol College wrote the Preface to the famous Book of Hereditary Right.[t] He said that Boerhaave has a brother,[u] a Minister in Leyden, reputed a dull man; the Physician dedicated a book to him wherein he mentions that he was himself designed for Orders.

On 8 June the *treckschuit* brought them to 'the best Inn in Holland', Mr Adams's Golden Lion at The Hague.

[5] Ezekiel Hamilton had two brothers who were Irish Archdeacons: William, of Armagh (d. 1729), and Andrew, of Raphoe, from 1690 to 1754.

[t] Hilkiah Bedford was imprisoned and fined on suspicion of having written *The Book of Hereditary Right to the Crown of England* in answer to Higden, but he was protecting the author, George Harbin. I can find no other evidence of the preface, which is unsigned, having been written by Theophilus Downes.

[u] Probably Marcus, half-brother of Herman Boerhaave.

The Hague has the most gentile [*sic*] buildings and the greatest number of 'em of any place in Holland; it abounds with shady Walks above all others, where of an Evening you may also see Persons of Quality airing in their Coaches. One fault we found in some of the chief houses – that the Door was not in the middle of the house, but much on one side. The Rooms belonging to the States-General are part of a Court of Old Buildings which make no figure on the Outside; but within, these Rooms are really fine; the Room in which the States meet is a Length adorned with five three-quarter pieces of Princes of Orange, one of these [William III with a dog] seems to be much about the same with that at Mount-Edgcumbe. Into this opens the Ambassadors' Room where are Lengths of the five Princes of Orange, the latter as King of England, all, I believe, painted at the same time. It was but just t'other day that they set a round table in this Room in order to prevent such Inconveniences as have often arisen on the score of precedence.

And so through the Admiralty Room and the Conference Chamber they passed, finishing with the hall where the many colours taken from the French in the last war were hung.

As they had two nights at The Hague they were able to make two excursions. One of these was to see the gardens belonging to Charles Bentinck[v] whose father, a courtier and diplomat, had gone to England with William and Mary and became the 1st Earl of Portland.

The Road to Scheveling, about two miles distant, is one of the fine walks about the Hague, for besides the Road between trees, there is a footpath on each side between Trees also. About half-way . . . are Mr Bentinck's Gardens. They are large, and, considering what a barren Soil lies about them, the Plantations of Oak &c are really to be esteemed; there is no Taste shewn in the Disposition of the Garden; the Orangery is well-disposed; Bentinck is half-Uncle to the Duke of Portland. Scheveling Village lies on a most beautiful Coast, a finer you can nowhere see; here they shewed us a fish, just caught, which corresponded with what our Painters give us for a Dolphin.

The Prince of Orange's house in the Wood[w] is another way out of town; the Wood does not belong to the Prince. Here again we saw Oaks – nowhere but here and in the Road to Scheveling since we have been in Holland. The house was built by the Widow of Frederick Henry.[x] Two large Wings were added in 1734 and the whole in some measure altered; the front of the main house only is of Stone. The fine Room all over

[v] John may have met Bentinck later as he married Lord Cadogan's niece in 1738. He was a son of the 1st Earl of Portland by his second marriage. His main estate later was at Nijhuisen. See Paul-Emile Schazman, *The Bentincks*, trans. S. Cox, 1974.

[w] The House in the Wood – Het Huis ten Bosch.

[x] Amalia, Princess of Orange.

painted with Frederick Henry's life or history was also done by his Widow
as the inscription round her picture in the Cupola informs us.

After describing the tapestries depicting Princes of Orange and their wives,
John concluded his account on a practical note.

> There is a Chappel, the Shell of one, above Stairs. What is furnished of
> this house is very handsomely done; the Chimney-pieces are elegantly
> neat. After all, for want of proper Offices, this house is too inconvenient
> to live in.

On the way back to Rotterdam they walked again through the city of Delft,
where two gibbets in the way reminded them of Tyburn, which they thought
was built in a similar manner – a wall running round three pillars in a triangular
form. Rotterdam was a most congenial place and they were soon in touch with
friends they had made on their first visit through introductory letters they had
brought with them.

> We found good friends in Rotterdam. Such was Mr Andrew, a Scotch
> Merchant and his Lady, whom we waited upon several times, and who
> with great goodness assisted us very much where Strangers want
> Assistance. Such in a high degree was Mr Pickfatt, an English Merchant;
> one of better breeding with all the marks of sincerity, one of greater
> good-nature and a stronger inclination to do real Acts of Service with an
> equal Power at the same time to do them, such a one we may despair of
> finding; this Gentleman entertained us most hospitably at dinner and
> favoured us with his Company at our Inn to the hour of departure,
> obliging us more and more. Mr Lowther, the English Minister is a
> sensible man; we were at his house and he with his Curate, Mr Ansty, at
> ours.

On Sunday 12 June they sailed in a *schuit* to Hertogensbosch where they spent
some time investigating the church. It was interesting enough and so was the
Museum:

> The repository of rarities which they call the Konst-Kamer contains
> several Curiosities like those in the Oxford Museum; among other Coins
> here is a Jewish Shekel; a large collection of Eggs of strange fowl, several of
> a very large size; several Cups, one within another, wonderfully cut (as I
> imagine) in Boxwood – they are as thin as Wafers; in the upper Room are
> many Skeletons and stuffed Skins of the Bodies of Men and Beasts,
> artificially disposed. Some of the Skeletons are dressed in a grotesque
> manner, so they were in the Anatomy-School at Leyden; thus the dignity
> of human nature is shamefully degraded.

On their journey due south to Maastricht in the Bishopric of Liège, the aspect
of the country changed and they found they were driving along causeways

which had been raised artificially over the fens. 'These Causeys turn and wind that they may be the better commanded by the forts here . . .' and later

the Countrey was like England; sometimes we had good Corn. The Road was now a deep Sand perhaps, but towards the last especially, we had wild Heaths, few houses anywhere.

At Eindhoven they saw flowers hung up over several of the doors and boughs over others to honour St John Baptist's Day.

It took two days to reach their destination and when they did they found that Maastricht was rather like Oxford with its towers and surrounding hills; but once they were in it they were disappointed.

Maastricht within does not answer what might be expected from the View of it at a distance . . . there are few, scarce any good houses here, they are covered with slatts. The place is dirty too, but so all places must appear to those that come from Holland.

The Stadhouse, however, was an elegant structure with a good library and a good view from the top and there was a most interesting 'quarry'.

Within Cannon-shot of the town is that amazing Quarry of Stone[y] which the Philosophical Transactions speak of. We walked in it near an hour by torchlight, nor do we believe that we went over the same ground twice; as the Stone is soft they have taken the occasion to smooth the high Roof workmanlike; we met Carts in the Quarry; as we came out of it at quite another Entrance than we went in at, we were near a Recollect Convent founded by J. de Hornes, Bishop and Prince of Liège, who died in 1505. The Father-Guardian, over above thirty Friars, shewed us with great civility the house and gardens; they are hanging-Gardens over the Water – the Maas, extremely pleasant, Maastricht in view on one side and a good Country across the River. The Garden excells in what we call Garden-Stuff; many Travellers come to see this most pleasant Convent. The fortifications of Maastricht are very considerable. They surprised us not a little. We entered the town by an underground Passage.

It was now that they had their brief excursion into Germany, arriving at Aix-la-Chapelle in a berlin – a four-wheeled carriage with a hooded seat behind. From Mr Florentine's inn, the Golden Dragon, there was a fine view to the east, but to north and south the hills seemed so close that they considered Maastricht, unclean though it was, to be the more beautiful.

The fortifications of Aix are old and slight enough; the stone-walls are very thin; the City is by no means well-built, most of the houses slatted.

---

[y] The famous catacombs of Maastricht.

The best front which is of Stone and large, is that to the Bath-house. The Waters are warm and look bluish in the Baths. Those which you drink have the taste of whites of Eggs, I thought; the houses hereabouts for the reception of the Company are the best in town.

There was plenty to see in the 'town-house' and the great church which reminded John of St Sepulchre's at Northampton. They walked out to a village close to Aix to see an unusual bath there.

The Borset has besides several Wells in houses, a common Bath exposed to the Air for the use of poor People; of this we experienced the Water to be quite scalding hot; you see it boil up from the Spring and a stream from the Bath runs reeking along the Street; this Spring is at the bottom of a steep hill. From the high hill North of Aix you see a Countrey which only wants a River to make it much admired . . . Our Baggage was slightly examined at this Inn when we entered the City, the *ne plus* of our intended Tour.

They left on 18 June, driving in the berlin to Spa and Mr Richard's establishment – the Court of London.

It was above half-way before we rode through Limburg, the most contemptible Metropolis of a Province called the Dutchy of L. 'Tis but a very small place, chiefly one short Street, that in ruins; here is the face of importance in a Guard at one of the Gates who asks you the usual questions, whether you carry Merchandize &c. Seated on a Rock, it overlooks all the Ground round about; if a City on an hill could be hid it would be no small advantage to Limburg in its present deplorable circumstances, though it has been of no small consideration for its strength . . . as for natural strength, that it has still – but what more? We fell-down (I may say) a very steep hill upon the Village of the Spaa.

Spa lay in a valley almost surrounded by hills green with brushwood. There were about 300 houses and most of them were old. It had long been famous for its mineral springs, which tasted to John like steel as well as white of egg, and was a fashionable resort. Here they found several English peers taking the waters, including Lords Lanesborough, Allen, Paisley and Cathcart.[z]

To one of the Fountains that is out of town the Company ride in the Mornings; they keep extreme good hours here; their chief publick Walk is in the Garden of a Capuchin Convent. Mr Alexander Hay keeps the public

[z] Lord Cathcart married as his second wife, Elizabeth, the famous Lady Cathcart who was imprisoned in Ireland for many years by her fourth husband, Colonel Hugh Macguire (Lord Cathcart was her third). She was descended from John's great-aunt, the eldest daughter of Michael North, who married into the Cox family – Southwark brewers. She and John became great friends in their old age. See p. 2 n.*e* and p. 452 n.*i*.

Rooms . . . A very ingenious manufacture is carrying on here, that of japanning Dressing-boxes, tooth-pick cases &c.

A seven-hour drive in a 'bye coach' took them to Liège on 22 June; it lay delightfully situated among the hills in Flemish Luyck. Mr Pierpoint (*sic*) was the host at the White Sheep Inn.

One of the bridges over the Maas is a magnificent wide Structure of six stone Arches, some of which are of the very widest, as is the Walk over the bridge. The town-house is very large and has many apartments above and below; 'twas built in 1714; the Cielings are of fret-work and the marble Chimney-pieces are very handsome . . . there is a Chappel also above-Stairs like that in Aix town-house. Smitsens, an inhabitant of this Place, has several excellent Paintings in the Rooms here, of flowers, birds and beasts. The Bishop's Palace that was burnt down is now rebuilding.

There are many churches to admire, but none struck John so forcibly as the modern Jesuit church which surprised them by having its tower at the east end and which was adorned with large silver busts as it was a holiday in honour of the Virgin Mary. Then they climbed up above the city to the College of the English Jesuits. In the library were a number of portraits of members of the Order and a very large 'armed magnet'.

Bolt of Warwickshire is the present Father Rector; the elder brother of Plowden of Worcestershire[a] is one of this house; we saw both these and were treated with great humanity and good nature by the Rector, a tall strong grey-haired man, above sixty years of age. An Uncle of Sheldon of Weston is a brother of this house. We also called at the English Nunnery upon Sister Dormer of Buckinghamshire.[b]

Baron de Crassier, an old Gentleman, with great Civility and good manners, shewed us his Rarities.[c] . . . In the Library are many MSS.—two Volumes of the Latin Bible in 4to, supposed to be the first that ever was printed; it is printed like Durandus without date, printer's name, paging or catch-letter. The Baron also has some very fine illustrated MSS. In one of the Rooms there is a Window just over the Chimney so that the Smoke is conveyed by two rounding funnels which meet at top of the house; have

[a] William Plowden of Plowden Hall was the youngest of four brothers; the others were all Jesuit monks of whom two had died. Edmund was rector at Liège in 1730, succeeded in 1734 by Father Henry Bolt.

[b] One of the daughters of the 5th Baron Dormer, all of whom remained single except Frances who had married William Plowden's son, William, in 1726. She was also connected with the Earl of Abingdon which may account for John's acquaintanceship with the Dormers.

[c] These also included coins, gems, busts and a picture entitled *Ecce Homo* of which John said 'The eyes must water, if not the heart bleed, at this exquisite representation.'

not I seen near the like of this at Wilton-House? Sure the Gentleman's name was Varnott who very civilly shewed us round his fine collection of Paintings.

They had to leave this interesting place regretting that they had only seen half of it, but they had a fourteen-hour journey to make by coach to Louvain in Imperial Brabant and the prospect of visiting another famous university was balm enough. They drove along a raised paved causeway, through wonderful corn country, to their destination.

> Louvain is one of the largest places in the Low Countries if you regard the circumference of its Walls; but then, within this circuit are many fields, orchards and gardens . . .
> The publick Schools of the University are now much different from what they were in Ray's time; the building is very large; the Schools, very handsome Rooms, are above Stairs; the Scholars attend the publick Lectures in their Cloaks and Hats, for Cloaks they all (however the Under-Graduates) wear at all times; black Cloaks the Students in Theology, of any other Colour those in other Faculties. The publick Library is upon the same Floor with the Schools, and this is a most noble Room of great Length and also Breadth. The Classes of Books do not project into the Room, as in our Libraries. The Classes are most elegantly made of Flanders-Oak, but they are not yet full filled with books, for this is a late Building; if it recalled any Library to my mind it was that of Trinity College in Cambridge. 'Tis the University that now maintains Louvain.

They saw another library in the Jesuit College where a looking glass appeared to increase the length of a very long room.

> At the other end, through a Door partly sashed with a Curtain before it, we saw a little Room full of Books, which you go down some Steps to out of the Library. This may possibly be the *Hell* where they shew heretical books. In their Church is a very noble Pulpit carved out of Oak, several very large figures about it, well worth seeing. Half a mile from Louvain is the Duke of Aerschot's house, an ancient extended front of Brick and the front-side is all that is now standing, so that the Duke uses it but seldom as a hunting-Seat. Near it is a pleasantly retired Cloister of Celestines founded by his Ancestors who are buryed in the Convent-Church . . .

They were shown all the monuments of this family 'with great modesty and good nature' by Father McCarty, an Irish Recollect who was the Professor of Divinity in the University and Confessor to the English convent. They had been recommended to him by Dr Robert Witham, the President of Douai College who was now infirm and living in Louvain.

In Mechelen, on 25 June, they made first for the Cathedral where they were particularly interested in the Archbishop's throne – an elbow chair standing under a high canopy of crimson velvet and resembling the state canopies in British palaces.

'It might be upon some particular occasion that the Church was so sett-off with bay trees; they stood on Pedestals between the Pillars in the Body and also again in the Cross-Isle. A Stage was erecting in the Body for the Reception of a large Silver Coffer, St Rumbold's Shrine, I presume; at last we saw it carryed with great solemnity and Music on the Shoulders of the Priests out of the Choir to this Stage and there left.

When they returned through Mechelen three days later John knew his guess was correct: there were no bay trees, nor shrine, nor stage in the Cathedral.

They now made a short detour to Antwerp, which John called 'noble and magnificent' for its wide streets and stone houses as well as the broad walks between rows of trees on the walls themselves. He had expected to see part of the Exchange covered with grass, but soon realized that this rumour merely meant that trade had diminished. He made notes on six churches, leaving barely enough time to see all the English people they wanted to meet. They called on Sister Chapman in the English convent, whose brother was the rector of Stratfield Saye in Hampshire,[d] and they were treated 'very generously and with great frankness and good nature' by Lord Dormer's[e] two brothers who were both merchants in the city. But the most interesting encounter was with the artist Pieter Snyers, who was a director of the Académie Royale.

Snyers is the greatest Master of Painting now at Antwerp. He did himself shew us his Works, the chief of which are distinct Pictures of the Months described by their different qualities; and a Sign of the Zodiac more plainly determines each Month; this Master's pieces are thoroughly finished; to do it the more exactly he has each fruit, each Green, every Basket that holds 'em, every person that holds the Basket – he has all these before him when he paints; he has some small Painting of a Plumb (perhaps) with a drop of Dew on it, or a fly, either so naturally expressed that one would be ready to take-off either.

An whole Street of Brewers is served with Water by a Machine, more like that in Moor-Park by Farnham than what we have a Cut of in Ray's

---

[d] The rector's name is given as Walter Chapman in F. T. Madge's list of clergy in the Winchester Diocese (1918) and in Coates's *History of Reading*, but as William in *Nichols's Literary Anecdotes*, vol. II and the *D.N.B.* under John Chapman). His daughter Margaret later married John Spicer, headmaster of Reading School.

[e] Charles, 6th Baron Dormer was in holy orders of the Church of Rome and did not actually assume the title.

Observations, for the Buckets are fastened to the Wheel and do not depend by a Chain. There is not a Corner-house in any Street of Antwerp but it has an Image with a Lamp before it.

They had an eight-and-a-half-hour drive in a coach to Brussels on 29 June, stopping briefly not only in Mechelen but before that at an Abbey of the Bernadines:*f* the Abbot's lodgings were

> as magnificent as any Nobleman's and as well-furnished; gilded leather is a main part of it; and indeed you have it in every Room, almost, of every Inn throughout the Countrey; there are several good Portraits of Abbots in the Apartments which are very large; but the Choir of the Church, particularly the Altar, demand attention; 'tis said that nothing can exceed the latter. It is all of Marble. Marble Pillars, Marble Statues, Marble Bas Relieves; the Steps up to it are of Marble; on the Marble Walls of the Landing-place above the Steps is on one side an Historical account of the foundation of the House, on the other a list of the Abbots engraved. The whole Altar and approach to it is very large; nothing can be more magnificent and at the same time more elegant. The Choir is paved in such a manner as in black and white Marble to form so many Tomb-stones, some of which are filled up with Epitaphs. Others are uninscribed as yet, designed for the future Dead; in Niches over the Stalls are very good Effigies in Wood, large as the life, of great Men that have been of their Order.

From Mechelen they drove on the paved way to Brussels, the chief city of the Brabant and the home of the Imperial Governor, Archduchess Marie Elizabeth, sister of the Emperor Charles VI, for whom she acted as Deputy. They stayed there for four days, putting up at the Great Looking Glass Inn.

> The houses here are most of them tawdry and some that are so are notwithstanding without Inbenchings, as some again are all of Stone with Inbenchings. Scarce an house here but that the lower Windows have bars or grates before them, as a good many at Antwerp had. The fine Palace, burnt-down a few years since, shews still very stately Ruins; it stands high (for Brussels is seated on a Decline) adjoining to a Park small enough, if in England, to have been called a Paddock. The ArchDutchess now resides at the Hotel d'Orange. The Ring, or more properly the Mall (for it is a Length) was on our right hand as we entered the Town; here the River or Canal . . . runs between two long Walks, on each side of which are rows of Trees; in one of these Walks the Coaches (which in all this Countrey are made to turn in a very narrow Compass) drive the Beau Monde about every Evening . . .

f The Cistercian Abbey of the Bernadines op't Scheldt on the river due south of Antwerp, dedicated to the Virgin Mary.

Their first visit was to the Town Hall where they saw the State rooms and especially admired two pieces of historical tapestry

framed like Pictures and might more readily be thought such than what they are, the colours so wondrous lively, each part so thoroughly finished. At Vander Borght's[g] we saw Tapestry in the Loom and his finished Sheets are excellent, no man weaves a face so well as this Artist.

There were many calls to be paid in Brussels where plenty of English people were staying.

There are two English Nunneries here; in the Dominican Nunnery we visited Dame Compton, a distant Relation of the Earl of Northampton's, an agreeable and conversable young Lady; – and Dame Blount, daughter of Mr Blount of Mapledurham and Dame Lucy Ireland in the Benedictine Nunnery . . . Father Yates, an Englishman, whose brother marryed the daughter[h] of Sir Roger L'Estrange, shewed us with wondrous good-nature the Chartreux, of which he is a Member; each Father besides his Bed-place, Study &c. has a Shop and a pretty Garden belonging to him.

On 2 July the Archduchess rode in state to the Flemish church of the Carmelite nuns and John and his friends were in the congregation.

She spent the day in the Convent where she dined. She is a large Woman, her Eyes fail her – she has a voracious appetite, but is extremely devout; an Abbot officiated at the Altar on this occasion; he had on a Mitre of Silver Tissue, as it seemed; he did not wear the cloven part foremost, but the broad, closed part.[i] In the Church of the Great Carmelites the Organ is over the high Altar, making a part of it; as in the Royal Chappel at Windsor the Organ is behind the Altar and visible through an Oval over it; it is also behind the Altar in the Duke of Chandos's Chappel at Cannons; but the Pulpit here is a great Curiosity; 'tis to imitate, and it does it sufficiently, a Rock with Trees growing wildly out of it, two of which support the Sounding-board; the Steps up to it are cleft and rough-hewn; such polishing however, and none other, a rude Rock will admit of. The bare-footed Carmelites have a Sacristy well-stocked with sacred Plates and Ornaments for their Altars on high days; some of the former are of massy Gold, very much of Silver; so also Silver Tissue for the Altar and a large Missal with more substantial Silver Ornaments than I have elsewhere seen . . .

[g] This family wove carpets in Brussels from 1676 to 1794. Gaspar owned the business in 1737.
[h] Sir Roger was greatly distressed by his daughter's conversion to Rome in or about 1703. His letters to Sir Christopher Calthorpe on this subject are mentioned in the D.N.B.
[i] John said that this contradicted John Anstis's assertion in the Appendix to Fiddes's Life of Cardinal Wolsey (1724).

The third Sunday in July (new style) is the Day of the most holy Sacrament of Miracle, in the Morning of which there is always a Procession about the City; the Streets through which it passes are lined with boughs of Trees on each side and strewed with Rushes. First of all came some of the Orders of Friars (for the Jesuites and bare-footed Carmelites were not there); these walked two and two and before each Order; there was a Banner with the Cross at top borne by one of the Order, I think a Lay Brother. After these Orders came the respective Parishes headed by their secular Priests in their Copes; so each Parish attended their respective Priests and a Banner separated Parish from Parish. After these came the Trades and Companies separated by their respective Ensigns; each Burger had a large wax-torch lighted in his Hand. Then followed the Magistrates; then (if I mistake not) the Secular Priests belonging to St. Gudule's in their Copes; these went on singing, as one of the Orders did; then the Host supported by some Priests, over which was carryed a Canopy. The ArchDutchess, could she have attended, would have come next, and her Court with her; but this was now omitted and only the Soldiers followed and these were a disgrace to the Solemnity, so poorly clad as indeed they all are in Imperial Flanders, a strange sight after the Dutch Soldiery who are admirably well cloathed, a Credit to their Governors.

In the great collegiate church of St Gudule a special altar of the most holy Sacrament of Miracle had been set up the day before at the entrance to the choir, so blocking it up –

the form of it is in a Picture prefixed to *Histoire du Jubilé à Brusselles*; the Materials are Wood Gilt, very bright and massy Silver, of which latter among other parts, is the noble Ballustrade surrounding the Altar.

It was on that Saturday that they were invited to dinner by the Earl of Ailesbury, a gentleman of over eighty years of age, whose conversation was so interesting that John wrote much of it down. Thomas Bruce, 3rd Earl of Elgin and 2nd of Ailesbury (by which latter title he was known in Brussels, his home for forty years) had been a courtier to James II, so close to the king that he had accompanied him on the barge to Rochester when he fled from London. Later he had been imprisoned as a Jacobite and non-juror, but released on condition that he lived abroad. The only daughter of his second marriage to a Flemish lady had married the Prince de Hornes in 1722. One of her daughters, whom John met at dinner, was to become the mother of the clever and sensible Louise, Princess of Stolberg, who made an unfortunate marriage to the dissolute Prince Charles Edward, the Young Pretender, in 1772. Another old gentleman present at dinner was Dr Henry Perrott who had represented Oxfordshire in Parliament since 1721 and continued to do so until his death in 1740.

On the Saturday we dined with the old Earl of Ailesbury; his two young granddaughters, the Princesses of Hornes, dined with us; the Earl is a large, tall Gentleman, his memory for his Age is very surprising; and, as he is a very fine bred Gentleman, he is very communicative. He said that on his knees he intreated James II (in the case of Magdalen College) not to touch the Freeholds or endeavour to alter their Constitution; rather than do so, to found a College in each University for Papists, to which he himself (the Earl) would be a Benefactor. He spoke of Archbishop Sancroft as his particular friend; he said that upon Sheldon's death the Bishop of London (Compton) was thought of to succeed him; but the King sent Chiffinch (I think) to the Dean of St. Paul's to bid him come to him. Dean Sancroft was his Chaplain, but had never the honour to speak to the King; when he came and kneeled down in the Presence, the King said, 'Rise up my Lord Archbishop of Canterbury.' This was all without application, nay it was what could not be at all expected by Sancroft. He said that Sancroft kept a noble Table at Lambeth and that even till the very time of his quitting the Archbishoprick; then he retired to very small Lodgings in London. Lord Ailesbury visited him. 'It is not without great concern, my good Lord,' says he, 'that I see this Alteration.' 'O! my Lord,' says the venerable Confessor, 'rather rejoice with me for now I live again.'

My Lord spoke of Vesey, Archbishop of Tuam, as one that did one day make very free in a public Company with Sancroft's Conduct, and very soon after paid him an hypocritical visit at Lambeth. He also spoke of Tillotson as a thorough good-natured man; of Tenison as an incomparable Parish-Priest, but as a very heavy man and very unequal to the high Post assigned him; of Hough as one that had acted an insincere false part by him, viz – the Earl, in his Troubles; for when, to try Hough upon his many professions, he desired him to apply to such and such Noblemen in favour of himself (my Lord) and by no means to apply to any other, which he promised; away goes Hough, says not a word to those Noblemen, but tells all that had passed to Lord Somers, a bitter enemy of the Earl's. He spoke of his Tutor, Stephen Penton, afterwards Head of Edmund-Hall, (to whom he gave a Living) as an odd behaved man.[j]

Henry Perrot found the three visitors so congenial that he spent the evening with them at their inn. Another traveller staying there was a Mr Wollascott on his way to the Spa; John had seen his house at Woolhampton in 1731 when he was taking notes for Hearne. The final callers

[j] This description of Penton was in keeping with Anthony Wood's who said he had 'a rambling head'. He was also Lord Ailesbury's chaplain in 1671. Ailesbury presented him to the living of Wath-by-Ripon in 1693 after he resigned the principalship of St Edmund Hall.

were Michael Blount's two elder sons who were being educated in Brussels and came to the inn to see John.

> On the Sunday Evening Stalls were opened in several Streets for the Kermays or Fair was begun . . . Queen Christina of Sweden's Cabinet is with a Bookseller here; the main Cabinet is itself by much the finest I ever saw; very large as it is, the main materials seem to be Tortoise-Shell and Brass; but there are many curious pieces of Marble inlaid in it and many smaller curious Stones, some of which have Busts in Relievo. The Contents of this are Coins ancient and modern, fine Stones and Gemms; here is also a Mandrake.
> N.B. English Giles is an admirable Guide for 2s.6d. per diem, finding himself in everything.

With this practical postscript John ended his account of Brussels for on Monday they had to leave for Ghent in the common Diligence.

Ghent was not a place to be recommended; its size was due to its covering so much vacant ground, said John. Its streets straggled and its houses were in the 'Inbenching Taste'.

> Some of the most ancient are of Wood; these Plank-houses in Flanders are differently built from those in Scotland where the Planks are laid breadth-ways, one lapped over the other; here the Planks are never (as I remember) breadth-ways, but generally are placed upright in lengths as they grew in the Tree. Walking through the Streets of Ghent will soon convince a man how great and flourishing a Place this once was and what a Nothing it is now; you see no one stirring, that is (to speak literally) you have here a great City with a small number of Inhabitants. . .
> The Clock-house or Bellefort Tower has in it the great Bell called Roland; if it be true that it weighs 14000 lbs and that ten men are required to ring it, yet Tom of Oxford weighs near 17000 lbs and the Clapper 342 and sixteen men must ring it. Note that some writers have very erroneously placed this bell in the Cathedral Tower. Every morning at a quarter after nine there are Trumpeters which blow at each corner of the Tower.

The Cathedral and most of the churches received due praise, with the exception of the College of English Jesuits under its Father Rector, a brother of the Plowden they had met at Liège – 'It has nothing to shew you.'

The house of the Bernadines[k] and St Peter's Abbey of the Benedictines both showed unusual objects: these were spitting boxes with sand in them placed in front of the stalls. John did not disapprove, realizing they were there 'to keep every thing clean'. He liked the 'neat' Abbey church and the lodgings, with good tapestry, built by the Abbot's predecessor. Finally they

---

[k] 'Abbatia B. M. de Baudeloo' (John Loveday).

visited an artist's studio to see the moving pictures, which were not unlike Pinchbeck's.

Wednesday July 6. Hence in a Coach to Lisle [Lille] in French Flanders at the 3 Kings, about 13 Leagues . . . We intended to have passed through Menin in Imperial Flanders also, which, though small, is one of the most noted Places for its fortifications of any in Europe; but our Intention was frustrated by an Accident of a bridge being broken-down in the way to Menin . . We travelled within 3 quarters of a League of it and, till we got into the great paved Road again we laboured through a deep Sand. Arrived in French Flanders, the Women and Children sat before their Doors all along the Road, spinning. Our Baggage was very slightly searched at the Inn at Lisle: It was no very great way from Ghent that we saw walking in the Road, Mr Egan, an Irishman; he is a young Student in the great College at Louvain and was very hospitable and obliging to us when the Father Lecturer carryed us to that College; we now had an opportunity of returning the Civility by taking him into our Coach. He went with us throughout, and was of great Service to us – a very modest man.

Lisle, the chief Town of Walloon Flanders is called Little Paris for its beauty . . . the houses are uniform and noble, many built of Stone, few of Wood; in general very unlike the Flemish and Dutch mode of Building. The fortifications and Citadel are truly noble. The Magazine is a very large Building of great Length and consisting of several Stories; in the Vaults are the Stores of Brandy; in the upper Lofts the amazing quantities of Corn. By the height of it 'tis certainly much exposed. In the Esplanade there are two foot-walks, one on each side of the Coach-Road. There are very many windmills about Lisle, the only thing which can here remind one of Holland. Here we waited on Mr Jennings Junior of Shiplake, his Lady and Miss Kent. We had his Company while we staid in town and also in good measure the company of an Acquaintance of his, Captain Clarke, an Irish Officer in the French Service, a young man and quite of a good Temper.

The Jennings family were well known to John and his mother. Henry Jennings had come abroad for his health, but died two years later at Aix. He and his wife Susannah (formerly Kent) had five children, the youngest of whom – a boy of six – grew up to be known as Henry Jennings the virtuoso.[1]

The stage coach took them to Ypres on 8 July – at that time in Imperial Flanders 'subject to the Emperor, but garrisoned by Hollanders'. They stayed at the 'Town-house' and they noticed particularly the painting of Christ's Resurrection in the Jesuit church, the image of the Virgin Mary with a black face called La Notre Dame de Lorette in the Cathedral and the 'good

[1] Elizabeth, daughter of Henry Constantine Jennings, the virtuoso, married William Lock of Norbury and became a friend of John's daughter, Penelope.

basin of water' in the market place. Next day they reached Dunkirk, conspicuous for its grey brick buildings and very large barracks, but there were few soldiers there now.

> Trading Vessels come to Dunkirk still. Mr Horesh an Englishman for so all of the three Nations are called abroad, was of great Service to us here.

The tour was almost over and the last day's journey took them into France itself, but only for a short time. Four leagues in six hours was faster than they had expected and was mainly due, said John, to the French leagues being remarkably short. Their baggage was searched at the Fort of Mardyke and again in the Customs House at Calais; with the formalities completed they set sail in a bye boat, the *Jacob*, Captain Boykett commanding, which left the port at seven o'clock in the evening. Thirty-two hours later they were in Dover.

So it was that early in the morning of 11 July they found themselves on horseback once again, riding out of Dover on the way to Canterbury. As a finale to the tour and perhaps to avoid a feeling of anticlimax they planned to stay at the Red Lion, visit the Cathedral and then go on to Rochester next day. And when John saw the beauty of the nave[m] once again, the colours of the glass, the splendid tombs and the fine proportions, he was full of praise. There have been relatively few changes since his day. Though few would agree that the door of the carved pulpitum should have been wider by two stalls on each side, other alterations he would have liked to see have in fact been made. The large iron gates dividing the nave from the transept must have been very frustrating and the altar east of the choir unnecessarily high.

> The plain Altar-piece, erected within these few years, is very lofty and has no Openings through it, so that the large part of the Church, east of the Altar, is entirely excluded from View. Indeed of ancient times, as well as of late, all methods have been used to block-up the View of this most noble Church; for the great Gates at entrance of the Cross serve to that end very egregiously; and again the entrance through the Screen into the Choir is very small . . . the Organ stands North in the Choir so distracts no view . . . The Walloons, driven from Artois, in the time of Queen Elizabeth, and the French who came over in Lewis 14th's time worship together in the Undercroft.

The first of their friends to hear all the news was William Lowth who, with John Oare, dined with them at the Black Bull in Rochester and then took them all back to his parsonage for tea and supper. Next day Jenner and Lluellyn made their farewells and went back to London, while John rode off to Maidstone for another dose of Hebrew and hospitality.

---

[m] John also said the nave was nobly lighted if the lower range of lights on the north side had not been stopped up, and that it wanted a good pavement.

One of his first tasks was to write down his impressions of Holland and Flanders, which he did in two separate accounts as he had found so many differences between them. They are of interest not only because of what he noticed but also because they show exactly what seemed unusual to English eyes in 1737.

Holland in General

The Countrey being on a flat, the Towns must be so too . . As to the Buildings there is very little of Stone; their Bricks are less than ours; except that their Windows are longer and larger, in other points the Outside of the houses that they build *now* is much like ours in England; those of longer standing (which make by much the greater part of their towns) are insufferably tawdry, built of brick (red brick, not Graystocks such as we found at first entering the Countrey). Towards the top there are several inbenchings or contractions pyramid-wise; at every one of these there is an Ornament of white stone, so over every window, sometimes in every of the many Stories. The form of the building had been ridiculously visible enough without the white Stone on a brick Ground to make it appear more glaring; but least this should not yet be perceived, the Shutters are Green perhaps, and the lower parts of the Windows have generally closed Shutters. The houses are generally built very slight, so that to support the Joists it is sometimes necessary to use Cramps at the very first, that what the thin Walls cannot support may be supplyed by Iron; you see many houses cramped and the Iron contrived very ornamentally. The Cielings are of Wood, hence an inconvenience that one man above you makes more Noise than many in a room English-cieled. Some houses have the dates in front; nay, their barns, which are neatly thatched (the thatch being shaved-off so close as to make a plain superficies), have the date in a strong relievo of Thatch. Their Parlor-Floors are covered with Matting and the Passages through their houses are lined with Dutch-tile chair-high; you have the Same in their Chimneys. They delight much in China-Ware, their Mantlepieces abound with it, and Shelves are put-up on purpose to receive it. Some Garden-Inclosures are of Planks, Openings in them opposite to the Walks in the Gardens.

For their Churches they are generally all of brick (old as well as new) . . . the Steeples at the West and the Steeples of the new Churches have generally Spires out of a Tower; by new Churches I would mean those which seem to have been built since the Reformation here. In many there are two Organs, one but small which stands on one side. By what I can understand, when an Hatchment has been a proper time over a Door of an house, 'tis removed into a Church;" . . . over the Arms you have very frequently something like a Coronet, as also on their Coaches . . .

" John said that there were no names on the hatchments, only the date and *Obiit* or 'O' with the coat of arms.

These Calvinists, in their Churches, keep on their Hats, except when the Minister prays; then they are bare-headed; but for the most part they do even then very irreverently keep their Seats, worshipping (may it be called so?) sitting. The Ministers bawl extremely loud and use much Action in their Preaching. They use no Service at burying a Corps and are determined that the Dissenters among them shall not by a contrary practice put them out of countenance. Hence in the Grant of a Church to the English Episcopalians, the use of a Surplice and the burying their Dead are excepted expressly, so that these are buryed in the same manner as and in the same place with, the Calvinists. In the English Churches they have an Altar at the East end, which is more than the Episcopalians in Scotland dare to have. With considerable alterations they use the first Collect in the Navy-Office . . . From the great regard the Dutch have to Storks it is that you see every now and then on the tops of their Churches &c. large wooden Vessels put up for them to build in.

On the Road you have at Inns very large Stables, which stand open at each end wide enough for any Carriage to enter, which they frequently do, and there feed the horses with fresh Grass and cold Water. 'Tis very uncommon to see anyone on horseback; the horse that draws the Hackney-boat (literally the drawboat) is reckoned to trot 3 miles an hour. At Amsterdam and elsewhere we saw Coach-bodies drawn on Sledges by one horse,° the Driver walking by the Coach-window with the Reins in his hand.

All the Druggists' Shops have a Gaaper at the Window – a Man's head gaping widely. Charity Children have one half of their Cloaths, that is the half of one and the same Garment, black, the other half red. The Domines, or Dutch Clergy wear bands and short Cloaks over a black Suit. The Dutch Laity dress as we do; they chiefly affect black Cloaths; bag-wigs seem more in repute in Holland than elsewhere; but indeed People seem to follow their own fancy in dress in this Countrey; strangers, perhaps, that come here, not thinking it worth their while to enquire after Dutch fashions. The Dress of the common Women is singular enough, that of their head comes very forward upon the forehead; and they wear short jackets over their Petticoats which are very short too. Some Women wear black Veils over them; sometimes they take it over their heads, sometimes slip it down about their Shoulders. We saw some few young folks of both sexes with wooden shoes and no Stockings, but some again go entirely barefoot; however slippers is the general Wear of the Women. Some of the Women are very fair; they have no Shapes; both sexes are very like the English. The men, nay boys, smoke very much, smoke in a morning; which may be no more than what this damp foggy Climate may absolutely require in the Winter. Peat is the general fuel here; it keeps-in an incredible while.

° John also said that dogs and goats drew 'burdens on little carriages'.

The Dutch Clocks strike every half hour; so, at half hour after 6 they strike 7 and if you then ask them what it is o'th'clock, they tell you half 7. For the Dutch money observe that an English Shilling goes for 11 Stivers. A Stiver comes nearest to our Penny, it is very base silver . . . the Silver is not good enough (this wise People know) to tempt any one to carry it out of their Countrey. The Ducat (a most thin Gold Coin) is 5 guilders and 5 schellings or 8 shillings and 9 pence in English money.

Flanders in General

The Thatch of some Buildings is furrowed all down at such distances, one would think it should lodge Rain. There is scarce a Latin Inscription on any Building throughout this Countrey, but what has some letters larger than others to constitute a poor Chronogram. Neither the Hollanders nor Flemish know how to make a pair of Stairs in a house; theirs are infinitely clumsy and in each Stair the Board on which you step projects a good way forward beyond the upright Board that supports it. Here and in Holland, there are Ordinaries[q] at the Inns and in Flanders the Ladies dine at them as well as the Gentlemen; the Ladies do not sit all together at Table, but a Gentleman and Lady sit together and then another Gentleman and Lady; the common Wine here is Burgundy, it was French Claret in Holland. There are open Stables here at Inns upon the Road as in Holland and here the horses have the same food as in Holland – sometimes they add black Bread.

. . . None of the Cathedrals[p] have any large and noble Steeples in the middle; we have Cathedrals in England that very far exceed any we have seen in grandeur of the Fabrick; but they are the fine Ornaments that so strike here, the number of their Altars set-off with Imagery, Painting &c, the Marble or Brass Ballusters dividing each Chappel from the Church; and as for Pictures, some that are hung-up in their Churches (consisting of Scripture or Legendary History) serve by way of Monument for some Persons deceased as the Inscriptions under them witness. Scarce any Church without a representation of the Trinity either in Statuary or Picture and it is generally over the high Altar . . . To every Pulpit there is a Crucifix fastened that is not barely a Cross but Jesus Crucifixus and here (by the bye) the finest Crucifix we saw in a publick Place was the very large gilt one upon the Maer in Antwerp; next to that another gilt one upon a bridge in Mechlin. There are no Pews in the Churches but forms or common Chairs and it is sufficient to kneel in a Chair. In the few Nunnery-Churches that we saw, the Nuns sit either in the West part of the Church, sufficiently divided from the other, or within a Room on one side of the Altar, which they can see through a Grate. The Cloisters in Religious houses are glazed and there is a Garden the inside of them. The

[p] John was also including churches in this category.
[q] Ordinaries were taverns or eating houses where regular meals were served or the dining room in such a house. A seventeenth-century term.

secular Clergy dress like the Dutch Domines, only their Bands here are blue. Nothing can be meaner than the Habit of the Recollects, 'tis of the coarsest brown Stuff; that of the Cordeliers (they call them Beggars here) differs nothing from this, but only that it is black. The habit of the Capuchins is precisely the same with the Recollects except that they have a very large white Patch behind and always wear long Beards. The upper habit of the Great Carmelites (when they are full dressed) is white; so the compleat habit of the Bernadine Monks is white underneath and over it the black habit hangs loose, both before and behind in the shape of an Archbishop's Pall. The Jesuites' is a most becoming Habit very like the English Cassock. The lower rank of Men retain the Spanish fashion of wearing Cloaks; blue is the most common Colour; they are often seen with the Cloak slipped off one Shoulder and held on that side under the Arm. Black Veils are more commonly worn by the Women here than in Holland; to hide their bad Shapes they all affect the French Sacks; in the two days' Journey from the Bosch we observed a very particular kind of Head-dress of the ordinary Women which did not prevail elsewhere; 'twas a kind of black Skull-cap, the Hair plaited together behind and run-through with a sort of Scewer, which at both ends is adorned with a large round Knob. Wooden Shoes without any Stockings is the common Wear of the Poor here. There is little Tobacco used in Flanders. This Countrey swarms with Beggars. Their Horses are ('tis well known) excellent for a Coach, but not for a Saddle. The Clocks strike every half hour as in Holland.

Mr Peareth tells me that among us the Clerks to Serjeants at Law of the first year only, wear a Jacket, one half of which is of a different shade of Purple from the other half.'

' This paragraph was added after John's return home.

Friends and Forays
1737 – 1738

John remained at Maidstone for three weeks. His old college friend James Webb, who had been his opponent in Austins and Determinations, lived at Town Malling (now West Malling), near enough for John to ride over for breakfast. He took with him John Oare, previously also a gentleman commoner of Magdalen though now, like Webb, in orders, and they saw the ruins of the ancient abbey, the gateway, refectory, one side of the cloisters and the west tower of its church. John had a great respect for Webb's judgment and continued to be on close terms with him when he became rector of Trottiscliffe.

During the second week Winchester and Whitehead arrived, the latter staying with John Oare while Winchester joined John at Mrs Bishop's lodgings. As he was always in demand as a preacher he obliged on the Sunday afternoon.

On 2 August John kept his promise of shaking hands with Bagshaw at Bromley and made further notes about the Palace there. Then he went off to Low Leyton for a week where he helped his aunt by putting her library into order and making a catalogue of the books. While staying with his grandmother at Clapham for two or three days he began to make notes on London buildings, a habit he kept up for several years. He made his first visit to St Bartholomew's Hospital and followed it with an expedition to Lambeth Palace.

'Tis a large irregular Brick Pile, some of it is of no great Age. The great

Hall is not made use of though there are Tables in it, as in College-Halls. The Chappel is plain and decent, an old Velvet Elbow-Chair stands within the Altar-Rails; they shew you how this Roof is supported like that of the Oxford Theatre. The Long Gallery here was the late Archbishop Wake's Library;[a] 'tis like that at Farnham Castle, which the Bishop of Winchester puts to the same use. What a fine View from the Leads need not be said. A Room in the Lollards tower has some Rings fastened by Staples into the wall.

While staying with his cousin Anne Bootle he went to see Westminster Abbey, St Margaret's Church close by, and St Paul's. In the Abbey, where most of his observations could be made today, he noticed that in Henry VII's chapel

the fine massy brass Gates to it are cleaned very bright, but not the Tomb, some of the fine work of which is also broke; here is a noble Stone Roof, almost flat, 'tis a segment of so large a Circle it reminds me of St. George's Chappel at Windsor; and here too hang the Banners of the Knights of the Bath, the Arms of their Esquires are fastened on the lower Row of Stalls; the side-Isles of this Chappel are quite separated from it by the Stalls; they also have a Stone Roof; in the Southern is the Royal Vault, in the Northern are the Monuments of some of the Royal Blood . . .

His notes on St Paul's were perfunctory.

As in the old Cathedrals, here are two small Rooms just within the West Door and behind the side-Isles; that on the North side is for early Prayers, that on the South is the Bishops' Court. The History of St. Paul is painted round the Cupola. A kind of Throne on the North side near the middle of the Choir among the Stalls is for the Lord Mayor, opposite sits the Bishop. He has another Throne on the same side Eastward of the Stalls (just where other Bishops' Thrones are) where he sits when he visits. The Doors of the Church are Lengths, not in the old form of an Arch . . .

Grosvenor Square. One side is entirely uniform, a Stone front in the middle, the other houses of brick, but those at the Angles higher than the other; the noblest house in the Square is unhappily placed at the end of one of the Sides.

St. James's Square. 'Tis paved throughout and has a bason in the middle; the houses on one side have their back-part towards the Square.

He returned to Caversham on 22 August and remained fairly stationary for the next two months. The first digression was a little trip down to Marlborough with Hopson, Winchester and Whitehead to see the Earl of

---

[a] Wake had died in January the same year, 1737. He left his books to Christ Church.

Hertford's garden and the ancient mound within it. The old castle had been given to the Seymours by Edward VI but had since been turned into a new house. Later in the century it became the Castle Inn and in 1843 Marlborough College was founded there. Lord Hertford, who lived at Marlborough until he inherited the Dukedom of Somerset (and Petworth) [b] was the second President of the Society of Antiquaries.

> The Earl of Hertford's house, near here, is built of brick, part of it not long since; 'tis a neat thing; 'tis called the Castle because the Castle stood here; the noble Mount was, in its primitive State, the Kepe of the Castle, – so Gibson;[c] the perpendicular height of it is 84 feet and they call it near a mile high from the very first rising to it; the Ascent is so easy as only just to be perceived; the Walks are wide; there's an Area at top 40 yards over, a Building on it and Rows of Trees; but then you have no View; the Hills are all round the Mount. 'Tis not long since that the beautiful Grotto has been made at the bottom of the Mount; part of the Materials are brought from the Glass-houses, part are Flints burnt white. There is also another smaller piece of Shell-work in the way up the Mount, opposite to St. Peter's Tower.

On his return he made his second visit to Cliveden[d] and the sixth recorded one to Windsor, with more notes on the paintings.

Thomas Potter, already mentioned by Hopson, must not be confused with his namesake and fellow barrister, the clever but unpleasant son of the new Archbishop of Canterbury[e] (translated this same year from the see of Oxford). He and John had been friends since 1729 when Potter, now of the Inner Temple, was at St John's College and they had spent much time together. He had been called to the Bar in 1732 but they continued to write and to meet. Many years later John's daughter Penelope wrote of him:

> Mr Potter was an early friend of my Father's who said that his wit and writings more nearly resembled Addison's than any person he ever knew. He died a young man.

After meeting John in London, Potter and Edward Lambert (by now a barrister of the Middle Temple) went to Paris and Brussels for a holiday, armed with various introductions from John who had found them so useful himself. A letter from Thomas Potter arrived at Caversham at the end of September.

> We are now at Brussels and find your Letters of great Service to us; I

---

[b] Lord Hertford succeeded the 6th Duke of Somerset in 1748 but died in 1750.
[c] In 1695 (second edition 1722) Edmund Gibson published a translation of Camden's *Britannia*. See also p. 98.
[d] See pp. 177–8. John's first visit was on 10 October 1734.
[e] Archbishop John Potter.

read them often and am as often reminded of the promise I made you before we left London. A Person who travels is never supposed to be in want of Matter, and I find the difficulty at present lies more in choosing than inventing. I could give you a list of what places we have seen, their distances from each other and the very days we passed through them, but I know you too well. The Observations of people when abroad are drawn for the most part from some similitude or disagreement which they find between the customs of the Country where they are and those of their own, or from something that seems to confirm or contradict the Accounts they have read or heard from others. This Agreement or Disagreement is the most observed in those things with which we are most conversant. A Man of Intrigue will enlarge upon the Conversation of the French Ladies and blame or commend their custom of painting, which is there carried to a pitch beyond any thing seen in England even upon the Stage. An Alderman will hold their Soops and Fricassées very cheap in comparison of Venison and Custard, at the same time that the Impartial Magistrate will have sense enough to prefer their Burgundy and Champagne to Port Wine and stale Beer. Ned, who is a Sportsman, despises every French Horse he sees and laughs in the face of a Hunter in Jackboots; as a Musical Man he ridicules their Musick while he is at an Opera and is convinced that there must be something in the Structure of a French Ear that would afford a curious dissection. 'Tis upon the same principle that both of us as Lawyers spent a morning at the Palais, and an afternoon to see an Execution; which is a very shocking sight and gave us an Opportunity of commending the Laws of England which for the most part exclude all manner of Cruelty from their punishments. And to crown all, as Lovers of old England, we climbed to the top of the Tower of Notredame to be satisfyed that Paris was not above three fourths as large as London; tho' Ned gives this a different turn and sais I did it merely as a City Counsel. – As to the Face of the Country 'tis much the same as that of England would be without its Hedges. The Vineyards, which I had heard so much of, did not answer my Expectation. The Vines are very low and are supported by sticks which are taller than themselves and by that means make a principal part of the prospect, which as you may imagine cannot be a very agreeable one. Upon my mentioning this I was told that the Vines in the Southern parts of France are very different and that the Country there deserves all that I had ever heard said in commendation of its Beauty. Such trifles as these drew our Attention who travelled merely to look about us any where else but in London during the long Vacation. As to Works of Art such as Painting, Statuary, Planting and Buildings it would be improper to give you a list of all we have seen, so I have no reason at present to determine me to pitch upon any particular one. Their houses excell the English chiefly in Magnificence. The Number of good Paintings and Statues which appear there, is owing to their Neighbourhood to Italy and the Encouragements given to the Masters of those Arts by their Kings. As to the people we know but little of them, but by what we could see and what we heard from others who were more conversant with them, they do not deserve to be so much distinguished as they have been from the rest of Europe upon account of their civility. Their Religion, Government &c and all that usefull part of Knowledge which Travellers generally set out with great hopes of attaining, never made part of my Enquiries, who went merely for a Trip; and who am still of Opinion that they are best learned from Books . . .

We are much obliged to you for recommending Gyles Anglois. he has shewn us Brussels very well. I am much pleased with the Entertainment we yesterday met with at Mr Robins's*f* and intend to go there again some time today. You never mentioned De Grijeck's Cabinet to me, though Gyles tells me that one of the Gentlemen (which by all description should be you) went to see it on a Sunday. Gyles has carryed us to Father Yates, we found him a good Catholick himself and very charitably inclined to make us so too; but as he is complaisant enough to allow that there is something in our Reasons to the Contrary, we are not as yet converted. He was a little busy the last time but has appointed us to be with him again this Afternoon when he will shew us the convent and chappel to great advantage this being the feast day of St. Bruno, the founder of their Order. 'Tis now Ten o'Clock; at Eleven I am to wait upon Miss Compton with your Compliments. – I had almost forgot to do Ned Justice who has behaved so well that we have been in but one Religious Scrape, which was the Beginning of our Journey at Bologne and which proceeded from no fault of ours. Our Guide had conducted a German Gentleman of our company and us thro' into the church during the most solemn part of the Mass; we suspected nothing of it by seeing the fellow walk before us and thought ourselves safe in following him; when a priest stepped out of a side-chappel and asked the German if he was an Englishman, who answered he was; upon that he bid him kneel down which the other refused. Ned stood by him all the time without knowing the substance of the Dialogue; I was at a little distance looking at a picture, but presently heard the words Retirez vous, Sortez vite, ne retardez pas. I understood the advice and from whence it came and followed it immediately without enquiring the Reason; my friends did the same and we all agreed when we came abroad that the open Air was best. My Letter begins to grow unconscionably long, therefore I will trouble you no further at present, but won't promise but that I may repeat it before I get to Dover. At Paris I left Brudon and Wragg, the former will

---

f While at Brussels John had written in his diary: 'We had no opportunity of seeing the paintings at Mr Robins's, a Gentleman of fashion.'

set out for Italy and the latter for London in about a fortnight. Ned desires his Service. Remember me to all Friends, particularly to Zinzan.

P.S. Since what I wrote above I have seen Miss Compton, she is still at the Dominicans tho' a high wind not long ago blew down the wall of their Convent; upon this Occasion, she sais, not a Soul offered to make their escape, so well satisfyed they are with their present Condition. She remembers you and your Civilities, makes an Apology for not seeing you the second time, hopes you won't take it amiss for she entered that day on her Exercise. Tho' the Father has not perverted my Religious principles she has got the better of my Honesty and will make me turn Smuggler as far as a piece of Muslin will go. I was afraid at first we should want for Conversation, but we held out very well till the Bell gave us notice to be gone. She is a Relation of Father Yates. We hear much of the King and Prince here. [1]

Potter's temperament was mercurial – cheerful and tolerant at times, at others profoundly dejected. A year later John received a very different kind of letter from him.

November 21.1738

What you mention of Friendship touches me to the quick. Were I ten years younger I would contract a friendship with every unexceptionable man that came in my way. The bad might easily be dropped and the valuable could not be overrated. Instead of this we generally pick up a few acquaintance, and have no sooner examined them and found them proof, but all of a sudden by the accidents of life they are gone. So that by the death of some, and the necessary avocations of others, a man at thirty finds himself almost destitute. And what is worse 'tis then too late to get new ones; for we soon grow old to commence friendships though they are designed as helps to the middle part of life, and comforts to old age. I must confess with you that I begin to find myself growing superannuated in this respect and that I can converse daily with numbers of men without looking upon any of them as my friend. The foundations of friendship should be laid in youth; and like those of buildings the lower they go the firmer they are, and the safer the superstructure. We easily place a confidence in each other in the undesigning season of our days, when we are open ourselves and think that others are so too; when we hate restraint and cannot believe that others will submit to it; in short when we look on the good qualities of men as the naked Indians did on the Spaniards' cloaths, not put on and off for convenience, but as a necessary and inseparable part of the person who appeared with them. These are melancholy and of consequence dull reflexions, yet I still have that comfort which some other superannuated gentlemen enjoy, I mean that of boasting of former successes; which I think I may do without any imputation of vanity, when I mention you and some others. But the chief use I would make of them is to remind you that you are a friend of my youth and to desire you to look upon that as a proof of the sincerity with which I am yours . . .²

Three years later Potter took his own life. John would not have subscribed to such pessimism about friendship after the age of thirty, but Potter's death was a cause of real grief to him – even if it may not have come as a complete surprise. Potter was buried in the grounds of the Temple Church in 1741. He was said to have destroyed himself in 'an unfortunate fit of mental derangement' which meant that his death was not considered to be *felo de se*.³ Writing to John Loveday on 29 January 1766, Dr A. C. Ducarel, the Lambeth librarian, said:

> Be not surprised at my desire of seeing you there [Doctors' Commons]; if you will please to recollect that the last time I had the pleasure was A.D. 1736 at the Chambers of poor Tom Potter in the Inner Temple, who made a fatal Exit a year or two after, by an unfortunate Self-suicide. for no other apparent Reason than an absolute Obstinacy not to bear Pain. For he left behind him a good fortune and a Character blemished only by his last rash Action.⁴

Whether Tom Potter knew he was dying of a painful disease or whether he took his life at a time of illness and deep depression, it was a sad ending to all that had seemed so full of promise. Shortly after his death his sister Elizabeth obtained leave of the Inner Temple to assign his chambers to a fellow barrister – none other than John Peareth.⁵

The year finished with visits to Blewbury and Horspath where on 29 December John saw the figures of London and his wife apparently holding up the tower.

> . . . a Man with Bag-pipes and a Woman; the Woman is still in her old situation, namely, on the South side of the Arch; on the building a Gallery they were obliged to move the Man from his Northern situation, but his figure was again fastened into the Wall not far off. In December 1729, John Palmer, then B.D. Fellow of Magdalen College and Minister here, told me that these were the figures of Thomas London, a Bag-Piper and his Wife. I add that to this day some Grounds in Horspath are called London's Lands by the Inhabitants. This man is said to have built the tower. Palmer also said that the Church was rebuilt by William Wainflete, but Mr Hearne said he feared this was without foundation. Horspath is a College-Curacy.

He described the church, noticing the Magdalen arms in one of the windows and the early date, 1499, in another.

> The Wake is kept on the first Sunday in September and the Church

(says Browne Willis) dedicated to St. Giles; Mr Hearne told me that he conjectured it . . . (for he had it not from any Papers) to have been dedicated to the Decollation of St. John Baptist, August 29 rather than to St. Giles, September 1; Churches dedicated to him being observed, in what Town soever, commonly to be placed at the uttermost end of it. (See *Textus Roffensis*) This Conjecture is further confirmed by what Dr Jenner mentioned viz. that the People of Horspath have a Notion, that the College-Lands in that Parish belonged to St. John Baptist's Hospital and it now appears from Tanner's *Notitia Monastica* that there is a Patent in the 30th year of Henry VI for appropriating the Church of Horspath to this Hospital . . .

He thought Willis was 'under a great mistake' in saying Horspath had been appropriated to the Knights Templar rather than to 'the Hospitalers of St. John Baptist of Oxford'.

Among his miscellaneous notes at the end of 1737 were two epigrammatical quotations which caught his fancy:

Cards make People easy by allowing them to be dull and superceding the necessity of their being entertaining; 'twas a stratagem of shallow people who could not converse to bring down to a level with themselves all who could.

In the human species alone the female is the most beautiful; the males of all other sorts of animals being the finest creatures.

The new Bishop of Oxford was the benign and scholarly Thomas Secker who was later to take an almost fatherly interest in the well-being of the delicate James Merrick. One of his first actions, in January 1738, was to ordain John Spicer a priest and Thomas Hiley a deacon in the Cathedral. This was very convenient for the Spicer family as young John was able to marry his father to the Widow Mapleton later in the year. Tom Hiley's pleasure on the other hand was short-lived. Tuberculosis was overtaking him and in April he had to give up his pupils and retire into the country near Swansea where his health continued to deteriorate.

Edward Holdsworth, a scholar who had resigned his demyship in 1715 because he would not take the Oath of Abjuration, was a guest at a dinner John gave in January. The President, Dr Jenner and William Haward were all invited and the company, which included one or two ladies, was so congenial that everyone stayed on for supper. Holdsworth was a charming and talented man who spent much of his time escorting young gentlemen on the Grand Tour. Though older, he had been an associate of John's since the pipe and tabor evenings at Eynsham and had become especially attached to one of the younger Fellows, Thomas Townson, after reading a number of his verses. A little later on he persuaded Townson to take a pupil and join him on one of his tours. John used to enjoy, in his old age, recounting the story of the unfortunate sequence of events when young Mr Dawkins, who had been placed under Townson's charge, behaved so badly that he had to be sent home in disgrace. Townson continued the tour to Italy without his pupil and with all his expenses paid.[g]

At the end of the month John rode out to Cuddesdon to see the Bishop of Oxford's palace. Recalling that it had been originally built by the seventh bishop, John Bancroft, and only completed in 1634, he wrote:

> The Draught of this House is painted in Bishop Bancroft's Picture in the Lodgings of University College for the house itself was, four years after the Bishop's death . . . burnt down by Colonel William Legg, Governor of Oxford Garrison, for fear of the Parliament Forces making it a Garrison. At the same time and for the same reason (we were told at Cuddesden) was Sir Thomas Gardiner's Mansion burnt,[h] the Ruins of which still make their appearance close to Cuddesden Church-yard on the South side. The Estate here that belonged to the Gardiners is now Mr Smith's, Son of Sir Sebastian Smith, who lives in an house Westward of the Church. But as to the Palace, it continued a Ruin till Bishop Fell rebuilt it on the old foundation at his own expence and with the assistance of Timber which Bishop Paul had laid-in for that purpose; the Outside was finished in 1679. The house is built of Stone in the form of an H. – Bishop Fell's Arms with those of his See over the Entrance. Bancroft's paternal Coat over a Portal at the Garden-front; the Chappel is a little Room, paved with black and white marble, below Stairs, not detached from the house but part of it; the Kitchen is very small; there is something singular in the placing of the Garret-Stairs . . . Bancroft is the only Bishop buryed at Cuddesden and he without Memorial.

An old Reading friend, Thomas Pearcey, son of a former Mayor, was now in charge of the parish of South Moreton in Berkshire. While staying there John had written to Richard Wooddeson and in February he received a reply reminding him of their mutual attachment to 'Sir Alexander Carbuncle' – their affectionate name for Pearcey. The letter began rather oddly, seeing that Wooddeson was aged thirty-four and John twenty-seven.

> I know not so sensible a pleasure as that of hearing from a worthy old Friend, it recalls better days to one's remembrance and methinks like the shipwrecked Philosopher on a barbarous Coast one reads the footsteps of Men. But nothing added more to the delight I received in yours than that

[g] The story was told by Benwell. Francis Drake had asked Holdsworth to include his friend Dawkins (almost certainly James Dawkins the archaeologist and Jacobite who was his contemporary). Holdsworth refused unless he could find another 'governor'. Dawkins finally paid Townson 'a handsome sum of money to carry him back to England' and young Drake, feeling responsible, invited him to continue the tour at no expense to himself.
[h] Sir Thomas is said to have burnt his house himself but after the King's death he retired to Cuddesdon where he died in 1652. See also *V.C.H., Oxon*, vol. V.

seat of honesty and plain-dealing from whence you date it . . . An Author
who thought it worth his while to record the jokes of the Ancients,
mentions as a celebrated one that of Lollius 'Ingenium Galba male
habitat', [i] but I don't know as times go whether one might not congratulate
Honesty even situated in the person of Sir A.C. and wish it everywhere as
warm and snug a residence as the Parsonage House of S. Moreton. Had I
Pope's Mantle, or Pope my inclinations, the Man of Ross [j] should not
make a more shining Figure to Posterity than honest Tom, but a Parson is
a Character that he never delights in but to abuse – and Poetry is no more
my Province than church principles are his . . .

After a spirited description of an imaginary temple for the Virtues on an
eminence 'surrounded on all sides with dirty Roads inaccessible to persons of
less Resolution than yourself' Wooddeson concluded

I had a thousand things to say and see my paper is almost out. I dare say
you rejoice with me upon Bonney's advancement, whom I verily
believe to be a very honest, virtuous young man. My Heart will, though
my Person cannot be with you on Tuesday night; I have at present no
Usher and have been sadly distressed lately for want of one, so that it is
impossible for me to leave the School. This Excuse, I doubt not, you deem
too reasonable to want any other apology. Believe me, dear Squire, I
would go twice as far at any time for the Gratification the Squeeze – the
Hugg – the Laugh would give your most affectionate Humble Servant
Richard Wooddeson. [6]

Another testimony to the heartiness of John's greetings.

Patty came of age on 20 March and duly received the sum of £2,000 under her
parents' marriage settlement. John does not seem to have been at Caversham
on this occasion and he was certainly in Oxford a few days later when he took
Peter Zinzan to have his portrait painted by Thomas Gibson who was visiting
the town. Gibson took a month to finish it and John then put it up in his own
room, having paid seven guineas for it including the frame. He was occupied
with the College manuscripts for the whole of that winter and spring, finishing
those connected with Sele Priory, a task he had begun before Hearne's death.
Apart from this he was sorting out his own 'Hearniana' and reading a great
deal.

It was while he was at the Sunrising, where he and Matthew Horbery had
gone to meet Audley, that Dr Merrick's son, Francis, died suddenly at his
house in Emmer Green, leaving a widow and a small daughter, Jane. He had

---

[i] 'Galba's intellectual ability is ill housed' – a jest by the Governor in Gaul at the expense of
the deformed Galba. Quoted by Macrobius – *Saturnalia, II*, 6,3. Galba was not then
Emperor. See *Macrobius: The Saturnalia*, trans. P. V. Davies, 1969.
[j] John Kyrle, the Man of Ross whose charitable and simple life was perpetuated by Pope in
Moral Essays, Ep. iii, 250 *et seq*.

practised as a doctor in the Haymarket in London and was popular with everyone both there and in Reading. This and the news that Tom Hiley was pining away in Wales cast a gloom on Reading society; but John did not go back there as his plans were all made for a visit to Boyton in Wiltshire with John Audley. Edmund Lambert had forsaken the Isle of Man on inheriting the property from his uncle[k] and had married and settled down there. So this was the basis of a June tour which was to take about three weeks.

After passing through the 'very pleasant and very small' village of Farnborough and spending a night at the Bear at Hungerford, they went on to Stonehenge and found the same elderly resident still living there.[l]

The old Man who has a Hut there and is about 82 years old, tells me that he has known it for 70 years and that there is not any the least Alteration in the face of it within that time, nothing fallen down now but what was so when he first knew it.

They spent a fortnight with the Lamberts. Ned was there for the first few days and there was plenty of company; of the manor house itself John wrote:

Boyton stands low, but pleasant in a Valley, on the hills are very fine Downs all about; the House (as all sort of houses in this Countrey) is built of Stone. It may be perhaps as old as Queen Elizabeth's time,[m] in whose Reign (as I find by the Writings of the family) lived Richard Lambert,[n] Alderman of London whose Son was Edmund Lambert Esqr., the Alderman was, as his Descendant at present is, Lord of the manors of Boyton and Corton both in the Parish of Boyton and also of the Manor of Sherington . . The Alderman had also other Estates in this and other Counties which are not now in the family . . . On the Staircase are some good paintings . . . the Gardens to this Seat are lovely hanging-Gardens, Terrace above Terrace; at the very top you have a View of the adjacent Countrey, with sheep feeding on it and here too you have shady Walks as retired as you please. In the Church (just-by) is a long recumbent figure cross-legged, bearing on his Shield 3 Lions with a Bar.

On 3 June Edmund went with them to see Lord Weymouth's house, Longleat. It was at the worst stage of its history, for the second Viscount would not live in it and the Dutch gardens, which had been the pride of his great-uncle, the first Viscount, were completely neglected. It was possible, however, to see round the house and inspect the pictures.

[k] Edmund Lambert (d. 1734). See p. 78 n.q.
[l] See p. 98.
[m] The house was rebuilt in 1613. See *Burke's Commoners*.
[n] Richard Lambert also bought the manor of Keevil from the Earl of Arundel in 1560. *V.C.H., Wilts.*, vol. IX.

Long Leat stands low, neither the grand or the garden-front commanding any thing of a Prospect. Did I ever see an house so old as this,
built in so elegant, so neat as well as magnificent a taste, without any
affectation of Gothic Ornaments and Niceties? At each end of the grand
front is a projection, then a Window, and then another projection; there
are Turrets at top of the house, the Stone 'tis built of shews well still; but
there are but three compleat fronts to the house; another is much wanting,
the Eye demands it. There cannot be finer walks on the Leads any where
than here, so spacious, and they are quite flat. On the right hand at
Entrance is the Hall, adorned with very fine large Paintings of Horses,
Dogs, Men &c all painted by Wootton, whose performances I had seen at
Newmarket.

They saw many family portraits in the apartments as well as those of various
noblemen and bishops. Looking at paintings of the Stuart royal family John
thought Lely had not flattered Charles II as he had his Queen –

but has in one sense daubed her Majesty, representing her very fair and
beautiful, nothing of the Portuguese complexion or turn of face. In a very
long Room above Stairs may be some of the Pictures already mentioned,
as most certainly there is a Portrait of a Man with Tintoret's name to it; the
Library (which, the Chaplain being absent, we could not see) is at one end
of what they call the Gallery, at top of the house; in this Gallery are a
Portrait of Sir Thomas Gresham, an old one, also head and shoulders of
Stafford, Duke of Bucks. One Room is hung with very good Tapestry of
four of the Cartons compleat and part of another; the four were made
abroad for King William, but in other Rooms there is a good deal of
antiquated faded Tapestry . . .
    'Tis said that the serpentine River in the Garden cost about £1,000; 'twas
made by this Lord, but surely does by no means answer the vast expence of
it; and as for a Garden, properly speaking there is no such thing now, this
Lord has laid every thing open so wildly and without any judgment.
Beyond the River some distance, you rise between an Avenue, advanced
to the top of which the View is beautiful on the house and adjacent
Countrey; but the Avenue is not wide enough to take in the whole of the
front.[o]
    We dined in the return at Mr Squire's, an Apothecary in Warminster, a
brother of whom wrote an Answer to The Independent Whig and Dr
Newcomb of Cambridge marryed his most ingenious sister.[p]

---

[o] Information kindly given shows that John Loveday's account of Longleat adds to
knowledge about the paintings and corroborates the belief that the fourth front (north) had
not been added at this date.
    [p] Mrs John Newcome, wife of the Master of St John's College, Cambridge, published *An
Enquiry into the Evidences of the Christian Religion* in 1728. Her brother, Thomas, the
apothecary, was the father of Dr Samuel Squire, Bishop of St. Davids. Francis Squire wrote

Audley and John left for Shaftesbury on 12 June. It was only a temporary parting, for Mrs Lambert and Miss Tull from Hungerford[q] (who had been at Boyton the whole time) promised they would come with Edmund to Wilton House on the 15th, meet again there and see the improvements that had taken place since John's last visit and then the whole party would go back to Salisbury for the night and stay at the Three Lions Inn.

Meanwhile there were some other interesting houses to see. They rode through Tisbury, where they had a look at the church. Shortly before this they had noticed a house lying in low ground with a good many workmen busy about the place. John said it belonged to Mr Cottington, and it was in fact the old Fonthill, built by Francis, Baron Cottington, a Royalist statesman. The family sold it to Alderman William Beckford, who rebuilt it after it was burnt down in 1755 and called it Fonthill Splendens. It was later destroyed by his son, William, who built Fonthill Abbey on a site higher up on the estate.

They did not go into this 'large old Seat of Stone' as they had a newer house to inspect, built opposite the ruins of an old one. These were the two Wardour Castles belonging to the 6th Lord Arundell.

Wardour Castle was defended by Lady Arundell for a week in 1643 with twenty-five against thirteen hundred Parliamentarians who greatly damaged it, contrary to Articles. This Castle had a regular front, there is still a Latin Inscription over it of the age of Queen Elizabeth; it now stands in the Garden, the front of it directly opposite to that of the present house which stands low, very damp and makes nothing of an appearance; though within it be an house as completely furnished as can anywhere be met with; yet the Rooms are low. On the Staircase is a Painting of Roman Charity; another and a very fine one of a dead Christ, the Virgin's Grief is expressed in very strong Colours, St. John's Sorrow is more temperate; both these are large Pictures. Above Stairs in a little Passage between two Rooms hang-up several silver framed Medals. One had on the obverse a Bust in Armour with a long Beard and the Legend in Capitals 'Henricus Comes Arundell' . . . the House is surrounded (and pretty near) with Hills all round except to the West, an odd situation for a Castle, but this surely was never meant as a place of defence (I speak of the old ruined Castle) but only as a Seat built castlewise, accordingly there are no Ditches about it; it formerly (I'm told) belonged to the Knights Templars. Lord Arundell's family bury at Tisbury.

They digressed a little between Shaftesbury and Blandford in order to visit

---

the *Answer to the Independent Whig* in 1723. Another brother, Samuel, was also a druggist.

 [q] Miss Tull may have been Mrs Anne Lambert's sister.

Eastbury Park, the Vanbrugh mansion which George Bubb Dodington had inherited nearly twenty years earlier with a fortune to match. His work at the Treasury (though he was not yet Treasurer to the Navy) kept him much of the time in London, but his country house was in very good order.

Mr Dodington's House at Gunfield [Tarrant Gunville] was designed by Sir John Vanbrugh and that not according to his clumsiest Model; the house is of Stone and so much like Blenheim that 'tis impossible not to think of it; the front is Rustic, there are 11 Windows in it, 6 Rustic Pillars of the Doric Order, support the Entablature; at each Angle is a square Tower; on each Side at right Angles from the front, runs on a low Cloister, higher and behind which is another building which does not either way reach to the end of the Cloisters, and in the midst of it is a very large square Tower, but not high; at the very extremity of each Wing is a low Pyramid; on one side behind the Wings are the Stables in some parallel lines to the Wings, on the other side are some offices to answer the Stables. There is a great flight of Stairs to the front; the great Door opens into the neat Hall, in it are two Staircases just the Same; the Apartments remind one of Rainham, the Lord Townshend's, for the Rooms are chiefly painted of the Olive Colour and gilded; so there are Pannels in the Cielings gilded round; the Chimneypieces are extremely elegant and various. There is great variety of most curious Marble-Tables. Over the Chimney in the State-room is a Painting of the Earl of Strafford and his Secretary; is this that which was in the Gallery at Kilkenny Castle?[r] There are two excellent Paintings of a Schoolmaster teaching his Boys to read and a Schoolmistress teaching her Girls to work; are not these painted by Chipari who painted the four large Pictures in Lord Cobham's Hall?[s] Here is a Painting of the Perspective of a Popish Church with Priests officiating in it – a very good Piece; in the same Room are two very fine and large blue and white china Jars. In a Room above, over a Chimney is a Clock, the Plate in Glass, the hand composed of diverse precious Stones; the Locks here are within the Doors and the Curtains are drawn back within a Cavity of Wood. The Kitchen, Servants Hall &c are really very good. After all there is no View, or very little, from hence; but within nothing can be grander and there sure nothing can be neater and more elegant throughout; a great taste is shewn in the fitting-up the Rooms and in the furniture. The Garden front is the lightest, here are the same number of Windows as in the grand front and the same number of Pillars, and of the same Order, but these are fluted, not rustic, and here the projection is very little. The

[r] See p. 160 for the painting John's uncle, Captain John Lethieullier, could remember at Kilkenny Castle.
[s] See p. 205 and John's visit to Stowe in 1735 when he saw four paintings by Cipper.

Gardens are very good; the Estate about here is but small; it was purchased to build this House upon.

They went on to Blandford which was built of brick and had suffered in the past from two major fires – one in 1713, the other in 1731.

. . . The main Street lies quite in the bottom, wide and airy; 'tis pity that the new erected houses were not built on one Plan, they are now as various as possible excepting that the Materials are the same and each house sashed. The Church of Stone is not quite finished, 'tis a neat structure supported by round Ionic Pillars, the bases of which are even with the tops of the Pews as in the great Church at Derby; it has a rounding East end. The Sufferers by the late fire received about 5s.9d. in the Pound for their Losses which amounted to 84, 348 £ over and above all Insurances.

Having reached Salisbury they went a little north of the town to visit Old Sarum. From Leland and Camden John knew how the old Roman town had looked in their days.

The present State of the Place is this; there is an half Moon before the East entrance of the Town, so that the way to this East entrance was not foreright, but on either side of the half Moon; at the West entrance there is also an half Moon, but so contrived as if by this way there could be no entering the Town but on foot, if even that were possible. The Ditch to the Town is truly very deep and strong;[7] on the North side is a great fragment of the Town-wall, very thick, some of the Ashler stone remaining in it and Holes through it to shoot from. The Castle, which is ditched round, stands perhaps in the very middle of the Town . . . though no turret of the Castle be now standing, yet at the East entrance of it there are several fragments of Stone or Flint still. Northwards from the Castle to the Town-Ditch runs a Cross-Bank of Earth; in like manner there seems to have been another such Rampart running Southwards, and this has a Ditch to it . . . Mr Audley conjectures that this Cross-Mound might be a sort of Boundary to the Cathedral Close. Grass and Corn grow where once the Streets run.

On 15 June they met the Lamberts as arranged at Wilton House. It was now seven years since John's previous visit in 1731 and there had been many changes. 'Old Pem', the eighth Earl, had died in 1733; he had been a collector on a grand scale and the wealth of sculpture and painting at Wilton, as well as the collection of valuable books, was largely due to his enthusiasm. His successor and eldest son, Henry Herbert, was especially interested in architecture in the Palladian tradition and in archaeology. Like Lord Hertford at Marlborough he was a friend of William Stukeley and belonged to the same antiquarian club. It was he who in 1736 had created the enchanting and already celebrated bridge across the river at Wilton to the south side of the house, and it was this which John and his friends particularly wished to see; but first of all they went back to the statues and pictures.

Under one of the Rooms of the house in a common Shore they found (about a year and a half since) the Tomb-stone of a Prior, his figure on it with the pastoral Staff, the lower end of it in a Dragon's mouth; the Tomb is broke in two and now lies in a bye place near the front of the house. The Window which is over one of the Chimney-Pieces is retired behind the Chimney, and not on the same Plane with it, as is the Window in Baron Crassier's house in Liège; there are two pillars of black Porphyry in a ground Room, which are so great Rarities that 'tis said there is but one more anywhere known; the Table of Lapis Lazuli is very thinly veneered, nay a great many pieces went to make-up the great superficies of the Slab. Of pictures that of Richard II is now in London . . in the State-Room is a 3 quarter of Charles I by Van Dyck, another of the same size of the Queen Henrietta Maria in a suit of yellow, and big with child, like that at Easton Neston, but sure not so fine a Painting as that. In one of the suit of small Apartments below which make a Vista and which were entirely fitted-up by this Lord, is a small Painting by 'Van Zyck 1410' of the Holy family'
. . . here also is 'Tabula antiqua ex templo Junonis', 'tis a very ancient Roman piece of Painting . . .

After seeing the pictures they investigated the many bas-reliefs and found that the one bearing the inscription which had puzzled Hopson and John had been

removed from the Station it held 7 years since, as are many other Pictures, Statues, &c into other places, and the late Lord's Observations on this Inscription are not now to be read on the wainscot. . . The Horns are now placed in the Porch of the great front.

As before, the busts fired his imagination; one had a perfect periwig, another – Julius Caesar – resembled John Locke.

M. Junius Brutus is extremely like Master Cockman [the Master of University College], King Pyrrhus has a Helmet on and the fiercest terrifying Look that is possible . . .

---

¹ The false signature of Van Eyck was added in the sixteenth or seventeenth century to this painting, *The Adoration of the Shepherds*, now attributed to Hugo van der Goes. John Loveday wrote Van Zyck in inverted commas either mistaking the 'E' for a 'Z' or because of verbal information. Surprisingly he did not change it when he read Van Eyck on p.64 of the catalogue compiled in 1731 by Count Gambarini of Lucca who probably recorded information given by the 8th Earl besides seeing the false signature. See *The Paintings and Drawings at Wilton House*, comp. Sidney, 16th Earl of Pembroke, 1968.

At length they went out into the gardens and there was the new bridge to delight them.

In the Gardens (all laid-open in the modern taste) is a serpentine River which runs with a good Current; over it this present Lord has erected a covered Bridge; 'tis a very light and most elegant Structure upon 5 rustic Arches; besides the beauty of it, this building serves two uses, that of a foot-bridge and that of a Summer-house on both sides the Water. You ascend the bridge by wide Stone Steps at the foot of which is an handsome Approach of Stone; the building is of the Ionic Order, under such an Arch you enter a square Room, passed which you are in an oblong Space supported on each side by four Ionic Pillars, not Arches; at the other End of this Space is such another square Room; a Ballustrade of Stone (for such the whole is built of) runs on each side of the Lengths of the 3 Rooms. The Roof is of brown Stucho in Pannels, old Busts adorn the Inside and some Statues the Approach. The whole Structure is leaded. On an eminence in the Gardens this Lord has built a thatched house, paved with rough bricks, – and window all round. Hence is a good Prospect, Salisbury Church looks nobly hence; from the house there is little or no View.

As it was his second visit to Salisbury John's attention was fixed mainly on the Cathedral.

They are now and have been many years very substantially repairing this Cathedral; the present Bishop" as Visitor of the Church has made them lay out large Sums upon the Roof in Beams &c . . . The Sermon is preached in the Body of the Church which is accordingly fitted-up with Pews . . .

The Choir is fitted up in a very decent, but not in the grave solemn manner; the Titles are wrote over each Stall, even those Titles which once belonged to this Church, but are now entirely alienated from it, or transferred into another Church . . . The Choir has long since been made irregular by a South Window to give light to the Altar-part; there is a great Beam runs across the more Eastern part to support it. An Inscription against the W. wall of the smaller N. Cross informs us that the three Tomb-stones on the floor over Bishops Wyvill, Ghest and Jewell were removed in 1684 from the Choir-floor when the Choir was paved with Marble by Dr John Tounson, son of the Bishop Robert Tounson; and still in the Choir there are Inscriptions just signifying where the Bodies are reposited . . . The small square Brass upon Bishop Jewell's Stone is gone so that nothing but the Stone remains; other Tombs in the Church are stript of Brass. Archdeacon Lambert and other of the Boyton family have Stones in the smaller North Cross . . .

" Thomas Sherlock.

'tis mighty well contrived for the beauty of the View, that at the very East end of both Isles of the Choir there are two large Monuments which in a Church abroad one might take for Altars . . . One – Helen Suavenburgh's,[v] a Swede's, who was Relict of William, Marquess of Northampton and afterwards marryed Sir Thomas Gorges. So in the South Isle at the East end too there is a noble and elegant Monument for the Duke of Somerset's family . . .

Even John had to admit that he had not transcribed the inscriptions to all the bishops, but he cannot have missed many. So he went round the Cathedral seeing it in its noble simplicity untrammelled by later Victorian additions which several generations either admired or endured, but which have now been swept away. With John the more negative the appraisal, the greater the compliment, so to say that 'the inside View of this Church presents us with a Symmetry not to be equalled every where' was meant as the highest praise.

The Lamberts had returned to Boyton on 16 June but John and Audley were well entertained by Mr Thompson, the organist, and his friends.[w] Next day they rode along the 'great Western road' to Winchester.

We did not see Winchester 'till we dropped into it through the West gate; to which Gate the Castle once, now the King's-house, joins hard on the South side . . over one of the Gates is a very small Church without any Steeple, which is called St. Swithin's. There is an old Cross, but not remarkably curious, in the Street we first came into which descends from West to East. Low on the South side of the Town is the Cathedral and Close . . The Cemitery is thick set with Trees which, however ornamental they may be in themselves, do entirely obstruct the View of the great Ornament the Cathedral, on the North and West sides of it. The Close is, within its Wall, locked up every night, and there are no houses within it but the Dignitaries and their Porters.

After discussing the history of the Cathedral at some length and describing the interior, he said:

Bishop Edyndon [Edington] begun to build [the Nave] and . . . William . . . of Wickham did at a prodigious charge carry it on and finish it; well it is, that so fine a Room is not cumbered with Pews or any impediments to the view of all its parts. Indeed there is an old Stone Pulpit against a South Pillar, but disused.

The screen which John saw (made to the design of Inigo Jones), has been replaced; he thought it lacked ornament to draw the eye to it.

[v] 'On the Tomb 'tis Snachenberg' (Diary).
[w] Thompson's friends were called Chauntrell and Israel Vander.

The Altar, and ascent to it, are beautifully paved with various Marbles. Bishop Fox's Altar-piece is erected against a beautiful Stone Partition or Screen, the upper part of which is as curiously wrought as any Lace can be; but as the whole is white-washed, it does not strike so much under the notion of Plaister-work, easy to be shaped into any Form, as it cannot fail to do in its undisguised stubborn shape of Stone. Restore it, Fuller says, that in venerable magnificence this Cathedral yieldeth to none in England; so the Choir is fitted up in the most solemn manner; and the View from the West door of the Church Eastwards is truly noble; for the Organ is placed North in the Choir, so that you look over the Screen (which is itself a close piece of work).

Whether or not he realized the transepts were part of the original Norman building, John disliked them intensely: they did not match the rest of the church and nothing could be imagined more 'vile' or 'beyond expression clumsy'. Here again his voice speaks from another age and with what seems now a limited scale of values as far as church architecture is concerned – yet with the utmost attention to detail.

In the Choir on a Sunday there are movable Pews placed in the middle; and on the Sunday Afternoon we heard the Sermon preached before the Prayers, for the benefit of the Winchester Scholars, who when the Sermon is over go out of Church and then the Prayers begin.

Some of the tombs were of special interest to him. There was the inscription to Bishop Mews composed by Robert Lowth's father, the effigy of the founder of Magdalen College, William Waynflete (literally lifting up his heart to God), and the recumbent figure of William of Wykeham. Then there was the more recent monument 'made by H. Cheere' for Bishop Richard Willis, the Visitor who had refused to let Zinzan keep his Fellowship. John thought it both beautiful and noble. It was the more interesting as only in the previous March he had watched Cheere's marble statues of Archbishop Sheldon and the Duke of Ormonde being erected in front of the Sheldonian Theatre in Oxford.[x]

On leaving the Cathedral they had another look at St Cross and spent the rest of their time with two old friends who had supplied them with a number of 'hints' about the places they saw – James Taggart, a minor canon, and Henry Stephens, late of Merton College, whom John had known for a number of years.[y] At Kingsclere they received a hearty welcome from

[x] In the *Inventory of Historical Buildings in the City of Oxford* these statues are only ascribed to Cheere. In his diary for 1738 John Loveday wrote: 'In March H. Cheere's Marble Statues of Sheldon and Ormond were erected in front of the Theatre.'

[y] Taggart, educated at Magdalen, was admitted Clerk in 1738, a year after becoming a minor canon at Winchester. Stephens had stayed at Caversham in 1730. In 1731 he sold John his translations of two of Bishop Edmund Gibson's Pastoral letters for the sum of a moidore (see p. 323). The third followed in 1732.

Jonah Chesterman and on 21 June they were back in Oxford for a brief three nights.

John Audley had to get back to Birmingham and as usual John and Richard Lluellyn rode with him as far as the Sunrising at Edgehill, their favourite inn. By now they were habitués of the place and the Frenches had become very much attached to them. Although they were innkeepers the Frenches mixed socially with some of the local gentry; they attended more than one of the neighbouring churches. On the Sunday, Lluellyn having departed to preach somewhere, Mrs French took the other two young men to hear Mr Lane's sermon at Radway in the morning and introduced them to Mr Seagrave, the parson at Tysoe, in the afternoon. Next day Tom French, thinking perhaps that some feminine society would not come amiss, invited them to ride with him to Avon Dassett to drink tea with Mrs Woodward at the Manor House. The easiest way was to go down Knowle End, the north-west slope of Edgehill, and through the tiny hamlet of Arlescote. John had looked down on the old house from the lane high above which led to Warmington and now riding so close to it he could see what extensive alterations had been made to the original Tudor building during the last fifty years or so. It was no doubt because of his inquiries about the house that Mrs Woodward began telling him about the family who lived there, Mr and Mrs William Goodwin and their four children.[z] There were two sons and two pretty daughters of whom the younger was still at her lessons; but the elder, Anna Maria, a girl of twenty-one, was considered by the neighbourhood to be a beauty. The father was very highly thought of, but was getting old. Mrs Goodwin, who was his second wife, had been Miss Abigail Bartlett of Upper Tysoe Manor. By his first wife, Abigail Booth, he had had one daughter, Abigail, who had married William Taylor of Williamscote, three miles north of Banbury, but had died in 1727. 'There heard of Miss Anna Maria Goodwin of Arlescote', wrote John in his diary and he kept her name in the back of his mind where it simmered gently for the next few months.

Summer at Caversham included long visits from Winchester and Townson. John took a big party to Windsor Castle and Eton and noticed that Mr Derham's catalogue was now out of date as so many paintings had been removed during the two Hanoverian reigns. On 8 August they rode over to Beaconsfield to visit the rector, Dr Thomas Collis, once a Fellow of Magdalen, and to see once again Hall Barn, the house belonging to the Waller family.

Beaconsfield, Dr Collis thinks, is so called from the many Beech Trees about it. It stands higher than Waller's Seat which was built by Dr Stephen

---

[z] The Woodwards of Avon Dassett were connected through marriage with the Goodwins, a Letitia Woodward having married William Goodwin's uncle, Thomas Goodwin of Radway. Richard Woodward had held the manor of Avon Dassett in 1738 and it was sold by Catherine Woodward, spinster, and seven other persons to William Holbech of Farnborough in 1744.

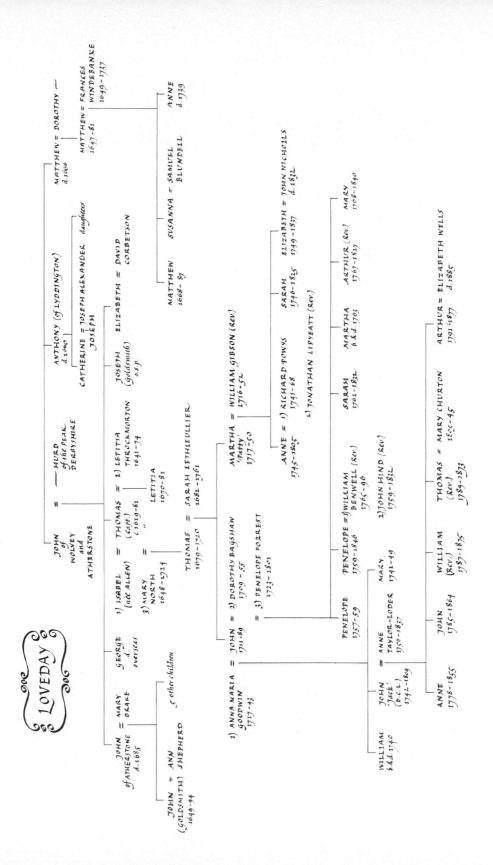

LOVEDAY

JOHN
of WOLVEY
and
ATHERSTONE
= — HURD
of the Peak
DERBYSHIRE
= ANTHONY (of LYDDINGTON)
d.1660
MATTHEW = DOROTHY —
d.1666
MATTHEW = FRANCES
1647-81   WINDEBANKE
            1649-1737

JOHN = MARY
of ATHERSTONE   DRAKE
d.1685

GEORGE
d.
overseas

1) ISABEL
(née ALLEN)

THOMAS
(Capt.)
c.1619-81

2) LETITIA
THROCKMORTON
1641-74

CATHERINE = JOSEPH ALEXANDER   daughters
JOSEPH

JOSEPH
(Goldsmith)
o.s.p.

ELIZABETH = DAVID
            CORBETSON

3) MARY
NORTH
1648-1724

LETITIA
1670-81

MATTHEW   SUSANNA = SAMUEL
1668-87   BLUNDELL

JOHN = ANN
(GOLDSMITH) SHEPHERD
1649-94

5 other children

THOMAS = SARAH ISTHIEUILLIER
1679-1720   1681-1761

1) ANNA MARIA = JOHN = 2) DOROTHY BAGSHAW
GOODWIN   1711-89   1709-55
1717-43
         = 3) PENELOPE FORREST
              1723-1801

MARTHA = WILLIAM GIBSON (Rev.)
'Patty'   1716-52
1717-50

ANNE = 1) RICHARD-POWYS
1745-1805   1741-68

        2) JONATHAN LIPYEATT (Rev.)

SARAH   ELIZABETH = JOHN NICHOLLS
1746-1825   1749-1837   d.1832

MARTHA   ARTHUR (Rev.)   MARY
b.&d.1763   1767-1827   1768-1840

SARAH
1761-1832

PENELOPE
1757-59

PENELOPE = 1)WILLIAM
1759-1846   BENWELL (Rev.)
             1765-96

          2)JOHN-HIND (Rev.)
             1759-1832

MARY
1741-49

ANNE
TAYLOR-LODER
1750-1837

WILLIAM
(Rev.)
1787-1875

THOMAS = MARY CHURTON
(Rev.)   1805-45
1789-1873

ARTHUR = ELIZABETH WELLS
1791-1877   d.1885

WILLIAM
b.&d.1740

JOHN
'Jack'
(b.&b.)
1742-1809

ANNE
1778-1855

JOHN
1785-1864

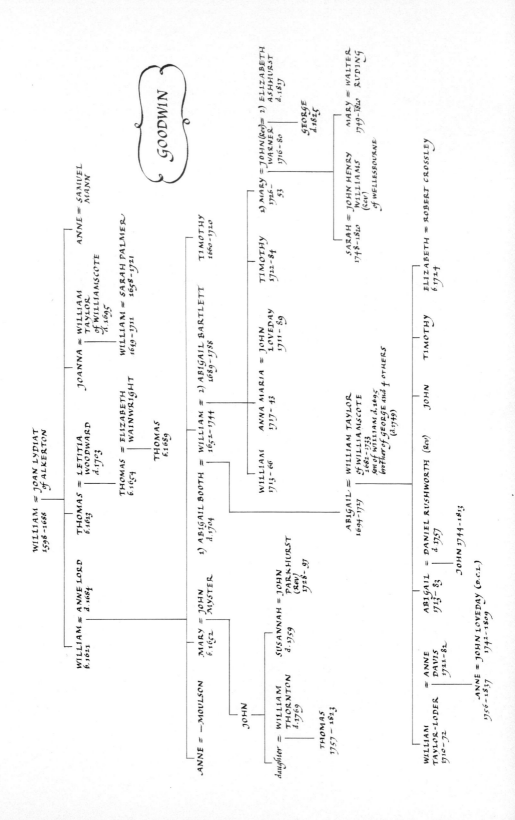

GOODWIN

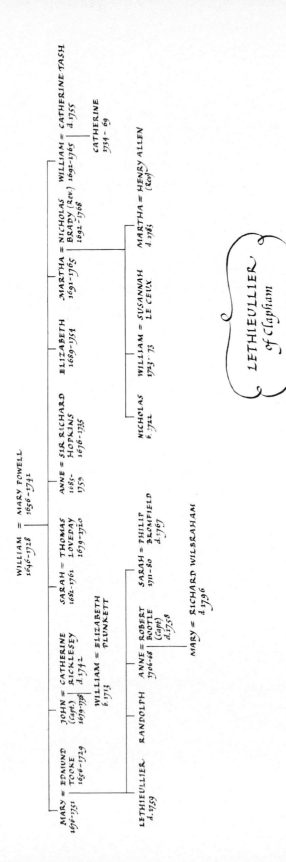

WILLIAM = MARY POWELL
1646-1728   1656-1741

MARY = EDMUND   JOHN = CATHERINE   SARAH = THOMAS   ANNE = SIR RICHARD   ELIZABETH   MARTHA = NICHOLAS   WILLIAM = CATHERINE TASH
1676-1751 TOOKE   (Capt.) BICKLESEY   1682-1761 LOVEDAY 1685-   HOPKINS   1689-1754   1691-1765 BRADY (Rev.) 1691-1765   d.1755
           1656-1729   1679-1738 d.1742   1679-1710   1759   1676-1735   1691-1768

                       WILLIAM = ELIZABETH   CATHERINE
                       b.1713   PLUNKETT   1734-69

LETHIEULLIER   RANDOLPH   ANNE = ROBERT   SARAH = PHILIP   NICHOLAS   WILLIAM = SUSANNAH   MARTHA = HENRY ALLEN
d.1759   1706-68 BOOTLE   1711-80 BROMFIELD   b.1721   1723-73   LE CEUX   d.1783   (Rev.)
                                   (Capt.)   d.1767
                                   d.1758

                         MARY = RICHARD WILBRAHAM
                                d.1796

LETHIEULLIER
of Clapham

Sir Peter Daniel's Great House in Clapham
Line drawing by Humphrey Stone

The Old Rectory, Caversham
Drawing by Barbara Seton

Arlescote House
Line drawing by Humphrey Stone

John Loveday in 1739, by Thomas Gibson

Thomas Hearne
Line engraving by G. Vertue

(Nº. 21.)

Dear Sir,

I make shift just to write, to thank you for yours of the
1st. inst. and to acquaint you, that tho' I am generally
pretty easy in the night time, yet in the day I am often painfull,
& I am really ~ tremely weak. I thank you for your ~~fresh~~ fresh
Marmalet, and am, Dear Sir,

     Your most obl. humble servant

      Tho. Hearne.

Edm. Hall
Oxford June
6. 1735.

Hearne's last letter

From a view of Magdalen College, published 1755

*A view of the old Caversham Bridge
'from the Meadow, the right of the Road'*

*Williamscote, by J. Skelton (courtesy of Ashmolean Museum, Oxford)
The wing on the left has since been removed; the road is now the drive*

Waller;[a] It had been a farm-house and is now called Hall Barn; the situation of the Mansion the Poet lived in was much preferable to this. In the house is an head of the Poet when young by Cornelius Jansen. The Poet's Room is esteemed one of the best proportioned in England; the Outside of it is not to be commended, 'tis starved for want of Ornament. Three antique Statues in the Garden are admirable for their Drapery, especially one of the Women; both the Women are without heads, the Man is not so much mutilated.

Bromley, Maidstone, Rochester, High Laver and Low Leyton – there were only two innovations to the usual September round of visits. John spent a night with the Revd John Fuller, whom he had previously met at Maidstone, in his old moated parsonage at Yalding and he saw a house he had wanted to visit ever since Hopson had described it in 1733 – the Duke of Dorset's mansion near Sevenoaks, Knole. He said very little about the house as he was preoccupied with the pictures, particularly the portrait of Endymion Porter and Lord Goring of which he had a fine copy at Caversham.[b]

Knowle seated on an hill (as the name would intimate) in a pleasant Park . . . The first Earl of Dorset,[c] *temp*. James I, new-furbished up the house and made some chargeable additions. The House is built of Stone, much in the collegiate way and consists of two Courts; there is nothing in the furniture unbeseeming the gravity of an ancient Mansion. Of Paintings there are many family pieces; also Lord Somers by Kneller – a Painting of General Monk as low as the knees and unlike any that I have elsewhere seen of him, with his Page; of Oliver Cromwell an handsome likeness . . . a full proportion of James I robed, sitting, much advanced in years; I

[a] This challenges the supposition, either that Hall Barn was built by the poet Edmund Waller, or the Garden Room for John Aislabie. It is unlikely that John Loveday could have been mistaken in 1733 and in 1738 when he referred to the poet's other house and said on both occasions that his grandson was living at Hall Barn which had been built by his father, Stephen, the poet's fourth son. John's friendship with the rector, Dr Collis, who must have known the owner well, is a further indication that the grandson, Edmund, was living there and built the Garden Room. His mother, Judith, married John Aislabie in 1713. Hall Barn belonged to her after Stephen's death in 1708, but Aislabie renounced any claim he might have had to the property in 1721, possibly the year when Stephen's son, Edmund, attained his majority. Colen Campbell who designed the Garden Room or Poet's Room at Hall Barn in 1724 worked later for Aislabie at Studley Royal in Yorkshire. Pevsner in *Buckinghamshire* (1960), *V.C.H.*, *Buckinghamshire*, vol. III (1925), and others offer alternative but indeterminate solutions.

[b] John preferred the Knole copy of the Van Dyck which though a little smaller was almost identical with his own. However in his the two Cavaliers were supposed to be the Colchester Martyrs, Sir George Lisle and Sir Charles Lucas, both Royalist generals and both shot after their defence of the town.

[c] The house was built orginally by Thomas Bourchier, Archbishop of Canterbury, in the fifteenth century and was granted by Queen Elizabeth to the poet and politician Thomas Sackville, 1st Earl of Dorset of the 4th creation.

have not seen one before so old of this Prince; a length of Henry Howard, Earl of Surrey who was beheaded; it is older and not at all like the Portrait of him in the lower Apartments at Windsor Castle; his name is wrote on *this* Picture. Here are good Copies of all the Cartons except that of St. Paul preaching, as large as the Originals. The Chappel is a venerable Room. The Gardens to this Seat are suffered to remain in the old Taste, shady Walks in the Woods.

During two days in London John managed to continue his explorations of old and comparatively new buildings. He saw the Temple Church, St Stephen's, Walbrook and St James's, Westminster as well as St James's Palace, Whitehall Banqueting House and two other great houses – Somerset House and Northumberland House. At St Stephen's he wrote:

This is Sir Christopher Wrenn's Masterpiece, though the Cupola does with the Church on the outside make no pleasing appearance. No Division between the Church and Chancel. The Pulpit is so commodiously placed that every part of the Church may plainly hear the Preacher; and pity it is that so fine a Church should have one of the smallest congregations in it of any in town, The Pedestals of the Pillars are (as I observed in two Churches at Derby)*[d]* as high as the Pews, but then the Pedestals are wainscotted all round. The Pillars are of the Corinthian Order and there are Ornaments against the Walls to correspond with (as they are directly opposite to) the Chapiters of the Pillars.

At St James's, Westminster, he saw in the vestry the portraits of all the rectors except Bishop Secker*[e]* and recognized the 'curious font of white marble adorned with passages of Scripture-History' from having seen the print of it in the first volume published by the Society of Antiquaries. Of the Banqueting House he wrote:

This light, elegant Building of Inigo Jones's contriving, is the lower part of the Ionic Order, the upper of the Composite. You ascend several Stairs into the great Room, which is now the Chappel. James I is the subject of Rubens's Paintings on the Cieling; it consists of three main Compartments; 'tis very unlike the Cieling-Painting of Verrio which has more glaring strong Colours than this great Master thought proper to make use of or else time has very much mellowed his Colouring, but indeed the

---

[d] At All Saints Church, Derby, on 13 September 1732, John had said the painted stone pillars stood on very high pedestals 'and do not look well at all'. On 25 May 1735 he noticed the pedestals as high as the tops of the pews in St Werburgh's Church, Derby, which was rebuilt in 1699.

[e] Secker held the rectory of St James's, Westminster from 1733 to 1750. He became Bishop of Oxford in 1737, Dean of St Paul's in 1750 and Archbishop of Canterbury in 1758.

Colours are evidently graver than usual on Cielings; this Painting is on Canvas. The fitting the Room for a Chappel has ruined the view of its symmetry and proportion.

At Somerset House[f] he admired the great stone staircase and the 'fretwork' ceilings but thought the gallery quite old-fashioned. None of the pictures there nor at St James's Palace nor Northumberland House took his fancy so much as one which he saw at Browne's Coffee House in Spring Garden –

a Painting of the decisive Battle between the Turks and Imperialists about Vienna; a work of infinite labour and Curiosity – very many hours' inspection would be necessary to gain a complete idea of this Piece in every part; the variety of the Armour; the variety of Deaths, where this Master has shewn great skill in Anatomy, and in every possible way of expressing the last Pangs . . .

A worthier recipient of benefactions from both the Universities than Don Lewis had been was the Revd John Checkley, a New England missionary who came to see John at Oxford during the autumn term. He brought a letter of introduction from Dr Waterland who described him as a man of learning and spirit who had suffered for his defence of Episcopacy some years ago; Cambridge University had raised contributions for him and John was chosen as his unofficial intercessor at Oxford. Having met him John wrote to the Doctor to say that he esteemed Mr Checkley as a clergyman and scholar and revered him as a confessor.

I have mentioned his Case to the good Governour of this Society,[g] who proposes this day to recommend it to the House, nor is there any reason to doubt of his success throughout the University.[8]

So Checkley received his M.A. degree at Oxford without paying any fee and parted from John with gratitude and a pleasant exchange of books.

As the year drew to a close there was more time for entertaining. A tea party in John's rooms attended by Browne Willis, Horbery, Townson, Lluellyn and Pennington was given as a farewell to Pennington who was going to take up his duties as curate at St Mary's, Reading – not a very serious parting. The new vicar there, who had just been inducted, was Robert Bolton, the Dean of Carlisle, a well-known theological writer who became a close friend of John. A week after the tea party Browne Willis came to dinner bringing his son Eliot, who was up at Trinity. However much John might disagree with him, Browne Willis was, after all, a great contemporary authority on all the cathedrals and John still had Bristol to visit. Although he would certainly not

_____

[f] The old Somerset House was later demolished and rebuilt to the design of Sir William Chambers in 1775.
[g] Edward Butler.

allow himself to argue with the older man about any of those rather dubious statements, dinner provided an excellent opportunity for a little discussion on subjects which interested them both.

For once Christmas was not to be spent at Oxford. Mr and Mrs Hiley, with one of their daughters, proposed to spend three weeks in Bath seeing their various friends and relations. John and Charles Hopson were invited to join them and gladly accepted. Rooms had been taken and all arrangements made when, just before the appointed date, there came the sorrowful news that Tom Hiley had died at Swansea. He was buried there on 15 December 1738.

A New Way of Life
1738 – 1739

The news came quickly but it was not possible to attend Tom's funeral. Mrs Hiley had already gone to Bath in the coach and John was at South Moreton on his way from Oxford. He went on, as arranged, to meet Mr Hiley at the Bear Inn at Hungerford. Peter Zinzan had thoughtfully escorted the stricken headmaster there; it was left to John to offer what comfort he could during the next two days. After spending a night at Sandy Lane they reached Bath on 17 December and went next day to Bristol to see Mr Hiley's relations, putting up at the Full Moon in Stokes Croft for a couple of nights. They then returned to Bath where they remained for Christmas and into the New Year of 1739.

During the first quarter of the century the development of Georgian Bath had been very slow and the only important group of buildings in recent years had been those in Queen Square, built to the design of John Wood the Elder. It still had the appearance of a small walled city surrounded by meadows and orchards and there was only the old bridge spanning the river to the south; but things were happening and there was a feeling in the air of pleasant anticipation, though no one could then have imagined the glories to come at the hands of John Wood's son. The Bath John Loveday saw was, as he said, enlarging every day – at that time a highly commendable state of affairs.

Bath is the Aquae Solis of Antoninus; one of the names the Anglo Saxons knew Bath by was Ackmanchester. It is built on a raised ground above the Meads, in a bottom environed with great hills out of which (says

Leland) many springs of pure Water are conveyed to Bath, which is small but compact, the Streets narrow but well paved. The Borough-Walls (for so they call the Town-Wall) *within* seem not high, but *without* are of a reasonable height. The Walls here are not entire; there are four Gates – the Westgate contains some of the best Apartments in Town. . . Leland queries whether divers notable Antiquities in Stone in the Walls betwixt the South and West and the West and North Gates were in the time of the Romans set thus in the Walls, or whether they were gathered out of old Ruins and since set up; other Stones of the same kind are in the low Wall built up at the East end of the Abbey-Church in the Grove; there particularly is the famous Bath Inscription which in 1708 was found at Walcote near Bath; indeed this Village joins to Bath, the London Road comes through it. . . . Walcote Church was damaged so much on Jany. 4 1739 by the dreadful weather in the morning that 'tis shut up and must be rebuilt.

Bath is built of Stone and is enlarging every day; the Square[a] is quite new; 'tis not on a flat, the sides are not built alike; the higher side is grand and shews like one house; one of the falling sides has the middle house retired far back behind the rest: this Square is in Walcote Parish and the new Chappel built here is served by the Minister of that Place; the front of the Chappel imitates that in Covent-Garden, London: within the roof is supported by Ionic Pillars, the Pedestals as high as the Pews.[b] The ecclesiastical state of Bath is this; the City present to the Abbey-Church, which is a Rectory, to which St. James's and St. Michael's are now Chappelries, as is also Widcomb, a Village near Bath. St. Michael's. commonly called Northgate-Church, is out of the City-Walls. Besides these three Churches and the Chappel in the Square, there is St. Michael's Chappel annexed to St. John Baptist Hospital; Walter Chapman, M.A. is now Master of the Hospital, no Relation of the late Master, John Chapman; this Hospital was founded in 1174 by Bishop Fitz Joceline; the Duke of Chandois has built Apartments over the Hospital to let-out for Lodgings.[c] The Abbey-Church is not so much frequented by the Company as the other Congregations because Service begins here at an inconvenient time for them. This great Church is dedicated to St. Peter and St. Paul whose large Statues stand in the West Front.

After discussing the history of the Abbey in some detail he continued:

[a] Queen Square.

[b] St Mary's Chapel, opened in 1734 and demolished about 1875. Other comparisons with St Paul's, Covent Garden are on pp. 345, 365.

[c] The Duke of Chandos had brought property with its rights to letting accommodation. His plans to rebuild were partly carried out by William Killigrew and continued in 1727 by John Wood the Elder. See Walter Ison, *The Georgian Buildings of Bath*, 1948.

The East Window over the Altar . . . is perfectly magnificent, very large and consisting of stained panes of Glass. The disposition of the Doors has made this Church extremely cold; there are five in all, three at the West End (a great Door and one on each side of it) and two at the East End, one to each side-Isle. South of the Altar is a Pew that appears once to have been a small Chantery-Chappel having a low Stone Roof.[d] The Altar-piece was given by General Wade;[e] and it is a very handsome one of Marble, containing a good Painting of the Wise Men's offering to Christ. The Vestry is entered out of the South Isle of the Choir . . . The Cross-Isle is quite spoiled by a Gallery and Organ-Loft erected quite over the Entrance of it; there are not above two or three Monuments extant before 1660, though six Bishops have anciently been buryed here. Against a South Pillar of the Cross is a Picture-Cenotaph for Lady Grace Gethin, an Irish Baronet's Lady; the Inscription says that there is such another Cenotaph as this for that Lady in Westminster-Abbey.[f] There is a Monument for Bishop Baker of Norwich against a Pillar in the South Isle of the Body; the Latin Epitaph talks of his *Morals* with approbation.

(Bishop William Baker, who had died in 1732, had also been Bishop of Bangor and was renowned for nepotism in both sees.)

John now looked at the exterior of the Abbey and having examined the whole building pronounced it 'a noble Church both inside and out – it strikes one very much'.

The Duke of Kingston is owner of the site of the Abbey-house;[g] this old building stands West and by South of the Church, just by it . . . the late Queen Anne lodged here. 'Prior W. Birde' occurs in Stone-work on the back part of the house.

Of the Baths, the King's-Bath is much the largest; the Queen's Bath is just by it and is supplyed with Water from it; in Leland's time Gentlemen resorted to the King's Bath, now it is more frequented by the meaner sort; the Pump-Room joins to it and 'tis from this Spring that they export Bath-Water. These two Baths then stand not far from the Cathedral, South-West of it. The Cross Bath, Hot Bath and Lepers Bath stand near St. John's Hospital; the first is now chiefly used by Persons of distinction; there is a Cross in the middle of it, whence its name. The Lepers Bath is very small and mean.

[d] Prior William Birde's Chantry chapel was begun in 1515.

[e] The altarpiece given in 1725 by Field-Marshal George Wade was sold and subsequently went to Grosvenor Villa, Bath.

[f] Lady Gethin, who died at the age of twenty-one, was actually buried at Hollingbourne (Kent) in 1697. Within six years three editions of her works were published, though many of the entries in her commonplace book were copied from Bacon's *Essays*. A sermon in her memory was instituted to be preached in Westminster Abbey on Ash Wednesdays.

[g] The Abbey House or Priory was demolished in 1755 to make way for the Kingston Baths.

The old Guildhall which John saw was inconveniently situated in the market place and was later replaced by the fine building designed by Thomas Baldwin.

The Town-house is an handsome Stone Building, supported on open Arches; the large Room above Stairs is adorned with many Pictures of the Aldermen and other Members of the Corporation, which their Member, General Wade, was at the expense of drawing to hang up here; they also have the General's Picture, a Length, at one end of the Room; in a smaller Room here is the Head of some Heathen Deity[h] in Brass gilt which was dug up in 1727 in Stallstreet. They also shew some Roman Coins found at the same time.

There is a Gate with a Stone Arch at the farther end of the bridge over Avon; so that the City is fortifyed with two Gates to the Southward; there is a long Street going up the rocky hill across the bridge, being a Suburb to Bath; it is called Holoway, the Inhabitants go to Widcomb Church; here is the Magdalenes, an Hospital for Idiotts in which at present there are but two; there has been no Service in the Chappel many years.[i] Dr Thomas, the Master, has a Fee for every Person buryed here, as the people of the Village are.

John ended his account of Bath by quoting Prior John Cantlow's inscription in four waved scrolls on the porch wall of this chapel and his own passing reflection, 'Bath abounds in beggars.' But there was still Widcombe to visit where the successful deputy postmaster, Ralph Allen, was building his new mansion, Prior Park,[j] and where he had already established a system for transporting stone from his quarries nearby on Claverton Down to the river-side wharf below.

The way to Allen's Quarries is by Widcomb; from them to Bath 'tis a gradual descent; the Stone-Carriages do not move here as the Coal-Carts in Newcastle, where two ranges of wooden grooves are fixed in the ways for the wooden wheels to move in, and then they go-on without horses, as they do here, where are no Grooves, but only lengths of Wood for the Iron Wheels to move upon, which are kept steady upon the Wood by means of the thin Iron-work on the innermost side only of the opposite Wheels being raised so high as to keep the Wheels moving without deviation upon the lengths of Wood. Mr Allen is building a very handsome Seat this way out of town.

[h] The head of Minerva was placed on a chimneypiece in the new Guildhall built in 1777.
[i] The Hospital was rebuilt in 1761. The Master was probably David Thomas who died in 1739. He was said to have been often absent and his integrity was in doubt. He was succeeded by Dr James Thomas. See Barbara Stone, 'St Mary Magdalene's, Holloway: The Oldest of the Bath Charities', Monograph, Bath Reference Library.
[j] Prior Park had been begun in 1735 and was not entirely completed until 1748.

There were walks to be taken to the village of Weston and on the hill to the north of Bath.

Of the two Downs about Bath, Clarkendown is but small; Lansdown is in good measure inclosed. The Monument there raised by the late Lord of that name for his gallant Ancestor[k] slain here in the Royal Cause is a poor clumsy unmeaning thing, the more unintelligible as the Inscription is not now visible; a plain Obelisk such as Mr Nash has reared in the Grove at Bath in memory of the benefit the Prince of Orange received from drinking the Waters, would have done much better.[l]

They had spent two more days at Bristol at the end of December and it was then that John made a comprehensive tour of the place. The Cathedral, 'commonly called the College', received as careful treatment as any edifice he had seen;[1] with his conversations with Browne Willis still fresh in his mind, he paced up and down, measuring the height and width of the choir and transepts and with only occasional slight criticism of his friend's pronouncements. Having dealt with the history and the proportions he turned his attention to the tombs and monuments with especial interest in two of them:

At present there is nothing Westward of the Great Cross . . .'[m] The Stalls were seemingly fitted-up, on its commencing Cathedral in 1542 by the first Bishop, Paul Bush, who built the Throne. His Sceleton on a low Tomb of freestone is at the upper end of the North side-Isle, between that and the Choir – not of the side-Isle as in B. Willis[n] . . . North of the Altar is a Tomb on which an Abbot, seemingly as old as the Church; 'tis likely for Knowle,[o] who dyed in 1322 and is said to have built the Church 'leaving Vacancies in the Walls in Arches, to contain the Effigies of his Successors'. So says Browne Willis[p] . . . On the floor of the North Cross . . . is an ancient gravestone in shape of a Stone Coffin-lid; there is a Cross on it, but above that a Man's Head, barely the head, no Neck, nor any Ornaments to the head, the Ears sticking out like those of a Diota; Willis says 'tis doubtless in memory of one of the most ancient Abbots or Priors; I can't recollect my having ever seen such another, though I may perhaps have seen a mitred head and shoulders over a Cross . . . The Chapter-house is

[k] Sir Bevil Granville was killed on the northern side of the hill and his grandson, Lord Lansdowne the poet, erected the monument to him in 1720.
[l] The most important of the three monuments, the obelisk in Queen Square, was erected by Nash in honour of the visit of Prince and Princess of Wales in 1738.
[m] The present nave was not begun until 1868.
[n] Cadaver monuments were usually erected during a bishop's lifetime and replaced after death by a vested effigy. Bishop Bush, who had resigned four years before his death, gave instructions in his will for a freestone tomb at the north side of the high altar. See The Friends of Bristol Cathedral Report, 1977, article by Arthur Sabin.
[o] Abbot Edmund Knowle built the choir.
[p] John was reminded of the Abbey of the Bernadines on the Scheldt.

in the East side, a good Room with a Stone-Roof where they meet on Church business. The Cathedral is in as good repair and kept as neat as any. The six Prebendal houses are upon the Green, but there are none for Minor Canons and Singing Men; the Dean's house too is at the West end of the Cathedral, the yearly value of the Deanery as good as the reserved Rents of the See. (See Willis.) . . . The College-Gateway, West of the Cathedral, was built by two Abbots in the time of Henry VIII. 'Tis a very curious piece of work, admirably preserved; sure the Stone must be more durable than ordinary, it is so bright and perfect; the Ornaments are very good, nor are they sparingly bestowed. The College-Green is an high, pleasant and wholesome Spot of Ground; in the middle the Cross is now erected which once stood in the City;[q] as it is placed in so large an area it wants elevation; an higher and broader Pedestal with steps up each side would have done the business; as it is new painted and gilded it has a gaudy appearance, but however in a View not too nigh has a very good effect, being very proper for an area adorned with three Churches; for besides the Cathedral there is another, St. Austin's, a Parish Church and also St. Mark's on the Green. B. Willis says it was made Parochial . . . how this Church should ever be Parochial, or when, I don't know; of late years it was a French Church, so continuing till 1722, when the Corporation, who used to go to the Cathedral, taking some offence at the Dignitaries, provided the French with a Tabernacle elsewhere and fitted this up for their own use; and 'tis now commonly called the Mayor's Chappel;[r] and here there is Service every Sunday morning, the Corporation now going to the Cathedral only on an high day or two in the year. In St. Mark's are several fine Monuments, one just North of the Altar is for Miles Salley, Bishop of Llandaff, who dyed in 1516, 'tis a recumbent length in Pontificalibus, mitred, the hands joined, two Cushions under the Head . . . Here are also the effigies recumbent of two Knight-Templars. The Vestry was once a Chappel; in it is a Confessionary differing from those abroad, as in them there are three Niches, the middle one for the Priest, the other two for the Penitent whereas in this there are only two Niches and a large square hole in the intervening Partition, one of these for the Priest, the other for the Penitent; 'tis all of Stone.

Redcliff Church is in a mean part of the Town: . . . There is a noble ascent of a great many steps to the Church, which (says Camden) far exceeds all Parish Churches in England; the Founder, William Canninges, five

---

[q] The Cross was taken down in 1762 and was later given to Henry Hoare by the next Dean, Cutts Barton (installed in 1763). It was taken to Stourhead in 1764 by wagon transport for which Hoare paid £300. See Annals of Bristol. T. (ST) 383.907, and Kenneth Woodbridge, *Landscape and Antiquity*, 1970. It was erected in 1765 and repainted in 1776 when Mrs Lybbe Powys thought it too bright.

[r] Now known as the Lord Mayor's Chapel. Bishop Miles Salley reconstructed the east end.

times Mayor here, then Dean of a College founded by himself at Westbury[s] in Gloucestershire, two miles from Bristol, lies against the South Wall of the Cross-Isle in both these capacities, both Effigies recumbent . . .

The outside view of the Church is very noble, except at the West-end which is very awkward; for there the Steeple is built not over the great middle Isle, but the North Isle and by the bulk of it we may be well assured that no other was designed to have answered it over the South Isle; this large Steeple then is a complete Tower with the beginning of a Spire, which that it may be looked upon as a finished Steeple, is ornamented at top with a sort of corona of carved Work; this Steeple too has spoiled the Inside of the Church, for at the West end of the North Isle there is one wide Arch to support this, as wide as two of the other Arches, and indeed there are two Arches in the South Isle exactly answering in space, as well as directly opposite, to this one Arch of the North Isle; nor is this all the deformity that the Tower has occasioned on the inside of the Church, for over this great disproportionate Northern Arch there is a large space of dead Wall, where, if the Tower had not run up, there should have been a Window; now all this incongruity might have been hid a few years since upon their erecting an Organ, which they have placed as far West as possible in the Church, whereas by bringing it forward a little, Redcliff Church would have been all of a piece. The Roof is throughout artificially vaulted with Stone; the great Isles and Cross are of the same height; the Cross has two side-Isles, but is too narrow. Out of the South Isle of the Choir you enter a low Chappel which is behind the high Altar; if you would go round the Outside of the Church, you go under this Chappel through an open Arch that supports it.

For 400 years St Mary's stood without its steeple which was not restored until 1872; had he seen it, John would have realized how important it was to the proportion of the church and would have probably been less biased about the effect of the tower on the interior.

'The Citizens have been very emulous of late years in adorning several of their respective Parish-Churches' was his general conclusion as he made a quick tour of as many as possible.

The Temple Church is an old fabrick; the Altar strikes wonderfully at the opening of the West Door of the Church; this is perfectly neat and elegant, of Mahogany, but the chapiters and other Ornaments are of Deal whited over, which has a very good effect with the above-said Wood. There is an old brass Branch in the Church set off with the figures of the

---

[s] The college of priests attached to the church at Westbury was rebuilt by Bishop John Carpenter. Canynges, the rich merchant who rebuilt St Mary Redcliffe, finishing the work begun by his grandfather, became a priest and Dean of the College, but was not the founder. The church was given Collegiate status in 1194. It had been a monastery since 961. See Henry Wilkins, *Westbury College*, 1917.

Virgin and Babe, and St. George (or is it not St. Michael?) and the Dragon.[t] At the West entrance there is a white marble Cross on the floor; this is new, but 'tis said that there was such an old one here.

Leland says that 'one Shepward a Merchaunt of Bristow made the right highe and costly Towre of St. Stephenes . . .', and (in truth) besides the great height of it, one can't but be amazed at the exquisitely curious work of it, as uncommon in the Plan as in the Execution . . . This Church is entirely fitted-up with Mahogany, Pews and all.

When John saw St. Nicholas's church its chancel stood over the gate at the lower end of High Street.[u]

St. Nicholas' Church stands on Arches, there is a Crypt underneath, where they bury and through which there is one way by Steps into the Church. The Altar is ascended by so many Steps, that 'tis higher than the Pulpit, which is the case at a Church in Exeter;[v] but here the flight of Steps is better proportioned to the space allowed for them; indeed this Altar stands over one of the City-Gates.

The whole of St. Leonard's Church is over another Gateway, which being the Entrance to three Streets is made with a face each way, and so takes up some Ground. The Steeple of St. John's Church stands also over another Gate. In All-Saints Church by the Tolsey is the Monument for Mr Colson;[w] his Effigies is said to be very like; all his publick Charities and benefactions are engraved upon the Monument; this is a costly thing, but a mural Monument just by for some Relations of his is very neat and elegant.

St. James's, with its tower to the east, was the last church he described and he now had time to observe the city itself.

The old buildings in Bristol are Wood and Plaster, very many of the new [are] of Brick. St. James's Square is very small; Queen's Square is larger than that in Soho, London; it is the same spot of ground that not long since was called the Marsh, a public Walk for the Citizens; in the middle is a noble Equestrian Statue of William III in Metal by Rysbrack. Near this is the Merchants Hall, to which there are excellent Kitchens. The Council-House is by the Tolsey – so they call the Exchange. Leland speaks of a pretty Church in the second Area of the fair Castle . . . this Castle was demolished in the Civil Wars; 'tis now turned into Streets and is

[t] The figures on the fine brass (or latten) chandelier are of St George and the Dragon below and the Virgin and Child above.

[u] It was rebuilt between 1762 and 1769.

[v] St Stephen's Church, Exeter, where in 1736 John had said 'The Altar is raised so high that the top of the rails is even with the top of the pulpit.'

[w] Edward Colston, a great benefactor to Bristol, died at Mortlake, his home for many years, but was buried at Bristol.

is extraparochial except with regard to Poors-Rates, in which respect the whole City is by Act of Parliament looked upon as one Parish.

The Bridge, on Stone Arches over the Avon, is close-set with houses on both sides, having no Opening to the Water as at London bridge; so that it may with great propriety pass for a Street. Frome is the other River here. Bristol is in the form of an horseshoe; there are very few Beggars here and as few Carts, instead of which they use Sledges, but they call them Drays: and they have reason for this Custom; the subterraneous goutes for carrying off the filth would be in danger from heavier Carriages.

Bristol's importance as a port received no mention from John, but he made a point of visiting the hot well and adding another highly regarded spa to his list.

The Hot Well is in the parish of Clifton in Gloucestershire but known by the name of the Hot Well at Bristol. Camden speaks of St. Vincent's Rocks; at the bottom of these romantic Rocks – for so they are on both sides the Water – is St. Vincent's Well as Dr Fuller calls it; 'tis very near the River and is affected by the Tide. In the Pump-Room is a good picture of an old man who had been Pump here: as to the public Rooms, below Stairs is a Billiard-Table Room and another Room; above, the Grand Room of 36 feet by 80, much superior to either of those at Bath, but wainscotted in a poor manner, unworthy of so noble an appartment.

He ended his account of the two cities by saying that in their language 'noblets' meant 'what we call round coals.' 'In these countries too,' said he, 'they perpetually use the expletives "do" and "did" and pronounce S like Z.'

Neither the poor weather nor the fact that they were in mourning prevented the Hiley family from making the most of their stay and seeing plenty of company; so that it was not until 12 January that John set off for home, leaving the others to follow next day. With no one to constrain him and his well-trained servant to carry the baggage, he managed to reach Hungerford on the first day.

There are but four Hills of remark on the Bath-road and all in this day's journey; the first is after the Stream that divides the Counties of Somerset and Wilts; the second is beyond Lacock . . . the third and most considerable hill is beyond Sandy Lane – viz. Beacon-Hill, of steep and rugged Ascent; the fourth of chalk or marl is beyond Marlborough. Lacock Nunnery, the Seat of John Ivory Talbot Esqr. stands on a flat at the farther end of Lacock. I saw the house some years since. Mr Styles is building a grand Seat on the hill above this.* It is very considerably nearer

---

* I am grateful to Miss Janet Burnett-Brown for information about Benjamin Haskin Styles, M.P. He moved between Moor Park, Hertfordshire, London and Bowden Park near Lacock. He began to build a great new house north of the present Bowden Park but it was never completed. He died the same year that John saw it being built.

to leave Avebury on the left hand and go close by Selbury [Silbury] Hill . . . this great round hill would make an appearance anywhere but where it is seated, like Marlborough Mount; it is on the lowest part of the Downs; it appears plainly to have been scooped out of the hole in which it stands. We rode too by several Barrows or Tumuli and many gray Weathers; so the Shepherds call the Stones which lie thick about here and at a distance may have the appearance of Sheep; some are now made use of in the Mounds.

John returned to Oxford knowing that his dreams about Anna Maria Goodwin, the girl he had heard of but never seen, had reached a critical stage; he must find out, whether the real person was as perfect as his image of her. The man to consult was Richard Lluellyn, who had various contacts in that part of the country and who understood the situation, although he had not heard Mrs Woodward's eulogies at the tea party. Lluellyn immediately hit upon the idea of writing to his friend Francis Lydiatt, the schoolmaster at Warwick, to ask him what he knew about the Goodwins and Anna Maria in particular. Lydiatt, a Fellow of Wadham, was a man of some reputation who had built up a flourishing school and was also a kinsman of the Goodwins. John sent his servant to Edgehill to prepare the way for all contingencies; then, on 7 February, the letter was dispatched. Mr Lydiatt's anxiously awaited reply came on the 12th. It was very satisfactory.

Now all that remained was to plan the strategy. No doubt, with Tom French's connivance, an invitation came to Lluellyn to preach the afternoon sermon on Sunday 18 February at Warmington, the parish church on a hill which the Goodwins attended. The two young men had arrived at the Sunrising two days earlier and at the appointed time they rode along Camp Lane, stopping to look down on the pretty hamlet below and the house which was Anna Maria's home. She too must have been in a state of curiosity, at least, for she must by now have heard of the young man who came so regularly to the Sunrising and knew so many of her neighbours. Surely the Frenches must have given her parents some warning of what might follow. No one knows exactly what happened or whether John was actually introduced to her after the service; certain it is that his mind was immediately made up.

He rode straight back to the inn and wrote a letter the same evening to Mr Goodwin. He also wrote three sentences in his diary:

Went in the afternoon to Warmington Church, Lluellyn preaching. There I first saw Nanny Goodwin. Wrote the letter to Mr Goodwin.

On Monday he rode over to Shenington, another Edgehill village, and spent the afternoon with a family called Diston who were cousins and close friends of the Goodwins. There he gleaned all the information he could, but then there was nothing for it but to ride back to Oxford and hope. He wrote at once to the President, perhaps to say he did not after all intend to spend the rest of his life at Oxford, and then tried to fill in his time as best he could. There was the Bodleian catalogue to annotate, a task he had begun the previous year. He also paid another visit to Blenheim on 10 March.

> The Gallery is 184 foot in length . . this Room, together with the Pew-Loft in the Chappel are the only parts of this House that are floored with Oak. The Statue of Queen Anne, Rysbrack has set-up in the Oval, opposite to the middle Door in the Gallery;[y] the Robing required a vast deal of Labour, which is fully bestowed on it; so much Work I never saw in any Statue. There are Glasses inserted in most of the Chimney-Pieces as at Dalkeith Palace in Scotland.

Mr Goodwin was not going to hurry himself to reply to a stranger, however well spoken of, who wished to pay addresses to his elder daughter without the proper preliminary advances. It was a month before his letter arrived, but it was encouraging enough to bring John back to Edgehill within two days – just at the moment when the University was rocking with horror at the appalling behaviour of the Warden of Wadham College, Dr Thistlethwaite, who was degraded and expelled for sodomy that very Sunday. John entered the facts in his diary, but he had more inspiring matters to consider as he and Thomas Townson travelled up the Banbury Road. Mr Goodwin had said he might call on him and after sending a note down to Arlescote and fortified by a good dinner at which Mr Diston joined them, he made his way down the hill. The meeting was pleasant, but he returned to Oxford still not knowing what was in store. After a week on tenterhooks he received another letter from Mr Goodwin accepting him as a suitor for the hand of Anna Maria.

A letter had been enclosed for his mother and he rushed down to Caversham to tell her the news and to ask for her approval. Back he went to Arlescote with the answer which Mr Goodwin must have been rather surprised to receive within four days. Payne and Lluellyn had come up with him, but this was a time when friends were superfluous and they went off to Warwick to appease Mr Lydiatt's curiosity. So John was alone and ready when young William Goodwin arrived at the inn to dine with him and escort him home to stay. Tom French, who would not have missed this meeting for the world, had also been invited down for supper.

William led them across the panelled hall where portraits of Mr Goodwin and his first wife, Abigail Booth, were hanging. The family was gathered to meet John in the parlour, a small panelled room furnished with tables, black

---

[y] I am grateful to Mr David Green for information on Blenheim. Queen Anne's statue was set up in the west bay of the Long Library (John's Oval). At some stage a new plinth was added with the date 'MDCCXXXX: VI:', possibly a year and four months after John's visit – but this is uncertain.

cane chairs and yellow cushions; and there it was that he met the two women to whom in different ways he was to be bound by true devotion – the beautiful and charming Anna Maria and her mother, Abigail Goodwin, who was to be his ally and counsellor for the rest of his life.

He stayed for five days, though he went up to the Sunrising to report progress to Lluellyn and Payne on their return, and to accompany Mrs French to church, a habit he continued through the summer. Otherwise he roamed the countryside with the young Goodwins on foot or in the saddle; it was a strange situation to be so intimately connected with people he scarcely knew and there was much to learn. The Goodwins had been small squires and landowners in the Edgehill country for a long time and by now were a considerable clan. Mr Goodwin's grandfather, another William, who owned property at Hornton and Alkerton, had wished to settle his sons on estates of their own. For the elder, William, he had bought Arlescote in 1646 from one Manasses Cooper; to Thomas he gave the Radway Grange estate.[z] The two Williams, unlike Thomas, had lived exemplary lives. The present one had married his second wife, Abigail Bartlett, in 1712, when he was in his fifties and she only twenty-three. Her parents, before moving to Upper Tysoe, had lived in Mortlake in Surrey. Mrs Bartlett, whose maiden name had been Abigail Ward, was a first cousin of John Ward, Professor of Rhetoric at Gresham College. In spite of their different generations he was only ten years older than Mrs Goodwin and was a frequent visitor at Arlescote, bringing with him a whiff of learning from the erudite London societies of which he was a most active member. Unlike her he was a Dissenter, but this made no difference at all to the deep trust she always had in him and his sister Abigail. She herself was a woman of strong and devout principles, a competent and practical housewife and a wonderful needlewoman. The year before John's arrival she had embarked on the colossal task of making an embroidered carpet in gros and petit point, which she did not complete until 1746.

The house was originally Elizabethan but had been extensively altered by Mr Goodwin's father. It had virtually been turned back to front so that the sitting rooms now faced south on to the hill, while the kitchen looked out northwards across the garden to the Burton Dassett escarpment, which bore on its brow an ancient beacon and windmill. This room had once been a parlour and it was there that the young princes, Charles and James, sat with their tutor Dr William Harvey during the Battle of Edgehill.[z] Other changes were made, such as introducing sash windows to the south front and replacing the two spiral or turnpike staircases at each end of the house with a central one. In the earlier house the bedrooms had led one into the

[z] Thomas Goodwin ran up debts and was in prison in 1694. His son and grandson eventually sold the Radway Grange estate to Sanderson Miller, father of the architect. The sale was completed in 1715.

other, the central chamber being occupied by the master and mistress. The sons slept in one adjoining room and the daughters in the other, while beyond each of these were bedrooms for the male and female servants respectively. Its only means of descent were by the staircases at each end, the parents could sleep peacefully, feeling, perhaps optimistically, that intercommunication between the other rooms was sufficiently hazardous. All that had changed and now the white room with its dimity curtains, the green room hung with calamanco[a] and the best chamber with its powder closet and yellow satin draperies were approached in the modern manner by passages. The servants had been relegated to the attics above.

The garden was and long remained typical of the late seventeenth century. At the time of the alterations four gazebos of Dutch origin, with ogee-shaped roofs, had been built round the house with great success, especially on the southern corners of the front lawns. At the back the garden was divided into four square sections planted with fruit trees, in the centre of which was a large mound with yews. The central walks were edged with roses set in grass paths and the others were bordered by filbert hedges. At the far end from the house a fishpond had been made, known as 'the canal', from which outlets were said to flow into the Severn and Thames. Close to it were a skittle alley and another of the fashionable mounds.

John spent the rest of the summer alternating between Arlescote and Oxford. Sometimes it seems that he only returned to his rooms in order to write a love-letter to Anna Maria and no sooner had she read it than he was back on the doorstep again. Though he usually travelled on horseback, as time went on he began to practise driving a chariot[b] in preparation for the days when he would be accompanied by his wife. (She was herself a good horsewoman, as indeed was almost essential in such a remote place.) Sometimes they would ride over to Williamscote, the home of her half-nephew William Taylor[c] (the son of Mr Goodwin's daughter by his first wife), who was a year older than John. He lived in a Tudor house which his family had purchased before the Civil War,[d] but as often as not he was at Arlescote. Many years later the only surviving child of Anna Maria and John was to marry William Taylor's daughter, thus cementing the links between the two families and estates.[e]

It was during one of their outings that John wrote some notes on Warmington church.

[a] Flemish woollen material with a fine gloss.
[b] A light four-wheeled carriage.
[c] William Taylor added the name Loder to his own in 1744 in order to inherit property at Lechlade from his uncle by marriage, John Loder, vicar of Napton, Warwickshire.
[d] Edward Taylor of Middleton Cheney and Banbury bought the property from Calcott Chambre in 1633.
[e] The marriage between Dr John Loveday, D.C.L. and Anne Taylor-Loder took place at Wardington on 7 October 1777.

You descend into this Church, which is not cieled. North out of the
Chancel is the Vestry, a Chimney in it as there is in the Room over it, the
floor of which is now taken up, so that the Vestry reaches to the Roof;
there was a necessary house as well as a Chimney, in the upper room, from
which through an Iron Grate there is a View to the Altar. Doubtless this
Room was a Cell or Hermitage for an Anchorite or Recluse who through
the Grate[f] might see the Host elevated and so join in Worship with the
Congregation. The Church stands upon an hill above the village and is
dedicated to St. Michael.

No well-conducted betrothal, however romantic, could be allowed to
proceed without attending to finance, with property as the prime consideration. Mrs Loveday at once made over the Feens estate to her son, which kept
Alexander Staples busy, and Mr Goodwin called in his attorneys, Lyne
Councer and his son from Bloxham, for conferences – with dinners included –
at Arlescote. When the day came for the two sets of lawyers to meet, John
and William Goodwin rode down to Caversham with the Councers
following discreetly a few miles behind. Mrs Loveday lodged the whole
party and provided a parlour for a legal battlefield. When all seemed settled
the attorneys were taken to see the Feens farms and then John and William
managed to shed them and went off to Eton and Windsor Castle to relax
among the paintings; but it was not until the end of June that matters were
finally agreed and then only after an Oxford lawyer, John Wright, had been
called in as arbiter. Meanwhile Patty had sent the family jewels to Oxford and
on 3 July John 'made the presents to Miss Goodwin'. All this was very
satisfactory to the families concerned, who followed every move closely
towards a seemly conclusion.

A cloud darkened their happiness in mid-July when Tom French suffered a
stroke. John, called up to the Sunrising one morning before breakfast, found
him alive but a very sick man and it was a long time before he was about
again.

A problem which had to be decided was where they were to live. Mrs
Loveday had promised to leave her old home and move to another house in the
village, but John would not hurry her and in any case he wished to make some
alterations to the rather uncomfortable house. The Goodwins pressed them to
stay in the neighbourhood, but there were few houses to rent. It was only four
days before the marriage that the whole family drove over to Little Kineton to
inspect Mr Bentley's manor house[g] which he wished to let for a year.
Everyone approved of it.

John's retirement from the bachelor scene was a subject of great interest

[f] John added a note later to say that Professor John Ward had 'the same notion of the use of
these barred windows north of the Altar in St Mary's Church, Warwick'.

[g] Little Kineton Manor was owned by Edward Bentley, who died four years later. The
Elizabethan house was pulled down in 1790.

among his friends, though most of them were to succumb eventually to matrimony themselves and in some cases, so strong were their ties of friendship, to marry each others' sisters or widows. Townson, Bagshaw and Audley stayed single; it was Townson who wrote some lines about John Loveday at the time of his marriage which show how he was regarded by them all.

> Must you, dear Honoured Friend, retreat
> From Oxford's calm and much-loved seat?
> [then, after the necessary classical allusions, continuing:]
> Loveday, whose side I oft have joyned
> (My idle business thrown behind)
> To roam where far-framed Bard[h] now grey
> By fourscore winters, tuned his lay
> With drum and pipe of sprightly tone,
> And pleased all ears, nor least his own . . .[i]
> For you the morning's Meditation,
> The noontide-walk, and recreation,
> For you the Day throughout shall grieve,
> But chief the social Hours of Eve.
> Oh Friend, tho' Nature's grace designed
> In you the deep reflecting mind,
> Of parts to search, of temper fit
> The sanctity of truth to admit;
> Exalted taste, with pure delight
> The Volume of the Book, our Light
> And Life, to read and mark aright
> And Memory firm, that holds in view
> The deeds of ancient time and new:
> Yet in one Bosom, mixt with these,
> Mirth, Humour, Wit and Fancy please
> That Passion there, whose gentle Sway
> All hearts, and most the best, obey,
> Soft entered on: the generous Sighs
> For charms of Worth and beauty rise; . . .
> Happy the Flame, which reason lighted!
> Happy with equal flame requited!
> Delights now round your married State
> Unfelt by vulgar hearts await;
> Love by Esteem not Fancy fed;
> And Friendship nursed in Love's soft bed

[h] John Boulton.
[i] Among the omitted lines is a reference to Thomas Pearcey – 'The scene . . . where Probity and Pearcey dwell.'

To tend'rest Joy: Fond-eyed Desire
That glows with still increasing fire,
Won by sweet converse void of guile
Endearing charms, and beautie's smile.
Oh may Time
Spare to cut short the virtuous bliss,
That dreads no other dart but His.[3]

Sadly the last prayer was not granted.

John Peareth, who could be guaranteed to hear all the rumours, false or otherwise, wrote late in August.

. . . I direct my letter to Oxford 'till I have a new address to you. I am told you have taken Ambrose Holbech's[j] house at Mollington, which I apprehended to be a mistake at first because I heard your own house at Caversham was beautifying for the reception of your Lady and that Mrs Loveday had taken the house Mrs Skirmore lived in in Causham Street, but since I received your last I have laid some circumstances together which make it not improbable but you have taken Mrs Finny's house. Mr Peareth will not be at Weston till the latter end of October or the beginning of November. I daresay Mrs Jennens will be glad to see you sooner. I was called to the barr [sic] last term; I have not yet made any great figure in Westminster-hall, for I took the oaths but the last day of the term, so I don't wonder you have not heard of my Fame in my profession. I did intend to have shewn my Phiz at the Newcastle Assizes, but when the time came I hardly thought it worth while to go four miles to open a declaration or so. I can't tell what Character Bourn's Antiquities[4] [of Newcastle] bear for I never heard any man of Judgment speak of them, but in my Humble opinion the Author was a dull fellow; there are several Charters of donations to religious houses some particularly relating to the siege of the town in Charles the Ist's time among which there is a letter of my great grandfather's[k] which shews him to be a bolder man than one of his descendants I could mention, but I forbear all scandal; in short the book may be worth looking into, but not reading. 'Tis a thin small folio printed, as well as I remember, within these ten years. I am at present four miles west of Newcastle,[l] where my Sister has a little hut to live in for the sake of her health in the summer and where she has brought a little girl into the world about ten days ago. The Picts Wall runs through the parish about a mile north of the river, there is no part of it standing hereabouts, but the grass is all grown over the rubbish yet 'tis very visible. There is a dry wall built for a fence out of the old stones on about a furlong of it and a trench dug, which happens to be close by the

[j] Ambrose Holbech died in 1701. His grandson, Hugh, was living there at this time.
[k] Sir John Marley. See p. 135.
[l] Newbourne.

old wall which shews it very plain; there are some stones which lie in this dry wall which seem pretty clearly to be cut in very small diamonds . . . but I don't see any with inscriptions on them; I am told there were some which were built into houses in Wall Battle, a little hamlett in this Parish. In all probability the wall is standing here two or three foot above the ground but the rubbish is fallen down on each side of it and the grass grown over it, so that it can't be seen. I beg my Service to all my Friends you see whether you receive this at Oxford, in Warwickshire or Barkshire. I shall be mighty glad to hear from you[5] . . .

They were married at Warmington on the morning of 3 September two days after Anna Maria's twenty-second birthday. Only the family were present at the quiet ceremony conducted by the Revd Robert Jackson. John paid him with a five-moidore piece, the equivalent of £6.15s. On their return to the house he immediately sat down to write to his mother and grandmother telling them the marriage had taken place. There was no question of their going away together, for the first week must be spent at Arlescote to receive callers. Headed by William Holbech of Farnborough, friends and relations began to make their bridal visits until on 10 October the newly married pair were able to drive away to Oxford – though not alone, for wherever they went young William Goodwin went too. They dined at Hopcroft's Holt, an inn renowned for highwaymen, and it is noticeable that John never took ladies there without being accompanied, or at least met, by one or other of the Williams, Goodwin or Taylor. On this occasion Professor John Ward was there and John and he took to each other at once. Ward, with his cheerful rubicund face, his engaging manner and his fund of knowledge of all kinds, had so much in common with John – even including a tour of Holland and Flanders (though some years earlier) on which he had written very comprehensive notes.

After a supper party at the Angel with Zinzan and Lluellyn and an equally sociable breakfast, they continued their way to Caversham where Mrs Loveday was waiting to receive her daughter-in-law. There, too, they must receive the polite calls from Lord Cadogan and the other neighbouring gentry, but in less than a week they were back in Oxford for a great reunion, bringing with them Anne Hiley and Patty. Mrs Costard let rooms in her house and John took them for his large party, for besides the five of them there was also the Arlescote contingent. Mrs Goodwin brought Mary, her companion Mrs Maria Walker, and Professor Ward and William Taylor brought himself. Only Mr Goodwin, who was to celebrate his eighty-seventh birthday in December, and Mrs Loveday, whose arthritis was beginning to cripple her, felt it was too much for them. Nothing could give John more pleasure than to show Oxford and Blenheim to the ladies and there they stayed for five days with dinners given in their honour by William Derham and Richard Congreve and with several other of John's friends in daily attendance. Chaperoned by Mrs

Goodwin, who entered into it all with as much alacrity as her son-in-law, the four girls and their escorts thoroughly enjoyed this unusual wedding party; but looking back at their happiness one cannot help reflecting on the appalling waste of young lives and even wonder that the girls were so anxious for matrimony. John and most of his friends attained reasonable old age, but within twelve years or so all four lovely girls were dead, three from the effects of childbirth and one of consumption.

No such sad thoughts were in their minds when they separated, Patty and Anne Hiley returning to Caversham and the Goodwins to Arlescote. With Tom Winchester in attendance, John drove Anna Maria to Beaconsfield and from there, joined by Dr Collis and Charles Hopson, he took her to see the paintings in Windsor Castle, the next stage in her advanced education. Then they went up to London for a month's holiday.

Their first engagement was to sup with Tom's elder brother and his wife. John Winchester[m] was a successful surgeon who practised in Norfolk Street and it was pleasant for Anna Maria to find another girl of her own age who would accompany them on expeditions. The next day was spent in Thomas Gibson's studio, where Anna Maria sat for the first time for her portrait. John's sitting followed, the two pictures costing him twelve guineas and '1.16s.0d for the frames'. While the sittings were taking place they fitted in visits to the family, Uncle William transporting them to Clapham in his coach as their own transport had always to be hired. On 30 September they attended a service at St Stephen's, Walbrook, where Winchester was preaching, and John noticed the beauty of the light on the top of the cupola as they ascended the steps at the west end of the church. He took his wife to many of the places he had seen before and also to the House of Lords where he confined his notes to the seating arrangements. The New Library in St James's Park was an obvious attraction for any visitor to London:

> The New Library or the Queens Library, for it was built by Queen Caroline; this beautiful Room is fitted up with all imaginable elegance, floored with Norway Oak – the Chimney-pieces elegant; over each is a Bust in white Marble by the hand of Rysbrack; one is of the late Queen, the other of the King and 'tis said to be more like him than anything he ever sat for to any Artist; he indulged the Statuary in point of time, sitting as long for the Model as could be desired; these have been but very lately put up; other Busts of Kings adorn the Room.

Of all their engagements two outshone the rest. One was an expedition to see Sir Gregory Page's house at Blackheath and the other was an invitation to dine with Dr Richard Mead and to see his collections. On the first of these they

---

[m] According to Ralph Churton, John Winchester was an eminent surgeon but declined business upon inheriting a wealthy estate in Kent, where he died in 1781. This was Nethersole House, near Canterbury. See *Magdalen College Register*, 1st series, vol. 1, 150.

were accompanied by the Winchesters and went first by coach to the King's Head Inn in order to see Greenwich Hospital. There they entered the room in which the pensioners dined and the great Hall above it painted by Thornhill. Then they drove up to Blackheath.

Sir Gregory Page was an immensely rich baronet whose father had made a fortune in the East India Company. Three years earlier, according to Lord Egmont,[n] he had tried to shoot himself after having failed to hang himself the day before. A fortune of several hundred thousand pounds had not prevented his life being so tedious that he had little to do but supervise the dusting of his treasures, which included some important paintings. Visitors to his house were allowed into Lady Page's boudoir, though whether this privilege was extended to gentlemen is uncertain; perhaps in Anna Maria John now had a scout who could investigate forbidden territory.

This House is built of Stone, is not grand, but on the contrary simple and neat. There are two lateral flight of Steps to the great Door terminating in one landing-place, reminding one of some houses in Amsterdam, of Wanstead, Earl Tilney's and of the Model of the Lord Mayor of London's Mansion-house. There is a Ballustrade on the House and there are nine Windows in front; the upper is an Attick Story as 'tis also in the Offices, which are at right angles from the Body of the House and connected to it by a low Doric Colonnade; this Colonnade is in a straight Line with the Body of the House; had it been made with a Sweep it would not have appeared disproportionably low; for then it might have been considered as having as near a Relation to the Offices as to the House, to the height of the former of which it is better proportioned; but now being in a line with the House and quite at right angles with the Offices, the Eye will always view it in a much nearer relation to the former than the latter.

The House within is high finished and furnished, Grandeur and Elegance were equally consulted, so remarkably beautiful and noble the Door-cases of Wood, the Chimney-pieces again so elegant; and the bottoms and cheeks of two Chimnies are entirely of Brass; there are such of silver at Cannons, the Duke of Chandois's. All the wooden Chair-frames and Tables in this House, except those that are gilt, are of that costly material, Rosewood. Lady Page's Toilet is furnished with a great variety of exquisite Apparatus, all double gilt. We did not see the Library but were sufficiently entertained with the fine collection of Paintings; here are several high finished Miniatures by Vanderwerff, all in curious rich frames; such were the Angels appearing to the Shepherds and the Roman Charity, but this in quite another expression from those at Windsor Castle and Blenheim; here is also a Bassan of the Angels appearing to the

[n] Sir Gregory lived to the age of ninety. See *Burke's Extinct Baronetcies* and the *Diary of the Earl of Egmont*, vol. II.

Shepherds, a capital piece reminding one of that by the same hand at
Burleigh-house. . . of Christ's Agony in the Garden. . . In the Gallery is
a Length Portrait by Van Dyck of the Duke of Guise that was murdered;
two Lengths of Rubens and his Wife together; a Van Dyck of Prince
Charles, the Duke of Gloucester and his Sister;° but none struck me more
than the Painting of the good Samaritan and the Man that fell among
thieves, the expression of his Illness is inimitable; a Rubens of Samson and
Delilah, she looks like a painted Strumpet; a large Piece by Rubens and
Snyders. In another Room is Peter denying Christ by Michael Angelo
Caravaggio.

At St Thomas's Hospital, on the way back, they saw the brass statue of
Edward VI, of especial interest since a few days earlier they had visited the
sculptor, Peter Scheemakers, and had seen his model for the statue in clay.

On the following day, 11 October, they went to dine with Dr Richard
Mead. He lived in Great Ormond Street and had built a gallery in his garden
to house his ever-growing collection. John had known him in the days when
he had been Hearne's consultant and already a famous collector as well as an
eminent physician. He was also renowned for hospitality and kept open table
for scholars who wished to study his paintings, sculpture and manuscripts;
though on this occasion the dinner was arranged. The other guests were
'Mr and Mrs Ward' (almost certainly the Professor and his sister), Thomas
Winchester, Hocker the librarian,ᵖ Dr Thomas Bentley, Fellow and
Librarian of Trinity College, Cambridge, and Councillor Mead, the Doctor's
brother.

This Gentleman admits nothing but what is truly curious, nothing
trifling, into his Collections, For Paintings, he has some old Roman ones
wonderfully preserved on plaster; other Pictures are Buchanan and T.
Hobbes, both small; Dr Harvey's; Mr Pope's – an high-finished Piece by
Richardson; Erasmus, the same with that in the Bodleian Gallery at
Oxford, but (in Thomas Gibson's judgment) the better piece; by the same
hand, viz. Holbein, is Petrus Aegidius, Erasmus's friend. He has a
remarkably sharp look; these are two excellent Portraits of the same size
and in the same manner. An original of Robert Boyle, a present from the
Earl of Burlington, 'tis just such another piece as at Ashhurst's of
Waterstock . . . A Magdalen, large built, by Van Dyck. Curiously
enamelled Pictures of Henry, Earl of Surrey, Mary Queen of Scots and

---

   ° The Van Dyck painting of the three eldest children of Charles I which was in Sir Gregory
Page's collection is now in the Suffolk collection at Ranger's House, Blackheath.
   ᵖ A printed list of the members of the Society of Antiquaries of London. . . 1717 to 19 June
1796 (1798), p. 10, shows that William Hocker, formerly librarian to Dr Richard Mead, was
elected on 16 March 1748 – 9 and 'now appointed to succeed Mr Holmes at the Tower' (as
Deputy Keeper of Records).

Queen Elizabeth; this last is the second Picture of that Queen in Hearne's Camdeni Annales.[6] Here is also some ancient Statuary, as well as Painting; the Drapery of the Goddess Salus is exquisite; a Bust of Geta; an head of Tully in a black marble called Basaltes; in my opinion the Engraver[q] has notoriously failed in the Print from the head of Theophrastus; the amiable humane turn of Countenance in the Original is much impaired in the Copy. Homer's head, among the Bronzes, has Hollows for the Eyes; In the same class of Antiques are the Pantheus, Cupid shooting the Muse Erato, a Bull, a Lamp once Cardinal Mazarini's &c. Here you have also a Consular Sceptre, here are Urns also and an Antique from another part of the World, viz – a Mummy. A wondrous Curiosity is the Temptation of Christ in Amber.[r]

Dr Mead gave me his five Prints. Professor Ward had given me the same.

It was a little hard to be given duplicates from such a store. The bronze which in Dr Mead's opinion represented Homer is now thought to be Sophocles. Similarly the painting of Petrus Aegidius which he regarded as a companion to his Erasmus is now said to be by Quentin Matsys.[7]

It was while they were with Aunt Hopkins at Low Leyton that John was able to make a second visit to Earl Tylney's house, Wanstead, and on this occasion he went indoors. The famous *Assembly at Wanstead* by Hogarth,[s] which he saw there and which was said to represent local society, had been painted in 1729. Although there can be no proof, two of the figures bear a resemblance to the portraits of Sir Richard and Lady Hopkins.

If you enter on the ground-floor you are first let into the Lobby; on this Floor are several good Apartments and by much the finest India Pictures that ever I saw; that of the great Mogul standing is very beautiful; a capital Piece; besides the India Pictures there are also Pictures at Wanstead of Fowl and Flowers; Kent has painted here, as well as Hogarth; of the latter is a Friar before a Crucifix; it may probably be a copy, as well as some others, one of which is the Virgin and Babe, Joseph and St. John, from Sion House, the Duke of Somerset's. The Conversation-piece of this family and the neighbourhood is also Hogarth's. Very good Tapestry here, especially in the fine Ball-Room; there the Colours are admirable; there is a fine and pretty large night-piece by Schalcken of Portia's Story; the Floors are fine, of Norway Oak; the Chimney-pieces neat and elegant.

They returned to Caversham at the end of October so that John could make a new will and then Townson came to stay and drove back with them to

---

[q] The engraver was Jonathan Richardson the Elder.
[r] John wondered whether it was not amber but ivory.
[s] This painting is now in the Pennysylvania Museum of Art, Philadelphia.

Oxford. All John's books and furniture had to be packed up but he had two enthusiastic helpers in his wife and her brother, who came over for the purpose. William Taylor met them as usual at Hopcroft's Holt and soon they were back at Arlescote in the bosom of the Goodwin family. They stayed there for a month receiving more bridal visits. Among the callers were Charles Fox of Chacombe Manor, a friend and neighbour of the Taylors at Williamscote, and Sanderson Miller with his mother and his great friend Henry Quartley, still at the University. John had already dined with them before his marriage and had struck up quite a friendship with the young architect, often meeting him on future visits to Arlescote. On 6 December they moved into the Manor House at Little Kineton – their first home – and William came too.

Christmas was a cheerful time for them all, with Winchester and Townson as guests and the pleasant news that Charles Hopson had been unanimously chosen Recorder of Reading.

An Unhappy Ending
1739 – 1743

They chose for their winter reading Steele's *The Tender Husband;*[a] the text may have been a little disappointing but the title was apt enough. To their great joy a child was expected in July; but happy as they were together, Anna Maria soon found herself playing hostess to a number of young gentlemen, mostly clerical, who had simply moved their headquarters twenty-five miles north of Oxford. Charles Hopson, Thomas Bagshaw and Matthew Horbery all came to stay in January and so it went on. Besides entertaining his friends John gave them numerous presents to celebrate his marriage and donated more books to Magdalen College Library.[1] To Deodatus Bye whom he had not seen for some time he was particularly generous, though, as in the case of Hearne and the marmalade, one of his gifts was most unsuitable. Bye wrote with gratitude on 1 March 1740.

> Within this hour I have received your most generous and friendly present of 4 dozen of Madeira Wine; be pleased to accept the best thanks my poor heart can give you in Return. Since I writt to you, I have been again laid up with the Gout, so that from the 26 October to this very day I have not been abroad much above a week; to morrow I propose (God willing) to gett down to Church. Dr Teel's behaviour towards me in my Illness, I am sure, will please you in hearing it; he carefully attended me; he kindly refused his Fees; he insisted upon my sending immediately to

[a] The play (1705) was not very successful.

him in any future Illness; and left me the other day with an offering of a piece of Gold, value £3. 12. 0 . . . God will provide is my confidence . . .[2]

Several people were distressed by the schoolmaster's poverty, but efforts to procure him a small living met with no success (even including an application to the Archbishop of Canterbury[b] by his own chaplain)[c] In September Bye was thinking of writing to Dr Merrick and Mr Hiley to thank them for their endeavours, but John advised him not to do so, saying he himself would make sure that they knew of his 'grateful sentiments'.[3] He described Deodatus in a letter to Dr Waterland in which he also explained his own changed circumstances.

> I divert to another [subject] only to relate a Matter of Fact of little Concern to any but myself and one other Person, that ever since September I have left the University, and that for the only Consideration that could have induced me to leave it, a Companion for Life, if God will; 'till Michaelmas I reside in my Wife's own Countrey and then hope to settle at an old house of mine at Caversham, near Reading . . .
>
> Mr Bye, a Curate at Maidstone in Kent . . . is upwards of 40 years of age, is Gouty and has nothing certain to depend upon; his Life has been remarkably exemplary; a more humble man I never knew, and one more resigned to the harshest dispensations of Providence; I can't think he has any Enemies; if he has they must for Shame conceal their Malice against his Character, which is so dear in the Esteem of very many Persons; I may add that his Learning is confessedly very great, especially in the Hebrew Language; by way of relaxation to his severer Studies, he amuses himself in the Northern Tongues; his Integrity and Judgment are so unquestionable, both at Reading (his native Place) and where he now lives, that he was and is often applyed to in Cases of Conscience.[4]

In the last of his many letters to John, Dr Waterland replied that he was much pleased with Mr Bye's amiable character and would spread it wherever he conceived it might be of service to him;[5] as it turned out, there was little time in which to do so for he died the following December. However Bye became headmaster of Maidstone School from 1741 to 1746 and was married by his friend John Oare to Mrs Mary Collison, the widow of a Maidstone attorney.[d]

Marriage had not diminished John's preoccupation with his studies. His love of books exceeded even his interest in places and it was through them that he chiefly devoted himself to discovering the past. He admired elegant

---

[b] Archbishop John Potter.

[c] John Chapman 1704–84.

[d] Frank Sheffield, *Account of the Grammar School in Maidstone*, 1915, gives the year of Bye's headmastership as 1741. In the *Marriage Registers of Maidstone* by the Revd J. Cave-Brown (1901) the date of his marriage is given as 15 January, 1741, but in the transcription of John's diaries it is 15 January 1742.

writing but was more interested in the actual use of words and was fascinated by derivations. Etymology, as he told Bye, was not only to be studied in books: 'You must know, I frequently run-over the Advertisements in News-papers and thence sometimes have extracted a little Knowledge.'[6]

Writing to him in April, Richard Wooddeson recognized this practical approach. He himself had been translating John Gay's *Fables* into Latin for amusement and sent John some examples, together with Greek transcriptions and quotations in French from Boileau.

> Upon a review of this long scroll, bless me! what a farrago do I find it of Latin, Greek, French and nonsense! What a mortifying view to see at once exposed the whole compass of a Man's Learning, and what is worse that it is sure to be disagreeable to you by the appearance of affectation, but be it so, it is an affectation of pleasing, and certainly therefore pardonable.[7]

Scholars they all were, but none the less averse to a little light gossip now and then. John's letter of 19 May to Bye concluded:

> You know that Tom Birt is dead; as is, I suppose, Mr Bond of Bradfield; Talbot of Burfield[e] hides his head for Debt. Mr Hiley's surviving Children, viz. two daughters,[f] are with us at Kineton; within these two Months we reckon my Wife will fall to pieces; we don't go to Causham 'till after that. Hopson is (at present) in London. Dolly Blagrave, who was once talked of for Zinzan, is married to an Apothecary . . .[8]

Some consternation had been caused in the family during March by the serious illness of Anna Maria's younger brother, Timothy, who lived in London where he was apprenticed to a brewer. He was now eighteen and for most of his life he spent an almost useless existence – to the constant concern of his mother, who could not understand his dilatory ways. There was no vice in him, and he displayed a certain charm of manner and a desire to please if it entailed no extra exertion. The only two memorable things he ever did were to be painted by Allan Ramsay and to go bankrupt. Ramsay may have been related to John Ward and possibly to Mrs Goodwin;[g] there can surely have been no other reason for his having agreed to paint Timothy.[h]

Ward, who was fond of him, wrote to John Loveday on 14 March:

---

[e] Talbot must have been related to the Earl of Shrewsbury whose name was Talbot and who owned the manor, but there is no record of a Talbot living at Burghfield Manor at that time.

[f] Anne and Mary Hiley.

[g] The only evidence of relationship is a tradition in the Loveday family, the words 'Also cousin of Allan Ramsay' on the back of Webster's portrait of John Ward and the fact that Mrs Goodwin called on him in London and evidently knew him. See p.418 and 418 n.s.

[h] Ramsay's portraits of Timothy Goodwin, Dr John Ward and his sister Abigail are now in the Warwickshire County Museum.

I have the pleasure to acquaint you that Timmy is so well recovered, that it is proposed he shall set out from London on Wednesday next, in order to meet his Mother that evening at the Crown at Uxbridge. For which purpose she designs, God willing, to come from Arlescote on Monday morning and perform this journey with her own horses. She is desirous to take him as soon as conveniently may be, into his native air, which she thinks will be best for him; and as she is not inclined to come to London herself this method of doing it is agreed upon.[9]

At the end of March John paid a second visit to Compton Verney but only added a note to his previous account to say that the portrait of Mr Verney was extremely like him and that

this Gentleman built the Stables which are very handsome and which above Stairs contain Lodging-Rooms, and Rooms for other uses.

He also went over to Warwick to see the new marble monument in St Mary's Church for Dr Hewitt, a physician who had written his own Latin epitaph 'full of the spirit of Christian Piety', and he visited the Priory which had belonged to Henry Wise, once gardener to Queen Anne and George I. It was now owned by his son Matthew.

North and by East of the Church is the Priory, Mr Wises's . . . this old Religious house is partly of brick, partly of Stone; the Prospect from the Gardens is really charming upon the Town, Castle and Church (which latter beautiful Structure you have in full View) and the adjacent Countrey.
There is a good Western View from the Garden belonging to Dudley's Hospital; the Chappel to the Hospital is very neat; the Master's Salary 50£ per Annum with Lodgings in the Hospital.

At the Castle once again, he described some of the miniatures and remarked on the very large offices and kitchen below stairs.

In the Wardrobe is the Armour which a Lord Brooke wore at the head of the Rebels before Lichfield Cathedral.[i] Some of the Castle Fortifications were dismantled upon the Restoration. Warwick is very ill supplyed with Water . . .

The Hileys joined their daughters at Kineton on 5 June. Knowing the headmaster's tastes corresponded with his own, John had arranged one or two treats. The first of these was Burton Dassett church, which,

dedicated to All Saints, stands on the side of an hill; the ground it stands on was never levelled, so that the floor of the Church ascends from West to East. There are Steps up to the Chancel where the ascent is steeper than in

---

[i] The 2nd Baron Brooke, a Parliamentary general, was killed by a musket ball in a successful assault on Lichfield.

the Body. There is a Cross-Isle to this Church, but the tower is at the West-end. Dugdale mentions Peter Temple Esqr. in the second [year] of Elizabeth as having the Estate here; it is now Lord Cobham's chief Estate. The Monuments for the Temples[j] are in the North Cross; the Church is large and extremely damp . . .

The old round Building of Stone by the Windmill is vulgarly called the Beacon; but, my Father Goodwin says, very improperly, for that the Beacon-hill is an higher hill nearer the Church and that round building was erected only for the Miller's use.

He returned in September and added some more notes:

The Beacon here was doubtless only an Iron Vessel or Pitch-Pan upon a Pole; for under the King's Arms, and just over the Entrance into the Chancel of the Church, is nailed a small Painting on a Board, which at the bottom has a green hill on which is fixed a Pole which gradually grows less and less to the top, where is a Vessel like a Basket full of fire; it has holes in the side of it for the Air the better to feed the fire; against this Pole stands a Ladder, which consists only of one Pole, the Steps drove through it and equidistant on each side from it; these are larger at bottom, diminishing gradually as they approach the top. On the right hand of the Beacon is an Escutcheon of Arms. Under both is the figure of some Animal, whether Dragon or Salamander, with a Coronet round the Neck . . .[k]

Mr Goodwin had at one time administered land for Lord Cobham on which a due was payable to Henry Seymer, son-in-law of William Wake, Archbishop of Canterbury. Seymer was dilatory, through ill health, in sending a receipt, and when at last he did so the Archbishop wrote himself to William Goodwin to say that if the form of receipt was unacceptable his son 'Seymour' would execute any other form Mr Goodwin cared to send and that future transactions should be made through him. This was fee-farm rent in 1725, an annuity of £80 charged nominally to Lord Cobham's estate at Burton Dassett. The Archbishop's letter had concluded:

You will be very kind in recommending a person in your place to take this trouble on his account, seeing you do not think fit to continue it your selfe. I am, Sir, your very loving Friend.[10]

---

[j] The Temple monuments were taken to Stowe to be cleaned and remained there. Only those of Peter Temple (d. 1577) and his son John (d. 1603) were left at Burton Dassett.

[k] John Ward also described this long lost hatchment. His notes were contained in the *Antiquary Transactions MS. No. XIX.* His account in the L.F.P. is in the hand of his amanuensis, James Nelson. (See p. 346 n.n.) He was with 'a friend' in September 1746, who was certainly John Loveday. In his own account John Loveday connected the beacon in the hatchment with the Belknap family coat of arms. The sexton had to get the hatchment down and wash away the dust. See also George Miller, *Rambles Round the Edge Hills*, 1896; ed. A. C. Wood, 1967.

Two days after visiting Burton Dassett they all went over to Adderbury to see the house which had once belonged to the dissolute Earl of Rochester and now to the 2nd Duke of Argyll.

This was once the seat of Wilmot, Earl of Rochester but is now (as it were) a new thing, nay it is altogether so in appearance; 'tis built of Stone. In the Hall, which is not large, are Busts of Pompey, Hannibal, Sappho, Jugurtha, Apollo and Nero with large Ears sticking out. In this House are very large Views in Painting of Aleppo, Persepolis, Jerusalem, Isfahan and Constantinople. There is wondrous Sweetness in the Countenances of two Cherubs who with great attention are looking over some musical notes together. The Gallery is very high-finished with all Elegance and equal grandeur; 'tis hung with green Damask; it has two Chimnies in it, the Chimney-pieces supported by Caryatides; the Bust of the Duke is in an Oval over one Chimney-piece as that of his Dutchess is over the other; so the King's and Queen's Busts are over the Chimney-pieces in the New Library in St. James's Park; just over the Door is a Bust of Condé; at the upper end of the Room there is a Portal to answer to the Door-way; within the nich of which is the Statue of a Muse, and over the Portal a Bust of Turenne; in the right-hand Corner at entering the Room is a Bust of Julius Caesar, the head of Porphry; in the left-hand Corner is the Bust of Oliver Cromwell; in the left-hand Corner at the upper end of the Room is the Bust of Edward, the Black Prince, and in the opposite Corner is the Bust of Alexander the Great with curled Hair . . . in the same Room are four Tables of rich Marble, each different from the other. In one Room is an old large Elbow-Chair which has entirely escaped the injuries of time; it is all of Wood and stands on 2 cross side legs and a bar runs from one leg to t'other athwart under the Seat; on one Elbow, on the Back and on the other Elbow (all on the inside) are carved these Words – 'Johanes Arthurus (monacus Glastonie) Salvet eu deus'; on the outside of one of the Elbows is carved 'Sit laus deo', on the outside of the other 'Da pacem d^{m}ne'.[1]

There is no grand Stair-case here. There are two Pictures of a Religious with a Crucifix; Pictures of the Duke and Dutchess, of several Officers; some fine Family Pieces, the Duke's Grandfather[m] has a resemblance of Sir William Temple . . .

After noting details of many more paintings John concluded his account by saying that the furniture of the house was 'Coffoy, Mohair, Sattin &c'.

As soon as the Hileys had left he sat down to write a long account of Kineton itself, having taken his guests to 'view the Antiquities' shortly after their

---

[1] 'John Arthur – Monk at Glastonbury – May God give him Salvation.' 'Praise be to God – Lord grant us thy peace.'

[m] Archibald Campbell, 9th Earl of Argyll.

arrival. In 1775 Sanderson Miller rebuilt the nave and transepts of the parish church of St Peter, but his work was destroyed in the latter half of the eighteenth century when further changes were made. The church, as John saw it, had stood as it was since 1315 when the monks of Kenilworth had rebuilt it, though he had some doubts about this.

This Town gives its name to the Hundred. The Tuesday's Market is as old as the 4th [year] of Henry III. They have a Fair on St. Paul's Conversion; but the chief day of Concourse is on St. Matthew, called Kineton Mop, a publick day for hiring of Servants. Dugdale . . . says that [the Church] was rebuilt about the beginning of Edward II's time; but this I take to be true only of the Tower (which stands at the West end) and the Body of the Church; for, as to the Chancel (which has no side-Isles) and the Cross-Isle, they appear to be a different sort of Building from the main of the Church; and with regard to the Cross-Isle, 'tis probable that the North and South parts of it were built at different times, as Chantry-Chappels perhaps. Such undoubtedly was the South Cross, in which is an holy Water place; this Cross belongs to Mr William Holbech's Estate at Brokehampton in this Parish. In the North Cross and against the North Wall, on a very low Stone, is the recumbent Effigies of a Religious, his shorn head lying on a Cushion, his hands joined: not any part of this Church is cieled; there is only a North side-Isle to the Body; there is an Epitaph on a Brass-plate inserted in a Grave-stone in the Floor as late 1728 or later; the Bentley family bury in the Chancel and are Patrons of the Vicarage; they first presented to it in 1624. So much for this Church, which was probably thus enlarged with the Chancel &c on the decay of the other Church; for Tradition says there was for the reception of the Inhabitants, another in Kineton[n] and that it stood Eastwards of the present Church on the Plat by the Banbury-Road, above (what still goes by the name of) Church-Well; on this Plat about eleven years since human Bones were dug up; a little farther on in the same Road and on the right hand of it, is Oxwell, near which the Tradition is that the Oxmarket was kept and that some Streets ran on thereabouts; this bears East and by South of the present Church . . .

Dugdale says 'there hath been antiently a Castle here, situate North-East from the town . . .' Now here is a very great mistake, for the Castle is situate full West of the Church . . .[o] It seems to have been a Seat built Castle-wise and no very large one; there is much higher Ground to command it just about it; the Kepe is very apparent with the Trench about it, as is another Trench that takes a larger circuit; but there

[n] John also said, 'Dugdale gives no hint of there having been more than one church.'
[o] John added a note saying that Gibson's *Camden* placed the castle north-west of the town.

is not one Stone upon another above ground. Besides Castle-hill Well, there is another much nearer the Kepe, which is known by the name of King John's Well. The Castle is on Mr Bentley's Estate, who is Lord of the Mannours of Little Kineton, Brokehampton and Cumbroke; Lord Brooke is Lord of the Mannour of Great Kineton . . . It belonged to the Berkeley family till of late years, says Dugdale . . . and since that time I find a Lord Berkeley in possession of it, for on June 9th, 1740, Mr Askell Venor, Apothecary in Great Kineton put into my hands a Parchment which belongs to him and is intituled 'A True Copy of the Custome of the Mannor of Great Kington, Little Kington, Comebroke and Brookehampton'[p] . . . Between the two Kinetons there is a bridge with two Arches over a Brook. The Tradition is now almost worn out for no one living has any remembrance of a Chappel that was anciently in Little Kineton; it stood a Length by the Road-side, in the South part of the village, on the site of a modern house where lives the Widow Savage who is 80 years of Age, but very intelligent, and has heard her Mother say that she remembered Divine Service to have been performed here every Sunday and moreover a Sermon to have been preached once a Month; here too they christened and the trough to a Grind-stone in the Garden belonging to this house is said to have been the Font-stone; they did not bury here; there was no Chappel-yard; the Chappel was thatched, and the house now on the site of it is held by Mr Bentley by the annual Rent of two Fowls; but whereas there are two Widows of the name of Savage which are next Neighbours, observe that the house here spoken of is that of the two which is nearest to Great Kineton. Butter is sold at Kineton, as in some other parts of this Countrey, by the Quart; here a quart is two Pounds and an half.

Though John did not describe Arlescote House he did write down a list of words and phrases he had heard in the hamlet. Some of those which were new to him are in common usage today, such as a spinney which he would have called 'a shaw', or 'by then' for 'by that time'. Among other curiosities of local speech he mentioned: to be 'perished' or 'fameled'[q] (starved with hunger); 'to go a glurring' (to go a-sliding); 'colled' (black with coal or soot); 'when time was' (formerly); 'the next way' (immediately); 'while Tuesday' (till Tuesday).

The common people call a goldfinch a proud Taylor. They call one that goes a courting a sprunter. To hayn the grounds – to take Cattle out of

[p] Further notes described the indenture between Henry, 7th Baron Berkeley and his tenants in the 'Mannour of Cheping Kington' dated 14 November 1605. Kington was the old name for Kineton.

[q] 'Fameled' or 'famelled' is the only item in John's list which is also in George Miller's list of local words and phrases in *Rambles Round the Edge Hills*.

them that they may produce mowing grass for hay. They call a kitchen the House.

The June visitors were Bagshaw, Lluellyn and William Johnson, the vicar of Teston in Kent. (Whether he was the same William Johnson B.C.L. of Queen's College who had helped with the defence of Hearne can only be surmised.) Then the entertaining ceased briefly as Anna Maria was about to 'fall to pieces', but there was no flippancy when the baby son was born on 18 July. John had only one word to describe his wife's experience – it was a 'shocking' labour. The child was christened William, but to their great grief he only survived two days and was buried at Warmington. While Anna Maria was recovering John devoted himself to his studies and when Richard Congreve arrived to stay at the end of the month he found him making additional notes to his Dutch and Flemish tours from the travels of John Ray[11] and Francis Misson.[r] Professor Ward, on holiday at Arlescote, also lent him his own manuscript notes of the tour he had made some years earlier.

One invited guest who did not turn up for a summer visit was Matthew Horbery. That handsome but diffident young man was not finding the prebendal seat at Lichfield quite as comfortable as he had expected; though this may not have surprised John who had noticed that Bishop Richard Smalbroke was ' in no good understanding with the Chapter' when he was at St Davids as long ago as 1730.[s] Horbery wrote to John on 9 August to explain the unfortunate dilemma which had prevented his visit and also sent him a piece of literary gossip which he had learnt from the Bishop's son-in-law. This concerned a well-known scholar and controversialist Dr Thomas Mangey, the vicar of Ealing, who – as everyone knew – had been editing his *Philonis Judaei Opera* for years. (He finally produced it in 1742.) But though in 1737 Dr Waterland had written to John 'Philo Judaeus, as I suppose you have heard, has long been in good hands, I mean Dr Mangey's',[12] others did not hold quite such a high opinion of him. Dr Bearcroft, chaplain to the Charterhouse, attacked his general character,[13] Lord Egmont accused him of manoeuvring a will[14] and Canon William Clarke of Chichester said that the Doctor liked business but not the appearance of it.[15] Horbery wrote from Eccleshall in Staffordshire:

> I have added to my Crime in not waiting upon you at Keinton in my way hither according to Promise, by neglecting so long to send you my Apology and ask your Pardon. I have thought of you I believe every Post-day this six weeks, but something or other either called me away, or else I was not in a Humour for writing . . . even now I fear you will think I rather justify myself than plead guilty. But the Case was this; my Lord's Secretary called upon me at Oxford, where if I had left him,

---

[r] Misson's *Voyage d'Italie*, published in 1691, contained advice for those wishing to make the same journey. He went via Rotterdam and returned through Brussels.

[s] See p.60.

or from which if I had hurried him, he would have thought I slighted
him. We left ourselves but just time for our Journey and so we took the
way we were best acquainted with, and made as much hast in it as we
could. We missed Birmingham so that I did not as much as see Audley; but
I hear since that he has lost his Mother. Dr Bateman is now here and has
been about a week. He seems a very good-natured man and makes my
time pass more agreeably and I hope will stay as long as my Lord is in the
Countrey. He tells an odd Story which he had at Oxford from Dr Fisher.
A Bishop in Sweden several years ago sent over a Philo Judaeus as he
thought ready for the Press, and Dr Mangey was recommended to him to
correct it. The Son of that Bishop is now in England (and had just been at
Oxford when the Doctor was there) to learn what is become of his Father's
Book; why it is not printed, when it will be, what Acknowledgments will
be made to his Father, and whether he is to be considered as the Editor, or
only as a small Contributor to the work? The Son may possibly over-rate
his Father's Performance; but it seems he looks upon it as a finished thing
when it was sent over, and wanted only a careful hand to correct the
Press.

   Dr Walker (Dr Bentley, Clarissimus)[f] is about an Edition of Arnobius
contra Gentes,[16] which may be expected very soon. A certain paltry
Scribbler, who however has the Honour of your acquaintance, has done
such another paper-Book as he troubled you with in the winter, which
carries him (as well as I remember) thro' the Acts. Its forty to one he'll
desire you to read it; which I hope will convince you that he had better be
quiet and sit still, and prevail with you accordingly to give him his
Quietus. I beg my humble Service to Mrs Loveday and Mr Goodwin.[17]

Horbery would always be welcome but this did not apply to everyone. A
clue to the way in which John divided the sheep from the goats may be found in
a letter he wrote to young James Merrick on 11 August.

Before Christmas I hope to be settled at Caversham; the doors of my old
house will always stand open to you, and such as you; the fewer of any
other stamp that do me the Honour of a visit, so much the greater my
obligations to 'em: but I tell you again that your company will always be
acceptable.[18]

The lease of Little Kineton Manor was up at the end of September and
after giving a final family party John and Anna Maria transferred not only
themselves to Arlescote, but all their servants as well. Mrs Goodwin
squeezed them all in for a month and then on 27 October they finally
departed for Caversham, accompanied as usual by the two faithful Williams.
They 'baited' at Aynhoe but did not enter 'Mr Cartwright's fine Stone Seat just

   [f] Dr John Walker, Fellow of Trinity College, Cambridge, was called 'Clarissimus' by Dr
Richard Bentley.

by the Church, commanding a distant View'. Of the church John wrote that it was new,[u]

all but the Tower, which stands at the West end; 'tis a neat Structure without Pillars, but not well built for the advantage of Hearing . . .

and he described the interior with the new monument to the last rector who had died in 1738, the classical scholar Joseph Wasse.

They spent the night at Islip where they were joined by Pennington, Winchester, Townson and Peter Zinzan, who was to travel down to Caversham with them next day. Anna Maria was by now quite used to being the only woman, the charming centrepiece of a jovial party. So on the following evening they arrived at Caversham to be greeted by Mrs Loveday, Patty and Aunt Betty who had come down from Clapham to help with the removal. John felt he was really at home at last and he wrote in his diary:

Arrived at my house at Caversham there to settle for life, God willing; my Mother at the same time removing thence to a hired house in the Village.[v]

One of his first purchases was a chariot and harness for four horses, which cost him £69. Now that he intended to settle down to a peaceful married life, he would be less in the saddle and, as often as not, driving sedately with his wife beside him. And so 1740 ended with no greater excitement than the Reading by election in November when both the candidates, awaiting results in the Town Hall, fainted away. 'It was remarkable,' said John, 'lite pendente.'[w]

Early in 1741 Dr and Mrs Merrick lost yet another son, William, a Fellow of St John's College, Oxford; but there was rejoicing in March when Charles Hopson married his cousin Anne Trevor, the daughter of Richard Hopson of Bracknell.[x] She and Anna Maria liked each other and the close friendship between the husbands soon also included the wives.

The winter's reading this year was Richardson's *Pamela*,[y] but in his study John was hard at work making notes for John Ward's *Lives of the Professors of Gresham College*,[z] a self-imposed task which he continued for the next two years. Dr William Richardson, the Cambridge scholar, also benefited from

[u] The body of the church had been rebuilt in 1725 but the fifteenth-century tower was retained.

[v] Zinzan had evidently come especially to accompany the ladies to their new home.

[w] 'While the contest hung in the balance.' William Strode had eleven more votes than John Dodd and was unseated on petition in February 1741. He recovered the seat at the General Election of 1741.

[x] Richard Hopson was described by Hearne as an 'honest gentleman'. *Collections*, vol. X, 18 July 1729.

[y] Published in 1740. It took John from 23 February to 14 April to read it.

[z] Though his book came out in December 1740, Ward continued to make corrections and amendments to it.

John's notes, sent to him through Ward, for his edition of Godwin's *De Praesulibus Angliae Commentarii* which came out in 1743. For his own use John was annotating works by Browne Willis and Le Neve.

A little girl was born to them on 28 June and this time all went well. It was the custom, as a mark of courtesy, to ask one's most elderly relations to stand sponsor and John had written to his grandmother to find out if she would undertake the responsibility. Replying on 30 June Mrs Lethieullier agreed to do so although she felt old and ill (she was in fact only three months from death).

> I am willing to be a God-mother to it, and as to the naim what you pleas, I am just going out of the world, so naim it as it pleasis you . . . I desier you to give the midwife and servants as is usuall and handsum, on the 28th of June which was last lords day I was eighty-four years old, but a poore gouty febil creture so live in great payn continually and wait my heavenly father's good pleasure to release me out of it, my love to my daughtar tel her I hartily wish her cumfort in you and all yours that she may live to see, I remain your loving grandmother – my love to your sistar if with you . . .[19]

The baby was christened in her name – Mary.

Apart from escorting Aunt Hopkins to the old lady's funeral at Clapham, John made no excursions in 1741 except for social visits with Anna Maria. One of these was to Whitchurch, near Pangbourne, where he had three good friends – John Whistler and his brother, and the rector, the Revd Samuel Walker. This little group, the nucleus of a small circle which included Dr John Burton and the Hockers, gave John a good deal of pleasure. John Whistler had been a schoolfellow at Reading and like the others was interested in antiquarian matters. It was not long before Professor John Ward was welcomed into their midst.

It was not until May 1742 that he added to his Windsor notes, remarking that the Duchess of York's portrait was not only like her father, the Earl of Clarendon, but also resembled Nanny Shirley, the daughter of his long-departed bookseller friend.

> In the Royal Chappel, the King's Loft is at the East end, the Altarpiece at the West; as there is a way into this Chappel through St. George's Hall which is at the East end of it, and one range of buildings with it, this extraordinary disposition of the King's Loft and Altar could not have been otherwise, without stopping up the said communication between the Hall and the Chappel.

James Merrick was so often at Caversham during the vacations that he was treated much as a younger brother. He not only consulted books in John's library but also used it to write in and for relaxation would spend hours arranging the interesting collection of coins. John had described him in a letter to Deodatus Bye written from Kineton in September 1740.

James Merrick, Scholar of Trinity College, the Doctor's youngest son, is a lad of astonishing Parts, Learning and Modesty; his Industry is immeasurable; he is upon publishing a new edition of Tryphiodorus in the Original,[a] and in an English Poetical Translation done by himself; this is an ancient Greek Poet; in all this young Gentleman's Studies he has in view the illustrating Passages of Scripture from profane Authors; I have with great delight seen some of his Labours that way; he has in a most sublime manner paraphrased the Benedicite in English Verse; he is capable of anything; I am acquainted with him and am glad that by the nearness of Causham to Reading I may expect to see him sometimes; he meets with wondrous Encouragement by the subscriptions to Tryphiodorous . . .[20]

James, who had written the English translation at the age of nineteen, had gone to great lengths in order to perfect it and he was soon corresponding with the foreign scholars, Reimar, Mencke and Montfaucon, about the edition in the original Greek which appeared in 1741. The delivery of these letters, with presents of his book, was arranged by the elderly classical scholar Michael Maittaire, a man who not only appreciated Merrick's genius but took an almost fatherly interest in his career. Being himself a protégé both of the great Dr Busby at Westminster and also of Dr South, he was anxious that James should keep to the path of pure classical learning, though aware that he might well choose to study medicine like his father and his only remaining brother, John. James, however, knew that when he was old enough he wanted to be ordained in the church, a decision to which Maittaire gave a rather grudging blessing on 22 January 1743.

Your elder Brother having embraced Physick is no objection against your embracing that Profession; the study of which requires most particularly the knowledge of Greek, a language you are so thoroughly acquainted with. I have nothing to say against Divinity, which your inclination prompts you to. I rather rejoice that you'll dedicate to God's Altar such a stock of learning, as very few of that Order are furnished with.[21]

An entry in John's diary for 8 June 1742 recalls one of those summer days which linger in the memory though nothing of great moment has occurred:

James Merrick here all the morning, breakfasting here. With my Wife to Powis's – then to Reading overtaking Lord Fane and Mr Hiley. Lord Fane went into my chariot, I walked with Mr Hiley to his house where we all met; James Merrick came there.

Though James did not go to Hardwick House on this occasion, he was in

---

[a] Merrick's English poetical translation of *The Destruction of Troy from the Greek of Tryphiodorus* came out in 1739. He brought out an annotated edition of the original Greek with a Latin version in 1741.

fact a first cousin of Mrs Powys, his mother having been born a Lybbe.[b] John had always been on friendly terms with Philip and his wife, but later on he saw less of the family and never referred in his diaries to Philip's daughter-in-law, Caroline Girle, who married his son Philip in 1762 and whose own diaries give such an excellent picture of Berkshire society in the second half of the eighteenth century. She was equally reticent about the Lovedays although her brother-in-law Richard (already dying of consumption) married Patty's eldest daughter, Anne Gibson, who was largely brought up at Caversham. One can only assume they did not like each other and indeed Caroline Lybbe Powys, intelligent and entertaining as she was, may well have represented those people 'of the other stamp' referred to by John in a letter to Merrick;[22] her values were more materialistic and worldly than his, though her brother-in-law Thomas Powys, rector of Fawley and later Dean of Canterbury, called him a 'valuable Friend whose extensive reading no good Author escapes'.[23] But all this was in the future and in 1742 the two families were close friends and neighbours.

They spent six weeks at Arlescote in the summer and Mrs Goodwin was at last able to meet her granddaughter. When he heard of their arrival Mr William Holbech invited the whole party to drink tea with him and inspect the fine terrace he had made at Farnborough, probably with the assistance of Sanderson Miller. With the exception of Mr Goodwin, who by now was too old to go out much, the family went over there on 24 July 1742 and were so much impressed by the terrace that Mr Holbech invited the gentlemen to ride on it three days later. John and the two Williams accepted with pleasure and may have been among the first people to sample the delights of a morning canter there.[c]

On 4 August John paid a visit to Baginton Hall, which had once belonged to the politician William Bromley, who had died in 1737. His heir, also William, was a boy of about fifteen whose mother had remarried after causing a scandal[24] and was now Mrs Richard Chester. There was a portrait of her; like John's grandfather's second wife, Letitia, she was a Throckmorton of Haseley. John had known William Bromley at Oxford, sometimes meeting him and his brother Francis in Hearne's room or at the evening gatherings in Cat Street.

> This Seat is on the right hand a little out of the Road between Warwick and Coventry . . . We saw also on the right hand of the Road before Bagginton, Stoneley [Stoneleigh] Lord Leigh's. The Manor of Bagginton was purchased by William Bromley Esqr. Anno 16. Jac. 1.

[b] The Lybbes had owned Hardwick House since 1527. Isabella Lybbe married Philip Powys in 1730 and the name became Lybbe Powys; later the family changed it to Powys Lybbe. I am grateful to Mr A. Powys Lybbe for information about his family.

[c] The date of the completion of the terrace is not known, but this is the earliest reference to its being used for riding.

according to Dugdale; the house stands high, has large Gardens but no water in them or considerable View from them except upon the City of Coventry; 'tis built of fine white stone, three Stories high, with a Parapet all round at top; there are 7 Sash Windows in Front; on each side of this and in a line with it and joining to it, is a blank Wall of the height of one Story, having on each side in the Stonework two spaces for Windows, but filled up; it is a meer blank Wall on the left hand, but that on the right hand has indeed the Kitchen behind it; on this Front we read (every Letter a Capital) 'Dii Patris Servate Domum 1714';[d] on the Garden-Front (every Letter also a Capital) 'Phoenix Resurgens'; both Inscriptions alluding to the old house that was burnt down. This Garden-Front, which is the handsomer of the two, has also seven Sashes in the front of the main house, and four in each of the Wings, which (as in the other Front) are in a line with it, and joining to it, and also one Story high; one of the Wings is the Library, the other the Chappel. In the great Parlour are several Portraits, as of the late Mr Bromley, of his Lady, a daughter and heiress of the Throckmortons of Haseley, now the wife of Mr Chester) also of his father, Speaker Bromley, of whom in this house there is another Picture when a much younger man; of the Lord Chancellor Bromley . . who was the Speaker's Grandfather;[e] of the old Lord Leigh, a fine Length Painting, he stands his hand pointing to a Scull . . .

Now came an opportunity of visiting Althorp at last. Their cousin Abigail, William Taylor's sister, had married the Revd Daniel Rushworth who held the curacy of Church Brampton, near Northampton. John had met them both and was interested in Daniel's account of his father, a well-known Northampton surgeon who had discovered the efficacy of cinchona bark for gangrene in 1721. Later in the century the Rushworths' son, John, settled in Banbury and became a close friend of his cousins at Williamscote.[f]

They now invited the whole Arlescote party, except Father Goodwin, to come and visit them, though being so many in number they would have to lodge in Northampton. Picking up William Taylor *en route*, John and his wife drove through Cold Higham where they stopped to look at the 'singular' steeple on the church.

---

[d] 'Gods of my father preserve this house.' 'The Phoenix arising again.'

[e] I am grateful to Lady Bromley-Davenport for information about the family and the paintings, some of which are now at Capesthorne. See also her *History of Capesthorne*. Baginton was rebuilt by William Bromley, the Speaker (d. 1732), to the design of Francis Smith, a fire having destroyed the previous house.

[f] Daniel Rushworth was rector of Culworth, Northants from 1731 to 1735. He was presented to the living of Saham Toney in Norfolk by New College in 1734, but possibly never lived there, though he held it till he died in 1757. His son, John, went into business in Banbury the details of which were never disclosed. However, I owe the information that he was a draper to Mrs P. Keegan of Cropredy.

It is a Tower on which from East to West is erected a Gothic Roof tiled; on the East and West sides 'tis faced up with Stone and has a Window in each of these Sides; in both these Views then, the Steeple ends pyramidically, but in the North and South View it has a Packsaddle Roof.

They rejoined the Goodwins and were shown the town of Northampton by Mr Rushworth before being taken back to the parsonage for supper. There they found William's unmarried sister Elizabeth,[g] who was staying with Abigail. Next morning she and the Rushworths arrived at their inn for breakfast – a pleasant eighteenth-century habit – and then Daniel took them to Althorp about five miles away. The owner at this time was the Hon. John Spencer to whose family it had belonged since 1508. His brother Charles, who had owned the house and estate for a short time, was the 3rd Duke of Marlborough.

The House is built in the form of an half H. – but the transverse line is very deep; 'tis built of Brick ornamented with Stone. The Hall is adorned with Paintings of Horses by Wootton (so he spells his name), as is the Hall at Long Leate in Wilts, Lord Weymouth's. These are some few of the great Collection of Paintings here – the Elevation of the Host in a Nunnery Church; the Nuns look through holes in the East Wall over the Altar;[h] Job and his Wife; her Countenance and manner say 'Curse God and die' as express as a Label out of her mouth . . A Venetian Nobleman by Titian, as I remember, as in the very habit of one of the Cornaros at Northumberland house. A Miniature Night-Piece by Schalcken being Solomon and his Concubines worshipping strange Gods; they all seemed surprised, perhaps at some inauspicious Omen; the fire on the Altar gives light to the Piece. There is a Painting in black and white (like two at Easton Neston) of a fictitious triumph of King Charles I. Another night-piece of Schalcken's pleases universally and is said here to be his Masterpiece; 'tis of a Boy blowing a Brand's end to light a Candle, which is in a Brass Hand Candlestick by him – Sparks fly-off from the Brand . . .

After describing more paintings he continued:

Twelve Marble Busts in one Room. The Stair-case here stands in a

<hr />

[g] Elizabeth Taylor later married Robert Crossley, an apothecary at Stamford.

[h] Information kindly given by the 7th Earl Spencer shows that this was really the painting of the statue of the Virgin and child, covered owing to its being so sacred. This was once attributed to Domenichino and now to his school. The Schalcken of Solomon and His Concubines is now called *Sacrifice at Night* and attributed to Jacob de Wet. This is one of the earliest accounts of the paintings by a visitor and is the only evidence of the vast plane tree. See also 'The Catalogue of Pictures at Althorp' comp. by K. J. Garlick, *The Walpole Society,* vol. 45, 1976 for other changes.

very large Room; 'tis formed like an approach of Steps to the front of an house; for there is a Landing-place in the straight Line of the Stair-case which is very singular; from the upper Landing-place there are Stairs turning right and left to the Apartments. In one of these Rooms are three Pieces of Tapestry from the Cartons . . . The well-proportioned Gallery is adorned with Portraits, several by Van Dyck; such is a Length of Charles I's Queen in white; she is breeding as usual in her Pictures . . . an Holbein of Henry VIII and his first Queen, Catharine . . . 'Tis observable that in this Picture also the top of the King's Ears are as high as his Eyebrows . . . There are other Heads in the Gallery and very many in the other Apartments; several of which have been purchased by the present Mr Spencer. In the Gallery are also the Beauties of Windsor Castle. The present Duke of Marlborough, in the few years he was Master of this Estate, built the Stables and Offices, all of Stone; they are on the left hand as you approach the House and form a quadrangular Court within; the Front to two of the Sides has in the middle of them a Portico like that to the Church in Covent Garden, London. [i] The Gardens are in the Mote which was stopped up in the Front of the House by the Duke, who also improved the beautiful Park (in a low part of which the House stands) with a round Basin of Water having an Eight in the middle and communicating with a short serpentine River; there is a vast Plane Tree in the Park and many fine Walks between Trees that arch together at top, reminding one of Ham Walk in Surrey.

At the end of August he went to see the tithe barn at Swalcliffe.

A Barn, belonging to Mr Loggin's house[j] is a very large one, beautifully and most substantially built of Stone and finely timbered within; there are two Porches in Front, lofty and wide for the uses of a Barn, not so incommodious as those at Coxwell Barn by Faringdon; to which Barn, however, this has some resemblance.

They returned to Caversham at the beginning of September in good time for Anna Maria to prepare for the birth of another child. Stopping at Adderbury House, John completed his notes there – which concluded his descriptions for 1742.

October saw the death of Thomas Brigham of Canon End near Caversham at the early age of thirty-eight. John had described him in letters[k] to Hearne as having inherited the suspicious temper of his father, a 'froward' county squire. His feelings about the Brighams may have softened, for he acted

---

[i] St. Paul's, Covent Garden. See p. 308, 308 n.b., and p. 365.

[j] The fifteenth-century tithe barn is in the grounds of the Grange or Rectory Manor House which was leased to the Loggin family in the seventeenth and eighteenth centuries by New College (*V.C.H., Oxon,* vol. X).

[k] See p. 14. and p. 27.

as a pall-bearer at the funeral in Caversham on 11 October, where the flags
of their respective families hung together above the altar. Brigham was
regarded with general respect as a landowner and Lord Cadogan was
another of the pall-bearers as well as Philip Powys of Hardwick.[l] Edmund
Lambert and his wife had scarcely concluded a visit to which John had
greatly looked forward, when the baby was born on 11 November, a little
prematurely. He was privately baptized by Mr Dryden and named John
and from then on he progressed normally. The godparents were Charles
Hopson, John's cousin Randolph Tooke and Mrs Goodwin, the two last
represented by proxies.

As if he knew it was a doomed year John's opening entry in his diary for
March 1743 was a little verse:

> Sooner or later since we must
> All of us moulder into dust;
> What matters it, if I today
> Do that which you tomorrow may.

It began sadly enough. Mrs Simon Walcroft, widow of the Caversham
parish clerk who had introduced John to the pipe and tabor, died on 22
March, two years after her husband. She had made John her executor, as he
learnt next day from his friend Richard Simeon who was now Reading's
leading attorney; and on the same day he heard the tragic news that Anne
Hiley had died early that morning from consumption, leaving Mary now the
only remaining child. The following month was more cheerful, enlivened by
visits from Richard Lluellyn and Robert Lowth. Lowth brought the
manuscript of his life of William of Wykeham and left it with John for his
comments.[m]

Correspondence with John Ward[n] was now cementing their friendship. The
ebullient professor seems to have answered the need John had in his youth of
some substitute for the father he had chosen to forget. Ward was a very
different character from those who had preceded him, having neither the
arrogance of Hearne nor the austerity of Waterland. His interests, too, lay in a
wider sphere so that he was able to enlarge John's world by bringing to his
notice all the latest news of the literary and artistic life of London. Besides being

[l] The other pall bearers were 'Temple Stanyan, Lydall of Ipsden and Mr Powell'. Temple
Stanyan, the politician and scholar, lived in Oxfordshire. John Lydall of Ipsden who had in
1736 married a widow, Elizabeth Toovey of Shirburn (owner of land at Britwell Salome)
was probably connected with the Lydall family who worshipped at St Laurence's Church,
Reading, in the sixteenth and seventeenth centuries. He may have been the John Lydall who
lived at Highmoor, near Ipsden, in 1766.

[m] It was not in fact published until 1758.

[n] Ward's letters to John Loveday (L.F.P.) were written in his own hand; many of those in
the British Library are in the hand of James Nelson in a beautiful script. He had known Ward,
who left him £50, since 1737. By profession he was a schoolmaster, but whether Ward
actually employed him as a clerk is not clear, though likely in view of the amount of work he
did for him.

a good scholar, Ward was genial, gregarious and immensely energetic, though always rather apprehensive about his health. With a finger in most of the antiquarian projects and a foot on everyone's threshold, he was in regular contact with such people as Dr Mead, James West or the various other well-known collectors. His vast correspondence, with the exception of most of his letters to John, was given to the British Museum by the younger John Loveday. Although the learned societies did have country members John never seems to have had any desire to become one; but through Ward he now received a running commentary on their affairs and could send messages or contributions by the same means.

Ward had still not had time to visit Caversham, but he wrote on 12 May to say that if it were convenient he would like to come for two weeks.

> You know my way of living so well that I promise myself you will consider me in a philosophical light, as one who shall no ways break in upon your other engagements, though indeed I have so many things to say to you that I know not whether I may not be like to prove a troublesome guest on that account.
>
> I presume it can be no news to inform you of the death of good Mrs Diston, whose funeral I attended with Coz. Timmy this day sevennight. And Mr William Diston her son set out yesterday on his journey for Shenington. Our public news is pretty much at a stand. And it is probable you may have heard of the observation lately made by a gentleman, that the house of Commons this last session have been so generous as to give more money for the public Service this year, than amounts to the weight of each member in solid gold, supposing him to weigh 15 stone . . .[25]

an interesting pointer to average weight in those days of hearty meals.

The younger William Diston was Mrs Goodwin's godson and like Timothy had been apprenticed in London, also very probably to a brewer. In an undated letter his godmother had made sure that if he were to come to any harm in the metropolis it would not be through lack of devout and practical instructions on her part. The affection which she had for all young people shines through the homily.

> You are now going into the World full of Temptations and Snares. I therefore can't forbear giving you some Cautions which I hope you'll sometimes read over and believe – they come from one who Loves you in piety and is truly concerned for the welfare both of your Soul and Body. What I first desire of you is to mind your Duty to God Morning and Evening and to keep strictly to the Sabbath Day for without a due regard of that many have run into great wickedness, for generally most of the evils that are Committed are begun by breaking the Sabbath. If you should be placed in a family that is in the Countrey in the Summer

(as I believe there is few now but what is) you will be out of your Master's eye of a Sunday and therefore you may think yourself secure, but be persuaded you are not out of God's who is always present and observes the actions of every person and takes an exact Account of them. I desire and hope you may be placed in a sober family that you may have a good example, but if should prove otherwise, (as I pray God it may not) you must not learn of your Master any evil but only your Trade, and you must endeavour to serve him, whatever Master you have, to the best of your power, and not wrong him in any thing, nor suffer any to wrong him, if you can prevent it, but be faithful to him in every particular and be as carefull of his interest as of your own; you must behave in an obliging way to all but don't make yourself too free with the Servants for that may produce great inconvenience to you, and has been the ruine of many a young Man and great sorrow to his Relations. One thing I must give you a particular Caution of the loose Women that walk the Street on purpose to entice and pick up Men and lead them into evil, shun them as you would the Plague and be sure never to hear what they would say to you, for they are like the Devil going about seeking whom they may devour. To prevent falling into their hands you must not drink to disorder your selfe for then you may be their prey for a Drunken Man is fitt for any thing and many times commits such things when drunk that he repents of all his Life, and never capable of atoning for his fault.

You must be sure not to get a habit of swearing or taking God's Name in vain nor of telling lies. I don't know that you are at present guilty of either – I pray God to give you his Grace to keep you from those or any other Sins. If you are at any time Guilty of a fault don't tell a lie to excuse it, but always tell the truth and that with persons of integrity will go a great way towards pardoning you, and now my dear Child I have only to recommend you to the Almighty protection of that good God that has hitherto preserved you and takeing so much care of you, and trust will continue to do so which is the hearty prayer of your affectionate Godmother . . .[26]

John Ward's visit took place at the end of June and, as he predicted, he had so much to say that John had to make a list of the subjects. Except for another visit to Windsor there were no more topographical notes during the rest of the year, though an excursion in August was worth mentioning when, with the Hopsons and Anna Maria, he went over to Luckley Park, just south of Wokingham. ·

Visited with our women at Dr Bolton's now at Luckley (Mr Palmer's house). With them we walked to the Gorrick Chalybeate; The Doctor rode a little in the way home with us.

When Robert Lowth came to see them early in September with his great friend Sir Edward Noel (Lady Byron's grandfather), they were able to entertain their guests in their newly restored parlour, in which they themselves had only recently sat for the first time. It seems to have been almost the only alteration John ever made to the house and probably did not affect the outer walls. William and Timothy Goodwin also arrived for a week or two and so did Thomas Winchester. Then there was an end to entertaining, for on 17 October Anna Maria gave birth to a stillborn daughter.

When John wrote to John Ward three days later he did not quite realize how ill she was. The first part of his letter was devoted to books and pictures. He concluded:

> Messrs Merrick and Winchester were not a little concerned that they should be absent from Oxford both the times when you called there; they are now each returned to their respective Cells; they, and indeed every one that had the pleasure of your Company in these parts, beg your acceptance of their heartiest Services. My Wife was t'other day delivered of a stillborn Child; we have a great reason to bless the divine Providence for throwing a skillful Man-Midwife in our way;[o] otherwise the consequences had been beyond measure shocking My little Girl first found your Oister-shell[p] in the table-drawer, and soon demolished it; next year I earnestly hope you will come and get another and we'll take more care of that. Recorder Hopson bids me tell you his design of waiting upon you at Gresham College some time in the next Month; he will safely convey to me the curious Particulars you have been so kind to procure for me . . .[27]

A week later, when she seemed no better, Hopson came over and together they went into the church and prayed. It was the celebration of St Simon and St Jude and the exact anniversary of the day she had been churched after the birth of their son John. Next day John wrote to the Bishop of Salisbury, Thomas Sherlock, perhaps to ask for his prayers. Reading was in his diocese and John had met him on his visitations. His friendship with Bishop Secker of Oxford was to come later.

While he was anxiously watching and waiting by his wife's bedside he heard of the death of Thomas Pearcey, a loss which affected him very much; Pearcey had often come over from South Moreton to give the Reading Lecture and had always seen John on those occasions. But now on his own anxieties superseded everything else as hopes began to fail. On 19 November, after

[o] Anna Maria's doctor, J. Hooper, who delivered the stillborn child, was a surgeon in Reading. His son opened the first hot and cold baths there in 1818.

[p] During Ward's visit from 27 June to 12 July he must have been taken to Catsgrove. He went to Oxford on 27 August 1743.

struggling to live for almost five weeks, Anna Maria died. Everything they had been to each other, all he had felt for her, was in the few words in his diary: 'The Delight of my Eyes vanished to the Father of Spirits a minute after 6 in the Evening.'

His mother was his closest comforter; the friends to whom he wrote were Hopson and Bye; the sermons to which he turned in his despair were those of Bishop Atterbury and Bishop Bull; there was also the grievous task of writing to the Goodwins at Arlescote. Then, on 25 November,

> My dear Wife, ever a great Lover and Promoter of Peace, buryed in a very peaceable quiet manner about 10 o'th'Clock by Mr Dryden.

He went through a period of great melancholy, finding his only consolation in books, especially the works of Sir William Temple and Jeremiah Seed, the Oxford divine who had been Waterland's curate and had preached his funeral oration. The only letter of condolence that he kept was from James Merrick, an earnest exhortation to believe it was all for the best, which although it seems out of place from a younger man was, as far as John was concerned, not only proper but indeed anticipated. But beneath the conventional exchanges the memories of four years of happy married life were so personal and so private to himself that neither then nor at any other time could he share them with others. Since he had scarcely left her side there were no letters and nothing remains of Anna Maria except her portrait and a sense of charm and goodness perpetuated by her husband's devotion. Many years later his daughter Penelope wrote:

> . . . she died after she had been married only four years to my Father, who loved her with the most ardent affection as is plain from his short expressive Memorandum of her death . . . Nor could he to the latest period of his life ever bring himself to recur in the most distant manner, to any circumstance concerning her; though he was in a frequent course of speaking of other departed and beloved friends.

Some of these friends were becoming anxious about him, the bachelors not quite understanding the depth of his grief. In mid-December John Ward wrote to James Merrick:

> I am much concerned for the great loss lately sustained by our good friend, Mr Loveday, and the melancholy state to which it has at present reduced him. But his own reflections, with the assistance of his friends, will, I hope, in time relieve him. [28]

Hopson came over again and then John Audley arrived to stay for several weeks; they passed some of the time going through all the letters from

Waterland and Bye. On Boxing Day his Reading friends decided that something must be done to winnow him away from a course of sermons and solemn verse. Robert Bolton came over to dine and they all three drank tea at the Hopsons'. This was followed by a visit to the Mitre in Reading where they were joined by Dr Merrick and Philip Whitehead. It was a successful plot which warmed his heart and in some measure brought him back to life.

Second Marriage
1744 – 1746

In the spring of 1744 John's sorrows were partly obscured by the news of Patty's betrothal. She had been staying at Low Leyton on one of her long visits to Lady Hopkins and with her mother's permission and her brother's approval had been receiving the addresses of a young clergyman, William Gibson, seventh son of the Bishop of London. In a letter dated 31 March William thanked Mrs Loveday for her consent to the marriage.

> I think myself obliged to return you and Mr Loveday my most sincere thanks for the part you have both contributed towards making me happy in an Alliance to so worthy a Family. I have received great Civility from my Lady Hopkins and through her Kindness I have been permitted to pay my Addresses to Miss Loveday; – whose Person, Temper and Behaviour have something in them so very amiable and agreeable, that I cannot but promise myself more and more Happiness from every Visit. It shall always be my utmost endeavour to answer the Character which you were pleased to say you had heard of me, and to shew myself deserving of so great a Favour, by all possible returns of Duty and respect to yourself and Mr Loveday and Love and Affection to the young Lady. The Bishop my Father desires his Compliments and Miss Loveday has been so good as to commission me to send hers to you and Mr Loveday. [1]

Any reservations John might have had about his new relationship with the son of a leading Whig spokesman on church affairs were quite overruled by his respect for the Bishop, both as a scholar and an administrator. His Tory upbringing, which had received every encouragement at Oxford, was not so extreme as to allow him either to support the cause of Prince Charles Edward the following year or to disapprove of the stringent measures which the Bishop of London authorized in his own diocese to oppose it – so giving a lead to churchmen all over the country. By men of John's intellectual calibre Bishop Gibson was held in high regard for his uncompromising stand against the licentiousness of the age, for his fight against the free-thinkers, and for his general sagacity and courage.

In January there appeared at Caversham the Revd Samuel Johnson, the vicar of Torrington in Devon. He was the son of a Reading councillor and brewer and in no way related to his celebrated namesake (though there was to be a connection with one of his friends when the second son, William, married Sir Joshua Reynolds's sister, Elizabeth). Johnson had published several sermons in 1740, but his last one had hung fire; he hoped, therefore, John would use his influence to get it printed by the Society for the Encouragement of Learning. John, being in two minds about it, did nothing for some time, so that Johnson, surprised at receiving no news of his 'Treatise on the Septuagint', became anxious and spurred him on with gifts – another pamphlet of his own and 'A Poem of the Honble. Mr Bridges*a* which will help to correct the extravagant Opinion that some entertain of Mr Pope's Writings.'[2] Somewhat against his will John did then write to Ward asking him to give himself the trouble of collecting the MS. from Will Parker, the bookseller at the King's Head in St Paul's Churchyard.

> If you find it fit to see the light the Author would rejoice to have the Society print it; how it will prove I can't divine; for however well performed, it may possibly be forestalled by other Works, which the Author (buried deep in Devonshire many Years) may never so much as have heard the names of; whether I have done wrong in this affair I cannot tell; if I have your Goodness will excuse it as the intention was not wrong . . .
>
> If I could flatter myself that your business and inclinations might give you to leave to see Causham in May, or whenever else you please, the thought would give me as much pleasure as I am now capable of receiving

---

a The poem was called *Divine Wisdom and Providence: An Essay Occasioned by the 'Essay on Man'*. It came out anonymously in 1736, but the author's name in the 3rd edition of 1738 was 'Mr Bridges'. There does not appear to have been any Hon. Mr Bridges or Brydges at that time except for an Hon. James Bridges whose death at Hampton in 1766 is recorded in *The Gentleman's Magazine* (27 January), *The Annual Register* (1 February) and *The London Magazine* (8 February). Possibly Johnson meant Robert or James Brydges, the nephews of the 1st Duke of Chandos who himself knew and admired Pope. Their father, the Hon. Dr Henry Brydges, Archdeacon of Rochester, died in 1728. The poem criticized the *Essay on Man* but not Pope himself. See also D. F. Foxon, *Bibliography of English Verse, 1701–1750*, B.443, 444, 445, where the name of Robert is mentioned.

and not only me but our friend Lluellyn also, who by Easter will be settled (we trust) in a Curacy at Reading . . .[3]

But Ward could not come and nor did Lluellyn, whose hopes of the curacy came to nothing. Old Mr Johnson also failed in his endeavours. He lived for two more years and then died in great pain and suffering 'too grievous to relate', as his son Samuel told John in March 1746. He too had faith in John's influence and requested him to support Lord Dupplin in an application to the Dean and Canons of Christ Church to grant him the living of Torrington. From the way the young man wrote John had evidently helped the Johnsons in the past:

As I hope I shall always retain a grateful sense of that Civility which my poor Father and Mother received from you at Caversham and the advantage secured through your means for the Family; . . . Thanks where an Ample return cannot be made may be well pleasing to so good a Benefactor.[4]

His inscription on a stone at the parish church of Great Torrington tells the end of the sad story: 'He, alas, having survived his Father 4 months and 28 Days, followed him the 8th of August, 1746, aged 26 years.'[b]

After Anna Maria's death a cousin of the Wards, Mrs Marey Cooper (as she was always known, though unmarried), had come from her home at Hampton to take charge of the house and children. Being so much older she was hardly a companion for John, but he liked her and had every confidence in her capability, so that in the spring of 1744 he felt able to leave her in charge and go with John Audley on a short visit to Maidstone and Bromley. While he was with the Bagshaws he met a friend of theirs called Steele who had known that unusual connoisseur of music and literature Thomas Britton, the musical small-coalman. In spite of the concerts he promoted and of his having aristocratic friends who consulted him on their purchase of books, Britton continued to sell his small coals in the streets of London until his death in 1714. Rumours had circulated that he was a Jesuit in disguise and Steele now added his testimony to the contrary.

Mr Steele of Bromley told me that he knew Britton – that he and many others believed him to be a Jesuit; that however he was married and had Children, and was a very inoffensive man, not concerning himself to promote the Romish Interest undoubtedly. Bishop Burnet in his Diary is made to mistake the Small-Coal-Man for a Romish Priest; query whether this may not hint at T. Britton who lived in the Neighbourhood.[c]

---

[b] See Susan Radcliffe, *Sir Joshua's Nephew*, 1930, which gives the epitaphs but says nothing is known of the two Samuels, father and son. The 'nephew' was Samuel Johnson of Pembroke College, son of the vicar's second son, William, and nephew of Sir Joshua Reynolds.

[c] Clerkenwell, where the Bishop also lived during his last years.

Early in June the whole family set off for Arlescote, John sending the children there in advance with Mrs Cooper so that he could spend a few nights at Oxford and see some old friends. The President gave a dinner party for him at Magdalen and he took the opportunity of returning to Lowth,[d] with his comments, the manuscript of *William of Wykeham* which he had only just finished. It was pleasant to spend an evening with him once again, with Merrick dropping in, and for the first time John also visited Merrick in his rooms at Trinity. Then he found William Goodwin waiting for him at Hopcroft's Holt and together they rode back to Arlescote and more affectionate greetings. Mr Hellier, a wool dealer from Cirencester who was also a guest in the house, must have been surprised by the number of callers in the next few days with the Holbech brothers closely followed by William Taylor and his uncle George. After a week John rode down to Boyton with William Goodwin to spend a few days with the Lamberts, leaving the children with their grandparents. By the time he had collected them again and returned to Caversham he felt more refreshed; on the other hand he was lonelier than ever and realized how much the children needed a younger woman to take their mother's place. Among those he knew one seemed particularly suitable; she was about his own age, she was pretty and intelligent and she was the sister of one of his closest friends, Thomas Bagshaw. He returned to Bromley in August and began paying his addresses to Dolly. It was the greatest mistake of his life, but at the time it seemed to them all to be an excellent arrangement.

The formal courtship took three weeks and was concluded to everyone's satisfaction. Mrs Gastrell, the widow of the Bishop of Chester, came to dine with her nephew Mapletoft and gave her approval as a senior member of the family.[e] Elizabeth would continue to look after her brother and Dorothy would marry John at the beginning of the new year, 1745. Cheered by this solution to his problems John began taking notes again in a rather desultory way. He saw the learned Mr Gilbert West's house at Wickham and Grove House at Chiswick, but both visits were social occasions and hs notes were brief.

> August 11. 1744. Mr Gilbert West's . . . A fine Painting of 3 Persons at length and as large as the life in Turkish Habits; one is Sir Humphrey Style of Kent. A Painting of Bishop Smalridge. A Vase beautifully made of Shells by Mr West in the Garden where are cut Hedges of Furze.

At that time West was chiefly known as a poet. His religious work was still to come and having visited Stowe three times John was probably more

---

[d] Lowth had been Professor of Poetry at Oxford since 1741.

[e] Elisabeth Gastrell was related to her husband whose mother was the fourth daughter of Edward Bagshaw (d. 1662) (see p. 70) and who was a first cousin of Harington Bagshaw. Nathaniel Mapletoft was the son of her brother John, rector of Broughton, Northants, which living he resigned for Nathaniel in 1753. The Gastrells' daughter, Rebecca, married Dr Francis Bromley (d. 1753).

interested in the fact that he was a nephew of Lord Cobham. The Grove (as John called it) at Chiswick was owned by Henry Barker whose son had been a friend of John for a long time.

In a summer-house is a Portrait by Hale (who dyed at 23 years of Age)*f* incomparably fine of my friend's Great Grandfather in the dress of the times, extremely like Mr Taylor of Williamscot. A Walk between a noble Eugh-Hedge in the Garden; several Eughs also here are of the common shape, but which end in a Tree. Mortlack in View from the Garden-Front.

While he was still at Bromley he received the news of the death of his 'father' Goodwin at the age of ninety-two. He made no attempt to go to the funeral and it was not expected of him. He had in any case to return to Caversham in order to receive William Gibson whose marriage to Patty was to take place in his own church at Bishopsgate on 20 September. He went round twice to his mother's house to bid his sister farewell but he did not go to the wedding, although he returned to London ten days later. His mother's absence is much more easily explained by her bad health and no doubt the marriage did not take place at Caversham or Low Leyton because of the inconvenience to Bishop Gibson who was to perform the ceremony. Mrs Loveday heard the news from the Bishop himself.

Madam, This morning, I have married your daughter to my son, very much to my satisfaction in all respects; and particularly on account of her own universal good character and the worthiness of the family to which she belongs. I am sure she will make my son happy; and if he also does not make your daughter happy, I must never pretend to make a judgment of any man's temper and disposition, as long as I live. Whenever Business bring you or Mr Loveday to town, I hope I shall have the favour of knowing it, that I may pay my respects to you. In the mean time, I remain his, and Madam, your faithful friend and Servant, Edmund London.[5]

Whatever he felt, or thought he felt, for Dorothy, John was an assiduous suitor; he was back again in November for another three weeks at Bromley and was becoming quite well known in the social life there. He was invited to dinner for the first of many times by the hospitable, if not particularly learned, Bishop of Rochester, Joseph Wilcocks, at his palace at Bromley – a party of ten gentlemen and four ladies. There he met the Bishop's son,

---

f The subject of the portrait by the unknown painter, Hale, was probably Thomas Barker, M.P. for Middlesex, who died at Grove House in 1630. Henry Barker died in 1745 and the house was subsequently sold to the Earl of Grantham who lived there from December 1746. Information kindly provided by Miss W. M. Heard shows that the Poor Rate accounts list a Henry Barker at Grove House in 1746 and the assumption must be that this was John's friend with whom he stayed at Chiswick in April 1746.

another Joseph, who, as Mrs Lybbe Powys said of him later, was 'curious in antiquity'.[6] He had to meet Dolly's friends too. She seemed happy and energetic, even arranging they should cross the Thames at Lambeth Bridge early one morning so that they could breakfast with her Aunt Busby in Hollis Street.

He went home for Christmas to find his cook was leaving, a situation he could not expect Mrs Cooper to cope with by herself. However, she was replaced by a woman with the comforting name of Christian Body and he contemplated with a sigh of relief the happy thought that Dolly would be there to deal with all such contingencies in the future.

They were married on 25 February 1745, at St Martin-in-the-Fields[g] by the Revd William Clements, a Magdalen man about a year younger than John, who like his cousin Daniel Prince, the Oxford bookseller, remained a friend of the family all his life. It was not thought seemly for John to be married from Bromley so he had taken rooms at the Golden Hind in Suffolk Street, a hostelry belonging to Christopher Seton, a seal-engraver whom he had lately met and found extremely interesting. Seton's wife, on the other hand, was not so much to his taste and it was on her account that the friendship did not thrive. In 1756 John wrote to his third wife (who had Seton connections):

> I hope you gave your mother a caution with regard to Christopher Seton (the seal-engraver's) family. I do not relish the woman of that house at all, and desire they may know nothing of our affairs.[h]

At the time of his marriage to Dolly, Mrs Seton's true colours had not become apparent and she and her husband and little boy were the only people present outside the family. After five weeks with the Setons the newly married pair left to stay for a week with the young Gibsons. John had not made any notes, except at the Griffin Inn at Holborn two days before the wedding.

> In the Griffin Tavern . . . is a Miniature-Length of the Princess (afterwards Queen) Elizabeth; here also they sell Faber's Mezzotinto from it, on which it is said 'Holben pinxit 1551.'[i] Faber has performed ill; the softness of the Countenance is lost in him, with whom she looks also older than in the Painting, and indeed (to my eye) the faces are unlike.

[g] The vicar of St Martin-in-the-Fields was Zachary Pearce, William Clements was then a lecturer at St. Stephen, Walbrook; later he became Librarian of Sion College. The organ given to St. Martin's by George I and just possibly played at the wedding ceremony is now in the parish church of Wotton-under-Edge.

[h] L.F.P., 4 January 1756. Evidently these Setons were distantly related to John Seton who was an uncle by marriage of Mrs Thomas Forrest (mother of John's third wife, Penelope) and whose daughter, Elizabeth, was the mother of Mary and Agnes Berry. Mrs Forrest was a daughter of the non-juring bishop Arthur Miller.

[i] Holbein died in 1543 when Elizabeth was ten years old. John Faber was evidently responsible for the mistake in the date on the mezzotint.

When they returned to Caversham on 6 March they were accompanied by Dolly's Aunt Busby. She remained with them for some time and was followed by Miss Vade,[j] a Bromley friend, who did not leave until 13 November – when John confided rather ruefully to his diary that this was 'the very first day that my wife and I have solus cum sola dined'.[k]

It could hardly be expected that their relationship should not be a little strained. Dolly was thirty-five and it was probably not until she was actually at Caversham that she realized she was replacing a beautiful girl with whom her husband had been deeply in love little more than a year ago. She had never had anything to do with children, nor even run a house. At Bromley it had seemed miraculous that she should now become the mistress of an establishment with the longed-for status which marriage conferred; but when she faced the cold reality of the situation it was daunting, however kind and attentive her husband might be. Her health suffered and her nervous system gradually deteriorated. At first she relied on her women friends, but soon John found it more and more difficult to leave her side. Ten long years of increasing frustration had begun. Yet disappointing though his marriage to Dolly proved to be, John's friendship with his brother-in-law grew even closer and Thomas became a beloved uncle to all the children, though his sister never had any of her own.

On 6 April more Roman coins were found on John's land at Feens.

My tenant Stroud says that last Summer in Feenes Field his Plough grated on foundations of a Building; at the same time he put into my hands 4 Roman Coyns of Brass which in 1744/45 were found upon the spot. I have also 2 others which were found in Feenes Field in 1743 and were also put into my hands by Stroud.[l] Mr Hearne in the Preface to Leland's Itinerary published in 1710 says that 15 or 16 years before as they were ploughing in a Field near the Manor of Feenes they grated upon the Ruines of an old Building, upon which Persons were imployed several days to dig; but that since the Place has been almost if not quite covered again with Earth, I presume the Ruines of an old Building are the same with the foundations of a Building grated-on so lately by my Tenant's Plough.

Two men contributed as much as any to his peace of mind that summer. One was Captain (later Admiral) Charles Fanshawe, who had settled his wife and family near Reading and had taken to calling regularly – often with his brother John, Archdeacon of Oxford and Regius Professor of Divinity and

---

[j] Miss Vade was either the daughter or sister of Bagshaw's assistant in parish affairs. 'Mr Vade', written in Bagshaw's handwriting, is frequently to be found in the Bromley parish register as the producer of affidavits in the case of burials. He is known to have had a son, John, born in 1720.

[k] 'Alone together.'

[l] Four more Roman coins were found there in 1747.

Greek. The other was the Archdeacon of Berkshire, Dr Samuel Knight, who was also a friend of Ward's. On his visits to the county he often dropped in on John with a store of anecdotes about bishops and other scholars which he had collected for his biographical works. So time passed until the Gibsons came to stay in August, shortly after the birth of their first child, Anne. Professor Ward was there too and it was then that John presented him with a copy of James Merrick's *Tryphiadorus* for the Gresham College Library. Ward was fond of Dorothy and as concerned about her as he had been in the past about his own cousin, Anna Maria.

In September Mary Hiley married Dr Anthony Addington, a young physician in Reading who moved later to London and acquired there a high reputation, especially in the treatment of insanity. He was a friend of the elder Pitt, and later, after his retirement, was called to Windsor by the Prince Regent to attend George III. He was also the father of a future Prime Minister, Lord Sidmouth. It was a great satisfaction to Mr and Mrs Hiley, after losing eight others, to see their only surviving child safely married. John was made a trustee of the marriage settlement, a sign of the deep affection the Hileys all had for him.

Soon after her husband's death Mrs Goodwin had packed up her things and removed to Warwick, where she rented a house in Jury Street for herself and her daughter Mary. It was a sensible decision, for she was a sociable person who liked to know what was going on and to meet her friends over the tea table. The isolation of Arlescote could be almost impenetrable in winter and while she had put up with it for her husband's sake she did not intend to become a housekeeper for a somewhat disagreeable son. For William unfortunately had a stubborn disposition and without Anna Maria's strong influence over him was not much of a companion to anyone except himself. His health was not good and she might have remained with him on that account, but she was barely thirteen miles away and he was quite happy to live alone and indulge his only passion, which was for the racecourse.

Mary was now twenty years old and hoping for marriage. So was a young clergyman called John Warner who had been looking for a wife for some time. In the spring of 1745, he had very nearly found one in the person of Miss Mary Waldo, who lived at Balliol College with her uncle, Dr Theophilus Leigh, to whom she acted as housekeeper. William Leigh of Adlestrop had written to his brother, Dr Leigh, on 25 April:

> I hear from undoubted authority that Mr Warner, the Divine, is mighty desirous to take to him a Wife. What think you of a Contrivance to Recommend him to Miss Mary or to Miss Emma Waldo?[7]

He had written again on 4 May:

> Mr Warner of Cherington dined with me last Thursday. Upon his telling me he was intirely at liberty, I mentioned to him your

Housekeeper. He seemed very well pleased, but desired time to consult his Father upon his Return from Buckinghamshire. The Father will Putt down at present, just as much as the Wife brings, be it one or two Thousand Pound; but whether he will think one sufficient, I shall know in a little time. I told him that was the most that could be expected. I am to dine with him on Tuesday the 14th instant, and am then to have my answer. I wish we may have success, for upon my Word it will be an advantageous Match in all Respects.[8]

Poor Miss Waldo seems to have had little say in the matter; the decision was left to John's father, Richard Warner, who lived at Ditchley and was a friend of Lord Litchfield. Evidently he turned the proposition down. Miss Waldo continued to minister to her uncle and aunt for forty years, neither she nor her sister ever finding a husband in spite of several efforts by their relations which always foundered on finance.

It can only be imagined what Mrs Goodwin would have done if she had known what a cold-blooded suitor John Warner really was when he made overtures for Mary's hand. What in fact she did was to invite John Loveday to undertake the negotiations with father and son on her behalf, preferring his advice to William's. John was only too glad to do her any service he could, so he rode up to Oxford with John Peareth to provide any necessary legal support and to keep him amused on the way. The interview was satisfactory and Mary's dowry was considered adequate. The marriage was not to take place until the following June which gave the young man time to fall in love if he had not already done so.

By October, with the Young Pretender installed at Edinburgh and with the defeat of Sir John Cope at the Battle of Prestonpans, the possibility of a successful rebellion could not be overruled. Meetings were held in the counties at which noblemen and gentry forgathered to affirm their loyalty to King and Country. John attended one of these at the Reading Town Hall on 12 October when, under the chairmanship of the Duke of St Albans, Berkshire proclaimed its allegiance. On the 15th he was at the Oxfordshire meeting where he could see in the council chamber the Earls of Jersey and Macclesfield, Lord Harcourt and Bishop Secker. The fighting, however, seemed fairly remote until he was given a front-line view of it in a letter from his friend Richard Lluellyn. Having failed in his attempt for a curacy in Reading, Lluellyn had temporarily forsaken Magdalen for an appointment as chaplain at Capesthorne in Cheshire, then owned by John Ward, father of Penelope Davenport.[m] He had been there since July and returned to Magdalen in 1749 on becoming Dean of Divinity. He wrote to John on 1 December having witnessed Prince Charles Edward's ill-fated march south which ended at Derby instead of London, its original objective.

---

[m] Penelope had died in 1737 and her son, Davies, was now the heir.

Dear Squire, Last Friday, at two o'Clock in the afternoon, the whole Rebel army entered Manchester, without observing any order, sometimes two, sometimes three, sometimes four in a rank. After passing in this Manner for about half an hour, came the Young Pretender attended by his Guards; soon after came a Coach & Six but there was no seeing who or what was in it, and immediately after a Chair drawn by two Horses in which were two Ladies. Afterwards came the remainder of their forces, by twos, threes, and fours, as before, and 13 brass Cannon drawn by two three or four Horses according to their different sizes, and after them three Carriages with Ammunition and Baggage, and one covered Carriage. The whole Procession took up about 3 hours and their numbers were computed to be about twelve thousand, but then full one fourth of them consisted of Boys, of 10, 12, or 14 years old, and of old Men and Women, so that, at the most, they have not above 9000 effective Men. The *Boys* are armed with a Musket, Sword and Target, and one or two brace of Pistols; they are chiefly dressed in Scotch Plads, and all of them seem to be in high spirits. About a thousand of them are well mounted; but then their Horses are more fit for travelling on the road, or for hunting, than for War; most of them being too slight to resist the weight of ours. The young Pretender has marched all the way from Edinburgh on foot, and declares he will not stride a horse 'till he gets to St. James's. The Bellman went about the Town ordering all Dealers in Tea, Candles &c. to pay six Weeks' Excise according to their last Receipts, which they were required to bring with them, and they likewise exacted half a Year's windows and Land Tax. They pay for whatever they call for and give notice to people to take care of their Sheets, Pewter &c. to prevent the Rabble from carrying them off, and do not knowingly suffer their Men to take any thing but Horses. There were Bonfires, ringing of Bells and Illuminations at Manchester and no other Mischief done than breaking those windows which wanted Lights . . .

P.S. I proposed sending the above by Monday's Post, the 2nd of December, but the Rebels having marched on Sunday from Manchester, have intercepted all letters to and from these Parts. I much suspect they did not pay for whatever they called for at Manchester, if they did 'twas more than they did at Macclesfield and the Neighbourhood thereof, for one Man told me he had forty Men and three Horses and all that he could get was about two shillings. They did not collect the Excise or Taxes at Macclesfield, but they issued out their orders to the Gentlemen of the Neighbourhood, to send in Hay and Corn; Mr Ward was ordered to send in 150 Measures of Oates and 5 loads of Hay and two of Straw under pain of military Execution. I thank God we have at last got rid of them for they went on Tuesday for Leek in Staffordshire and from thence they went on Wednesday to Darby, and on Thursday set out for Leicester.

From all the Accounts I can meet with, and one I had from a Gentleman who stood in one Spot and told them, they are not above 9000 effective men and I verily believe that number of regular forces would give a good Account of them. I went about 3 miles to see them go by but was an hour too late for seeing the Main Body and only saw about 50 Horse. Sixty joined them at Manchester, not one since, but I believe several have deserted when they have had an opportunity; I am sure as to two for they left their Plads and Bonnetts at Capesthorne. The main Body lay at Darby on Wednesday Night. As Darby is quite cross the Country I expect to hear no more of them but by the publick Papers. December 7th 1745. I have lost nothing by them. I hear the Duke's army is about Lichfield but can hear nothing of that under Mr Wade.[9]

As Lluellyn thought, the Duke of Cumberland had reached Lichfield. Wade had been hemmed in by snow in mid-November and had allowed Carlisle to fall to the rebels. They reached Derby on 4 December but their ranks were thinning from desertion and the English Jacobites had not given the support that Charles Edward expected. On 6 December he was persuaded by his own officers to retreat northwards and it was then that a lack of discipline in the troops, which had not been evident on the more orderly march down, lost him much of the support he had acquired. There had been very few recruits at Manchester, as Lluellyn explained in a further letter dated 28 December.

I told you that 60 Persons had enlisted with the Pretender at Manchester, but was informed on the Spot that he had not half that number. I should not have thought it worth while to set you right in this Matter, but for its being a convincing Proof of the Nation's being well affected and attached to the present Establishment. I suppose in your travels, you have heard Manchester spoken of as one of the most disaffected Places in the Kingdom, and I can't help congratulating my Country, that a Place so reputed, and consisting of 35000 Souls, should furnish out no more than 29 Rebels, and all those Men of desperate Fortunes.[10]

Dorothy's health took a turn for the worse at the end of the year, so much so that John wrote in his diary 'Begun the uncertainty of the signs of death', but whatever these were they had disappeared by the end of January 1746, when Ward congratulated them both on her improvement. The letter was chiefly devoted to comments on Dr Zachary Grey's new edition of *Hudibras*[11] with interesting interpolations of his own, as for instance:

He has no note upon sweating lanthorns . . . but I have been told by some of our Physicians and Surgeons, that in Salivations persons are

sometimes put into a large wooden box, made round at the top like a
lanthorn, with a blanket over them and spirits of wine underneath, which
makes them sweat very plentifully.[12]

Although he had recently lost his sister Abigail, Ward was as busy as ever.
He took the opportunity not only of thanking John for his just remarks upon
his own book on the Gresham Professors but of sending George Vertue's
acknowledgment to John of two corrections to his life of Wenceslaus Hollar,[n]
which would be printed with others on a single leaf. Meanwhile Thomas
Winchester was providing Dr Mead with a general index to all the volumes in
the new edition of Leland's *Itinerary* and Deodatus Bye also was entering
Ward's scene for the first time.

In April John decided that five weeks at Bromley would be good for Dolly
and the children. Picking up his friend Mr Barker at Turnham Green, they
drove to Gunnersbury House, once the home of John Maynard, King's
Sergeant to Charles II, and now belonging to Henry Furnese. Later in the
century its owner was Princess Amelia.

Lord Hobart sold it to the present Possessor, Henry Furnese Esqr. There
is a glorious view from this high situation; and though high, a fine piece
of Water in the Gardens, which are not large, nor is there any occasion
they should be so, the Garden-Wall being so waved as to let-in the most
beautiful Country; and such a built Wall has by no means any bad look of
itself; but if it had, would be excusable for the noble end it so perfectly
well answers. The House is equally grand and convenient; not a
Chimney could be placed more commodiously; all the Rooms except
Garrets are floored with Norway Oak. As to the great Staircase, the
Stairs are now Mahogany, though the old form be retained, which is
such as reminds me of Belvoir Castle, the Duke of Rutland's; entering
the Room in which is the Staircase, it first of all (after a sufficient distance)
occupies the middle space ascending foreright to a Landing Place, from
whence on each hand it turns at right angles; either flight of Stairs
landing you in one common Gallery above. Of the Paintings, one is by
Carlo Maratti of St. Andrew about to be crucified, seven figures in the
Piece. In the grand Room which is full as elegant as it is magnificent, are
two Chimnies; Termini not Caryatides, making part of the Ornaments
of them. Here are many Paintings, such as a Rubens of one of his Wives
and a Bassan of Christ driving the Buyers and Sellers out of the Temple;
but the two much valued Pictures are of a large size and in full
proportion; one is by Andrea Sacchi (Carlo Maratti's Master) of Apollo
(a Nudity) crowning a Youth who has one hand on a musical Instrument

[n] A *Description of the Works of Wenceslaus Hollar* was published in 1745 and reprinted in
1759. In his letter Ward said that Vertue proposed to print John's corrections 'with some
others made by himself or his friends in a single leaf; which he designs to give to all those who
purchased the book, there being in the whole but 200 copies . . .'

> . . . the other large Picture we looked upon (contrary to what th :y say in the house) to be the capital Painting, indeed a very capital one; 'tis a Guido of Liberality and Modesty, two graceful Females, in the loveliest Attitudes . . .

He described both paintings in great detail and much later on he added a note to say they had been bought by Mr Spencer for Wimbledon House.

While he was at Bromley he made several expeditions. He went to Eltham in search of the old palace, where

> The approach through what were once Offices reminds one of the Palace at Hampton Court; past these you come to the Porter's Lodge; the hindmost of all the buildings is the lofty hall, which has a curious cieling of Irish Oak . . .

Of St Botolph's in Bishopsgate which had not long been rebuilt and where his brother-in-law was the rector, he wrote:

> The Steeple is placed on Arches over the Altar; otherwise it had made no shew to the Street, for 'tis the East end of the Church that is next the Street.

And at Pinners Hall

> a Dissenting Meeting House, so first used in 1672, was once ('tis said) as long again as at present; the Roof is Irish Oak, looks very fresh, is much carved and very elegantly; in one place it is carved 1550.

The best likeness he had ever seen of Charles II was at Vintner's Hall and he then went to Apothecaries' Hall to see the portrait of James I which his great-grandfather, Michael North, had presented to the Society – 'a Portrait upon which they set a very high value'. It was then that he left the receipt for £20, given by the Master and Wardens to his grandmother, folded in his notes, where it remained for the next 230 years.[°]

On 3 May John paid the visit to Bishop Gibson that had been suggested. William Gibson took him to call on his father at Whitehall and he then went on with William and his brother George to Fulham Palace. There he saw the famous tortoise, as he told Dṛ Ducarel, the Lambeth Librarian, in October 1775 when a gardener had killed it by hitting its neck while it was emerging from the ground.

> The tradition is that Bishop Laud had two tortoises at Fulham; one he left there, the other he carried with him in 1633 to Lambeth. I saw the Fulham tortoise in the garden there on May 3, 1746. It had the only mark of age discoverable in a tortoise, that of dimness of sight.[13]

By then he had become a keen tortoise keeper himself.

[°] See p. 3.

They returned to Caversham on 4 June, stopping at Chiswick to see the Earl of Burlington's famous house and gardens. Surprisingly John said very little about that superb example of Palladian architecture, concentrating – as he was apt to do nowadays – on the pictures.

The Gardens are said to contain about 45 Acres; from a Terrace you have the view of Mortlack. Great Taste shewed in the disposition of the Gardens, wherein is a fine serpentine River. Several Buildings here, one has the Portico of Covent Garden Church; among Termini, Statues &c. are three of the latter Antiques, being Brutus, Sylla and Scipio which are said to have been brought from Hadrian's Garden. Antique Busts again in the House itself, as in that Room under the Cupola, where is a Length Painting of Lewis XIII of France, another Length of his Queen and a Picture of Charles I sitting with his son Charles and of his Queen with young James in Arms; it seems to be a Copy from that at Kensington. There are many admirable Paintings in this most elegant Cabinet of an house . . . Kent has Paintings here, one is an head of Mr Pope, a Profile, but a different side of the face from what I have before seen . . . Here are two Porphyry Vases as we take it. Two Tables of various Marbles inlaid in a white Marble, another such much more beautiful in a black marble Slab. Lady Burlington's Dressing-Plate is of Silver-Gilt.

Mary Goodwin and John Warner were married at Barford on 17 June. John received an account of the nuptials from the bridegroom while pondering over a letter from James Merrick who had been told by a mutual friend, Griffith Lloyd,[p] that John had heard that he disapproved of Christians reading ancient or heathen writers. James was apt to make heavy weather of any problem and he took this as a serious accusation. In a long letter he explained that he had merely said that he had not the same taste as formerly for those performances, but then he had been studying Divinity for the last year. 'I should think it great arrogance and presumption in me to censure the study of Heathen authors, as inconsistent with a course of piety.' Indeed, he added, he was apt to believe that the present growth of infidelity might in some measure be owing to a neglect of classical studies which would furnish solutions to several difficulties with regard to the sacred writings.[14]

But John knew how easily Merrick could torture himself. Only a year before he had threatened to expel himself from Trinity College because he thought he

---

[p] Lloyd was headmaster of Archbishop Harsnett's Free Grammar School at Chigwell, but left under a cloud. Writing to Merrick (L.F.P. 29 November 1763), Dr George Scott, Derham's cousin and Bishop Gibson's son-in-law, said Lloyd had suffered from the destructive conduct of a very bad woman. Of his successor, the Revd Peter Burford, he said he had raised a large school 'though so deficient in Point of Learning as to occasion my resigning my Trust as a Governor'. Lloyd left between 1761 and 1753. He came originally from Sonning. See also *Nichols's Literary Anecdotes*, vol. IX, p. 490. George Scott, D.C.L., was then living at Ingatestone Hall and wrote from Crown Court. From 1768 he lived in his family home, Woolston Hall, Chigwell. See also *V.C.H., Essex*.

had been over the age his scholarship allowed when he had been elected Probationer-Fellow – on his own interpretation of the statutes read after his election. He had written to this effect to the Visitor, Bishop Benjamin Hoadly. Meanwhile John had consulted his friend Samuel Weller of Maidstone, who replied sternly that Mr Merrick should consider it his duty to be cautious in giving way to scruples and that for a private Fellow to expel himself would be an unwarrantable thing, since it was for the Visitor to explain the statutes which must always be understood in their most favourable sense.[15] Bishop Hoadly, never having had much difficulty with scruples of any kind, had begged James not to hurt himself and had assured him that he was truly a scholar as long as the President and Dean thought fit to account him and treat him as one and so he would continue in all eyes, including the Bishop's, until someone made a complaint.

> Whatever should be my opinion, it cannot, as far as I can see, and ought not to have a Retrospect to any thing that is past; but must only look forward to what is to come, léaving all the Consequences of what has been already done to take place in their natural and usual Course.[16]

Merrick could not really understand this complaisant interpretation of a statute which appeared to forbid his retention of his scholarship after his twenty-fourth year, but he bowed to the Bishop's authority. Now this new accusation had, he felt, damaged his reputation still further. Everyone felt he had behaved 'very singularly' over the statutes and now he appeared to be acting with 'extraordinary preciseness' in his views on the Classics. Tiresome as his long-winded *apologiae* could be, John believed his genius and knew it must be reconciled with his conscience. He must use his influence with tact.

> . . . I am confident [he replied on 28 June] you will continue to make use of that variety of talents committed to your trust, in such manner as that all and every of them may turn out to account; 'tis in your power (in some sense) to become all things to all men; they are few that may not be won by your conversation; . . . directly or indirectly Divinity doubtless will be the scope of your studies arîd a practice suitable to it the business of your life; yet will human learning still be subsiduary to divine; discoursing freely upon the former you catch your hearers with guile, and craftily lead them to the latter; from humble speculation they are by degrees led to the heights of practice; and can such a train, fired by you, be called idle sport and trifling away time? No, it is no trifling, if even by riddles, by merry tales, you engage the attention of others of lower abilities and attainments and having engaged it, insensibly (as you well know how), divert it to more interesting themes . . .

Go on then [he wrote in conclusion] and prosper; mix with the world;

the salt of your conversation may do something towards stopping the increase of corrupt manners.[17]

During the following vacation Merrick began his practice of giving tracts to soldiers stationed at Reading and at least one young subaltern received a letter of advice from him. This was quite a courageous undertaking and through the years he had a good deal of success. In 1746 there was a detachment[q] of the 1st Foot Guards there from July until the end of September under the command of Sir James Foulis, who had joined the regiment as an ensign in 1743. This Scottish baronet was by nature really more of a scholar than a soldier and with the Earl of Buchan (David Steuart Erskine) was largely responsible for the foundation in 1780 of the Society of Antiquaries of Scotland. John waited on him and his officers at the Black Bull in Reading and finding that his wife was with him, took Dolly to call on them at their lodgings with Legg the carpenter. When the Foulises returned the visit they were accompanied by Miss Legg, one of those unexpected facts which so often defeat generalizations on eighteenth-century status and etiquette, for the class boundaries were not as severe as is often supposed. By the time Sir James came to take his leave a very great friendship had sprung up between himself and John, one which survived until the end of their lives – in spite of a misunderstanding that caused a long interval of separation. As William Benwell put it:

> Though they have been many years at a great distance from each other, Sir James residing at Edinburgh and Mr Loveday at Caversham, the warmest correspondence has been kept up and to read the letters that pass between them is to see one of the sweetest mixtures of literature and friendship that was ever known.

This testimony is borne out by such fragments as remain of the correspondence. The Earl of Buchan tried every conceivable tactic to retrieve Foulis's letters from John's son after the two friends had died, as he wished to publish them; but Sir James in his old age had become suspicious of Buchan and had made the younger John promise he should never have them. He also forced a promise that they should be burnt and in spite of his own regrets Dr John Loveday consigned them to the flames and salvaged his conscience. His father's replies to Foulis have not been traced and were perhaps fuel for another deplorable bonfire.

'My new great gates were put-up and the Earl of Kilmarnock and Lord Balmerino were beheaded,' wrote John on 18 August.[r] Whether or not there

---

[q] There is no proof either at the Ministry of Defence Office or the Public Record Office that this regiment had a detachment at Reading at this time, but there is a record of Foulis's appointment in 1743. John's diaries prove that he was in Reading with his men.

[r] They were both executed on Tower Hill on 18 August 1746, having been handed over to the Duke of Cumberland after the Battle of Culloden.

was a macabre innuendo in this reference to the Scottish rebels it did at least signify some improvement to his property. However much he admired the alterations he saw in other men's houses, he did very little about his own. Meanwhile little Mary and Jacky, now five and four years old, were being brought up according to his sensible theories, based partly on his own childhood. He explained his methods in a letter to Mrs Goodwin shortly after Mary's marriage, a letter in which he also described a terrifying incident which shocked him so much that he often referred to it, later on putting it at the head of a list of God's blessings, all of which were deliverances from near-disasters to himself or his relations.

Honoured Madam, I have my Mother's express commands to congratulate you in her name on my Sister's Marriage; my Wife and self join with her, and wish you all the solid satisfaction upon the occasion that is possible; may this satisfaction encrease with time and no abating circumstances ever intervene! may you be happy also in your Childrens' Children! My lovely Babes are in incomparable health; they go every day to an excellent School at Reading; if the weather be bad, each are carryed on horseback, otherwise they walk; the exercise is not at all too much for them, and I hold it to be the best Physick they have ever taken. They were happily visiting at Mansfield's on the Afternoon of Midsummer day, when a ball of fire broke into my Study, burst-open a Book-Press, singed the backs of several Bookes; the wire of the Bell there being heated, the heat was communicated along the said wire through the length of the passage to my Study and then turning the corner through two thirds of the length of the Gallery, the wire melting and burning into the Chairs or Floor wherever it fell; not two minutes had I been gone out of my Study, when the fire from heaven came down upon it; I went into the great Parlour where my wife and a friend[5] were sitting; the former was going to seat herself (had I not desired the contrary) in a place, which, a minute after I entered the room, was forcibly torn and split; attended with a report full as loud as any Cannon, and the house was full of Sulphur and Smoke; yet here we are all to glorify the Providence of God so marvellously exerted for our Preservation; and you, Madam will, I am confident, join with us in thanksgivings to heaven on this occasion. Mrs Addington has brought her husband a fine Girl, which is all the news occurring to, dear Madam, your dutiful Son and obliged Servant.

Tom French had died and he added a postscript to say that he had heard that Lord Northampton had written very kindly to the widow. As for national news:

[5] Dr John Burton had arrived for breakfast, but this was probably a female friend.

Lord Lovat[1] is allowed to be the greatest Villain of the pack, having plaid double with all parties; so all give him up with pleasure.[18]

He did not mention the fact that his son walked the three miles to school in his petticoats, but this imposition was finally removed in September and it was a special occasion when 'Jackey was breeched'. Professor Ward took a great interest in this ceremony and wrote a little while after it had taken place:

Liberty is so natural to the human species, that I doubt not but Master Jackey is much pleased with his new breeches. I am glad to hear of the continuance of his health and Miss's and especially that Mrs Loveday is better than when I left Caversham.[19]

Sarah Loveday was, of course, devoted to the children and a lock taken from her grandson's head is still wrapped up in a scrap of paper marked with the words 'My little fellow's Hare'.

As usual John was contributing to or benefiting from other men's research. In September, for instance – as a letter from Ward reveals – Martin Folkes, the President of the Royal Society, intended to put an impression of his Philip and Mary shilling into his new series when Vertue had engraved it; Thomas Birch, the scholar and antiquary, was examining his paper on an error in the life of Robert Boyle; John Whiston was unable to produce the Latin 'catalogue of the Eton foundations' as the College had none left; Dr Mead put up a slight resistance to information on the effect of a tarantula's bite for the new edition of his book on poisons.[20]

I informed him of what you told me from Mr Holdsworth but he seemed thoroughly satisfied with the authorities he has given in proof of the fact. And Mr Ramsay,[u] who was present, appeared to add some weight to them. Who said, that when he was at Naples, his landlord coming one day into his room told him, that if he would go into the Toledo, which was the adjoining street, he might see a person affected in that manner. But not being dressed he omitted it, not doubting from what he had heard of its being a common case, but some other opportunity would offer to satisfy his curiosity.[21]

John also had news of Captain Robert Bootle who was on dry land at the moment and busy with his collections to which he had so many opportunities of adding on his voyages. Writing to George Vertue in 1752, the numismatist George North said of him:

Captain Bootle I have the pleasure of knowing and some years ago of

---

[1] *The Memoirs of the Life of Lord Lovat* came out in 1746. Lovat was found guilty of high treason on 18 March 1747, and executed on 18 April, ten months after this letter.

[u] Allan Ramsay was shortly to paint Mead's portrait for the Foundling Hospital. He must have been referring to his first visit to Italy (1736–8).

seeing his collection; which as his industry is indefatigable, and almost inimitable, must be greatly increased.[22]

I saw Captain Bootle at the Society last Thursday [wrote Ward on 5 November] who it seems found so much business at Oxford as kept him there three days, which necessarily prevented his return by Caversham . . . when I shall receive by Mr Hopson the gold coin of Queen Elizabeth, I shall take care to deliver it to the Captain. Good Sir James [Foulis] was lately so kind as to call on me; but I am unable to return the visit without your assistance, having forgot his family name. This I should take for a great instance of my decay of memory, but that upon asking the Captain about it, I found the case was the same with him, which gave me some Consolation . . .[23]

Sir James, however, like most of John's friends, was soon one of Ward's circle.

M. Giles Bellai, the volatile old French master, was buried at St Laurence's Church on 22 November, attended from his lodgings to his grave by his three executors, Dr Merrick, Mr Hiley and John, and by Dr Addington. It was sad to say goodbye to this old friend and happier to remember him as the man who had taught his pupils the beauty of the French language and as the founder of the French Club. Tinged with their affection was also a slight sense of ridicule. Peter Zinzan had expressed the two sentiments a few years earlier in some irreverent verses.

BELLAY TO MRS GODFREY

Vat be de cause, dear Madmoiselle,
Dat I, who at Parnassus' Well
   Nere took a single Sipping
Now feel such woorkings in my brain
As if Dan Phoebus and his Train
   Deir revels dere were keeping?

Madam, You see how Love pour vous
Can all his Prodigies outdo
   And greater Wonders show yet,
For who, begar, could e're have t'ought
Dough Jove was Bull and Pan was Goat
   Dat I should have been Poet.

When I wid wide extended view
Your mighty Com'liness pursue
   Soft to myself I say,
Alas, in dat capacious Breast
Is no bye Corner unpossess'd
   No room for poor Bellay?

When you dat copious Magazine
Of beauty, wondrous to be seen,
        In its full Pow'r display,
Strait Cupid shoots me t'rough and t'rough
And in each vein from Top to Toe
        He dances en Français.

Oh Madam peety all my pain
And as you read dis tender Strain
        Let not your Brow grow rougher
If Love at last has found de skill
A Heart as old as mine to drill
        Den why should yours be tougher?

Warm'd by your Smiles I'll cast my skin
And should some marks of Age be seen
        Your Charms will soon repair 'em
T'ink not dat I'm declining yet
For par ma Foy I'll Children get
        As fast as you can bear 'em.[24]

Mixed Fortunes
1747 – 1754

The children were ill with smallpox during the winter of 1747, but recovered in time to take their grandmother Loveday's spring purge for the young (assuming John allowed it), consisting of rhubarb, wormseed, senna, stoned raisins and lavender cotton steeped for several days in a mixture of ale and small beer. Dolly too felt better in the spring and was able to go over to Silchester with John, Zinzan and her brother Thomas, 'eating our dinner at Farmer Pottinger's'. The following day, 4 April, they drove to Henley to see a cousin, Frances Bagshaw, and, leaving the ladies to chat, John took Thomas to Phyllis Court which the Freemans of Fawley had inherited from Bulstrode Whitelocke.[a]

> Phyllis Court at the end of Henley Town and upon the banks of the Thames, is a large and old house but a very good one. In a parlour over the Chimney is a very valuable perspective of the inside of a large house; the door is on the Spectator's right hand, King Charles and his Queen have just entered it . . .

After describing this painting in which there was a miniature picture of the altarpiece in the chapel of St John's College, Oxford, he continued:

[a] Fawley Court, once the seat of Bulstrode Whitelocke, was sold to the Freemans after the Restoration. It had been ruined by Prince Rupert's troops and Whitelocke went to Phyllis Court. He was British Ambassador to Sweden from November 1653 to July 1654. Queen Christina abdicated on 6 June 1654 and was succeeded by Charles X. Whitelock's *Memorials of English Affairs* came out in 1682. His final home was Chilton Park, Wiltshire. See *D.N.B.* and the diaries of Mrs Lybbe Powys.

In a long room above Stairs, among other pictures of the Overbury family, is one of Sir Thomas . . . several pictures of the Whitelock family, one said to be Bulstrode Whitelock . . . his hair is black and he has some resemblance altogether of Will Champ, and of Turner the Tallow-Chandler in New Inn Hall Lane, Oxford; 'tis said to have been painted in Sweden and to have been given him by Queen Christina together with her own picture which is of the same size and in the same sort of frame, and represents her with very large eyes and a most alarming turn of her eyes, which makes her sudden appearance not a little startling, and upon further consideration she has a rampant lewd look. 'Tis observable that Whitelock in his *Memorials* takes no note of these presents, but says 'The Queen and the new King[b] were pleased to honour me with their Pictures set with Diamonds.' This was in the year 1654 when the Queen was considerably under thirty years of age.

William Gibson had been installed as a canon of Windsor in place of his brother who had resigned and this meant that he and Patty were much more accessible. After staying with them in May and after dining with Lord and Lady Cadogan on the occasion of the marriage of their son, Charles Sloane, with the Hon. Frances Bromley, John and Dolly took the children for a long holiday to Warwickshire. At last he felt able to face the necessary but painful duty of taking her to Arlescote. Fortified by a night at the Greyhound in Oxford and the usual reunions, they made their way to the house of some friends in Banbury called Tatam, whose son, Robert, a Magdalen demy, was just about to be ordained deacon. William Goodwin brought his housekeeper, Mrs Maria Walker, to greet them there, a kind and sensitive thought. He was devoted to John with whom he had so often made one of a trio. They made formal presentations of books to each other and so did Sanderson Miller who gave John a history of Byzantine architecture by Charles Du Fresne.

The only outing was to Culworth to visit Mrs Lord and her daughters, who were cousins of the Goodwins,[c] and a sixteen-year-old baronet, Sir Harry Danvers, whose family had lived there since 1439. He and his mother showed them the house and garden and they found plenty of family and other matters to talk about. Only the year before Sir Harry's aunt Martha had married John's old schoolfriend Daniel Rich and the Danverses were related both to the Rushworths and to the Courtenays of Powderham. After this there were twelve days at Warwick with Mrs Goodwin who had also invited John Audley. Finally they went to Cherington to see the Warners' first baby, Mary, and stopped on the way to look at Charlecote church where John described admiringly the beautiful tomb erected for Sir Thomas Lucy and his wife. They returned to Arlescote for twelve more days, but the house, once

---

[b] Charles X.
[c] Anna Maria's paternal grandmother was Anne Lord.

so full of bustle, was very quiet now and John spent a good deal of the time visiting the great mansions within riding distance. At Ditchley Park he described the dominating portraits of Charles II and the Duchess of Cleveland, which he had not mentioned before.[d] Of the house itself he only recorded Cheere's 'elegant and high-polished Chimney-pieces'. On 23 July he returned to Cherington in order to visit Weston House nearby which belonged to William Sheldon.

> This magnificent large old house, built of stone, has a noble Gallery well-proportioned. In the great Parlour are the celebrated Tapestry-Hangings, being spatious and very distinct Maps of several Counties in England.[e]

After describing a number of portraits of well-known men, he concluded:

> But in the great Parlour are Paintings of several of our Princes and contemporary Monarchs, such as Francis 1st of France, together with several of our great men. . . Henrys 5, 6 and 7 begin the collection and are just like those in the Provost's Great Parlour at Eton. Besides many family-pictures, here are admirable good ones of some Popes and Cardinals.

The old enthusiasm had returned and the next day he rode to Wroxton Abbey where Sanderson Miller had begun to make extensive alterations for the Earl of Guilford. The architect was there to explain to John exactly what was being done and on this occasion he gave him another book – Fletcher's *Purple Island, or the Isle of Man,* . . ., published in 1633.

> This old, but unfinished, Stone Mansion, has several Paintings worth notice; such is particularly a fine Riley of Lord Keeper Guilford sitting. Sir Owen Hopton's face reminds me of my father Goodwin's – Sir Thomas Pope, Founder of Trinity College (of which Society his Lordship holds this Place), by Holbein. . . The Picture of the Founder in the Refectory of his College is but a Copy . . . The Gardens have the approbation of all judges, consisting of a piece of water admirably shaded with trees, of a Cascade, of a serpentine River &c. much of it made out of a bog. In the Church is a Monument for Sir William Pope, Earl of Down[f] and his Lady; the Canopy over their recumbent figures is truly admirable for the neatness and perfect elegance of it.

[d] See p. 173.

[e] John saw both sets – 1588 and mid-seventeenth century. Those bought by Richard Gough in 1781 were bequeathed to the Bodleian Library, those purchased by Horace Walpole eventually became the property of the Yorkshire Philosophical Society and were sold in 1960. The two Worcestershire maps now hang together at the Victoria and Albert Museum. The Oxford and Berkshire map is privately owned and on loan at Oxburgh Hall.

[f] The Earl of Downe built the house on the site of a medieval priory. He entertained James I there.

He rode the next day to Sir Clement Cottrell-Dormer's fine house, Rousham Park.

'Tis a good old Stone Seat, augmented with two Wings in the same old taste by the late General Dormer; the Library, a very fine room in one of the Wings, has a good threequarter-piece of the General sitting with the proper attributes of the Soldier and Scholar; here is also an head of Lord Falkland; but the supellex libraria is, as it ought, the main recommendation of the room; an head of Ben Johnson[g] in another room. The marble Chimney-pieces in this house are very neat. But they are the Gardens that make Rousham so celebrated; they contain about 35 Acres, have a remarkable concave Slope in front, are bounded some ways by the Charwell and here there is a beautiful meadow on t'other side of it; of the three jetteaus, one rises 55 foot high;[h] the buildings up and down here are all rural and unornamented; the Pyramid, among other Antiques, has a Roman Marble with a sepulchral Inscription.

He went on the same day to Kirtlington Park,[1] a new house built for Sir James Dashwood and not far from Rousham.

This magnificent house is so spacious as to contain 14 Lodging-Rooms on a floor with a Dressing-Room to each. The Stair-Cases have Sky-Lights only. The floors are of Norway Oak; the Garrets have floors of Stucho. The Offices are truly noble. But, after all, the place is but ill supplied with Water, that upon the spot being very hard indeed.

They returned to Caversham at the end of August and shortly after that the Gibsons came to stay, to be entertained with a lively party which included Phanuel Bacon, William Lowth, Zinzan, Thomas Bonney and John Burton. They were back in Windsor when William sent John news of the death of the Archbishop of Canterbury, Dr John Potter, and the subsequent events as they affected his father.

October 13. 1747. Dear Brother, I trouble you with this account which I have just received from Whitehall in regard to the Arch-Bishoprick of Canterbury, to furnish you with an Answer to any questions that may be asked you on that head, as far as the Bishop of London is concerned. The Arch-Bishop died on Saturday, and on Monday his Majesty was pleased to send the Duke of Newcastle to Whitehall to let my Father know that he would not suffer any thing to be said to him concerning that Promotion 'till he knew what his resolution was; which gracious offer the Bishop answered with a dutifull excuse. Upon his refusal, it is imagined that the Bishop of Salisbury will have it and that Llandaff[i] will come to Salisbury.

[g] Ben Jonson.
[h] Mr T. Cottrell-Dormer kindly gave me information about his house. He thought there was some exaggeration at the time by the gardener as to the height of the fountains.
[i] John Gilbert, Bishop of Llandaff, was translated to Salisbury in 1749 and became Archbishop of York in 1757.

My Wife continues to drink the Sunning-hill Waters with very good success. We hope that your journey hither stands fixt for the beginning of November and joyn in Duty to my Mother and love to all your Family. My sister Wilson is surprisingly recovered by Tar-Water. I am your affectionate Brother . . .[j]

Sherlock refused the Primacy and succeeded Gibson at London. It was accepted by Thomas Herring, the Archbishop of York.

At Christmas time the Revd William Sharpe left Caversham to return to Christ Church and later to become Principal of Hertford College. The change was a happy one for John as the Revd Peter Vatas, who arrived when the Thames was bursting its banks, was to remain as perpetual curate for over fifty years. A good scholar and a helpful friend, he became virtually one of the family.

Nothing very dramatic occurred in 1748 and yet several events had some hidden significance. It was the year in which Charles's ill health caused the Hopsons to leave Reading and return to Beenham; the year in which John deposited little Mary at a school in Dorchester, Oxfordshire, with tragic results. Bishop Gibson died in the autumn leaving all his children in comfortable circumstances, so that William's income was over £1,000 a year, clear of taxes. Dick Simeon married Elizabeth Hutton and made John a trustee of his marriage settlement and the Warners produced a second daughter, Sarah. Also John met for the first time three rather special people – the Revd William Markham, George Ballard, the antiquary, and the girl who was to become his third wife.

Dorothy and he went to Bromley again at the beginning of May and revisited Kensington Palace on the way. He particularly wanted to look at the original paintings of kings of England which George Vertue had engraved for Rapin's *History of England*, produced by the Knapton brothers in 1736. His notes on other paintings were quite extensive although they were on a journey.

Leaving Dolly and the children with her family he went straight down to Maidstone to spend a week with Deodatus Bye and on 9 May he visited Otford to see what was left of the Archbishops' palace.

The chief remains of the Palace are a Tower which carryed three floors, but is now unroofed and is the westermost building in front; from this Eastward is continued a long range of Building, much lowered but

---

[j] The late Dr Norman Sykes was shown William Gibson's letter (L.F.P. 13. October, 1747), and wrote to Dr Thomas Loveday (L.F.P. 13. November 1957) pointing out that it disproved the theory that the primacy was offered to Bishop Joseph Butler (*D.N.B.* and the *Life* by Thomas Bartlett, 1839). Archbishop Potter died on Saturday, 10 October and the oral message sent to Gibson on the 12th shows that the King approached him first. Sherlock was offerd the Primacy later on the 12th but declined twice. It is known that Butler was not approached between the refusal of Sherlock and the acceptance of Herring.

lately, and now chiefly used for a place to put their implements of husbandry in. Within the memory of man a great deal of the house has been taken-down and the tower also was inhabited. The Ruins abovementioned are of Brick, though the Coins are carryed up with Stone. The utmost extent of the building Southward may be about 25 or 30 Rods from the Church; and these Back-buildings of which one may almost say *periere ruinae,*[k] were ('tis highly probable) part of the old house mentioned above which Warham found here and indeed I concluded them to have been of a much more ancient date than the brick front before I had read anything of the History of the Place, these having very evident marks of an elder antiquity; and besides, here the materials seem to have been chiefly Stone. There have been no vaulted Cellars to this Palace; for the situation is so low that the Springs are almost level with the surface, nor is there any fall to draw the water off by sewers. The Place was never moted. An escutcheon of Arms in Woodwork, taken from the Ruins, is fixed up by way of ornament to the Entrance of a farm-house just by; it contains the Arms of the See of Canterbury, impaled with the paternal bearing of Warham . . . St Thomas Becket's Well. . . is a long Square, 5 yards perhaps one way and 10 another; 'tis paved with Stone and has a stone Wall about it.[l]

On his return to Bromley he went with Thomas to the Foundling Hospital which Captain Coram had established in 1739. Apart from his interest in Ramsay's portrait of Dr Mead, who was one of the Governors, he saw a number of others presented by those artists themselves who had also become Governors. He was critical of Highmore's offering,[m] 'meanly performed', and of Hogarth's painting of Moses being brought before Pharaoh's daughter:

> The child is not so beautiful as the sacred text describes him − . . . the Princess is English all over.
>   The marble Chimneypiece by J. Devall; the Bas Relief over it exhibiting the various employments of children is by M. Rysbrack. The curious frame of figures carved in Wood supporting a Table, by John Sanderson.

It was on 2 June, at the second of two dinners given by the Bishop of Rochester in a week, that John met William Markham, a future Archbishop of York. He was about eight years the younger and working for his D.C.L. The meeting was of no particular importance to either of them, but of some

---

[k] 'The ruins have perished.'

[l] Only the tower still remains of the ancient palace of the Archbishops of Canterbury.

[m] Genesis 21, v.15, *The Angel Calls Abraham*. The four great biblical paintings were by Hogarth, Hayman, Highmore and James Wills, all given by the artists. John was kinder in his assessment of Wills and Hayman. This was the Foundling Hospital's first address in Hatton Garden.

interest to two of their direct descendants who joined their families through matrimony nearly 200 years later.

John took his little daughter to Mrs Price's school at Dorchester in September and then went once more to the Abbey to look at a monument which Leland had described but which, he said, neither Hearne nor Anthony Wood had ever been able to find.

> . . . but some Months since on taking up a Stone that made part of the floor in the North Isle of the Nave, it proved to be a Monument turned with the face downwards; it is a painted figure and perfect (except that the hands are wanting) of a Bishop recumbent . . . habited and mitred . . . I call it the figure of a Bishop and not of an Abbot . . . and we can assign it to no one with higher probability than this Aeschwine who dyed about 995 according to B. Willis in his 2nd Quarto of Cathedrals.[2]

It is still thought likely that the effigy represents Bishop Aeschwine or Aescwig, but the problem has not been finally resolved.[n]

John went on to Magdalen for two nights and this time he visited George Ballard, whom – surprisingly, since Hearne had liked him – he had never met. Ballard, who came of humble Gloucestershire stock, had earned the respect of scholars by his antiquarian efforts. Influenced particularly by Browne Willis and William Talbot, vicar of Kineton, Dr Jenner, the President, gave him a position in 1750 as one of eight clerks at Magdalen. In 1748 he was displaying his collection of manuscripts and coins at Clements's Coffee House in Oxford. John, who became increasingly tied to Dorothy's demands, never saw him again, but they carried on a regular correspondence from this time – Ballard always a little obsequious (as he felt befitted his station in life), John friendly and courteous. He gave Ballard a good deal of help with his *Memoirs of Several Ladies of Great Britain*[o] and was repaid with gifts of copies of various manuscripts which had come into the antiquary's possession.

Later on in October he took Dorothy to call on Captain and Mrs Arthur Forrest who had come to The Grove at Emmer Green nearby. When they returned the call they brought with them the Captain's sister, Penelope, a quiet and charming girl with impeccable manners. This could not be said of the Captain's wife, to whom John took an immediate dislike: Mrs Arthur was selfish, imperious, extravagant and almost impossible to live with, amusing as her eccentricities seemed later to William Hickey[3] and some of her other

---

[n] *V.C.H., Oxon*, VI, p. 60 gives Aeschwine (the Saxon bishop whose effigy had disappeared when Anthony Wood visited the church in 1657) as a possibility. I am obliged to Mr Percy Beak for the information that although this is a favoured interpretation, the problem lies in the fact that there is no knowledge of a bishop having been buried there after the transfer of the see to Lincoln.

[o] The book came out in 1752. John sent many suggestions about learned ladies between 1751 and 1753 (Bodl. MSS. Ballard. 37).

friends. Captain Forrest had inherited property in Jamaica from his father, Thomas, and they would have been substantially well off but for his wife's increasing prodigality. His mother, who often stayed with them though her home was in London, was a daughter of Arthur Miller a non-juror Bishop of Edinburgh and later on she became a frequent and much-loved guest at Caversham.

Mary was not the only one to be packed off to school, for on 9 February 1749

> Breakfasted at Hiley's, putting my Son under his care – under the same excellent Master who brought me up.

Jacky was also under the charge of Mr Dore, once the dancing master; but Mr Hiley was only to be there for two more years – in 1750 he retired and went with his wife to his living at Saltford. John was raising his children on the lines which had been prescribed for himself and Patty, but Dolly's health may have had something to do with the fact that Mary was sent much further away and that Jacky sometimes went to stay with his grandmother Sarah for as much as two months at a time. On the other hand the girls' school run by the Misses Eades had apparently by now been closed.

With his account of Silchester being read before the Royal Society in February and his notes on the image at Dorchester awaiting the comments of the Society of Antiquaries, John, with Ward's lively assistance, was developing his own reputation as an antiquarian. He had also become interested in the history of some of the Huguenot families, especially, of course, that of the Lethieulliers. Lady Hopkins had been provided with a good deal of information on this subject by a cousin of theirs, James Burrow, and John now began to correspond with him as well.

Burrow, who was also a member of the learned societies, had been Master of the Crown Office since 1733. He became well known for the excellence of his law reports and was later knighted. His grandfather, Sir Christopher Lethieullier, who had married Jane Du Cane, was a brother of John's grandfather, William Lethieullier of Clapham. According to his epitaph[p] James Burrow was an easy and convivial character who liked others to be informal and cheerful. In a letter to John dated 7 June 1749 he gave further information about himself.

> I honour Sir Christopher for his exact Punctuality. For I am myself very accurate in Things of small Consequence; the sure Mark of a small Genius! (Not that I think the Reverse to be a certain Indication of a great one.)[4]

There was very little he did not know about this large and complex family and John acknowledged his indebtedness to him. It was often very difficult in those days to trace one's own pedigree and many people could not prove their

---

[p] The epitaph is in Lingfield church. Burrow was buried in the chancel (D.N.B.).

descent further back than the lifetime of their grandfathers. However, his acquaintanceship with the Revd John Fortrie of Washington, Sussex, enabled him, by filling a gap in Burrow's rendering of the family tree, to link the Lethieullier and de la Forterie families in 1627.[q]

He managed to get away for three days in July when he and Thomas Winchester rode through Basingstoke on a journey to inspect the tomb of William of Wykeham in Winchester Cathedral which had been repaired since his last visit. He made a good many notes at Basingstoke where he admired the church except for the chancel, which he called

> a very incoherent Botch, low and mean . . . consisting of a Body and a South Isle only . . . the South Isle of the Chancel is inclosed from the rest; the East part of it is a Vestry; the larger remainder a Library . . . Very many of the Books are embezzled . . .

He was more interested in the ruined chapel and the school founded by the first Lord Sandys[r] They had been closed and allowed to decay during the Civil War and now little remained of the chapel but the south and east walls with a hexagonal turret at the angle.

> The East end of the Chappel is triangular, a Window in each of the three sides; there are three Windows in the South side, then a door with a square Window over it, then the turret . . . the materials of the Chappel are brick faced with free stone and curiously ornamented; there are Niches for Statues with Canopies and with Pedestals supporting the Niches between each of the long Windows, and again at each angle of the Turret.

Nothing remained of the roof which Camden had described.

> Just West of the Chappel is a large regular room, deplorably out of repair, which says Loggon, p. 19.[5] is the only Chappel and School-room that has been of use of late years; I suppose we may say from the year 1670, agreeably to the Latin Inscription printed in Loggon. . which is on the West wall of the room, on one side the Window, specifying that in that year by Bishop Morley's care the Estate belonging to the Chappel was restored; and I presume from the very time of the Civil Wars to that year there had been no Schooling at all. . . Mr Loggon is the Chaplain and Schoolmaster, but there has not been a Scholar for some few years past. There is a stipend of 10£ per Annum left to the Schoolmaster on condition that he be appointed by the Corporation.

[q] The link was through the marriage of John Lethieullier of Lewisham and Jane, daughter of John de la Forterie, a London merchant whose likeness, drawn in 1622, now belonged to his great-great-nephew, Thomas Chiffinch of Northfleet, Kent, according to a de la Forterie pedigree which James Burrow gave to Lady Hopkins. (L.F.P.) Chiffinch was the great-nephew of William, closet-keeper to James II. See p. 275.

[r] Lord Sandys was buried in 1540 in the now ruined Chapel of the Holy Ghost.

So far the year had been happy enough. Dolly had been able to go about once the spring had come and to entertain John's friends, including Dr Jenner who had been President of Magdalen since the death of Edward Butler in 1745. Patty's third daughter, Elizabeth, was born in August, but that same month brought great sorrow to John with the death of Charles Hopson at the early age of forty. Of all his many friends, this one had always been the closest and dearest from the days of their boyhood; it was a bitter loss. It was also in August that his mother came to dine for the last time: the arthritis from which she suffered finally prevented her from moving again, though she lived on for a number of years. September was only memorable for the fact that he saw two ostriches on the Thames at Purley, an occurrence so inexplicable that it cannot be commented on. (Had it been a few years later they might have escaped from Medmenham where Sir Francis Dashwood is said to have received some unusual birds and beasts.)

On 26 November Dr Winchester left Oxford to ride down to Caversham and it occurred to him that he might stop at the school at Dorchester to see Mary and take any message she might have for her father. To his unutterable horror he was told the little girl had died at eleven o'clock the previous night of a bilious attack. There was nothing for it but to ride on, the bearer of the terrible news to the unsuspecting family. Their anguish can be imagined: Dolly was distraught and to John the news was the worst blow he had ever experienced, except for the death of Mary's mother. Now this frail link with Anna Maria was tragically broken and there was only Jacky left. Mary was buried at Caversham five days later. 'My truly affectionate and beloved daughter was buryed in the Family-Vault in the Evening.'

A few days later he wrote to Mrs Goodwin. He had not seen her since the day he had gone to Oxford after leaving Mary at school, when she had come down from Warwick and they had supped together at the King's Head in the Cornmarket and taken leave of each other rather sadly. No one could understand better than she the thoughts he could not bear to set down as he reaffirmed his loyalty and devotion.

Honoured Madam, Your very affectionate letter contains very cogent arguments for a total submission to the divine Will; God grant they may have a proper effect on the hearts of all concerned! The good Professor advises us to turn our thoughts to the Blessings still vouchsafed us, and there he says (and with great truth) we shall still find room for abundant thanksgiving. These things are surely designed to loosen us from the earth we so cling to, reminding us that we are but sojourners here, and should not therefore be so fond of this great Inn the lower World, as though it were our home, our abiding Place, which we trust is in Heaven; there, in that great Society, of which the souls of men made perfect is a part, we (if we fall not from God's grace and are wanting to ourselves) shall again meet our departed friends, they amazed at our glorified appearance, we equally congratulating theirs; this must be part of the meaning of 'Thy Kingdom come', a Kingdom in which we shall reign together with Christ. Let us then join with one heart and voice in the following Petition, – may, our Father, thy will be done on earth as it is in heaven!

My Boy and yours sends his Duty to his dear Grandmother; he increases in health, strength and intellectual faculties. Dolly's poor Nerves have received such a shock as cannot be got over soon; she desires her unfeigned compliments to you. Don't think it possible, Dear Madam, that any event can ever diminish the extreme affection I bear towards you; I shall ever honour and esteem you as a Parent, and am convinced you will ever look on me as your Son; this is too tender a subject to dwell upon; a line more would mingle my tears with the ink.[6]

He ended his letter with titbits of local news which she loved to hear. She took an intense interest in events in Reading and Caversham, whether it was a son and heir for the young Cadogans or a dozen cows carried off by distemper; indeed in normal times there was nothing she liked better than letters from her young friends and relations, and three in particular did their best to gratify her curiosity – John Loveday, John Warner and a great-niece of her husband's called Susannah Myster.[5] Susannah's father had lived at Hornton, near Banbury, made a fortune and moved to Epsom. Her sister had recently married the Member of Parliament for York, William Thornton, a man of parts who had raised a troop of volunteers against the Young Pretender and who later became Colonel of the West Riding Militia. Thornton was a great sportsman, father of the Thomas Thornton who is said to have revived falconry in England and whose *Sporting Tours* are well known.[7] He lived at Cattall, near York and Susannah had gone there with the newly married couple. She had written to her great-aunt on 12 September 1749, but it was not the wedding she sat down to describe as much as the trousseaux of both bride and groom, which seem to have been of paramount importance. She had been delayed in writing, as at each attempt

so sure am I to be called upon to go a fishing, setting, coursing or some such diversion; for Mr Thornton will not be easy without we are both with him from morning till night; except those letters I wrote to my Papa I have not been able to write one since I left Epsom . . . You will perhaps be glad to know about the Wedding which I will readily give you; the courtship lasted not long, every thing proving to the entire satisfaction of the parties concerned. My Papa in this, as he has always done, shewed himself one of the best of Fathers – he gave with my Sister ten thousand pounds down besides three hundred pound for Cloaths; I

---

[5] Mary Goodwin, sister of William Goodwin (d. 1744) married John Myster, yeoman of Hornton in 1686. Their son, John, became a wealthy merchant at Epsom. Susannah was his younger daughter.

don't know whether I should have mentioned this, therefore hope you will keep it as a secret; the settlement my Sister has is a thousand pound per annum. Her best suit is a gold Stuff, a very handsome one – it cost fifty guineas; the second is pink and silver, a lustring Sack, a white and silver night gown, a flowered one, a pink tabby; and washing ones besides; a Point Head &c. two other dressed suits and the rest undressed; all the laces are very good. My Papa divided the jewels he had between us, my Sister's share went towards making a diamond cross which is very large, and is so contrived that she can wear it, in Stars down her Stays, and in other shapes besides; her Ear-Rings are very handsome. My share of the jewels are the earrings which were new set for me; the cloaths I had for the occasion are a blue and silver suit, and a plain yellow suit. Mr Thornton's cloaths are a light-coloured flowered velvet turned up with a gold Stuff, and a gold waistcoat; and a brown cloth trimmed with silver and several embroidered waistcoats. My Papa made a blue coat trimmed with gold. The writings being signed and the cloaths made, nothing remained but to tye the knot for which purpose on the 11th of July the Bride and Bridegroom elect, with my Papa and self, set out from Charterhouse Square at 8 in the morning and went to Beddington where the ceremony was performed and from thence we went to Epsom where we staid three weeks; during our stay there we were fully engaged in receiving and paying of visits and in then shewing Mr Thornton the places thereabouts. At last the fatal day arrived when I was to bid adieu to my dear Papa for four months . . . and I shall not be happy till I see him again; it is certain one don't know the value one has for a Parent, till one is parted from them . . .[8]

Susannah's own husband, to whom she was married in 1754, was very different from Mr Thornton. The Revd John Parkhurst, a Biblical lexicographer, was short, studious and of sedentary habits. It was a happy marriage, blessed by three children, but Susannah died of cancer in 1759. A letter from her husband shows that she died very courageously, locking the door so that he should not be too distressed, and gives the impression of a very sweet woman.[9] She was survived both by her father and by her husband, who remarried and lived for another forty years.

Charles Hopson's widow, Anne, was a great favourite with everyone and her friends in Caversham and Reading made a point of driving over to Beenham to cheer her up. Peter Zinzan was one of the most frequent callers and, finding each other's company infinitely more desirable than a solitary life, they were married in February 1750. To the Lovedays this union of two such great friends was a matter for quiet rejoicing, knowing that Charles had known and liked Zinzan all his life and would have wished his young wife to have a happy and secure future.

With the coming of spring John, though never a great horticulturist, began to examine his garden. He did not like the damage the snails were doing, living happily in the high wall between the garden and the church, so at the cost of £1.0s.11d. (or 2d. a hundred) he had as many as possible destroyed, noting in his diary that some 12,550 had been accounted for. Later in the year he widened a walk in his 'warren', formerly the old rectory rabbit warren. Spring, too, brought a number of visitors to Caversham, including Ward, Winchester and Payne, and he enjoyed the chance of taking them to see his neighbouring friends; Dolly's health had not improved this year and she preferred people to visit her. But just as he was becoming reconciled to the horror of Mary's death and his natural resilience had even begun to lift him up, he received another terrible blow. Patty, finding the effects of the waters at Sunninghill were disappointing, had gone to the Bristol spa, where, before her marriage, they had been beneficial. She had not been well since the birth of her last baby, but it was a completely unexpected shock to hear on 4 May from poor William that she had died there suddenly, far from her home and children. John did not cancel a visit from the other two Williams, Goodwin and Taylor, a fortnight later, but for the rest of the year he spent most of the time in his study.

His chief correspondence at that time was with that eccentric figure Dr Richard Rawlinson. John had known him since he first went to Oxford, but the renewal between them of letters and gifts of books was partly due to his own friendship with William Derham, now President of St John's College, of which Rawlinson was a Fellow. Rawlinson was now about sixty years of age, unmarried and extremely touchy, not at all the sort of man to cope with the embarrassing situation in which he had recently found himself. Derham had told John about it in December 1749, when writing to him about a manuscript from Rawlinson's vast collection.

I prevailed with one of our young Gentlemen to transcribe the Anecdote relating to the good Arch-Bishop, who drew his first Breath in your neighbourhood, though at first Sight of it he looked as shy as if I had been entrusting him with some of the Treasures of the Levant. However he has by his great Sagacity extricated it from the Arabico – Britannick Characters in which you saw it at Caversham. The poor Doctor from whom I had it, is under great affliction for the loss of a Nephew' abroad, by which four young Ladies are thrown upon his Hands. You are no Stranger to his generous Intentions towards our University and in particular towards this College, and will not therefore wonder, that he should in his Letters to me and others very pathetically lament this Interruption of several very agreeable Schemes he had formed, some (Take his own Words) for the 'Benefit of the Publick.'[10]

' Richard Rawlinson was one of fifteen children and family trees do not give details of them all. The name of the nephew who died abroad may not have been Rawlinson.

The Doctor's 'generous intentions' were handsomely realized on his death in 1755. Derham (who survived him by two years) received on the College's behalf not only the legacies but the donor's actual heart. It is preserved in the chapel.

While John was spending the summer of 1750 at home, the Warners had suddenly, to their surprise and delight, found themselves whisked away on a magical tour by the young and popular Lord Litchfield and his wife Diana. Although they knew them fairly well, since John Warner's father lived at Ditchley, it was not really to be expected that such an invitation should come their way. After three years of marriage, punctuated by the births of two daughters and harassed by a long tussle with brother William Goodwin's uncompromising attitude towards their marriage settlement, they were quite ready to leave the parish of Cherington to its own devices, at least for a short spell. Lord Litchfield, at the age of thirty-two, was known as a jovial companion and a man of the world. Warner explained to Mrs Goodwin how it had come about and described their journey in two letters in July. It was only as appendages to their aristocratic friends that they could ever have had the entrée to so many houses, not as tourists but as guests. That Lord Litchfield was interested in gardening is indicated by his choice of places to visit, culminating with the hospitality of the King's gardener. Pains Hill, Woburn Farm, and Oatlands were among those where the grounds were of particular renown.

Guild Hall, July 10th. 1750

You will wonder to see a letter from me dated from this place, but I found that the scheme was to entice us to Oxford and then to press us to undertake the future expedition. On Monday, the third of July we set out for Oxford and in the afternoon were entertained in the Theatre with an elegant speech from the Orator" wherein he commemmorated the benefactors to the University which being finished there was an elegant piece of Musick performed to the satisfaction of a Numerous Audience. On Tuesday morning my Lord and Lady declared they would not part with us, and as there were two places in the Landau, he insisted upon it that they should be filled by us; this being the case I could no longer resist and having sent our horses to Cherington, we set out on Tuesday last for Mr Powis's woods' which gave great satisfaction to our company; from thence we proceeded for the Crown at Reading, and in our way stopped at Caversham where my wife and I staid for about an hour; Mr Loveday was so overjoyed to see us, and made so much Noise, that the drums of our ears were almost broke, he is pure well as is the little fellow – Mrs Loveday but indifferent. On Wednesday we set out for Sir Harry Englefield's'" which I think is very well worth seeing, from thence we

" The Public Orator was Roger Mather.
' Hardwick House, Oxon.
'" Whiteknights.

went to the Orkney Arms at Maidenhead bridge, and there we saw
Taplow,[x] and did intend to visit Cliefden, but the Prince's being there
put a stop to our design; in the afternoon we visited Windsor Castle and
lay at the Windmill at Slough. On Thursday morning we saw my Lord
Lincoln's,[y] dined at Weybridge, in the afternoon saw Mr Hamilton's at
Cobham,[z] lay there and the next morning went to Clermont,[a] Esher,[b]
and dined with Mr Southcote at Woburn Farm, which is the most
elegant place I ever saw in my life. On Fryday night we lay at Hounslow;
the next morning we saw the Duke of Argyle's[c] and from thence
proceeded to Hampton Court where we dined with Mr Lee, the King's
Gardener, and in the Evening arrived at this place. On Sunday brother
Tim and the Professor met us here, they are extremely well and send
duty and respects to you. On Monday we dined with my Lord and Lady,
and in the Evening went with them to Vauxhall, where Uncle [d] and Tim
met us, supped with our company and restored us hither in his Coach
betwixt 1 and 2 in the Morning. Tim is now here and will be so for this
whole day. My wife is brave and well and I think the Journey has been of
Service to her. On Thursday we set out from the great Town and in our
way home we are to see Mr Waller's at Beaconsfield,[e] Mr Drake's at
Amersham,[f] Sir William Stanhope's[g] and Sir Francis Dashwood's,[h] so
that it will be uncertain what day we shall arrive at Cherington. We
visited the Milliner's yesterday, and whilst I was laying out Money
there, I could not help sending you a small though sincere testimony
of our love, of which I beg your acceptance. My Uncle desires his
Compliments . . .[11]

The next letter was written from Cherington on 20 July.

. . . after I had sent you my account, we went to Vauxhall and the next
evening to Ranelagh and Marybone Gardens, but my Uncle was so

[x] Although Cliveden was owned by Anne, Countess of Orkney and her husband, the 4th
Earl of Inchiquin, their home was Taplow Court at this time and Cliveden was leased to the
Prince of Wales.
[y] Lord Lincoln (later 2nd Duke of Newcastle) lived at Oatlands, near Weybridge.
[z] Pains Hill, Surrey, an early example of landscape gardening, was laid out by the Hon.
Charles Hamilton in 1729. He was the sixth son of the 6th Earl of Abercorn.
[a] Claremont was the seat of the 1st Duke of Newcastle.
[b] Esher Place belonged to the Hon. Henry Pelham, younger brother of the 1st Duke of
Newcastle.
[c] Known then as the Duke of Argyll's House, it was later called Whitton Place. The 3rd
Duke's main seat was Inveraray.
[d] Miles Man, Town Clerk of London.
[e] Hall Barn.
[f] Amersham Manor was the seat of William Drake.
[g] Sir William Stanhope, second son of the 3rd Earl of Chesterfield, lived at Eythrope
Manor, Buckinghamshire.
[h] West Wycombe Park.

careful of my Wife that he would not suffer her to go upon the water, which deprived her of a good deal of pleasure she proposed from that scheme. Brother Tim and the Professor spent their whole time with us whilst we were in Town; Tim gives us some small hopes of visiting you this Summer, but they must not be depended upon. After we left Town which was on the 12th of July, we came to Mr Waller's at Beaconsfield, saw his gardens and lay at High Wycomb, and the next day we went to Sir Francis Dashwood's at West Wycomb, which is indeed the most delightful place and my Lord and the rest of the company were so captivated with it that Sir Francis would not part with us till Monday last, when we dined at Tetsworth, went to the Musick meeting at Oxford, lay there that night and the next day we arrived at Ditchley, and on Wednesday we all paid the Wedding visit to Mr and Mrs Brown[i] and returned here in Mr Sheldon's coach in the Evening. I need not tell you how agreeable home is to us, we found our children perfectly well and in great spirits. My Wife joins with me in duty to you, she is very well . . . and, I do think upon the whole, is a good deal better for the journey.[12]

Ill health had by now forced James Merrick to return permanently to Reading and to devote himself to his studies at home. Kind Bishop Secker continued to take a great interest in his work, (being a fine scholar himself) and also in his physical well-being; he believed that riding cured most ailments and was out on his horse at six o'clock every morning.[13] He adjured Merrick to do the same and wrote to this effect from Cuddesdon on 3 August.

Good Mr Merrick, I heartily thank God that you are so much recovered and pray him to perfect his work. I am glad too that you do not neglect riding. I fear you did before you apprehended the importance of it. But now I am persuaded that you will think it your Duty to do whatever you are directed to; and your Business to be idle in respect of study, that you may apply afterwards to better purpose . . .

I here send you a list of such little Books,[14] as, amongst those that have fallen my way, seemed to me the properest for my Parish and Diocese. But others may be fitter for other places. I suppose you know that a subscriber member of the Society for promoting Christian Knowledge[j] may have them at half price. Your two noble pupils did me the Honour and pleasure of dining with me on Thursday. I hope to return their visit before they go to Wroxton.[15]

The two noble pupils were Lord North, the future Prime Minister, and his

---

[i] George Browne of Kiddington succeeded to the baronetcy the following year. William Sheldon was a brother of the bride, Mrs Fermor. Weston House, his home, was close to Cherington.

[j] The S.P.C.K. was instituted at the end of the seventeenth century.

stepbrother, William Legge, who became the 2nd Earl of Dartmouth later that year. They had matriculated at Trinity College in 1749, North receiving his M.A. degree in 1750, Dartmouth in 1751. There is no record of Merrick having taught them in the list of matriculands and their tutors in the College, but writing to Jacques d'Orville in 1758[16] he mentioned the 'two young persons of quality' who had been his pupils at Oxford. It is clear from their own letters to him that the young men were and remained extremely fond of him. Lord North's father, Lord Guilford, spoke of the sincere regard and esteem in which he held Merrick when he wrote to him as a subscriber to his metrical version of the Psalms.

> . . . I am extreamly sensible of the obliging things you are so good as to say with respect to the young Men of my Family. I have been so fortunate as to put them into very good hands, and they have answered the care and pains bestowed upon them. They make me very happy; and it is a Blessing of which I am truly sensible . . .[17]

Bishop Secker occasionally came to preach at Caversham and it was in August 1751, when he was staying with Lord Cadogan, that an amusing incident took place, described later by John's daughter Penelope. She began by discussing her father's admiration for the Bishop on account of his 'exemplary goodness' and his 'unwearied efforts to do all the good he could to others'. John had also admired his sermons as being 'universally useful'.

> He remarked that South and Secker comprised more in their Sermons than was sometimes spun out into a volume by other writers; and thought Secker's manner of introducing passages from Scripture particularly beautiful. He lamented that the language was not better, the length of sentences often making the style perplexed to those who were not in the habits of reading it; but he said whoever heard him preach found all as clear as possible from his manner of being plain and impressive and suited to this style. My Father spoke with the highest indignation of Pope's insolently protecting line, in which he merely says of this pious and excellent Prelate – Secker is decent.

It was Pope's verdict in *Epilogue to the Satires* which gave rise to some merriment on the afternoon of Secker's visit. Having given them all dinner the night before, Lord Cadogan and his son Charles brought the Bishop, Dr Burton and the Revd Samuel Walker of Whitchurch to call on the Lovedays next morning. After the service the three clergymen stayed for dinner. It was a beautiful day and there at the bottom of the garden was the river. It is still possible to stand beside the old boathouse, now known as the gazebo, and to see in the mind's eye three middle-aged gentlemen embarking in their boat and taking it out on that wide and tranquil stretch of the Thames – the slight figure of the youngest, John Loveday, the burly form of Dr Burton and the tall commanding presence[18] of the future Archbishop of Canterbury.

My father [wrote Penelope] was on the water with the Bishop when Dr John Burton, Vicar of Mapledurham, chose to assist in rowing and was throwing off his coat for the purpose; the bishop pleasantly exclaimed 'No, learned Doctor, remember that Secker is decent'; he added 'What a sight would this be to those who might be inclined to say that "the proud Prelate of Oxford was rowed by one of his Incumbents."'

John's own efforts in 1751 were largely directed towards his correspondence with George Ballard which began in May. He took Dolly and Jack to Warwickshire for the usual round of visits, finishing with a few days at Wexham where William Gibson lived with his daughters, having just 'accumulated his degree in Divinity going out Grand Compounder'. Apart from Honington Hall, where he described some pictures, there were no visits recorded to country houses. In July he spent a day or two with his friend John Cleeve at High Laver and a week at Low Leyton, during which he took his Aunt Hopkins to Hackney where Aunt Mary Tooke was failing and where she died in September.

Everyone was distressed about James Merrick's health and old Dr Merrick eventually consulted his son John, who was in practice at Isleworth. The nervous disorders and spasms of fever had not reduced his appetite, but he rose feeling ill, lax and fit for nothing. His mother thought he should not sleep under such a great pile of bedclothes, but his brother considered this beneficial and prescribed Glauber's Salts, though confessing he could not diagnose the trouble. John Loveday's remedy was to invite James to stay for a month in January 1752 and try a mixture of Caversham food and conversation. In March he managed to escape for a few days and rode down once again to the West Country. He picked Mr Hiley up at his Saltford rectory and together they made their way to Newton Park for a short visit to the Langtons who lived in the old house.[k] His notes began at Chippenham and continued at Bath where the Zinzans were staying.

> Chippenham Church Yard is very pleasant with a Walk round it. . . .
> Gilbert Lake, the Vicar here, who was Hearne's correspondent, dyed in 1730 and his Monument is in the Chancel. North in the Chancel is a Loft, made like a Balcony, which they call a Rood Loft, but it is not in the right situation for that; I should have taken it only for a family-gallery, had not the stone staircase to it been so narrow; after all, it has been conjectured to be a pulpit . . .[l]

[k] Joseph Langton rebuilt the house during 1762–65. See Graham Davis, *The Langtons at Newton Park*.
[l] The chancel was largely rebuilt in 1875–78. A broad Norman arch originally supported a fourteenth-century staircase which did not lead to the rood loft but perhaps to a minstrels' gallery. See also Revd J. J. Andrews, *History of Chippenham*.

Bath Square[m] is built on uneven ground for the expense would have been too great to have levelled it; both of the falling sides should have been alike; that which should have been the model to the other consists of three distinct roofings each lower than the other, in conformity to the slope of the ground, and has no bad effect in my eye . . .

Newton Park, Mr Langton's old Seat; though there be no park at present. It is in the parish of Newton St. Lo.

March 16. Badminton, the Duke of Beaufort's, is in a very damp situation on a cold clay, but the view from every window is delightful. It is a grand modern house of stone, exceedingly well furnished; one room has two Chinese Looking-Glasses. The Stairs are of Spanish Oak inlaid with a fillet of Mahogany. They have just made a light fretwork cieling of Paper[n] to the Library; it appears like stucho. The most beautiful Sarcophagus was a Present from Cardinal Alberoni to the late Duke; the great variety of figures on it are justly proportioned; there is no leaf or flower over the Nudities of the human figures nor is there any bust in an Oval — the sculpture goes round the front and two ends without any division into different compartments; it stands at one end of the hall (where are pictures by Wotton[o] of horses &c) upon four balls of marble, which are elevated upon a marble tomb or altar, but these were added when the Sarcophagus was put up here. Another grand observable is a very large Cabinet, amazingly magnificent and elegant; the ground of the main part is touchstone, inlaid with other stones in their native colours, so disposed as in the most lively manner to represent Birds, Flowers &c. Much of the Ornaments consist of lapis lazuli and porphyry; the Drawers are rosewood with ebony borders; a clock crowns the whole. There is a gallery of family pictures beginning with John of Gaunt. But the best pictures, with the cabinet and several very fine marble tables (one, though|not|very|large,|of porphyry), were the late Duke's purchases at Rome. Here is a Roman Charity in a different taste from that at Windsor or the other at Blenheim; it did not strike me much. But the Carton pencilled with charcoal deserves extraordinary regard; it is of St. Paul curing a boy possessed with a devil . . . 'tis great pity that the piece is damaged and some of the figures vanishing. This carton of Raphael represents the lower part of his Transfiguration-piece, the most capital and most highly celebrated picture of all those in the churches at Rome, the design of which is so well-known by the prints. The Carton belonged to one of the Cardinals of the name of Albani . . .

He returned on 20 March in good time to welcome his next guest, Dr

[m] Queen Square.

[n] A note added later reads 'papier mâché'. A patent for making papier mâché was not taken out by Henry Clay until 1772. See Elizabeth Burton, *The Georgians at Home*, 1967.

[o] John Wootton.

Edward Bentham,[p] and to prepare for a spring visit to Bromley. Meanwhile Thomas Bagshaw had, on 26 March, officiated at a funeral which would ensure his own name for posterity – the burial of Mrs Samuel Johnson.[q] The old church was destroyed in the Second World War and very little survived, but her memorial and his signature in the register confirming his involvement can still be seen. To Bagshaw this was an episode of great interest, increasingly so as the Doctor's reputation grew. Two letters to Thomas from Dr Johnson, one in connection with her epitaph and the other concerning his *Dictionary* are quoted in Boswell's *Life*. He had, besides, a personal connection through his friendship with John Hawkesworth who lived in Bromley and through whose good offices it probably was that Tetty's burial took place there.[19] While they were staying with the Bagshaws John spent an afternoon and evening at Hawkesworth's house for the first time. They had much in common, including an affection for the *Gentleman's Magazine* of which John Hawkesworth became literary editor in 1756 and to which John was to be a frequent contributor. No doubt they often met on his future visits until Hawkesworth's death in 1773 and it was probably on a later occasion than this that he gave John an amusing impression of Dr Johnson which he in turn recounted to Penelope.

> I recollect my Father's mentioning Dr Hawkesworth having, in conversation with him, remarked on Dr Johnson's very singular manner and appearance; and saying that he called on him one morning and that on hearing he had not yet risen he was on that footing of intimacy with him as to go to his chamber, which he entered unobserved by Johnson, who was reading in his bed, the collar of his shirt open, and, in the place of a night cap, a wig put on nearly hind part before – he was full of contortions whilst his eyes were steadily fixed on his book. This afforded Hawkesworth the opportunity of so far abstracting himself as to consider himself in the situation of a stranger viewing this extraordinary appearance and to deliberate on whether he was to consider the object before him as a fool or a madman; – and he decided on the former.

After staying a night with Richard Lluellyn at Saunderton in Buckinghamshire, where he now held the living, they arrived home in time for John Spicer's marriage to Miss Margaret Chapman. Spicer had returned from Cork, where he acted as chaplain to the late Colonel Hopson's regiment, in order to take over the headmastership of the school on Mr Hiley's retirement in 1750. He had been both a pupil and an usher under his predecessor, whose faith in his abilities was justifiable. But for the Lovedays there was more sorrow and trouble ahead. William Gibson's career had flourished and he had become Archdeacon of Essex, but his health had deteriorated. In August he sent his

[p] Later Regius Professor of Divinity.
[q] I am grateful to Miss Muriel H. Hughes for information about Bromley and for showing me the parish registers. See also p. 358 n.*j*.

three children, Anne, Sarah and Elizabeth, to stay at Caversham and they were still there when on 31 October John received a letter, sent by hand from George Gibson in Kensington with 'the fatal news'.

> It is with inexpressible concern that I acquaint you with the Death of our dear Brother Dr Gibson, which happened about 11 this Morning attended with such a degree of true Christian Patience and Resignation as could not but administer much comfort to all about him.[20]

He went up to London for the funeral at Fulham where William was buried in the Gibson family vault. Next day he went to stay with George in Whitehall to discuss the future of the three little orphans. A week later they went down to Windsor together where they were received with great kindness by the Dean, Dr Peniston Booth, and some of William's fellow canons and were also visited by John Burton who was at Eton at the time. Everyone was shocked by the tragedy. Dolly met them at William's home, bringing little 'Nancy', now seven years old, for a last night there. It was agreed that she and her sisters should spend most of their time with George and his wife at this stage of their lives, but should take long holidays at Caversham as well. It was a terrible grief to them to lose two such good parents in two years but they could not have had kinder uncles to care for their future.

As soon as this sad business was settled John became deeply engrossed in a political cause, an unusual diversion for him. The campaign for the famous Oxfordshire election of 1754 – the first county election there for nearly fifty years – had begun in August 1752 with a meeting attended by the principal freeholders who supported the Old Interest, namely the Tories. At this meeting Lord Wenman, the member for the city, and Sir James Dashwood, one of the present members for the county, had been elected as candidates. There is no evidence of John being present – he would not have qualified as a principal freeholder as far as his residence was concerned' but he had taken note of what was going on. Knowing that Lord Cadogan supported the New Interest and would not be representing the Tory freeholders in Caversham, he felt himself to be the right person to organize them. As has been seen, he was no Jacobite though he was a Tory by upbringing and inclination. Charges of connivance with their Roman Catholic neighbours, levelled against supporters of the Old Interest by the Whigs, could not be maintained, though in John's case his relationship with them was perfectly amicable. On the whole his own University friends favoured Wenman and Dashwood, with the exception of the Christ Church contingent who followed the Whig Bishop Secker. There was some animosity among the dons but not in the country, except from a few quarrelsome squires; John would continue to dine with Lord Cadogan or entertain Bishop Secker, regarding politics as outside the normal obligations

---

' This was on a Christ Church lease.

of hospitality and polite behaviour. He wrote to Lord Wenman on 21 November to offer his services. That he chose Wenman was probably due to his kinsmanship with the Bertie family; indeed it was his old acquaintance Norrys Bertie[5] – the present member with Dashwood for the county – who, not wishing to continue, had suggested his cousin Lord Wenman in his place. A reply arrived within three days, written on 22 November from Thame Park.

> I received the favour of yours on Sunday last in my way to Sir James Dashwood's or otherwise should have returned you my thanks by the bearer. We are both of us extremely obliged to you for the great assistance you have given us and shall take proper care of all our friends as soon as possible, for which purpose I have deposited some money in Mr John Clerke's hands (who has been an exceeding good Friend of ours) and will, I believe, véry soon call on you to consult what will be proper to be done till I can have the pleasure of seeing you, which I hope for the beginning of next week. Sir James Dashwood desires his compliments and thanks, as does your much obliged and Humble Servant, Wenman.
>
> PS. If anything of consequence should happen before I can wait on you I shall take it as a particular favour if you'll acquaint me with it.[21]

He appeared in person at Caversham six days later to be followed by his agent, Browne, who stayed for three nights and came back after a few days. Altogether it was a very prompt and thorough investigation, considering that Caversham only had about sixty freeholders all told. John had probably sent a preliminary list with his first letter and during the next year he went into the matter with all his natural efficiency. It was not always easy to determine whether a man was a freeholder at all and he had to include those who lived in Caversham but whose property was elsewhere and those who held land in the parish but were not resident. Then there was the question of the names being disqualified by the opposing candidates and he had the satisfaction of getting one removed by Lord Wenman and saving two Old Interest voters from the claws of Sir Edward Turner and Lord Parker.[t] He found one freeholder who had land in Caversham and lived in Henley, but it must be a matter for conjecture as to whether John's was one of the fifteen coaches which followed Wenman and Dashwood into that town on 15 December accompanied by trumpets, drums and French horns, not to mention 568 banners.[22].

The election was still many months away and besides making his lists and doing some canvassing he had plenty of other things to engage his attention. The first and worst of these was the death in April of Mary Warner, most probably in childbirth. 'Dyed my sister . . . something under twenty-eight

[5] A son of James Bertie of Springfield, Essex.
[t] Candidates in the New Interest.

years of age and was buryed in Guildhall Chapel,' wrote John in his diary
and the simple words reflect a bewilderment that this should have happened
again. Except for Mary Addington and his cousins Anne Bootle and Sarah
Tooke, now Mrs Philip Bromfield, she was the last and the youngest of the
girls he had known best and it was another link broken with the memory of
Anna Maria. Now there were two more little motherless girls, but these at least
had a father. John Warner mourned his wife sincerely enough but he had a
palliative in his enthusiasm for collecting old glass and placing it in the
windows of Cherington church. When the dining-room windows at the
Brownes' house at Kiddington were altered in 1750 he had been allowed to
remove some beautiful armorial shields for this purpose and he was gradually
accumulating more glass.[23] In 1755 he took a second wife, Elizabeth Ashhurst
of Waterstock." It was a happy marriage which brought them a son, George,
and she was a particularly charming person to whom John Loveday's children
became completely devoted; but John Warner was never entirely *persona grata*
with Mrs Goodwin.

John had hoped to visit Oxford with Ward in April 1753, but was prevented
– as he explained in a letter to George Ballard:

> The dread of Small-Pox will infallibly keep Professor Ward at a proper
> distance from Oxford during the Easter-holydays; otherwise it was much
> his intention to have paid you a visit at that time and I had promised myself
> a great deal of pleasure in bearing him company to you; but so it is that this
> pleasure must necessarily be postponed; and he and I must rest contented
> in drinking your better health at above twenty miles distance from you.[24]

Ballard had still not been able to overcome an apparent lack of confidence in
himself, of which a letter in March had been typical.

> When you do me the honour of reading my Book be so good, Sir, as
> note down the mistakes you find and transmit them to me at your leisure. I
> doubt not but your Candour and good-nature will make proper
> allowances for the want of Learning, Capacity and Judgment in worthy
> Sir, your most devoted humble Servant.[25].
>
> I beseech you [replied John] to lay aside your so great diffidence
> concerning the reception the knowing world will give it, of whose suf-
> rages you are secure.[26]

He reiterated the 'high entertainment and real instruction' he had received
from his valuable work; but towards the end of the year Ballard was becoming
increasingly ill with 'the stone' and John did not like to bother him with
many letters. He received one in January 1754, apologizing for the lack of a
frank.

" The names of John and Elizabeth Warner can be seen in the centre of the beautiful
window containing the coats of arms of the Ashhursts and allied families in Waterstock
church.

I am sorry I can't have the pleasure of seeing you here; Whenever you will do me that honour I will promise for your entertainment a larger set of Antiquaries than you can meet with at their Club at London. .[27]

In his last letter in February John replied that he begged Ballard once for all to take notice 'that no man living sets less by a Frank than I do' and that his letters would always abundantly overpay the postage;[28] but there were no more and eventually the sick man returned to Campden. The enjoyment they had both received from the exchange of manuscripts, books and information was over. In July 1755 John heard from the vicar of Kineton – William Talbot, Ballard's friend and patron – that he had died.

I don't know whether the News of poor Ballard's Death has yet reached your Ears. He finished a painful Life on Tuesday 25th and was interred on Friday. The Torture he underwent for some months before his Death made us all who were witnesses to it rejoice at his Release . . . never was there a more just Behaviour under Sufferings than he manifested, as indeed all his Life has been exemplary from his Youth, and now he is gone according to his own assured but humble Expectation to reap the Reward of it. I helped to close his Eyes, having just finished the recommendatory Prayer as he expired.[29]

John's share of the bequests Ballard had left to his friends was a beautiful old missal and two rare books. 'I daresay you will receive the Legacy with an Esteem of it much beyond its intrinsic value,'[30] said Talbot and indeed it was the kind of gift which touched John's heart and would always remind him of this kind and trusting soul.

One of the copies Ballard had sent him was from a manuscript which has not been traced in his collections.[31] It was of especial interest to John both because of a new glimpse of history and for its connection with Lathom House, the mansion in Lancashire which Captain Bootle's brother, Sir Thomas, had bought in 1722 from Henry Furnese. Thomas Pennant[32] relates the tale that the 9th Earl of Derby had refused to sell him a house at Bootle, thinking that as he had made a fortune as a successful lawyer he was a 'new man'. Sir Thomas 'with proper spirit' sent word that if he could not be a Bootle of Bootle he was resolved he'd be Bootle of Lathom; but the Earl died twenty years before this came about and the house had already been sold once to Furnese in 1717 by the Earl's daughter, the Countess of Ashburnham. Bootle, who became Chancellor to Prince Frederick and was knighted in 1746, was no upstart; his family had been 'gentlemen of the county' near Bootle for generations.[v] He rebuilt Lathom House and on his death in January 1754 it passed to his brother and then to his niece Mary, a woman of

[v] V.C.H., Lancs., III, p. 246. Sir Thomas himself was surprisingly called a 'dull and confused man' by John Croker, editor of Lady Suffolk's correspondence (John Murray, 1824). See Letters to and from Henrietta, Countess of Suffolk, vol. I, p. 342 (edited anonymously).

as redoubtable a spirit as his own. John Ward mentioned the Bootles in December 1753:

> Your letter . . . brought with it one directed to Sir James Foulis of Bombay[w] – to be delivered to Captain Bootle for a proper conveyance. I soon after waited on the Captain, who very readily undertook it. But at the same time he informed me, that in writing to those parts, it is usual to send a duplicate of the same letter by a different conveyance, for fear of a miscarriage. And as other ships will be going thither towards the latter end of February, if you think proper to take that method, he will then, as he said, take care of a proper conveyance for that letter in the like manner . . . When I saw Captain Bootle he told me that he was to set out the next morning for Oxford, to meet his brother, who was confined there by illness . . . As it has pleased God to visit your town with the distemper at this Season of the year, I would hope it may be well over by the time I promise myself the pleasure of paying you and Mrs Loveday my usual visit.[33]

Ballard had sent John the copy of the old letter in July 1753 saying that it contained a piece of history which he did not remember to have seen in print. Though it was unsigned it was evidently written by a son of Samuel Rutter, chaplain to the 7th Earl of Derby, whose wife Charlotte had so heroically defended Lathom House during the first siege.

> Sir, In pursuance to my promise, I have sent you the Story you desired of me when I saw you last. Sir, after the late King was beheaded (if I mistake not) Latham House which belonged to the Earle of Darby (who was also beheaded at Leverpoole) was surrendered to my Lord Fairfax upon promise of having quarter, at which surrendry my father being in the House and Chaplaine to the Earle, was taken prisoner with the Earle of Darby's Children, who were imprisoned in Leverpoole Gaoll, where he was kept close prisoner in the Dungeon, tho' the rest were permitted the liberty of the Gaoll yard; where I believe he would have layne till the King's returne or till death had set him at liberty, if it had not been his fortune to be freed by the following accident. The Patriarchs of Greece, hearing of the unparalled [sic] murder of our late King, by his own subjects, sent one of their own body as an Envoy over here into England, and his errand was this, to know of Oliver Cromwell and the rest, *by what Law either of God or Man, they put their King to death* – But the Patriarch speaking no other language, but the common Greek, and coming without an interpreter, no body understood him; and tho' there were many good Grecians (whose names I have forgott) were brought to him, yet they could not understand his Greek. Thereupon Lentale[x] who was speaker to

[w] Sir James served in India until 1753.
[x] William Lenthall.

the House of Commons, told them that there was in Prison one of the King's Party that understood the common Greek, who would interpret to them what the Patriarch said, if they would set him at liberty, and withall promise not to punish him if what he interpreted out of the Patriarch's words *that* reflected on them; which at last they were forced to do, tho' much against their Will. At last the day was set for hearing, where was present Cromwell, Bradshaw, and most of the late King's Judges, if not all; when the Patriarch came he wrote in the common Greek the aforesaid Sentence and signed it with his hand, after which my father turned it [into] other Greek, which when it was writ, he did (tho' with much adoe) understand, and set his hand to it; then my father turned it into Latin and English, and delivered it under his hand to Cromwell; that that was the business of the Patriarch's Embassy, who then returned him this answer, that they would consider of it, and in a short time send him their answer; but after a long stay, and many delays, the Patriarch was forced to return, as wise as he came. Upon the Patriarch's departure, they would have sent my father to prison again, but Lentale would not let them; saying that it was their promise that he should be at liberty; whereupon they sent for him, and commanded him to keep the Patriarch's Embassy private, and not to divulge it upon pain of imprisonment, if not of death. Then Lentale made him Preacher of the Roles, and my father bought him a Chamber in Grays Inne; which Chamber he afterwards parted with to Mr Barker, who now has the possession of them. This is the Relation which I have heard my Father oftentimes tell, and to the best of my knowledge, I have neither added nor diminished any thing.[34]

Love and War
1754 – 1762

Dolly was so unwell during the early months of 1754 that John became very anxious. As he explained to Ballard in February:

> I frequently wish myself with you, though the ill-health of Mrs Loveday has hitherto confined me at home: but as everyone that knows her, wishes her better health, who can say but their prayers may at last prevail?[1]

However, when he took her to Bromley in June she had rallied so much that she was able to go out with John in the evening, accompanied by Thomas Townson's delightful sister, Lucretia, who lived with their mother in Bromley College.

> July 1. With Bagshaw my wife and Miss Townson to London; with the first I breakfasted at Dr Nicholls;[a] then to see wild beasts, the Foundling Hospital and Reynolds's the Painter's; then to dine at the Star and Garter in Pellmell; then to the late Lord Archibald Hamilton's[b] and to Rysbrack's; with my wife and Miss Townson to Vauxhall.

[a] Dr Frank Nicholls, Richard Mead's son-in-law, was a lifelong friend of Thomas Bagshaw. His son, John, a less attractive character, married Patty's third daughter, Elizabeth Gibson, and was a constant source of annoyance to Jack (her trustee) and to Mary Wilbraham-Bootle.
[b] Probably a sale of books and prints. Lord Archibald, a widower, had died on 5 April 1754.

On his return from a visit to the Byes he found her well enough to join a family expedition, which included the twelve-year-old Jack, to William Lowth's parsonage at Rochester and she even came with her sister Elizabeth to call on Bishop Wilcocks before they left. This was a last farewell, though they were unaware of it, to the friendly old man who had always had a special interest in John, partly because he had once been a Fellow of Magdalen. He died in 1756 and was succeeded by Bishop Zachary Pearce who proved to be equally hospitable.

Another visit John made was to see the treasures of Dr Joshua Ward, a quack doctor who had made a fortune from his very dubious remedies.

June 11. 1754. Dr Ward's, Whitehall. A marble statue of Cupid sleeping surely nearer to the life than anything I have met-with in statuary. Among the many fine paintings is a Guido [Reni] of Apollo fleaying Marsyas who roars horribly. The holy family by Raphael's Master, Pietro Perugino. . . has much of the Flemish air.

He was particularly interested in a picture he saw the same day at the Princess Dowager's home, Leicester House.[c]

One of the capital paintings here is of Jacob's departure by F. Lauro [Lauri], whose pencil was exercised on small figures and histories in little. T. Major has engraved this, but has by no means hit off the sensibility in the face of the principal female figure . . . Here are Ivory Models of Rowe's and Shakespeare's monuments.

He had made very few notes since his visit to Badminton two years earlier. He had been back to Rochester Cathedral where the chancel had been 'new-fitted' since his last visit and he had criticized the house built against the front of the edifice and occupied by the Provost of Oriel as Prebendary of Rochester.

It is surprising that part of a prebendal house should ever have been suffered to erect itself against the grand front of the Cathedral, yet so it is; the house . . . curves so as to block up the face of the small southern of the two towers [which are] unlike each other . . . Observe that though the Prebendaries shift Stalls, they never do houses, here.

This house was demolished about 1820 and the two west towers were dismantled in 1763 and rebuilt later.[d]

He had examined brasses at Chigwell, ancient stone coffins at St Mary Overy in Southwark and the paintings at Goldsmiths' Hall. It was the pictures too which interested him at Sir Robert Ladbroke's house, West

[c] The widowed Princess Augusta lived here with her younger children until it was taken over for the use of the Prince of Wales in 1756.

[d] The Provost of Oriel moved to a new house next to The Vines about 1820. I am grateful to Canon P. A. Welsby for information about Rochester Cathedral.

Hatch, and on another visit to Wanstead House where he also noticed quantities of curious old china.

In September came the sad news of Mr Hiley's death.

27th. Dyed my honoured Master, the Revd. Mr Haviland John Hiley at Bristol and was buryed at his Rectory at Saltford, Somersetshire to which he was presented in 1713.

Mrs Hiley lived for another sixteen years. Their memorial hangs on the north wall of the sanctuary in the beautiful little church and the earliest parish records from 1750 to 1754 are in Mr Hiley's handwriting.[e]

Two weeks later Aunt Elizabeth Lethieullier also passed away, a nice woman who had always been ready to help her brothers and sisters and who had been a generous aunt. She was buried in the family vault at Clapham, now becoming so full that Lady Hopkins remarked ominously to her nephew by marriage, Philip Bromfield, that after her sister Betty was buried there would only be room for one more.

The Oxfordshire election took place in April 1754 and was nominally a victory for Lord Wenman and Sir James Dashwood. These two gentlemen, with a party of supporters, had arrived at Caversham the previous summer to give John their personal encouragement. It had been a very close contest locally, the Old Interest topping the New by only three votes – thirty-one to twenty-eight and three 'neuters'. The news later on that the victors had been unseated as they could not maintain their claims came as a great disappointment to their followers. It was while the House of Commons was still debating the issue that John wrote once more to Lord Wenman and received an immediate reply dated 20 January 1755,[2] in which he regretted he was unable, owing to bad health, to undertake an important trust which had been suggested by John – who evidently pressed him to reconsider the matter. Wenman wrote again on 17 February:

I should have answered your letter by the return of your Servant, but at the time had so much business that I was unwilling to detain him. I own myself under great Obligation to you and my Friends for thinking of me in an Affair of such Consequence, and if, other circumstances concurring, I could persuade myself that *my Services* would be acceptable to the University, I should very readily embrace the Honour you intend me. But whatever may be the consequence of this your friendly proposal, I must desire that nothing *at this time* may be mentioned, least it may give occasion to some to interpret my non-attendance, which proceeds only from the troublesome disorder in my eyes, to my disadvantage; and represent me as neglecting one point in hopes of another. I can give you no certain account of our affair at present, but intend being soon in Town,

---

[e] I was able to confirm this from a letter from H. J. Hiley to John Loveday (L.F.P., October 1748) on a grammatical subject. This was the only letter of Hiley's to be kept.

and will then trouble you with a Line if I can send you any intelligence that may be depended on . . .[3]

There is no conclusive evidence as to the nature of the proposal, but it has been suggested[f] that it could only have concerned the highest honour the University could give, commensurate with Lord Wenman's rank and standing in the county – the Chancellorship. Lord Arran held the office since 1715 and there was frequent discussion as to his successor. Whether it was originally John's idea or, as is more probable, came from conversations with his friends at Oxford, he was evidently thought the most suitable person to sound Wenman on his willingness to have his name put forward. 'Give me leave, Sir, to assure you I am truly sensible of your friendship,' Wenman had written and they may have known each other for a considerable time through the Berties and Courtenays. However his health and his fears of prejudicing his cause in the House prevented Wenman from taking any further steps. He died in 1760, only two years after Lord Arran, who was succeeded by the Earl of Westmorland.

John Warner's second marriage took place in April 1755 and was followed in May by that of Mary Bootle and Richard Wilbraham of Rode Hall, Cheshire; Sir Thomas had died and Lathom House now belonged to her father, the Captain. On his death in 1758 Mr Wilbraham had to add Bootle to his name so that she could inherit and she called him Mr Bootle for the rest of her life.

Dr Rawlinson died in April, prickly to the last – only two days before the end Sam Speed was writing to John about his 'awkwardness'[g] – and in July came the news of the death of George Ballard. Meanwhile at home Dolly's condition seemed to improve after her bad winter, but John thought it best to ask John Ward to postpone his usual visit till September. The good Doctor,[h] clearly put out, wrote back to say he was pleased to hear Mrs Loveday was better, but

You will give me leave to beg the reason why you are pleased to suspend my being witness to this agreeable circumstance till the entrance of September . . . as you intimated your design of continuing at home all this summer; so you was pleased to propose some things, which were to be done by us in August. This led me to conclude that some part of that month would be most agreable to you . . .[4]

The reason for the fuss was a very attractive invitation he had received from

[f] The late Dame Lucy Sutherland kindly gave me her interpretation of Wenman's letters. There is no other record of this offer and there is no known collection of Wenman's correspondence.

[g] L.P.F., 4 April 1755. The argument was as to which should buy volumes off the other to make a set, but Rawlinson would only write to Speed through John.

[h] Ward had received a Doctor of Laws degree at Edinburgh University in May 1751.

that well-known astronomer, the President of the Royal Society, to visit Shirburn Castle and to see his laboratory.

> My Lord Macclesfield had more than once formerly given me an invitation to his seat at Sherborn, where I have never yet been. And at the breaking up of the Royal Society this last month, the last words he said to me were to ask me whether he should not see me this Summer if I came into that country; to which my answer was that I hoped to be there before the end of August and should not fail to do myself that honour. I have received so many civilities from his Lordship as oblige me to pay him the greatest regard and would upon no account have him entertain any other thoughts of me. My Scheme therefore was, after I had been a few days with you, to have gone from thence in a post-chaise to Sherborn . . .⁵

John felt he must accommodate his friend as he made such a point of it. Macclesfield's son was Lord Parker, one of the opponents in the recent election, but he had no hard feelings of any kind and besides he was a friend of Merrick's. So Ward came in August, bringing with him the new catalogue of Dr Mead's pictures; and so it turned out that he was in the house at a time when he would have preferred to be elsewhere, for it was on 18 August that Dolly died.

> About ½ hour after 10 departed to her God and my God my dear wife, who had been a real blessing to me and mine.
> August 25. After 9 was buried my wife, who had as honest an heart as any mortal. Vatas performing the ceremony.

Her illness has never been explained and the only known symptoms besides her nervous temperament were her arthritic hands. She seems a lonely figure, within reach of all she desired yet never able to attain it. She was only forty-five when she died, having been dogged by ill health through all the ten years of marriage. John was sincerely fond of her and would have continued to be a kind and protective husband; that he felt nothing more was certainly not because he was incapable of loving a woman after Anna Maria. Even while he mourned Dolly's passing he knew exactly what he was going to do. It was little more than six weeks later that he wrote in his diary on 11 October: 'P.F. aged 32 years complete this day. Born in Scotland and brought thence at little above 4 years of age.' Three weeks later Penelope Forrest came over from Emmer Green and he asked her to marry him. It was barely two months since Dolly's death and he could not set down this momentous event in ordinary words. He called it 'the thing'.

> October 31. P.F. here; the thing mentioned and at once agreed to.

However much he disguised it there was no doubt at all that he was rapturously in love again. Only one other person had to be consulted besides Pen's mother and that was his own.

November 18. Drank tea at my Mother's; the thing mentioned and at once agreed to.

They could not be married for a year and for much of that time Pen was in London which meant that their courtship had to be carried on by means of letters. Whereas he had survived Anna Maria and Dorothy and had destroyed such letters as they may have written, his own letters to Pen were carefully preserved. They explain so much about his character – the humour, the kindness and the charm which had captivated his first two wives as surely as Pen. He wrote straight from the heart, not bothering to mince his words yet with such command of them that she must have found his letters enchanting.
First of all he wrote a prayer which before long they shared.

O gracious God, my Creator, Preserver, Redeemer and Comforter, Grant that in the weighty affair depending wholly upon my determination, I may be directed from above to what will be best both for the bodies and souls of myself and the intended partner of my life. Oh may thy blessed Will be done in me and by me, now and forever. Amen. [6.]

His first letter on 24 November was formal but definite.

Dear Miss Forrest,
    Be pleased to let the bearer know whether you are in expectation of any company this afternoon: if so, I will wait on you some other day. But if quite alone I shall do myself that pleasure before 5 of th'clock, and shall trouble you till 8. And 'tis much my desire that we may have two hours of that space of time for a private conversation between you and me only. I beg my compliments to Mrs Lynch; and am, Madam, for life, hand and heart Yours, John Loveday. [7]

Three days later he began to feel unwell and within a week had become seriously ill with 'an asthma'. This was succeeded by more problems when he was 'wracked with a stranguary'. Bagshaw and Winchester were staying in the house but left before Christmas and on the latter's return he pronounced the invalid improved. It was more than John thought himself, but he was able to renew his letters to Pen and even to see her when she came back from London.

    . . . We will talk this over on Thursday when I propose to spend much of the larger part of the day in a private confabulation with you, the joy of my heart and (under God) my chief support: I sink if you do not swim. so no wonder I pray that God may hold you up. [8]

It was his first serious illness since childhood and it was very frustrating to feel low as such a time. He tried driving:

    . . . The beginning of last week we had good weather; which I made use of to flourish-about in a Postchaise for 12 or 13 miles; this was of singular benefit to the proprietors of the said chaise; but my breath being in no degree helped by it, I am convinced that sitting in my Study (a room I have heard you mention with regard) will improve my inward man more, and be as good as post-chaising for the outward man . . .⁹

By 4 February 1756 he was able to go to church and was glad to see that Pen's mother was with her for it was no secret that life with Mrs Arthur Forrest, her sister-in-law, could be quite uncomfortable.

> God sanctify every affliction to you and me [he wrote]. I shall write to you again on the eleventh day of the month, having a particular superstitious affection for that said number eleven; you may suppose it is because eleven is an odd number and I am an odd fellow: I own myself odd, dear Pen, but by your assistance I hope to be made even; no single man but a double one.¹⁰

Jack was now thirteen and a great comfort and companion to his father in the holidays. He too had been captivated by Miss Forrest.

> My boy is charmed with your letter; he says he never saw such a letter in his life; tears came into his eyes; pray, Pappa, says he, my most humble service to Miss F. with a great many thanks. He thinks this is a properer answer for him to make, than to attempt a fuller answer in writing. And indeed my lovely Pen, true enough it is, that your excellent good heart appears in every line of the letter, accompanied with such a sensible head, that I know not where else to meet with the like; but what does it signify whether I do or no? I have met with you, and if it pleases God will hold you tight now I have got you . . .¹¹

All the same Jack did manage a little letter that month.

> Honoured Madam,
> I hope to be your dutiful son ere long; for at present I can only subscribe myself, Your very humble Servant, John Loveday Junr.¹²

On 11 March Pen went away with her mother to pay a visit to friends and John wrote to her the same day.

> My Dear, What a delightful day was yesterday for travelling! I would flatter myself that you have found the benefit of it. Is it not clear to every gossip, male and female, in Caversham, that we were married yesterday? Attend to the proof; Mrs and Miss F. were seen going over the bridge in the coach pretty early on Wednesday morning; no vast length of time after, followed a clergyman that is at Mr L's; his name is Lluellyn, Newellyn, Quellyn, or some such name; very quick upon his horse's heels were seen Mr L. and master in a postchaise; 'tis demonstration so I wish you and myself joy . . . Madam Zinzan says I look better than when she saw me last, which was yesterday fortnight. Give me an occasion, my Pen, to say as much of and to you at your return; that is, do your best to

improve in health by a proper attention to it and trust God with the consequences. After so much motion 'tis probable you have some uneasy remembrance of your fall down stairs, if so do not neglect to acquaint Mr Robinson with it.[13]

Unfortunately Pen's illness was not only due to a fall. She had been very worried about the true character of a woman she had befriended who turned out to be a fraud. In trying to discover the truth she had walked too far in all weathers and become unwell. Time and again the day of her return was postponed and John's letters were full of concern and advice.

. . . do not injure yourself, and me of consquence, by coming down a moment too soon for your health; if you do not arrive till Saturday, I will be with you on the afternoon of Easter day, for my patience will not hold out till Monday morning. I never tell my mother any ill news; so she has not the least notion of your being ill; to your kind inquiries after her health I am able to return a chearful answer and she returns you her thanks.[14]

But Pen, who had been in London for some time, did not come back. John wrote on 4 April:

If my writing to you will give you spirits you shall not want for letters . . . No doubt, my girl, it was a most happy circumstance that you did not come down the day after perspiring so copiously; had you attempted it, probably it would have killed you and then I should have been a candidate for Bedlam; I, that as Lady Cadogan told Mr Vatas on friday, looked better last Sunday than I had done since my illness.[15]

A little note from Lady Cadogan shows her concern for her neighbour in his wifeless state:

Lady Cadogan has known such wonderfull good effects from the inclosed Method of Infusing the Bark (so preferable to any Decoction) that she sends it to Mr Loveday wishing he would try this Prescription which has taken off many Feverish disorders that nothing else would relieve.[16]

And she enclosed the instructions for infusing an ounce of Peruvian bark for forty-eight hours and adding four teaspoons of brandy to the strained liquor to be taken three times a day before meals – 'Dr Berry's method'.

Dr Anthony Addington had left Reading two years before and was now practising in London. John implored Pen to see him.

Let me beg and intreat you by all the love that is between us, not to think of returning to Caversham till your health shall be established sufficient for such an enterprise; run no hazards I beseech you. Surely you now see the expediency of consulting Dr Addington; let him attend you; and think, as I do from the bottom of my heart, that you can lay out no money so discreetly as for the security of your health. I have been complimented to day by no less than three people on my gaining flesh, but what is that to the purpose? I am not yet one flesh with her that I call *my own girl*, since we are of one mind. Never were colds more in fashion; and I warrant you, my Pen thought that as long as she was a virgin she would be in the fashion; since she would have little chance to be so afterwards when united to a very old-fashioned wight indeed.[17]

There was no false modesty between them and he wrote to her as easily as the thoughts came into his head. Quoting some lines of verse in which unfeigned Innocence and most engaging Virtue, free from pride or artifice

> Promise long joys
> To th'honest nuptial bed, and to the wane
> Of life a mitigation of its ills ,

he had written on 21 March:

My dear, These lines struck me the other day in reading; and why should not I communicate to you anything that pleases me? I cannot place anything of that sort elsewhere, so naturally as with you; for truly, you please me beyond all things. On Friday evening came in here most unexpectedly, but most welcome, my brother Bagshaw, and stays with me till Monday se'ennight. On Monday, tomorrow, Dr[i] and Mrs Zinzan dine and lie here. Such friends would make a man well if he was ill before; but I thank God, I have now no pretence to talk of illness; can my dear Pen say as much for herself? – then am I happy indeed. And with better grace I can press you to take care of yourself, as this morning I did myself stay away from church on account of the raw damp weather . . . I am all alive when in any shape employed about you, the darling of my heart . . .[18]

Towards the end of April he decided to go up to London to see for himself how she was.

If you have an opinion of your physician you should undoubtedly be punctual in following his advice; otherwise you neither give him nor yourself fair play; I know this much, that Dr Nicholls prescribes the hot bath in these cases. 'Tis not unlikely but that on Sunday next day I may hear from Lady Hopkins that she is coming down here speedily; in which case you will imagine that I shall be busied preparing for her . . . but if I hear nothing from my aunt I propose being with you on Monday, about one o'th'clock . . . You must describe your house so that we may have some idea where it is we are to stop. I must beg you to provide me a warm lodging somewhere near you for that one night . . . 'Tis to be hoped we

---

[i] Zinzan was practising in Reading at this time and attending John.

shall be left together the main of Monday; for it is for your company wholly and solely that I set out from home . . . I shall take a four-wheel postchaise and Mr Vatas will go with me; he will look-in and ask how you do and learn at the same time where he is to call for me on the Tuesday morning . . .[19]

By May she began to recover and plans were made for her return as soon as the weather was mild enough. John took over the arrangements with his usual attention to detail.

To be sure the journey from Knightsbridge to Caversham will be too long for you without some previous jaunt. Or, however, you must make two days of it, thus; a postchaise carries your good mother and yourself as far as the Windmill at Slough; where Mr Vatas and I give you the meeting; there we lodge that evening and the next day come-on for Caversham; you will meet with carriages at the Windmill, an house where I have spent many a pound, and where you will be at home. But I charge you, do not give in to this scheme, except it be altogether commodious and agreeable to you; for I'll assure you, among all my infirmities, I have not that of huffing[j] if other persons think they have at least as good a right to think for themselves, as I can possibly have to think for 'em. I also take it for granted, that, as the Doctor thinks you have sweated enough, you do not therefore any longer make use of means to procure a sweat, except when you find yourself uneasy for want of one. As to diet, Dr Nicholls was against persons in your case eating much fish; but as to lobsters and crabs he absolutely forbad them . . . Pray keep that song you shewed me on Valentines; I hope to hear you sing it ten thousand times. Mrs Whistler of Bristol, once Mrs Harris of Reading, tells Mrs Zinzan that she will like a Lady that I am laying close siege to, very much; in short it is much the fashion to like the said Lady . . .[20]

A week or so later the plans were completed. John had thought of everything, including the gossips:

Lo, here is a dawning of good weather, to be made good use of by a good girl . . . you might hire a postchaise to take Mrs Forrest (who has a right to my best services) and yourself as far as Hounslow; if you set out at eleven from home you will be there by half an hour after twelve; there you might take a light dinner and from thence hire a fresh postchaise to the Windmill, where we all drink tea and sup together. In my next you shall have the sign of the Inn at Hounslow, where (to my knowledge) you will be well accommodated, and get a good carriage and driver onward in

[j] In a letter to Pen in March, John wrote: 'I am none of your huffy sort of fellows that are angry, they don't know why.' (L.F.P.)

your journey. On our second day get-up as late as you will; we will dine at
Hare-Hatch, the breakfasting place for the Reading stages; where I shall
bespeak a dinner the day before. From Salthill to that place your honoured
mother and Mr Vatas will fill one postchaise, you and I the other; but from
thence home, perhaps it may be as well for you and me to travel separate,
to prevent bell-ringing &c . . .[21]

His next letter told her that the inn at Hounslow was the Rose and Crown
and exhorted her to grudge herself nothing conducive to her health and ease.

> Exercise, my dear, will do you much good; but fatigue a deal of harm;
> so I intreat you to not to take a two-wheeled, but by all means a
> four-wheeled postchaise . . . you will have time to rest yourself
> thoroughly at Hounslow, for the postchaise cannot be two hours in
> going from thence to the Windmill; I wish it was in motion now, I
> would be as alert in a sympathizing vehicle. If they bring you indifferent
> wine at an Inn, for they are sometimes base enough to serve the women
> so, qualify it with some warm water and then sure you need not be afraid
> of it.[22]

The whole manoeuvre took place as planned and Pen crossed Caversham
bridge on 21 May under the protection of the cloth as provided by the amenable
Mr Vatas. The precision of John's arrangements was entirely typical of him;
indeed he himself was sometimes amused by his own careful habits, as he told
Pen in a letter written to her at Emmer Green in June. Four children were
staying with him – Anne and Sarah Gibson and two little girls called Bigg
whose father was also a widower.[k]

> How you will laugh at my formality when I tell you that I have just now
> settled most minutely the very day on which my four little folks are to
> leave Caversham – viz. St. Peter's day, June 29! What a stiff, precise blade
> are you like to encounter with! Many will pity you not a little. But take
> courage, my girl; I doubt not but to make you a tolerable good husband, as
> the world goes; if I do not, I shall be an intolerable scoundrel in my own
> opinion and that will be a far greater grievance to me than the ill opinion of
> the whole world besides. But however, I shall be truly anxious always to
> preserve your good opinion; for without it life will have no relish for me,
> you may venture to believe; and I hope to live a life of a high relish with my
> Pen, I can assure you that.[23]

It was understandable that the thought of illness should haunt him. He
himself had been plagued by a cold ever since his visit to Knightsbridge in
April, but by July he felt better, though still taking care of his health.

[k] Mr Bigg was about to remarry but died well before 1764. He was a friend of Ward and
Bagshaw and lived in Bromley. His sister was Mrs Halcombe.

Thomas had the discretion to bring my galoches and great coat to church to me; or how I should have got home I know not . . .[24]

He rode down to Mattingly, south of Reading, on 15 July to visit some great friends of the Forrests, Mr and Mrs Baker. They had gone to live there within the last year and it was to their comfortable home that Pen and her mother had driven together over Caversham bridge in March. The date of the wedding was now drawing near but there was a problem as to where it should take place. Pen did not want to be married from her brother's house on account of her sister-in-law's unpredictable ways and John fully supported her. Though he avoided the lady as much as possible he occasionally felt he should wait on her, visits which were 'unedifying enough' unless he could see Pen too. There was always the problem of how to pay a morning call on someone who was never dressed before the afternoon. Mr Baker came to the rescue and suggested that the marriage should take place from his house, to the great satisfaction of all concerned, including Mrs Arthur, who would certainly not have wanted the bother of it in her own. Jack went off on visits to his Warwickshire relations while his father made preparations for receiving the bride, whom strangely enough he introduced to his mother for the first time when he took her to drink tea there on 2 September. Now the months of letter writing were over, for in John's words –

As great a lottery as life is, if you live and I live, I am sure of a benefit-ticket in you; let us be always imploring the blessing of heaven upon our design, nor doubt its answer to our utmost wishes . . .[25]

On 20 September he dined with her and drove her to Mattingley. Next day he wrote in his diary:

Between 10 and 11 married to Miss Forrest at Heckfield Church by Vatas; present Mrs Forrest Senr. and Junr., Miss Biddy Forrest,[1] my son, Miss Owen, Miss Love, Mr and Mrs Baker; all the company dined at Baker's as did also the Revd. Mr Henchman of Basingstoke and Monsr. du Moulin, taken aboard the Alcides.

He also made a note of the expenses which had fallen to him.

The marriage articles		£11. 10.	0.
The Licence and commission		16. 16.	0.
The certificate		5.	1.
The Minister who officiated	(5 moidores)	6. 15.	0.
The Minister of the parish		1. 1.	0.
The clerk		5.	0.
The ringers		1. 1.	0.

[1] Bridget married the Hon. John Byng, later 5th Viscount Torrington, in 1767.

The Clerk of Caversham   10. 6.
The ringers of Caversham   2. 2. 0.

A week later they returned to Caversham, went at once to drink tea with his mother and lived happily together for the next thirty-three years.

All John's friends, not least Thomas Bagshaw, were charmed with Pen. John Ward sent her an ornament for her watch as a present, but was not entirely happy with a gift of rob, a conserve made from elderberries, honey and sugar, which he received from them.

> The elder rob came safe to hand, for which I return you my hearty thanks. But upon tasting of it I have found it not so sweet and warm to the stomach as some I have had from you formerly. And therefore I should be glad to be informed whether boiling it up afresh with sugar might not help it; or if there be any other method of giving it that comfortable relish.[26]

It is clear that while Ward was as busy as ever himself he had not had the usual number of commissions to execute for John; but by the time he wrote again in March 1757 the Caversham study had resumed its usual routine and he was particularly pleased to see that his friend was submitting information and corrections to the *Gentleman's Magazine*. One of these was to point out an error in the 'Parliamentary Transactions' in the October number and John Hawkesworth rectified this in January, 'though', said Ward, 'I could wish it had been done, somewhat more explicitly for the sake of some of his readers.'[m] Meanwhile the continuous exchange of books and pamphlets between John Loveday, Ward, Winchester, Merrick, Audley, Bagshaw, Burton and others had never abated.

In April old Dr Merrick died with a quip on his lips which John copied into his diary.

> Said he to his brother physicians on their visiting him in his illness 'Non habui febrem, Symmache, nunc habes.'[n] Dr John Merrick was Father of the Corporation of Reading. He resigned his gown on January 26. 1756.

He was buried by the font in Caversham church, but John was not invited to the funeral. James sent him a brief note explaining the reason.

> It has pleased God, in his infinite wisdom, to take my dear Father from us. His devout preparation for eternity, his earnest desire of his

---

[m] From *The Gentleman's Magazine Supplement*, 1756. 'Physical and Astronomical Observations to be concluded in January when Article XVII will be reprinted, a mistake having been made in copying the inscription, which mistake has somewhat embarrassed the sense of the whole article.' An explanation was given that Article 17 (October, p. 477) was an account of a Roman inscription found by Ward at Malton, and that it had been printed wrongly. The correction was made in January 1757, with no further explanation.

[n] 'I have not had a fever, Symmachus, now you have.'

Dissolution, and the gentle manner in which he departed, have afforded
me great consolation on this trying occasion. Among the last orders he
gave me, one was that his Love should be presented to you. As he was
desirous of being buried in an extremely private manner, he hoped you
would think that a sufficient apology for not inviting you to his funeral.
He desired that you would take the trouble of chusing a place for his
grave.[27]

To which John, ever the most rational of men, replied:

I have with all the punctuality in my power fulfilled the intentions of your
most friendly, most affecting letter. I sympathize with Mrs Merrick and
all her family very feelingly on this melancholy occasion, but think with
you that the circumstances attending your excellent parent's exit are very
reasonable alleviations of Sorrow.[28]

Although he had handed over the housekeeping duties to Pen, John still
maintained some interest in them, having performed them for so long by
himself. Like many other people he had taken to eating the new refined loaf,
though still using the wholemeal bread in the household. 'For three weeks in
June an Gallon loaf of the second bread cost 8d. Of the fine bread 9d.' Mutton
was 4d. a pound in April, but the biggest increase was in malt and he noted its
inflationary prices for the rest of his life. In October, 1757 he had to pay 4s. 9d. a
bushel compared with 2s. 9d. in 1745. In 1763 the price was 5s. rising to 6s. 3d.
by April 1783. He did not live long enough to see the steeper rise in prices after
1790 in food and other commodities.

He made one or two very brief topographical notes during the summer and
occupied himself with John Hocker's account of Catsgrove, but outside the
study it was life with Pen, who was expecting a baby in November, which
absorbed his time and thoughts. After a 'tedious labour' a daughter, Penelope,
was born, but she was not the Penelope who grew up and married William
Benwell. This little girl lived for only two years. Thomas Bagshaw was her
godfather and the two grandmothers were her godmothers, Mrs Loveday
being represented, rather surprisingly, by Mrs Arthur Forrest.

In March 1758 John received a letter from Phanuel Bacon. He wrote from
Balden in Oxfordshire, where he was now rector, to explain his reasons for the
production of his latest book, *The Humourous Ethics*, which consisted of five
short plays. Phanny had been quipping and punning his way through life for
thirty years or more – he was now fifty-eight – and still had a reputation as a wit.
His biographer in the *Dictionary of National Biography*, Joseph Knight, who
died in 1907, could not understand his popularity with his contemporaries and
dismissed his *Humourous Ethics* as having no significance. Without pretending
that it had great literary merit, significance in fact was what it was all about, so
let Phanuel Bacon make his own *apologia* and explain his reasons for writing in a
humorous vein at all. He began by depending on John's friendship and good
nature:

As I live in the Country, Leisure and Rainy Days tempted me to write – the Follies of the Age soon furnished me with a Subject; and my taking it for granted, that to set them in a ridiculous Light would be more likely to contribute to their cure than any other Method I could use, determined me to treat my Subject in the manner I have done. I thought it better to attempt to make People serious by laughing than to give them the opportunity of shewing themselves greater fools by laughing at what was serious – and I must tell you upon Honour, that the vanity of being an Author was the least of my motives to the commencing one; – if I know my own Heart, the whole is owing to my sincere Wishes that Mankind was better – neither after all, could I be tempted to give it a Pass and send it out into the World, without first taking the opinion of my Friends; whose openness and sincerity I never found reason to question, and whose Judgment I hope I was not deceived in; – and upon Supposition I was rightly advised, as Justice could never be duly administered unless Judges were to take their Cirquits; and as all our Itinerant Physicians have their Stages in all Publick Places, I came to a Resolution not to keep *mine* Idle and out of Business; when I was conscious that in taking their Progresses they would be likely to meet with such a number of Culprits, who deserve Correction, and such Heaps of Patients who want Prescriptions . . . I should be obliged to you if you'll do me the favour to communicate to any Friend who is as yet a Stranger to the Performance, that he is not to expect so close and regular a system of Morality as that of the Schools – and yet as regular one as the Plan will admit of . . .

He went on to explain the significance of each play in the book. Two must suffice – the two which Joseph Knight perhaps underestimated as far as their meaning was concerned.

The *Timekillers*, by setting the fashionable ways of misspending Time in a ridiculous Light, is just censure of the little Regard that is shewn by People in high Life for the good of the Community and lastly to reform such abuses the Bad Citizen is considered in the *Insignificants* as a Dead Person, fit only to be consigned over to the Undertaker, and lodged in the Repository I have erected for him.

He concluded with further civilities and asked John to procure admission for some copies of the book into his bookseller's shop at Reading.

Perhaps some of my Friends won't think the worse of me for designing well and I hope a trifling Purchase will help to keep me in their Remembrance.[29]

Jack had been confirmed the previous August by Bishop Secker. In answer to a letter from Sir James Foulis, many years later, in which he said that tears were 'ambiguous evidences of our sensations that attend deep sorrow and exquisite joy',[30] John replied:

> What happened in my pew at Caversham Church above thirty years since, is still fresh upon my mind. Dr Secker, then our Diocesan, preached that sermon on Confirmation, which has since appeared in print; when he opened and dilated upon the answer comprised in two words only, which the persons to be confirmed are directed to give to the Bishop's very solemn demand; a thorough conviction of the high importance of the subject, and the undoubted truth of his paraphrase upon it, pregnant with matter, yet utterly unadorned, struck so forcibly upon Dr Merrick, Mr Powys and your humble servant, that we burst with one consent into a flood of tears.[31]

It was not until the July of 1758 that Jack received the Holy Sacrament for the first time (though it was not so long an interval as between his father's confirmation and first Communion). This was partly due to the fact that he had become ill in April with a miliary fever which kept him upstairs for three weeks and a little over a month later he was back from school with smallpox, which he was supposed to have had as a child. His father, besides being extremely worried, was in bed himself with some sort of fever. When they recovered he wrote in his diary: 'The Hand of God remarkably upon me and mine; may I never forget it! It was for good. Deo Gratias.'

During this miserable time came the news of the death of Deodatus Bye, 'that worthy, good man – fourteen years older to a day than my unworthy self'. Describing the circumstances of his death a friend of them both, John Russell of Maidstone, told John that Bye had indicated his wish that he should have his interleaved Bible in four volumes and Anthony Wood's history of Oxford. He had also made it clear that both he and Jack were to accept any other books they pleased, including a small edition of Tully for the boy.[32]

John Ward came to stay for two months in August accompanied by his faithful servant Catherine Jones. He was still there when Jack took the part of Davos in Terence's *Andria* on 5 October. The whole Caversham party, which included John Peareth, was in the audience, having first been entertained by the headmaster. Ward left four days later, apparently in good health, and it was a great shock to them all to hear that he had died suddenly ten days later, having supped well before being taken ill in the night. The news came from one of his executors, Thomas Tredway, a glover of Leadenhall Street who was in business with a partner called Bailey. He had been in Portsmouth when the Doctor died and hoped John had not already seen the news in the paper. Ward had bequeathed to John all his silver and copper coins that were not current money and his globes and some books to Jack. He was to be buried beside his sister Abigail in Bunhill Fields.

The other executor, a bookseller also called John Ward but unrelated, wrote to tell John the contents of the will. Mrs Goodwin had been named residuary legatee; the library was to be sold by auction and a catalogue would be prepared. He asked John to commend Catherine Jones to Mrs Goodwin so that she might receive the furniture Ward had intended for her as well as a legacy of £50.[33] This John was glad to do, for she had been a good housekeeper to his friend and was a very intelligent woman. Mrs Goodwin soon made it clear that she would hand over all her cousin's papers to John[34] and they should be delivered to him by the executors. When Bagshaw came to stay in December he brought presents which the old gentleman had asked him to give to John the day before he died. It was all very affecting, but so far everything appeared to be proceeding in good order. No one was sorry to say goodbye to 1758, a year of tribulations. It was also a year in which, according to John, there were

> Immense quantities of wild fruit, and extremely large of the kind, such as haws, acorns, beechmast &c, but a very mild and open winter followed.

The New Year opened with tragedy – the death of their daughter. 'My delightful little girl was pursued so with fits that she breathed her last about a quarter before 6.' Two days later, on 18 January, 'my lovely babe buried about 4 in the family-vault.'

Were all the sorrows to be repeated? It seemed so when only a month later he was called to London where Lady Hopkins was dying. 'My honoured aunt and benefactress expired at her house in New Broad Street, London and on February 26 was buried at Low-Layton.' Her large estate was divided as evenly as possible between her nephews and nieces and education trusts formed for their children. Of the four executors, most of the work was bound to fall on John, the others being his mother, Anne Bootle and James Burrow's elder brother, Christopher, who died himself the following year.

Life was happier again in June when the second Penelope was born. Jack stood godfather, a duty he performed at his father's wish for Sarah, Martha, Arthur and Mary in due course 'as a pious additional bond between us'.[35] After emulating his father by taking the part of Cato in the school play that autumn he left at the end of the year and went up to Magdalen as a gentleman commoner in February 1760.

The only other incident of much importance in 1759 was entered in the diary for 12 May: 'Sealed up the notes on Mr Walpole's book, for him.' By this time John's standing as an antiquary was matched by his reputation as a traveller and connoisseur of painting. Walpole may have heard of him through George Vertue or possibly through Dr. John Merrick of Isleworth. Walpole had bought Vertue's manuscripts from his widow in 1758 and began to look them over in September 1759. He used them for his *Catalogue of Royal and Noble Authors* which he began to write in January 1760. However, the possibility that John's notes were for the *Anecdotes of Painting* which appeared in 1762 (and to which he frequently made references) cannot be excluded.[a] His diary shows that Walpole sent him 'Letters from Edw. VI to Barn. Fitz Patrick qto. pamphlett 1772' on 29 March 1773, but there is no record of their ever meeting and by the time Pen's cousins, Mary and Agnes Berry, had become Walpole's close friends, John was in the last year of his life.[p]

Although a fight over Dr Ward's papers occupied a great deal of his time during the years 1760 to 1761, there were also some family events. Captain and Mrs Forrest moved from Emmer Green to Binfield but they were still near enough to be constantly in touch with Caversham. The Captain had come back from Jamaica in his ship, the *Augusta*, in August 1759, and after paying her off the following April he joined the Grand Fleet in the *Centaur*, a ship he had commissioned. Having moved the family in October he was delighted to be sent back to Jamaica in the New Year of 1761 – 'Jermacio – the place most agreeable to him', as Mrs Goodwin observed. While he was there his admiral died and upon being left as senior officer he promoted himself commodore and commander-in-chief. His family saw rather more of him after he had been sent back in a passenger ship in 1762. As far as they were concerned his conduct had been exemplary, but it was not until 1769 that he achieved the rank of commodore legitimately and returned to Jamaica as commander-in-chief. He died on active service in 1770.

After having suffered a paralytic stroke the previous summer, Sarah Loveday died on 3 February 1761 – two days before John's fiftieth birthday. 'My dear Mother – my best of Parents' he called her, and so she had indeed been to him all his life, caring constantly for his welfare, offering counsel when required, but making few demands for herself and never interfering or dissuading him from any of his enterprises. Nor could she have wished for a more loving son:

> I have often heard my Father enlarge [wrote Penelope] on the excellence of her understanding, on her lively and active mind, her liberality of sentiment and generosity of heart; and talk of the cheerful tranquillity she possessed even in the few closing years of her life when the loss of the use of her limbs by the palsy confined her to her chair. She read a good deal and had written much.

Another change in family life took place the following May when Anne and Sarah Gibson came to live at Caversham 'altogether' as John put it. George Gibson now had a young son and Elizabeth stayed with them. With the arrival of the next baby, Sarah, in July John's family had now virtually increased to seven. Writing to wish Pen 'a good breeding' Mrs Goodwin had offered her services.

---

[o] The late Dr W. S. Lewis kindly gave me this interpretation of John's entry.
[p] Penelope Hind met Walpole much later on and referred to him as 'Lord Orford, the calumniator'.

. . . if you should be at a loss for a Sponsor for the little Stranger, be pleased to accept of me, who will do it with satisfaction for you, but am not desirous of making the offer to any other person . . .[36]

She was a little wary as she had made a similar offer to Susannah Parkhurst a few years earlier and had been turned down with profuse apologies, an old lady on the husband's side having got her offer in first.[37] This time she was more successful.

From the beginning of 1760, the battle for Dr Ward's papers had been warming up. John had received the greater part of them on Mrs Goodwin's instructions, but it was clear that they were not all there. The opposition was made up of Thomas Tredway and a formidable lady, Mrs Ann Ward, the mother of John Ward the bookseller, who had died early that year. John directed his forces from a distance, attacking from unexpected angles. Mrs Goodwin was second-in-command and even made one foray alone. The officers in the field were Thomas Bagshaw and John Hocker, who went up to Bedford House regularly on business; and Tim Goodwin was a most unreliable lieutenant. After a long and fruitless campaign John eventually brought in strong additional support from Dr Robert Vansittart of the Inner Temple. The foe was then soon routed, but the victory had an unexpected twist.

It all began with a minor skirmish when John received a very polite letter from Ward's successor at Gresham College, Joseph Whateley.

Since I have had the Honour of succeeding Dr Ward at Gresham College, I have been informed that he left several manuscript Books which are now in your possession, relating to the affairs of the College. Any thing written by him must undoubtedly be very curious and useful, but the Subject of these Books render them more particularly so to us, and for that Reason as well as upon account of the Respect we bear to the memory of Dr Ward, we should think ourselves very happy if we could obtain the Favour of having them in our Library, where they would always be preserved with the greatest Care and might be referred to on any occasion; and I am therefore desired by the rest of the Gentlemen of the College to present you our most respectful Compliments and to acquaint you that if you would be so good as to favour us with them, we should think ourselves very highly obliged to your Generosity, and the more so as we know not how it can ever be in our power to return the obligation; though we should be very glad to do it; either by a present to Dr Ward's residuary Legatee, or if that would not be acceptable, by any other Method that you would be so good as to point out to us.[38]

John's intransigent reply must have surprised the College.

Last week Mr Ward of Cornhill and myself had a conversation on the very subject of your letter; when I told him (who well knew the purport of the manuscript volumes in question), that as they mention so freely the names of many persons still active in life, it would be highly inexpedient to let them go out of the private hands they are now in, for some years to come; and that then the properest place for them would undoubtedly be the British Museum, to which foundation Dr Ward bore an hearty good will, and on which his residuary legatee has engaged to bestow *The Lives of the Gresham Professors*, very much augmented by the Author. For, to say the truth, as your respectable society is at present constituted, I mean with regard to the Committee, I must beg leave to differ from you and the rest of the gentlemen of the College, (to whom my compliments are due) as to the safe custody of any such papers in your library. You will be pleased to accept of this as the answer, it being indeed the fixed resolution of, Sir, Your very humble Servant, John Loveday.[39]

Ward must have passed on to him some misgivings about the library but even so his letter was scarcely civil. He had always been able to say no in an unequivocal manner and it was a talent which improved with age and which Jack inherited. Cordial, kind and friendly as they both were, they had no difficulty at all in responding in a blunt, negative way to people they did not respect or to requests of which they did not approve. Their uncompromising honesty, praiseworthy as it was, engendered as they grew older a kind of torpor on occasion which was not in keeping with their active minds or generous instincts. Such frankness could be genuine but sometimes it was used as the simplest way out of a dilemma.

John was sure there were a few papers about Gresham College which he had not received and he was even more concerned about a small folio book half-bound in marbled paper containing all the printed papers relating to the management of the Society for the Encouragement of Learning.[q] In September 1760 he wrote to Tredway asking him to deliver them up. Mrs Goodwin was staying at Caversham at the time and as no reply was received she decided to take matters into her own hands and to confront Tredway and Mrs Ward. She had a further problem in that she had made over the copyright of Dr Ward's manuscript 'Dissertations upon Several Passages of the Sacred Scriptures' on certain conditions which would bring in some money and she wished to encourage Mrs Ward to publish it. She also wanted to see Tim, who seemed to have become quite feckless. She wrote to John on her return to Warwick, thanking him for her kind reception at Caversham.

Mrs Loveday, who though I was a stranger treated me as an old friend . . .
My Grandson, I conclude, is gone to the residence.[r] I shall rejoice to hear of

[q] This society, founded in 1736, was dissolved in 1746. Ward and Thomas Birch were keen members.
[r] Magdalen College.

all your healths, [including] Miss Pen. I suppose by this time she is quite a foot-woman, as it will not be long before her tongue is as active as her feet . . .

She had seen Tredway, but he had absolutely refused to give up the book or some copperplates which John wanted and she now thought he meant to present them to the British Museum himself; he was a most impertinent man, she declared, and she had had no better luck with Mrs Ward who had just come back from Margate and had so much company that she could not listen to any instructions. As for Tim, she had last seen him at Peel's Coffee House and she doubted if he would send on an old will and codicil which she had forced from Tredway. She had inquired after Allan Ramsay[5] at his house, but had not seen him.[40]

Tim, in fact, wrote almost at once, sending the will and some effects of John Ward's, but not the other papers. John immediately sent him instructions to present 'our old friend Mr Tredway who has refused to do me justice' with an expression of his astonishment at the refusal to deliver up the book half-bound in marble paper, et cetera – 'But let the conscientious man answer it as he may.'[41]

Tim replied:

I spoke to him to deliver up the Papers you mentioned in yours; he returned me the same answer as he had done to my Mother, that if no body made any claim on him, or that he should not hear of any body that had a just claim, that then in a proper time he should deliver them up, and not before. I am very sorry that I cannot acquaint you that I was got into Business, which gives me much uneasiness . . .[42]

It gave even more to his mother that he had not written to her since her return to Warwick. Worse than that, he had disappeared from the respectable lodgings in which she had left him. He was traced back to Peel's Coffee House from which he would not move. At the same time William's health deteriorated, and as for the Warners, she had not seen them for months. She wrote on 1 December:

I hear he and Mrs Warner have been at Waterstock and are now at Charlbury, to which place he has sent for the children, where he will stay till near Christmas. I know he does not love his own house at this time of the year and as he must be somewhere, he is in the right of it to let the old Gentleman keep him . . .[t]

₅ Mr Willot said Ramsay had returned; this was probably from Edinburgh where he had been in September 1760. Mrs Goodwin was considering whether to consult him on pictures which had belonged to Ward – 'his own and of the Spanish Carton'. She had already received Ramsay's portraits of John and Abigail Ward, now in the Warwickshire County Museum. The sentence remains an enigma; there is no proof that it refers to Ramsay's self-portrait for many years owned by the Loveday family and thought to have been purchased abroad in the nineteenth century.

_t Richard Warner may have moved to Charlbury, a few miles from Ditchley.

She ended on a more cheerful note:

What a mercy it is, that we have such a Prospect of our young King as his Declaration, Proclamation and Speech gives us.[43]

She wrote to Mrs Ward herself in December, having heard through Bagshaw that Richardson, the printer, was extremely busy.

. . . Why not publish it yourself, which you will certainly set about immediately, if you consult either your own interest or mine; as I have a respect for you I would advise you to it; I have nothing to do but to insist upon your fulfilling the ingagement of your late Son, who to be sure was so well acquainted with his own business, as to know how to make a Bargain . . .[44]

But she had met her match in Mrs Ward, who thereupon wrote to John suggesting to his astonishment that he should publish the book. Mr Hocker or Mr Bagshaw would have told him that she was winding up her business. John replied to this piece of presumption in January 1761:

Had I ever been in trade, or particularly in your trade, I should not have wondered at your desiring me to take the work off your hands and publish it myself. Whereas being a plain country gentleman, altogether unacquainted with selling, having all my life been a buyer, I am as unqualified for taking such an affair upon myself as I am for succeeding to your business in Cornhill.

He suggested that she should offer better terms to Richardson or Field.

Oh, Madam, had this work been published by yourself some months since, you would have saved yourself a deal of trouble; no abatement of your profit would have ensued and every thing would have been just as it should be. I protest to you that I have by my two friends served you unfeignedly to the best of my powers.[45]

There was another reason for refusing which he did not divulge to Mrs Ward, one which even if he had been in the trade would have made the project impossible. He made a careful note after having consulted Bagshaw and Audley, as priests of the Church of England,

whether [the 'Dissertations'] do not contain principles of Anti-paedobaptists, such as would ill become a son of the church of England to publish . . . this then shall not be published by me . . .[46]

His letter evidently impressed Mrs Ward as shortly after this she found a publisher called William Johnston to take on the book. John sent him explicit instructions, expressing his pleasure and even referring to 'good Mrs Ward'.[47] This new opinion did not last long. In April he heard from Bagshaw that she would not send some more papers she had found unless he would let her off paying the money she owed Mrs Goodwin until Johnston had paid her – and this he would not do until he had raised the money by the sales of the book. Hocker, said Bagshaw, was out of all patience with her.

> But don't copy after him if you have a mind for the MSS. Any thing I can do in this troublesome affair will be done with great pleasure . . . she is now removed and lives in St. Paul's Church Yard opposite the North Door of the Church.[48]

Even the conciliatory Bagshaw lost patience on his next visit to her, as she persisted in whining and sighing and putting off the matter and could be brought to no conclusion. She had also told him that when she last saw Mr Timothy Goodwin he had made a very mean appearance indeed.[49]

Meanwhile it transpired through Bailey, who gave the game away while his partner was out, that Tredway was now consulting Dr Thomas Birch, rector of St Margaret Pattens, secretary to the Royal Society and a respected scholar, as to what course he should take. This really annoyed John who regarded Birch as a friend and a man of his own standing. He had already told Johnston to send Birch a copy of the *Dissertations* and was at present discussing with Ducarel, the Lambeth librarian, the possibility of asking him to write a short life of Ward. He had been a member of the Society for the Encouragement of Learning until it disintegrated in 1746. John decided to write to him at once telling him the story of his dealings with Tredway and including every detail –

> and if Mr Tredway, on application to you, should be inclined at last to do me justice, a line from him to Mr Bagshaw (with whom he is not unacquainted) might soon put an end to this affair.[50]

Evidently Birch's sympathies were with Tredway for nothing happened. John decided he must now put the whole business into the hands of Dr Robert Vansittart whose family home was at Shottesbrook, close to Feens. Tall, thin and urbane, Robert was the second son of a large family of which his younger brother Henry, Governor of Bengal at the age of twenty-six, is the best known. George, the youngest child, had been a schoolfellow of Jack's and was probably the closest of his lifelong friends; he had now gone to join Henry with the express intention of making his fortune with the East India Civil Service. Robert himself was a few years later to become Regius Professor of Civil Law at Oxford. He has been accused of leading a debauched and licentious youth,[51] perhaps because, like his brothers, he was a member of the Medmenham fraternity;[*] but had that been so he would hardly have been such a close friend of John Loveday, for he was only thirty-three years old in 1761.

He went straight into the attack, visiting Mrs Ward on 28 November and

---

[*] The proceedings of the Hell-fire Club seem to have been a good deal exaggerated. See Betty Kemp, *Sir Francis Dashwood*, 1967.

telling her she must fulfil her contract, which she agreed to do through complaining she had lost money on it.

I represented to her that these complaints, however they might raise compassion, could have no effect upon a contract already made; she was not to expect that Mr Loveday would commence bookseller – that she knew very well that the copy money was due upon the printing the work; that it would be very unfit for Mr Loveday to keep a correspondence in order to be informed of the sale of Books . . .[52]

He had also seen Dr Birch and Johnston, who had not been quite open about his receipts. He wrote next on Christmas Eve, 'thursday night and a rainy evening', to say that he had again seen Mrs Ward who was difficult to be brought to honest payments. Being a man of the world he had also made a discovery which John's more innocent friends had missed.

[Mrs Ward] seemed more reasonable than the old Lover who sat by her fireside and was suggesting many difficulties that took up much time . . . she is advised by the old Lover, whom I found always at her house . . .[53]

Between them they had put up so many objections that even Vansittart could not complete the matter at once. He wrote again in the middle of January 1762.

I am just returned, my dear friend, from St. Paul's Church Yard, the Habitation of the Dead and of Mrs Ward. You will see by the inclosed receipt that I have thought proper to conclude her controversy . . . I think Mrs Goodwin will be satisfied with the payment considering that the old lady will not be very soon reimbursed the expenses she has been put to by the publication; which she does insist was undertaken for the honour of Dr Ward, the profit to the Booksellers upon that article being small, because as Mrs Ward informs me 'Divinity is amongst the Trade a mere drug'.[54]

So Mrs Ward was dealt with at last, but there was still Mr Tredway. When Vansittart saw him again he found a man in a quandary and therefore easier to manage. He had, in fact, a good many more manuscript volumes than the one John had sought for so long and they did not all concern the Society for the Encouragement of Learning.

Vansittart wrote on 13 February:

He said he had had a message from Lord Macclesfield, in relation to a minute of Entry in the Books of the Royal Society, and that he had returned for an answer that the Minutes might be inspected by any Gentleman of the Society who was disposed to examine them. He expressed some doubts of the claim to papers which related to the transactions of those Communities of Learning to which Dr Ward was Secretary; and it was on these accounts that he wished to have an acknowledgement of the receipt of such papers by you and of 'your engagement to give inspection of them on request to any parties concerned'; I praised his assiduity as far as I might do without flattery, and found him not unwilling to give you possession of the MSS upon your signing any paper, tending to the purpose above mentioned. I wait now for some such note . . .

Wishing to allay any shock John might have received he turned to lighter topics.

I am sorry my time is so bounded, that I cannot by this post send you my Commentaries upon Mr Mason's measurement of verses and Mr Sheridan's exceeding Attic Ear . . .[v] Shery tells me that his Father died before Dr Swift; it was in 38 or 39; he could not well by memory fix the time . . .[55]

He wrote again on 23 February in reply to a letter from John.

I expressed myself improperly when I said that Dr Ward was Secretary to any of [these] Societies. I wrote in haste, and wanted a word to signify the same as the French chargé d'affaires; I only meant that Messrs. Tredway and Bailey thought that the papers and Minutes now received to your use, might possibly be demanded by some one of those Communities of Learning; as having been taken by their Order and recording their proceedings, in which case a question is moved, that I would rather find to be answered by the delivery of the papers, than by litigating the right to them, and setting up Mr Loveday's title against that of somebody or nobody that might chance to demand them this year or ten years hence; . . . I examined into the general Contents of each Book and took the whole upon the assurances of Mr Tredway that he had no more; they were packed up in a box and I sent my servant to conduct them to the Bell in Warwick Lane; they were directed to be left at Mr Hocker's for you; and I believe you are indebted to my servant eighteen pence for the box in which the said eleven books were reposited. Quod felix sit faustumque.[w] We are ready to give you credit and a helping hand in any Order you shall favour us with . . . What a sad affair is this that I hear from the mouths of all the Polite world and the whispers of Court. Lord P[embroke] (comes Wiltoniensis)[x] run away with

---

[v] Thomas Sheridan, father of the dramatist, a successful actor-manager and lecturer on elocution, brought out a book on English grammar in 1762. His father, a friend of Swift, died in 1738.
[w] 'And let this go well and successfully.'
[x] 'The Earl or Count of Wilton.'

Miss H . . .^{y} I am not surprised at it, considering the accounts I have received of his behaviour to Lady P. – the gentlest and most delicate of Women! who yet once in her life plucked up spirit enough to tell my Lord who was railing at the shackles of Marriage in her company and at table 'My Lord, you should not complain of any ties that sit so easy upon you.' No man has had less honour in that relation of life than his Lordship . . . I have looked over Mason's book upon Poetical numbers; it makes me laugh to see such a work made about Iambus and Trochee; he quite mistakes Poetical measures; there is no creature speaks or sings in true Iambus, except a Jack Ass; and he does it universally, except in the close of his periods, which is always done with an Anapaest – you shall see my Asinine Ode, it is set to Music . . .[56]

Vansittart's quips could not disguise the fact that the victory was an embarrassing anticlimax. On opening the box John found himself the possessor of five books and two portfolios relating to the defunct Society for the Encouragement of Learning and four more portfolios containing, respectively, papers concerning the Royal Society, The Society of Antiquaries, Gresham College and the British Museum. He looked at the form Tredway had sent for him to sign. If only this tiresome man had explained the problem at the beginning how much time and trouble might have been saved. Not only was he tiresome but, as Mrs Goodwin had said, impertinent. Tredway had written:

Received this day of Thomas Tredway and James Bailey, Executors of Dr J. Ward, sundry Books and papers relating to [the various Societies] which I promise to be accountable to produce when called by either of the said Executors.[57]

Slowly he crossed out the final lines and replaced them with 'all which particulars I do engage myself on application to me, to grant the inspection of, to any of the parties concerned.'[58] He sealed it up and sent it back, but he was not happy; he knew what Vansittart thought and in his heart he agreed. What moral right had he, who had never belonged to any of these institutions, to their private papers? A few weeks later he packed them up again and directed them to Dr Birch with the following note:

These Papers, lately received from Mr Tredway of Leadenhall Street, an executor of the late Dr John Ward, are thought by Mr Loveday much fitter to be lodged in the hands of Dr Birch than to be retained in his own. The Doctor is therefore desired to accept of them.[59]

The Doctor also agreed to write a short life of John Ward and much time

^{y} Lord Pembroke met Kitty Hunter, daughter of a lord of the Admiralty, in January 1762 and eloped with her. He was reconciled with his wife the following year. See Tresham Lever, *The Herberts of Wilton*, 1967.

and energy was spent in collecting the facts for him. He himself was in touch with Mrs Goodwin and with Catherine Jones who wrote him an extremely well composed and intelligent letter.[60] His pamphlet came out in 1766,[z] but not until after his untimely death from a fall from his horse. Grave and correct, it failed to rekindle Ward's warm and lively flame or even to reflect his own. Dull his writing may have been, but much must be forgiven a man who invariably dressed up as a tree when he went fishing.[61]

John still had a huge quantity of Ward's manuscripts and most of these (though not his letters to John) were given by Jack to the British Museum. The gift included the majority of the letters which with other papers made up the saga of the battle with Tredway.

Mrs Goodwin was delighted to receive her money, which she really needed as she had practically to support Tim. William had gone to Bath in the January of 1761, accompanied by Hugh Holbech's servant, but he was still 'a poor weak Creature'[62] and would not help her.

> I pray God incline his heart for I can't press him, as he has been such a Sufferer already and it is morally impossible the other should continue without Assistance . . .[63]

John Warner, though she had asked him to help, was a broken reed,

> so taken up with his own Affairs that he has not once taken a ride over to ask me how I do. I have not seen him since his Son was innoculated . . .[64]

> He gives me no advice, but I desired he would see whether he could persuade my Son to take his Brother in, which he has attempted but could not succeed . . . what has turned him I can't tell, for he used to be a most fond brother; to be sure he has suffered a good deal upon his Account, but I offered to do what was in my power to bear part of the expense. I think Warwick not a proper place, or he should come to me directly, as to his diet I think I could bear, but Cloaths and all, I cannot . . .[65]

John came to the rescue when Tim was declared bankrupt and received grateful thanks from his mother. Tim continued to meander through life in his amiable, aimless way until William's death in 1766, when he inherited Arlescote. He lived there on reasonable terms with his neighbours, but was the despair of his lawyers and of any tiresome tax-gatherer who happened to cross his path. It was inevitable that he should be sued for not paying his tithes. Yet when he died in 1784 at his mother's house in Warwick, it was due to pneumonia caught while attending a special jury to past midnight and not taking care of himself afterwards. Mrs Goodwin survived him by four years,

---

[z] The brief pamphlet was edited by his executor Matthew Maty, who sent a copy to John Loveday.

dying at the age of ninety-nine without a grey hair. By then she had become a legend and there were many eulogies at her passing. 'This my dear Relation was honoured in her generation and has left a name behind her' wrote John in his diary, one year before his own death. Arlescote had come into her possession and was left to her grandson, Jack.

Peaceful Conclusions
1760 – 1789

Uncle William and Aunt Martha Brady were the last of the senior members of the Clapham branch of Lethieulliers. John had always been mildly attached to his uncle, but it could not be denied that ever since the death of his wife in 1755 his existence had become even seedier and his friends shadier, though he still had plenty of money. His only daughter, Catherine, was as wild as he had been in his youth, keeping peculiar company and with a penchant for the bottle. In 1760 she had mysteriously vanished and her father, as anxious for the safety of her wordly goods as he was for her person, deluged the press with advertisements:

> Whereas on Tuesday the 15th of July instant, as a young Lady and her Father were going to Vauxhall Gardens, they called at a house near Walnut-Tree-Walk, Lambeth, and while her Father went into the Yard, the said young Lady either voluntarily absconded or was taken away by Force; this is earnestly to desire the said young Lady, if she has any Regard for her unhappy and disconsolate Parent, that she will send a Letter, or by some other Means give him Intimation whether she was forced from him, and whether it is through Choice or Restraint that she still keeps from him; if through Choice the reason why? This will ease his present afflicted Mind, as he is in dreadful doubt, as she had Things of Value about her, whether she may not have been plundered and murdered . . .[1]

Anyone with information was to inform Mr Welsh at his office in Long

Acre and would receive a reward of twenty guineas, but there was no news and a final advertisement appeared in the *Whitehall Evening Post* that her father had good reason to think she had got into

> some such Hands as were reported to sell a great B . . . r's Daughter, or with some of the secret Friends of a certain great Man, that was sent into the Fleet Prison for a like Crime some Time ago, who, he imagines, have seduced her, in order to make the most of her . . .[2]

and he was determined to prosecute the betrayers and their abettors with the utmost severity of the law. Early in 1761 John received a cry for help from his afflicted uncle:

> I am credibly informed that my Daughter is now removed into Lodgeings by Cavindish Square, to the same house that Miss Young is now in, who was at the Bagnio with the unfortunate Miss Bell, Sir William Fowler[a] and Mr Sutton, the last lately tryed for wounding Miss Bell; and that she, my Daughter, is a going speedily to be married to one Kelly, an Irishman now in Prison for Debt, but will soon be let out on the late Act. What to Doe I know not to save her Life and fortune, both which she is in great Danger of speedily Loseing, and in that case you and the rest of our family will Lose what would otherwise come to you and them – I wish I could see you, for I can't write what I have to say.[3]

John replied at once with his usual good sense and no illusions at all about inheriting anything from that quarter. But he may have been mistaken in assuming that Anne Bootle or Sarah Bromfield could influence their wayward cousin at the age of twenty-seven.

> It is a strange world we live in. There are many that delight in making others uneasy; perhaps some such persons may be working in the dark, and raising stories to disturb your peace. If indeed it should not be so, but all true as you are informed, why then the question is, *what is to be done?* And here very sure I am, that the lady's fortune already in her own hands, and also that larger part of it depending on her parents' marriage-settlement, when it shall come into her hands, – both these, I am sure, must be at her absolute disposal, as much as her own person is. All that can be done must be by the gentle methods of persuasion and none can make use of these methods with so much probability of success as persons of the same sex. And who of those so proper as the relations? Was I the parent here, to such I would undoubtedly apply; nor can I think there is any that

---

[a] Sir William Fowler, Bt. was a cornet in the Dragoon Guards who died in Germany the same year, 1760. His sister Lucy married John Jones of Cavendish Square and they were presumably the owners of the house mentioned. They came from the family of Fowlers of Harnage Grange and were related to Lady Cadogan. The bagnios were the high-class brothels of the Covent Garden district.

would not willingly engage to do their utmost. No better advice than this could I give was I upon the spot. Women always manage best with women, as they are the best judges of what arguments are reckoned most conclusive with the sex. Very cordially do I wish you an happy exit to this momentous affair; nor shall my prayers be wanting on the occasion.[4]

Father and daughter were reconciled but did not live together again. On his death in 1765 she sent John a long account of his last hours. He had been ill but was, she thought, improving and they had planned to take a villa in Greenwich for the summer. Then one morning Jim the barber, who ran his errands, came with the news that he had died in the arms of his two maids. She went at once to the house and was furious to find he had been laid out, as she had promised this would not be done for twenty-fours hours.

> I always thought the Barber would do justice by him for his own sake at least, as he would lose a very good friend when ever he died – he having saved him from being arrested many times and given ten guineas when Jim was not very well; however they ought to have informed me of his illness at first . . I have at least the satisfaction to have been certain that he did not die through carelessness or neglect . . .[5]

No will could be found and Catherine inherited his whole fortune. The Bradys and Bromfields were equally disappointed when she died in 1769, the first cousins only getting £200 apiece, though her maternal relations fared rather better. Sending the details to John, the Bradys' son-in-law, Henry Allen, told him that the rest of the money was left to a small boy called John Crook now in the care of an Essex shopkeeper, with instructions for his education. 'He is said to be the son of Persons now dead, but is supposed to be a very near Relation of her own.'[6] And so, eight years later, the mysterious disappearance was explained.

Mrs Brady's interment a few months earlier than her brother's had been quite discreditable, according to a shocked Philip Bromfield. He was responsible to John for the upkeep of the Clapham vault and on hearing that Uncle Brady had unauthorized designs on it, he made inquiries of the stonemason who confirmed his worst suspicions. Mr Brady had ordered the vault to be opened and 'therein deposited the remains of his late Wife'. He had also ordered the stone with Aunt Tooke's epitaph to be removed and replaced by another with his wife's name carved on it. This had been done, but it could not be replaced without John's permission.

> As to what alterations he may have ordered within the Vault I have not enquired, but I have often heard your Grandmother had always given a strict charge not to have one Coffin put upon another . . . 'Tis natural to suppose that he either has or will Contrive to make room for himself to lye with his Wife . . .[7]

It was an awkward problem for a dutiful nephew; after all both ladies were his aunts and it seemed reasonable for Martha Brady to have the last place. He solved it by saying that Aunt Tooke's epitaph must be returned to the top and Aunt Brady's placed on the side with the family arms at the other end.

> But as my Grandmother might express herself in conversation . . . that may be carefully observed with regard to her own coffin. But surely it need not influence the placing of other coffins for a husband and wife; as it is highly probable that matter was all talkt-over between my late deceased Aunt and her surviving husband.[8]

It was all very different from the decent way these things were done at Caversham. As for the unpopular Mr Brady he did very well for himself, for

> he has sometime since gott his Son and Daughter to relinquish the Articles by which means he now comes in for the whole Income of your Aunt's fortune for his Life.[9]

Philip Bromfield died himself in 1767 with no aspirations to a place in the Clapham vault. The responsibility for that mausoleum eventually fell upon Jack and Mary Wilbraham-Bootle jointly, which necessitated many additional letters to their long and lively correspondence.

When Jack went up to Magdalen in 1760 it was to a life which he was to find as enjoyable as his father had before him. He was already much involved in John's own studies, often acting as his secretary, and he knew so many people at Oxford that he was in no need of introductions. Though many of them were older than he they treated him as a friend, at first for his father's sake and then for his own. He had the same capacity for making and keeping friendships among his own generation and a better aptitude for letter writing. He was studious, meticulous and reliable; no one could have been more good-natured or readier to put himself out for others; all he really lacked was that quality of resolute determination and the magnetic touch which distinguished his father's character.

His first tutor was Thomas Winchester whom he regarded almost as an uncle; but this only lasted for a year, as in 1761 Winchester married Lucretia Townson. After the wedding ceremony they drove to Caversham with her two brothers, Thomas and John, and stayed there for a few days with their dearest friends, John and Pen Loveday. Winchester had been presented to the living of Appleton in Berkshire on resigning his Fellowship.

Thomas Bagshaw was devoted to Jack and often wrote to him. In a letter dated, 22 February 1760 he gave him a description of his father as he had appeared to his companions thirty years earlier.

> This ingenious and steady temper makes me expect the greatest things from you and almost envy my old friend, your tutor; who will have the pleasure of seeing the youth of the father reflected in the son, whilst he

is diligently pursuing, perhaps in the same manner, the same laudable ends.

If your morning guests should be allowed no more than an hour for breakfast and conversation; or if you should at any time refuse to open your door when an impertinent Lounger knocks; should you constantly attend chappel believing it your duty; and with generous emulation perform Exercise in the Hall from which Gentlemen of your Gown are too frequently exempt – the Doctor[b] will with pleasure recollect that these things have been all done before by one of the same name, and that *there is nothing new under the sun*. But I will not trouble you with a review of past times and by talking of old things betray the garrulity of age. You invite me kindly to your chambers and so acceptable an invitation it will be difficult for me to decline . . . the ladies you mention will not at all interfere, I can only admire them from a distance and shall have never the courage to approach, now that their keeper is withdrawn.[10]

The ladies about whom Jack had warned him were Catherine and Gertrude, the matronly twin daughters of Browne Willis, known as the 'Lambs' because they were so much sillier than their younger sisters, the 'Lions'. Their old father had died two weeks earlier and they were left on an unpredictable course. Fortunately, however, it was not long before they went back to their house at Whaddon.

Bagshaw was secretly delighted when Jack asked him to contribute some Latin verses to a collection being assembled to commemorate the accession of George III. 'It is like requiring an old decrepit man to dance briskly and gracefully,' he demurred;[11] he was no longer quite the exponent he had been in the days of his youth when many of his friends had consulted him in the art, and in fact the two Johns had to use a little tact in order to procure some alterations. But Bagshaw was always modest and easy; his verses were included (though anonymously, on his instructions), as were Merrick's. He was told by Daniel Prince that it was a greater collection than had ever been published by the University on a like occasion.[12]

Among a number of Reading schoolboys who came up to Oxford while Jack was there was Arthur Dodwell, son of the Archdeacon of Berkshire and a nephew of the controversial Henry. He was elected a demy of Magdalen in the summer of 1760 at the astonishingly early age of thirteen. One of the Fellows, Gilbert Swanne, who was also Dean of Divinity at the time, described the scene to Jack.

As I often take the liberty of calling you my laughing Friend, I cannot observe to you that our Election has in every respect been such as need not give the least check to your indulgence of that chearful disposition. We have . . . elected Parr and Dodwell. But as I know you are not less capable of Anxiety and concern for any distress of your Friends than of

[b] Thomas Winchester.

J. L.'s mother, Sarah (née Lethieullier)
By T. Murray

Thomas Loveday (J. L.'s father)
By T. Murray

Martha Loveday, aged four
By Schwartz

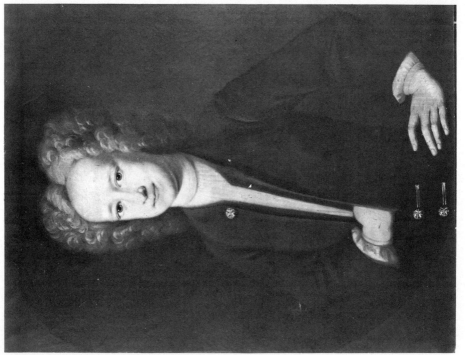

John Loveday, aged ten
By Schwartz

Abigail, second wife of William Goodwin
John Loveday's mother-in-law

William Goodwin
Father of John Loveday's first wife

Dr John Ward
Pastel by Joseph Samuel Webster

Engraved by James Fittler. A.R.A.

Daniel Waterland, D. D.
Engraving by James Fittler

Timothy Goodwin (J. L.'s brother-in-law) by Allan Ramsay
(courtesy of Warwickshire County Museum, Warwick)

A present to Penelope and Sarah Love=
:day of the likeness of beloved and revered
Mr. Bagshaw, one of their dear Father's
highly prized friends. Given them by
Mr. Bagshaw at their earnest request, &
received by them Nov. 6. 1785.

——————

Thomas Bagshaw in old age

Penelope, John Loveday's third wife

John Loveday in old age

rejoycing in their good fortune and Success, I'm sure you'd have had full experience of the former of these Sensations had you sate perdue in some Corner of the Election Chamber, when little Dodwell came to be examined. He had gone through the rest of his Exercises very well; but the Solemnity of having a Book delivered to him for Examination before the Officers, so afflicted him that the Tears flowed apace down his modest Cheeks, and his Sobs frequently interrupted his Expression. – But when you had found that his Modesty only served to adorn and recommend his very sufficient Attainments, and that he hardly mistook or misconstrued a single Word, how would you have been affected with such a Scene as this? . . .[13]

Little Dodwell was at least elected on his merits, but when William Lord, a protégé of Thomas Bagshaw, received a similar honour in 1764, it was entirely on the strength of a recommendation from Jack, who did not even know him. Robert Tatam, now curate of Fenny Compton, had been present when Lord and a Reading boy, William Etwall, were elected as demies.

Mr Etwall will acknowledge his obligations to you and so must all Lord's Friends. The President nominated Lord and his nomination was strongly opposed. But Mr Hoole and your humble Servant voting with the old Gentleman, brought him in. You see the weight of your Interest with me, for I should certainly have joined in the opposition, had you not desired me to espouse the Cause of Lord . . . I hope for your own sake you will write to your Uncle Bagshaw and let him know that the success of Mr Lord was intirely owing to your application on his behalf.[14]

James Birch had a stormier passage to a Fellowship next day, competing against Coningsby Sibthorp, the son of the botanist.

Birch came off triumphant with a Majority of seventeen Votes to ten; Mr Kent with his usual malevolence of heart, instead of assisting Birch in his construing the Books, several times put him out and confounded him by saying 'That's wrong, – Now he has construed three words, &c.' I sharply remonstrated with Mr Kent and told him that he acted an ungenerous and ungentleman-like Part and was seconded by Johnson, Gardiner and many others. Mr Kent could not justify his ill-natured Proceeding, and so declined any further Altercation. I am glad we have finished the whole so much to the Satisfaction of every good and honest man . . .[15]

except of course to Ambrose Kent's, a Fellow who was admittedly awkward, but this time not entirely without reason.

John Spicer, who took a great interest in his former pupils, had two reasons for writing to Jack in July 1763. The Reading poet Mary Latter, who had already dedicated a book of verse to Pen in 1759, had now published her

tragedy *The Siege of Jerusalem* with an ode on the birth of the Prince of Wales.
Jack was to tell the subscribers that Fletcher, the bookseller, had received their
copies from London.

> She has lately wrote a Burlesque Poem on Liberty and Interest[16]
> which is far the best Composition she ever made. It abounds with true
> Wit and Satyr; and the Numbers are so correct and harmonious and the
> Imagery so lively and well painted, that you would take it to be
> Swift's.
>
> I am heartily glad to hear that you intend to mount the Rostrum; could I
> know for certain on what Day you exhibit, I would willingly attend you,
> being well assured that *your* Applause and *my* Satisfaction would keep
> pace together. I hope Powney and Hanger are to be formed by old Roscius
> as well as yourself, lest they should sink into the sleepy Hum and Bagpipe
> Elocution of Queens. Go on and prosper . . .[17]

Being so considerate and polite, Jack was much in demand as an escort for the
ladies, as his former headmaster well knew:

> Mrs Bromley has been so good as to admit Mrs Spicer to be of her
> party; I find you are to be their Palinurus and think them happy in that
> respect; though the Direction of two seasoned Vessels and two spruce
> Frigates is, I think, rather too much for a young Pilot.[18]

Penyston Powney (a lifelong friend) did read English verse for Queen's on
the same day that Jack spoke a Latin dialogue with Thomas Delves – 6 July.
Bagshaw received an account of the Encaenia from a friend who heard this
dialogue in the Theatre and told him it was excellent and had received universal
applause. Jack could now put a silver tassel in his cap.' He sent a copy of
'Mercator and Civis' to be delivered to the Chancellor, Lord Litchfield, and
went straight off to Arlescote and then to Cherington. He was under orders to
bring back his Uncle Tim from the Warners so that he could be reunited with
his mother who was spending four months at Caversham.

In the same year, 1763, Jack completed the work for which he is most
remembered – the indexes to Richard Chandler's great tome, *Marmora
Oxoniensia*.[19] It is well known that the University had engaged Chandler to
produce this illustrated record of all their marbles and archaeological
possessions and that it was partly because of the success with which the work
was received that he was commissioned by the Dilettanti Society to join an
expedition to Turkey the following year. The great friendship which lasted all
their lives began at Magdalen and Chandler never failed to send an even livelier
account of his travels than he wrote in his books. Jack never went abroad

---

' From the transcription of his own diaries for 1763 by his daughter Anne. Tufts in the cap
were allowed to students who had performed an exercise in the Theatre. See Buxton and
Gibson, *Oxford University Ceremonies*, p. 32, a note on irregularities in 1689. Gold tufts could
only be worn by the sons of noblemen.

himself, but was provided with the vicarious excitement of their adventures by such friends as George Vansittart in India, Penyston Powney in the army and Chandler on his explorations. He was then twenty-six years old, an amusing, informal individual. After the Encaenia was over and Jack had gone off to Warwickshire he had chanced to look at the indexes.

. . . I was resolved to leave a line for you, dear Jack, in order to let you know what I have done in your absence. One Page of the Index then is composed, but not corrected, since you went; Swinton's Translation is printed off, Dr Browne's[d] is now receiving his last corrections, I am dead asleep and am to set out early tomorrow morning, so a good night to you, my sweet Johnny. But I have forgot to tell you that I go to meet Mr Godwin at the Hercules Pillars and that we are to go together to Ranelagh. What the deuce do you laugh at? . . . I have got a letter from the Vice-Chancellor to Mr Secretary Wood . . . and will give you an Account of my Reception on condition you will write to me, Richard Chandler, at Hampton, Middlesex, and if you do not, may you oversleep yourself every Morning till you are worse than myself, may the edges and bindings of your Books you take in your Portmanteau be damaged irreparably, may your Dictionaries and Lexicons fail you when you want them most . . .[20]

So, with his introduction by Robert Wood – the Under-Secretary of State and himself a renowned traveller – to the Dilettanti Society, he was set on a career which resulted in Chandler's *Travels in Asia Minor, Travels in Greece*[21] and other notable books.

The first important function Jack attended was undoubtedly the Coronation of George III in 1761. No one knows how he managed to be included in that august assembly or whether he just stood in a crowd, but he was certainly in Westminster Abbey from six o'clock in the morning until six o'clock in the evening, lodging at night with Peter Vatas's brother.

As he was reading Civil Law he remained at Oxford and in October 1764 had an interesting encounter in the Magdalen Common Room when he was 'in company with the great Mr Samuel Johnson'. This seems to be the only indication that Johnson, who received his Dublin doctorate the following year, was at Magdalen or even at Oxford that time. He may have been pursuing inquiries in connection with his edition of Shakespeare[e] – as he did the following year at Cambridge – and possibly at the same time visited his protégé, George Strahan, son of the King's Printer, at University College to which he was admitted at this time.

No one was more delighted than James Merrick to have such a useful friend

---

[d] Joseph Browne, Provost of Queen's College, Oxford; Vice-Chancellor 1759–65.

[e] Published in 1765. Both with this and the *Dictionary* Bagshaw and the two John Lovedays played a postal game, cutting out with scissors words on which they disagreed. These snippets are with the L.F.P.

at Oxford. Cut off from University life as he had been for many years on account of his health,^{f} he had been under some difficulties; but here was someone who could order books, arrange for his publications and help in various other ways. A less good-natured youth than Jack might have found the onslaught of queries and instructions little short of merciless, but he understood the tenacious 'Jemmy' and took it in good part. In 1764, just at the time their mother was dying, his brother John came back from Isleworth to face a lingering death. James gave him every care and six months later mourned him, not only as a brother, but also as a man of intellect and taste. He had left a fine Flemish painting to Horace Walpole in his will, but had insisted on his taking it before he left Isleworth. James received a letter from Walpole, written on 1 December 1764, in which he described his feelings for John Merrick.

> It was a very sensible affliction to me to hear of your Brother's death, for whom I had a real and very great value. His worth, humanity and good sense were very uncommon, and are a peculiar loss to any man whom he honoured with his friendship, as I flatter myself he did me; and nobody would have done more willingly than I would to preserve so valuable a life. His consummate knowledge in his profession convinced him *that* was impossible; and his philosophic resignation and tranquillity made *that* conviction no pain to him. He was so kind as to insist on my taking the picture before he left Isleworth, much against my inclination, and only upon condition that he would let me restore it if he lived to return; a condition I heartily wish coud have been accomplished! I shall now presume it in memory of him with the highest esteem; but should you ever, Sir, come to Twickenham or to London, I hope you will give me an opportunity of showing my regard to Dr Merrick's memory, by expressing my satisfaction in seeing any body so nearly related to him . . .[22]

His years of hard work were now about to bring James's name once more into the public eye. He had brought out *Prayers for a Time of Earthquake and Violent Floods* in 1756, of which Bishop Secker had observed when thanking him for a copy –

> It may be feared that even Earthquakes are now in great measure disregarded, though the Repetitions of them continue. Much less do we think of Floods . . .[23]

He had contributed to all the Oxford collections of verse honouring the Monarchy and his *Poems on Sacred Subjects* came out in 1763. The following year saw the appearance of the first part of his *Annotations on the Gospel of*

---

^{f} Writing to Bishop Secker in 1767 (copy, L.F.P.), James Merrick said that for the last seven years he had scarcely been free from pains in the head for two minutes together. He could often neither read, write nor sleep.

St John. His most important work, a metric version of the Psalms, was published in 1765 and his notes for it three years later. He acknowledged the great assistance he had received by being able to work in two good libraries nearby, those of Dr Robert Bolton in Reading and of John Loveday at Caversham. John's help had been invaluable, especially through his proficiency in the Hebrew tongue. Other scholars to whom James was greatly indebted were Robert Lowth and Bishop Secker, who firmly refused to be referred to by name. Thomas Hunt, the Orientalist, Richard Pococke, the Bishop of Ossory who knew Egypt, Charles Morton of the British Museum, George Jubb and Warren Hastings were among those who supplied him with information. The labour involved in a work of this kind was not only in the composition and research, but also in finding enough subscribers to make its publication practicable and profitable. That he could throw his net so wide is a tribute to his popularity. Nearly eighty letters are preserved from friends and acquaintances willing to draw up subscription lists after receiving the draft copy, many testifying to their affection for him. Of the peers who promised help none was more assiduous than Lord Dartmouth, visiting him in Reading and providing packets of franks. Some people asked for as many as thirty or more receipts, no small matter as it entailed collecting the money and depositing it with one of the named booksellers. Even Dean Patrick Delany took six – and his wife another two – although he told Lord Dartmouth that, though he was no stranger to Merrick's character and literary merit,

> I am not in general a friend to Paraphrases on the Sacred Text, because it is scarce possible in that case not to vary from, or add to the original . . . therefore I should be shy of engageing in the encouragement of any such work, except in the case of such men as Mr Merrick, whose Piety will, I am sure, keep him within the strictest bounds of decency . . .[24]

Some of his correspondents took the opportunity of asking James to compose epitaphs or congratulatory verses for their friends. Others sounded warning notes:

> I have not been able to succeed with the Illiterati of this County; our rustic Genius's delight more in the culture of the apple tree than of the Bay . . .[25]

wrote Thomas Symonds Powell[g] of Pengethly, Herefordshire, sending James two atrocious epitaphs to improve on 'friends so negatively good that neither afforded me one shining quality to rouse my Muse'. Another observed that a version of the Psalms would not raise the curiosity of the multitude 'in this

---

[g] The letter is signed Thomas Symonds Powell, but it seems from John Duncumb, *History of Hereford*, vol. 6, that unlike his brothers he changed his name to Powell Symonds later and his descendants followed suit. He was a contemporary of Merrick at Trinity.

Profligate age',[26] but in spite of all the forebodings the subscriptions lists were longer than James had dared to hope. By the autumn of 1764 they were 'flocking in', as he told Jack, and finally he had between six and seven hundred subscriptions at half a guinea apiece, well over a hundred coming from ladies. One of these was Mrs Thrale who wrote on behalf of her husband and mother;[h] she had not yet met Dr Johnson and it was probably Bennet Langton who persuaded him on to his list.[i] A wide section of society was covered, but in spite of the many illustrious names it was the approbation of the scholars which pleased James the most. They, like everyone else, praised the depth of his scholarship and the purity of his verses, yet he still suffered from those fears which had always plagued him. When Jack told him that Robert Tatam had written

> Every body reads with pleasure and approbation Mr Merrick's Para-phrase. Mr Holbech is particularly fond of it and says he could sit up the whole night to hear it read,[27]

he replied, with a primness caused by genuine consternation, that he hoped Mr Holbech's favourable opinion proceeded from his

> having found it in some degree serviceable to the purposes of Religion, a circumstance which Mr Holbech has, I am persuaded, the good sense to value beyond any poetical excellence.[28]

Even before the work on the Psalms was completed, with all it involved, and with all his family commitments besides, this semi-invalid was absorbed in what, to him, was an even more exciting endeavour. Although there were reliable indexes to Latin classical authors and to Greek poetry, Greek prose was quite lacking in this respect. With all the enthusiasm and tenacity of which he was capable James set about rectifying this deficiency. He began by making a list of the books and editions which should have indexes. It was obviously a far greater task than he could attempt alone, and he needed a substantial number of volunteers. He found it easy enough to persuade John Spicer to give such an exercise to some of his senior boys and they became the first of Merrick's indexers; but it was soon apparent that he must look farther afield. His thoughts turned to Magdalen College School where his old friend, Robert Bryne was the Master and where he knew two of the ushers.[j] Jack was the

[h] L.F.P., 1 December 1763. The letter begins: 'Mr Thrale favours me with his Commands to answer your letter in the manner I would most wish.' Mr Thrale rejoiced to find himself remembered by so valuable an acquaintance &c. She wished the undertaking the success it deserved 'less perhaps on your Account, than on that of the tasteful Few who have long wished to see so commendable a design begun with so strong a probability of success.' Mrs. Thrale's mother was Mrs Salusbury.

[i] L.F.P., 15 August 1764. Langton wrote at some length approving Merrick's work and saying he would not wish to see a modern translation of the Psalms. He took seven subscriptions, six to be delivered to him by his friend Robert Vansittart.

[j] Richardson Wood and John Rawbone.

emissary with full instructions as to how the indexes were to be made and which was to be attempted first.

Very soon a number of clergymen in and around Reading found themselves cutting up sheets of paper and manufacturing wooden boxes with twenty-four partitions. The system was quite complicated, but approved by various scholars whom he consulted while inviting their subscriptions to the Psalms. Only one, Nathaniel Lardner, disapproved the method and advanced his own, which he had taken from John Locke, but this had no effect at all on James Merrick. He wrote a long open letter, printed in pamphlet form, to Joseph Warton, the Headmaster of Winchester, asking him to set some of his boys on to this exercise and pointing out how beneficial it would be to their education. Warton, who liked and admired Merrick, replied a little evasively that he would not fail

> as far as lies in my power to recommend this Scheme to some of the young men with whom I am concerned, as far as is consistent with the System of School-business established here . . .[29]

According to James at least one of Warton's pupils became an indexer. One of his aims was to restore the proper study of Greek to the schools and he felt that a cause of its neglect was the lack of practice in writing it. He held the accepted view that a thorough classical education was of inestimable value to clear thinking and he was convinced that the actual writing was a great aid to the memory. His star performer (though not the youngest, who was only eleven) was undoubtedly William Etwall, who before he left Reading School for Magdalen at the age of fourteen had made several indexes, including one for Forster's edition of the *Select Dialogues of Plato* – of which he himself brought out an edition when he was older.[30] Writing to Jack about the election of demies already described, John Spicer said

> Was a Stranger to see Etwall and guess at his Country, the Greek Digamma is so vividly stamped on his Forehead that I have no doubt but that he would pronounce without the least Hesitation that he came from one of the Islands of the Archipelago, but I am authorized to assure you that he is a Native of Berkshire.[31]

Having motivated his indexers like spinning tops in various parts of Southern England, James wondered where next to promote the good work. His choice of Russia, incongruous as it may seem, was not without good reason, for the Empress Catherine the Great was already renowned for her interest in learning and education. An old college friend, the Revd Daniel Dumaresq, had lived in Russia for seventeen years, while keeping his living in Somerset. On his return to England the Empress had instructed the British Ambassador, the Earl of Buckinghamshire, to invite him to come back and to take on the task of establishing schools of classical learning. She had then written to him herself, but as her letter had miscarried it was not until his return that he found to his dismay that she expected him to apportion different studies to various scholars as best suited the country and nation.[32] The study of classical knowledge, he told Merrick, writing from St Petersburg on 5 August 1764, had improved but was seldom carried far; however, he was hopeful of finding some young scholars who could adapt themselves to James's methods. Moreover,

> The Empress being desirous that some of the young Russians, bred up in the Seminaries or Episcopal Schools of this Country should study at Oxford and at Cambridge, she has ordered 12 to be chosen for that Purpose; and 6 more have offered of their own accord, who will probably be joined to them. They are just arrived here and were presented to me about 3 Days since. It is thought they will imbark for England in one of the last Ships this Autumn.[33]

Dumaresq was also popular with the young King Stanislaus II of Poland, a reformer like Catherine, whose lover he had become when she was Grand Duchess. When James saw in the newspapers that he had invited Dumaresq to his court to discuss education, he wrote to his friend to suggest that His Majesty might like to institute indexing in Poland. Distances dwindled in his mind as he informed him that before his accession Stanislaus had stayed with Dr Thomas Hunt in company with the Attorney General, the Hon. Charles Yorke; and he recalled that Yorke's brother,[k] the vicar of St Giles's, Reading, had told him that the King's letters had been very elegantly written in English.[34] Visions of his scheme being supported by a King of whose 'condescension and abilities' he had heard such pleasing accounts and an Empress of 'such distinguished genius' excited James so much that Jack wrote in amusement

> I find that you are determined to make the Russians perfect Grecians; may success attend you![35]

There was no further news of the Russians for the next two years though James optimistically sent to the British Museum eighteen copies of his open letter to Joseph Warton for Charles Morton, the Librarian, to deliver to them on arrival. Then, in August 1766, he heard again from Dumaresq, now back in England.[36] Six students had arrived earlier that year and had been given Merrick's letter before going to Oxford, but the other twelve, on hearing that they could not be matriculated in either of the Universities, had gone to Leiden and Göttingen instead. Dumaresq himself had suffered a reverse of fortune when the sketches of plans he had made for the Russian schools were not adopted. He had come back through Poland and Stanislaus had given him a letter of recommendation to George III; but apart from being given a common

---

[k] The Hon. James Yorke, Dean of Lincoln, was vicar of St Giles', Reading 1756–68, when he exchanged livings with William Talbot. Subsequently he held three bishoprics.

prebend at Salisbury, nothing happened and he had no choice but to return to his parsonage.

The indexing in England was never completed for James died in 1769 and no one took over the organization of the project. All his papers came eventually into Jack's possession and he presented the indexes to the University of Oxford, with a letter to the Vice-Chancellor, [37] in 1802. They have remained in the Bodleian Library ever since. [38] Those compiled at Magdalen College School have been described as 'a painful and meaningless exercise', [1] but the mechanics of the procedure were probably less painful than construing. They were certainly of great significance to James Merrick, who directed the progress of the students to the last detail, though only from a distance. Sending Jack some books for Mr Bryne, he wrote:

I am greatly pleased with the Alacrity which his young Scholars discover in their application to our new Method of Study and find that a Greek Volume, when thrown into his School, is likely to be as soon demolished as a Loaf tossed into a Carp-pond. [39]

Whatever present-day opinion may be as to the merits of James's ideas at a time when very little Greek was being taught, he had the fullest support of such men as Robert Lowth, James Harris the grammarian, William Blackstone and many others. They were also united in their respect and affection for him, so that when he had the bit between his teeth he was very hard to resist. However austere he was in his personal life he had an attractive and engaging personality.

Mr Rose, who really loves you and will deserve your affection [wrote Gregory Sharpe, Master of the Temple, of a young protégé], offers his most humble and diligent Services in attempting to make an Index of any Book you shall please to recommend to him. [40]

His single-minded enthusiasm may have been tiresome at times, but it is hard to complain of a man who wrote as he did to Jack:

I beg my Compliments may be presented to Mr Bryne, and hope (to use an expression of Cicero's relating to Isocrates, the Author in which his Scholars are now engaged,) that as many Grecians will come out of his School as issued from the Trojan Horse: were that Horse in being, and I in possession of it, (which as Translator of Tryphiodorus I might perhaps have some right to expect) I would willingly split it into Index-Boxes, and distribute them as presents among his young Operators . . . [41]

Since Jack mixed happily with men of all ages he was frequently used as a messenger by those wishing to consult his father. John, for his part, watched

---

[1] R. S. Stanier, *Magdalen School*, 1958. Evidence in L.F.P. indicates that Bryne was very well liked and respected.

his son's progress with great satisfaction, approving his decision in 1762 to 'enter upon the law-line' under another tutor, Benjamin Wheeler. Three years later he 'put on his Civilian's gown'.''' John allowed him the same freedom he had enjoyed himself, never questioning his comings and goings and encouraging him to bring his friends to Caversham. He gave him a reasonable allowance according to his expenses, £224 in 1764 being above the average. Like Merrick he appreciated the strengthened links with the University, but he felt things were going a little too far when he received a provoking letter from Robert Vansittart. It was gratifying that he wanted Jack to stand for a Fellowship at All Souls and that he thought he would be an honour to the Society – 'I believe they have taste enough to think that the Election of him would to themselves be an acquisition of new pleasure'[42] – but the means whereby it was to be effected were very questionable. In those days Founders' kin had first claim to Fellowships.

> . . . I once mentioned the subject to you and said, I believe, that I had no doubt but your Family was as much related to the Founder as the families of many who had claimed and had succeeded as Kinsmen of the Founder; I wished to have a paper of the descents, that I might compare your Genealogy with the pedigrees in College, and prove your Son to be of the blood of Chicheley, or of some who had been admitted as partaking of that Stock; this search is by no means too late even for this year; I still wish that such a paper might be directed to me at All Souls College.[43]

John left it to his son to practise the delicate art of refusal without causing offence. Saying that as it related solely to him it was incumbent on him to write, he replied on 11 August 1764:

> . . . My Father is certain that no pedigree can be made out except from the side of the Lethieulliers. And I believe it has upon examination fully appeared, that they cannot claim any kindred with the family of Chicheley. Charles Lethieullier, who was Fellow of your College, did not, as you yourself informed my Father some time since, come in as Founder's kin. But, waiving all this, I would by no means choose to appear a Candidate for any preferment, at the same time, where a friend and fellow collegiate of longer standing than myself, and an old schoolfellow, had any thoughts of offering themselves. This is the case now and I heartily wish them Success. Was I to act contrary to these Sentiments, I should never think myself intitled to the character of a gentleman. After returning my best thanks . . . for your very kind recollection of me, I must beg leave to decline all pretensions to the honor you designed me. We hope to have the pleasure of your good company whenever you come into this part of the world . . .[44]

''' He read Civil Law.

He wrote from Caversham very much in his father's manner, as the future Regius Professor of Civil Law no doubt observed when he received this rather daunting reply from a very junior aspirant to his own profession.

John's reaction to a request from the minister of the Baptist church at Castle Hill, Warwick, was less easy to understand. John Knight was a scholarly man with whom he liked to talk when he stayed with Mrs Goodwin. He wrote in confidence in September 1765, asking for assistance in becoming an ordained priest of the Church of England – partly through inclination after having read many theological works, and partly because of

the odd Sentiments and Dispositions of the People I serve, who for the most part are very rigid and bigotted Calvinists of a censorius, narrow, froward Temper; very ignorant – no Lovers of Learning or judicious Discourses, but on the contrary of rambling, nonsensical, enthusiastic preaching which I cannot come into, and which is really too much the Case with the Baptists especially those in the Country . . .[45]

Having put his case at great length, Knight thought that no bishop would refuse him and felt sure all the local clergy would support him. He begged John to use his influence in these directions as well as with the heads of Oxford colleges. But the reply he received, though polite, was negative and unexpected.

As to the main purport of your letter I can do no more than applaud it. My acquaintance lies in a very narrow compass. Particularly as to the clergy, I do not visit any of the incumbents in the neighbouring town. I do not know a bishop. It has occurred to me that in the application to any of them for the purpose, it is possible he may say: 'Sir, if I ordain you and in consequence thereof you christen a child, may not the said child, when come to years of discretion, have a scruple concerning its baptism; as that was administered by a person who was never himself baptized by an episcopal minister' . . .

He suggested that Mr Knight should be baptized 'hypothetically' and that he should consult a clerical friend in Warwick.

Depend upon it, nothing in your letter shall get air from me, God direct you in the whole.[46]

Why was John's refusal to help so final? He may have thought Archbishop Secker or Bishop Pearce too remote and it is true there were two new vicars in Reading, one of whom, Charles Sturges at St Mary's, was to become a close friend. Why did he not suggest Merrick who would have welcomed a convert and who had closer contacts with Secker? It can only have been this growing desire not to become involved with anything outside his immediate family and friends or the special studies he enjoyed. The opportunity was lost and John Knight remained at Castle Hill for the next ten years or more.

It may have been this reluctance to play a prominent part, as well as the prevailing fashion for pseudonyms, which prevented him from publishing books or articles under his own name. Writing to Jack in 1774, Thomas Bagshaw referred to what he called a 'Pot folio' which he said had been published by John thirty years earlier, observing that it was generally thought that nothing had ever appeared under his name. No trace of this work can be found nor was such a book mentioned in the eighteenth-century catalogue of his library." .

His kindness to the Caversham parishioners and his willingness to give all possible aid to writers and scholars – not to mention the hospitality of his table – were the primary reasons for his great reputation for benevolence. His friends invariably acknowledged his help, though not always by name, knowing his wishes for privacy in that respect. One of these was James Granger, the author of the *Biographical History of England*,[47] a near neighbour in his parish at Shiplake and a man to whom John became really devoted. Another regular correspondent was Roger Huggett, the conduct and chaplain at Eton, who through his wide researches into medieval history, his access to the resources of the College Library and his friendship with Ralph Bigland, the Somerset Herald, gave as much as he received. He got on very well with John, but the Provost and Fellows took a less favourable view of him and tried to eject him in 1760 by the simple expedient of boarding up the door to his chambers without any warning.° In 1763 he was given the living of Hartley Wespall (very near John's friends, the Bakers) through the good offices of George III. Writing on 20 May, he said:

> I have to thank you on your kind congratulatory Letter on account of my succeeding to the Rectory of Hartley-Waspaill, which you observe was in a way of Honour, to which I must add, and in a way of singular Providence which put it into the Heart of the King to be at the first as particular in his Inquiries about, as he was afterwards in his interposition for me . . . among the many agreeable circumstances which attend the said Preferment, I must not omit the mention of this one, that it places me but at the distance of eleven measured miles from Mr Loveday and in a good Turnpike Road . . .[48]

Throughout the 1760s the man who most surely filled the gap left by the deaths of Ward and Ballard was the brilliant young Keeper of the Ashmolean, William Huddesford, who was under thirty years of age when he first came to know

---

" L.F.P., 2 November 1774. Bagshaw said it was most correctly printed. Nothing is known of such a work at the Bodleian or British Libraries nor in the eighteenth-century catalogue of books now in the Pennsylvania State University Library.

° Huggett's lengthy letter of protest to the Provost, Dr Stephen Sleech, and Fellows of Eton, B.L. Add. MSS.4839–4844, though repetitive and pathetic, is not without entertainment value. The King's interest may have been due to the fact that Sleech was his chaplain.

John. For eleven years until his early death in 1772, his letters were interspersed with visits to Caversham. Being nearer in age to Jack (of whom he was very fond), his amusing self-deprecatory style reveals a natural deference as well as a cheerful affection.

> I wish myself dayly in your Study [he wrote not long before his death] – but that is no Compliment to the Ladies – I add, therefore, in your Parlour at proper Times; to say the Truth, from the Parlour all along the Passage, through the Gallery, into the Study, my best wishes attend you and yours . . . I forgot the Museum at the end of the Gallery.[49]

He was the only man John considered able to draw up an acceptable life of Hearne and he begged him to undertake it. Huddesford's letters to John show that he planned to do so, but he did not live to carry it out. Although he called the text 'vile' he did supply notes for a life of Hearne published in 1772 by Fletcher of Oxford and Pote of Eton (whom he disliked intensely). He was much more involved with Anthony Wood's autobiography which Fletcher and Pote published with the lives of Hearne and Leland. The first part of it had appeared in Hearne's *Thomae Caii Collegii Vindiciae Antiquitatis Academia Oxonienses* (1730). Writing to John in March 1771, Huddesford described an editor's dream come true.

> We have discovered a great Prize. Among Rawlinson's MSS. is one entitled 'Passages of A. Wood's Life from his Papers'. It is wrote in Dr Rawlinson's hand and seems to be extracted from A. Wood's private pocket Almanacs . . . The Passages themselves are so like my friend Tony's that there can be no doubt that they were his own. But we cannot among Rawlinson's Books find the Almanacs themselves; nor does the Doctor give any account of them. This puzzles us much, However they will so nicely fit into the former part of the Life that we are determined to print them as a continuation of it, leaving out only some very obnoxious things and those which are quite foreign to our Purpose.[50]

On 16 July he explained how he had filled an unfortunate gap.

> We shall soon be at a loss for no Diaries or Pocket-Books are to be found between 1683 and 1692, Some part of the Chasm I shall supply by publishing some curious Account of the Scholars training in Arms during Monmouth's Rebellion from A. Wood's Papers in M. Ashm.[P][51]

[P] See vol. II, p. 332, footnote (Fletcher and Pote). 'Mr à Wood's Diaries from 1683–1695 being lost, at least not transcribed by Dr Rawlinson . . .' Wood's MSS. in the Ashmolean were transferred to the Bodleian (where there were already a good many) in 1858. In the preface to vol. I, *The Life and Times of Anthony Wood* (1891), Andrew Clarke explains that these almanacs (1657–95) disappeared and were not seen by Huddesford nor by Philip Bliss. They were found, eventually, in a drawer in the Gough Room at the Bodleian by the Revd W. Dunn Macray and then carefully bound.

In 1768 Huddesford decided to repair Hearne's tomb, which needed a new marble slab and inscription. The only possible corroboration for Daniel Prince's assertion, made forty years later, that John repaired the tomb in 1750[52] might be in the fact that he told Huddesford to turn up the stone in order to find the genuine epitaph on the other face of it.[53] He now contributed a guinea to the cost of the repair; the mason's bill was only £3.18s.9d. – which was just as well, as all Huddesford could raise was £1.11s.6d. from a few Oxford antiquaries.[54]

Writing to him much earlier when Huddesford was depressed by the poor reception his Latin catalogue of Wood's library was receiving, and wishing he could help, John revealed something of his own outlook on life:

> I never wish myself a man of consequence but upon such occasions as this; otherwise, a retired private life is not more my lot than my choice . . .[55]

Certainly it amounted to a state of bliss in the study to be one of the protagonists in an exchange of letters and books when Huddesford, Granger, Ducarel and Thomas Warton were the others. Writers not only consulted John on material for their work but also on the work itself, as when Warton sent him the proofs of his *Life of Sir Thomas Pope* to examine in 1771.[q]

Meanwhile his young family grew and prospered. The death of little Martha in 1763 was the last of the personal tragedies. Undeterred by Mary's fate at Dorchester, John and his wife sent their elder daughter to boarding school at a Madame Latuffière's establishment two weeks before her sixth birthday. Fortunately Madame left England at the end of the year and Pen had to come home.

The days of the rambles had long been over when suddenly in the summer of 1765 John decided to make a long journey with Jack as his companion. The diaries of his tours had been quite neglected except for a few notes made the previous spring when he had seen Drapers' Hall, the College of Physicians and Rush's Vinegar Yard.[r] The excuse now was to pay a visit to Thomas Townson at Malpas and they arranged the journey so that they could see Richard Congreve on the way there and John Audley at Birmingham on the way back. Setting off from Warwick on 1 July, they rode to Castle Bromwich Hall, a 'noble old house' as Jack called it.[s]

> In Sir Henry Bridgeman's Seat are many portraits; such as the Lord Keeper of that name, of whom this gentleman is the representative; he has a very sedate look, is sitting robed . . . Charles I in armour; a full face but

---

[q] Enclosed in a letter from Huddesford (L.F.P., 15 December 1771).

[r] Rush's Vinegar Yard was in Southwark. John described a vessel containing 1,341 barrels at the rate of 36 gallons to the barrel. There were 3 tons of iron in the hoops and it cost £500 exclusive of key hoops (Diary, 24 May 1764).

[s] L.F.P. The diaries of Dr John Loveday (d. 1809).

thin–. . . his right hand is upon a helmet that lies on a table, on which is the
Sceptre tipt with a dove, an emblem of his inclination to peace . . . Good
tapestry in this house, some by Vandrebanc.

They looked at the excellent portraits in the long gallery and rode on into
Staffordshire the same day, stopping for the night at Shenstone. Next morning
they rode 'over Cannock Heath to Leacroft Hall, the Revd Mr Congreve's
where we breakfasted'. The house had come into Richard Congreve's
possession through his first wife, the widow of William Byrche, the previous
owner.

> In this old large timber seat of the Byrche family is a picture, though but
> an indifferent one, of Mrs Jane Lane[t] – who after the death of her husband,
> Sir Clement Fisher of Packington . . . retired to her Sister Byrche's, and
> died in Leacroft Hall, but is buried at Packington. . . . We travelled upon
> the Streetway this day, before Leacroft, but especially after it when it was
> much upon the ascent, but very easy.

They rode past Weston Park[u] which had belonged to the late Earl of
Bradford and close by Woodcote, 'the very handsome seat' of Colonel
Cotes.

Beyond Newport is Chetwynd Hall, the seat of [George] Pigott, Esq., an
old house in the bottom on the right hand, his walled Park across the road
on the left . . .[v] We first got sight of [the Wrekin] yesterday, just as we
were beyond Weston.

> Whitchurch is a very considerable town; the old houses of timber, the
> new of brick . . . The church and tower, all built in this century of hewn
> stone, and a very beautiful church it is; But was it worth while to make the
> stone-pillars appear like wooden ones for the sake of ever so fine a
> deception of fluting? Indeed the painter by his performance that way has
> made all the amends possible for the disguise. It is regularly pewed; the
> pulpit, with the back to the communion-table, has a sounding board
> suspended over it by an iron rod,[w] its only support. Over the front of the
> Organ-loft are the Queen's arms in needlework[x] . . . The Earls of
> Shrewsbury were the old patrons of this church; the 1st Earl's recumbent
> effigies of stone is in the South wall; but the epitaph, preserved by
> Camden, is omitted in the new church . . . The Duke of Bridgewater

[t] Jane Fisher was celebrated for having helped Charles II to escape after the Battle of
Worcester.
[u] Weston Park now belonged to Sir Henry Bridgeman on a division of the late Earl's
estates.
[v] The house is Elizabethan.
[w] The sounding board was later made into a table.
[x] The church of St Alkmund was rebuilt 1712–13. The silk royal arms, preserved
elsewhere in the church, formerly hung behind the Speaker's chair.

now the patron ... The present Rector, Bishop Newcombe of St. Asaph, has built a very good parsonage-house. There is a brass plate as late as 1742 inserted on a tomb-stone in the cemetery. Not long since as many of the inhabitants here as were willing to pay the price, were enfranchised by the Duke of Bridgewater.

They arrived at Malpas that night to be greeted by Townson whose rectory was in the lower part of the town. There they stayed for eight enjoyable days. They visited Chester Cathedral, saw the salt works at Northwich and admired the fine views from Mr Egerton's terrace at Broxton. They listened to sermons in the 'fine old church, excellently well lighted ' . . . very elegant pillars'; and one wonders whether Townson showed them the grammar school where they might have seen a bright boy of eleven at his books – a boy from a neighbouring farm[y] of whom the rector thought so highly that he later on recommended him to Brasenose College and paid half his University expenses; one who was to think of Caversham and Williamscote almost as second homes and whose daughter would one day marry Jack's son, Thomas. How astonished they would have been, if they had noticed the small Ralph Churton, to be told that he would be the man to write their obituaries and those of several of their friends.

They left after breakfast on 11 July, Townson accompanying them as far as Hawkstone, the seat of Sir Rowland Hill, the first baronet. They were shown round the house and grounds by his second son, John.

There is a very fine room in this house, but that may be paralleled elsewhere; not so the improvements out of doors, where nature indeed has done so much that not to have helpt it somewhat by art would have been unpardonable in a man of fortune. The ground rises behind the house in fine lawns, topt by thick shaded woods. Ascended the heights you are on a terrace, whence the view every way is grand beyond compare; Shrewsbury is to be seen from hence, Beeston Castle also and mountains all round; however we are so high upon this spot, that in truth the Wrekin makes no distinguished figure here. But the wonder of the place are the great rocks in so cultivated a country, rocks decked in green, nay supporting oaks. The ruins of Red Castle just by, mentioned by Leland as 'all ruinus and decayid many a Day'. A grotto is now making, to be entered one way through arched passages under ground, turning many ways. The whole of this fine place takes a great circuit.

Here they parted from Townson and went on to Newport and, next day to Wolverhampton. They stopped to look at Tong church on the way, noticing its steeple rising from the centre.

Stalls in the chancel and a grand lofty monument for Sir Thomas Stanley,

[y] Upper Snabb Farm, Bickley, Cheshire.

second son of Edward Earl of Derby, elbows God's altar in an extraordinary manner, being just close to it on the North side,[z] and exhibits three recumbent effigies large as the life. But this is modern in comparison of many fine monuments in the church, some with recumbent figures on raised tombs, others of brass laminae . . .

The stones of the college which stood just by are now making use of at Tonge castle, not far off. – a very large mansion of brick, belonging to [George] Durand Esq., late the Duke of Kingston's.

Riding down Tettenhall hill they could see Wolverhampton, 'a town of account . . . spreading itself on a considerable rise'. At the bottom of the hill lay Tettenhall Green, a pleasant shaded spot where Sir Richard Wrottesley was both patron and incumbent of the living. Wolverhampton, with its brick buildings and narrow streets, reminded John of some quarters of the City of London. In the church they noted the 'curious stone-pulpit' in the nave, the stalls in the chancel which were made use of 'only for a chapter act' and the solid brass statue of Sir Richard Leveson in a niche in the south wall – 'a frezo in 1588'; but appropriately enough, since it was the last church he was to describe, it was that lifelong interest of his, the stipends of the clergy, which preoccupied him. William Gibson had told him that the prebends of this collegiate church must be given to the canons of Windsor in seniority, if they chose to accept them, but the only such name on the list he copied was that of a minor canon and friend of Dr Waterland, Isaac Chapman.

Dr Gibson set the reserved rent of the deanery at 30£ per annum, they say here it is more; the prebends are of unequal value, the best of them is called the golden prebend; the houses and estates of all these are leased out, as is the deanery just by. The duty is done by the Sacrist, here vulgarly called the Minister, and three readers. The former is appointed by the dean; he reads the early prayers and he administers the Sacrament, as he has the cure of souls; it may be worth to him about 60£ per annum . . . the three readers have 10£ per annum each, which with the surplice fees may amount to 30£. These are put-in by some of the prebendaries, as are the three singingmen and six choristers; notwithstanding whom there is at present no choir-service . . .

Within this extensive parish are five chapels of ease; one of them a late and elegant building of stone[a] within the town; it has an handsome well-toned organ and stands in a large cemetery; and as the Earl of Stamford gave 1000£ towards the fabric, his lordship has the nomination of the minister. There is a notoriously public mass-house in the town; and a mile off, on Lord Dudley and Ward's estate, a great Popish school. The 'fre schole made by Syr Stephane Jenning[b] Maire of

[z] The monument to Sir Thomas Stanley was moved to the south transept.
[a] St John's Church was built in 1755.
[b] Sir Stephen Jenyns. Quotation from Leland's *Itinerary*.

London' in 1508 is a handsome building, and a modern one. William Wood, so well known in Ireland, lived in this town and was buried in the great church, though without memorial.[c] Jonathan Wild was a Native here.[d]

No one who was interested in houses could ride this way without stopping to see the Hermitage at the Wombourn Wodehouse or The Leasowes at Halesowen.

Womborn Woodhouses. Sir Samuel Hellier's – The woods here are laid-out in true taste and give us views into the country that are really pleasant. Lines out of English poets inscribed on tablets, that are hung upon trees up and down, are well suited to the places assigned them. But the Hermitage here is curious indeed, consisting of several apartments, moss and roots the materials; by springs the hermit, formed very naturally, has motions that surprize his visitants who suppose him inanimate. The Music-room in another part is an instance of its master's elegance, both in the fabric itself and its furniture. Lord Dudley and Ward's Park comes up close to these improvements.

Dudley Castle, a ruin on a hill, is on the left hand as you enter the town; which is no inconsiderable place . . . the castle is in Staffordshire as well as the ruin of the Cluniac cell in the bottom as we came into town.

Half a mile from Halesowen is The Leasows, late Mr Shenstone's, now by purchase Captain Joseph Turnpeny's who has vamped up the house.[e] Before Shenstone's death, Lord Ward – now Viscount Dudley and Ward – was the main contributor to the building of the Brerely chapel, on an eminence for the use of the colliers; which proves a fine point of view from this improved farm, the walk round which is above two miles. Woodhouse's[f] poems describe the place, the propriety of the mottos cannot enough be admired and some views here are inscribed to noble friends of Mr Shenstone.

From this memorial to the poet and landscape gardener, William Shenstone, they went next day to Hagley Hall, the splendid house which had been rebuilt by Sanderson Miller for its present owner, George, 1st Lord

[c] By dubious means Wood, an ironmaster, received a patent from George I for coining farthings and halfpence and disposing of them in Ireland, causing controversy in which Swift and other satirists joined.

[d] Wild set up a business as a thief and informer in London and after an exciting career was hanged at Tyburn.

[e] Two years after William Shenstone's death Captain Joseph Turnpeny was the third owner, since him, of the Leasowes. Five others followed in fairly quick succession over the next few years.

[f] James Woodhouse, known as the poetical shoemaker, sent an elegy to Shenstone in 1759 which the latter printed with his own poems. He became well known and his *Poems on Sundry Occasions* had come out in 1764.

Lyttelton, and only completed two years before. John had ridden past the old house in 1730 on his way back from Wales. They stopped for two nights in Kidderminster in order to spend as much time as possible in this beautiful place.

> This palace of a house is not upon the same spot with the old one; it is built of a beautiful stone from a quarry three miles off. Were it not for the size it might appear a lodge in the park; for all the offices, though just by, are intirely hid; so the house stands by itself in a lovely lawn. Use is equally consulted with ornament throughout the fabric; and the furniture is peculiarly elegant and grand . . .

The paintings were a revelation as he recorded them in the supping parlour, the saloon, the bedchambers, the dressing-rooms, the library, the withdrawing-room with its 'elegant cieling in compartments by Cipriani' and 'fine English tapestry by Saunders'[g] and in the gallery – 'a noble room above 83 foot long and proportionable every way'. All the floors were of English oak and the chimneypieces were all different and very elegant.

> The church is in the park near the house, but hid by trees; in it a monument for Mrs Lyttelton, my Lord's first wife, another for his father, Sir Thomas. The church, though old, owes much to my Lord. The kitchen-garden and shrubbery deserve distinct notice. Who can describe the perpetually varying scenes in the park of about five miles compass, enriched with noble forrest-trees, and viewing the Wrekin among other mountains? It runs up hills and abounds with lawns. The great high road is so sunk and overlooked, that the country beyond it seems altogether a part of the Park. In the Park is a tower and adjacent ruins, so placed by his Lordship as to terminate several views and at the same time to afford a commodious habitation to the keeper and his family.

Although it is not mentioned it is likely that Lord Lyttelton met these particular visitors. He too was a friend of his architect, Sanderson Miller, and his brother, Dr Charles Lyttelton, had been closely associated with John Ward through the Royal Society.

The tour ended on 16 July and was followed by further visits to Warwick Castle and Weston House, the home of William Sheldon. It was really Hagley

---

[g] The ceiling of the tapestry room at Hagley Hall has been attributed to James Stuart because of a letter written by Lord Lyttelton in October 1758 saying 'Stuart has engaged to paint for me a Flora and four pretty little Zephyrs.' Edward Croft-Murray, in *Decorative Painting in England*, 1970, says there is a problem which cannot be resolved from a stylistic point of view and quotes two contemporary sources who attributed the ceiling to Cipriani. John Loveday's is a third contemporary voice. The tapestry at Hagley is by Joshua Morris and there is no record of tapestry there by Paul Saunders. However this does not preclude the possibility that there was Saunders tapestry there in 1765 and John must have had some reason for saying so.

which made such a splendid finale to the tours of John Loveday. That he was back in the folds of the family was brought home to him at Arlescote when he heard of the death of old Paul Mansfield who had served his grandmother, his mother and himself for over half a century. He and Jack were reunited with Pen and the Gibson girls at Cherington and on 7 August 'we got home about noon, safe and sound'. Two days later little Pen and Sarah were fetched back from friends, to be followed by Jack and John Audley from Oxford. They were all together again and at home.

It had been a good ramble, but it was the last. Perhaps, at fifty-four, John had found it a little tiring. They had kept up the traditional daily mileage and he was after all out of practice and getting older – it was time to hang up his silver spurs. In any case there was not the same excitement he had known in the old days. He had been one of the pioneers, exploring the countryside, clambering over mountain passes, toiling along the dusty or sandy roads long before many of the new turnpikes were built. He had seen the country houses before their owners had transformed them and had watched the growth of new buildings with interest and approval. Reared in the tradition of Hawksmoor and Vanbrugh he had never lost his taste for the Baroque, but had welcomed equally the Palladian influence which had reigned throughout his adult years. Of the Greek classical revival now emerging he had nothing to say, for it had hardly made itself felt when he closed the diaries of his tours. Nor had he ever pretended to an expert knowledge of architecture. Writing to Huddesford in 1767, he said, 'When in the cathedral with you, you observed upon the forms of the arches; it is a subject I am not master of,'[56] and he mentioned difficulty in distinguishing between Norman and Saxon round arches as an example. In all his tastes, and especially in his dismissal of Elizabethan houses as 'old retired places' and his dislike of anything earlier than Gothic in cathedrals and churches, he was a man of his times, reflecting the general opinion of his contemporaries. Now younger men were following in his footsteps; indeed anyone who could not afford the Grand Tour of Europe could at least ride round Great Britain. It had become a fashion and he had never been a competitor. His pleasure would still be to read from time to time the accounts of his rambles and to add to them appropriate notes from his extensive reading. The days of discovery were over.

Antiquity was no deterrent as far as manuscripts or books were concerned and he became increasingly enthralled with church history. When Gilbert White came to stay in October 1777 the conversation on the history of Selborne Priory so fascinated them both that it was continued by correspondence. There were still many years in which to enjoy these more leisurely preoccupations and it was not until 1788 that he resigned himself to having reached old age. In 1766 he was appointed to a grand jury in Oxford for the first time and thereafter had to visit the beloved city more often; but gradually the story of his life becomes inextricably interwoven with those of his children, apart from his influence on the work of other scholars.

Jack practised law in London from 1772 until 1777 when he married Anne Taylor-Loder and settled at Williamscote, devoting the rest of his life to his family, friends and scholarly pursuits. His four sons were all sent to school at Reading. Penelope and Sarah, almost inseparable from their Forrest cousins, grew up to play their part in the society around them until, after their father's death, they moved with their mother to a different part of the country. Arthur was ordained and remained at Magdalen almost all his life. Mary, a victim to introspection, preferred to spend most of hers with her cousins. Long before that Anne Gibson fell in love with the attractive but consumptive brother-in-law of Mrs Lybbe Powys who had lost his first wife after a Gretna Green marriage. Her bewildered uncles corresponded about her 'infatuation' but allowed her to marry him in 1768 from George Gibson's house since[57] 'neither the young lady nor himself could be prevailed upon'.[58] Girls did sometimes get their own way, but sadly Richard Powys died a few days later. After a discreet interval Anne retrieved her reputation for common sense by marrying a suitable clergyman, the Revd Jonathan Lippyeatt. Sarah Gibson stayed single and Elizabeth married John Nicholls.

Inevitably the years took their toll of John's friends and his diary reflects his assessment of what each had meant to him. One of the first to go was Lady Cadogan, in 1768 at the age of sixty-six. She had known him since his childhood and had been ever 'my staunch and able friend'. Of her husband eight years later he wrote 'who surely could never have made himself an enemy'. In 1769 the loss of James Merrick, to whom he had been almost an elder brother, deprived him of a companion of intellectual prowess.

> January 5th, about 2 in the morning, died the Revd. James Merrick, M.A., one of the most extraordinary men this age has produced; but not more so in regard to his abilities, both natural and acquired, than for the real goodness of his heart, as far as it is possible after a long and intimate acquaintance, to form any judgment of the heart of man.[h]

John was the last survivor of the Magdalen friends of his early youth. Thomas Bagshaw, who lived until 1787, wrote to him after Audley's death:

> You and I, now the only two left of an happy knot of friends, are like two old timber trees, once surrounded by others which have been occasionally rooted up by the Lord of the soil. Both have now strong marks of decay, and so close do they grow, with their roots intermingled and intwined, that one cannot be probably taken-down without drawing after it the other.[59]

Two of that group had been Winchester and Zinzan, both of whom had remarried after losing their much-loved wives – Winchester re-strengthening

---

[h] Penelope Hind, writing on Merrick composing his Paraphrase of the Psalms from her father's recollections of him, said: 'If any alteration was proposed in regard to the metre or the rhyme, he could with as much facility turn the thoughts into a fresh set of words as if it had been prose instead of verse . . .'

the knot some years later by marrying the widow of Richard Lluellyn. After a long interval Sir John Foulis came back into John's life and their revived correspondence gave them a great deal of pleasure in their old age. The house at Caversham was as hospitable as ever, filled now with young people and its doors always open. Bridget Forrest married John Byng, who was soon a welcome and frequent guest, joining John on his favourite walks and discussing the changes in those parts of the country which the older man had described long ago and the younger was now discovering. [60] William Benwell, John's scribe and protégé, reminded him in some ways of the young James Merrick. He watched his excellent progress at Trinity College with fatherly interest and welcomed him into the family, but, it seems, never imagined he would one day marry Penelope. Jack returned often to the fold, sometimes with his family, but John did not visit them at Williamscote. It was just a little too far for someone who had decided never again to sleep outside his own bed. [i] When at last the time came for him to go he directed his own death with courage, as calmly and devoutly as he had directed his life. Penelope recalled later that Lord Braybrooke had remarked on 'the general grief expressed in Berkshire':

> It is something new to hear an old person lamented with as much warmth as could be expressed for one equally worthy cut suddenly off in the prime of life –

and she remembered some words of her cousin Mary Berry,

> When I was lately with Miss Berry, she was speaking of my Father with that warm affection and respect with which he had justly inspired her, and she said – 'When I first saw Mr Loveday I expected to find a grave theologian, given up solely to such studies; and to my surprise and delight I found him entering with animation on all subjects of refined literature, shewing a polished taste, and appearing just as I have pictured to myself that a gentleman of high blood and high breeding of the last age must have done.'

The concluding words are his own:

> Of all books I abominate those where matter of fact and fiction are indiscriminately interwoven. I am content if they give me all Truth or all Romance.

---

[i] Accepting an invitation from his cousin, Lady Cathcart of Tewin Water, for his family, but refusing for himself, John wrote on 2 August 1783 (L.F.P.): 'As many of them as can be spared from me (who have not lain out of my own bed for years, and so have never once made a visit to my Son living in the same County) will do themselves the honour of waiting upon your Ladyship . . .' See p. 268 n. z.

Envoi

In March 1789, just before he died, John Loveday adapted some lines by Alexander Pope which 'aptly delineate some circumstances attending J. L. and his mansion at Caversham':

> Let me on Thames's banks recline at ease,
> And see what friends, and read what books I please;
> I was not born for courts or great affairs:
> I pay my debts, believe, and say my prayers.

Bibliographical and Source Notes

CHAPTER I

1. Goldsmiths' Company records.
2. Harleian Society, vol. XXIII. *Allegations for Marriage Licences, 1558–1699.*
3. Michael North's will.
4. Christ Church Library, MS. Estates, 65, fol. 20, 8 September 1702.
5. Ibid., fol. 23. South to John Brooks, 17 September 1702.
6. Ibid., fol. 25. South to William Stratford, 20 November 1711.
7. L.F.P., Dr John Loveday's accounts.
8. L.F.P., 1696.
9. First published 1724–27.
10. Published by William Derham, Senr., 1726.
11. *A Companion for the Festivals and Fasts in the Church of England,* 1704.
12. Hearne's *Collections,* vol. IX, 20 February 1728.
13. Charles Coates, *The History and Antiquities of Reading,* 1802.
14. Ibid.
15. L.F.P.
16. Bodl. MSS Rawl. lett. D.682. f.34. John Loveday's information.
17. L.F.P., probably late April 1756.
18. Jeremy Collier, *Short View of the Immorality and Profaneness of the English Stage,* 1697–98.
19. Bishop Richard Cumberland published this essay in 1686 and dedicated it to Samuel Pepys.
20. Published in 1714 by the Revd John Walker.
21. Coates, *The History and Antiquities of Reading.*
22. Bodl. MSS. Rawl. lett. 15.f.123, 23 April 1727. (Published in *Letters Written by Eminent Persons in the Seventeenth and Eighteenth Centuries . . from the Originals in the Bodleian Library,* 2 vols.)
23. L.F.P., copy of letter, 15 February 1724.

CHAPTER 2

1. *Ductor Historicus, or, A Short System of Universal History* was published by Hearne in 1704.
2. Bodl. MSS. Rawl. lett. 7 f.177, 9 January 1728. L.F.P., John Loveday's copy.
3. L.F.P., 17 January 1728.
4. Published in 1727.
5. Hearne's *Collections,* vol. IX, 20 February 1728.
6. Ibid., 23 February 1728.

7. *Liber Niger Scaccarii* was published in 1728.
8. *Magdalen College Register*, first series, vol. VI, pp. 161, 206.
9. Hearne's *Collections*, vol. X, 26 August 1730.
10. Ibid., 10 October 1728.
11. Bodl. MSS. Rawl. lett. 7.f.178, 28 September 1728. L.F.P., John Loveday's copy.
12. Bodl. MSS. Rawl. lett. 28.f.123, 3 October 1728. L.F.P. John Loveday's copy. An extract from this letter, taken from a draft in the Bodleian, is quoted in Hearne's *Collections*, vol. X.
13. Hearne's *Collections*, vol. IX, 2 October 1725.
14. *D.N.B.*, William Oldisworth.
15. W. R. Ward, *Georgian Oxford*, 1958.
16. L.F.P., 15 January 1729.
17. L.F.P., 22 January 1729.
18. Bodl. MSS. Rawl. lett. 7.f.182, 12 February 1729. L.F.P., John Loveday's copy.
19. Hearne brought out *Johannis de Trokelowe Annales &c.* in 1729.
20. L.F.P., 20 February 1729.

CHAPTER 3

1. Hearne's *Collections*, vol. X, 5 February 1729.
2. Ibid., 21 March 1729.
3. Bodl. MSS. Rawl. lett. 15,f.125, 20 March 1729, L.F.P., John Loveday's copy, 20 March 1729.
4. L.F.P., 27 March 1729.
5. Hearne's *Collections*, vol. X, 24 February 1729.
6. Bodl. MSS. Rawl. lett. 7.f.181, 9 April 1729.
7. Hearne's *Collections*, vol. X, 19 April 1730.
8. Ibid., 21 March 1729.
9. William Roper's *Life of Sir Thomas More* was first published in 1626.
10. Hearne's *Collections*, vol. X, 17 June 1729.
11. L.F.P.
12. Bodl. MSS. Rawl. lett. 15.f.126, 25 August 1729. L.F.P., John Loveday's copy.
13. L.F.P., 4 September 1729.
14. Leland's *Collecteana*, 1715.
15. L.F.P., 18 September 1729.
16. Hearne's *Collections*, vol. X, 23 October 1729.
17. John Bearblock's account of Queen Elizabeth's visit to Oxford in 1566 was printed by Hearne as an appendix to his edition of *Historia et Vita Ricardi II* in 1729.

CHAPTER 4

1. L.F.P.

CHAPTER 5

1. *Autobiography* of Edward Gibbon, first published 1796.
2. *Magdalen College Register*, first series, vol. I, p. 143. Also *Nichols's Literary Anecdotes*, VIII, p. 520. 'He was a most elegant scholar and the most amiable of men.'
3. Published anonymously in 1773.
4. B.L. Add. MSS. 42160–42173. The MS. diaries of Caroline Lybbe Powys. Also Emily Climenson, *Passages from the Diaries of Mrs Philip Lybbe Powys*, 1899, p. 60.

5. It was written on the back of a copy of a letter to Hearne, dated 30 August 1730, informing him of his planned tour.
6. L.F.P., undated. See n. 5.
7. *The Commonwealth of Oceana* was published in 1656.
8. Published 1714–25.
9. Anthony Wood, *Athenae Oxonienses*. See ed. P. Bliss, iii, 1158.
10. L.F.P., 17 September 1730.
11. L.F.P., 10 October 1730.

CHAPTER 6

1. *Correspondence of Horace Walpole*, Yale edition, vol. II. Walpole to William Cole, 12 July 1778.
2. Bodl. MSS. Rawl. lett. 27c.f.70, October 1731.
3. *Historia Ecclesiastica Novi Testamenti*, first printed in 1655.
4. This was a *Cordyale* (1479), now in Mr Paul Mellon's collection.
5. See Leslie Gardener, *Stage Coach to John o'Groats*, 1961.

CHAPTER 7

1. G. C. Boon, *The Roman Town, Calleva Atrebatum*, 1972.
2. Leslie North, 'Stormy Times for the Bulldog Alderman', *Mercury Country Tales*, no. 6.
3. L.F.P., 14 April 1805.
4. South's will – Oxford University Archives. Proved in the Chancellor's Court.
5. The last five volumes were not published until 1744, two years after Henry Smith's death. Writing to George Ballard on 12 August 1752 (Bodl. MSS. Ballard 37.f.34), John Loveday said, 'No great while ago I had the satisfaction of collating the five additional volumes of his Sermons with the original Manuscripts.' His collations were entered into his own copies of the five additional volumes. These are now in Pennsylvania State University Library.
6. Bodl. MSS. Rawl. lett. 27c.f.32, 21 August 1731.
7. *Diary of the Earl of Egmont*, vol. III, Historical Manuscripts Commission, 1923.
8. L.F.P., 26 August 1731.
9. Bodl. MSS. Rawl. lett. 27c.f.134, 15 September 1731. L.F.P., John Loveday's copy.
10. L.F.P., 21 September 1731.
11. Hearne's *Collections*, vol. X, 10 October 1731.
12. Ibid., vol. X, 19 October 1731.
13. Ibid., vol. X, 11 January 1730.
14. Ibid., vol. X, 9 December 1731, footnote pp. 482–3.
15. Ibid., vol. XI, 10 January 1732, footnote p. 15.
16. Ibid., vol. XI, 10 January 1732, footnote pp. 15–16.
17. Now in Pennsylvania State University Library.
18. *The Grub Street Journal*, Thursday, 9 December 1731.
19. Hearne's *Collections*, vol. XI, 14 January 1732.
20. Hearne's Autobiography, *Collections*, vol. X, p. 478.
21. Bodl. MSS. Rawl. lett.7.f.184, 30 March 1732. L.F.P., John Loveday's copy.
22. L.F.P., 6 April 1732.
23. Hearne's *Collections*, vol. VI, 24 August 1717.
24. *Diary of the Earl of Egmont*, vol. II.

CHAPTER 8

1. The subject of *Diary of a Tour in 1732*, edited by J. E. T. Loveday and published privately for the Roxburghe Club, 1890.
2. Hearne published *Walteri Hemingford, Historia de Rebus Gestis Edwardi I, II, III*, in 1731.
3. *Nichols's Literary History*, vol. I, p. 310.
4. Bodl. MSS. Rawl. lett. 27c.f.36, 1 June 1732.
5. *Mona Antiqua Restaurata*, an archaeological discourse on the antiquities of Anglesey, was published in Dublin in 1723.
6. L.F.P., 7 June 1732.
7. Bodl. MSS. Rawl. lett. 15.f.129, 9 July 1732.
8. L.F.P., 13 July 1732.
9. L.F.P., 28 July 1732. This is the original letter which John must have retrieved after Hearne's death.
10. L.F.P., 30 August 1732. Also the original letter.
11. L.F.P., as p. 132, n. 10.
12. L.F.P., 5 August 1732.
13. L.F.P., as p.132, n. 10.
14. L.F.P., 6 September 1732.
15. L.F.P., 16 November 1732.

CHAPTER 9

1. L.F.P., 31 January 1733.
2. Hearne's *Collections*, vol. XI, 11 May 1733. John Loveday's copy of Derham's catalogue is now in Pennsylvania State University Library.
3. Ibid., 9 March 1733.
4. *Thomas Otterbourne*, published by Hearne in 1732.
5. 'On painting in the *Philosophical Transactions*.' John Loveday's note.
6. Hearne's *Collections*, vol. XI, 6 July 1733.
7. Ibid., 5 July 1733 gives price of 5 shillings for a ticket.
8. Bodl. MSS. Rawl. lett. 27c.f.134, 28 July 1733.
9. L.F.P., 7 August 1733.
10. L.F.P., 27 June 1733.
11. See A. D. Godley, *Oxford in the Eighteenth Century*, 1908.
12. L.F.P., 1 December 1733.

CHAPTER 10

1. John Ray, *Wisdom of God in the Creation*, 1691.
2. Hearne's *Collections*, vol. XI, 13 June 1734.
3. *Robert of Gloucester's Chronicle* was published by Hearne in 1724.
4. Norman Sykes, *Edmund Gibson*, 1926.
5. Published in 1730.
6. L.F.P., probable date 16 December 1734. John Loveday's copy.
7. Although most of Waterland's letters to John were printed in Van Mildert's book, these extracts are taken from the original MSS. and from John's copies of his replies, which were not published, except for a few brief extracts.
8. L.F.P., 1 January 1735.

9. L.F.P., probable date 6 January 1735. John Loveday's copy.
10. L.F.P., 23 January 1735.
11. L.F.P., 18 March 1735. Extract not published.
12. L.F.P., 28 March 1735. Not published by Van Mildert.
13. L.F.P., 7 April 1735. John Loveday's copy.
14. L.F.P., 30 March 1735. John Loveday's copy.
15. L.F.P., 2 April 1735. Extract not published.
16. L.F.P., 7 April 1735. John Loveday's copy.
17. L.F.P., 2 July 1735. John Loveday's copy.
18. L.F.P., 6 July 1735. From Cambridge.
19. L.F.P., 10 July 1735. John Loveday's copy.
20. L.F.P., 15 July 1735.
21. L.F.P., 18 September 1735.
22. L.F.P., 17 January 1735.
23. *Diary of the Earl of Egmont*, vol. II, p. 328.

CHAPTER 11

1. H. E. Salter, Preface to vol. IX, Hearne's *Collections*.
2. On twelfth-century etymology.
3. L.F.P., 4 May 1735.
4. Bodl. MSS. Rawl. lett. 7.f.186.
5. Loveday to Tanner, 9 October 1735. This transcription is taken from an Appendix to *The Lives of John Leland, Thomas Hearne and Anthony à Wood*, published by Fletcher and Pate in 1772.
6. L.F.P., 19 June 1735.
7. L.F.P., 28 June 1735.

CHAPTER 12

1. L.F.P., 18 May 1736.
2. Daniel Defoe, *A Tour through the Whole Island of Great Britain*, 1724–27.
3. L.F.P., 20 November 1736.
4. See Elizabeth Burton, *The Georgians at Home*, 1967.

CHAPTER 13

1. L.F.P., 22 March 1736.
2. L.F.P., 26 February 1735.
3. L.F.P., 6 October 1736.
4. L.F.P., 9 November 1735.
5. L.F.P., 27 October 1734.
6. L.F.P., 8 November 1734.
7. L.F.P., undated.
8. L.F.P., undated.
9. *Whitehall Evening Post*, 24 March 1737. Signed 'A.B'.
10. L.F.P., 23 April 1737.
11. L.F.P., 18 May 1737.
12. The last sentence was added a little later.

13. See John Dunton's eulogy of Buckley in *The Whipping-Post*, 1706; also quoted in *Nichols's Literary Anecdotes*, vol. IX, p. 708.
14. *Observations Made on a Journey through Part of the Low Countries, Germany and France*, 1673. See p. 337.
15. L.F.P., 30 May 1737.

CHAPTER 14

1. L.F.P., 24 September 1737.
2. L.F.P., 21 November 1738. The letter was not kept but was copied by Penelope Hind into her 'Family Book'.
3. From information kindly given by the Librarian of the Inner Temple.
4. Bodl. MS. Eng. lett., c.6, f.10.
5. As p. 289 n. 3.
6. L.F.P., 16 February 1738.
7. *The Itinerary of John Leland*. See ed. L. Toulmin-Smith, vol. I, p. 261.
8. L.F.P. 20 November 1738. John Loveday's copy.

CHAPTER 15

1. Part of the description of the Cathedral and the Lord Mayor's Chapel appeared in an article by the author in *The Friends of Bristol Cathedral Report 1970 – 71*.
2. See *Aubrey's Brief Lives*, ed. O. Lawson Dick, 1949 and Peter Young, *Edgehill, 1642*, 1967.
3. L.F.P., Thomas Townson, 1739.
4. *The History of Newcastle upon Tyne* was published in 1736, three years after the death of the author, the Revd Henry Bourne, who left it in an indeterminate state.
5. L.F.P., 27 August 1739.
6. *Gulielmi Camdeni Annales* was published by Hearne in 1717.
7. See Mary Webster, 'Taste of an Augustan Collector', *Country Life*, 29 January 1970 and 24 September 1970.

CHAPTER 16

1. An edition of *Longinus* edited by Zachary Pearce and *Histoire Romaine* by Catrou and Rouillé in 20 vols.
2. L.F.P., 1 March 1740.
3. L.F.P., 19 May 1740. John Loveday's copy.
4. L.F.P., 25 June 1740. John Loveday's copy.
5. L.F.P., 6 July 1740.
6. L.F.P., 19 May 1740. John Loveday's copy.
7. L.F.P., 25 April 1740.
8. L.F.P., 19 May 1740. John Loveday's copy.
9. L.F.P., 14 March 1740. Addressed to Caversham where John Loveday must have been on a visit.
10. L.F.P., 6 November 1725.
11. See p.261 n.14.
12. L.F.P., 24 March 1737.
13. *Diary of the Earl of Egmont*, vol. II, p. 250.
14. Ibid.

15. *Nichols's Literary Anecdotes*, vol. IV, p.436.
16. Dr John Walker died the following year (1741) and left material for this work to Dr Richard Mead.
17. L.F.P., 9 August 1740.
18. L.F.P., 11 August 1740. Benwell's transcription.
19. L.F.P., 30 June 1741.
20. L.F.P., 24 September 1740.
21. L.F.P., 22 January 1743.
22. L.F.P., 11 August 1740. See n. 18 above, Benwell's transcription.
23. L.F.P., 22 November 1763. T. Powys to James Merrick.
24. *Diary of the Earl of Egmont*, vol. II, pp. 218, 366–7.
25. L.F.P., 12 May 1743.
26. L.F.P., undated.
27. L.F.P., 20 October 1743.
28. B.L. Add. MSS. 6226. f.41–2. 14 December 1753.

CHAPTER 17

1. L.F.P., 31 March 1744.
2. L.F.P., 7 March 1744.
3. L.F.P., 13 March 1744.
4. L.F.P., 25 March 1746.
5. L.F.P., 20 September 1744.
6. *Passages from the Diaries of Mrs Lybbe Powys*, p. 175.
7. The late Mrs Gwen Beachcroft kindly gave me transcripts of these letters from the Leigh correspondence on which she was working. I am grateful to Mr S. P. Beachcroft for permission to use his family letters in print.
8. Ibid.
9. L.F.P., 1 December 1745. A short extract from this letter appeared in the *Manchester Guardian* on 28 November 1757.
10. L.F.P., 28 December 1745.
11. Published in 1744 with cuts by Hogarth.
12. L.F.P., 23 January 1746.
13. *Nichols's Literary History*, vol. III, p. 672, 9 October 1775.
14. L.F.P., 17 June 1746. Penelope Hind's transcription.
15. L.F.P., 18 April 1745.
16. L.F.P., 4 May 1745. Merrick's copy, the original letter having been deposited by him with the President of Trinity College, George Huddesford.
17. L.F.P., 28 June 1746. Penelope Hind's transcription.
18. L.F.P., 29 June 1746.
19. L.F.P., 5 November 1746.
20. The new edition of Mead's *A Mechanical Account of Poisons*, which first came out in 1702. 'Now printing' – Ward.
21. L.F.P., 18 September 1746.
22. *Nichols's Literary Anecdotes*, vol. V, p. 447.
23. L.F.P., 5 November 1746.
24. L.F.P., Zinzan. Several verses omitted.

CHAPTER 18

1. John's descriptions appeared in an article by the author, 'Unpublished Notes on

Heythrop House and Kirtlington Park', in *Cake and Cockhorse*, vol. VII, no. 4, after visits by the Banbury Historical Society to these houses.

2. Published in 1730.
3. *The Memoirs of William Hickey*, ed. Alfred Spencer, 1925.
4. L.F.P., 7 June 1749.
5. *The History of the Brotherhood of the Holy Ghost in the Chapel of the Holy Ghost at Basingstoke* came out in 1742. John gave a copy to George Ballard in 1752.
6. L.F.P., 9 December 1749.
7. Thornton's *Tour of Northern England and Scotland in 1786* came out in 1804, his *Sporting Tour of France* in 1806.
8. L.F.P., 12 September 1749.
9. L.F.P., 12 December 1759.
10. L.F.P., 6 December 1749.
11. L.F.P., 3 August 1750.
12. L.F.P., 20 July 1750.
13. Bishop B. Porteus, *The Life and Character of Archbishop Secker*, 1770.
14. The list of twenty 'little books' began with *The Whole Duty of Man* and included four by Bishop Gibson, *The Christian Monitor* and Wake's *Commentary on the Church Catechism*.
15. L.F.P., 3 August 1750.
16. L.F.P., dated 1758. Merrick's copy.
17. L.F.P., 27 December 1763.
18. *D.N.B.*
19. See James Clifford, *Dictionary Johnson*, 1979.
20. L.F.P., 31 October 1752.
21. L.F.P., 21 November 1752.
22. R. J. Hobson, *The Oxfordshire Election of 1754*, 1949.
23. See Thomas Warton, *History and Antiquities of Kiddington*, 1782.
24. Bodl. MSS. Ballard 37.f.36, 3 April 1753.
25. L.F.P., 15 March 1753.
26. Bodl. MSS. Ballard. 37.f.36, 3 April 1753.
27. L.F.P., 8 January 1754.
28. Bodl. MSS. Ballard f. 38-9, 5 February 1754. John kept no copies of his thirteen letters to Ballard now in the Bodleian Library.
29. L.F.P., 2 July 1755.
30. Ibid.
31. The original manuscript letter which Ballard copied (L.F.P.) is not in the Ballard Collection in the Bodleian and is not known in the British Library. Ballard considered it to be the first draft of a letter.
32. See Thomas Pennant, *A Tour from Downing to Alston Moor*, 1801.
33. L.F.P., 27 December 1753.
34. L.F.P., 27 July 1753. Copied by Ballard into his letter.

CHAPTER 19

1. Bodl. MSS. Ballard 37.f.38-9, 5 February 1754.
2. L.F.P., 20 January 1755.
3. L.F.P., 17 February 1755.
4. L.F.P., 15 July 1755.
5. Ibid.
6. L.F.P.
7. L.F.P., 24 November, 1755.

8. L.F.P. (early 1756).
9. L.F.P., 4 January 1756.
10. L.F.P., 5 February 1756.
11. L.F.P., February 1756.
12. L.F.P., 7 February 1756.
13. L.F.P., 11 March 1756.
14. L.F.P., 15 March 1756.
15. L.F.P., 4 April 1756.
16. L.F.P.
17. L.F.P., April 1756.
18. L.F.P., 21 March 1756.
19. L.F.P., 22 April 1756.
20. L.F.P., 2 May 1756.
21. L.F.P., 11 May 1756.
22. L.F.P., 15 May 1756.
23. L.F.P., 6 June 1756.
24. L.F.P., 2 July 1756.
25. L.F.P., 18 July 1756.
26. L.F.P., 4 November 1756.
27. L.F.P., 6 April 1757. Benwell's transcription.
28. L.F.P., 7 April 1757. Benwell's transcription.
29. L.F.P., 10 March 1758.
30. L.F.P., undated. Penelope Hind's transcription.
31. Ibid. As these letters are undated it is not certain (though probable) that John was referring to Jack's confirmation. Penelope Hind's transcription.
32. L.F.P., 28 April 1758.
33. L.F.P., 21 October 1758.
34. L.F.P., 2 November 1758.
35. Penelope Hind's Diaries.
36. B.L.Add. MS. 6265.f.17, 17 January 1761.
37. L.F.P., 7 July 1760.
38. L.F.P., 11 March 1760.
39. LF.P., 13 March 1760. John Loveday's copy.
40. B.L.Add. MS. 6265.f.6, 13 October 1760.
41. B.L.Add. MS. 6265.f.8, 27 October 1760.
42. B.L.Add. MS. 6265.f.9, 25 November 1760.
43. B.L.Add. MS. 6265.f.10, 1 December 1760.
44. B.L.Add. MS. 6265.f.17, 31 December 1760. Mrs Goodwin's copy.
45. B.L.Add. MS. 6265.f.16, 8 January 1761. John Loveday's copy.
46. B.L.Add. MS. 6265.f.86, undated.
47. B.L.Add. MS. 6265.f.20, 25 February 1761.
48. B.L.Add. MS. 6265.f.22, 15 April 1761.
49. B.L.Add. MS. 6265.f.23–4, 24 May 1761.
50. B.L.Add. MS. 4312.f.246, 14 July 1761. B.L.Add. MS. 6262.f.29, 14 July 1761. John Loveday's copy.
51. D.N.B.
52. B.L.Add. MS. 6265.f.36, 24 November 1761.
53. B.L.Add. MS. 6265f.38, 24 December 1761.
54. L.F.P., 19 January 1762.
55. B.L.Add. MS. 6265.f.46, 13 February 1762.
56. B.L.Add. MS. 6265.f.48, 23 February 1762.
57. B.L.Add. MS. 6265.f.50, undated.

58. Ibid. John Loveday's copy.
59. Ibid. John Loveday's copy.
60. B.L.Add. MS. 6265.f.41, 21 November 1765.
61. George Colman, *Circle of Anecdote and Wit*, 4th edn. 1823.
62. B.L.Add. MS. 6265.f.17, 17 January 1761.
63. B.L.Add. MS. 6265.f.25–6, 1 June 1761.
64. Ibid.
65. B.L.Add. MS. 6265.f.31, 18 July 1761.

CHAPTER 20

1. L.F.P. Press cutting sent by William Lethieullier.
2. L.F.P. Press cutting – *Whitehall Evening Post*.
3. L.F.P., 31 March 1761.
4. L.F.P., 2 April 1761. John Loveday's copy.
5. L.F.P., 23 June 1765.
6. L.F.P., 14 April 1769.
7. L.F.P., 20 April 1765.
8. L.F.P., 21 April 1765.
9. L.F.P., 13 April 1765.
10. L.F.P., 22 February 1760.
11. L.F.P., 10 November 1760.
12. L.F.P., 19 January 1761. Bagshaw to John Loveday, Jnr.
13. L.F.P., 28 July 1760.
14. L.F.P., 28 July 1764.
15. Ibid.
16. Published in 1764.
17. L.F.P., 3 July 1764.
18. Ibid.
19. Published in 1763.
20. L.F.P., 8 July 1763.
21. Published in 1775 and 1776 respectively. *Ionian Antiquities* appeared in 1769.
22. In private possession. A copy was given to Dr Paget Toynbee in 1913 by Dr Thomas Loveday. It appeared in the *Supplement* to the *Letters of Horace Walpole*, 1918. The original spelling was not used. The reference in the *Yale Edition of Horace Walpole's Correspondence* is vol. XL, pp. 368–9. The picture was described by Walpole as 'The inside of a Church, a very good Flemish picture'.
23. L.F.P., 22 April 1756.
24. L.F.P., 10 April 1764. Delany to Dartmouth.
25. L.F.P., 23 May, 1765.
26. L.F.P., 10 September 1763. Edward Willes to Merrick.
27. L.F.P., 11 November 1765. John Loveday, Jnr. to Merrick.
28. L.F.P., 19 November 1765.
29. L.F.P., 28 October 1765.
30. Nathaniel Forster's *Platonis Dialogi Quinque* . . . had come out in 1746. Etwall's *Platonis Dialogi*, with a Latin preface by Merrick (though anonymous), came out in 1771.
31. L.F.P., 18 February 1764.
32. L.F.P., 5 August 1764.
33. Ibid.
34. L.F.P., Merrick's undated copy of his letter to Dumaresq.
35. L.F.P., 11 November 1765.

36. L.F.P., 14 August 1766.
37. Dr Michael Marlow's acknowledgement. L.F.P., 21 June 1802.
38. Bodl. MSS. Auct.V.I. subtus 16–29ª,30. (S.C.27987–28002.)
39. L.F.P., 15 November 1765.
40. L.F.P., 5 December 1765.
41. L.F.P., 11 December 1765.
42. L.F.P., 4 August 1764.
43. Ibid.
44. L.F.P., 11 August 1764. John Loveday, Jnr.'s copy.
45. L.F.P., 12 September 1765.
46. L.F.P., undated. John Loveday's copy of his reply.
47. Granger's *Biographical History* was published in 1769.
48. L.F.P., 20 May 1763.
49. L.F.P., 31 March 1772.
50. L.F.P. Undated but received 19 March 1771.
51. L.F.P., 16 July 1771.
52. *Nichols's Literary Anecdotes*, vol. III, p. 708.
53. Bodl. MS. Ashmole 1822.f.206, 19 July 1768.
54. L.F.P. 9 July, 1768. See also *Jackson's Oxford Journal*, 22 October 1768.
55. Bodl. MS. Ashmole 1822.f.154, 21 January 1762.
56. Bodl. MS. Ashmole 1822.f.203, 19 November 1767.
57. BL.Add. MSS. 42160–42173, the diaries of Caroline Lybbe Powys. This entry is not included in Emily Climenson's *Passages* from the diaries (1899).
58. Ibid.
59. L.F.P., 1782. Penelope Hind's copy of Bagshaw's letter.
60. See *The Torrington Diaries*, vol. I, ed. C. Bruyn Andrews, 1934.

Principal Manuscript Sources

Bodl.   The Bodleian Library
B.L.   The British Library
L.F.P.   Loveday Family Papers

Ballard, George, Letters from John Loveday, Bodl.: MSS. Ballard 10, 37 (S.C. 10796, 10823).
Bryne, Robert, Diary and collections on Magdalen College, Bodl.: MSS. Gough Oxon. 10, 32–36 (S.C. 18128–33).
Christ Church Library, MS. Estates 65, (Caversham Old Rectory).
Delafield, Thomas, MSS. Bodl.: MS. Gough Oxon. 31 (S.C. 18151).
Ducarel, A. C., Letters to John Loveday, Bodl.: MS. Eng. lett. c.6 (presented by Dr Thomas Loveday).
Hearne, Thomas, Letters from John Loveday and others, Bodl.: MSS. Rawl. lett. 7, 15, 27^c, 28, (S.C. 15578, 15585, 14917).
Hearne, Thomas, Pocket books, Bodl.: MSS. Hearne's diaries 1–162, 164–77, 182–5, 186^{a-c}, 187–92 (S.C. 15124–285, 15287–300, 15301–13).
Huddesford, William, Letters from John Loveday, Bodl.: MS. Ashmole 1822.
L.F.P., in private possession.
L.F.P., Deeds on deposit, Bodl.: MSS. D.D. Loveday.
L.F.P., Deeds and other MSS. on deposit, Warwickshire County Record Office.
L.F.P., Correspondence of James Merrick on deposit, Bodl.: Dep. c.254/1–2.
Loveday, John, Caversham freeholders, list of. Reading Central Public Library, RH/HA (presented by Dr Thomas Loveday).
Loveday, John, MSS. connected with, B.L.: Adds. MSS. 4189, 6206, 6230, 6287. (See also Ward, John.)
Loveday, John, MSS. and notes in books, Pennsylvania State University Library.
Lybbe Powys, Caroline, Diaries, B.L.: Add. MSS. 42160–42173.
Mackenzie, G. O. W., 'Caversham Park: A Retrospect', Reading Central Public Library RH/NW.
Merrick, James, Correspondence in private possession. (See also L.F.P.)
Merrick, James, Indexes (classical), Bodl.: MS. Auct. V.I. subtus 16–29, 29a, 30 (S.C. 27987–28002) (presented by John Loveday, Jnr.).

Pearce, Zachary, Correspondence, Westminster Abbey Library (presented by Dr Thomas Loveday).

Rawlinson, Richard, 'Tour of Oxfordshire in 1718', Bodl.: MS. Rawl. B.400F.

Ward, John, Letters and other papers relating to the disposal of his MSS., B.L.: Add. MSS. 4284, 4312, 6265 (presented by John Loveday, Jnr.).

Williamscote deeds and other Loveday estate papers, Bodl.: MSS. Ch. Beds. Berks, Derbys., Glos., London & Msex., Northants., Oxon., Rutland, Surrey, Warwicks., Worcs.; MSS. Top. Oxon. b.259, c.596–7.

Select Bibliography

GENERAL

Banbury Historical Society publications.
Berkshire Family History publications.
Berry, William, *County Genealogies.*
Burke, John, *Burke's Commoners,* 1826.
Burke, John and Burke, J. B., *Extinct and Dormant Baronetcies,* 1844.
Burke's Dormant and Extinct Peerages, 1883; reprint, 1969.
Burke's Irish Family Records.
Burke's Landed Gentry, various edns.
Burke's Peerage, Baronetage and Knightage, various edns.
Calendar of State Papers (Domestic).
Cockayne, G. E. and Gibbs, Hon. Vicary, edd., *The Complete Peerage,* 2nd edn., 1910.
[*D.N.B.*] *Dictionary of National Biography, The*
Encyclopedia Britannica, The, 14th edn.
Foster, Joseph, *Alumni Oxonienses,* 1887–91.
Foster, Joseph, *Lancashire County Pedigrees,* 1873.
Foster, Joseph, *Yorkshire County Pedigrees,* 1874.
Gentleman's Magazine, The.
Hector, L. C., *The Handwriting of English Documents,* 1966.
Le Neve, John, *Fasti Ecclesiae Anglicanae,* ed. T. D. Hardy, 1854.
Le Neve, Peter, *Pedigree of Knights,* Harl. Soc., 1873.
Macray, W. Dunn, *Annals of the Bodleian Library,* 1890.
Musgrave, Sir William, *An Obituary Prior to 1800 &c.,* ed. George Armitage, Harl. Soc., 1899.
Newspapers: *The Grub Street Journal, Jackson's Oxford Journal, St James's Chronicle, The Reading Mercury, The Whitehall Evening Post.*
Northamptonshire Record Society publications.
Notes and Queries articles.
Oxfordshire Family History Society publications.
Powicke, F. M., *Handbook of British Chronology,* 1939.
Venn, John, *Alumni Cantabrigienses,* 1922.
[*V.C.H.*], *Victoria History of the Counties of England, The.*
Warwickshire Local History Society publications.

HISTORY

Birley, R., *The History of College Library*, 1970.

Brooke, John, *King George III*, 1972.

Burton, Elizabeth, *The Georgians at Home*, 1967.

Carpenter, S.C., *Eighteenth Century Church and People*, 1959.

Carson, Patricia, *The Fair Face of Flanders*, 1969.

Carter, Alice Clare, *The English Reformed Church in Amsterdam*, 1964.

Drew, Bernard, *The London Assurance*, 1928.

Foley, Henry, *Records of the English Province of the Society of Jeṡus*, 1877–83.

Green, David, *Queen Anne*, 1970.

Krieger, L., *Kings and Philosophers*, 1971.

Lathbury, Thomas, *History of the Non-Jurors*, 1845.

Marples, Morris, *Poor Fred: The People's Prince*, 1970.

Moorman, J. R., *History of the Church of England*, 1953.

Stavely, Thomas, *History of the Churches*, 1712.

Styles, Philip, *Studies in Seventeenth Century History*, 1978.

Sykes, Norman, *Church and State in the Eighteenth Century*, 1962.

Trevelyan, G. M., *English Social History*, 1948 edn.

Turbeville, A. S., *English Men and Manners in the Eighteenth Century*, 1926.

Underdown, David, *Royalist Conspiracy in England, 1649–1660*, 1971.

Wakeford, Geoffrey, *The Princesses Royal*, 1973.

Warne, Arthur, *Church and Society in Eighteenth-Century Devon*, 1969.

Williams, Basil, *The Whig Supremacy*, rev. C. S. Stuart, 1962.

Young, Peter, *Edgehill, 1642*, 1967.

OXFORD

Bilstone, John, ed., [*Thomas Hearne's Letter of Vindication (1700)*], 1731.

Bliss, Philip, ed., *Reliquae Hearnianae*, 1857.

Bloxam, J. R., ed., *The Magdalen College Register*, 1853–85.

Buxton, L. H. D. and Gibson, S., *Oxford University Ceremonies*, 1935.

Chandler, Richard, *Marmora Oxoniensia*, 1763.

Clark, Andrew, ed., *The Life and Times of Anthony Wood*, 1891–1900.

Curll, Edmund, *Life of Mr Thomas Hearne*, 1735.

Doble, C. F., Rennie, D. W. and Salter, H. E., edd., *Remarks and Collections of Thomas Hearne*, 1885–1921.

Fletcher, J. J. and Pote, Joseph, *Lives of John Leland, Thomas Hearne and Anthony à Wood*, 1772.

Godley, A. D., *Oxford in the Eighteenth Century*, 1908.

Hobhouse, Christopher, *Oxford*, 1939.

Hobson, R.J., *The Oxfordshire Election of 1754*, 1949.

[Hurdis, James], *A Word or Two in Vindication of the University of Oxford*.

Macray, W. Dunn, *Register of Magdalen College, Oxford, New Series*, 1894–1915.
Oxford Council Acts, Oxf. Hist. Soc. publications, from 1928.
Pointer, John, *Oxoniensis Academia*, 1749.
Stanier, R. S., *Magdalen School*, 1958.
Ward, W. R., *Georgian Oxford*, 1958.
Warton, Thomas, *Companion to the Guide*, 1760.
Wilson, H. A., *Magdalen College*, College Histories, 1899.
Wood, Anthony, *Athenae Oxonienses*, 1691–92.
Wordsworth, Christopher, *University Life in the Eighteenth Century*, 1874.

JOURNALS AND BIOGRAPHY

Abbott, J. L., 'Samuel Johnson, John Hawkesworth and the Rise of *The Gentleman's Magazine*', *Studies on Voltaire and the Eighteenth Century*, CLI, CLV, 1976.
Abbott, J., L., 'John Hawkesworth', *Eighteenth-Century Studies*, 3, 3.
Allen, D. G. C., *William Shipley*, 1968.
Barnard, E. A. B., *The Sheldons*, 1936.
Beresford, John, ed., *The Diary of a Country Parson by James Woodforde, 1758–81*, abr. edn., 1935.
Birch, Thomas, *An Account of the Life of John Ward, LL.D.*, 1766.
Boswell, James, *The Life of Samuel Johnson LL.D.*, ed. G. B. Hill, rev. L. F. Powell, 1934–64.
Bray, William, ed., *John Evelyn's Diaries and Correspondence*, 1818.
Chown, C. H. I., 'The Lethieullier Family of Aldersbrook House', *Essex Review*, vols. XXXV, XXXVI, 1939.
Clifford, James, *Dictionary Johnson*, 1979.
Climenson, Emily, ed., *Passages from the Diaries of Mrs Philip Lybbe Powys*, 1899.
Coleman, George, *Circles of Anecdote and Wit*, 3rd and 4th edns., 1823.
Croker, J. W., ed., *Letters to and from Henrietta, Countess of Suffolk*, John Murray, 1824.
Davenport, John M., *Lords Lieutenant and High Sheriffs of Oxfordshire, 1086–1868*, 1868.
Dickens, L. and Stanton, M., edd., *An Eighteenth-Century Correspondence*, 1910.
Egmont: *Diary of 1st Earl of Egmont* [ed. R. A. Roberts], Historical Manuscripts Commission, 1916–23.
Eland, G., ed., *The Purefoy Letters*, 1931.
Fellowes, E. H., *Minor Canons of Windsor*, 1945.
Ford, Edward, *Tewin-Water: The Story of Lady Cathcart*, 1876.
Gibbon, Edward, *The Autobiography*, ed. Lord Sheffield, 1907; repr., 1972.
Green, David, *Sarah, Duchess of Marlborough*, 1967.
Green, V. H. H., *The Young Mr Wesley*, 1961.
Grimble, Ian, *The Harington Family*, 1957.

Hamilton, Elizabeth, *The Backstairs Dragon*, 1969.

Hamilton, Elizabeth, *The Illustrious Lady*, 1980.

Ilchester, 6th Earl of, *Lord Hervey and his Friends*, 1950.

Jenkins, J. G., *The Dragon of Whaddon*, 1953.

Ketton-Cremer, R. W., *The Early Life and Diaries of William Windham*, 1930.

Lawson Dick, O., ed., *Aubrey's Brief Lives*, 1949.

Lever, Tresham, *The Herberts of Wilton*, 1967.

Lewis, Lady Theresa, ed., *Journals and Correspondence of Miss Berry*, 1865.

Lewis, W. S., ed., *The Yale Edition of Horace Walpole's Correspondence*, 1937–.

Linnell, C. L. S., ed., *The Diaries of Thomas Wilson, 1731–37 & 1750*, 1964.

McClatchey, Diana, *Oxfordshire Clergy, 1777–1869*, 1964.

Malcolm, J.P., ed., *Letters between the Rev James Granger and Literary Men of His Time*, 1805.

Meade, Richard Hardaway, *In the Sunshine of Life*, 1974.

Melville, Lewis, *The Berry Papers*, 1914.

Mildert, William Van, ed., *The Works of the Rev Daniel Waterland*, 1823.

Newton, Thomas, *Lives of Zachary Pearce, Skelton, Pococke and Newton*, 1782.

Nichols, John, *Illustrations of the Literary History of the Eighteenth Century*, 1817–58.

Nichols, John, *Literary Anecdotes of the Eighteenth Century*, 1812–15.

Pemberton, W., *Lord North*, 1938.

Porteus, B., *A Review of the Life and Character of Dr Thomas Secker*, 1770.

Schazman, Paul-Emile, *The Bentincks*, trans. Steve Cox, 1976.

Scott Thomson, Gladys, *Letters of a Grandmother*, 1943.

Sheridan, G., *The Early Career of Alexander Pope*, 1934.

Spencer, Alfred, ed., *Memoirs of William Hickey*, 1913–25.

Stokes, F. G., ed., *The Blecheley Diary of the Rev William Cole, 1765–67*, 1931.

Sykes, Norman, *Edmund Gibson, Bishop of London*, 1926.

Sykes, Norman, *William Wake, Archbishop of Canterbury*, 1926.

Tanner, Lawrence E., *Recollections of a Westminster Antiquary*, 1969.

Valpy, R., 'Some Account of the Life of the Rev William Benwell', in *Reading School: Poems . . .*, 1804.

White, R. J., *Dr Richard Bentley*, 1965.

Wooll, John, *Biographical Memoirs of Joseph Warton, D.D.*, 1806.

THE ROAD

Andrews, C. Bruyn, ed., *The Torrington Diaries*, 1934.

Camden, William, *Britannia, 1586*, ed. Edmund Gibson, 1695.

Cartwright, J. R., ed., *The Travels round Britain of Dr Richard Pococke (1750–51)*, 1888.

Defoe, Daniel. *A Tour through the Whole Island of Great Britain*, 1724–27; repr. (J. M. Dent), 1962.

Gardener, Leslie, *Stage Coach to John o'Groats*, 1961.

Kay, George, *Royal Mail*, 1951.

Loveday, J. E. T., ed., *Diary of a Tour in 1732*, 1890.

Moir, Esther, *The Discovery of Britain*, 1964.

Morris, Christopher, ed., *The Journeys of Celia Fiennes*, 1947.

Ogilby, John, *A Pocket Book of The Tables of the Road*, 1721.

Pearse Chope, R., ed., *Early Tours in Devon and Cornwall*, 1967.

Simmons, J., *Journeys in England: An Anthology*, 1951.

Toulmin-Smith, L., ed., *The Itinerary of John Leland*, 1907–10.

Wright, Edward, *Observations Made in Travelling through France, Italy . . . 1720–30*, 1730.

TOPOGRAPHY

Bell, J. J., *The Glory of Scotland*, 1932.

Besant, Sir Walter, *London and the Eighteenth Century*, 1925.

Birch, Clive, *The Book of Beaconsfield*, 1976.

Boon, G. C., ed., *The Roman Town Calleva Atrebatum at Silchester*, 1972.

Brett-James, Norman, *Middlesex*, 1951.

Carpenter, Barbara, *A History of Hampshire*, 1963.

Climenson, Emily, *A History of Shiplake*, 1894.

Coates, Charles, *The History and Antiquities of Reading*, 1802; Suppl., 1810.

Cooper, J. J., *Some Worthies of Reading*, 1923.

Corbett, E., *A History of Spelsbury*, 1931.

Chancellor, E. Beresford, *The Eighteenth Century in London*, 1920.

Cussans, J. E., *A History of Hertfordshire*, 1870–80.

Dickens, Margaret, *A Little History of Cherington and Stourton*, 1934.

Ditchfield, P. H., *Memorials of Old Oxfordshire*, 1903.

Draper, Warwick, *Chiswick*, 1923.

Drive Publications, *Treasures of Britain*, 1968.

Dunbar, Janet, *A Prospect of Richmond*, 1966.

Dunn, Ronald, *Devon and Cornwall*, 1966.

Fellows, Arnold, *The Wayfarer's Companion*, 1937.

Gepp, H. J., *Adderbury*, 1924.

Gwynn, Stephen, *The Charm of Ireland*, 1927.

Hervey, Alfred, *Bristol*, 1906.

Higham, Roger, *Berkshire and the Vale of the White Horse*, 1977.

Hoare, R. Colt *A History of Modern Wiltshire*, 1822–44.

Horsley, P. M., *Eighteenth–Century Newcastle*, 1971.

Hutchins, John, *History of Dorset*, ed. R. Gough, 1813–15.

Jessup, Mary, *A History of Oxfordshire*, 1975.

Kemp, Brian R., *Reading Abbey*, 1968.

Kift, Mary, *Life in Old Caversham*, 1980.

Little, Bryan, *Bath Portrait*, 1961.

McGrath, Patrick, ed., *Bristol in the Eighteenth Century*, 1972.
Mann, J., *The History and Antiquities of Reading*, 1815.
Markham, Sarah and Arnold, H. Godwin, *A History of Caversham Court, Reading*, 1978.
Mee, Arthur, ed., *The King's England Series*.
Miller, George, *Rambles Round the Edge Hills*, ed. Anthony C. Wood, 1967.
Millson, Cecilia, *Tales of Old Berkshire*, 1977.
Morris, A. Clifford, *The Rycote Yew*, 1976.
Morton, John, *Natural History of Northamptonshire*, 1712.
Perkins, Angela, *The Book of Sonning*, 1977.
Pevsner, N., *Buildings of England Series*.
Potts, William, *A History of Banbury*, ed. Ted Clarke, 1978.
Rees, William, *Cardiff: A History of the City*, 1969.
Richards, Melville, *An Atlas of Anglesea*, 1972.
Savory, E. W., *Guide to Cirencester*, 1889.
Smith, E. E. F., *Clapham*, 1976.
Taverner-Perry, John, *Memorials of Old Middlesex*, 1901.
Williams, M., *Cardiff: Its People and its Trade*, 1963.
Williams, Stewart, ed., *South Glamorgan: A County History*, 1975.
Williamson, Ross, *Ackerman's Cambridge*, 1951.
Wittich, John, *Discovering London Villages*, 1976.
Wright, Louise and Priddey, James, *Cotswold Heritage*, 1977.

ARCHITECTURE, CHURCHES AND HOUSES

Angus, W., *The Seats of the Nobility and Gentry in England and Wales*, 1787.
Clifton-Taylor, Alec, *The Cathedrals of England*, 1972.
Colvin, H. M., *The Biographical Dictionary of English Architects, 1660–1840*, 1954.
Cornforth, John, *Pyne's Royal Residences*, 1976.
Country Life articles.
Davis, Graham, *The Langtons at Newton Park*.
Delderfield, E. R., *West Country Historic Houses and Their Families*, 1968.
Dodsley, R., *A Description of The Leasowes*, 1764.
Fedden, Robin and Kenworthy Browne, John, edd., *The English Country House Guide*, 1979.
Girouard, Mark, *Life in the English Country House*, 1978.
Gloag, John, *The Englishman's Castle*, 1949.
Grant, Arthur, *The Grey Shrines of England*, 1927.
Green, David, *Gardener to Queen Anne*, 1956.
Grimston, Hon. Charlotte, *A History of Gorhambury*, c. 1821.
Guidebooks to various churches and houses.
Hadfield, Miles, ed., *A Book of Country Houses*, 1969.
Harris, John, *The Artist and the Country House*, 1979.

Harvey, John, *English Medieval Churches*, 1954.
Hassell, J., *Seats near London*, 1804.
Heely, Joseph, *Descriptions of The Leasowes [and] Hagley Park*, 1777.
Hymans, Edward, *Capability Brown and Humphry Repton*, 1971.
Ison, Walter, *The Georgian Buildings of Bath*, 1948.
Jourdain, Margaret, *The Work of William Kent*, 1948.
Lees-Milne, James, *Earls of Creation*, 1962.
Lees-Milne, James, *English Country Houses: Baroque*, 1970.
Morris, Richard, *Cathedrals and Abbeys of England*, 1979.
National Trust Reports and guidebooks.
Neale, J. P., *Views of the Seats, 1818–1829.*
Sandby, P., *A Collection of One Hundred and Fifty Select Views*, 1783.
Spencer, Noel and Kent, Arnold, *The Churches of Norwich*, 1970.
Walker, G. G., *Churches of the Banbury Area*, 1975.
Waterson, Merlin, *The Servants' Hall*, 1980.
Winn, Colin G., *The Pouletts of Hinton St George*, 1976.
Yarwood, Doreen, *The Architecture of Britain*, 1976.

HISTORY OF ART

Bénézit, E., *Dictionnaire de Peintres, Sculpteurs . . .*, 2nd edn., 1949.
Burke, Joseph, *English Art*, 1976.
Croft-Murray, Edward, *Decorative Painting in England*, 1970.
Hamelman, H. and Boase, T. S. R., *Book Illustrators in the Eighteenth Century*, 1975.
Haskell, Francis, *Patrons and Painters*, 1963.
Havinden, M. A., *The Soho Tapestry Makers,* G.L.C. Survey of London, St Anne's, Soho, 1966.
Kelley, F. and Schwabe, R., *Historic Costume*, 1925.
Killanin, Lord, *Sir Godfrey Kneller and his Times*, 1948.
Millar, Oliver, *The Queen's Pictures*, 1977.
Northcote, James. *Memoirs of Sir Joshua Reynolds*, 1813.
Orpen, Sir William, ed., *The Outline of Art*, und.
Plumb, J.H. and Weldon, Huw, *Royal Heritage, 1977.*
Smart, Alistair, *The Life and Art of Allan Ramsay*, 1952.
Thieme, V. and Becker, F., *Allgemeines Lexikon d. bildenden Künstler*, 1907.
Thomson, W. H., *Tapestry Weaving in England*, 1915.
Walpole, Horace, *Anecdotes of Painting*, [1780], ed. R. N. Wornum, 1888.
Walpole Society, volumes XVI, XVIII, XXXVII, XLV.
Wilenski, W., *Flemish Painters*, 1960.

Other books are mentioned in the notes.

Appendix

(Records from the published tour of 1732 not included)

1 **Adderbury House** 12 June 1740

PAINTINGS

Gallery

The Marriage of the Virgin, by Luca Giordano – 'an old one'. Later note – 'This was purchased by Lord Cadogan [but this might refer to the next picture]'.

'The Virgin mourning over the dead Christ' – a fine painting.

Gallery and elsewhere

Views of 'Aleppo, Persepolis, Jerusalem, Isfahan and Constantinople' – 'very large'.

Two Cherubs 'who with great attention are looking over some musical notes together'.

'A Religious with a Crucifix.' Two paintings.

'Bathsheba bathing, her Women attending; King David viewing her from his Palace roof.'

St Jerome – 'The flesh of an Inhabitant of the Deserts is well painted'.

[2nd] Duke and Duchess of Argyll. Two paintings.

[9th] Earl of Argyll – 'has a resemblance of Sir William Temple'.

Duke and Duchess of Lauderdale. Two paintings.

General Talmash – 'her Grace's second Husband'.

1st Earl of Shrewsbury. Length.

Sir Charles Lucas – 'An Head as the Painters would call it'.

Henry VII – 'a length which may easily be taken for Erasmus'.

Henry VIII – 'his ears higher than his eyebrows'.

Portraits of several officers.

Views of Venice, Ruins of Rome etc.

SCULPTURE

Hall

Busts of Pompey, Hannibal, Sappho, Jugurtha, Apollo and Nero.

Gallery

2nd Duke and Duchess of Argyll in ovals over two chimneypieces. Busts.

Prince de Condé. Bust.

Vicomte de la Turenne. Bust.

Statue of a Muse in a niche below.

Julius Caesar. Bust in the right-hand corner on entering – 'the head of Porphyry'.

Oliver Cromwell. Bust in the left-hand corner on entering.

Alexander the Great. Bust in the right-hand corner at the upper end of the room.

Edward, the Black Prince. Bust opposite Alexander.

11 September 1742

PAINTINGS

The Good Samaritan – 'extremely fine'.

Manius Curius Dentatus Refusing the Gold of the Samnites – 'Miniature copy of Godfrey Flinck's fine Painting at the Stadthouse at Amsterdam'.

2 Aix-la-Chapelle: Church of the Recollects 17 June 1737

PAINTINGS

Relating to St Francis 'as at Maastricht'.

Altarpiece in two parts – 'the upper of Christ taken from the Cross, the lower of the Crucifixion'.

3 Aix-la-Chapelle Town Hall 17 June 1737

PAINTINGS

The Emperors: Charlemagne, Leopold, Joseph, Charles VI ('the present Emperor').

Charlemagne Granting a Charter to the Burgesses. An older picture above the Emperors.

Chapel above stairs 'a large room'

Pope Alexander VII. Head and shoulders – 'A great benefactor to this city'.

STATUE

Charlemagne, on the fountain in front of the 'Town House'.

4 All Souls College, Oxford 12 May 1733

Chapel

The Ascension of the Founder, by Thornhill. Altarpiece. 'Another designed for All Hallows.'

5 **All Souls College, Oxford: Dr George Clarke's House** 17 March 1733

PAINTINGS (John Loveday recorded all the bequests later)

The 'first' room

Dr (John) Radcliffe, by Kneller. Length. – 'the only one that was ever sat for' . . . bequeathed 'to his Library when built'.

Dean (Henry) Aldrich . . . Half length – 'Hearne tells me he was grey at thirty.'

Dr (Richard) Blechynden. Half length.

[1st] Duke and Duchess of Marlborough. Half lengths – 'She excessively like her length at Dalkeith House.' [*Diary of a Tour in 1732*, p. 158.]

Admiral George Churchill. Half length.

Sir Kenelm Digby, his Wife and Two Children. Miniature.

A room below stairs

Charles I (in black velvet), sitting. Comparison with a copy at Caversham and a 'wretched' copy at Baron Hill. Later reference to Walpole's *Catalogue of Engravers*, p. 51.

Study

Prince George of Denmark and Dr George Clarke, sitting, by Kneller – 'I don't admire it'.

'The Doctor's father, mother and himself, an infant . . . an odd piece.'

A room below stairs and on the staircase

Eight heads from the Cartoons – 'well-painted'.

At foot of staircase

'Hans Holbein's picture.'

On staircase

Queen Margaret of Scotland – 'by Hans, I take it'.

Mary, Queen of Scots – 'an ordinary Copy from the Original at Duway [Douai] or I mistake'.

William III, robed. Length.

Queen Mary, by Kneller.

Henry VII and his Queen – 'two small old pieces, both perhaps by Holbein'.

Top of staircase

(Isaac) Fuller – 'the Painter of Magdalen Altar-piece, and at All Souls, drawn by himself – a very remarkably ugly man'.

Archbishop Ussher. Half length.

A room above

'The late Lord Torrington [George Byng]', leaning on a cannon.

General Ginkel, Earl of Athlone – 'a fine Painting'.

Ben Jonson. Oval head and shoulders – 'like to but better than that in the Picture-Gallery'.

The Duke of Ormonde, by Kneller – 'many years ago, a fair handsome man'.

A little room above

'Duchess of Somerset (who was no Beauty), daughter of Robert, Earl of Essex' by Van Dyck. Half length.

6 **Althorp** 19 August 1742

PAINTINGS

Gallery

Paintings of horses, by Wootton.

Hall and elsewhere

'The Elevation of the Host in a Nunnery Church'. [See p. 344 n.*h*.]

Job and his Wife.

A Venetian Nobleman, by Titian 'in the very habit of one of the Cornaros at Northumberland House'.

'Solomon and his Concubines worshipping strange Gods', by Schalcken – 'Miniature Night-Piece' . [See p. 344 n.*h*.]

'A fictitious triumph of King Charles I . . . in black and white like two at Easton Neston.'

The Bacchanals – 'of which there is also a Print in this House'.

St John the Baptist – 'a very fine head'.

Samson Rending the Lion – 'by Rembrandt surely – a large piece'.

'A Boy blowing a Brand's end to light a Candle', by Schalcken – 'pleases universally and is said here to be his Masterpiece'. Later reference to Walpole's *Anecdotes*, III, 140.

Two other night pieces by Schalcken.

Gallery

Henrietta Maria (in white), by Van Dyck.

William Russell, Duke of Bedford and George Digby, Earl of Bristol, when young, by Van Dyck. Later note – 'from hence you have the heads of each among *Heads of Illustrious Persons*. v. Walpole's *Anecdotes*, II, 161.'

[1st] Earl of Sunderland, by Van Dyck. Length.

1st Earl Spencer.

[1st] Earl of Shaftesbury.

Sir Kenelm Digby.

Henry VIII and Queen Catherine, sitting at a table, by Holbein.

Henry VII, when young, by Holbein. A small head – 'his face is much longer than usual'.

Philip of Spain.

Monsieur St Evremont. A head – 'exactly like the Prints of him'.

'The Beauties of Windsor Castle.'

'Other heads in the Gallery and very many in the other Apartments; several of which have been purchased by the present Mr Spencer.'

SCULPTURE

In one room

Twelve marble busts.

TAPESTRY

In an upper room

Three pieces from the Cartoons of Raphael:
  Ananias and Sapphira.
  The Man held by Peter and John.
  Christ's Charge to his Disciples (without the full number of figures).

7 Amsterdam Stadhuis 28 May 1737

PAINTINGS

Council Chamber

Jethro's Advice to Moses.
Solomon Asking Wisdom of God.

Other rooms

Manius Curius Refusing the Gold of the Samnites, by Flink. [See also under (1) Adderbury House.]
Burgomaster Witzen's Company, by van der Elst.
The City Watch or Militia, by Rembrandt.
Paintings by Bol, Rubens, Van Dyck, Rembrandt and van der Elst.

8 Antwerp: Academy of the Painters 'over part of the Exchange' 26 – 28 June 1737

An old man 'by one of the de Vos pleases us very much'.

9 Antwerp Cathedral 26 – 28 June 1737

'The very many Chappels and Altars in this Church exhibit numberless Paintings by the greatest Flemish Masters, such as Rubens, Van Dyck, Quentin Matsys.'

Christ Taken Down from the Cross, by Rubens 'the capital Painting in the South Cross, in a Case'.

'Another against one of the Pillars of the North Isle is very fine . . .'

10 **Antwerp: Church of the Carmelites** 26 – 28 June 1737

'The history of their Order in several good Paintings hung up against the
North and South walls of the Nave's Isles.'

'At an Altar in the North Cross is a Painting shut-up; the Painter is not
known. It is the Head only of Christ . . . a much admired piece.'

A Prospect of Antwerp and The Siege of Antwerp. Two bas-relief panels in
'a North Chappel out of this [north] Cross . . . all lined with Marble'.

The Apostles Curing a Cripple. A copy of Raphael's Cartoon 'South in the
Choir'.

11 **Antwerp: Church of the Jesuits** 26 – 28 June 1737

Painting on clouded marble 'about the Altar . . . the Painter has frequently
made the natural veins of it subservient to his design'.

12 **Antwerp: M. de Licht's Collection** 26 – 28 June 1737

PAINTINGS collected by 'the late Mr de Licht, a Priest' included:

Albert, Archduke of Austria, by Rubens.

Small paintings in Still Life by van der Goes – 'the chief curiosities here . . .
his fruits and flesh are admirable'.

13 **Antwerp: St Michael's Abbey of Praemonstratenses** 26 – 28 June
1737

Church

Bust of Abraham Ortelius on a mural monument – 'very well performed'.

Refectory

Lined with paintings on canvas.

14 **Antwerp: St Walburgh's Church** 26 – 28 June 1737

Altarpiece of The Rearing of the Cross, by Rubens.

15 **Antwerp: Snyers's Studio** 26 – 28 June 1737

See p. 271.

16 **Apothecaries' Hall, London** 5 May 1746

James I, by Matthew Snelling. [See p. 3.]

17 **Avebury** 18 July 1729

The Catherine Wheel Inn

Drawings by William Stukeley with his descriptions on them, all signed
'Stukeley delin.':

1. 'A View of the Cell of the Celtic Temple at Abury.' 16 August 1721.
2. 'A View of the South Entrance into the Temple, at Abury.' August 1722.
3. 'View of Lord Hartford's House at Marlborough.' 29 June 1723.

18 **Badminton** 16 March 1752

PAINTINGS

'The best pictures were the late Duke's purchases at Rome.'

Hall

Paintings of horses, by Wootton.

Elsewhere

Family portraits beginning with John of Gaunt.

The Roman Charity – 'in a different taste from that at Windsor or the other at Blenheim'.

Raphael's 'St Paul curing a boy possessed with a devil . . . pencilled with charcoal'. It belonged formerly to Cardinal Albani. ''Tis a great pity that the piece is damaged and some of the figures vanishing. This carton represents the lower part of his Transfiguration-piece. . . .' Reference to Wright's *Travels*, pp. 251, 266, 312, 471.

'Joseph with the Babe, large as the life . . . it seems to be in Rembrandt's manner.'

A SARCOPHAGUS *at one end of the Hall.* A present to the [3rd] Duke from Cardinal Alberoni. [Described on p. 390.]

19 **Baginton Hall** 4 August 1742

PAINTINGS

Great Parlour

William Bromley [d. 1737].
William Bromley, the Speaker [d. 1732].
Mrs Richard Chester [Formerly Mrs Bromley].
Sir Thomas Bromley, Lord Chancellor.
[Thomas 1st Baron] Leigh – 'the old Lord Leigh'. A fine length, 'his hand pointing to a Scull'.
[Edward] Lord Stawell.
Sir Benjamin Bathurst.
Lord Bolingbroke. A head 'in the Painter's style'.
Edward, 1st Earl of Oxford. The 'same size' as Lord Bolingbroke.

Another parlour

General Monck [Duke of Albemarle].

Another room

Cardinal Wolsey – 'a profile as usual'.

Elsewhere

William Bromley [d. 1732] 'when a much younger man'.

20 **Bath Abbey** January 1739

The Wise Men's Offering to Christ. Altarpiece 'given by General Wade . . .
a very handsome one of Marble, containing a good Painting . . .'.

21 **Bath Guildhall** January 1739

Large room above stairs

Portraits of Aldermen and other members of the Corporation drawn and
hung at General Wade's expense.

A smaller room

Head of a heathen deity in brass gilt 'dug up in 1727 in Stallstreet'. [See p.
310 n.*h*.]

22 **Belvoir Castle** 7 June 1735

PAINTINGS

Gallery

'Lengths of Peers of this House' from the 1st Earl of Rutland to 'the present
[3rd] Duke'.

Staircase

Some 'mean performances'.
Copies of 'eminent Originals' including:
   'Peter, James and John from Michelangelo at Windsor Castle.'
   Charles I on horseback with the Earl of Pembroke from the Van Dyck in
   Kensington Palace or the painting in the hall of the Middle Temple.

Elsewhere

Charles I, when young. Half length. 'I never before saw a Picture of that
Prince in his green years.'
Dukes of Devonshire and Rutland, Lord Howe, Lord William Manners
and Henry Archer Herbert, by Philips (1732). 'Conversation-piece in
miniature.'
Paintings in Still Life.

TAPESTRY

The Cartoons.

23 Bernardines (Cistercian Abbey): Op't Scheldt 29 June 1737

In the Apartments
Portraits of the Abbots.

Chapel (in the Choir)
Lifesize effigies of great men of the Order in niches over the stalls.

24 Beverley: St Mary's Church 3 June 1735

'The mid-Isle of the Chancel has a roof painted with the effigies of several of
our ancient Kings, but the old Painting on the roof of the South side-Isle
of the Chancel is yet more curious, containing the Story of St Katharine,
in several Pannels.'

25 Blackheath: Wricklemarsh House (Sir Gregory Page's) 10 October 1739

PAINTINGS 'A fine collection'

Gallery
[3rd] Duc de Guise, by Van Dyck.
Rubens and his Wife. Two lengths.
'Prince Charles, Duke of Gloucester and their Sister', by Van Dyck.
The Good Samaritan.
Samson and Delilah, by Rubens.
'A large piece' by Rubens and Snyders.

Another room
Peter Denying Christ, by Caravaggio.

Elsewhere
The Angel Appearing to the Shepherds, by van der Werff among several
'high finished Miniatures . . . all in curious rich frames'.
The Roman Charity, by van der Werff, another of the miniatures – 'this in
quite another expression from those at Windsor Castle and Blenheim'.
The Angel Appearing to the Shepherds, by Bassano – 'a capital piece
reminding one of that by the same hand at Burleigh-house [Burghley
House] . . . of Christ's Agony in the Garden'.

26 Blenheim Palace 23 October 1733

PAINTINGS

Gallery 'with the Loves of the Gods'.

Charles I on a Dun Horse, by Van Dyck. Later reference to Walpole's
Anecdotes, II, 99.

Faith, Hope and Charity, by Rubens – represented by his three wives. The fruit in the same picture by Snyders.

The Roman Charity, by Rubens, 'in a different way from Tintoret's in Windsor Castle which I prefer'. Later reference to Walpoles *Anecdotes*, II, 93.

Saloon 'Sallon . . . Marble chair-high . . . Door-cases of Marble'

A Concert, by Caravaggio.

'A Gipsey telling fortunes', by Veronese. Later note – 'by . . . Caravaggio – so said in 1762'.

Mary, Queen of Scots – 'not handsome enough'.

Earl of Strafford with his Secretary, by Van Dyck.

Other rooms

[1st] Duchess of Marlborough, by Kneller. Length.

[1st] Duke of Marlborough, by Kneller. Length.

Ladies, by Lely.

'A fruit piece', by Michelangelo di Campidoglio.

A painting by Snyders and Bassano.

'Mary de Medices, by Van Dyck.' Later note – 'Rubens, so said in 1762.'

'Katharine de Medices, by Rubens.'

The Woman Taken in Adultery, by Caravaggio.

The Children Brought to Christ, by Rubens.

The Adoration of the Wise Men, by Rubens. Later reference – 'Walpole'.

Lot and his Family Going from Sodom, by Rubens.

A Madonna, by Van Dyck.

Isaac Blessing Jacob, by Rembrandt – 'very fine'.

The Holy Family Journeying into Egypt, by Rubens – 'living colours'.

Venus and Adonis, by Rubens.

Painting of his own Family, by Dobson.

Rubens's Wife, by Rubens.

Rubens's Family, by Rubens.

SCULPTURE

'King Lewis's [Louis] Bust over the Garden-front, from the Gates of Tournai – but 'tis said that the original is abroad.'

7 May 1734

PAINTINGS

'All the Paintings in the Sallon by Laguerre who personates the Frenchman as Dean Jones does the English. The German is much admired.' Reference to Kettlewell's *Life*, p. xxxv. Later reference to Pope on the *Epistle to Lord Burlington*.

BAS-RELIEF at the bottom of Count Tallard's monument, representing his capture at the Battle of Blenheim.

22 October 1735

The Children Brought to Christ, by Rubens – 'He is himself one of the fathers there and it is thought that the whole is from the faces of his own family.'

10 March 1739

'The Statue of Queen Anne, Rysbrack has set-up in the Oval, opposite to the middle Door in the Gallery.' Drapery much admired.

3 June 1762

PAINTINGS

The Holy Family, by Rubens.
St Jerome, by Carracci.
Paracelsus. A head, by Rubens.

27 Blythburgh Church 8 May 1731

'The roof of the middle Isle is admirably painted with flowers . . . and farther beautified with Angels and Coats of Arms, carved and painted.'

28 Boyton Manor 12 June 1738

PAINTINGS

On the staircase 'Some good Paintings.'
The Vulture Feeding on Prometheus, the upper part of the body and face 'well-described'. A large painting.
The Virgin, Babe and St Anne – 'probably by Hans Holbein'. A small painting on wood.
'A fruit piece . . . excellent.'

29 Bretby Hall 24 May 1735

PAINTINGS

'Reading of Derby painted some of the Cielings.'
'There are many excellent Paintings here, but who painted them or of whom the Portraits are, we could get no information.'
Many paintings of birds, beasts and flowers, 'excellent in their kind'.
The Duchess of Portsmouth.
Anne, Duchess of York.
Charles I.
'King William's father.' Later note 'I'm satisfied 'tis not his father, perhaps 'tis his grandfather . . . like Van Dyck'.
'The Duke of Florence and Machiavel his Secretary.' One of the best

paintings. Later note – 'the same I saw on April 2, 1736 at Mr Lenthall's of Burford, again at Ditchley, Northumberland House and Sion House'.

30 Bristol: College Green December 1738

The High Cross in the middle of the Green – 'a gaudy appearance'.

31 Bristol: Pump Room December 1738

'A good Picture of an old man who had been Pump here.'

32 Bristol: Queen Square December 1738

William III. Equestrian statue in metal, by Rysbrack.

33 Bromley: Bishop's Palace 'The House to which, under the Bishop of Rochester, belong the Great Tythes' 2 August 1737

A painting by Dürer expressing melancholy. Also an old print of the picture. 'Some of the particulars want a note to shew their propriety.'

34 Bromley Church 1 September 1730

'The portraiture of Bishop Wendover is not now, I think, lying in the Church-wall.' Reference to Weever, p. 338.

35 Bromley College 1 September 1730

Chapel

Portrait of Bishop John Warner kneeling – unlike those at Magdalen College.

36 Browne's Coffee House, Spring Gardens, London 20 September 1738

'A Battle between the Turks and the Imperialists' at Vienna. A painting 'of infinite labour and Curiosity'.

29 September 1739

PAINTINGS

Charles II, when young. A head in watercolours.
The Siege of Vienna, as above.
Five young people 'engaged in some holy exercise' – possibly the Ferrars family of Little Gidding. 'Very agreeably grouped.'

37 Brussels: Collegiate Church of St Gudule 29 June – 3 July 1737

Altarpiece of L'Histoire du Jubilé à Bruxelles.

38 Brussels: Flemish Church of Carmelite Nuns 29 June – 3 July 1737

Archduke Albert and Archduchess Isabella. Two paintings.

39 Brussels Town Hall 29 June – 3 July 1737

Chamber of the Imperial Provinces
Emperor Charles VI. Portrait.

Two pieces of historical TAPESTRY, framed.

40 Brussels: Van der Borght's Workshop 29 June – 3 July 1737

Tapestry in the loom.

41 Burford Priory 2 April 1736

PAINTINGS

Sir Thomas More and his Family. – a 'noble Picture . . . it does not in all respects answer to the description of Mr Roper's Picture . . .'. References to *Athenae Oxonienses,* I, 40, 41, and Hearne's Preface to Roper's *Life of More.*
Sir Thomas Tanfield, robed. Length.
Lady Tanfield. Length.
Earl of Pembroke, by Cornelius' 'Jansen' [Johnson], thought to be William, 'a relation of the Lenthalls'. Three-quarter length.
The Earl of Abercorn, by Kneller.
'Speaker Lenthall [Sir John] in his Robes, but drawn at different times of life.' Three paintings.
'The Duke of Florence and Machiavel his Secretary' or so 'supposed'. 'The same as at Bretby Hall.' Reference to Northumberland House and later to Syon House.

42 Burghley House 9 June 1735

PAINTINGS 'all most excellent in their kind'
The finest apartments painted by Verrio, but not floored nor fitted up. Later reference to Walpole's *Anecdotes,* III, 39.
Few portraits except family pieces.
Hall
The Salutation of the Virgin, by 'Carlo Marat' [Maratta].

The Holy Family, by Andrea del Sarto.

Another room hung with paintings of the history of Christ chiefly by Carlo Maratta.

'Tarquin the Proud's Wife driving her Chariot over her father's Corps', by Carlo Maratta.

Europa and the Bull, by 'Jordain' [Jordaens].

St John the Baptist about to be Beheaded, by 'Jordain' [Jordaens].

Christ and the Samaritan Woman at the Well, by Carlo Maratta.

Seneca, by Jordaens. Very large. Later note – 'Rubens's Seneca at Lord Derby's [Knowsley Hall, *Diary of a Tour in 1732*, p. 87] seems to be nearer death than in this piece.'

Paintings of 'Beasts, Birds and Fish', others of Flowers by 'Baptist' [Monnoyer].

The Four Elements – 'Four curious Miniatures.'

In the closets 'some of the most incomparable Paintings'.

Christ's Agony in the Garden, by Bassano – 'so dark that it requires a strict attention to find-out the distinct figures in it; which done it improves upon the Eye. . . .'

The Institution of the Sacrament, by Carlo Dolci. 'Half-piece of Christ only.'

The Adoration of the Wise Men, by Carlo Dolci.

Chapel

Paintings of Scripture history.

Elsewhere

Miniature 'Statues in Box . . . esteemed Master-pieces' were attributed to Gibbons in a later note and also the 'curious Carving' in the house.

43 **Burley on the Hill** 8 June 1735

PAINTINGS

Hall

The Labours of Hercules in watercolours.

Hall and ground floor

[2nd] Earl of Nottingham and his Wife, sitting. Full proportion.

[6th] Earl of Thanet.

James I, sitting. Half length.

Charles I – 'a good Painting'.

William, Earl of Pembroke, 'Chancellor of Oxford'. Length.

George Villiers, Duke of Buckingham – 'a singular look'.

Charles II, sitting and robed. Length. 'Much the best piece that ever we saw of [him].'

James, Duke of York, with his Admiral's truncheon.

Henry, Duke of Gloucester.

Christ Taken Down from the Cross – 'admirable'.

'The Virgin fainting' – 'admirable'.

Family portraits.

Above stairs

A magnificent room painted by Lanscroon in 1711 with the History of Caesar.

TAPESTRY

The admirable coloured tapestry, some of the Cartoons, was covered from view.

44 **Bushey Park** June 1733 and 7 September 1736

Painted canvas caves – 'Ts. Carwitham fecit. 1736.'

45 **Cannons** June 1733

PAINTINGS

Ceilings in the house painted by 'Bolusis' [Bellucci].

Third room

Duke of Chandos, by Kneller.

Queen Anne, by Van Dyck.

Charles I. Three half-lengths 'in different habits' ['In Three Positions']. Later references to a Van Dyck at 'Bertie's [Low Leyton]' and *Letters between Pope and Hill*, p. 5.

Lord Middleton, by Van Dyck.

[John] Lacey 'in his three Postures as at Windsor'.

Winter's Frost, by ? Van Dyck. [The MS. is not clear.]

A Satyr 'by the same'.

Antony and Cleopatra – 'a neat Marble Bathing-Room'.

The Crucifixion of Peter – an old piece with many figures.

Four Heads. Separate paintings by Raphael.

A Madonna and Babe, by Raphael.

'Mother, Babe and Baptist', by Raphael.

Christ Taken Down from the Cross, 'by Van Dyck they say . . . ill performed'.

'Above' Miniatures of the Cartoons in watercolours.

In a closet

Some of the Duchess's painting.

Duke of Chandos's Private Study
The Apostles Finding Money in the Fish.

The Grand Apartments above 'All the rooms but small'
Prince Charles, by Van Dyck 'they say'.
The Duke of Buckingham's Family, by Van Dyck.
The Marriage of the Duke and Duchess of Chandos – 'ill-performed, the
    Duke very ugly'.
[1st] Earl of Godolphin, by Lely. Length.

A large room – the ceiling painted by Thornhill – 'very well'.

Chapel
Ceiling painted by 'the same Italian hand [Bellucci] as those in the house,
    but it is better, gilded also and stucho'.
Windows 'painted' by J. Price.

SCULPTURE
Hall
Oliver Cromwell. Bust over the chimneypiece 'to the right'.
Plato. Bust over the chimneypiece 'to the left'.

Gallery over the entrance 'where sits the Duke [of Chandos]'.

TAPESTRY
Good Brussels Tapestry.

Grand Apartments above
The Cartoons [presumably tapestry but not stated]:
    The Creation.
    God Making Man in His own Image.
Two others 'now repairing at London':
    God Conveying Adam to the Garden of Eden.
    'God pronouncing his Curse against fruit.'

46 **Castle Bromwich Hall** 1 July 1765

Long Gallery Many portraits.
Henry VIII. A head, full face.
Edward VI. 'Its companion.'
Sir Henry Spelman. A head exactly corresponding with the print.
Earl of Derby in armour. Three-quarter length.
Bishop Bridgeman, standing 'advanced in years'.

Elsewhere
Sir Orlando Bridgeman, sitting, robed.
Earl of Strafford. A head.

General Monck.
Charles I in armour. Full face.
Archbishop Laud, standing. Three-quarter length.
Bishop John Bridgeman of Chester, sitting.

TAPESTRY

Good tapestry, some by Vanderbank.

47 **Castle Durrow** 6 August 1733

PAINTINGS

Oliver Cromwell.
'The old Duke of Ormonde.'
The Virgin Kneeling at the Cross. A fine Spanish painting, formerly an
     altarpiece, with 'nails and tools &c'.

48 **Caversham: The Grove** 4 October 1733

PAINTINGS

Hall

Charles I on horseback. Miniature.
Fish. A large painting.

Best Parlour

'Perspective of a Romish Church' as at Brancepeth Castle [*Diary of a Tour of
     1732, p. 181*].'
Infanta of Spain 'to whom Charles I made his addresses', by Cornelius
     'Jansen' [Johnson].

15 June 1741

Sir John Cotton, by Lely.
Dr South's mother, by William Dobson, 1640.
Admiral Berry [Dr South's grandfather], by Cornelius 'Jansen' [Johnson],
     1616.
Colonel Berry [Dr South's uncle] 'slain at Edgehill', by William Dobson,
     1640.
Dr South when a young clergyman, 'homely and sickly'.

September 1742 [probably]

'Whereas 'tis said on Dr South's picture that it was painted by Dobson in
     1640 – that must be a mistake for South was not elected to Christ Church
     till 1651.' The note emphasizes that Dobson died in 1747 while South was
     a boy, with other reasons for the error.

49 Caversham: The Old Rectory

'Taken from my father's mouth, 1763.' [Note by John Loveday's son John.]

PAINTINGS

The Study

Peter Zinzan, by Thomas Gibson. 1738.

Passage outside Gallery

Edward VI, 'purchased at Lady Hopkins's sale'.

Gallery

'Mr Powell, my mother's uncle.'

Thomas Loveday, 'my father when a child'.

William Daniel [John Loveday's great great-grandfather].

Mary Daniel, formerly Delanoy [William Daniel's second wife].

Henry Powell [John Loveday's great-grandfather].

Susan Powell, afterwards Lady Thompson [John Loveday's great-grand-mother].

Charles I 'when in confinement', with his son James. 'Probably by Lely who painted the fellow of this at Sion house.'

Archbishop Laud. Purchased by John Loveday.

Prince Charles. 'Probably from a painting of Van Dyck's at the late Lord Cornbury's, afterwards Hyde [Cornbury Park].'

Dr Curle, Bishop of Winchester. Purchased by John Loveday.

Henrietta Maria. Copy from a portrait by Van Dyck at Windsor Castle.

William Herbert, Earl of Pembroke 'whose statue is in the Bodleian Library'.

Archbishop Whitgift. [Later note, not by either John Loveday, calls this Arsenius of Thebes.]

Edward Sackville, Earl of Dorset. Purchased by John Loveday.

Edward Hyde, Earl of Clarendon. Purchased by John Loveday.

Sir Charles Lucas and Sir George Lisle. Reference to '*The History of the Rebellion*'.

Thomas and Sarah Loveday [John Loveday's parents]. Two portraits by Murray.

Queen Anne 'consort of James I'. [This is doubtful.]

The Best Parlour

John and Martha Loveday as children by B. Schwartz. Two portraits.

Edmund and Mary Tooke [John Loveday's uncle by marriage and aunt], 'by Kneller'. Two portraits.

Sir Richard Hopkins [John Loveday's uncle by marriage], painted before he was knighted.

Anne Hopkins [John Loveday's aunt].

Bishop Arthur Miller.

Tapestry Room

'Mr afterwards Captain John Lethieullier, my uncle and godfather, by a woman abroad.'

[The portraits of John Loveday and his first wife, Anna Maria, by Thomas Gibson were at that time kept by him 'in a case in the garret'.]

Room over the Best Parlour

William Busby of Marsh Gibwen. [A relation of the Bagshaw family.]

John Loveday's bedchamber

Mrs Frances Bagshaw [formerly Harington]. 'A Copy from Lely at Bromley College.'

Clement Throckmorton of Haseley.

On the staircase

Herman de Wilda, Archbishop and Elector of Cologne, 'given me by Mrs Hiley'. Reference to Jortin's *Life of Erasmus* and later to Cellarii, *Hist: Universal,* ii, 103.

Charles I.

The Satyr and Nymph, engraved by Alexander Voet from a painting by Rubens.

Passage below stairs

Paul Mansfield [the gardener], by John Seton.

Anne Wright, 'an old Servant in the family at Bromley College', by John Seton.

Elsewhere

Mrs Nodes [formerly Elizabeth Harington], by Verelst.

50 **Chatsworth** 27 May 1735

Hall, painted by Verrio, who painted several ceilings.

Chapel

The Miracles of Christ painted by Verrio.

PAINTINGS 'few paintings here'

Judith and Holofernes.

William, [3rd] Earl of Pembroke. Length.

Members of the Cavendish family. Length portraits.

Henry VIII, on wood. Half length – 'less than the life'.

'A strange picture on paper of Henry VII and Henry VIII, lengths; it looks like a Print.' Later reference to Walpole's *Anecdotes,* I, 81.

'Sir James Thornhill has some Performances here upon Stucho; he also painted the Wonders of Castleton.'

SCULPTURE

Gallery
Philip of Spain. Marble bust.
Some antique busts.

TAPESTRY
Excellent tapestry of several kinds. Some from Raphael's Cartoons.

CARVING
'Curious carving in Wood here, but the Pen in the Inkhorn is a very
masterpiece.' Later addition – 'by Gibbons'.

51 **Chichester Cathedral** 15 September 1730

Heads of the Bishops of Selsey and Chichester, from Wilfrid, 1st Bishop of
Selsey to Robert Shirburn, are painted on Wood. Opposite to them the
Kings from William the Conqueror ending with Charles I. The Pictures
of the Kings since are hung-up on painted Canvas.' Reference to
Bingham, VIII, 8, and later to Walpole's *Anecdotes*, I, 190 and *Archaeolo-
gia*, III, 270.
Cedwalla, King of the S. Saxons. 'Large old Painting on Wood . . .' Later
reference to *Mercur. Rustic.*, p. 201.

52 **Chippenham, Cambridgeshire** 13 May 1731

PAINTINGS

Hall
'Kings and Queens and Queen-Consorts from Edward VI to George I.'
'Some of the Rebels, as Cromwell, Ireton &c.'

Room below
Jane Shore – 'tall and red-haired'.

'Another Hall on t'other side the Green-house'
'Piece representing at full length the Earls of Orford and Hallifax, Duke of
Devonshire, Lord Sommers, Lord Wharton and the Earl of Sunderland.'

TAPESTRY
'A great deal of Tapestry with small figures.'

53 **Chirk Castle** 17 July 1733

PAINTINGS 'Tillemans and Dahl have Pictures in this house.'

Gallery
Views of the Castle.

Sir Orlando Bridgeman, 'Lord Keeper', sitting.
Sir Thomas Myddelton.
Many family pictures.

Dining room

'Charles I on a dun horse.' 'A small life-piece . . .' as at Brancepeth [*Diary of a Tour in 1732*, p. 181.]
Prince Rupert in Garter Robes.
Jane Shore. Half length.

A closet

A Burgomaster Meditating, by 'Brugen' [Ter Brugghen].
Grapes 'full ripe' by Schalcken.
Lady Myddelton.
Lady Denham.
Lady Whitmore. [See p. 155 n.*p*.]
An Altarpiece.
'A fine Cascade in one of Mr Myddelton's Lordships.'

54 **Chiswick House** 4 June 1746

PAINTINGS

Room under the Cupola

Louis XIII of France. Length.
Queen Anne [wife of Louis XIII].
Charles I and Henrietta Maria with their young sons. 'It seems to be a Copy from that at Kensington.'

'About the house'

'Date obolum Belisario', described in detail. 'There is another representation of this story at Rainham.' References to Pope VI, 55, and Mason's *Elfrida*, p. xi. Later references to Walpole's *Anecdotes*, II, 101 and *Catalogue of Engravers*, p. 129, etc.
Alexander Pope, by Kent. Profile.
Other paintings [unspecified] by Kent.
Charles I.
Mary, Queen of Scots.
The Holy Family, 'miniature'. 'The exquisite touches . . . might incline one to think Carlo Dolci was the Author.'

SCULPTURE

In the house

Antique busts, some in the room under the Cupola.

In the garden

Three 'Antiques, being Brutus, Sylla and Scipio' said to have been brought from Hadrian's Garden.

Other statues [not named].

55 **Christ Church, Oxford** 10 October 1734

Library

Print of a 'night piece' by Schalcken, 'drawn by himself, the Print taken at London in 1694'.

Archbishop Sancroft. A small picture set in gold.

56 **Cliveden** 10 October 1734

PAINTINGS

Many family portraits.

'The Duke of Hamilton that was beheaded. It looks exactly like that Piece at Windsor Castle which Hanneman painted.'

The Earl of Orkney and the Duke of Hamilton.

Prince Rupert. Length.

The Prince Elector Palatine. Length. 'I take it to be Charles, elder brother of Rupert.'

The Duke of Northumberland. Length.

Queen Anne when Princess of Denmark. Length.

King William [III], when a child.

The Earl of Pembroke with the Golden Key.

Edmund Spenser [with a query].

The Countess of Orkney. Later reference to Swift, XVII, 247.

TAPESTRY

'I know no Tapestry that excells Lord Orkney's; 'twas made at Brussels on purpose for him.' Historical and mythological scenes.

57 **Compton Verney** 20 May 1735

Gallery or Dancing Room

Family Pictures, 'well painted'.

'Sir Foulk Greville' when old. Three-quarter length.

Charles I and Charles II.

Another room

Charles I with a son. Three-quarter length.

Henrietta Maria with another son. Both copies but 'ill done of the large Painting at Kensington Palace'.

Robert Harley, Earl of Oxford, 'the lower part of whose face resembles Lord Fane'.

'The heads and shoulders of three very young persons, probably . . . Charles II, James II and the Duchess of Orleans', reminiscent of the families of Henry VII and Henry VIII at Wilton House and Windsor Castle.

Jane Shore, veiled – 'an old piece'.

27 March 1740

'The present Mr Verney [John] and extremely like him.'

58 **Cornbury Park** 11 July 1733 [See also *Diary of a Tour in 1732*, pp. 1–3]

PAINTINGS

The Judges' Room

Judge Coke. One of the twelve judges.

Another room

Lord Goring, in armour. Head and shoulders.

A room above stairs

The Duchess of Orleans. A length, sitting. 'A sprightly look.'
Charles I and Charles II.
The Duke of Saxony and the Reformers.

Another room

Lord Cottington. Length. 'A facetious look.'
The Earl Holland. Length.

A room above

'Cecil [Lord Salisbury].'
Lord Buckhurst.
The Earl of Northumberland.

Another room

Duke of Ormonde. Length.
'The Earl of Derby, his Countess and Son when a Child.'

The study

Archbishop Wareham.
Lord Ellesmere 'as in the Picture Gallery at Oxford'.
'Lord Keeper Coventry.'
William Camden, 'unlike him'.

Elsewhere

'Le Cardinal de Chatillon.' Head and shoulders.
'Le Cardinal de Loreinne.' Head and shoulders.

59 Coventry 15 June 1730

'The Town Cross (made like that formerly at Abbingdon) is now in the main compleat – a Statue or so belonging to it have been added of late years.'

60 Ditchley Park 24 June 1734

PAINTINGS

Hall

Lord Litchfield '. . . uncommon to find the Nobleman's Picture in his Hall.'

A lower room

James II when Duke of York with the Duchess and their daughters.
'Wolf-hunting.' – A 'fine painting'.
Courtesans. – 'Two good Pictures.'

Elsewhere

Family portraits. Some admirably painted.
Henry VIII. Length. – 'His Beard would have been shaved closer by our modern Painters.'
Charles I, sitting in a red velvet chair, 'Prince Charles standing by . . . it is but half a Painting which I have seen in two places.' Reference to Newbottle House [described in *Diary of a Tour in 1732*, p. 155].
The Duchess of Cleveland and her Daughter – 'in miniature'.
Queen Elizabeth. Two lengths. – 'In one she treads on a Carpet Map of England.' Later reference to *Gul. Neubrigens*, III.
A Maid of Honour to Queen Elizabeth. Length.

Chapel

Altarpiece of the Dead Christ.

TAPESTRY

'Good coloured Tapestry here.'

21 June 1747

PAINTINGS

Henry VIII, by Holbein.
Charles II, sitting. Full proportion.
The Duchess of Cleveland. Length.
James II when Duke of York, with the Duchess and their two daughters.
Prince Arthur, eldest son of Henry VII. 'Very remarkable . . . grotesque.'
The Duke of Florence and Machiavelli. 'The same as at Bretby Hall, Burford Priory, Northumberland House and Sion House.'

61 **Drapers' Hall, London** 24 May 1764

PAINTINGS

Mary, Queen of Scots, in black, with her son James.
Sir Joshua Sheldon – 'by Gerard Soest called Zoust'. Later reference to *The Gentleman's Magazine,* 1778, p. 589.
Sir Robert Clayton.

62 **Dublin Castle** 25 – 27 July 1733

PAINTINGS

The Duke of Bolton. Length. – 'very ill painted'.

Another room

Queen Anne. Length.
Good tapestry in this room and also in the Presence Chamber.

63 **Dublin: Parliamentary House** 25 – 27 July 1733

Good tapestry of the Battle of the Boyne, designed for the House of Lords.

64 **Dublin: Royal Hospital** 25 – 27 July 1733

Hall

Twenty length paintings including:
   Archbishop Boyle, Earl Coningsby, Sir Cyril Wyche, etc.

65 **Eagle Hall, Gloucester** 31 March 1736

Summerhouse ceiling painted by Casteels in about twenty-four hours – 'great skill'.

In the house

Two paintings of Still Life by Casteels.

66 **Eastbury Park** 13 June 1738

PAINTINGS

The State Room

Earl of Strafford and his Secretary 'over the Chimney. . . . Is this that which was in the Gallery at Kilkenny Castle?' [See p. 296.]
'Schoolmaster teaching his Boys to read.'
'Schoolmistress teaching her Girls to work; are these not painted by Chipari [Cipper] . . .?' Reference to Stowe.
'Perspective of a Popish Church' with priests officiating.

67 **Easton Neston** 20 May 1731 [There is an augmented account in *Diary of a Tour in 1732*]

PAINTINGS

Gallery

Good family paintings, not by Lely as were others in the house.

Other rooms below stairs

'Pieces by Snyders' of dogs and fowl.

Sir Paul Rycaut, by Lely.

Shepherds Worshipping Christ, after Titian. See 12 June 1735.

Duke and Duchess of Richmond, by Rubens.

'The Duke his Son', by Van Dyck.

'A fine Magdalen, by Linto [Lint] but damaged. . . .' See 12 June 1735.

Pieces of Still Life, by 'Rostretto' [Roestraeten].

Lord Vaux, by Van Dyck.

Charles I and Henrietta Maria. Two miniatures. Later note attributes them to Rottenhammer – after Van Dyck and Cornelius 'Jansen' [Johnson]. See 12 June 1735.

Shepherds Worshipping Christ, by Peter 'de Petro' [de Pietro]. See 12 June 1735.

Christ and the Virgin with Tobias and the Fish, by Titian.

Henrietta Maria, by Van Dyck.

The Union of the Two Houses of York and Lancaster, by Holbein.

Death of Germanicus, by Nicolas Poussin.

'Many more pieces by great hands.'

Staircase painted by Sir James Thornhill.

Above stairs

A cabinet with the history of Moses painted on copper by Rottenhammer.

SCULPTURE

In the house

'An Antony, mutilated.'

'Statue of C. Marius.'

Some 'antique busts'.

The Garden Front

'Set off with antique Statues, Busts and fine Bass Relieves.'

Statues of the Muses 'imperfect'.

In the garden – house

Tully 'declaiming'.

Archimedes 'with a Square . . .'.

Bacchus 'fine'.

'A very large Pallas, much repaired.'

'Camilla, Melpomene, Clio, the Sphynges [Sphinxes] &c.'

In the park and garden

'In the Green before the house Q. Fab. Maximus.'

A Terminus.

The two Scipios in armour.

An Apollo on a fluted pillar.

TAPESTRY *above stairs*

The Labours of Hercules, The Temple of Victory, etc. 'from the design of
    Raphael'.

'Good Tapestry of Alexander's History.'

12 June 1735

PAINTINGS

Hall

Cimon and Iphigenia, by Lely, 'Miniature'.

Landscape, by 'Bolognese' [Grimaldi].

'A Dead Christ', by Schiavone.

Lord Vaux, by Dobson.

'John the Baptist, not the Magdalen by Linto' – see 20 May 1731.

Charles I and Henrietta Maria. 'Remy [Remi] painted the miniatures . . .
    from . . .' [See 20 May 1731. Presumably 'from' Van Dyck and Cornelius
    Johnson.]

The Union of the Two Houses of York and Lancaster. 'The Union was
    drawn before Holbein's time; but quaere if it be Holbein's. Sure it was
    not drawn at the time of the Union.'

Christ and the Virgin, by Titian.

Boy with a Bustard on his Back, by Cooke.

The room 'next to that where hangs the Union'

Henrietta Maria, in yellow, by Van Dyck. 'Incomparable . . . the same size
    as that at Windsor.' 'In my MS. Folio [see *Diary of a Tour in 1732*, p. 223]
    I mention 2 pictures of the Queen in this house besides the miniature; it
    must surely be a mistake.'

'There is but one Painting of The Shepherds Worshipping Christ in this
    house; the Person that shows this house varies each time in her account of
    the Painters' names, as is evident from comparing this with the former
    Papers.'

Below stairs

James I and Queen Anne. Miniature head and shoulders.

Miniatures of the Fermor family by Cornelius 'Jansen' [Johnson].

Ruins of Athens, by 'Penini' [Panini] – 'admirably described'.

In a Closet

Louis XIII and his Queen. '2 very surprising Pieces . . . half-pieces, less than the life, extremely lively and performed in black-and-white Oil colours to imitate Prints.'

On the staircase

The History of Cyrus in watercolours, by Thornhill.

SCULPTURE

Hall

Statue of Antinous – 'naked, the right hand off'.

Elsewhere

A Terminus.
An old stone chair with a Greek inscription.
Tully, damaged by cleaning.
'V on the Pedestal of Fab. Max.'
Judith. 'However bad. . . . Death is well-expressed in Holofernes' face.'

68 **Ely Cathedral** 14 May 1731

'On the North Wall of the Choir, next the Church, are 7 scarce visible Paintings of Anglo-Saxon Noblemen and Bishops, the people call them the 7 Ringers.'

69 **Englefield House** 4 October 1733

PAINTINGS

Hall 'hung with good Lengths of the twelve Apostles'.

Small Parlour

Sir Nathan Wrighte, sitting.

Another room

The Priest of Jupiter Sacrificing to Paul and Barnabas – ' 'tis a miniature . . . very valuable'.

Duchess of Somerset. Three-quarter length – 'whose length is at Fawley Court'.

Family pictures.

TAPESTRY

Small Parlour 'has in it very ancient and uncommon Tapestry'.

Diningroom 'hung with Tapestry'.

70 **Eton College** 8 June 1733

Chapel

'Behind the Wainscot all along were painted in Water-Colours the figures of Saints, Fathers &c. They are now up and down in the fellows' houses whereas they should have been in the Anti-Chapel.'

[Monuments to Sir John Murray and Lady Collins were shut up behind the wainscot.]

14 May 1747

PAINTINGS

The Provost's 'great Parlour'

Portraits of Henry V, Henry VI and Henry VII.

Portraits of several Provosts including 'Sir Henry Savile, a length like that in the Bodleian gallery.'

Sir Henry Wotton – 'an excellent piece, from whence the Print before his Remains.'

Francis Rous in his Speaker's Robes, sitting.

71 **Euston Hall** 12 May 1731

Ceilings painted by Verrio.

PAINTINGS

Hall

Charles I, length – 'Habited for walking, his Page and Groom attending'. A copy from Van Dyck – 'The original at his Grace's house in London' [The Duke of Grafton].

In one room

'A Painting in several divisions, said to be done as a Trial of Skill by several painters.'

On the staircase

'The Great Mogul's [later alteration "The King of Morocco's"] Ambassador who was here in the time of Charles II. The Earl of Arundel, whose Seat this was, had it taken.'

Elsewhere

Charles I and Henrietta Maria.

The Stuart Royal Family.

Christ and Nicodemus – said to be by Van Dyck.

Other paintings by Van Dyck.

TAPESTRY

The Duke of Newcastle instructing his son in horsemanship.

The gallery was being repaired.

72 **Exeter College, Oxford** 24 October 1733

Hall
Archbishop Marsh.

73 **Faringdon House** 13 April 1732

Good family paintings.

74 **Fawley Court** 2 November 1732

PAINTINGS *in one room*
The Usurers. A copy from Windsor Castle.
Other copies from Windsor Castle [not specified].

SCULPTURE

Hall
Three antique statues, one of a man with a modern head and hand.
'The Drapery of one of the others very easy, 'tis a Woman in a sort of *tenuis toga.*'

In a garden ruin representing a chapel
Antique and mutilated figures.

An arched room behind the ruin
'Busts of Antiquity' in niches outside.

TAPESTRY *in the house*
'Good and lively.'

24 September 1733

PAINTINGS *in one room*
The Duchess of Richmond 'whose Wax-work figure is in Westminster Abbey'. Length. Later reference to Granger, II, 419.
Juno and Venus with Cupid and Pallas, 'well performed. . . .'

4 June 1734

An upper room
John the Baptist in the Wilderness.

21 February 1738

A painting by 'Jordanius' [Jordaens]. 'It seems to be designed for a Kitchen and Larder and a family going to dinner in it.'

75 **Forde Abbey** 29 June 1736

PAINTINGS

'Chancellor Clarendon and his Son the Earl of Rochester.'
Sir Edward Seymour in Speaker's Robes. Length.
Judge Popham 'as at Cornbury house'.
'A View of Mequinez.'

TAPESTRY

The 'grand Room' above stairs sometimes hung with tapestry of the
Cartoons.

76 **Foundling Hospital** 14 May 1748

PAINTINGS

A room 'adorned gratis by the Artists'
St Mark 10, v. 13, by James Wills. 'The Painter has shewn a very good
fancy in the disposition of the piece.'
Genesis 21, v. 15, by Joseph Highmore – 'meanly performed . . .'
Exodus 2, v. 8–9, by Francis Hayman. 'The countenances . . . speak their
characters strongly.'
Exodus 2, v. 10, by William Hogarth. The figures criticised [see p. 377].

BAS-RELIEF *over Devall's marble chimneypiece*
'The various employments of children', by Rysbrack.

1 July 1754

'In the same room where is Dr Mead and his goddess Salus, by Ramsay, is
The March to Finchley, by Hogarth.'

77 **Ghent: St Peter's Abbey of Benedictines** 4 – 5 July 1737

Portraits of the present Abbot and of his predecessor who built the
Lodgings.
Rooms partly hung with tapestry.

78 **Ghent: Abbey of Bernardines** 'Abbatia B. M. de Baudeloo' 4 – 5 July
1737

Painting of the Abbot and his Society.

79 **Ghent: Cathedral of St Bavo** 4 – 5 July 1737

In a chapel on the south side of the nave
St Sebastian 'shot with Arrows'.

80 Ghent: St Michael's Church 4 – 5 July 1737

Chapels hung with painted leather but few of the paintings good.

81 Ghent Town Hall 4 – 5 July 1737

PAINTINGS
Charles VI, Emperor.
Prince Eugene.

82 Gloucester 1 April 1737

Statues of 'our Monarchs', all 'deplorable'.

83 Goldsmiths' Hall, London 6 July 1753

PAINTINGS
Six Aldermen at Blachford's, by Hudson.
Sir Hugh Myddelton. 'The projector of the new-river-water.'

84 Gorhambury 5 May 1731

PAINTINGS

Hall
Lord Bacon. Length.
'Sir Thomas Methouse.' Later note: 'perhaps Meautys v. Lord Bacon's
    epitaph.'
A Duke of Norfolk.
George I on horseback.

Gallery 'Pictures at length in every Pannel'
Queen Elizabeth – 'a good one'.
George, Lord Carew.
Earl of Totnes.
Duke of Buckingham.
Earl of Portland, Lord Admiral.

The painted glass in the windows described. Later reference to 'Heylin's'
    Journeys, p. 61 [Peter Heylyn].

One room
Sir Nicholas Bacon and his Wife. Later reference to Ballard's *Memoirs*,
    p. 193.

In a closet
'A very beautiful Mary Magdalene (they said) reading.'

Another room
'The Cook-maid of the house . . . a Fellow behind her . . .', by Sir Nathaniel
Bacon. Later references to Walpole's *Anecdotes* and Granger, I, 196.

A room above stairs
The Prophet Fed by Ravens.

Library
Paintings of the Grimston family.

85 **Greenwich Hospital** 10 October 1739

Great Hall painted by Thornhill.
Painting of George II when Prince of Wales – 'in the most conspicuous
point of Light . . . glaring disproportions'. Later references to Wren's
Parentalia and Chamberlayne's *Present State of Great Britain*, p. 455.

STATUE
George II. Marble. 'In the area of Colonnade.'

86 **Grove House, Chiswick** 24 August 1744

The Summerhouse
Portrait of [Thomas] Barker [d. 1630], by Hale, who died aged 23.

87 **Gunnersbury House** 24 April 1746

PAINTINGS
On or just above the stairs
St Andrew about to be Crucified, 'seven figures', by Carlo Maratta.

The Grand Room
'One of his Wives', by Rubens.
'Christ driving the Buyers and Sellers out of the Temple', by Bassano.
Apollo Crowning a Youth, by Andrea Sacchi.
Liberality and Modesty, by Guido Reni. This and the Sacchi said to be
much valued. Contrary to opinion in the house, John Loveday considered
the Guido to be the 'capital' painting. Later reference to *Aedes Walpol.*,
p. 60, and note: 'These two pictures have since been purchased by Mr
Spencer for Wimbledon House.'
Mercury Offering a Purse to Minerva. Reference to Spence's *Polymetis*.

88 **Guy's Cliff House** 17 June 1730

In the chapel 'now a woodhouse' the mutilated statue of Earl Guy, against
the wall.

89 **Hagley Hall** 13–14 July 1765

PAINTINGS

Library

Pope and his Dog, Bounce, by Richardson.
Gilbert West. A head.
James Thomson, the poet.

Saloon

Charles I's 'little family and the dog', by Van Dyck. A note says the print
    was said to be taken from the original Van Dyck at 'the Earl of
    Portmore's' [Portmore Park, Surrey].
James Hay, Earl of Carlisle, by Van Dyck. Reference to his miniature 'in the
    farther room at Warwick Castle'.
The Countess of Carlisle, by Van Dyck. Length.
Jacob and his family 'travelling to meet Esau', by 'Giacomo Bassan' [Jacopo
    Bassano].
'Venüs reconciling herself to Psyche', by Titian. Venus 'just the figure of
    the Marchioness del Gasto at Windsor Castle'.
The Marriage of Neptune and Cybele, by Rubens.

The Withdrawingroom

'Elegant cieling in compartments by Cipriani.'
Five heads – 'distinct paintings of illustrious persons in our own time':
    [Sir William] Pulteney, Earl of Bath, by Ramsay.
    Sir Richard Temple, Viscount Cobham, by Van Loo.
    Lord Hardwicke.
    Henry Pelham.
    The Earl of Chesterfield, by Van Loo.

Gallery

Sir Christopher Minnes. Three-quarter length.
The Princess of Orange, 'mother of King William'. Three-quarter length.
James, Duke of York, by Lely. Three-quarter length.
Lord Brouncker, by Lely. Three-quarter length.
Mrs Stuart, afterwards Duchess of Richmond, by Greenhill. A head.
General Fairfax, in armour, by Stone.
The Duchess of Buckingham, by Van Dyck. Three-quarter length.
The Virgin and Babe, by Van Dyck.

The Supping Parlour

[Sir Edward] Lyttelton, Lord Keeper. Three-quarter length.
Sir Thomas Lyttelton. 'Resembles my Lord, his son.'

The best bedchamber

The Dead Christ, by Van Dyck.

A dressing room

Heads by Cornelius 'Jansen' [Johnson] including:
  The Queen of Bohemia.
  Sir Alexander Temple – 'admirable indeed'.
  Prince Maurice when young, by Dobson. A head.
  Lord Lyttelton. A head – 'much the air of the late John Merrick MB'.

Another dressing room

A Dutch Woman, by 'Blosinart' [Bloemeart] – 'very natural'.
'A Boy in the Character of Bacchus', by Dobson.
'The history of Pompey's head brought to Caesar', by 'Dr Wall of Worcester [John Wall]'.
Many family pictures about the house, but none of the 'great author of the Tenures [Sir Thomas Littleton, 1422 – 81] but what is a copy from one of the Temple Halls'.

TAPESTRY

The Withdrawingroom

Fine English tapestry, by Saunders.

90 The Hague: Government Buildings 9 June 1737

Ambassadors' Room

Five Princes of Orange. Lengths. William III as King of England. 'All, I believe, painted at the same time.'

Conference Chamber

'Several curious small Paintings said to be by Holbein, but surely they are by a later hand. They contain a Series of the History of Petilius Cerialis. . . .'

State Room 'in which the States meet'

Five pictures of the Prince of Orange. King William as a young man with a dog similar to a painting at Mount Edgcumbe. Three-quarter lengths.

91 The Hague: Het Huis ten Bosch 9 June 1737

PAINTINGS

'The fine room' painted all over with the history of Prince Frederick Henry of Orange.

Princess Amalia, his widow – in the Cupola.

Family portraits in the house.

TAPESTRY

'In one room'

Three pieces, the first the best:
    William II and his Wife, on horseback. 1641.
    William III, when Prince, and his Wife, on horseback, 1688.
    William III and Queen Mary, on horseback. 1690.

92 **Hall Barn** 9 June 1733

'The Poet's Room', or Garden Room

Heads of the Poets 'fronting' the water.

In the garden

Several mutilated statues.

8 August 1738

In the house

Edmund Waller, the poet, when young, by Cornelius 'Jansen' [Johnson].

In the garden

Three antique statues – two women without heads, and a man. Later
    references to *The Gentleman's Magazine,* 1769, p. 351, and R. Gough,
    p. 730.

93 **Hampton Court Palace** 1 September 1730

PAINTINGS

Ceilings painted by Thornhill and Verrio.
Staircase painted by Verrio.
Triumph of Julius Caesar. Later note: 'by Andrea Mantegna'.
James I and his Queen [Anne] – 'two fine pieces'.
Henry, Prince of Wales. Later reference to Walpole's *Anecdotes,* II, 99 n.
Charles I, standing, by Van Dyck.
William III on horseback, by Kneller. Later reference to *Aedes Walpol.,*
    p. 45, and *Anecdotes,* III, 115.
Raphael's Cartoons were being copied by Thornhill and Le Blon. Later
    reference to Walpole's *Catalogue of Engravers,* p. 133.

June 1733

PAINTINGS

Staircase, by Verrio. Later references to Walpole, III, 39, Wanley on
    Painting in the Philosophical Transactions and Defoe, p. 358.
James I and His Queen, by van Somer – 'different but preferable to those at
    Windsor'. Later reference to Walpole's *Anecdotes,* II, 4.

Room painted by Verrio throughout
Prince George of Denmark, High Admiral.

Another room
'Mary, Queen of Scots, a Monkey in her hand exactly the same as the half
    length of her at Dr Clarke's [All Souls].'
Duchess of Lennox.
'Duke of Brunswick; His Daughter; a Marchioness of Brunswick.' Three
    portraits. Later references to Walpole's *Anecdotes*, II, 9.
Earl of Nottingham, by van Somer – with a query.
Destruction of the Spanish Armada, by van der Velde – 'in eight pieces'.
Marquess of Hamilton, by van Somer.
Christian IV of Denmark, by van Somer – 'like Whiteside'.
The Queen of Bohemia [daughter of James I]. Later reference to Walpole's
    Anecdotes, II, 99.
Madonna, by Correggio.
Anne, Duchess of York, by Lely.
Fine paintings of 'Fowl and Flowers', by Buckdown.
David with Goliath's Head, by Feti – 'well expressed'.
The Holy Family, by Correggio.

A Gallery
The Triumph of Caesar, by Mantegna.

The Beauty Room
'King William's Beauties', by Kneller. Lengths.
Queen Mary, by 'Wisson' [Wissing]. 'Half-piece, ill-performed.'

Another gallery 'too low and narrow for a proper view'
The Cartoons in watercolours. Sketched for tapestry. 'Le Blon the Copier.'

TAPESTRY
Very fine, after Raphael. 'The very same sort as at Windsor Castle.'

7 September 1736

PAINTINGS
'In one room'
The Countess of Lennox, daughter of Margaret, Queen of Scots.
Louis XIII when young. Later reference to Walpole's *Anecdotes*, II, 127.
'A Painting of Guzman.'
A painting 'supposed by some to be Gundamore – a sly-looking man'.
Count Mansfeld. Length.
Philip II of Spain, when young. Length.
'A length of his second Wife [Isabella].'
The Burning of the Armada, by Van de Velde.

The Admiral's Gallery

Portraits of fifteen admirals, by Dahl and Kneller – 'Sir Cloudesley Shovel and Sir Thomas Hopson are two of them.' Later reference to Walpole's *Anecdotes*, III, 119.

Below stairs 'out of the Beauty Room'

'Constantine's Battle', by Giulio Romano, 'who copied it'.
Joseph and Potiphar's Wife, by Gentileschi.

On the new staircase

Charles I and Henrietta Maria, etc. Later addition 'by van Honthorst'. A large emblematical painting. Later reference to Walpole's *Anecdotes*, II, 126.

Elsewhere

'Some Perspectives of Rosso's [Rousseau].'
Charles I. 'Mr Vertue says (as I am informed) [this] is the only one of that Prince in his Parliamentary Robes. It is said to be the last that he sate fore.' Later reference to Walpole's *Anecdotes*, II, 99.
Paintings of Flowers, by 'Baptiste' [Monoyer].

In the garden

The Brass Gladiator – 'admired . . .'

TAPESTRY 'in the same Room as Guzman'

'A piece of Tapestry from the Carton of Sergius Paulus. Raphael is said to have painted himself in St John healing the impotent man.'

Elsewhere

Rich tapestry of the 'history of Abraham'.

CARVINGS by Grinling Gibbons.

94 **Hatfield House** – almost unfurnished 5 May 1731

'In one room', not the gallery

'The late [6th] Earl of Thanet.' Later reference to Granger, I, 219.

95 **Hinchingbrooke Castle** 18 May 1731

TAPESTRY

In a room above stairs

'Very lively Tapestry' of the Cartoons, 'more exactly taken than any Copies either in Colours or on Copper-Plates which I have yet seen'.

96 **Hinton House** 30 June 1736

PAINTINGS

The Grand Room below stairs

Charles I and Henrietta Maria – 'miniature'.
William, Earl of Pembroke.
Philip, Earl of Pembroke. Later references to Walpole's *Anecdotes*, II, 112
 and [William] Montgomery.
The Holy Family.
The School of Athens.
'A Woman shifting herself, the same is at Shotover.'
Boys with a Pitcher. Two paintings. 'The same are at Mr Baber's of
 Sunninghill.'

The Grand Room and elsewhere

Portraits of the Poulett, Herbert and Bertie families.
Edward VI. Length.
Queen Anne, when a girl.
Later note – 'Gibson has several Portraits here. Some are Copies.'

In a closet

'The Virgin sleeping with the Child in her arms.'
A Grecian Wedding – 'As at Shotover house'.

TAPESTRY

'Very good Tapestry of Darius's Tent is formed (as I take it) upon the
 design of Le Blon.'

97 **Holborn: The Griffin Tavern** 23 February 1745

Princess [afterwards Queen] Elizabeth. Length. Faber's mezzotint was sold
 here 'on which it is said "Holbein pinxit 1551"'. John Loveday thought it
 was 'performed ill'. [See p. 357 n *i*.]

98 **Honington Hall** 4 June 1751

The Prodigal Son, by Teniers – 'high-finished, a capital piece'. Later note –
 Professor John Ward said it cost 150 guineas.
'An old Shoemaker smoking and working at his trade', his 'good woman'
 blowing the fire.
Inigo Jones. 'A good head in the Painter's style.'

99 **Houghton Hall** 11 May 1731

Salon

Paintings by Snyders.

TAPESTRY
Representing rural life at Houghton.

100 **Hull** 4 – 5 June 1735 [see also *Diary of a Tour in 1732*, pp. 202 – 3]

William III. Leaden equestrian statue – 'very unlike him'.

101 **Hull: Trinity Church** 4 – 5 June 1735

Altarpiece of The Last Supper, by Parmentier – 'the same that painted the Alter-piece at St Peter's, Leeds'.

102 **Hurst: Walter Pryse's House** 12 September 1734

The Parlour
Walter Devereux, Earl of Essex. Three-quarter length on wood.

103 **Ipswich** 7 May 1731

The Butchery – 'of Cardinal Wolsey's erecting . . . carved about it a Man's Head with a Knife in his Mouth which I was told was the Cardinal'.

104 **Kensington Palace** June 1733

Staircase and some ceilings painted by Kent.

PAINTINGS in the rooms above stairs.

The 'long room'
King William and Queen Mary, by Kneller. Two lengths. 'He was made a Baronet for these Pictures.'
James II as Duke of York with the Duchess [Anne], by Lely.
James II and Queen Mary [of Modena], copied from Van Dyck. 'I fancy from Hampton Court.'
Queen Elizabeth at Woodstock – 'very singular'. Later reference to Walpole's *Anecdotes*, I, p. 151.
Henry VIII, by Holbein.
Queen Catherine and her little daughter, Mary, by Holbein.
Queen Mary, by Holbein.
Philip of Spain. 'An original.'
Charles I and Henrietta Maria, she in yellow, 'a dog between them', at one end of the long room.
Charles I on a white horse, at the opposite end of the room.
The Muses, by Tintoretto.

Christ and the Samaritan, by Bassano.

Ahasuerus and Esther, by Tintoretto.

A Deluge, by Bassano.

The Duc d'Espergnon. Later reference to Walpole's *Anecdotes*, II, p. 99.

Another room

Queen Mary and Queen Elizabeth when young. Head and shoulders. Two
   pictures.

Henry VIII when young, by Holbein. Head and shoulders. Later reference
   to Walpole's *Anecdotes,* I, p. 81.

'Charles [?] and his Queen', by Van Dyck. Half lengths.

Queen Anne when young, by Lely. Head and shoulders.

Nurse to James II, by Riley – 'fine'.

A Dead Christ, by Titian.

Crucifixion, by Titian.

A Skirmish, by Holbein.

Another room

The present [1733] Queen of Prussia.

Cupid Inspiring the Painter, by Guido Reni.

Another room

A Magdalen, by Carlo Dolci.

Four 'pieces' of the Holy Family, by Veronese, Palma, Bassano and
   Rubens.

The Daughter of Herodias with the Head of John the Baptist, by Carlo
   Dolci.

Edward VI, by Holbein. Length.

A back staircase out of the long room

Henry, Prince of Wales. Half length.

Henry, Duke of Gloucester [son of Charles I], by Van Dyck.

Erasmus, by Holbein, 1537. A head.

SCULPTURE

'In one room'

'Antique' statue of Venus with an apple.

'An antique mutilated statue.'

5 May 1748

PAINTINGS

The Queen's Gallery

Full length portraits of monarchs including:
   Queen Mary.
   Philip of Spain.

Henry VIII from which 'Vertue engraved the Head for Rapin's *History*'. Later reference to Walpole's *Anecdotes*, I, 81.

Another room

Edward IV. Engraved by Vertue for Rapin's *History*.

'Here are woful heads of other Kings and their Consorts':

[Another] Edward IV; Queen Elizabeth [Woodville]; Edward III; Richard II; Henry IV, full face. Reference 'v. Vertue'.

Henry V; Henry VI; Henry VII; 'from these Vertue has engraved the heads in Rapin. These three the same with those in the Provost of Eton's Lodgings and at Sheldon's Seat at Weston.'

'The Queen of Henry VII; Henry VIII; his first Queen Catherine; his Queen Anne Bullen; Edward VI.'

James V of Scotland 'a kind of miniature' with the Scotch Escutcheon of Arms. Later reference to van der Doort, p. 154, with a query. Attributed by John Loveday to Holbein.

Another room

Sir Kenelm Digby, by Van Dyck. Later note 'engraved among *Heads of Illustrious Persons*'.

The Two Sons of the Duke of Buckingham – 'both these brought hither from Windsor Castle'. Later reference to Walpole's *Anecdotes*, II, 103.

'Three beautiful females, perhaps the Graces, all differently employed in dressing Venus.' John Loveday thought it was probably by Titian at the time. Later note gave the title: 'Venus attired by the Graces is by Guido Reni. See Whitehead's *Venus Attiring the Graces*, pp. 5, 7.'

Edward VI, by Holbein. Later note says that Vertue engraved the head for Rapin's *History*.

Another room

Henry VIII – 'doubtless by Holbein'. A red velvet cushion bearing a scroll of parchment.

A Knight of the Garter, 1547, *aet.* 49 – 'probably Sir Henry Guilford'. John Loveday thought it was painted by Holbein. Later reference to Walpole's *Anecdotes*.

Henrietta Maria, full face – 'a Van Dyck no doubt'.

The Prince of Denmark's staircase

The Duke d'Alva. An equestrian painting.

A back staircase out of the King's Gallery

Two Van Dyck paintings, engraved by Baron.

Henry, Prince of Wales.

Several good paintings.

Many good heads throughout the house.

A long note on the painting of Henry VIII and Emperor Maximilian then at Whitehall. Reference in 1773 to Sir Joseph Ayloffe, p. 6, when the painting was in a private apartment at Kensington Palace.

105 **Kiddington House** 28 June 1734

PAINTINGS

Rooms below stairs

Some good family pictures.
William Cecil, Lord Burghley – 'if I mistake not'.
Herodias and her Daughter with the Head of John the Baptist, by Van Dyck
– 'a very fine Painting'.
Lord Carrington. Half length.
'A Nun of this family [Browne].' Half length.

In the garden

Edward the Confessor's font from Islip.

106 **Kilkenny Castle** 17 August 1733

The Earl of Strafford and his Secretary. This painting mentioned as having been 'one of the fine Pictures' which had hung in the Gallery of the Castle and which might now be at Blenheim or Eastbury Park. [See also *Diary of a Tour in 1732* for a brief description of Kilkenny Castle.]

107 **King's Lynn: Guildhall of the Holy Trinity** 11 May 1731

Sir Thomas White, among other unspecified pictures.

108 **Knole** 1 September 1738

PAINTINGS

Many 'family pieces'.
Lord Somers, by Kneller. Length.
General Monck, 'as low as the knees and unlike any that I have elsewhere seen of him'.
Oliver Cromwell – 'an handsome likeness'.
Two 'night-pieces', by Schalcken, one of a monk tempting a woman with money.
'Silenus drunk . . . by some great Master.'
Lord Goring and Sir Endymion Porter, 'said to be a Copy from Van Dyck'. John Loveday preferred it to his own similar painting, thought to be Sir Charles Lucas and Sir George Lisle.
Archbishop Bancroft 'in a Room where are many of the same size and age and perhaps by the same hand'.

Sir Kenelm Digby, by Van Dyck.

Henry VIII, by Holbein – 'in a very close Dress'.

James I, in old age, sitting. Full proportion.

Henry Howard, Earl of Surrey – his name on the picture. 'Not at all like the Portrait of him in the lower Apartments at Windsor Castle.'

The Cartoons. Good copies of all except St Paul preaching – 'as large as the Originals'.

In a letter to John Loveday dated 27 June 1733 Charles Hopson mentioned two night pieces by Schalcken, one a copy from that in Windsor Castle of a friar tempting a nun, which he called a fine painting, and of a Bacchus 'in his Cups' by Titian – as well as the copies of the Cartoons and family portraits. Whimsical figures were painted on the wainscots [all seen at Knole in 1733].

109 Lanhydrock House 14 June 1736

One family picture only.

110 Leacroft Hall 2 July 1765

Jane Lane (Lady Fisher) – An 'indifferent' portrait.

111 Leeds: St John's Church 31 May 1735

A portrait of the founder [John Harrison] in Corporation robes, over his monument. Length. 'A very good look.'

112 Leeds: St Peter's Church 31 May 1735

Altarpiece of The Last Supper, by Parmentier.

113 Leicester House 11 June 1754

PAINTINGS

Jacob's Departure, by 'F. Lauro' [Lauri]. Engraved by Major, but lacking the sensibility of the original.

St Martin on horseback. Later reference to Walpole's *Anecdotes*, II, 94.

Philip of Spain on horseback, by Holbein 'as it seems'.

Thomas, Duke of Norfolk. Later reference to Walpole's *Anecdotes*, I, 82 n.

IVORY MODELS of Rowe's and Shakespeare's monuments.

114 Leiden University Library 7 June 1737

Portraits of Lips, Scaliger, van Erpe, Heins, Casaubon, Sir Thomas More and others.

115 Liège: Baron de Crassier's House 21 – 22 June 1737

PAINTING

'Ecce Homo.' Christ's Agony, dated 1113 – 'an exquisite representation'.

GEMS with the heads of great men – 'those of Pompey . . . unlike the Bust at Wilton-house'.

116 Liège: College of English Jesuits 21 – 22 June 1737

In one room
Two Garnetts among several pictures of Jesuits.

117 Liège Town Hall 21 – 22 June 1737

PAINTINGS
'The finest room', at the upper end
'The present Prince and Bishop.'
Elsewhere
'Flowers, birds and beasts', by Smitsens. Several paintings.

118 Liège: M. Varnott's Collection 21 – 22 June 1737

Many fine paintings.
A Dead Christ, by Van Dyck. Half-closed eyes unusual.

119 Lincoln Cathedral 5 June 1735

'The pictures of the four Bishops in the Cross were painted by Damini.'

120 Longleat House 12 June 1738

PAINTINGS
Hall
'Horses, Dogs, Men', by Wootton. Large paintings.
Long room above stairs
Portrait of a Man, by Tintoretto.
Charles I, when young. Length.
Charles II, his Queen and James, Duke of York, by Lely. Three length portraits said to be originals. The Queen flattered, 'fair and beautiful'.
Gallery
Sir Thomas Gresham.

'Stafford, Duke of Buckingham . . . an old one.'

The long room and elsewhere – Many family pictures.

Henry VIII, aged 54. An original. Head and shoulders.

Marquis del Gasto and his Family. A copy from Windsor Castle.

Lord Lansdowne.

Archbishop Juxon.

Bishop Kenn when old.

Charles Brandon, Duke of Suffolk. 'Old head and shoulders.'

'Villiers, Duke of Buckingham.'

[1st Baron] Coventry, Lord Keeper.

The Holy Family. Five children including, possibly, those of the painter.

The King and Queen of Bohemia. Two paintings.

TAPESTRY

One room hung with very good complete tapestry of four Cartoons and part
   of another. The four were made abroad for King William.

In other rooms

Antiquated, faded tapestry.

121 **Low Leyton: The Great House** 17 September 1736

Statues in the garden

122 **Low Leyton: Leyton House** so called later 14 September 1736

PAINTINGS

Staircase

Charles I. 'Full Face and both Profiles [In Three Positions] as at Cannons;
   the Original is said to have been at Whitehall.' Later reference to
   Walpole's *Anecdotes*, II, 57, after Carte's *Ormonde*, II, 55.

Parlour

Moses in the Bulrushes.

Delilah Cutting off Samson's Hair. Both good pictures.

123 **Maastricht: The Franciscan Church** 14 – 15 June 1737

The Life of St Francis. Large paintings.

124 **Magdalen College, Oxford: Divinity Lodgings**

A portrait of Dr Richard Zouche by Sir Peter Lely hung there during John
   Loveday's period of residence. It belonged to Robert Lydall, son of

'Richard Lydall, Warden of Merton College, who married Zouche's daughter. It was left to Robert's nephew, William Walker, who sold it to John Loveday in 1774 for 4 guineas.

125 Magdalen College, Oxford: Thomas Hecht's Music Room
February 1732

Lady Isabella Turnor with five other persons and three dogs. A large painting seen in 1738 in the rooms at Salisbury of Hecht's nephew, Edward Thompson, organist.

126 Mapledurham Church 14 September 1731

'As the Plaistering wears off the Walls of this Church they discover odd Paintings in fresco. A Procession of Persons riding upon strange Beasts . . .' Described and compared with Holbein's 'Dance of Death' at Basle.

127 Mapledurham House 23 September 1733

PAINTINGS

Hall
Philip of Spain and Queen Mary. Two small half lengths.

Best parlour
Family pieces by Lely, Holbein and Van Dyck.
Sir Thomas More, by Holbein, 'over the Chimney . . . not much more than the head'.

Withdrawingroom
St Jerome and an Angel, by Dürer.
An enamel of Galba's bust.

Chapel in the house 'in which are Paintings'
Altarpiece of the Dead Christ, by 'Paul Lorain'.
Christ with the Crown of Thorns, by Van Dyck.

9 September 1745

On the staircase
'Fabian Smith; agent for the English Merchants to the Emperor of Muscovia' – a head. 'An old Picture, much damaged.'

128 Marsh's Library, Dublin July 1733

Archbishop Narcissus Marsh, sitting. Length.

129 **Dr Richard Mead's House, Great Ormond Street** 11 October 1739

PAINTINGS

Old Roman paintings 'wonderfully preserved on plaster'. Later references to Mason's *du Fresne*, p. 9; *Polymetis*, p. 207 [Spence]; *Museum Meadianum*, p. 241.

[George] Buchanan. Later note: 'Engraved among the Heads of Illustrious Persons.'

Thomas Hobbes. Hobbes and Buchanan were small pictures.

Dr Harvey.

Alexander Pope, by Richardson – 'high-finished'. Later note says that Richardson also etched this picture.

Erasmus, by Holbein. Thomas Gibson thought the one in the Bodleian the better piece. Later reference to Knight, p. 309, and to an Erasmus in a closet at Windsor Castle.

Petrus Aegidius, by Holbein – of the same size and manner as the Erasmus. Later reference to Knight, p. 314. Later note – 'purchased by Viscount Folkestone. v. Walpole I, 68 n'. See p. 327 n. 7.

Robert Boyle 'an Original'. Later note 'by Kersseboom' – ''Tis just such another piece as at Ashhurst's of Waterstock.' It was a present from the Earl of Burlington. Later note – 'who once again was the owner by purchase; engraved among the Heads of Illustrious Persons'.

A Magdalen, by Van Dyck – 'large built'.

Henry, Earl of Surrey; Mary, Queen of Scots; Queen Elizabeth – 'curiously enamelled Pictures; the last is the second Picture of that Queen in Hearne's *Camdeni Annales*'.

SCULPTURE AND 'ANTIQUES'

The Goddess Salus – drapery 'exquisite'. Later note: 'purchased by the Earl of Litchfield for Ditchley'.

Geta, a bust.

Tully. Head in black marble. Later note: 'called Basaltes'.

Theophrastus. A head, The engraving from it was considered by John Loveday to be a failure.

Homer. A bronze head. Later reference to 'Walpole's Painters', II, 84, and to Granger, I, 349.

The Pantheus. Later reference to Horsley, pp. 243, 348.

Cupid shooting the Muse, Erato.

A Bull.

The Temptation of Christ in amber or possibly ivory.

Urns and other curiosities.

130 **Mechelen: Church of the Beguines** 25 June 1737

The Murder of St Rumbold.

Other fine paintings [unspecified].

131 Melbury House 1 July 1736

PAINTINGS

Hall

Portraits of Charles I, Charles II and James II, with their Queens.
The [5th] Duke of Hamilton.
Other family pictures.

132 Melcombe Church 2 July 1736

Altarpiece of The Last Supper, by Thornhill.

133 Moor Park, Surrey 24 August 1736

PAINTINGS

Parlour

Sir John Temple, by Lely. Half length.
Sir William Temple, by Lely. Half length.
Lady Giffard, by Lely. Half length – 'judged to be a finished Piece'.
   Reference to Swift XIX, 331.
The Earl of Northumberland [Admiral], with an anchor. Half length.
   Reference to a portrait of him at Cornbury Park.

Above stairs

Sir William Temple, when younger. Half length.

SCULPTURE

Hall

Bust of a Moor, the face and neck of touchstone – 'antique'.

Room next to hall

Marble busts placed there by Sir William included: Miltiades, Theocritus,
   Mark Antony, Pomponius Atticus, Geta, Titus, M. Marcellus, P.
   Decius, M. Brutus, Julius Caesar, etc.

A withdrawingroom

'A small Busto in Ivory of Tully, as we imagine.'

In the garden

Two 'antique' statues of boys, 'much admired'. *'Papirius'* written on one
   pedestal and *'Comes Papirii'* on the other.

134 Mount Edgcumbe 22 June 1736

PAINTINGS

Hall – among other unspecified paintings

Prince Rupert in a black wig with a truncheon.' Three-quarter length. Later reference to a similar one at Cliveden.

William III, when Prince of Orange, armed and 'in his own hair'. Three-quarter length.

135 The New Library, St James's Square 12 October 1739

George II and Queen Caroline. White marble busts, by Rysbrack.
'Other Busts of Kings adorn the Room.'

136 Newbury Church 3 August 1731

PAINTINGS IN THE VESTRY
'The famous Twisse [William] once Minister here.'
Richard Cowslade [d. 1718].

137 Newmarket 14 May 1731

Duke of Bolton's 'brick box'
Paintings of famous racehorses, by Wootton.

138 Northampton Sessions House 12 June 1735

'Lengths of our Sovereigns beginning with William III.'

139 Northumberland House 29 September 1738

PAINTINGS
The Cornaro Family, by Rubens – much admired. Later reference to Walpole's *Anecdotes,* II, 104.
'A naked woman lying along they call Jane Shore.'
The Earl of Northumberland [Admiral].
Sir William Temple.
Daniel, Earl of Nottingham.
Henrietta Maria – 'copied, but not exactly, from Windsor Castle'.
Paintings by Van Dyck [unspecified].

1 October 1739

In the same room as the Cornaro Family
Self-portrait, by William Dobson. Half proportion.
Sir Charles Cotterell, by Dobson. Half proportion.
Sir Balthazar Gerbier, by Dobson. Half proportion.

Above stairs

'Queen Christina of Sweden in her younger years.' Full proportion.
'King William's Mother in Weeds, sitting.' Full proportion.

140 Oxford: Sheldonian Theatre March 1738

The marble statues of Archbishop Gilbert Sheldon and the Duke of Ormonde, by Henry Cheere, were erected outside the Theatre.

141 Peterborough Cathedral 10 June 1735

'Robert Scarlet, the Sexton.' An old picture on canvas in full proportion 'against the West wall of the mid-Isle'.
Thomas Deacon. A 'modern Monument'.

142 Phyllis Court 4 April 1747

PAINTINGS

Parlour – over the chimney

'A very valuable perspective of the inside of a large house.' Miniature figures of King Charles, the Queen, William Earl of Pembroke and Philip, Earl of Montgomery. The altarpiece at St John's College represented. Reference to Clarendon, I, 46, and to a picture at Hinton House, without explanation.

Long room above stairs

Portraits of the Overbury and Whitelock families.
Sir Thomas Overbury.
Oliver Cromwell, in armour. A head 'in the Painter's style'.
Elizabeth Cromwell [wife of Oliver]. Later reference to *Biblioth. Topograph. Britan.*, no. XXXI, p. 23.
Bulstrode Whitelock. A portrait said to be of him and to have been painted in Sweden and given to him by Queen Christina.
Queen Christina. A matching portrait – both in similar frames. References to Whitelock's *Memorials,* p. 594, Misson, vol. 2, p. 141, and later to Mannerschiedius [*Miscellan. Lipsiens,* II, 703].

143 College of Physicians, Warwick Lane, London 24 May 1764

The long room
Dr Richard Mead. Marble bust.

144 Plymouth Town Hall 23 June 1736

Sir Francis Drake. An old portrait.
Other paintings, unspecified.

145 **Portsmouth** 18 September 1730

William III. A statue, 'Brazen (as I take it)'.

146 **Powderham Castle** 26 June 1736

PAINTINGS

'Sir William's best Paintings are at Ford, by Newton Bushel . . . yet here are
    some well worth noting.'
The Duke of Albemarle in armour, robed.
'Charles II, a Child with a Dog.'
Peregrine Bertie. Length.
The Duchess of Suffolk, 'his Wife'.
Lady Anne Courtenay, by Kneller.
'Two or three very good Perspectives' including:
    'A long Cloister by lamplight . . . a Person represented studying in it,
        possibly St Jerome.'

147 **Raynham Hall** 11 May 1731

One room

'Hung with the Pictures of famous Admirals in Queen Elizabeth's reign.'

Another room

'Blind Belisarius' – 'given to Lord Townshend . . . by the King of Prussia'.
    Later note: ''Tis by the hand of Salvator Rosa and engraved by
    R. Strange in 1757.' Reference to *Catalogue of Engravers* and *Aedes
    Walpol.*, p. xxvii. [See Chiswick House.]

148 **Richmond Gardens: The Hermitage** 21 September 1736

Marble busts of Robert Boyle, William Wollaston, George Clarke, John
    Locke and Sir Isaac Newton.

149 **Rousham House** 25 July 1747

Library

General Dormer, sitting.
Lord Falkland. A head.

Another room

Ben Jonson. A head. Later references to Walpole's *Catalogue of Engravers*,
    p. 25.

Outside

'The Pyramid, among other Antiques, has a Roman Marble with a
    sepulchral Inscription.'

150 **Rycote** 15 – 17 February 1736

PAINTINGS

Long gallery and billiard room

'The chief of this family from Richard Bertie . . . no personable man.'

Long gallery

Baroness Willoughby de Eresby. Length.

Montagu, 2nd Earl of Lindsay with his wife, Elizabeth [formerly Baroness Norris].

James, 1st Earl of Abingdon.

Lord and Lady Williams of Thame.

James Stewart, Duke of Richmond and Lennox, standing, by Van Dyck. Full proportion. 'A fine Portrait.'

Mary, Duchess of Richmond and Lennox, sitting, by Van Dyck. Full proportion.

General Monck [Duke of Albemarle] – 'a remarkably sleepy, dull look'.

Colonel John Cromwell. Later references to Burrow's *Anecdotes,* p. 11; Nickoll's *Original Papers Addressed to Oliver Cromwell,* p. 45; Echard, p. 658; MSS. Harleian 2311; *Glastoniensis,* p. 609.

Robert, 1st Earl of Lindsay. Head and shoulders.

The Prodigal Son. John Loveday thought it was in the manner of Michelangelo Caravaggio.

Christ Walking on the Water. A small picture.

The Holy Family. A small piece, 'very well touched'.

'Droll' small paintings by Heemskirk including:

A Sessions in Oxford Town Hall, 1637.

Still Life of a glass mug half full of liquor, a lemon and a knife.

Portraits of the (Norris) Earls of Berkshire.

Billiard room

Baroness Willoughby de Eresby. Half length.

Peregrine Willoughby de Eresby [11th Baron], 'compleatly armed'.

Robert, 1st Earl of Lindsay. Head and shoulders. Later note: 'That in the Billiard–Table–Room is a Copy by Tellschaw.'

151 **St Albans Cathedral** 4 May 1731

Above the altar

Painting of the Last Supper given about twenty-seven years earlier by Captain Polehampton, coach-stainer of Cow Lane, London, and 'by his own hand'. 'A good Painting.' [See p. 84 n.*h.*]

The ceiling of the church

Ancient painting of Coats of Arms.

At the foot of Duke Humphrey's coffin
Wall painting of the Crucifixion 'much defaced'.

152 St Albans: Crown Inn 4 May 1731

'The Martyrdom of Amphibalus in Stonework.' Three figures described.
  Discovered at Verulamium in 1729.
Other curiosities included a large urn containing ashes, with a 'surprising
  large Kneepan' taken from it; a lesser urn, Roman and other spurs; a
  complete Roman tile; a 'well-turned' arch over the heads of Offa and his
  Queen. Later reference to Gough's *Anecdotes*, p. 198, vi. A large stone
  crucifix had been dug up two weeks earlier. 'The curious in Stones would
  admire a Flint here.'

153 St Bartholomew's Hospital, London 12 August 1737

PAINTINGS

The Great Staircase
The Pool of Bethseda, by Hogarth.
The Good Samaritan, by Hogarth.

The Great Hall at the top of the stairs
Henry VIII in 1544. Three-quarter length.

5 October 1739

Henry VIII. A query as to whether this was a different painting from that
  seen in 1737 or the same 'new-vamped'.

154 St James's Church, Westminster 29 September 1738

Vestry
Portraits of the rectors, except 'the present one', Bishop Secker. Tenison,
  Wake, Trimnell 'like the Picture in the Palace at Winchester', Clarke and
  Tyrwhitt.
Lord Lanesborough's Column in the churchyard.

155 St James's Palace 29 September 1738

PAINTINGS

'Two very good Rooms'
Edward IV. Length in profile – 'in a night gown'. Later note – 'by Van
  Belcamp'. Later references to Walpole's *Anecdotes*, I, 46; II, 127, his

Engravers and Vertue's print of Edward IV from the picture at Kensington Palace.
Andromeda.
Judith with the Head of Holofernes.
The Head of John the Baptist on a Charger.

156 St John's College, Cambridge 15 May 1731

PAINTINGS

Library

Bishop Morton, Archbishop Williams, Sir Ralph Hare. Matthew Prior, an original – unlike others seen of him, Lord Wentworth, Lord Malton, Dr Gower – 'not an Original', The Countess of Richmond, Bishop Gunning, Edward Benloes and others.

157 St Paul's Cathedral 20 August 1737

The History of St Paul painted round the Cupola.

2 October 1739

Library
Bishop Compton. A head.

158 St Thomas's Hospital, Southwark 10 October 1739

Edward VI. Brass statue – lately erected. The model for it in clay seen at Scheemaker's Studio on 4 October.

159 Salisbury Cathedral 31 July 1731

'The Cross-Isle and Choir adorned with oval Paintings from the Scriptures with the Months of the Year &c.'

160 Salisbury Town Hall 17 June 1738

PAINTINGS

Sir Thomas White.
Bishop Henchman.
Bishop Ward. Reference to Pope's *Life of Bishop Ward*. The portrait unlike his bust in the Cathedral.
Bishop Burnet.
Bishop Talbot.

161 **Shellingford House** 13 April 1732

PAINTINGS

Hall

George Villiers, Duke of Buckingham, in armour – 'The Navy out at Sea'.

Another room

John Winchcombe [son of Jack of Newbury].

St Matthew at the Receipt of Custom. A small picture. John Loveday thought St Matthew seemed to be 'imitated' from the painting by van der Hagen at Sonning House which was a large picture.

A Church and a Sacred Procession. A good perspective.

162 **Shotover House** 12 November 1731

PAINTINGS

In one room

Queen Christina of Sweden, sitting.

'The 1st Lord Brereton.'

Laurentius Priolus, Doge or Patriarch of Venice, d. 1559. Later reference to Bodleian *Catalogue,* vol. II, p. 363.

Sir Timothy Tyrrell.

Colonel [later Lt. General] James Tyrrell.

James Tyrrell, the historian.

Archbishop Ussher – 'an old face'.

Charity with her Children. 'No mean Performance.'

'Nymph extracting an Arrow from another's Breast.'

Elsewhere

Earl Cadogan. Length.

Anne Boleyn. Half-piece on wood.

A Duke of Buckingham.

'James I, his Queen and Prince Henry.' Three lengths. They 'seem to be good Copies from those at Hampton Court'.

Prince Henry, when a Boy. 'I never saw before.'

Thomas Smith, in armour with inscription – 1579.

TAPESTRY

'Good Tapestry here.'

15 June 1735

John of Gaunt – 'an ordinary looking man'.

163 **Somerset House** 30 September 1738

PAINTINGS

Long Gallery 'an old-fashioned Room'.

Charles I and the Duke d'Espergnan on horseback. The painting 'belongs to Kensington Palace'.

Elsewhere

The Dead Christ. A small painting.

TAPESTRY

In the Long Gallery

'Concerning the Spanish Armada which came from the House of Lords [and also] belongs to Kensington Palace.'

164 **Sonning House** 30 March 1731

Hall

Christ Calling Levi from the Receipt of Custom, by D. van der Hagen, 1652. A large painting with six or more figures.

165 **Stowe, Buckinghamshire** 20 May 1731

PAINTINGS

Room below stairs

Oliver Cromwell in Armour with his Page. Original.

Van Dyck and his Wife. Two paintings both by Van Dyck.

Joan of Arc.

TAPESTRY

Another room below stairs

'A Battle Lord Cobham was engaged in.'

13 June 1735

PAINTINGS

'Rubens's Wife', by Rubens.

Joan of Arc, 'supposed by Albert Durer'.

Moses Burying the Egyptian, by Nicolas Poussin.

The Marriage in Cana, by Bassano.

Duc de Sully, by Van Dyck. Length.

Four pictures 'in low life' by 'Ciperi, now living' [Cipper].

Oliver Cromwell and his Page, 'copied by Richardson from a Painting at the Earl of Oxford's [Wimpole Hall, Cambs.]'.

SCULPTURE
Cyrus's Camp. Bas-relief in marble.

TAPESTRY
'Excellent Tapestry of the Battle in the Wood, the old Miller appearing in
it.' It differed slightly from the tapestry at Cliveden.

166 Stowe House, Cornwall 10 June 1736

PAINTINGS

In one room
Sir Bevil Granville.
Charles II, when young, 'very likely by Van Dyck'. Half-piece as at
Windsor.
Several family portraits.

Another room
'Charles II Riding over the Sea in a triumphal Car.' John Loveday thought
there was a similar painting on a ceiling at Windsor Castle.
Christ's Agony in the Garden, painted in the same way 'perhaps by the
same hand as that much more complete piece of this History at . . .
Burleigh house [Burghley House]'.
The Holy Family.
The Roman Charity – 'not the best I have seen'.
Paintings in Still Life.

The Grand Staircase
Views of Stowe House, Plymouth and Bideford 'on the three broad sides'.

167 Sunninghill Park 1 October 1734

PAINTINGS

Hall
'The oldest Church in Rome' with a procession. 'A good Perspective.'
'Two Hucksters, Man and Woman with their Wares', by Kincheller, 1585.
'Fowl, Rabbets, Pumpkins &c.'
Lady Ranelagh, by Dahl – 'I think'.

168 Syon House 11 September 1736

PAINTINGS

Long Gallery
'Duke of Tuscany and his Secretary Machiavel, as at Bretby Hall and

Burford Priory.' Later note adds Northumberland House and Ditchley. The Duke was 'not pourtrayed so well' at Syon House as at Bretby Hall and Burford.

'The Princess of Orange, King William's Mother', by Lely.

Charles I and James, Duke of York 'presenting to his Father a pair of Scissars', as at Caversham but with different expressions. The picture at Syon House 'much damaged'. Later reference to Walpole's *Anecdotes*, III, 17.

'Joseph and Mary with the Babe Travelling into Egypt . . . certainly by a great Master.'

Earl of Essex [Robert Devereux].

Countess of Essex.

William III, when young – inferior to that at Mount Edgcumbe.

Charles II and his Queen. Half proportion.

Queen Mary, when young.

A Madonna on copper.

Hall

James II, when a boy. Good head and shoulders.

Elsewhere

The Earl of Northumberland, Admiral. Head and shoulders.

The Virgin and Babe in the Stable. Several 'anachronisms'.

Portraits of the Percy family.

169 **Thomastown** 8 August 1733

SCULPTURE *in the garden*

Lead Statues 'very well performed'.

Stone busts of poets.

Two little boys 'in Lead are deservedly admired'.

'Gladiator in the front of the house', also admired.

170 **Trinity College, Cambridge** May 1731

Library

'A Lord Hallifax.'

Bishop Hackett.

Dr Barrow.

Other portraits [unspecified].

171 **Twickenham: Pope's Villa** 12 September 1736

The garden

Nymph sleeping, in stone.

172 **University College, Oxford** – undated but referred to at Cuddesdon 26 January 1738

In the Lodgings

Bishop Bancroft. 'The Draught of this House [Cuddesdon Palace] is painted in Bishop Bancroft's Picture. . . .'

173 **Vintners' Hall, London** 5 May 1746

Charles II. Full length. 'The handsomest likeness of him when King.'

174 **Walsingham Abbey House** 10 May 1731

PAINTINGS

Bishop John Warner – 'the finest Picture I have seen of him . . . the face exactly like that in the Picture at Bromley College'.
Dr Lee, Archdeacon of Rochester.

175 **Wanstead House** 18 October 1739

PAINTINGS 'Kent has painted here as well as Hogarth.'

Room on the ground floor

'By much the finest India Pictures that ever I saw.'
'The Great Mogul standing is very beautiful.'
'A Friar before a Crucifix', by Hogarth. Possibly a copy.
The Virgin and Babe with St Joseph and St John. A copy from that at Syon House.
'Conversation-piece of the family and the neighbourhood [The Assembly at Wanstead]', by Hogarth.
Paintings of Fowl and Flowers.

Ballroom

'Portia's Story' . . . 'a fine . . . night-piece', by Schalcken.

TAPESTRY

'Very good Tapestry here especially in the fine Ballroom . . . Colours are admirable.'

30 June 1753

Sir John Glynne – 'Sergeant at Law but in the habit of a Judge'.

176 **Dr John Ward's Collection at Whitehall** 11 June 1754

PAINTINGS

Apollo Flaying Marsyas, by Guido Reni.

The Holy Family, by Pietro Perugino – 'much of the Flemish air'. Later reference to Fresnoy, p. 225.

Many fine paintings.

SCULPTURE

Cupid Sleeping. Marble statue.

177 **Wardour Castle** 12 June 1738

PAINTINGS

Staircase

The Roman Charity. Large.

The Dead Christ. Large – 'very fine'.

Passage above stairs

Medals of the Arundell family, framed in silver. Inscriptions and decorations described.

178 **Warwick Castle** 16 June 1730

PAINTINGS

James Hay, Earl of Carlisle, by Van Dyck. Miniature length.

Other paintings by Van Dyck which were being copied by Bodwyn of 'near Green's Brew-House, Westminster'.

TAPESTRY

A room hung with tapestry, 'curious for its small Figures and the Variety of them'. ' "Franciscus Spiringius [Frans Spirinx] Fecit 1604" at the edge of one piece.'

21 May 1735

PAINTINGS

'The third Room'

Henrietta Maria. Miniature.

A Nun, 'daughter to the Earl of Bristol'. Head and shoulders. 'Excellent miniature.'

Phineas Fletcher.

Charles Lennox [1st] Duke of Richmond, 'the late Duke'. Head and shoulders.

Anne, Duchess of York.

17 – 18 April 1740

PAINTINGS

William Russell, 1st Duke of Bedford – among other miniatures.

Sir Philip Sidney. Three-quarter length. 'Original' written on it.

10 July 1747

PAINTINGS

Lady Whitmore. 'One of the Beauties at Windsor Castle.'

'The last Wilmot, Earl of Rochester [Charles, 3rd Earl].' A small oval – 'like his Father'.

In a farther room

'Capital heads in small squares.' Later reference to Walpole's *Anecdotes*, II, 7. They included:

The [5th] Earl and 1st Duke of Bedford. Opposite profile to that in the *Heads of Illustrious Persons*.

'A Nun of the Digby Family [as on 21 May 1735].' Full face. 'Commands the attention of every body.'

22 June 1762

PAINTINGS 'brought of late years into Warwick Castle'

Robert Devereux, Earl of Essex, by 'Fed. Zucchero' [Zuccari]. 'A very fine Head.'

Sir Fulke Greville, when old.

Lady Catherine Grey and her Child. An oval. Reference to Fuller's *Worthies in Leicestershire,* p. 127.

Lady Anne and Lady Mary Boleyn. Miniature heads – 'distinct paintings of 2 sisters'.

22 July 1765

PAINTINGS *in the Cedar room*

St Peter and St Paul in Debate, by Manfredi.

Christ's Agony in the Garden, by 'old Bassan' [Francesco Bassano].

The Virgin and Babe with Elizabeth and St John, by Andrea del Sarto, Painted on board.

'A Flemish young woman of fashion leaning out of window', by Rembrandt.

Elsewhere

Sir Fulke Greville – 'It is a copy from Lord Willoughby de Broke's [Compton Verney].'

Anne Boleyn – 'like Mrs Warner' [Elizabeth Ashhurst].

179 **Warwick Priory** 14 July 1747

PAINTINGS

William, Earl of Pembroke, standing, with white Staff. Three-quarter length.

Duke of Shrewsbury, sitting in Garter Robes with white staff. Three-quarter length.

Henry VIII – 'large head and neck . . . filling the Canvass'.

16 June 1762

Hall

Sir Henry Puckering. Length. References to Birch's *Life of Prince Henry*,
  pp. 328, 375, and 'Catalogue MSS, Angliae'.
Sir Henry's Two Concubines – 'also at length, distinct pieces, wonderfully
  fine women, both big with child'.

180 **Waterstock House** 29 October 1733

PAINTINGS

Hall

Christ and the Apostles. Thirteen good paintings.
William III. Length. Original.
Philip of Spain.
Duke d'Alva.

In other rooms

Family paintings, several belonging to the Earl of Uxbridge's family 'which
  are Relations; one of him that was Ambassador to the Porte [William, 6th
  Baron Paget]'.
Robert Boyle, sitting with a book. 'It is said on the Picture that the first Sir
  Henry Ashhurst of Waterstoke was Executor to him.'
Earl of Holland.

TAPESTRY

Colours 'wondrous lively. See Caius, p. 581.'

181 **Wentworth Woodhouse** 29 May 1735

PAINTINGS

Conversation Piece of thirteen persons including 'the present Lord Malton'.
Charles I. Length.
Henrietta Maria, in a black hat, with a dwarf.
James [7th] Earl of Derby.
The Countess of Derby [his wife].
Thomas Wentworth, 1st Earl of Strafford – 'the finest Picture of him is in
  the Dining-room, which we did not see.'
The Duchess of York.
Jane Shore.
A Magdalen – 'incomparable'.
The Virgin and Christ. A 'night-piece'.
The Cartoons. Copies in miniature.
Christ Taken from the Cross.

182 **West Hatch** 5 July 1753

Sir Robert Ladbroke's collection of paintings 'left him by Mr Peck'.
A Musician, by Teniers.
Other paintings, by Teniers.
A Drawing, by Holbein.
Fruit and flower pieces.

183 **Weston House, Warwickshire** 23 July 1747

PAINTINGS – 'a multitude'

Great Parlour

Paintings 'of our Princes and contemporary Monarchs'.
'Henry 5, 6 and 7 begin the collection and are just like those in the Provost's
    Great Parlour at Eton.'
Francis I of France.
'Lord Cromwell.'
'Wolsey.'
Paintings of Popes and Cardinals – 'admirable good ones'. Later references
    to Granger's *Supplement*, pp. 335–7.
Paintings of great men and family pictures.

Elsewhere

Nicholas Heath, Archbishop of York. Later reference to *Athenae
    Oxonienses*, I, 705.
Oliver Plunket, titular Primate of Ireland.
Lord Burghley.
Sir Nicholas Bacon.
'Lord Petre and the learned Ralph Sheldon when a young man.'
Ralph Sheldon 'when in years'.

TAPESTRY *in the Great Parlour*

'The celebrated Tapestry-Hangings.' Maps of several English counties.

27 July 1765

PAINTINGS

John Selden.
Sir Harry Spelman 'like that at Hagley and the prints of him'.
Sir William Dugdale.
Ben Jonson.
Sir Henry Saville.

A bedchamber

'A fine Descent from the Cross probably Albert Durer's.'

TAPESTRY

'The Map-Tapestry here was the very first made in England.' Later reference to Walpole's *Anecdotes,* II, 22. Later note: 'This I understand to be the very Tapestry for which the earl of Harcourt is now [1787] preparing a fit reception at Newnham [Nuneham Park].'

184 Whitchurch Parsonage, Oxfordshire 3 April 1741

Gilbert Ironside the Elder, Bishop of Bristol, holding a book.

185 Whitchurch Church, Shropshire 3 July 1765

The Queen's arms in needlework, over the front of the organloft.

186 Whitehall: Banqueting House 29 – 30 September 1738

The Great Room 'now the Chappel'

[The Apotheosis of] James I. Rubens's painting 'on canvass' on the ceiling. Later references to Gambarini, p. 6; *Polymetis*, p. 296.

187 Wickham, Kent 11 August 1744

Three Persons in Turkish Habits – one Sir Humphrey Style of Kent. Lengths – 'as large as the life . . . a fine Painting'.
Bishop Smalridge.

188 Wilton House 30 July 1731

PAINTINGS 'many by Lely and Van Dyck'

Staircase
The Holy Family – 'a curious Piece'.

Above stairs
Henry VIII's Family, by Holbein, 1495. Small.
Edward VI, by Holbein. A head.
'His Children', by Rubens.
A Woman Holding a Candle, by Schalcken – 'an incomparable night-piece'.
The Chief Reformers [including John Wycliffe]. 'Not remarkable.'
A 'Family Piece', by Van Dyck – 'which Lewis XIV would fain have purchased'.
Charles I and Henrietta Maria, by Van Dyck. Two paintings, 'by no means the best'.
A small altarpiece with 'King Richard on his Knees'. Reference to Preface to

Hearne's *Historia Ricardi*, II, and later to Vertue's *Hollar*, pp. 3, 124, Walpole's *Anecdotes*, I, 26, Coudry, p. 66, Anstis, II, 112, Van der Doort, p. 173.

The Cube Room

'On the bottom pannels is painted the Countess of Pembroke's *Arcadia* written by Sir Philip Sidney.'

SCULPTURE

Lower room

Marble bas-relief with Greek inscription.
Caracalla. Bust in bas-relief – 'large and valuable'.

Staircase

Livia.
Didia Clara.
Manlia Scantilla, sitting.

At foot of staircase

Egyptian sepulchre – 'most expressive Faces in Bass Relievo'.
Urn of Probus and Claudia. Later reference to Coudry, p. 34.
Sesostris – granite head.

Above stairs

Many antique busts, mostly on marble pedestals, including:
Severus.
Germanicus. 'A handsome likeness (in my opinion) of Somner.'
Constantine the Great – 'a larger bust'.
Pyrrhus 'in Porphyry'.
Pompey – 'indeed an ordinary face. . . .'
Brutus Junius – 'something desperate Countenance. . . .'
'Masinissa the Son . . . the Drapery [of this and others] gives us the exact colour of the Cloaths.'
Ptolemy, brother to Cleopatra.
Vesta, sitting.
The Ephesian Diana – 'her Face, Neck, Hands and Feet being black'. Reference to Dr [Thomas] Shaw's *Travels*.
'A Black Egyptian Isis sitting on her heels.'
Hercules 'with the golden fruit curiously performed in Mosaic-work'. Later reference to Coudry, p. 90.
Messalina. Later reference to Coudry, p. 53.
Urn of Horace. Later reference to Coudry, p. 86.

The 'two fine upper rooms' including the Cube Room, 'ceilings painted'

'Busts of the Caesars all but Otho and Tiberius.'
Busts of 'lawgivers', philosophers, historians, poets, etc.

Horace 'in porphyry'.
Cicero 'in a kind of Touchstone'.
Socrates. Reference to Burnet's *Letters*, p. 24.
A Sibyl.
'Marcus Aurelius on horseback in alto relieve.'

A third upper room

Tiberius, Otho – both 'of Closet-size'.

Cube Room (specifically)

Hercules supported by Paeas.

At foot of another staircase

Urania.
Cleopatra with Caesarion in her arms.

Room below

Two Apollos.
Antinous. A statue and a bust.
Mercury.
Autumn.
Silenus and Bacchus.
Bacchus alone.
Flora – 'exquisite Drapery'.
Saturn holding Jupiter.
Hercules – 'large'.

Building in the bowling-green

Jupiter Hammon with ram – 'ill-proportioned'. Later reference to Gough, 529.
Three fine sepulchres.

Upper end of 'plain Garden'

'Equestrian Marcus Aurelius in Lead, like that in the Capitol.'

TAPESTRY *above stairs*

Two of Raphael's Cartoons in tapestry. 'I can't think them comparable to those at Hinchinbroke.'
'No great quantity' of other tapestries – all small figures.

15 June 1738

PAINTINGS

The painting of Richard II was now in London.

The State Room

Charles I, by Van Dyck. Three-quarter length.
Henrietta Maria (in yellow). Three-quarter length – 'like that at Easton Neston, but sure not so fine a Painting'.

'In one of the Suit of small Apartments below'

The Holy Family 'by Van Zyck [Van Eyck] 1410' [now attributed to Van der Goes]. Later reference to Gambarini, pp. 4, 64. See p. 298 n.*t*.

Tabula Antiqua ex Templo Junonis – 'ancient Roman piece of painting' representing gods and goddesses.

Chiaro Oscuro of Polydore – 'the Story of Hector dragged round Troy Walls by Achilles'. Reference to Gambarini, p. 44.

The Reformers – 'neatly done enough. Not like the grotesque Groupe at Cornbury-house'. Reference to Gambarini, p. 66.

Elsewhere

'The Night-piece', by Schalcken.

SCULPTURE

Many busts and statues (and also paintings) had been moved to different positions since 1731.

Lower apartment

Marcus Aurelius. Equestrian figure in alto relief.

Busts, many on pedestals of 'curious marbles'.

Julius Caesar.

Julia Domna.

'M. Junius Brutus is extremely like Master Cockman.'

King Pyrrhus.

Socrates.

STATUES

'Silenus and Bacchus out of one piece of Marble is admirable.'

A Queen of the Amazons defending herself against a horse which had now 'all gone save for one hoof . . . the Queen's right arm is much admired'. Later reference to Coudry, 183.

On the bridge

'Old Busts adorn the inside and some Statues the Approach.'

189 **Wimbledon House** 10 September 1735

PAINTINGS

Salon

Family portraits of the 1st Duke and Duchess of Marlborough, their children, sons-in-law and grandchildren.

The 'present' Duke and Duchess of Bedford, by 'Wood' [Whood].

Other portraits by Seymour.

Elsewhere

Sidney, Earl of Godolphin.

Queen Anne.

Daniel, Earl of Nottingham.

1st Earl of Macclesfield, 'Lord Chancellor'.

St Matthias in a painting.

'Above' St Matthias 'an old Painting from the Flemish School, as I presume; I take part of it to be Cardinal Bona reflecting on Eternity. *Respice finem* is wrote on the piece.'

SCULPTURE

'Two fine rich Statues of Blacks made of different kinds of Marble.'

TAPESTRY

Excellent tapestry 'wherein Lions, Camels, Crocodiles seem alive'.

190 **Winchester Cathedral** 2 August 1731

Library (over the door)

Bishop Morley. A painting 'designed by himself for this place'. Reference to Bingham's Preface to his *Origines Ecclesiasticae*.

191 **Winchester College** 2 August 1731

Statue of the Founder over the door.

192 **Winchester: Samuel Speed's House or Rooms** July 1749

John Speed, the historian 'from which the Print is taken prefixed to his Chronicle. The Print makes him a larger man than the Painter has portrayed him.' Reference to Ames's *Catalogue of English Heads*, p. 145.

193 **Windsor Castle** 4 September 1731

PAINTINGS

Gallery 'One side hung a considerable way with Paintings of Saints and Jesuits'

James I and Queen Anne – 'not comparable with those at Hampton Court'. Later reference to Walpole's *Anecdotes*, II, 4.

A Magdalen with a Candle, by Schalcken – 'small night-piece'.

Two Userers, by 'a Smith of Antwerp'. Later addition: 'Quentin Matsys.'

Henry VIII, 'not at length – The Bataille of Spurrs, 1513. So on the Picture.'

Elsewhere

Henrietta Maria, in a grey dress with rose-coloured ribbons. A copy of this painting was at Caversham. Later reference to Walpole's *Anecdotes*, II, 100.

Prince Henry, son of Charles I.

Peter, James and John, by Michelangelo – 'not Paul as in the Catalogue'.

Room 'hung with the Beauties of Charles II'

A closet

Henry VII's Family. 'This probably drawn before that at Wilton-house.'

Erasmus, by Holbein – 'like that at the Picture-Gallery at Oxford'.

'The Countess of Desmond, who is mentioned by Sir Walter Raleigh, p. 66, has a Painting here.'

Another room

Charles II 'when a lad', by Van Dyck – like a painting seen at Euston Hall.

[The needlework of Mary, Queen of Scots, was in this room.]

The Royal Chapel

'Verrio has painted . . . The Miracles of Christ and among the Multitude has drawn himself, his features hard.' Later references to Wright's *Travels*, 73, 153, 470, etc.

St George's Hall 'represents':

'King William, sitting. The Steps of the Throne very natural.'

Edward III 'creating the Knights of the Garter' on one side of the room.

'The Black Prince's Triumph and Entry, by Verrio.'

28 – 29 March 1733

PAINTINGS

Ceilings by Verrio.

Guard Chamber

Prince George on a White Horse, by Dahl.

Gallery

Prince George, by Dahl – 'an ordinary Painting'.

Judith and Holofernes, by Guido Reni. Two paintings 'in a different manner'.

'Yet a third in another taste, which is done after the same great hand.'

The Stoning of St Stephen, by Rottenhammer. Later reference to *Aedes Walpol.*, p. 54.

The Roman Charity 'in Tintoret's manner'. Later reference to Taylor's *Elements of Civil War*, p. 374.

Duns Scotus by 'Spagnaletto' [Jusepe de Ribera] – 'from whence doubtless Ashfield took the hint of that Painting in the Picture-Gallery at Oxford'. Later references to Otterbourne and Whethamstede, p. 793, and *Aedes Walpol.*, p. 78.

Lot and his Daughter, by Michelangelo.
The Massacre of the Innocents, by Giulo Romano – 'The Innocents slain'.
The Wise Men's Offerings, by Veronese – 'a large Piece'.
Still Life, by Verelst – with a query.
Aretino and Titian, by Titian.
Paintings of Saints and Jesuits including:
  'Paul the Hermit [and] . . . St Charles Borromeo.' Later reference to
    Addison's *Travels*, p. 29.
Henry VIII aged 'about forty . . . like the Picture of a Chinese'.

Closet out of the Gallery

Erasmus 'seems the very same as that in the Picture-Gallery at Oxford'.
Sir Thomas More – 'or is it Frobenius, Erasmus's friend?'

China closet out of the Gallery

Henry VII's Family, by Holbein.
Cupid Sleeping, by Carracci.
Charles II, when a boy, armed, by Van Dyck.
Sir Kenelm Digby, sitting, by Van Dyck. Later removed to Kensington.
'Francis Couplet, a Jesuit Missionary in China', by Kneller – 'Kneller's
  Masterpiece'. Later reference to Walpole's *Anecdotes*, III, 115.
'Four Figures singing by Candle-light', by Schalcken. 'Another Night-piece
  . . . very large, no Miniature. It is not known that there is any such other
  of this size by the same hand.'
Prince Henry of Gloucester, son of Charles I.

SCULPTURE *in the Gallery*

'A famous Statuary by Michelangelo – some imagine 'tis of himself.'

[Of Gibbons's 'carving in limetree throughout' John Loveday admired most
  the folds of a curtain for a canopy to the royal seat in the chapel.]

TAPESTRY

China Closet out of the Gallery

'Excellent good' tapestry.
Needlework of Mary, Queen of Scots, when in Fotheringay Castle.

8 June 1733

PAINTINGS

'The greatest Likeness, they say, that ever was drawn of Charles II is on one
  of the Cielings by Verrio.'

A water closet in the Gallery

Luther and his Wife. So called in the Catalogue, p. 11, 'and said to be in
  "Holbein's manner". By some said to be Holbein and his wife.' Later
  reference to Walpole's *Anecdotes*, I, 82.

The Guard Chamber

Charles XI, King of Sweden.

St George's Hall

A carpet representing St George and the Dragon painted above King William.

'Lord Delaware presenting the captive Kings to Edward III.'

The Royal Chapel

'Lanscroon, who worked under Verrio and Sir Godfrey Kneller in Wigs. Sir G. drew Verrio and Verrio drew Sir G.K.' [Walpole refers to Sir Godfrey Kneller and Baptiste May in the painting of The Healing of the Sick.] John Loveday thought Verrio succeeded better on ceilings than on canvas.

9 April 1734

PAINTINGS

Massacre of the Innocents. 'The Innocents slain . . . said to be done by Julio Romano.'

Madonna with St John – 'over the Chimney' . . . said to be by Raphael.

Judith, 'said to be done after Guido [Reni]'.

'The Queen's private Eating Room – No. 7'

Lady Byron.

The Gallery – No. 10

Judith and Holofernes, by Veronese. Later references to Misson, 132; *Aedes Walpol.*, pp. 54, 63, 66, 71, 80.

31 August 1734

PAINTINGS

The Apostles Worshipping at the Sepulchre, by Schiavone.

St George's Hall

Further descriptions of Verrio's painting.

The Royal Chapel

The Miracles of Christ, including Lazarus Raised from the Dead. 'One of Verrio's prime excellencies was the projection of his figures; of this sort are amazing instances in Windsor Castle, as in the first Guard-Room &c.'

30 September 1737

PAINTINGS

The Queen's Withdrawingroom – No. 5

'Marc Antony and Cleopatra and their family is really the Painter and his Wife and Family. The Children are what make the Picture admired.'

'Hercules at the Distaff, and Omphale . . . Cupid and the Ball of Twine are much admired.'

'A Family being Ten Figures, p. 10, line 2 of the Catalogue. This hangs in a dark place yet each figure glows. . . . A Dutch or Bohemian family according to the Quarto History, p. 421.'

TAPESTRY

'Though old retaining its Colours remarkably well, being originally in dark Colours . . . said to be Brussels Manufacture . . . "Everaert Leyniers fecit".'

7 August 1738

PAINTINGS

'Many of the Castle-Pictures have been removed since the Hanover reigns to Kensington, such as Sir Kenelm Digby, The Duke of Buckingham and his Brother when young. v. the Catalogue 6 & 7.'

Room in the Lower Lodging

Henry Howard, Earl of Surrey, when young, 'in a red habit . . . over the Chimney-Piece'. Length. ' 'Tis said to be Henry VIII in my Catalogue, p. 12, but 'tis surely a mistake. . . .'

Henry VIII, Queen Catherine Parr, Prince Edward, the two Princesses and others, by Holbein. Later references for 'this Whitehall piece' to Van der Doort, p. 118, Sir Joseph Ayloffe, p. 43.

'Henry VIII going by Sea to Boulogne [Embarkation of Henry VIII]', by Holbein. Later reference to Lord Herbert, p. 513.

'Henry VIII's . . . Passage and Entry into Boulogne. [Field of the Cloth of Gold]', by Holbein.

'These three Holbeins are said to have been brought from Whitehall Banqueting-House.'

SCULPTURE in 'the open Room at the bottom of the great Staircase'

Antique busts in niches.

31 May 1739

PAINTINGS

A closet

The Countess of Desmond.

Henrietta Maria 'in craons. This is what the Catalogue, p. 4, calls "The Queen Mother in little by Gibson" as I take it.'

China closet out of the gallery

Magdalen, squeezing a sponge – 'Catalogue, p. 10'.

'Dutch Woman with a Dog', by Titian.

St George's Hall

'The Canopy over St George and the Dragon is much admired, as swelling and projecting in a bold manner.'

TAPESTRY

Some of it 'of the same sort with that I have seen at Cornbury-house'.

24 September 1739

Lower Lodgings

Cupid Sleeping. A statue 'over a Chimney-piece'.

28 May 1742

Anne, Duchess of York. Painting. 'Catalogue, p. 3.'

19 July 1743

PAINTING *'in the same room as the needle-work of Mary, Queen of Scots'*

'Winged Contemplation', by Carracci. 'Attributed to this Author in the Catalogue, p. 6, under the Title of Cupid with a Bow.'

The Tomb House

Painted ceiling by Verrio of James II, full proportion, with Charles I and Charles II, head and shoulders, in ovals. 'This Cieling is much decayed.'

19 August 1743

Beheading of Mary, Queen of Scots, by 'Jennet' [Clouet].

15 August 1746

Room with needlework of Mary, Queen of Scots

Artimisia, Orazio Gentileschi's Daughter, painted by herself – 'Vulgarly said to be Titian's Daughter'.

13 May 1747

Closet 'where the Blenheim Banner is lodged'

'A small St Jerome said in the Catalogue, p. 3, to be painted by Mieris' [van Mieris].

Boy with Fruit, by Michelangelo – 'another admired piece'.

Miniature of one of Christ's Miracles, by Rottenhammer – 'raising from death the widow's son at Naim'. 'Christ and Lazarus' in the Catalogue.

14 March 1750

Magdalen at her Devotion, by Lely – 'hands very bad indeed'.
Magdalen Reading in her Book, 'much admired'. 'Catalogue, p. 13.'

194 **Windsor Castle: Charles Hopson's Account** 1 December 1733

A Room hung round with half-lengths of heroes, by Lely.

Princess Royal's Apartments

The Infanta of Spain 'whom Charles I was to have married . . . a peculiar odd dress'.

A Venetian 'who would have made a complete Bacchus'.

Mary, Queen of Scots, 'dressed as Eachard has described her . . .'.

195 **Windsor Castle: St George's Chapel** 4 September 1731

The Last Supper. A fine altarpiece.

8 June 1733

The Altarpiece damaged 'It was, they say, turned the other way and made a carpet of in the time of the Civil Wars.'

Edward IV's monument also damaged.

196 **Worcester: Edgar Tower** 13 July 1733

Statues 'painted lately' of King Edgar with his two Queens.
Bust of George II on the west side of the gate.

197 **Worcester Guildhall** 18 June 1730

PAINTINGS

Queen Anne, when Princess. Original given by Sir John Packington.
Lord Coventry [Lord Keeper].
[2nd] Earl of Plymouth, 'the late Earl'.

'The Room for Mayors' Feasts' – above stairs

Sir Thomas White.
Portraits of White's contemporaries.

13 July 1733

Lower room

Four length portraits including that of Lord Coventry.

The room above

Lord Somers. Head and shoulders.

Over the Great Door

'A Groupe of warlike Instruments well carved.'

198 **Wroxton Abbey** 24 July 1747

PAINTINGS

Lord Guilford (Lord Keeper), by Riley. Three-quarter length, sitting.

Sir Owen Hopton. Later reference to 'Sir Thomas Pope's *Life*'; 411, Ed. 1.

Sir Thomas Pope, by Holbein. Later reference to *Life*, 414, Ed. I. Later note: 'The Picture of the Founder in the Refectory of his College [Trinity] is but a Copy. v. Athenae Oxonienses, II, 612.'

Henry, Prince of Wales – 'very remarkable'.

A portrait of a Harrington [*sic*], 'as appears by the Arms'.

199 Yarmouth Town Hall 8 May 1731

George I. Painting.

200 Ypres: Church of the Jesuits 8 July 1737

Altarpiece of The Resurrection of Christ.

The Publishers and the Author gratefully acknowledge the generous assistance of The British Academy in making a grant towards the cost of the Appendix.

Places Mentioned in the Appendix
(other than as numbered entries)

Index of Artists
Mentioned in the Appendix

General Index

References in bold type are to descriptions in the text. P, S, T: portrait, sculpture, tapestry of subject. Counties are as preceding recent changes. References to the Appendix (separately indexed) are not included.